# Electronic Signatures in Law

Stephen Mason

*of the Middle Temple, Barrister*

OBserving Law – IALS Open Book Service for Law

First published by LexisNexis Butterworths, 2003
Second edition published by Tottel, 2007
Third edition published by Cambridge University Press, 2012
Fourth edition published by the Institute of Advanced Legal Studies for the SAS Humanities Digital Library, School of Advanced Study, University of London, 2016



This book is also available online at http://ials.sas.ac.uk/digital/humanities-digital-library/observing-law-ials-open-book-service-law.

ISBN 978-1-911507-00-0 (paperback edition)

Institute of Advanced Legal Studies
University of London
Charles Clore House
17 Russell Square
London WC1B 5DR
http://ials.sas.ac.uk

# Contents

# Preface

With this fourth edition, the time is right to separate out the different forms of electronic signature, giving each a separate chapter. I anticipate that this approach will enable the reader to have a better understanding of the different forms in which an electronic signature can be manifest.

The case law on the topic has increased – in fact it has increased to such an extent that I have not been able to incorporate as many cases in this text as I have discovered after cursory searches in electronic search engines. If I have missed a particularly important case, please let me know. I have begun to prefer citing case law from appellate courts. I have also removed the extensive list of legislation on the basis that I maintain a table of world legislation that is updated and published in the *Digital Evidence and Electronic Signature Law Review* occasionally. This list in turn now relies on lawyers and legal scholars from across the world to help keep it up-to-date.

This leads me on to consider the purpose and structure of this book. A number of issues arise, such as whether the book should be as comprehensive as possible, or a more selective approach might be considered; whether to include examples from as many jurisdictions as possible, or to restrict the citing of examples. In addition, the question also arises as to how individual chapters for each type of electronic signature is structured – that is, whether a country by country analysis is appropriate, or if the analysis by legal topic is more helpful, together with a breakdown by jurisdiction.

Another concern for this edition are the suggestions by my good friend Timothy S. Reiniger in his review of the third edition.[1] Tim, who is a principal author of the Electronic Identity Management Act of Virginia,[2] suggested:

> In a future edition, the reviewer hopes that Mason will add discussion and analysis of cybernetics, information theory, and entropy in the context of various proposed forms of electronic signature and identity credential strategies. This would be a great addition to policy discussions around federated identity management, access control, trustworthy computing, and identity theft.

We have discussed these issues on occasion. One consideration will be to extend the book to include identity and authentication. Unfortunately, the timetable

1 *The Journal of Law, Science and Technology*, 53 (2013), pp. 239-47.

2 Chapter 483 An Act to amend the Code of Virginia by adding in Title 2.2 a chapter numbered 4.3, consisting of sections numbered 2.2-436 and 2.2-437, and by adding in Title 59.1 a chapter numbered 50, consisting of sections numbered 59.1-550 through 59.1-555, relating to electronic identity management; standards; liability. [S 814]. Approved 23 March 2015.

leading up to the preparation of the fourth edition did not permit such an extension. Perhaps readers will kindly offer their opinions on this suggested change.

I agreed with the Institute of Advanced Legal Studies to host the *Digital Evidence and Electronic Signature Law Review* online under open source, and I have now decided that this book is better available online under a Creative Commons licence as well. I am delighted to take part in this project with the School of Advanced Study, University of London and the Institute of Advanced Legal Studies. I sincerely hope that by putting the book online and making it available as open source, it will become more widely available – and in turn, I hope to encourage others to take part in the next edition – for which see the manifesto.

Finally, I have an observation regarding the types of electronic signature that are listed in this book as 'electronic signatures'. For many jurists across the world, the act of ticking an icon in the shape of a box to accept the terms of a contract can hardly count as a form of signature. In the physical world, that must be right. Similarly, it might be questioned that a personal identity number (PIN) can also be considered to be an electronic signature. Here is the analysis I offer in my book *When Bank Systems Fail: Debit cards, credit cards, ATMs, mobile and online banking: your rights and what to do when things go wrong* (2nd edn., St Albans: PP Publishing, 2014), pp. 50–1:

> Arguably, the PIN combines two functions. Before considering the two functions, consider the requirements of the bank. The bank needs to satisfy itself that:
>
> 1. The card is legitimate (this is difficult to achieve, as the reports about fraud demonstrate), and
>
> 2. The card is in the possession of the customer to whom it was issued, or a person authorised by the customer to use the card.
>
> If the bank satisfies itself that its computer systems are interacting with the card issued to the customer (which is not always the case), then the computer system requests the purported customer to undertake one further act to confirm they (or a person authorised by them) have physically inserted the card into the ATM or the point of sale terminal, by keying in the correct PIN. Generally, if the computer systems receive positive results from both interactions, then the bank will permit the person at the ATM or the point of sale terminal to undertake whatever activity they are permitted to do within the terms of the mandate.
>
> *The first function of a PIN*
>
> The first function of the PIN acts as a means of authentication. The PIN purports to demonstrate that the person that keyed in the PIN knew the correct PIN (there are some forms of attack that do

> not need the correct PIN – any combination of numbers will act to deceive the card issuer that the correct PIN has been keyed in).
>
> *The second function of a PIN*
>
> Once the computer systems of the bank are satisfied that the card is legitimate and the PIN is the correct PIN of the customer, then the person at the ATM or the point of sale terminal can undertake any activity on the account that is permitted within the mandate and within the limitations of the technology.
>
> The PIN, even though it is offered to the machine before a transaction is effected, acts as a signature to verify a payment or other form of transaction. This means that the presentation of a card to an ATM, and the input of a PIN, is similar to a cheque that is written out by the account holder, signed, and then presented to the cashier at the bank. The customer completes the action necessary to request a payment in advance of the payment being made by the cashier, and then signs the cheque in the presence of the cashier – all before receiving acknowledgment that a transaction has been authorised. This means the PIN is a form of electronic signature.

It might be considered that the action of clicking the 'I accept' icon or box, or typing in a PIN are merely a means by which the person agrees to conclude the contract, but the act is not that of appending their electronic signature.

This analysis might be right, but we must recall that the digital world is different to the physical world. Conceptually, some of the forms of electronic signature may not strictly be considered 'signatures' in the physical world. Nevertheless, it is a convenient shorthand to refer to some forms of agreeing to enter a contract as an 'electronic signature' – at least we can all understand the meaning behind these words, even if the form is not quite what we expect.

Stephen Mason
stephenmason@stephenmason.eu
Langford, Bedfordshire
September 2016

# Acknowledgments

As always, I thank the members of staff at the Institute of Advanced Legal Studies for their help with obtaining various law reports from the bowels of the building. I also thank the Institute of Advanced Legal Studies for continuing to renew my Associate Research Fellowship, which permits me unlimited use of the IALS Library and Information Services.

I remain indebted to John Mitchell, PhD, CEng, MBA, of LHS Business Control Limited and Professor Fred Piper, Department of Mathematics, Royal Holloway College, University of London, both of whom reviewed the technical chapters for the first edition. I am responsible for the text, which remains the same.

With thanks to Steve Whittle, the IALS Information Systems Manager and Emily Morrell, Publications Officer, School of Advanced Study and Senate House Library, University of London for all their help and patience in preparing the text for publication.

# Table of cases

## Argentina



## Australia

### Federal



### New South Wales



### Northern Territory




S. Mason, *Electronic Signatures in Law* (London: Institute of Advanced Legal Studies, 2016), Table of cases, pp. ix–xxxix

## China



## Colombia



## Czech Republic



## Denmark



## England and Wales

## Estonia



## European Patent Office



## Finland



## France



## Germany

## Lithuania



## Netherlands



## New Zealand



## Norway



## Papua New Guinea



## Poland

## Portugal



## Russian Federation



## Scotland



## Singapore



## Slovenia

## South Africa



## Sweden



## Switzerland



## Turkey



## United States of America

### Federal

**Alabama**



**Alaska**



**Arizona**



**Arkansas**



**California**

**Indiana**



**Iowa**



**Kansas**



**Kentucky**

**New Hampshire**



**New Jersey**



**New Mexico**



**New York**

**North Carolina**



**North Dakota**



**Ohio**



**Oklahoma**



**Oregon**



**Pennsylvania**

**Rhode Island**

# Table of legislation

## Table of statutes

### Antigua and Barbuda



### Argentina



### Australia

#### Commonwealth



#### New South Wales



#### Northern Territory



#### Victoria



S. Mason, *Electronic Signatures in Law* (London: Institute of Advanced Legal Studies, 2016), Table of legislations, pp. xli–lvii

## Estonia

## Saint Vincent and the Grenadines



## Saudi Arabia



## Singapore



## South Africa



## Switzerland

## Taiwan



## United States of America

### Federal



### Alabama



### Alaska



### Arizona



### California



### Connecticut

# Table of Statutory Instruments



# Table of European Legislation

## Secondary Legislation

### *Decisions*

## *Implementing Decisions*

## *Directives*



## *Regulations*

# Table of International Legislation

## *E*



## *U*

# Table of Other Enactments

## England & Wales



## European Patent Office



## Singapore



## United States of America

### Michigan



### Ohio

# 1
# The signature

**1.1** The purpose of this chapter is to put the concept of the signature into a broad legal context; to set out the purposes that can be attributed to a signature and to explain the functions a signature is capable of performing. In order to appreciate what constitutes an electronic signature, it is helpful to understand the function a signature performs and how judges have responded to changes in technology over the generations. It is for this reason that this chapter sets out a brief history of how judges have responded to changes in technology and the different methods that have been used to indicate how a signature can be made manifest. The function a signature performs remains as valid in the electronic age as when the use of an impression of a seal was considered to be the best means of authentication before the advent of widespread literacy, although seals, as with all other forms of evidence, were forged.[1]

**1.2** It should be acknowledged that many of the cases referred to in this chapter refer to statutes that may well have been amended or appealed. However, this does not detract from the problems that lawyers and judges faced when applying legal principles to new forms of technology. As most of these cases illustrate, judges applied the underlying legal principles to the facts of the case, leaving the technology to one side, because the technology does not affect the legal principles. That judges and lawyers have had to deal with new technologies is hardly unique, and to suggest that judges are dealing with technological change for the first time in history is erroneous. Judges have always been required to apply the law, regardless of the technology used, and the development of the networked world is no different.

## The purpose of a signature

**1.3** Legislation providing for electronic signatures has, essentially, been directed to provide for the authenticity of the person using the signature, although various statutes provide for additional uses, such as providing for the integrity of a message or document. Authentication can be the process by which a person or legal entity seeks to verify the validity or genuineness of a particular piece of information. Alternatively, it can mean the formal assertion of validity, such as the signing of a certificate: we authenticate what it certifies. In certain circumstances, there may also be a need to verify the identity of an individual or legal entity, although what is meant by 'identity' will also depend

1 R. G. Johnston, D. D. Martinez and A. R. E. Garcia, 'Were ancient seals secure?', *Antiquity*, 75 (2001), pp. 299–305.

S. Mason, *Electronic Signatures in Law* (London: Institute of Advanced Legal Studies, 2016), chapter 1, 'The signature', pp. 1–94.

on the reason for ascertaining the identity.[2] With a cheque, the signature serves to link the name of the person printed on the cheque with the person that claims to have the authority to draw money from the account indicated on the cheque. The existence of the cheque guarantee card with a manuscript signature on the reverse serves to reinforce the link between the card and the cheque, although the signature, even if the signature on the reverse of the cheque guarantee card matches the signature on the cheque, does not necessarily identify the person signing the cheque.[3] In cheque cases, the printed name on a cheque is not necessarily accepted as a form of signature, although it can contribute to authenticity. For instance, Lawton LJ considered the issue of authenticity in relation to a cheque with a name printed on it, and suggested that 'A printed name accompanied by a written signature was prima facie evidence that the cheque was being drawn on the account it purported to be drawn on',[4] although in the South African case of *Akasia Finance v. Da Souza*,[5] Leveson J indicated why, at 338 G-H, he did not consider the name printed on the cheque could be a signature:

> At the foot of each cheque, where the signature of the drawer is normally to be found, appear the words, 'Domestic Homes (Pty) Ltd, Registration No 73/0541'. The words are printed and are plainly printed by machine.
>
> It is well known that for several years past banks have been issuing cheque books to their customers with the customer's name machine-printed thereon in the same space as the cheques in the present case. The printing is usually computer-controlled. This is done as part of a design to facilitate the modern banking system. Of importance is the fact that the printing is not done by the customer. It is therefore not the company's signature in the sense that, if put there by a person authorised by a corporate customer, it would constitute the company's signature or seal under the provisions of the Companies Act 61 of 1973.

2 N. Bohm and S. Mason, 'Identity and its verification', *Computer Law & Security Review*, 26 (2001), pp. 43–51; for a technical response, see R. E. Smith, *Authentication: from password to public keys* (Boston, Mass., 2002).

3 A website cited in previous editions of this text (http://www.zug.com/pranks/credit_card/) illustrated how little people relied on a manuscript signature for the many millions of transactions conducted every day. The illustrations included the use of variations of their signature with a number of transactions, including evidence of the transaction slips. Alas, this website is no longer available.

4 *Ringham v. Hackett* (1980) 124 SJ 201 at 202(a). In *Central Motors (Birmingham) Ltd v. P A & S N P Wadsworth* [1982] CAT 231, 28 May 1982; (1983) 133 NLJ 555 Court of Appeal (Civil Division), a second account holder was held jointly liable for a cheque that he did not sign under the provisions of the Bills of Exchange Act 1882.

5 1993 (2) SA 337 (W).

**1.4** The function of a signature is generally determined by the nature and content of the document to which it is affixed.

**1.5** It is thought that the act of a person fixing their name to a document is well understood by lawyers and non-lawyers alike. However, a consideration of the case law demonstrates the range of issues that have arisen in relation to what seems, at first glance, a relatively simple concept. The means by which judges have tested the validity of a signature has altered over time. From concentrating on the form a signature takes, judges went on to question its validity by considering the function the signature performs.[6] The analysis in the move from form to function applies equally to the analysis of electronic signatures. The perceptive comments from the sound dissenting judgment of Bell J in 1855 in the South African case of *Van Vuuren v. Van Vuuren*,[7] at 121 provides a useful summary with which to begin:

> ... the expression 'to sign' a document has no strict legal or technical meaning different from the popular meaning, viz., to authenticate by that which stands for or is intended to represent the name of the person who is to authenticate. If you say to the most illiterate person 'Sign this paper,' if he cannot write, he will put a cross to it, and if he do not know how to do this the most experienced man of business cannot tell him to do more. If the party have learned a little writing, or if rheumatism of hard labour have cramped the nerves of his hand, and you ask him to sign a document, he will put the initial capital letters of his Christian and surname, while he will not venture upon writing the other more minute and therefore more difficult to be executed letters of these names, and he will feel satisfied that he has 'signed'. If the man of business doubt this, and, seeing he can write so far as to be able to make the capital letters, think it will not be sufficient without the smaller letters, and insist upon his making them, should the party say he cannot, the lawyer will be content. On the other hand, should the party make the attempt and produce a scrawl more or less legible, so again the man of business will be content – whether the scrawl be legible or illegible, he will be satisfied that the man has 'signed'. Such is the popular and professional practice, and the decision of the Courts had been conformably to it.

6 C. Reed, 'What is a signature?', *Journal of Information, Law and Technology*, 3 (2000), http://www2.warwick.ac.uk/fac/soc/law/elj/jilt/2000_3/reed/.

7 2 Searle 116.

## Dictionary definitions

**1.6** The *Oxford English Dictionary* offers a number of definitions of the word 'signature' as a noun and a verb.[8] The earliest references relate to signatures of a public nature that are intended to have legal effect. The first definition of a signature as a noun is that of 'A writing prepared and presented to the Baron of Exchequer by a writer to the signet, as the ground of a royal grant to the person in whose name it is presented'. An illustration for 1534 refers to 'To pass with writings and signaturis to be subscrivit be the Kingis grace'. The remaining references for this entry also relate to royal signatures in the public domain. The second and third definitions continue with the same meaning. Item 2(a) is defined as 'The name (or special mark) of a person written with his or her own hand as an authentication of some document or writing', and is illustrated from Hollyband of 1580, referring to 'the signature or marke of a Notaries', with the next illustration from Coke dated 1633 referring to 'A bill superscribed with the signature or signe manuall, or royall hand of the King'. The third reference, item 2(b), 'The action of signing one's name, or of authenticating a document by doing so', is also illustrated by an early reference to Lord Keeper Williams from 1621: 'Some things wee must offer to the kings signature when the clarkes are not to bee found'.

**1.7** The law dictionaries vary in their treatment of the definition of 'signature'. Some provide a definition that is similar to that offered by the *Oxford English Dictionary*, such as:

> Signature. A sign or mark impressed upon anything; a stamp, a mark; the name of a person written by himself either in full or by initials as regards his Christian name or names, and in full as regards his surname, or by initials only ... or by a mark only, though he can write ... or by rubber stamp ... or by proxy.
>
> A person signs a document when he writes or marks something on it in token of his intention to be bound by its contents. In the case of an ordinary person, signature is commonly performed by his subscribing his name to the document, and hence 'signature' is frequently used as equivalent to 'subscription'; but any mark is sufficient if it shows an intention to be bound by the document; illiterate people commonly sign by making a cross.[9]
>
> 1. A person's name or mark written by that person or at that person's direction. 2. *Commercial law*. Any name, mark, or writing used with the intention of authenticating a document.[10]

8 *Oxford English Dictionary* (2nd edn. on CD-ROM, version 4.0, 2009).

9 *Jowitt's Dictionary of English Law* (4th edn., London: Sweet & Maxwell, 2015).

10 *Black's Law Dictionary* (10th edn., n.p., West Group, 2014).

**1.8** Other legal dictionaries provide judicial examples of the meaning to be attributed to a signature, with case examples.[11]

## The manuscript signature

**1.9** The epitome of a signature is the act of an individual writing their name in their own hand on a document, usually in the form of a manuscript signature.[12] More widely, it is the action of a person affixing a permanent imprint upon a document. In the world before the invention of electricity and computers, an imprint was required to have the characteristic of permanency because it was necessary to retain tangible evidence of intention. In addition, the parties to the document may consider it necessary to retain the evidence for a sufficient length of time in order to enforce any rights or obligations evidenced in the record. Before the development of the telegraph, a document would normally be considered something written onto a material, mainly paper. Although a number of people may be involved with the framing of a document and its subsequent manifestation in its final physical form, the document will have been created physically. Thus if an instruction was passed from one party to another by means of the operators of a semaphore, the sending operator could give evidence of the instructions received from the instructing party and the signals they used to transmit the message, and the receiving operator could give evidence of the signals they observed and noted down on paper. With the development of communications over the electric telegraph, the same principles would apply as with the semaphore, but the electronic pulses would be interpreted in the light of the code used by the sending and receiving operators. The use of the telegraph meant that the message was encoded into electronic pulses, but the pulses were not stored. The receiving operator transferred the evidence of the message to a carrier. In contrast, software code transmits and stores the data in digital format, but the data are not visible to the human eye. It requires a combination of the interpretation and use of hardware and software to make the data visible to the human. In a world that relied on physical and permanent evidence of proof of intent, the requirement for an enduring record is understandable. While the legal consequences of a signature will differ when fixed to artefacts, such as items of pottery, paintings, sculpture and carvings on surfaces such as stone, marble, glass and wooden furniture, nevertheless a signature is capable of establishing the identity of the

11 *Stroud's Judicial Dictionary of Words and Phrases* (8th edn., London: Sweet & Maxwell, 2015). The entry in this dictionary is of useful length, separating out different areas of law with good discussion. *Words and Phrases legally defined* (4th edn., London: LexisNexis Butterworths 2007; supplement 2010).

12 Although the *tuğra* (a cipher or imperial monogram) of the Ottoman sultans that served as the signature of the sultan was drawn up by a court official and affixed to official documents. Over time, it was also carved on seals and stamped on coins, and artists illuminated later *tuğra*.

creator of the article and is also capable of authenticating the provenance of the object.[13]

**1.10** A document usually exists on a carrier, typically paper. The carrier is marked permanently with content, usually with ink, either in the form of handwriting or by means of a printing press. This process alters the carrier physically. The content imprinted on the carrier may include a range of information, depending on the nature of the document, including information about the person that created, issued or initiated the content. Over time, the carrier will include additional information as it is handled, including coffee or tea stains, scratches, additional content, fingerprints and DNA. Finally, a person or legal entity might sign the carrier with a signature. The reason for signing the document will depend on the nature of the document and the purpose for which the person is signing. When brought together, these components comprise the document in its entirety.[14]

## Writing

**1.11** In England and Wales, writing is defined in s5, Schedule 1 of the Interpretation Act 1978, and 'includes typing, printing, lithography, photography and other modes of representing or reproducing words in visible form, and expressions referring to writing are construed accordingly'. This definition emphasizes the need for the writing to be in visible form, which excludes information in a digital format. This means that information in digital format will only come within this definition if it comes within the method set out in the definition, 'and other modes of representing or reproducing words'.[15] In his conclusion of whether information in digital format will amount to writing, Professor Reed suggested there were two possible approaches to this problem:

> The distinction is not between information affixed to a carrier or not, but between informal speech and formally recorded information, in the same way that the content of a message was recorded by means of telegraph, although the problem with this analysis is that there is no distinction between the use of the technology in a formal or informal capacity.
>
> The second possibility is to suggest that the requirement of 'writing' is merely evidential in nature, although the courts continue to

13 The copy of a painting with a false signature painted on it with the intention of passing off the painting as by the genuine painter was determined to be a cheat at common law by Cockburn LCJ and his fellow judges in *Regina v. Thomas Closs* (1858) Crown Cases Reserved 460, Dears & Bell 460.

14 For the meaning of a 'document' in a digital context, see S. Mason (ed.), *Electronic Evidence* (3nd edn, London: LexisNexis Butterworths, 2012), ch. 10.

15 C. Reed, *Digital Information Law: Electronic Documents and Requirements of Form* (London: Centre for Commercial Law Studies, 1996), 83–4 for other statutory definitions and further comments.

> maintain the position that tendering oral evidence cannot rectify the lack of formality.[16]

**1.12** It is useful to note the range of functions that writing performs in relation to a physical carrier, as considered in the UNCITRAL Model Law on Electronic Commerce:[17]

> the following non-exhaustive list indicates reasons why national laws require the use of 'writings': (1) to ensure that there would be tangible evidence of the existence and nature of the intent of the parties to bind themselves; (2) to help the parties be aware of the consequences of their entering into a contract; (3) to provide that a document would be legible by all; (4) to provide that a document would remain unaltered over time and provide a permanent record of a transaction; (5) to allow for the reproduction of a document so that each party would hold a copy of the same data; (6) to allow for the authentication of data by means of a signature; (7) to provide that a document would be in a form acceptable to public authorities and courts; (8) to finalize the intent of the author of the 'writing' and provide a record of that intent; (9) to allow for the easy storage of data in a tangible form; (10) to facilitate control and subsequent audit for accounting, tax or regulatory purposes; and (11) to bring legal rights and obligations into existence in those cases where a 'writing' was required for validity purposes.[18]

**1.13** For the position in Scotland, the reader is referred to the Requirements of Writing (Scotland) Act 1995.

## Statutory definition of signature

**1.14** There does not appear to be a statutory definition of the term 'signature', and Ashman J commented in 1892 in a case regarding probate that there was no judicial formula either:[19]

> Exactly what constitutes a signature has never been reduced to a judicial formula ... The principle upon which these cases proceeded was that whatever the testator of grantor was shown to

16 Reed, *Digital Information Law*, 94–102.

17 The Model Law on Electronic Commerce was adopted by the Commission on 12 June 1996, following its 605th meeting, which in turn was adopted by the General Assembly in Resolution 51/162 at its 85th plenary meeting on 16 December 1996, and includes an additional article 5 *bis* as adopted by the Commission at its 31st meeting in June 1998.

18 Guide to Enactment paragraph 48.

19 Mitchell J quoted these comments of Ashman J (whose decision was reversed) in *In re Plate's Estate*, 148 Pa. 55, 23 A. 1038.

> have intended as his signature was a valid signing, no matter how imperfect or unfinished or fantastical or illegible, or even false, the separate characters or symbols he used might be, when critically judged.

**1.15** The Interpretation Act 1978 does not provide a definition, although Professor Reed noted there were fifteen statutory definitions of 'signature' or 'signing' in force in 1996, eleven of which adopted an identical or similar variation to the following: '"signature" includes a facsimile of a signature by whatever process reproduced'.[20] This particular definition is sufficiently general to include a representation of a signature in electronic format. The most obvious example is that of a manuscript signature that is scanned and converted into digital form. Such a representation can be attached to a document produced on a computer, or it could be the image of the signature as sent and received by a facsimile machine. It is estimated that there are in the region of 40,000 references to the requirement for a manuscript signature.[21] However, whether a personal signature is required depends upon the wording of the statute or from the context of the requirement.[22] With respect to legislation, Professor Reed notes that the statutory provisions relating to the provision of a signature fall into three broad categories:[23]

> Where documents that have been signed are admissible in evidence, or create evidential presumptions. The evidential presumptions are either that the document is conclusive proof of its contents, or it is clear evidence of the facts set out in the document.
>
> Where documents have to be signed for the purpose of authentication, either expressly or from the context of the requirement.
>
> Where a signature is required to exercise a statutory power.

## The functions of a signature

**1.16** In summary, a signature can serve a number of functions, each of which can have varying degrees of importance.[24]

20 Water Resources Act 1991 (c 57) Schedule 4, Part II, Proceedings of Flood Defence Committees, quoted in Reed, *Digital Information Law*, p. 225; Table 5.1, pp. 262–3 for the full list.

21 HC Official Report (6th series) col 41, 29 November 1999; note also Reed, *Digital Information Law*, p. 239 and n. 41; Reed, 'What is a signature?', 3.1.2 and n. 68.

22 Reed, *Digital Information Law*, pp. 233–4 and nn. 23 and 24.

23 Reed, *Digital Information Law*, pp. 240–1. Professor Reed provides examples in nn. 42–52.

24 L. L. Fuller, 'Consideration and form', *Columbia Law Review*, 41 (1941), pp. 799–824 refers to the evidentiary, cautionary function and channelling functions; M. Sneddon, 'Legislating to facilitate electronic signatures and records: exceptions, standards and the impact on the statute book', *University of New South Wales Law Journal*, 21 (1998), part

## *The primary evidential function*

**1.17** It is suggested that the primary purpose of a signature serves to provide admissible and reliable evidence that comprises the following elements:

> (i) To provide tangible evidence that the signatory approves and adopts the contents of the document.
>
> (ii) In so doing, the signatory agrees that the content of the document is binding upon them and will have legal effect.
>
> (iii) Further, the signatory is reminded of the significance of the act and the need to act within the provisions of the document.

**1.18** The nature of the act of signing differs between the application of a manuscript signature and the use of an electronic signature. This is because a manuscript signature, if authentic, is biologically linked to a specific individual, but cryptographic authentication systems bind signatures to individuals by way of software code and procedural mechanisms.

**1.19** With electronic signatures, the person does not physically sign anything, but causes software to sign electronically using an untrustworthy machine for knowing what document has been signed[25] – even when using a biodynamic version of a manuscript signature. This is significant, because the act of signing using an electronic signature has a different symbolic meaning to that of a manuscript signature, and suggests a weaker sense of the involvement of the person in the process of signing, as noted by Professor Chou.[26]

---

2 II A (i)–(iv), http://www.austlii.edu.au/au/journals/UNSWLJ/1998/59.html; 'Digital signature guidelines' (Judicial Studies Board, 2000), p. 3; J. Dumortier, P. Van Eecke and I. Anné, *The Legal Aspects of Digital Signatures* (Leuven: Interdisciplinary Centre for Law and Information Technology, 1998), Report 1, Part III, p. 50; ISTEV, 'Legal and Regulatory Issues for the European Trusted Services Infrastructure – European Trusted Services' (2007), para 3; *Digital Signature Guidelines* (n.p.: American Bar Association, 1996), pp. 4–9; A. McCullagh, P. Little and W. Caelli, 'Electronic signatures: understand the past to develop the future', *University of New South Wales Law Journal*, 21 (1998), p. 56; UNCITRAL Model Law on Electronic Commerce with Guide to Enactment 1996 with additional article 5 *bis* as adopted in 1998 (New York: United Nations, 1999) paras 48 and 53; UNCITRAL Model Law on Electronic Signatures with Guide to Enactment 2001 (United Nations, New York 2002) para 29; 'Protections of the acknowledgment' in 'A Position on Digital Signature Laws and Notarization', a position statement from the National Notary Association, September 2000, 3 – 5; *Promoting confidence in electronic commerce: legal issues on international use of electronic authentication and signature methods* (Vienna: United Nations, 2009), pp. 1–8; for a similar overview of the same topic and discussion of the development of signatures, see L. Brazell, *Electronic Signatures and Identities: Law and Regulation* (2nd edn, London: Sweet & Maxwell, 2008), 2-001–2-043.

25 S. Mason and T. S. Reiniger, '"Trust" between machines? Establishing identity between humans and software code, or whether you know it is a dog, and if so, which dog?', *Computer and Telecommunications Law Review*, 21 (2015), pp. 135–48.

26 E. Y. Chou, 'Paperless and soulless: e-signatures diminish the signer's presence and decrease acceptance', *Social Psychological and Personality Science*, 6 (2015), pp. 343–51. Professor Chou also provides further citations.

### *Secondary evidential functions*

**1.20** A signature can also provide evidence of identification and proof of the following:

(i) The signature can authenticate the identity of the person signing the document. One example would be to reinforce the causal link between the signature and a name printed on a document, such as a name printed on a chequebook or credit card.

(ii) The identity of a particular characteristic, or attribute, or status of the person such as a government minister or company director.

(iii) Where a person signing acknowledges, verifies or witnesses the record, but does not necessarily agree to be bound by the content of the document.

(iv)The existence of the document provides a record of the intent of the signatory, and, in turn, physical evidence of the originality and completeness of the document itself, including the time, date and place of the act of the affixing of the signature to the document.

(v) Where a person is a witness to the signing of a document, the signature of the witness can provide for the authenticity and the voluntary nature of the signature of a third party.

(vi) It can demonstrate that the content of the document has not been altered subsequently to the affixing of the signature.

(vii) A signature can provide evidence that the record is a true copy of another record.

### *Cautionary function*

**1.21** This function acts to reinforce the legal nature of the document, thereby encouraging the person affixing their signature that they should take care before committing themselves to the contents of the document.

### *Protective function*

**1.22** As a corollary to the cautionary function, the party receiving the document containing a manuscript signature recognizes that the other party affirms the content of the document and they have given their full attention to the content of the document. They can also be assured of the identity of the signatory, and are consequently in receipt of the proof of the source and contents of the document. This function is linked to the evidentiary function.[27]

27 Sneddon, 'Legislating to facilitate electronic signatures and records', Part 2 II A (ii).

### *Channelling function*

**1.23** The formality of a manuscript signature helps to clarify the point at which a person recognizes the act has become legally significant. Also, the content of the document, by being recorded on a durable form, serves to concentrate the mind on the legally binding nature of the document, thus reducing the risks associated with oral recollections. This function is also linked to the evidentiary function.

### *Record keeping function*

**1.24** Closely related to the evidentiary function, a document contained on a carrier manifest in physical format serves as a durable record of the terms of the agreement. It also enables governments to impose taxes on documents and permit audits based on the existence of documents having a physical existence.

# Disputing a manuscript signature

## Defences

**1.25** A manuscript signature cannot be disputed unless the following defences can be established: the signature is a forgery;[28] the signature was conditional; the signature was obtained as a result of misrepresentation; the signature was obtained in such circumstance that it was not the act of the person signing (*non est factum*); mental incapacity; mistake; where one party unilaterally added material terms to the writing after the other's signature; where the person signing the document did not realize the document they signed was a contractual document; by statute as being unreasonable or unfair. These defences are not dealt with in this text, other than a brief consideration of the disputes where a manuscript signature has been at issue. The reader is referred to the standard textbooks on the subject. It is well known that manuscript signatures are forged. To prevent this problem, and to test both the validity and the effectiveness of a manuscript signature, some documents require the signature to be affixed in the presence of a witness or an authorized official, such as a notary.

## Evidence of the manuscript signature

**1.26** Where a manuscript signature is challenged on a document, evidence

28 In the case of *Brown v. National Westminster Bank Ltd* [1964] 2 Lloyds Rep 187 QBD Commercial Court, the bank paid sums of money on 329 cheques that were alleged to have forged Mrs Brown's signature. The bank admitted to paying out on 100 cheques that were forged, but put Mrs Brown to proof that the remaining cheques were forged. This was because the bank took measures, through the branch managers, to question Mrs Brown on a number of cheques that passed through her account. Mrs Brown failed to prove that she did not sign the remaining cheques. For similar facts in Australia, see *Tina Motors Pty. Ltd. v. Australia and New Zealand Banking Group Ltd.* [1977] VR 205.

will need to demonstrate the issues discussed below. It should be noted that the evidentiary burden is a factor in considering the precise nature of the signature. In the Canadian case of *Regina v. Blumes*,[29] the signature on a vehicle registration document, issued by the Insurance Corporation of British Columbia, was challenged. It was alleged that the document was not admissible because it was not clear whether the signature was a manuscript signature, a rubber stamp or a facsimile signature. This document was afforded the presumption of regularity, which meant that a mere challenge was not sufficient to avoid the operation of regularity.

## *The identity of the person affixing the manuscript signature*

**1.27** Evidence will have to be adduced to show the signature affixed to the document is that of the signatory. In such cases, the signature in question will have to be compared to samples of the same signature. A signature may be forged or the signature could be that of the signatory, but they may have attempted to disguise their handwriting. Thus a handwriting analyst[30] will need to have two kinds of samples: 'request samples' which are produced for the examination and duplicate the material in question, and naturally occurring samples, made by the signatory without realizing the example will be examined. Two main factors can then be examined, that of pictorial impression, which includes matters such as slope, size, margins, spacing and the position of the writing in relation to lines. Second, the construction of the letters can be examined, such as the direction the letter 'o' is formed, the way the letter 't' is crossed, and the way in which the person has written letters that require more than one movement. Forgers tend to concentrate on the pictorial impression and fail to copy details of the way letters are constructed. Likewise, people trying to disguise their handwriting also concentrate on the pictorial impression, rather than changing the formation of their letters. Further analysis can be undertaken by considering the relative proportions of letters, the spaces between letters, pressure variations. Also, the attributes of the instrument used to affix the signature to the document can be considered, such as how smooth the signature has been signed, whether it is jagged or confident, whether there is a pause and where the instrument lifts off the surface. Further, the carrier itself can be examined, from the type of material used (physical properties, optical properties), any security features (watermarks),

29 2002 BCPC 0045.

30 Recent research has demonstrated that the findings of experts across all forensic disciplines can be subject to bias as the result of cognitive factors, such that the same expert has reached the opposite conclusion with the same evidence, for which see I. D. Dror, C. Champod, G. Langenburg, D. Charlton, H. Hunt and R. Rosenthal, 'Cognitive issues of fingerprint analysis: inter- and intra-expert consistency and the effect of a 'target' comparison', *Forensic Science International*, 208 (2011), pp. 10–17 and the references cited therein. Apparently the US Secret Service uses a software program called Forensic Information System for Handwriting (FISH) that enables document examiners to scan and digitize text writings such as threatening correspondence.

the printing process used (the use and identification of a photocopier, computer or printer) and other evidence such as perforations and microscopic analysis that might reveal imperfections that may link the carrier to the person. Further examination can include the comparison of typescript; impressions by means of Electrostatic Detection Apparatus; whether more than one type of material was used to affix information on the carrier; whether any alterations were made or entries obliterated, and the sequence in which intersecting lines have been written.

**1.28** Where the party relying on the authenticity of the manuscript signature successfully demonstrates the similarity of the manuscript signature to the sample signatures, the evidential burden will then fall upon the alleged signatory to prove the signature was forged. Although this point was made in *Saunders v. Anglia Building Society*[31] in relation to the defence where the signature was obtained in such circumstance that it was not the act of the person signing, the principle applies to a forged signature.

## Intention to authenticate and adopt the document

**1.29** Where a person affixes their manuscript signature to a document, it must be shown that they intended to sign the document. The case of *L'Estrange v. F Graucob Limited*,[32] which pre-dates the modern legislation, serves to illustrate the point. In this case, Miss L'Estrange carried on the business of a café. The defendants manufactured and sold automatic slot machines. In early 1933, Miss L'Estrange agreed to buy an automatic slot machine for cigarettes for a total of £81 5*s* 6*d*, payable over 18 months. She signed a form, printed on brown paper headed 'Sales Agreement'. This document included a number of contract terms written in very small print, one of which included 'This agreement contains all the terms and conditions under which I agree to purchase the machine specified above, and any express or implied condition, statement, or warranty, statutory or otherwise not stated herein is hereby excluded'. The machine was installed on 29 March 1933. However, it failed to work, and she eventually initiated an action in the county court to recover the payments she had made. Judgment was made in her favour. The decision was reversed in the Divisional Court because Miss L'Estrange had signed the written contract, and in doing so acknowledged that she was bound by the terms. There was no misrepresentation that induced her to sign. It was irrelevant that she did not read the contract or know its contents.[33]

31 [1971] AC 1004.

32 [1934] 2 KB 394 Divisional Court; J. R. Spencer, 'Signature, consent, and the rule in *L'Estrange v. Graucob*', CLJ, pp. 104–22, notes at p. 104 that this was not the first case in which the rule was laid down, although it was the case that made the rule famous; see *Parker v. The South Eastern Railway Company* (1877) 2 CPD 416, *The Luna* [1920] P 22 and *Blay v. Pollard and Morris* [1930] 1 KB 628.

33 This decision, and the discussion of a fourth defence, that the signatory did not agree to the term, is discussed in Spencer, 'Signature, consent, and the rule in *L'Estrange v. Graucob*'.

**1.30** This was not the case in *Pryor v. Pryor*.[34] Anthony Pryor made a will on 5 November 1859. One of the attesting witnesses was his daughter. The testator wanted his daughter's husband to sign the will as a witness, but because it was not known when he would return, he asked his daughter to sign her husband's name instead of her own. She did so. Sir C Creswell refused to admit the will to probate because the subscription was not intended to represent her signature.

**1.31** Although a manuscript signature on a document may not be in dispute, the person signing the document may wish the other party to infer they had the authority to sign the document, as in the case of *Ringham v. Hackett*.[35] The presumption may be rebutted by evidence. In this case, the name printed on the cheque in *Ringham* was that of a partnership, and the signature by one of the partners on the cheque was deemed to be sufficient evidence to intend the recipient to infer the cheque was drawn on the partnership. In the case of *Central Motors (Birmingham) Ltd v. PA & SNP Wadsworth*,[36] Central Motors required a cheque for the payment of a motor car in the name of the firm. In accordance with this request, Mr Wadsworth gave Central Motors a cheque with his signature beneath the name of the firm, which was printed on the cheque, below that of the names of the defendants. It was held that by handing over a cheque signed in this way, Mr Wadsworth provided sufficient evidence from the circumstances to personally authenticate the document as being a cheque of the firm. By signing the cheque, Mr Wadsworth had the requisite intent to adopt the cheque as that of the firm.

# Methods of authentication before manuscript signatures

## Objects as a means of authentication

**1.32** Before the use of written charters became common, objects would be used to preserve memory and provide evidence of an act, especially when obtaining title to a property. The object served to act as a symbol of the conveyance. For instance, Earl Warenne gave a gift to Lewes Priory in 1147, and both he and his brother had hair from their head cut off by Henry of Blois, bishop of Winchester before the altar for retention by the Priory as evidence of the gift,[37] although by the reign of Henry II, judges began to refuse to take cognizance of symbolic objects, other than sealed writings. However, the production of an object could still be adduced as evidence, and knives were used for this purpose, especially for a conveyance.[38]

34 (1860) LJR 29 NS P, M & A 114.

35 (1980) 124 SJ 201.

36 [1982] CAT 231, May 28, 1982; (1983) 133 NLJ 555 Court of Appeal (Civil Division).

37 M. T. Clanchy, *From Memory to Written Record: England 1066–1307* (2nd edn., London: Blackwell, 1993), p. 38, where further examples are given.

38 Clanchy, *From Memory to Written Record*, pp. 39, 257–9 indicating knives were often used to convey land, and the blade had to be broken in the process.

## The sign of the cross

**1.33** The presumption about what constitutes a signature is predicated on the concept of literacy. Evidence from anthropological studies of non-literate societies and sociological studies of people living in deprived areas of the industrialized world suggest that literacy itself is primarily a form of technology.[39] This is reflected in the history of literacy, because in medieval society, it was rare for the most educated people to write. There was no value placed on a personal signature. Documents were ratified with a cross, because the cross was a solemn symbol of Christian truth. This method of authentication was retained after the conquest by the Normans,[40] and is illustrated in a grant dated 1068–76 by Waleran, of property at Bures St Mary, Suffolk, to St Stephen's Abbey, Caen, attested by William I, Queen Matilda, John of Bayeaux, bishop of Rouen, and Roger and Robert Beaumont, with their names added by the scribe next to each cross.[41]

## The seal and chirograph

**1.34** There was a time when a personal signature was not accepted as a lawful mark of authentication on a document unless the person signing the document was a Jew. A Christian was required to sign with a cross, or their signum was affixed to the document in the form of an impression of a seal.[42] Seal impressions were made in malleable metals, such as gold or silver, while the papacy used lead. The use of metals prevents the impression from being attached directly to the document, which means the seal must be attached to the document in some other way, such as a piece of string. Sealing wax began to be used, which is an amalgam of beeswax and resin. The beeswax becomes malleable when gently heated, and the resin acts as an adhesive. In the sixteenth century, shellac was introduced as a material, and remains popular today. By 1300 in England, the use

39 Clanchy, *From Memory to Written Record*, p. 7.

40 W. S. Holdsworth, *A History of English Law*, III (3rd edn., London: Methuen), 231.

41 P. D. A. Harvey and A. McGuinness, *A guide to British medieval seals* (Toronto: University of Toronto Press, 1996), figure 1. Museums across the world display early documents, and it is fun to seek such documents out to note the various designs of a cross that people adopted. Two documents from the state archive of Dubrovnik are in display in the Dubrovnik maritime museum with a variety of crosses: a contract between Dubrovnik and Termoli from 1203, signed in Termoli on the mutual exemption from port duties and taxes; an agreement on the renewal of friendship between Dubrovnik and Molfetta from 1208, confirming mutual exemption from port duties and taxes as stated in the previous contract from 1148.

42 Clanchy, *From Memory to Written Record*, p. 233; Harvey and McGuinness, *Guide to British Medieval Seals*, p. 1; P. M. Barnes and L. C. Hector, *A Guide to Seals in the Public Record Office* (2nd edn., London: HMSO, 1968) illustrate, on p. 3, that the meaning of 'seal' is the actual impression that was attached to a document, and the 'matrix' or 'die' is the implement which makes the impression. However, in this text, the word 'matrix' and 'die' will not be used for fear of making the subject far too technical.

of seals had permeated society to such an extent that serfs and villeins were using documents, especially to convey property. The use of seals have a long history in China, Japan and Korea, and continue to be used daily in these countries.

**1.35** Sometimes two copies of a document, whatever the subject, would be produced. This form of document was known as a chirograph, dating from the ninth century or earlier. A chirograph might record an agreement between two parties, including a marriage settlement, conveyance of land or repayment of a loan. The text is written twice, usually on two sides of the same parchment. When written on the same parchment, the two halves were separated by being torn or cut into two pieces, usually with a wavy line or a zigzag as a precaution against forgery or alteration.[43] In addition, the scribe would add text across the division, such as the word CHIROGRAPHUM.[44] Each party would be given one of the halves of the parchment, duly authenticated by the impression of the seal of the other party, and each piece served to authenticate the other. This practice was so popular that chirographs became known as indentures. Tripartite chirographs were also widely used in England for drawing up wills in the tenth and eleventh centuries.[45]

## Witnesses and scribes

**1.36** Clanchy has observed that there would be occasions when the addition of the sign of the cross or the impression of a seal on a charter was not considered a sufficient means of authentication. Hence documents would include a list of witnesses attending the event in which the promise was made. In such cases, the emphasis would have been on the public ceremonial attendant upon the transaction.[46] It was also possible that parties would rely on the particular handwriting of a scribe to establish the authenticity of a document. The test of distinctive handwriting was acknowledged in the Statute of Merchants of 1285, requiring all merchants to have their debts recorded before the mayor of London, or before similar authorities in other cities and towns, as designated. Each bond

43 In a similar fashion, after being notched with the amount received, tally sticks were cracked open lengthways by splitting the stick vertically into two. The tally-writer then inscribed the smooth sides with the details of the person to whom the tally was given, and the reason for the payment. As a record, they were light, small and virtually impossible to forge. To make space in the rambling buildings making up the Palace of Westminster, the Treasury ordered the tally sticks, no longer used as records, to be destroyed. In burning the tally sticks in the furnaces that heated the House of Lords, the heat generated was so great as to cause the House of Lords and House of Commons to burn to the ground (C. Shenton, *The Day Parliament Burned Down* (Oxford: Oxford University Press, 2012), pp. 14–15; 50–3, 240).

44 Clanchy, *From Memory to Written Record*, p. 87; for an example of an agreement between Colchester Abbey and the burgesses dating from 1254, see plate VII, in the Harvard Law Library MS 87, 2.254.

45 P. Chaplais, *English Diplomatic Practice in the Middle Ages* (London: Hambledon and London, 2003), pp. 40–41.

46 Clanchy, *From Memory to Written Record*, p. 295.

was to be written by a nominated clerk, and the bond had to be enrolled in the hand of the clerk who was known.[47]

# The format of the signature

**1.37** In England, an early record of a manuscript signature is that of Edward III of 1362, who signed a document with his name. It is suggested it was already the custom to do this in Castile, and because he was writing to the king of Castile, he also appended his manuscript signature. The manuscript signature acted to confirm his recognition of the contents of the document, but not to replace the seal.[48] Although politicians enact statutes with a view to regulating human affairs, human ingenuity always manages to circumvent procedures and rules laid down in an attempt to provide for certainty. As a result, judges have been required to exercise their powers to test the definition of a signature, and what is acceptable in the legal context. The case law illustrates that in general, judges assessed the validity in relation to the functions a signature performed. Different factual problems required a broader understanding of the function a signature performed. Whatever the form a signature took, judges looked to the intent behind the use of the signature. Thus the range of forms a signature can take is wide, as demonstrated by the following discussion.

## Manuscript

### *A mark*

**1.38** A mark can be in the form of any shape, including the sign of the cross, an 'x', a shape or a number of lines that intersect. An example is the mark on a memorandum dated 16 October 1666 of words spoken by Elizabeth Daniel of Eyam in the County of Derby as her last will and testament. Rebecca Hawksworth appended her mark on the memorandum as a witness to what was spoken and written down. Probate was granted on 24 April 1667. Her mark consisted of an incomplete line that is roughly in the shape of a heart, intersected with a further horizontal line.[49]

**1.39** **Bills of exchange** A case dating from 1798 is that of *Adam v. Kerr*,[50] where a mark on a bill of exchange included an argument over whether the particular mark used by custom in Jamaica was acceptable as a valid signature, and in 1830, *George v. Surrey*[51] dealt with the validity of a bill of exchange in which Tindal

47 Clanchy, *From Memory to Written Record*, p. 307.

48 Harvey and McGuinness, *Guide to British Medieval Seals*, p. 2 and n. 2.

49 A copy of this document is on display in the museum at Eyam, together with another document with the marks of three men; each of these marks is different in shape.

50 1 B & P 360; 126 ER 952.

51 1 M. & M. 516, 173 ER 1243.

CJ accepted a bill with a mark which included the endorsement 'Ann Moore her mark'.[52]

**1.40 An interest in real property** In respect of the transfer of property, a general warranty deed conveying property and signed with affixing a mark to the document before a notary public and witnesses was a sufficient signature,[53] as was the sale of an erf in South Africa, where the mark was considered an act of the signer, and signified assent to the content of the document.[54]

**1.41 Wills** Before the majority of people could read and write, the provisions of some statutes meant that where a person could not write their name, they were still required to provide a mark on a will,[55] even when the will was signed with a signature, but the codicil was signed by a mark;[56] and where the will is signed by a mark where the testator was able to write.[57] This also applies to a witness,[58] and where a witness signs a will by marking the document with a cross.[59] Where an interested person adds a mark to a will, the presumption is

52 In the South African case of *Hanse v. Jordan & Fuchs* 1909 19 CTR 530, the sum of £21 4*s* was due on a promissory note. The defendant claimed not to have added his mark. The magistrate at first instance, having heard the case, believed the plaintiff's account of the facts. On appeal, Buchanan J commented, at 530, 'The defendant denied this [adding his mark to the note], but the mere fact that he can write, and only signed by his mark, is not sufficient ground upon which the Court can upset the finding of the Magistrate upon the fact'.

53 *Mitchell v. Mills*, 264 S.E.2d 749.

54 *Chisnall and Chisnall v. Sturgeon and Sturgeon* 1993 (2) SA 642 (W). For Scotland, see M. C. Meston and D. J. Cusine, 'Execution of deeds by a mark', *Journal of the Law Society of Scotland* (1993), pp. 270–2.

55 Although in the case of *Crosbie v. Wilson* (1865) 3 M. 870 in Scotland, a will which was attested, but only had the testator's name at the end in words only, with the statement 'her mark'. This was held to be ineffective as a signature.

56 *Baker v. Dening* (1838) 8 AD & E 94; 112 ER 771; Patterson J indicated that when a document is signed by a mark, an enquiry may be undertaken as to the circumstances of the signing to ensure a will was properly attested. See also *Re Field's Goods* (1843) 3 Curt 752; 163 ER 890, although note *Hindmarch v. Charlton* (1861) 8 HL Cas 160 and *Re Holtam, Gillett v. Rogers* (1913) 108 LT 732.

57 *Taylor v. Denning*, 3 Nev. & P. 228, where the illness of the testator made it difficult to write. In the 1929 New York case of *In the Matter of the Estate of Stegman*, 133 Misc. 745, 234 N.Y.S. 239, probate was denied where a testator, who was able to write, subscribed a third will with a mark. The proponent failed to prove the third and final will was valid. Evans S indicated, at 747 'This manner of execution is not rare but it is unusual, for a person to sign by a mark that is able to write. This fact in itself does not invalidate a will but it is obvious that it calls for greater scrutiny on the part of the court'. For a contrary decision in Wisconsin in 1925, see *In re Mueller's Will*, 188 Wis. 183, 205 N.W. 814, 42 A.L.R. 951, where the testator made her mark, even though she could write, and where a witness added the words 'her' above, and 'mark' below the cross.

58 *Harrison v. Harrison* (1803) 8 Ves Jun 185; 32 ER 324.

59 A will was held to be sufficiently signed where a testatrix signed with a mark without her name appearing on the document in *Re Bryce's Goods* (1839) 2 Curt 325; 163 ER 427.

that the will is not valid.[60] The act itself is not invalid, but strict proof is required, as noted by Lord Watson in the case of *Donnelly v. Broughton*[61] where he pointed out, at 442, that 'the onus of proof may be increased by circumstances, such as unbounded confidence in the drawer of the will, extreme debility in the testator, clandestinely, and other circumstances which may increase the presumption even so much as to be conclusive against the instrument'.

**1.42 United States of America** In the United States of America, the case law has covered a wider range of examples where judges have been required to determine the legal implications of various forms of mark and other signs, including fingerprints and an account number. A mark on a bill has been held sufficient as a means of authentication,[62] as on deeds,[63] fingerprints,[64] on insurance documents,[65] notices of appeal,[66] under the relevant Statute of

60 *Paske v. Ollat* 2 Phill 323.

61 [1891] AC 435 PC.

62 Federal: *Zacharie v. Franklin*, 37 U.S. 151, 12 Pet. 151, 1838 WL 3945 (U.S.La.), 9 L.Ed. 1035 (the mark of Joseph Milah in a bill of sale comprising slaves, their children, and stock and household furniture had the same effect as a signature) (1838).

Indiana (1867): *Shank v. Butsch*, 28 Ind. 19, 1867 WL 2925 (Ind.).

New Hampshire: *Willoughby v. Moulton*, 47 N.H. 205, 1866 WL 1982 (N.H.) (a promissory note signed by a mark may be valid against the person signing, even though there was no subscribing witness).

New York: *Brown v. The Butchers & Drovers' Bank*, 6 Hill 443, 41 Am.Dec. 755 (a person writing '1. 2. 8.' on the back of a bill of exchange as a substitute for his name served to endorse the bill) (1844).

Tennessee: *Brown v. McClanahan*, 68 Tenn. 347, 1878 WL 4292 (Tenn.), 9 Baxt. 347, 2 Leg.Rep. 59.

South Carolina: *Zimmerman v. Sale*, 37 S.C.L. 76, 3 Rich. 76, 1846 WL 2269 (S.C.App.L.) (a mark that is not accompanied by the name of the person making the mark remains a signature) (1864).

63 Carolina (1891): *Devereux v. McMahon*, 108 N.C. 134, 12 S.E. 902, 12 L.R.A. 205.

Kentucky: *Blair v. Campbell*, 45 S.W. 93, 19 Ky.L.Rptr. 2012 (a deed signed with a mark and acknowledged before the county clerk was held to be sufficient as a signature) (1898); *Stephens v. Perkins*, 273 S.W. 545 (in the conveyance of property, the marks of nine heirs was sufficient signature on the conveyance) (1925).

Georgia: *Horton v. Murden*, 117 Ga. 72, 43 S.E. 786 (A deed signed 'I, J. R., sign my hand to it X here' is sufficiently signed) (1903).

64 Illinois: *Matter of the Estate of Deskovic*, 21 Ill.App.2d 209, 157 N.E.2d 769, 72 A.L.R.2d 1261 (1st Dist. 1959).

New York (1937): *In the Matter of the Estate of Romaniw*, 163 Misc. 481, 296 N.Y.S. 925.

65 Georgia: *Thurmond v. Spoon*, 125 Ga.App. 811, 189 S.E.2d 92 (a mark affixed to a beneficiary card is a sufficient signature) (1972). Dissenting, Evans J articulated the view that the name of the person must be affixed to the document as well as a mark.

Pennsylvania: *Tomilio v. Pisco*, 123 Pa. Super. 423, 187 A. 86 (it is a signature where the person signing is too weak to sign their name, but makes an undecipherable series of curves and strokes) (1936).

66 North Carolina: *State v. Byrd*, 93 N.C. 624, 1885 WL 1753 (N.C.).

Wisconsin: *Finley v. Prescott*, 47 L.R.A. 695, 104 Wis. 614, 80 N.W. 930 (appeal papers

Frauds (including a trade mark),[67] with respect to trover and conversion[68] and wills.[69]

## *Illegible writing*

**1.43** It is rare for illegible writing to be the subject of legal proceedings, although in 1862 the surname on a notice of objection was disputed because it was not legible.[70] The appeal court reversed the decision of the revising barrister, and held the notice of objection was sufficient. Earle CJ observed, at 39:

---

may be signed by a mark, and there is no statutory requirement to have the signature of a person in the form of a mark witnessed) (1899).

67 Federal: *Bibb v. Allen*, 149 U.S. 481, 13 S.Ct. 950, 37 L.Ed. 819, 50 L.R.A. 240 (telegrams containing orders in the form of Shepperton's Code, and directed the sales delivery for account of designated names, such as 'Albert,' 'Alfred,' 'Alexander,' 'Amanda,' 'Andrew,' 'Winston,' were intended and understood to represent the firm name of B. S. Bibb & Co., held to be sufficient as a signature) (1893); Federal 4th circuit: *Barber & Ross Co., v. Lifetime Doors, Inc.*, 810 F.2d 1276 (4th Cir. 1987), 3 U.C.C. Rep.Serv.2d (CBC) 41 (trademark printed on a written sales brochure met the requirements of the Statute of Frauds and signature requirement).

Missouri: *Defur v. Westinghouse Electric Corporation*, 677 F.Supp. 622 (E.D.Mo. 1988) (writings with the defendant's trademark printed on them constituted signed writings).

68 Massachusetts: *Foye v. Patch*, 132 Mass. 105, 1882 WL 10891 (Mass.) (adding a mark to a written agreement is a satisfactory signature).

69 Illinois: *Cunningham v. Hallyburton*, 342 Ill. 442, 174 N.E. 420 (1930); *In re Westerman's Will*, 401 Ill. 489, 82 N.E.2d 474 (1948) (the will of Minnie Westerman (her maiden name) dated 13 April 1942 revoked an earlier will dated 9 April 1942 and executed under her married name of Wilhelmina Frederichs, when both wills were signed with her mark, notwithstanding she was not authorized to resume her maiden name in her second divorce proceedings).

New York: 1809 case of *Jackson v. Van Dusen*, 5 Johns 144; 1847 case of *Butler v. Benson*, 1 Barb. 533; *Jackson v. Jackson*, 39 N.Y. 153, 12 Tiffany 153, 1868 WL 6249 (N.Y.) (after trying for some time to apply the pen to the paper to sign his name, the hand of the deceased trembled so much that he made a cross on his will); *In the Matter of the Estate of Galvin*, 78 Misc.2d 22, 355 N.Y.2d 751 (a mark added to a will by the daughter and at the request of the deceased was a valid signature of the deceased) (1974).

Pennsylvania: *Main v. Ryder*, 84 Pa. 217, 4 W.N.C. 173, 1877 WL 13243 (Pa.) (signing a will with a mark while touching the writing instrument held and controlled by another person) (1877). Note: in Pennsylvania, a new Act was enacted in 1833, requiring the manuscript signature of a testator, and a mark was no longer permitted, for which see *Assay v. Hoover*, 5 Pa. St. 21 (1846); *Grabill v. Barr*, 5 Pa. 441, 5 Barr. 441, 1846 WL 5049 (Pa.), 47 Am.Dec. 418; but see *Long v. Zook*, 13 Pa. 400, 1850 WL 5764 (Pa.), 1 Harris 400 where Gibson CJ, in applying the revised Act of 1848, commented that the 1833 Act probably defeated more true wills than false ones; also note the comments of Gibson CJ in the earlier case of *Greenough v. Greenough*, 11 Pa.St. 497, 1849 WL 5732 (Pa.).

Texas: 1934 case of *Short v. Short*, 67 S.W.2d 425; 1937 case of *Mortgage Bond Corporation v. Haney*, 105 S.W.2d 488.

Wisconsin: *Will of Susan Jenkins*, 43 Wis. 610, 1878 WL 3217 (Wis.).

70 *Trotter v. Walker* 13 C.B. (N.S.) 29; 143 ER 12.

> Lastly, it is one thing to say that the statute enjoins a legible signature, and another thing to say that such legibility is a condition precedent to the validity of the notice. Were we to hold this notice bad, questions would arise on the notice or claim of every man who might have written his name very badly or spelt it incorrectly. The object of the act of parliament, which calls to its aid persons of very imperfect education, might be defeated by adopting a rigorous construction, and furthered by a more benignant one.

**1.44** In Scotland, an illegible signature by the testator on a codicil was accepted as a signature in *Stirling Stuart v. Stirling Crawfurd's Trustees.*[71] In this case, Mr Crawfurd was not able write, even his own name, without becoming affected with a tremor, which meant that his writing was shaky and irregular. The Lord President made an interesting observation at 625 and 626 on the issue of illegible writing:

> ... it is said that if you examine this particular signature without reference to any other signature of the testator, it is utterly illegible, and that the Court is not entitled to give effect to an illegible signature. That proposition is stated a great deal too broadly. Illegible signatures are not uncommon even when the writer is not suffering from the infirmity under which Mr Crawfurd suffered, but from other infirmities altogether. The infirmity of affectation is perhaps, of all others, most productive of illegible signatures. Many persons of the highest ability and skill in penmanship sign in such a manner that it is impossible for anyone seeing their signatures for the first time to say what is meant by them. Now, are all those illegible signatures to be disregarded? I think that a very dangerous doctrine, and I am not prepared to accede to it. Does it then make any difference if the illegibility arises from an infirmity such as Mr Crawfurd suffered from? I think not. If it is clear that this is written by him, and if it is made out that that is the kind of writing by which he was in the habit of representing his name in deeds, how does the case differ from illegibility arising from other causes? You require evidence in both instances to enable you to say what the writing is; here you require someone to tell you that what is written stands for "William Stuart Stirling Crawfurd," while in the other cases I have referred to you require to be instructed that that is the ordinary way in which the writer signs his name.

**1.45** In Ireland, two scrawls that were undecipherable but intended to be initials were accepted as a mark under the Wills Act 1837,[72] and in Canada, it was held that a manuscript signature of a Justice of the Peace does not render the

71 (1885) 12 R. 610.

72 *In the Goods of Kieran*, deceased [1933] IR 222.

information invalid if it is not legible, because of the presumption of regularity.[73] In the United States, judges have also been required to consider illegible scrawl,[74] and the 1890 Pennsylvanian case of *Appeal of Knox*,[75] it was held that a note written by the deceased and signed with her first name 'Harriet' was a signature. Mitchell J remarked, at 1023, that 'Custom controls the rule of names, and so it does the rule of signature'. He went on to note, in relation to the difficulty in reading a signature:

> So the form which a man customarily uses to identify and bind himself in writing is his signature, whatever shape he may choose to give it. There is no requirement that it shall be legible, though legibility is one of the prime objects of writing. It is sufficient if it be such as he usually signs, and the signatures of neither Rufus Choate nor General Spinner could be rejected, though no man, unaided, could discover what the ragged marks made by either of those two eminent personages were intended to represent. Nor is there any fixed requirement how much of the full name shall be written. Custom varies with time and place, and habit with the whim of the individual. Sovereigns write only their first names, and the sovereign of Spain, more royally still, signs his decrees only, 'I, the King,' (Yo el Rey). English peers now sign their titles only, though they be geographical names, like Devon or Stafford, as broad as a county. The great Bacon wrote his name 'Fr. Verulam,' and the ordinary signature of the poet-philosopher of fishermen was 'Iz: Wa'. In the fifty-six signatures to the most solemn instrument of modern times, the Declaration of Independence, we find every variety from Th. Jefferson to the unmistakably identified Charles Carroll, of Carrollton. In the present day it is not uncommon for business men to have a signature for checks and banking purposes somewhat different from that used in their ordinary business, and, in familiar correspondence, signature by initials or nickname or diminutive is probably the general practice.[76]

**1.46** In South Africa, Murray J concluded in the case of *Van Niekerk v. Smit*[77] that a letter on headed notepaper with the name and address of the firm was

73 *R v. Kapoor* 52 C.C.C. (3d) 41.

74 Alabama: *Dew v. Garner*, 7 Port. 503, 1838 WL 1335 (Ala.); Mississippi (1896): *Sheehan v. Kearney*, 82 Miss. 688, 21 So. 41, 35 L.R.A. 102; Pennsylvania (1936): *Tomilio v. Pisco*, 123 Pa. Super. 423, 187 A. 86; Wyoming (1929): *In re Iverson's Estate*, 39 Wyo. 482, 273 P. 684, 64 A.L.R. 203.

75 131 P. 220, 18 A. 1021, 6 L.R.A. 353, 17 Am.St.Rep. 798.

76 Note his comments at 1022 about *Vernon v. Kirk*, 30 Pa.St. 222; *Assay v. Hoover*, 5 Pa. St. 21 and *Grabill v. Barr*, 5 Pa. 441, 5 Barr. 441, 1846 WL 5049 (Pa.), 47 Am.Dec. 418 and the subsequent change of the law.

77 1952 (3) SA 17 (T).

properly signed, even though indecipherable marks were made with a lead pencil, perhaps representing initials, over the concluding words in type 'Ferreira en van Zyl'. In *SAI Investments v. Vander Schyff NO*[78] it was held that extrinsic evidence was admissible to indicate the identity of an illegible signature on the agreement where the signature of the person signing as purchaser on the last page was indecipherable, as were the names of the two witnesses who attested to the signature. A similar finding was made on appeal in the case of *Van der Merwe v. Kenkes (Edms) BPK*,[79] where the appellant was clearly identified in an agreement as the purchaser, but the signatures of both the purchaser and the seller were illegible. Extrinsic evidence to indicate that the illegible signature was that of the appellant or her husband was admissible.

## *Assisted signature or mark*

**1.47** The problems associated with people that are too ill or too weak to sign a document are well illustrated in the South African case of *Matanda v. Rex*,[80] where a boy of thirteen could not write. He made a statement to a magistrate, described at 436:

> My practice, which we adopted in this case, is for the witness to come up to me, I hand the pen to him, he touches the pen and then I make the mark for him. I hold one end of the pen and he holds the other, after he is told to what he is deposing. He is not actually holding the pen at one end while I am making the mark. I hand him the pen, holding it myself. He fingers it. Then I take it and I make the mark. That is what happened in this case.

**1.48** A similar point was discussed in *Fulton v. Kee*,[81] where the members of the court of appeal distinguished between a will signed by the testator with assistance or by direction. In the 1975 New York case of *In re Estate of McCready*[82] and the 1927 Pennsylvania case of *Brehony v. Brehony*,[83] the mark of a person who was blind that was made with the assistance of another was considered a signature.

**1.49** **Wills** Where a person is too ill to sign a document, one question might be whether there is any evidence to demonstrate the person intended to sign. In the case of *Wilson v. Beddard*,[84] the testator made a will dated 7 September 1826

78 1999 (3) SA 340 (N).

79 1983 (3) SA 909 (T).

80 1923 AD 435 (B).

81 [1961] NI 1, CA (NI).

82 369 N.Y.S.2d 325, 82 Misc.2d 531.

83 289 Pa. 267, 137 A. 260.

84 (1841) 12 Sim 28; 59 ER 1041.

and died the following day. The will was signed by the testator's mark, his hand being guided by another person. Before making the mark, the testator made faint strokes on each of the sheets containing the will. On the motion for a new trial, the Vice-Chancellor, Sir L. Shadwell, agreed with the trial judge, Parke B, that the will was signed by the testator. It was decided that the act of making the faint strokes provided evidence that the testator intended to sign the will, and the fact that he was helped by another person to place his mark on the document did not make the mark any less of a signature.

### *A name without a signature*

**1.50** There are occasions when a person makes a promise that they later refuse to fulfil for some reason. Such was the case in *Knight v. Crockford*,[85] where Crockford agreed to sell a public house to one Knight. Given the evidence in this case, Eyre CJ determined that the draft agreement was a sufficient agreement, and although only Knight had affixed his signature to the document, the words 'I, James Crockford, agree to sell, &c' written by Crockford were considered a signature within the meaning of the Statute of Frauds 1677.

### *Mistake as to the name*

**1.51** **Wills** Sometime humans make mistakes, and in circumstances where the better response is to render an equitable result, judges have, on occasion, disregarded minor issues in respect to wills. For instance, in *Re Clarke's Goods*[86] the testatrix was described as 'Susannah Clarke', and executed the will with a mark, against which was written 'Susannah Barrell, her mark', Barrell having been her maiden name. Sir C. Cresswell was satisfied that the mark was that of Susannah Clarke, and thought the additional words next to the mark did not matter.[87]

### *Variations of a name*

**1.52** **Voting** Administrative mistakes tend not to be considered an adequate reason for preventing people from casting their vote. In *R v. Thwaites*[88] the names of a number of men entitled to vote were listed on the burgess roll incorrectly. When they voted, they signed the voting papers with their correct names. It was held that the men had a right to vote, and although they voted with different

85 1 Esp 190; 170 ER 324; the insertion of names into a document that the parties intend to sign is not signed: *Hubert v. Treherne* 3 Man. & G. 743, 133 ER 1338.

86 (1858) LJR 27 NS P & M 18; 1 Sw & Tr 22; 164 ER 611.

87 *Re Douce's Goods* (1862) 2 Sw & Tr 592; 164 ER 1127 where the deceased was mistakenly described as John Douce, but his name was actually Thomas Douce.

88 22 LJQB 238.

names in comparison to the names listed on roll, they were the men mentioned in the burgess roll and this was a mere case of misnomer within the provisions of s142 of the Municipal Corporation Act of 5 & 6 Will. 4 c76 1853.

**1.53 Wills** There are times when some people will adopt alternative names for a variety of reasons. For instance, they may forget to write their present name, as in the case of *In the Goods of Glover*,[89] where a woman signed her will with the name of her first husband, 'Susan Reeve' and then placed the will into an envelope marked by her 'The will of Susan Glover'. Alternatively, a person might use a substitute name.[90] In Scotland, a letter written and sent from one sister to another was capable of constituting a holographic will, and the subscription of her Christian name 'Connie' was also a sufficient authentication.[91]

**1.54 United States of America** A range of variations of a name have been tested in the US courts, including the use of a fictitious name on deeds,[92] and using the name of another without permission on a promissory note.[93] More commonly, mistaken or partial names have appeared in matters relating to a lien,[94] the Statute of Frauds,[95] mortgages,[96] the name of a partnership on an

89 11 Jur. 1022, 5 Notes of Cases 553.

90 *Re Reddings Goods* (1850) 14 Jur 1052; 2 Rob Ecc 338; 163 ER 1338. The two law reports differ whether the testatrix signed her first name with the initial 'C' or 'Charlotte'.

91 *Draper v. Thomason* 1954 SC 136, 1954 SLT 222.

92 Arkansas (1947): *Walker v. Emrich*, 212 Ark. 598, 206 S.W.2d 769.

New York: *David v. Williamsburgh City Fire Insurance Company*, 83 N.Y. 265, 38 Sickels 265, 1880 WL 12653 (N.Y.), 38 Am.Rep. 418 (where a person adopts a fictitious name with intent to covey title, he is bound by the name he adopts when executing a conveyance of the property).

93 New Hampshire: *Grafton Bank v. Flanders*, 4 N.H. 239, 1827 WL 744 (N.H.) (a person putting the name of another on a promissory note without authority from any person of that name is liable for the note).

94 Federal 2nd circuit: *In the Matter of Excel Stores, Inc.*, 341 F.2d 961 (1965) (the name 'Excel Department Stores' instead of the correct name 'Excel Stores, Inc' was a minor error and not seriously misleading when the contract was properly signed by an appropriate officer of the company).

95 Massachusetts: *Fessenden v. Mussey*, 65 Mass. 127, 1853 WL 4969 (Mass.) (the name 'Benj. Mussey' as recorded at the time of the auction held to be a signature, even though it omitted the middle letter of the defendant's name); *Walker v. Walker*, 175 Mass. 349, 56 N.E. 601 (a marriage contract was deemed to be signed where the defendant signed the document with her first name only) (1900).

Missouri: *Great Western Printing Co. v. Belcher*, 127 Mo.App. 133, 104 S.W. 894 (the words 'Guaranteed. Belcher' written in lead pencil across the face of the original account is a signature, even though the signature did not include the first name) (1907).

96 California: *Middleton v. Findla*, 25 Cal. 76, 1864 WL 629 (Cal.) (a grantor that signs a deed by a wrong name (Edmund Jones) with his correct name in the body of the deed (Edward Jones) does not invalidate the conveyance).

Indiana: *Zann v. Haller*, 71 Ind. 136, 1880 WL 6236 (Ind.), 23 Am.Rep. 193 (a woman signing a mortgage deed with her first name only, accepted as a signature).

arbitration bond[97] and on a writ,[98] and it is not surprising that the range of human behaviour is more widely reflected in the cases of wills,[99] although the liberal approach in extending the meaning of a signature was not extended to the 1914 Pennsylvanian case of *In re Brennan's Estate*,[100] where a testamentary paper ending with 'your miserable father' was held not to have been executed correctly.

## *The use of initials*

**1.55 Statute of Frauds** The use of initials has been held sufficient to be a mark or signature to indicate the intent of a party under the provisions of the Statute of Frauds, as in the case of *Phillimore v. Barry*.[101] Messrs Fector and Minet of Dover stored a quantity of rum, the cargo of a Danish prize, which was to be sold by auction in various lots on 28 April 1808. Before the day of the sale, the defendants wrote to Fector and Minet to buy thirteen puncheons of the rum. As a result, Mr John Minet Fector of the firm bid for several lots, which were duly knocked down to him. The auctioneer wrote down in the printed catalogue the initials 'I.M.F.' opposite each lot sold to the defendant. On 11 May 1808, the defendants subsequently wrote a letter to Fector and Minet, recognising and approving the purchase. The warehouse accidentally caught fire on 18 May 1808, and a quantity of gunpowder stored in the building exploded (that is, it burnt rapidly at a subsonic speed), destroying the rum. There was no evidence that the deposit was paid. The defendants claimed the contract was void under the Statute of Frauds on the basis that there was no memorandum in writing. It was also submitted that the auctioneer was not the authorized agent of the defendants, and even if he were, the inclusion of the initials against each lot could not be considered a memorandum of agreement. It was also contended that the rum remained at the risk of the sellers for thirty days, and the property did not vest with the defendant. Lord Ellenborough held that Mr Minet was the agent to the defendants, and that his initials as written by the auctioneer in the catalogue, together with the defendant's letter confirming the sale, constituted a sufficient memorandum in writing to satisfy the Statute of Frauds. He also held that the property vested absolutely in the purchasers from the moment of sale, and the provision of storage for thirty days was part of the consideration for which the purchase money was to be paid. While the finding by Lord Ellenborough was not

97 New York: *Mackay v. J. and L. Bloodgood*, 9 Johns. 285 (the affixing of the name and seal of a firm by one partner binds the other partner) (1812).

98 Maine: *Sawtelle v. Wardwell*, 56 Me. 146, 1868 WL 1770 (Me.) (the surname of attorney on the back of a writ of endorsement is a sufficient signature), although note the dissenting judgment of Kent J.

99 Kentucky: *Wells v. Lewis*, 190 Ky. 626, 228 S.W. 3 (the signature 'Ant Nanie' appended to a letter as a testamentary writing is a sufficient signature) (1921).

100 91 A. 220, 244 Pa. 574.

101 1 Camp 512; 170 ER 1040.

relevant to whether the initials represented a signature, nevertheless they were considered part of the evidence to demonstrate a contract existed between the parties.

**1.56** In *Chichester v. Cobb*,[102] the defendant wrote a letter to Mary Ann Williams, as follows:

> Kensington, 21st July 1865
>
> My dear M. A. – So soon as all pecuniary and necessary arrangements are made to constitute an unquestionable legal marriage as proposed, I will be prepared to pay over for your behalf 300*l.*, and concur in every practicable measure by which an equitable share, or its equivalent, in the settled property can be assured to you. I shall expect to see Edward here this evening, as requested in my note to him of last evening. – Yours ever affectionately, E.C.

**1.57** After the marriage, the defendant refused to pay the £300. Blackburn and Shee JJ in the Queen's Bench agreed that the initials constituted a sufficient signing of the contract or memorandum to satisfy the Statute of Frauds.

**1.58** **Judicial use** There is a case where a judge in England and Wales signed a bill of indictment with his initials. In *R v. Morais*,[103] a bill of indictment was signed in manuscript 'Cor. The Honourable Mr. Justice Roch' and underneath, in the judge's handwriting, the words 'Leave to prefer' and his initials, 'J. R.', with the date '23.9.87' and the words 'A Justice of the High Court'. This form of signature was held not to be a signature by Lord Lane, CJ in the Court of Appeal. A new trial was ordered.[104] Judicial officers in the United States have used initials, although the decisions do not always indicate approval of the use of initials in the absence of a full signature.[105] In the 1933 Federal case of *George A. Ohl & Co., v. A. L. Smith Iron Works*,[106] the use of a judge's initials followed by 'D. J.' was held as a signature authenticating a bill of exceptions, and the initials 'D. J.' were added for the purpose of indicating his judicial office. Hughes CJ commented on the use of initials at 176–77:

102 (1866) 14 L.T.N.S. 433.

103 [1988] 3 All ER 161, CA.

104 Surprisingly, no case law on signatures appeared to have been cited or referred to in the appeal, which is particularly interesting, bearing in mind the comments by Buxton and Brooke LJJ in *Copeland v. Smith* [2000] 1 WLR 1371.

105 Federal: *Origet v. United States*, 125 U.S. 240, 8 S.Ct. 846, 31 L.Ed. 743 (the initials 'A.B.' held not to be a signature of the judge, nor sufficient authentication of a bill of exceptions) (1888); *Kinney v. United States Fidelity & Guaranty Company*, 222 U.S. 283, 32 S.Ct. 101, 56 L.Ed. 200 (a paper in the record styled 'Exceptions to the Charge to the Jury' upon which the initials 'J. P. McP., Trial Judge' are placed is not a bill of exceptions) (1911).

Kentucky: *Wurts v. Newsome*, 253 Ky. 38, 68 S.W.2d 448 (there was no signature where a judge signed a ballot with his surname and initial, or with his initials) (1934).

106 288 U.S. 170, 53 S.Ct. 340, 77 L.Ed. 681.

> Signature by initials has been held to be sufficient under the Statute of Frauds and the Statute of Wills, and in other transactions. It has been held in some states that a different rule obtains in the case of the official signature of certain judicial officers, but the Congress has not established such a rule for the judges of the federal courts. Nor, in the absence of special statutory requirement, is there a uniform custom in relation to official signatures. It may be assumed that a requirement of the officer's signature, without more, means that he shall write his name or his distinctive appellation; but the question remains as to what writing of that character is to be deemed sufficient for the purpose of authenticating his official act. There is no rule that he shall adhere to the precise form of his name as it appears in his commission. The full name of the officer may or may not be used. Not infrequently Christian names are omitted, in part or altogether, or are abbreviated or indicated by initials. In some of the most important communications on behalf of the federal government, only the surname of the officer is used. When an officer authenticates his official act by affixing his initials he does not entirely omit to use his name; he simply abbreviates it; he uses a combination of letters which are part of it. Undoubtedly that method is informal, but we think that it is clearly a method of 'signing'. It cannot be said in such a case that he has utterly failed to 'sign,' so that his authentication of his official act, in the absence of further statutory requirement, is to be regarded as absolutely void.

**1.59** The cases of *Origet v. United States*[107] and *Kinney v. United States Fidelity & Guaranty Company*[108] were neither cited nor referred to as being overruled, although the comments by Hughes CJ appear to indicate that initials are acceptable. The initials of a judge on a judgment were held to be sufficient in the Illinois case of *Robertson v. Robertson*,[109] and in the 1905 Nebraska case of *Griffith v. Bonawitz*,[110] the initials of two judges, written on the back of a number of ballots, were also held to be signatures.

**1.60 Wills** Initials have been used in wills, as in the case of *Re Savory's Goods*,[111] where the testatrix executed the will by writing her initials in the presence of two witnesses who duly attested. See also *In the Goods of Clark*[112] where the deceased, who was too ill to sign his will, requested his wife to sign for him, which she

107 125 U.S. 240, 8 S.Ct. 846, 31 L.Ed. 743.

108 222 U.S. 283, 32 S.Ct. 101, 56 L.Ed. 200.

109 462 N.E.2d 712 (Ill.App. 5 Dist. 1984).

110 73 Neb. 622, 103 N.W. 327.

111 15 Jur 1042.

112 2 Curt. 329, 163 ER 428.

did, with her mark. This was a sufficient compliance with the Act, although the executrix lost a legacy that was granted to her under the terms of the will. In the case of *In the Goods of Christian*,[113] H. H. Christian, a rear admiral in the Royal Navy, left a will that included the signature of a witness in the form of initials, which was also a sufficient subscription. For a line of cases in England with respect to wills, see *Re Blewitt's Goods*,[114] and in Scotland, initials were considered a form of signature in *Speirs v. Speirs or Home Speirs*.[115]

**1.61** In South Africa, a will signed with initials was signed in the case of *In re Trollip*,[116] in which the decision in *Van Vuuren v. Van Vuuren*[117] was overruled, and the decision in the case of *In re Ebden's Will*[118] approved. De Villiers CJ observed, at 245, that 'If a mark is a sufficient signature, *a fortiori* initials must be sufficient'. A modern example of a will in which initials were accepted as sufficient evidence of a signature is that of the Canadian case of *Re Schultz*.[119]

**1.62** **Rights in property** In respect of rights in property, the initials of a landlord in a rent book served to renew a lease and enable an option to buy to be exercised,[120] and directors adding their initials to a clause providing a guarantee in a contract were bound by the guarantee under the provisions of s2 of the Contracts Enforcement Act 1956 in the New Zealand case of *Doughty-Pratt Group Limited v. Perry Castle*.[121] Although it was accepted that initials can be considered a signature in *Newell v. Tarrant*,[122] in the particular circumstances of the case, the initials in question did not amount to an execution and authentication to create an equitable charge over Chase Farm, and the initials also failed to comply with the strict requirements of s2(3) of the Law of Property (Miscellaneous Provisions) Act 1989.

**1.63** **Voting** In the 19th century voting papers had to be signed with the name of the burgess voting under the provisions of s32 of the Municipal Corporation Act of 5 & 6 Will. 4 c76. In 1852, in the case of *R v. Avery*,[123] it was held that a person can sign as they ordinarily write their signature, such as, in this instance, the surname and initial of the Christian name.

113 2 Rob. Ecc. 110, 163 ER 1260.

114 (1879–81) 5 PD 116.

115 (1879) 6 R. 1359.

116 1895 12 SC 243.

117 2 Searle 116.

118 4 Juta 495.

119 (1984) 8 DLR (4th) 147.

120 *Hill v. Hill* [1947] 1 Ch 231.

121 [1995] 2 NZLR 398 (CA).

122 [2004] EWHC 772 (Ch), 2004 WL 741782.

123 21 LJQB 430.

**1.64 United States of America** In the United States of America, decisions relating to the use of initials covers a range of situations, including bills,[124] cheques (checks),[125] the Statute of Frauds,[126] trusts[127] and wills,[128] although the evidence does not always indicate the initials served as a means of authentication, as in the 1945 Wisconsin case of *North American Seed Co., v. Cedarburg Supply Co.*,[129] where the initials 'H. Z.' for Harvey Zirtzlaff were placed in such an odd position, that it was determined they did not serve as a signature in accordance with s207 of the Restatement of Contracts. Attempts are made on occasions to retrieve a small scintilla of hope from an otherwise impossible position, which is what was attempted in the federal eighth circuit case of *Vess Beverages, Inc., v.*

124 New York (1845): *Palmer v. Stevens*, 1 Denio 471.

125 New York: *The Merchants' Bank v. Spicer*, 6 Wend. 443 (the initials of the defendant on a check held to be a sufficient endorsement) (1831).

126 Federal: *The Salmon Falls Manufacturing Company v. Goddard*, 55 U.S. 446, 14 How. 446, 1852 WL 6760 (U.S.Mass.), 14 L.Ed. 493 (the initials 'R.M.M.' and 'W.W.G.' were sufficient to be signatures) (1852); Federal 5th Circuit: *Jones v. Fox Film Corporation*, 68 F.2d 116 (the initials 'J.T.J.' for John T. Jones held to be a signature) (1934); Federal 7th Circuit: *Monetti, S.P.A. v. Anchor Hocking Corporation*, 931 F.2d 1178 (7th Cir. 1991) (the initials 'SS/mh' typed by a secretary held to be the signature of Steve Schneider, who dictated the letter to the secretary).

Iowa: *Burns v. Burrows*, 196 N.W. 62 (the initials 'R.A.S.' held to be a signature of R. A. Santee) (1923).

Massachusetts: *Irving v. Goodimate*, Co., 320 Mass. 454, 70 N.E.2d 414, 171 A.L.R. 326 (the initials 'RL/s' of the president of the company were typed at the bottom of a letter); *Sanborn v. Flagler*, 9 Allen 474, 91 Mass. 474, 1864 WL 3510 (Mass.) (initials of both parties, 'J.H.F.' and 'J.B.R.' were signatures) (1946).

Michigan: *Archbold v. Industrial Land Co.*, 264 Mich. 289, 249 N.W. 858 (an instrument signed 'Approved: J.S.L.'. and 'O.K. with me: O.T.B.' and 'O.K. with me: O.T.M.' held to be signed by O. G. Bowker and J. S. Lille, respectively president and vice-president of the Industrial Land company, and O. T. Morse, vice-president of the American Blower Corporation) (1933); *Borkowski v. Kolodziejski*, 332 Mich. 589, 52 N.W.2d 348 (defendant signed his name with the initials 'L.S.' after it) (1952).

Missouri: *Kamada, M.D. v. RX Group Limited*, 639 S.W.2d 146, (Mo.App. 1982) (initials on a lease sufficient).

New Jersey: *Smith v. Howell*, 11 N.J.Eq. 349, 1857 WL 4462 (N.J.Ch.), 3 Stockt. 349 (the initials of Walter Kirkpatrick used by him as his signature to form a trust) (1857); *Crabtree v. Elizabeth Arden Sales Corporation*, 305 N.Y. 48, 110 N.E.2d 551 (the initials of Robert P. Johns, executive vice-president and general manger subscribed to a payroll card, is a signature for the purposes of establishing an employment contract) (1953).

Washington: *Degginger v. Martin*, 48 Wash. 1, 92 P. 674 (the initials of an agent added by him in his own hand underneath his typewritten name, contract held to be sufficiently executed) (1907).

127 California: *Weiner v. Mullaney*, 59 Cal.App.2d 620, 140 P.2d 704 (the initials of George J Mullaney typed at the end of several letters to his sister comprised a signature sufficiently signed in the formation of a trust) (1943).

128 Virginia: *Pilcher v. Pilcher*, 117 Va. 356, 84 S.E. 667, L.R.A. 1915D 902 (a will written by the testator 'I give to my wife, Alice McCabe Pilcher, all of my property, real and personal. E.M.P.' held to be sufficiently signed) (1915).

129 247 Wis. 31, 18 N.W.2d 466, 159 A.L.R. 250.

*The Paddington Corporation*,[130] where the initials of those attending a meeting that were added by the person who took a note of the meeting did not constitute individual signatures, and thus did not qualify as a means of authentication.

## *The use of a surname*

**1.65 Statute of Frauds** People use many variations of their name when signing a document, and the use of first name or family name is not unusual. In the context of the Statute of Frauds, the question about what could be construed as a signature was argued before Lord Denham CJ and Patteson, Coleridge and Wrightman JJ in the case of *Lobb and Knight v. Stanley* in 1844.[131] Interestingly, the comments made both by counsel and Patteson J in this case seem to imply that contemporaries would have preferred to reverse the liberal approach relating to the meaning of a signature. However, the authorities were too well established to be reviewed or ignored. In this instance, one Stanley, a certified bankrupt, gave a written promise signed by him after his bankruptcy. Three undated letters were produced, one of which read:

> Mr Stanley begs to inform Mr Lobb that he will be glad to give him a promissory note or bill for the amount of Mr Stanley's account, payable at three months, as Mr Stanley has of late been put to heavy expenses, and hopes this arrangement will be satisfactory to Mr Lobb. 3 Crescent. Thursday morning.

**1.66** At the trial before Lord Denman CJ, a verdict was found for Lobb, and leave was given to appeal. Whately, counsel for Stanley, submitted that all the previous decisions relating to what was meant to be a signature were not correct. He argued: 'Those decisions, however, are scarcely to be defended on principle; and, if the question were new, probably a different doctrine would be adopted'.[132] This view was noted and commented upon by Patteson J:

> It is true that the word 'signed' occurs in the statute: and, if this had been the first time that we were called upon to put a construction on that word, and if the decisions on the Statute of Frauds had not occurred, I should perhaps be slow to say that this was a signature.[133]

**1.67** Lord Denham CJ agreed, that in one sense the letters were not signed. However, he then considered the intrinsic evidence of the documents, and pointed out that

130 941 F.2d 651 (8th Cir. 1991).

131 (1844) 5 QB 574; 114 ER 1366; *Law Times*, 2 (1843–4), p. 366.

132 (1844) 5 QB 574 at 579.

133 (1844) 5 QB 574 at 582.

> ... it is a signature of the party when he authenticates the instrument by writing his name in the body. Here, it is true, the whole name is not written, but only 'Mr Stanley'. I think more is not necessary.[134]

**1.68** Coleridge J reinforced the significance of the mechanism by which the document was authenticated, when he pointed out that:

> Is it not enough if a party, at the beginning of a document, writes his name so as to govern what follows? Does he not then use his name as a signature?[135]

**1.69** It was unanimously agreed that Stanley signed the documents. Stanley wrote the letters himself. He identified himself by surname in the body of the letters. By identifying himself in this way, he demonstrated his intention that the recipient should rely on the promise contained in the letter. The signature was, in effect, his assertion, by writing his surname within the text of the message, that the contents of the letters are to be acted upon by the recipient.

**1.70** A note written in the third person was accepted as a signature in the 1811 case of *Morrison v. Turnour*,[136] as was an unsigned statement that began 'Mr Wilmot Parker has agreed,' in an action for specific performance in respect of a contract for the purchase of a leasehold house.[137]

**1.71** **Deeds** In Scotland, Lord Dervaird held that a deed executed by the subscription of the granter's surname alone is not of itself improbative or invalid in the case of *American Express Europe Ltd v. Royal Bank of Scotland plc*,[138] following the decision in *Gordon v. Murray*,[139] where it was upheld that the subscription to an assignation, being 'Fullerton of that Ilk' without a Christian name, was valid. The case of *Traquair (Earl of) v. Janet Gibson*[140] in which the use of initials was used, was also canvassed. For the modern position in Scotland, see s7(2) of the Requirements of Writing (Scotland) Act 1995.

## *The use of a trade name*

**1.72** The use of a trade name by a party may be sufficient to indicate an intention to enter into a contract, as in the case of *Johnson v. Dogson*,[141] where an agent for the plaintiff signed a memorandum retained by the defendant

134 (1844) 5 QB 574 at 581.

135 (1844) 5 QB 574 at 582.

136 18 Ves. 175, 34 ER 1204; 18 Ves. Jun. 175, 34 ER 284.

137 *Propert v. Parker* [1830] 1 Russ & M 625; 39 ER 240.

138 1989 SCLR 333, 1989 SLT 650, OH.

139 (1765) Mor. 16818.

140 (1724) Mor. 16809.

141 (1837) 6 LJ Ex 185; 1 Jur 739; 2 M & W 653; Murp & H 271, 150 ER 918.

'for' Johnson, Johnson & Co. In *Cohen v. Roche*,[142] the printed name of the firm on the front page of the auction catalogue was held to constitute a signature by Mr Roche. In reaching his judgment in this case, McCardie J considered that the insertion of the name in the catalogue served to authenticate the catalogue, and this authentication was reinforced 'in that the defendant himself wrote down in his auctioneer's book the price realized by lot 145, and also entered the names of the purchasers'.[143] However, the mere insertion of the name of the seller in a memorandum where the sale of the property was subject to the approval of the seller, even where the buyer signed the document with his mark, does not indicate the authentication of the document, and the inclusion of the name of the auctioneer on the particulars of sale only acted to announce that he would sell the premises.[144] In the 1842 New York case of *Miller v. Pelletier*,[145] the clerk to the auctioneer wrote down the name of the highest bidder for 7 Barclay Street, New York, in the sales book. The successful bidder subsequently took action to recover the deposit, because the seller claimed they had not subscribed to the contract. The Vice-Chancellor concluded that the purchaser was bound by the addition of his name to the sales book by the clerk to the auctioneer, but in the absence of the seller's name or subscription in the sales book, the contract was void, and the deposit returned to the buyer.

## *A partial signature*

**1.73 Wills** Sudden changes in life expectancy can cause a person, as they near the end of their life, to review the arrangements for the disposal of their worldly goods. On such occasions, ensuring the disposition is made in the proper form can be overtaken by the imminent demise of the testatrix. In *Re Chalcraft's Goods*,[146] as Mrs Chalcraft's life ebbed away, her doctor administered greater doses of morphia to alleviate the pain she was experiencing. She wanted to sign a codicil to her will, and took hold of a pen and wrote 'E. Chal', but never completed her name, because she died, and the signature came to an abrupt end. One of the issues before the court was whether what the deceased wrote was intended to be her signature. Willmer J found that making a decision as to whether the partial signature could be considered to be her signature within the provisions of the Wills Act 1837 to be a 'very difficult point to decide'.[147] He suggested that there must be a question of degree involved in any decision, and he interpreted the words used by the Lord Chancellor in *Hindmarch v. Charlton*[148] broadly. Taking

142 [1927] 1 KB 169.

143 [1927] 1 KB 169 at 175 and 176.

144 *Dyas v. Stafford* [1882] 9 LR Ir 520.

145 4 Edw. Ch. 102.

146 [1948] P 222, [1948] 1 All ER 700.

147 [1948] P 222 at 232.

148 (1861) 8 HL Cas 160 at 167 'I will lay down this as my notion of the law: that to make a

into account the circumstances the deceased found herself in at the end of her life, he decided that the mark she made did amount to a signature.

**1.74** In comparison, in 1892, Mitchell J concluded that there is no signature where a testator began to sign a codicil, but stopped after making a stroke of the pen resembling the first part of the first letter of his name, and said to those present 'I can't sign it now'. Given the nature of the evidence, the judge concluded that the testator did not intend the scrawl on the document to be a signature.[149] The Outer House in Scotland reached the same decision in the case of *Donald v. M'Gregor*,[150] where the matron of the hospital, at the request of the deceased, wrote a codicil on a post card. The deceased tried to sign it, but desisted after writing 'Mary T. M'Gr', adding a cross as her mark. Two witnesses appended their signatures. Lord Ashmore noted, at 105, that 'the deceased did not herself subscribe the codicil; for although she began to write her name she did not complete it, probably because she was too weak and too ill to write more than she did, and no one executed the writing for her' and went on to indicate that in Scotland, 'as regards the cross which she added – signing by a mark is not sufficient in law'. Thus neither her partial signature nor the cross acted as a signature.

## *Words other than a name*

**1.75** **Wills** Occasionally, people will not refer to each other by name, but by reference to their relationship with each other, such as between parents and children, where a child may call their parents 'mum' and 'dad', 'mater' or 'pater' or some other form of address. Equally, parents may well do the same with their children, especially when writing to them. They may not sign a letter or card with their name, but with the words 'mother' or 'father'. In the case of *Re Cook's Estate Murison v. Cook*,[151] the testatrix drew up a holograph will on two sheets of notepaper, which was duly properly attested by two competent witnesses. The document ended 'Please Leslie be kind to Dot. Your loving mother'. Leslie was her son and Dot referred to one of her daughters. The question was whether the words 'Your loving mother' constituted a signature within the meaning of the Wills Act 1837. Collingwood J, having cited various authorities, came to the conclusion that the testatrix intended the words 'Your loving mother' to identify herself as the person attesting.[152] This case illustrates the concern that judges have in establishing whether the person signing the document intended the words they used to apply to the terms of the document they signed, and in the United States,

valid subscription of a witness, there must be the name or some mark which is intended to represent the name'.

149 *In re Plate's Estate*, 148 Pa. 55, 23 A. 1038.

150 1926 S.L.T. 103.

151 [1960] 1 All ER 689.

152 The most persuasive comment to support his decision in this context was the opinion of Lord Campbell LC in *Hindmarch v. Charlton* (1861) 8 HL Cas 160 at 167.

there is a line of case law to illustrate the use of similar words and phrases,[153] although the 1940 Californian case of *Berdan v. Berdan*[154] demonstrated this liberal approach can only be taken so far. In this instance, a father wrote a letter to his son on a typewriter, and his wife added further handwritten script on the reverse of the letter: 'Dad signed this with his signature and also "Dad" below. The signature in case you might want to use it. Lawfully. Mother'. The word 'Mother' was capable of being a legally binding signature, but taken not to be because it was assumed, in the absence of any evidence, that the language illustrated that she did not believe the word 'Dad' was a legally binding signature.

## *An identifying phrase*

**1.76** In contrast to the previous examples above, the use of the phrase 'mother' was not held to be a signature in an earlier case of *Selby v. Selby*[155] where a letter addressed to the son, beginning 'My Dear Robert' and ending in the words 'Do me the justice to believe me the most affectionate of mothers', was not sufficiently signed within the meaning of the Statute of Frauds 1677. The Master of the Rolls held that it was not sufficient that a party to a document can be identified in such a way, because the Statute required the document to be signed. He rejected the proposition that where the writer of the document has been identified, it could therefore be construed that there was a signature within the meaning of

153 Arkansas (1906): *Arendt v. Arendt*, 80 Ark. 204, 96 S.W. 982 (after William Arendt shot himself, a letter addressed to his wife was discovered, including the statement 'Whatever I have in worldly goods, it is my wish that you should possess them'. At the end of the letter, he signed with a shortened version of his first name, 'Will'. Held to be a signature by the members of the jury and affirmed on appeal); *Boone v. Boone*, 114 Ark. 69, 169 S.W. 779 (testator omitted the letter 'n' in his signature in writing his first name, Emanuel, on one of the sheets of the will; this does not affect the validity) (1914); *Cartwright v. Cartwright*, 158 Ark. 278, 250 S.W. 11 (a letter sent by an American soldier killed in action on 14 October 1918 to his wife, part of which was testamentary in its effect, and signed with the abbreviation of his first name 'Lus', held to be a sufficient signature) (1923).

California: *In re Henderson's Estate*, 196 Cal. 623, 239 P. 938 ('From A Loving Mother' a sufficient signature) (1923); *In re Button's Estate*, 277 P. 758 *reversed* 287 P. 964 ('Love from Muddy' a valid signature) (1930).

Kentucky: *Word v. Whipps*, 28 S.W. 151, 16 Ky. Law Rep. 403 (in the absence of fraud or suspicious circumstances, the misspelling of a name does not affect the validity of a signature, 'A. J. Whpps' written instead of 'A. J. Whipps') (1894); *Wells v. Lewis*, 190 Ky. 626, 228 S.W. 3 ('Ant Nanie' appended to a letter as a testamentary writing is a sufficient signature) (1921).

Pennsylvania (1890): *Appeal of Knox*, 131 P. 220, 18 A. 1021, 6 L.R.A. 353, 17 Am.St. Rep. 798; *In re Kimmel's Estate*, 278 P. 435, 123 A. 405, 31 A.L.R. 678 (a testamentary letter ending with 'Father' held to be signed) (1924).

Texas: *Barnes v. Horne*, 233 S.W. 859 (a letter by the deceased to his brother considered a will, and signed at the end with the shortened version of his name 'Ed' accepted as a signature) (1921).

154 103 P.2d 622.

155 (1817) 3 Mer 2; 36 ER 1.

the Statute. Lord Skerrington also concluded, in *Pentland v. Pentland's Trustees*,[156] that a holograph codicil signed 'Yr Loving Mother,' was not signed. The basis of the objections to accepting such terms as a form of signature were set out by Interim Sheriff-Substitute Kermack in *Allan and Crichton, Petitioners*,[157] where a witness had subscribed as 'Mrs Bernard' without adhibiting her Christian name or initial, was not considered to form a signature.

**1.77** It is instructive to compare the decision of the Master of the Rolls in *Selby v. Selby* to that of the comment made by Maule J in *Morton v. Copeland*, that a 'Signature does not necessarily mean writing a person's Christian and surname, but any mark which indicates it as the act of the party'[158] and the decision by Lord Hunter in *Rhodes v. Peterson*[159] from Scotland. In this case, Mrs Dorothy Macandrew wrote a letter to her daughter in her own handwriting, and signed it 'Lots of Love. Mum'. Lord Hunter was required to determine whether the word 'Mum' was sufficient to establish the holograph will was duly signed. He noted some latitude in the law of Scotland towards the meaning of what is meant by a signature, and went on to observe, at 100(a):

> It clearly is not essential that the subscription should consist of a surname preceded by either an initial or initials or a Christian name or names, nor is it essential that the surname should appear at all or, indeed, that there should be comprised in the subscription or signature any of the Christian names or surnames written in full.

**1.78** Lord Hunter also indicated that the use of a familiar or pet name could be a valid signature provided it was proved that the writer signed their name usually in such a way. He went on to suggest, at 100(b), that the use of such a form of signature was 'as apt to signify that the writing is the completed and concluded expression of the writer's intention as a signature by initials or by abbreviated Christian name'. In particular, he considered it settled authority, that where a holograph writing consisted of a name other than the Christian name or names or initials followed by the surname of the writer, that there must be sufficient evidence to identify whatever name was used by the writer (in this case, 'Mum'), was used regularly. The form by which a person identify themselves does not necessarily affect the validity of the document, especially where a person writes a document with their own handwriting and uses a phrase as a means of identification. The facts of these cases do not appear to offer any features to distinguish them.

156 (1908) 16 S.L.T. 480.

157 1933 S.L.T. (Sh. Ct.) 2.

158 (1855) 16 C B 516 at 535. A footnote was added to this comment: 'Provided it be proved or admitted to be genuine, and be the accustomed mode of signature of the party', 139 ER 861.

159 (1972) SLT 98.

## *Abbreviation of a name*

**Solicitors Act 1974** Professional firms tend to accumulate long names over time, although the present fashion is to adopt a shortened version. Long names can be tedious, and one partner in the firm of Bartlett Gluckstein Crawley & de Reya sought to reduce the requirement of signing the firm's name in full, and a client decided to challenge this practice.[160] Mr Byrne was sent a bill of costs. The bill had a printed heading with the full name of the partnership, its address and the names of the partners. The bill was signed 'Bartletts' by a partner. The full name was printed below the signature, but not immediately beneath it. The bill was sent with a letter headed with the firm's full name, which was also signed in the same abbreviated name. Mr Byrne refused to pay because the signature on the bill did not comply with the requirements of s69(2) of the Solicitors Act 1974. The firm brought an action to recover the costs. McDonnell J gave judgment for Mr Byrne. He accepted the sum was owed, but agreed that the bill was not signed in accordance with the required form. On appeal, Fox LJ determined that the bill was properly signed, and offered the following comments:

> There had been legislation relating to solicitors' bills of costs over several centuries. The question was whether as a matter of construction it could be said that the bill was signed 'in the name of the firm'.
>
> Those words could not require that the whole name of the firm, which in the present case was a long one, had to be set out in full. If a solicitor was required to sign in his own name he did not have to sign all his names in full nor write all his initials.
>
> If the name of the firm had been printed immediately below the signature 'Bartletts' it could hardly have been doubted that the bill was signed in the name of the firm.
>
> There was a signature on the bill of costs by a solicitor of the Supreme Court. That signature was intended to authenticate the bill and the defendant treated it as a bill issued with the authority of the firm itself....
>
> The signature could only be regarded as a signature in the name of the firm, and anyone reading it would take it to be a convenient and obvious contraction of the full name of the firm.[161]

**1.79** Bush J agreed with this analysis and the appeal was allowed. Interestingly, between the trial and the appeal, a fresh bill of costs was prepared and delivered

160 *Bartletts de Reya v. Byrne* (1983) *The Times* 14 January; (1983) 127 SJ 69, Court of Appeal (Civil Division).

161 (1983) *The Times* 14 January.

to Mr Byrne, signed with the full name of the firm. It was paid before the hearing in the Court of Appeal.

## Impression of a mark

### *A seal imprint*

**1.80 Wills** The impression of a seal on documents has a long history, especially on wills, and their use continues today. An early case after the passing of the Statute of Frauds where a seal was the subject of a decision is that of *Lemayne v. Stanley*,[162] where the devisor wrote his will in his own hand, and added his seal to the will, but did not sign it. It was unanimously held that this was a good will, because he had written it himself and identified himself in the will by name. However, there was disagreement as to whether the imprint of the seal was sufficient to satisfy the requirement for a signature. Three members of the court, North, Wyndham and Charlton JJ, considered signing was no more than a mark, and sealing was a sufficient mark. However, the report is ambiguous, and states the majority held the mark was sufficient because 'for *signum* is no more than a *mark*, and sealing is a sufficient *mark* that this is his *will*' (italics in the original). The second part of this sentence may be construed either to mean the sealing was sufficient to authenticate that it was the devisor's will, or that the sealing was sufficient because the devisor wrote the will in his own hand and clearly identified himself.[163] However, this decision may well not have been acceptable to many judges, for in *Smith v. Evans*,[164] Lord Chief Baron Parker and Clive and Smythe BB denounced this decision as 'a very strange doctrine'. It was considered that signing with a seal would open the possibilities of forgery, a comment that reflected a change in judicial attitude from the middle ages, indicating the reduced importance given to a seal in England and Wales. In a later case, that of *Warneford v. Warneford*,[165] Raymond CJ ruled that the sealing of a will was also a signing within the Statute of Frauds 1677. The report of this case is merely a statement of the decision, which does not make it a persuasive authority. This case predated the comments made in *Smith v. Evans*. The reporting of decisions such as this were clearly in the mind of a later Chief Justice when he commented upon this issue in *Ellis v. Smith*.[166] That a seal could be a substitute for a signature was quashed by Willes CJ:

162 (1681) 3 Lev 2; 83 ER 545.

163 In the case of *Dormer v. Thurland* (1728) 2 Eq Ca Abr 663, 22 ER 557; 2 P Wms 506; 24 ER 837, a will had to be signed and sealed to be effective, and because it was signed but not sealed, it was declared void for want of being sealed.

164 (1751) 1 Wils K B 313; 95 ER 636.

165 (Easter 13 Geo 1) 2 Strange 764; 93 ER 834.

166 (1754) 1 Ves Jun 11; 1 Ves Jun Supp 1; 30 ER 205; 34 ER 666.

> Nor do I think, sealing is to be considered as signing; and I declare so now, because, if that question ever comes before me, I shall not think myself precluded from weighing it thoroughly and decreeing, that it is not signing, notwithstanding *obiter dicta*, which in many cases were *nunquam dicta*; but barely the words of reporters; for upon examination I have found many of the sayings ascribed to that great man, Lord Chief Justice *Holt*, were never said by him. (italics in the original).[167]

**1.81** Two arguments were put forward to distrust a seal. In *Grayson v. Atkinson*,[168] the Lord Chancellor suggested that it was not possible to determine whose seal was used:[169]

> ... how can it be said, that putting a seal to it would be a sufficient signing? For any one may put a seal; no particular evidence arises from that seal: common seals are alike, and one man's may be like another's; no certainty or guard therefore arises from thence.'

**1.82** Another reason for rejecting the use of a seal was given by Sir John Strange,[170] suggesting that the nature of a seal was such that it cannot act to identify an act:

> ... that sealing is signing, I am not convinced; for sealing identifies nothing; it carries no character ... and most seals are affixed by the stationers, who prepare the paper.

**1.83** It seems the court in the case of *Ellis v. Smith* had sufficient weight of authority, comprising, as it did, the Lord Chancellor, Master of the Rolls, Chief Justice and Chief Baron, to prevent future submissions that a seal could be a substitute for a signature. A further variation of the use of a seal occurred in the case of *Re Emerson's Goods*,[171] where a hand written document ended with the words 'Signed, sealed, and delivered by me, the first day of February, 1881'. The seal marked, with his initials, was added in the presence of the subscribing witnesses, and the testator also placed one of his fingers on the wax impression and stated before the witnesses 'This is my last will, and this is my hand and seal'. Warren J granted probate on the basis that the testator used the words 'this is my hand', intending this statement to be his signature. This decision was followed by Warren J in the case of *Re Lemon's Goods*, [172] where the testator was too ill

167 (1754) 1 Ves Jun 11 at 13.

168 (1752) 2 Ves Sen 455; 28 ER 291; Ves Sen Supp 382; 28 ER 556.

169 28 ER 556 at 292.

170 *Ellis v. Smith* (1754) 1 Ves Jun 11 at 13, at 15.

171 (1882–3) 9 LR Ir Ch 443.

172 (1896) 30 IrLTR 127.

to write, so he stamped his initials in wax on the paper in the presence of the witnesses.

**1.84 Interest in real property** Seals used to be attached to an indenture respecting an interest in property, and Lord Eldon LC took up the discussion relating to the use of a seal in the case of *Wright v. Wakeford*,[173] where indentures were signed, sealed and delivered. However, the memorandum of attestation only stated that they were signed and delivered. Bearing in mind the value of the estate, at £15,988, this became a technical issue of great importance to both parties. After the death of Thomas Wood the elder, who was a party to the indenture, the two attesting witnesses endorsed a further memorandum, stating they witnessed the signing at the same time as the original document was sealed and delivered. Eldon LC rejected the proposition that a subsequent attestation was acceptable. He accepted that the document may have been signed, sealed and delivered, but it was not attested to this effect. As a consequence, he held that the members of a jury could not presume that the act of signing was done in the presence of the attesting witnesses. In comparison to the other cases cited in relation to whether a seal is sufficient as a signature, the decision in this case was decided upon the technical issue of regularity of the attestation. Lord Eldon took the opportunity, at 458–9, to make further observations about the use of a seal as a means of authentication:

> It is true, at one time it was decided, that sealing was signing (*Lemayne v. Stanly*, 3 *Lev*. 1. *Warneford v. Warneford*, 2 *Sir*. 764); and when it was urged, that the Legislature meant more than sealing, first, from the circumstance, that sealing is not mentioned as to Wills: secondly, as the Legislature must have proposed some evidence from the hand-writing of the party, the objection was, that a person may sign by his mark: an act affording no material testimony; and upon such reasoning it was decided originally, that sealing was signing: but upon a review of that the contrary has been held for a long time; and, so far as sealing from being equivalent to signing, that it is determined, that sealing is not necessarily; and that sealing without signing is not a sufficient execution of a Will (see *Ellis v. Smith*, 1 *Ves, jun*. 11; and that attestation by a mark is good, *Harrison v. Harrison*, *Addy v. Grix*, 8 *Ves*. 185, 405): the converse holding as to a deed; which cannot be without sealing and delivery: if signed, it may be a writing: but, if delivered, it may be a good deed, whether signed, or not, and, if it is to be executed under a power with signature and sealing, both are required.

173 (1811) 17 Ves Jun 455; 34 ER 176.

**1.85** This decision may have been unique to the facts of the case, given the value of the estate in question, and can be distinguished from *Re Emerson's Goods*[174] for this reason.

**1.86** By comparison, another technicality arose in *Lord Lovelace's Case*,[175] where a swaynemoote roll was authenticated with one seal by an officer of the forest by the assent of all the verders, regarders and other officers. In this instance, it was held that a single seal was a good obligation of them all. Similarly, in *Ball v. Dunsterville*,[176] one partner executed a deed for himself and his partner, by authority of the partner and in his presence. This act was a sufficient execution, even though only one seal was used. In *Cooch v. Goodman*,[177] two people entered into a lease in their capacity as governors of a hospital. The defendant signed the lease and added his seal, and the lessors affixed a common seal to the lease, but did not sign it. No decision was made, because the seal was that of a corporation, not of the individuals, which meant the wrong parties initiated the action. Lord Denman CJ commented, at 598, that a single seal may serve a number of people:

> It is true that one piece of wax may serve as a seal for several persons, if each of them impress it himself, or one for all, by proper authority, or in the presence of all, as was held in *Ball v. Dunsterville* (4 T.R. 313), following *Lord Lovelace's Case* (W. Jones, 268).

**1.87** More recently, the case of *First National Securities Ltd v. Jones*[178] considered the effect on a legal charge sealed with a circle printed on the document containing the letters 'L.S.' with the signature of the first defendant affixed across the seal. It was held to be sufficiently executed where the seal has been placed with the intention of serving the purpose of a seal. Buckely LJ indicated at 118 C-D:

> ... it is a very familiar feature nowadays of documents which are intended to be executed as deeds that they do not have any wax, or even wafer, seal attached to them, but have printed at the spot where formerly the seal would probably have been placed, a printed circle, which is sometimes hatched and sometimes the letters 'L.S.' within it, which is intended to serve the purpose of a seal if the document is delivered as the deed of the party executing it.
>
> In the present case there is not only the circle with the letters 'L.S.' within it upon the document, printed as part of the printed version of the document, but also there is the feature that the mortgagor

174 (1882–3) 9 LR Ir Ch 443.

175 W. Jones, 268, 82 ER 140; W. Jones, 270, 82 ER 141.

176 4 TR 313; 100 ER 1038.

177 (1842) 2 QB 580; 114 ER 228.

178 [1978] Ch 109, [1978] 2 All ER 221, CA.

> has placed his signature across the circle. In my judgment those features and the attestation, in the absence of any contrary evidence, are sufficient evidence to establish that the document was executed by the first defendant as his deed.

**1.88** Goff LJ emphasized at 119E that the intent behind the act was important: 'In my judgment, in this day and age, we can, and we ought to, hold that a document purporting to be a deed is capable in law of being such although it has no more than an indication where the seal should be', and Sir David Cairns suggested at 121B what the modern view might be on the use of seals: 'Moreover, while in 1888 the printed indication of a *locus sigilli* was regarded as being merely the place where a seal was to be affixed, I have no doubt that it is now regarded by most business people and ordinary members of the public as constituting the seal itself'. The decision reached in this more recent case mirrors the approach taken by the members of the court in *Re Sandilands*,[179] where a deed had pieces of green ribbon attached to places where the seals should be, but no wax or other material to receive an impression. It was held there was sufficient evidence that the deed was sealed. Bovill CJ observed at 413 'Here is something attached to this deed which may have been intended for a seal, but which from its nature is incapable of retaining an impression', while Byles J also offered the opinion at 413 that 'The sealing of a deed need not be by means of a seal; it may be done with the end of a ruler or anything else'.

**1.89** **Court records** However, despite the reluctance by some judges to accept a seal as a signature in the 18th century, the members of the Exchequer of Pleas in the 19th century decided a seal was sufficient in relation to office copies from the Insolvent Court, being a court of record, in the case of *Doe d Phillips, Jones and Morris v. Evans and Lloyd*.[180] It was possible for an office copy to be adduced as evidence without further proof, although it had to be signed by an officer of the court. Having discussed the relevant statutory provisions in his judgment, Bayley B came to the conclusion that where an office copy was sealed with the seal of the Insolvent Debtors' Court, 'The seal of the Court then becomes the signature of the Court and of the officer'.[181] It seems that this decision provided for the authentication of the insolvent petition either where the document contained the signature of the officer or his deputy and the seal of the court, or where the document only contained the seal of the court. Given the comment by Bayley B, it appears that the seal of the court was sufficient for the purpose of authentication. In *R v. St Paul, Covent Garden Inhabitants*,[182] relating to the settlement of an illegitimate child, it was not considered necessary that an order of the justices be sealed with wax. Two Justices of the Peace signed the order. The order was made

179 (1871) LR 6 CP 411.

180 (1833) 1 C & M 450; 149 ER 476; (1833) LJ Ex 2 NS 179.

181 (1833) 1 C & M 450 at 461.

182 (1844) 5 QB 671; 114 ER 1402; (1845) 7 QB 232; 115 ER 476.

on a pre-printed form. From time to time the parish officers of St Martin in the Fields caused a printer to print a large number of the forms, and on each sheet a stationer was employed to impress two marks in ink with wooden blocks, and these impressions, when made at the foot, were intended to serve as seals for the justices when they signed such orders. The court in the Quarter Sessions held that the impression in ink made by such blocks was a sufficient seal to make the order, and when signed and delivered by the justices, it constituted a good and valid order.

**1.90** In the United States of America, seals have generally been upheld, although there seems to have been a divergence between adopting the word 'seal' as an acknowledgment that a document has been sealed, and refusing to accept a document has been sealed unless an impression of a seal has been affixed.[183] Recognition of the Japanese seal is illustrated in the Pennsylvanian case of *Zenith Radio Corporation v. Matsushita Electric Industrial Co., Ltd.*,[184] where Becker DJ commented, at 1224, that a Japanese seal 'should be given weight equivalent to a signature'. The 1916 New York case of *Matter of the Probate of the Will of Severance*[185] dealt with an unusual form of seal. The testator affixed a holiday seal (containing the inscription 'Merry Christmas. American Red Cross, 1912 Happy New Year') to his will and inscribed it with his initials. It was held to constitute a subscription where the testator intended the holiday seal and inscription as a signature.

## *The use of a fingerprint*

**1.91** In the same way that a mark is accepted as a form of signature, in what seems to be a unique case in England, the impression of a thumb smeared in ink was accepted as a signature, although Langton J commented that the method did not commend itself to him.[186] Thumb prints are also accepted in South Africa,[187] and in China, where a party affixes a fingerprint to a contract, it has the same effect as a signature or stamp.[188]

## *The use of a printed name*

**1.92** **Statute of Frauds** The legal constraints relating to commerce were gradually amended during the 19th century, and the case of *Saunderson v.*

183 For a list of cases relating to the adoption of seals, see R. A. Lord, *Williston on Contracts*, I (4th edn., n.p.: Thompson West, 1990), 2:2.

184 505 F.Supp. 1190 (1980).

185 96 Misc. 384, 161 N.Y.S. 452.

186 *Re Finn* (1935) 105 LJP 36; both parties accepted a thumb print was capable of being a signature in the case of *In the Estate of Parsons, Borman v. Lel* [2002] WTLR 237.

187 *Putter v. Provincial Insurance Co. Ltd.*, 1963 (3) SA 145 (W).

188 'Supreme People's Court, interpretation on several issues concerning the application of the PRC contract law', *China Law & Practice*, 23(2009), pp. 41 and 69.

*Jackson*[189] at the turn of the century serves to illustrate how the judges began to deal with the practical issues relating to contractual disputes where the 'signature' was affixed by the use of technology. In this instance, a bill of parcels was delivered, part of which was printed as follows: 'London. Bought of Jackson and Hankin, distillers, No 8 Oxford Street' and there followed in manuscript writing '1000 gallons of gin, 1 in 5 gin £350 7*s*'. A dispute occurred, and Lord Eldon articulated the single question as follows: 'Whether if a man be in the habit of printing instead of writing his name, he may not be said to sign by his printed name as well as his written name?'[190] In this instance, the bill of parcels was not considered to be of sufficient evidence on its own to be viewed as a note or memorandum of the contract, although a subsequent letter signed by one of the parties acted to connect the two documents, and thus took the matter outside the Statute of Frauds. The later case of *Schneider v. Norris*[191] distinguished the facts in *Saunderson v. Jackson.*[192] In this instance, Messrs John Schneider bought cotton yard and piece goods from Thomas Norris, who acted as agents. The bill of parcels read as follows: 'London, 24 October 1812. Messrs John Schneider and Co bought of Thomas Norris and Co, Agents. Cotton yard and piece goods. No 3 Freeman's Court, Cornhill', all of which was printed, except the words 'Messrs John Schneider and Co', which were hand written by an agent or employee of the defendant. The defendant refused to deliver the yarn. At the subsequent trial, the defendants did not accept that a contract had been formed, and relied on the absence of a note or memorandum in writing of the contract, as required by the Statute of Frauds 1677. Lord Ellenborough CJ overruled this objection and Schneider and Co obtained a verdict. On appeal, Lord Ellenborough reiterated his opinion at the trial, and considered that the printed name of the defendants, as it appeared on the bill, was recognized as a signature. This occurred when the name 'Messrs John Schneider and Co' was added to the bill of parcels that included the printed name of Norris and Co. By writing the name of the firm on the bill, Schneider's identified themselves with the other party to the transaction. Le Blanc and Bayley JJ concurred with this decision, and Dampier J added that the act of a person handwriting the name of the plaintiffs on the bill served to authenticate it as a memorandum of the bargain struck between the parties, and went on to explain, at 290: 'The defendant has ratified the sale to Schneider and Co by inserting their name as buyer to a paper in which he recognizes himself as seller'. Thus the names of the two firms on the same bill provided evidence of the agreement. There is a fine distinction between these two cases. The additional manuscript comments to the bill of parcels in *Saunderson v. Jackson* referred to the price and quantity of the order. This was not considered sufficient evidence, in the absence of the later signed letter, to demonstrate a contract existed. In comparison, the additional manuscript comments to the bill of parcels in

189 (1800) 2 Bos & Pul 238; 126 ER 1257.

190 (1800) 2 Bos & Pul 238 at 239.

191 (1814) 2 M & S 237; 105 ER 388.

192 (1800) 2 Bos & Pul 238; 126 ER 1257.

*Schneider v. Norris* contained the name of one of the parties to the contract. This meant that both parties to the contract in *Schneider v. Norris* were identified in the bill of parcels, and this was sufficient to establish a commercial relationship between the parties.[193]

**1.93** At the same time as these cases were being determined, another problem occurred of a similar nature in circumstances where one of the parties retained evidence of the orders they received in loose cases and memorandum books. The 1809 case of *Allen v. Bennet*[194] illustrated the problem. Wright, the agent for Bennett, agreed to sell goods to Allen, writing the orders into a book owned by Allen. The book was described as 'a sort of waste book, containing various memoranda of different natures'. Mr Allen's name was not written upon or in any part of the book. Bennett failed to deliver the goods. It was considered that the orders entered by the agent for Bennett were made in that capacity, and in conjunction with the exchange of correspondence between the parties, this was sufficient as a memorandum and a signature by Bennett. Mansfield CJ observed a wider question that occupied the courts on this issue at the time when he said, at 176:

> ... every one knows it is the daily practice of the Court of Chancery to establish contracts signed by one person only, and yet a court of equity can no more dispense with the statute of frauds than a court of law can, there is no reason therefore to set aside the verdict, and the rule must be discharged.

**1.94** A similar set of facts occurred in 1856 in the case of *Sarl v. Bourdillon*,[195] where the defendant, about to proceed to India, ordered goods from the plaintiff. Having selected the goods, a list was entered into an order book retained for the purpose, with the words 'Order Book' printed in gold letters on the outside and the names 'Sarl & Son' written on the flyleaf at the beginning. At the foot of the entry, the plaintiff wrote the name and address of the defendant. The defendant failed to pay for the goods, and claimed there was no sufficient memorandum of the sale as required by s17 of the Statute of Frauds. It was held that the names of the contracting parties sufficiently appeared to satisfy the statute.[196] The judgments did not explain the reasoning for this decision. Jervis CJ indicated at the end of the submissions by counsel that there was only one point worth considering at length, and merely commented, at 195, that 'We also think that

193 In *Hubert v. Treherne* 3 Man. & G. 743, 133 ER 1338 the names of the parties appeared in the body of a draft agreement that neither party signed: it was held that the agreement was not signed. Both *Saunderson v. Jackson* and *Schneider v. Norris* were cited, and Tindal CJ indicated, at 754, that the decision in *Saunderson v. Jackson* depended 'for its authority more upon the subsequent recognition than upon the printed names'.

194 3 Taunt. 169, 128 ER 67; the spelling of Bennet differs as between the name of the case and the description of the firm in the report.

195 1 CB (NS) 188; 140 ER 79.

196 *Jacob v. Kirk* 2 M & R 221; 174 ER 269 was argued on different facts.

the names of the contracting parties sufficiently appear, to satisfy the statute of frauds'. Cresswell J proceeded to deliver the judgment of the court more fully at a later date, and he said, at 195:

> In this case, inasmuch as the defendant declined to go to the jury, and insisted that there was no evidence of a memorandum to satisfy the statute of frauds, it may be assumed that the defendant wrote his name in the plaintiff's book, intending it as a signature to an order to the plaintiffs, whose order-book it was, and whose names were written in the beginning of it in the usual way. This, with the observations made in the course of argument, disposes of all the objections raised.

**1.95** It is interesting to note that Cresswell J mentioned that the name 'Sarl & Son' was written in the beginning of the order book 'in the usual way'. It might be inferred from this comment that Cresswell J was referring to the usual method of taking an order, and that it was common knowledge that note books containing pages to enter orders were widely used. If this was the case, the importance of this decision should not go unnoticed, because a decision the other way would have caused business people to alter the way they conducted business, and it is usually the case that judges in England and Wales looked to the common custom in reaching a decision.[197]

**1.96** The use of a printed name was also challenged in the case of *Evans v. Hoare*[198] where an employer authorized a clerk to draw up a contract of employment, which was signed by the employee, as follows:

> 5, Campbell-terrace, Cannhill Road, Leytonstone, E. Feb 19, 1890. Messrs Hoare, Marr, and Co., 26, 29, Budge Row, London, EC. Gentlemen, In consideration of your advancing my salary to the sum of £130 per annum, I hereby agree to continue my engagement in your office for three years, from and commencing January 1, 1890, at a salary at the rate of £130 per annum as aforesaid, payable monthly as hitherto. Yours obediently, George E Evans.

**1.97** The members of the jury found a verdict for Mr Evans, but the assistant judge of the Mayor's Court did not accept there was a memorandum signed by the firm in accordance with s4 of the Statute of Frauds, so gave judgment for the defendants. This decision was reversed upon appeal on the basis that the clerk

197 In *Joshua Buckton and Co. (Limited) v. London and North-Western Railway* Company (1917–18) 34 TLR 119 a contract signed with the printed name of the firm 'Joshua Buckton and Co. (Limited)' was accepted by Astbury J as a regular business practice at 121: 'having regard to the long practice of signing these consignment notes and to the fact that notes so signed have been accepted and recognized by the Court as fulfilling the requirements of the section', the printed name was a signature under the provisions of s7 of the Railway and Canal Traffic Act 1854.

198 [1892] 1 QB 593; (1892) 66 LTRep NS 345.

was authorized by the firm to draw up the document.[199] Reference was made to the firm by the use of 'your' in the text and the name of the firm was included at the top of the document. The comments by Cave J reflected the difference in procedure between the passing of the statute and the time this case was heard:

> The Statute of Frauds was passed at a period when the legislature was somewhat inclined to provide that cases should be decided according to fixed rules, rather than to leave it to the jury to consider the effect of the evidence in each case. This, no doubt, arose to a certain extent from the fact that in those days the plaintiff and the defendant were not competent witnesses ... No doubt, in attempting to frame a principle, one is obliged to depart somewhat from the strict lines of the statutes.[200]

**1.98** A variation of this theme, which also indicated the way people conducted their daily business, is illustrated by the case of *Jones Brothers v. Joyner*,[201] where an order for hops was written down in a note book owned by the Jones Brothers, and Joyner signed the order. The paper book in which this order was placed was, in turn, slipped into a leather cover, upon which the name 'James Jones' was stamped. When the paper memorandum book was full, it could be withdrawn and a fresh one inserted in the same leather cover. Mr Joyner contended there was no sufficient memorandum to satisfy s4 of the Statute of Frauds, as re-enacted by s4 of the Sale of Goods Act 1893, because the name of the plaintiff did not appear in the memorandum signed by him. Jones Brothers contended that the name on the cover constituted a sufficient signing. Sir Richard Harington held that the cover and the book were two distinct articles, distinguishing the decision in the case of *Sarl v. Bourdillon*. The decision at first instance was reversed on appeal before Darling and Bucknell JJ. In reaching his decision, Darling J focused on the relationship between the note book and the cover, at 769:

> ... when the memorandum was made they were only one. Take the case of the letter and envelope. First of all the letter is written, it is placed in an envelope, and the name of the other person appears on the envelope. In such a case there may be two distinct articles, which are used as one. Further, I think it makes no difference that the words "order book" do not appear. In fact, the orders were placed in a book which was used for that purpose.[202]

199 A hop factor is capable of acting as the agent for both parties to a contract: *Durrell v. Evans* (1862) 1 H & C 174; 31 LJ Ex 337; 9 Jur NS 104; 10 WR 665; 7 LT 97; 158 ER 848, Ex Ch; an auctioneer is an authorized agent for the vendor where the auctioneer enters the name of the vendor on a printed agreement form for the sale of real property: *Leeman v. Stocks* [1951] 1 Ch 941, [1951] 1 All ER 1043.

200 [1892] 1 QB 593 at 597. For a more robust and less polished version of this part of the decision by Cave J, see (1892) 66 LTRep NS 345, 347.

201 (1900) 82 LTNS 768.

202 Compare the decisions in *Champion v. Plummer* 5 Esp. 239; 170 ER 798; 1 Bos. & P. (NR)

**1.99 Real property** The principles set out in *Schneider v. Norris*[203] were subsequently followed by Hall VC in *Tourret v. Cripps*,[204] where Mr Cripps wrote in his own hand on a sheet of memorandum paper an offer to lease property. The memorandum was not signed, but contained, at its head, the words 'From Richd. L Cripps' and his address. Tourret accepted the offer, and was subsequently granted judgment for specific performance. The letter was in the handwriting of Cripps, it contained his name and it was actually sent by him, thus the court inferred that his intention was to grant the lease, and his name at the head of the letter authenticated this intention. In Ireland, the members of the Supreme Court reached a similar conclusion in the case of *Casey v. Irish Intercontinental Bank Limited*,[205] where a memorandum for the sale of a property was typed on the headed notepaper of the auctioneers, with the names of the directors printed at the bottom of the letter. The only manuscript signature was that of the buyer.

**1.100 Public notices** The use of a printed name was beginning to be used by local authorities in the late 19th century. In the case of *Brydges* (*Town Clerk of Cheltenham*) *v. Dix*,[206] the Cheltenham council required the town clerk to execute certain works. When the owner of the property refused, the council sent a notice to the owner on a printed form, duly filled in, with the name of the town clerk printed at the foot of the notice. The council subsequently undertook the work and then sought to recover their costs. Matters dealing with the authenticity of the notice were set out in s266 of the Public Health Act 1875, as follows:

> Notices, orders, and other such documents under the Act may be in writing or print, or partly in writing and partly in print, and if the same require authentication by the local authority the signature thereof by the clerk to the local authority, or their surveyor or inspector, shall be sufficient authentication.

**1.101** An objection was taken that the signature of the clerk was a requisite and that it should be affixed by hand. The magistrates accepted this argument and refused to make an order for payment. Pollock B and Charles J heard the appeal in the Queen's Bench Division. They allowed the appeal and came to the conclusion that if a signature was required, a manual signature was not necessary: 'all that was necessary was that the notice should be authenticated as coming from the town clerk, and that sufficiently appeared in this notice'.[207] The printed signature was held to be sufficient. This observation was also to be noted by Romer LJ in

252; 127 ER 458; *Allen v. Bennet* 3 Taunt. 169, 128 ER 67; *Jacob v. Kirk* 2 M & R 221; 174 ER 269.

203 (1814) 2 M & S 237; 105 ER 388.

204 (1879) 48 L J Ch 567; 27 WR 706. These cases were reviewed by Buckley J in *Hucklesby v. Hook* 82 LT 117.

205 [1979] IR 364.

206 (1890–1) 7 TLR 215.

207 (1890–1) 7 TLR 215 at 216(a).

*Goodman v. J Eban Limited*,[208] where he pointed out that the recipient could verify the authenticity of the notice by confirming its contents directly with the clerk.

**1.102** Generally, judges in the United States of America, in combination with the approach adopted in various model acts to provide a degree of uniformity to the law, have agreed with their brethren in England. The range of illustrations includes printing on bank notes,[209] bills of lading,[210] bonds,[211] brokers contracts,[212] court papers[213] (although printed names have not always been accepted),[214] and a printed name can be the subject of forgery (including a name

208 [1954] 1 QB 550 at 564; [1954] 1 All ER 763; [1954] 2 WLR 581, CA.

209 Federal, 7th circuit: *Hill v. United States*, 288 F. 192 (the facsimile signatures of the governor and cashier of the Federal Reserve Bank of St Louis on bank notes are true and genuine signatures) (1923).

210 Pennsylvania: Carna t/d/b/a/ *T.C. Trucking Company v. Bessemer Cement Company*, 558 F.Supp. 706 (1983) (the pre-printed company name on bill of lading held to be a sufficient signature).

211 California: *Pennington v. Baehr*, 48 Cal. 565, 1874 WL 1399 (Cal.) (a bond signed by a printed facsimile of the President of the Reclamation Fund Commissioners held to be sufficient) (1874). It is reported that the Attorney-General argued, at 567, that 'A printed *fac simile* ... could be more easily forged than an autograph; and such a signature would be no more protection than no signing at all'; *Williams v. McDonald*, 58 Cal. 527, 8 P.C.L.J. 23, 58 Cal. 527, 1881 WL 1946 (Cal.) (a resolution of intention with the printed name of the clerk affixed was sufficient because he intended the printed name to be adopted).

212 Nebraska: *Berryman v. Childs*, 98 Neb. 450, 153 N.W. 486 (where the plaintiffs signed a contract with their printed name, they are entitled to the benefit of the contract) (1915).

213 California: *Hancock v. Bowman*, 49 Cal. 413, 1874 WL 1548 (Cal.) (a judgment is not void because the name of the plaintiff's attorney is printed on the compliant) (1874); *Ligare v. California Southern Railroad Company*, 76 Cal. 610, 18 P. 777 (a summons signed with the printed signature of the clerk accompanied with the seal of the court held to be sufficient signature) (1888); *Smith v. Ostly*, 53 Cal.2d 262, 1 Cal.Rptr. 340, 347 P.2d 684 (a name printed on a notice of appeal can be adopted as a signature providing the petitioner intended to authenticate the document) (1959).

Indiana: *Hamilton v. State*, 103 Ind. 96, 2 N.E. 299, 53 AmRep. 491 (it is sufficient that the name of the prosecuting attorney appears in print on an indictment) (1885).

Iowa (1908): *Cummings v. Landes*, 117 N.W. 22, 140 Iowa 80 (an original notice is signed when the name of the attorney is printed thereon).

Minnesota: *Ames v. Schurmeier*, 9 Minn. 221, 1864 WL 1409 (Minn.), 9 Gil. 206 (a summons in a civil action is void where the name of the plaintiff or their attorney is printed where handwriting is required); *Herrick v. Morrill*, 37 Minn. 250, 33 N.W. 849, 5 Am.St.Rep. 841 (a summons in a civil action may be subscribed by the printed signature of the plaintiff or his attorney) (1887).

New York: *Barnard v. Heydrick*, 49 Barb. 62, 32 How. Pr. 97, 2 Abb.Pr.N.S. 47 (a summons issued by an attorney with his name typed at the end is subscribed by him within the meaning of the provisions of the Code of Procedure) (1866). Note the cases cited and discussion of the decision of Ingraham J in *The Farmers' Loan and Trust Company v. Dickson*, 9 Abb.Pr. 61).

Wisconsin: *Mezchen v. More*, 54 Wis. 214, 11 N.W. 534 (a summons in a civil action with the printed names of the attorneys is subscribed) (1882).

214 Arkansas: *Lee v. Vaughan Seed Store*, 101 Ark 68 (1911), 141 S.W. 496, 37 L.R.A.N.S. 352 (a printed name was not accepted as evidence of authentication); California: *Marks v. Walter*

on a rubber stamp),[215] promissory notes (subject to suitable evidence),[216] public documents,[217] Statute of Frauds (with rare exceptions) generally,[218] with respect

*G. McCarty Corporation*, 33 Cal.2d 814 (1949), 205 P.2d 1025; New York: *The Farmers' Loan and Trust Company v. Dickson*, 9 Abb.Pr. 61 (a summons issued by an attorney with his name typed at the end was a nullity) (1859).

215 Massachusetts: *Commonwealth v. Ray*, 3 Gray 441, 69 Mass. 441, 1055 WL 5701 (Mass.) (a printed or engraved name can be forged) (1855); *Wellington v. Jackson*, 121 Mass. 157, 1876 WL 10902 (Mass.) (a person who knows a signature is forged on a promissory note, but who acknowledges it as his own, assumes the note to be his as if it was signed with his authority).

Oklahoma: *Boyer v. State*, 68 Okl.Cr. 220, 97 P. 779 (a person can forge a name if they use a rubber stamp) (1939).

216 Illinois: *Weston v. Myers*, 33 Ill. 424, 1864 WL 2948 (Ill.) (a printed name adopted on an instrument for value).

Minnesota: *Brayley v. Kelly*, 25 Minn. 160, 1878 WL 3577 (Minn) (a printed name on a promissory note was not admissible as the act of the party without further evidence).

Oregon: *Toon v. Wapinitia Irrigation Co.*, 117 Or. 374, 243 P. 554 (a printed signature attached to an interest coupon payable to bearer is sufficient to authenticate the instrument) (1926).

217 North Carolina: *State of North Carolina v. Watts*, 289 N.C. 445, 222 S.E.2d 389 (the mechanical reproduction of the name of an authorized officer placed on a public record is properly authenticated where the officer intends to adopt the mechanical reproduction as his signature) (1976).

Wisconsin: *Potts v. Cooley*, 13 N.W.Rep. 682 (a tax certificate with the words 'Assigned May 19, 1877. J P. Carpenter, County Clerk' partly written by hand and partly printed on the face of the certificate is sufficient for the purposes of the statue) (1882).

218 Arizona: *Bishop v. Norell, doing business as Al Norell Company Realtors*, 88 Ariz. 148, 353 P.2d 1022 (a name and address printed on a listing agreement is signed in accordance with the statute provided it is done with the intention of signing) (1960).

Georgia: *Kohlmeyer & Company v. Bowen*, 126 Ga.App. 700, 192 S.E.2d 400 (the name of a securities brokerage firm printed on a confirmation statement for the sale of securities was held to be intended as a means of authentication and thus met the signature requirement under the Statute of Frauds) (1972). Note the dissenting judgment of Evans J and his comments in respect of *Evans Implement Company v. Thomas Industries, Inc.*, 117 Ga.App. 279, 160 S.E.2d 462.

Illinois: *Prairie State Grain and Elevator Company v. Wrede*, 217 Ill.App. 407 (the name 'Ben. B. Bishopp, Grain Broker' printed on a memorandum is adopted and signed by him, especially because he had used such a signature for years as if it had been personally placed on the memorandum) (1920).

Kansas: *Southwest Engineering Company, Inc., v. Martin Tractor Company, Inc.*, 205 Kan. 684, 473 P.2d 18 (the name 'Ken Hurt, Martin Tractor, Topeka, Caterpillar' printed on a memorandum with the details of specifications for a generator written by hand was sufficient authentication) (1970).

Michigan: *Grieb v. Cole*, 60 Mich. 397, 27 N.W. 579, 1 Am.St.Rep. 533 (a warranty printed on the back of a purchase order with the vendor's printed signature binds the warrantor) (1886).

Missouri: *Defur v. Westinghouse Electric Corporation*, 677 F.Supp. 622 (E.D.Mo. 1988) (a Relocation Policy/Home Sale Program had the defendant's name printed on every page, held to constitute a writing signed by the defendant).

New York: *Vielie v. Osgood*, 8 Barb. 130 (names printed at the foot of a contract held not to be a sufficient subscription within the Statute of Frauds) (1849); 1913 case of

to letterheads[219] and in matters pertaining to voting.[220] The burden of proving a printed name was adopted is on the party asserting the nature of the signature, as illustrated by the 1949 Californian case of *Felt v. L. B. Frederick Co., Inc.*[221] In addition, care must be taken over proving the link between the printed name or letterhead, and the intent to authenticate, as in the 1949 Californian case of *Marks v. Walter G. McCarty Corporation*,[222] where the letterhead stationery of the

*Goldowitz v. Henry Kupfer & Co.*, 80 Misc.Rep. 487, 141 N.Y.S. 531; 1920 cases of *Pearlberg v. Levisohn*, 112 Misc. 95, 182 N.Y.S. 615 and *United Display Fixture Co., Inc., v. S. & W. Bauman*, 183 N.Y.S. 4.; *Cohen v. Arthur Walker & Co., Inc.*, 192 N.Y.S. 228 (the printed name of the defendant corporation on an order for goods is sufficient compliance with the statute) (1922); *Mesibov, Glinert & Levy, Inc., v. Cohen Bros. Mfg. Co. Inc.*, 245 N.Y. 305, 157 N.E. 148 (no proof of intent is demonstrated when a paper with the name of a firm is printed at the top and not signed) (1927); *Reich v. Helen Harper, Inc.*, 3 UCC Rep.Serv. 1048, 1966 WL 8838 (N.Y.City Civ.Ct.) (sales confirmation sent on stationery imprinted with the name of the seller's agent upon which the name of the seller's principal was handwritten was signed within the meaning of the UCC) (1966).

219 Federal 3rd circuit: *Associated Hardware Supply Co. v. The Big Wheel Distributing Company*, 355 F.2d 114 (1966).

Federal 7th circuit: *Monetti, S.P.A. v. Anchor Hocking Corporation*, 931 F.2d 1178 (7th Cir. 1991).

Connecticut: *Merrill Lynch, Pierce, Fenner & Smith, Inc., v. Cole*, 189 Conn. 518, 457 A.2d 656 (Conn. 1983).

Georgia (1974): *Evans v. Moore*, 131 Ga.App. 169, 205 S.E.2d 507.

Georgia: *Troutt v. Nash AMC/Jeep, Inc.*, 157 Ga.App. 399, 278 S.E.2d 54 (the seller's standard printed form, with the seller's company name, address and other information on the letterhead amounted to a signature) (1981).

Illinois: *Automotive Spares Corp. v. Archer Bearings Company*, 382 F.Supp. 513 (1974) Bauer, J at 515 'This Court recognizes the need to use common sense and commercial experience in regards to this signature question. Often times merchants exchange documents which control the transaction that do not bear their signature'.

Maryland: *Drury v. Young*, 58 Md. 546, 1882 WL 4502 (Md.), 42 Am.Rep. 343.

Mississippi: *Dawkins and Company v. L & L Planting Company*, 602 So.2d 838 (Miss. 1992) (a letter on the buyer's letterhead with the name of the sender typewritten at the bottom of the document is a sufficient signing to meet the merchant's exception to the Statute of Frauds).

New York (1980): *B & R Textile Corp. v. Domino Textiles, Inc.*, 77 A.D.2d 539, 430 N.Y.S.2d 89, 29 UCC Rep.Serv. 396.

Ohio: *Alarm Device Manufacturing Company v. Arnold Industries, Inc.*, 65 Ohio App.2d 256, Ohio App., 417 N.E.2d 1284 (the letterhead on the seller's invoice was sufficient to satisfy the Statute of Frauds) (1979).

220 Kentucky: *Lamaster v. Wilkerson*, 143 Ky. 226, 136 S.W. 217 (trustees caused their names to be printed on a notice prepared by them of the time and place of holding an election to issue bonds: the printed names were sufficient providing they authorized the printing of their names and adopted them as their legal signatures) (1911).

Massachusetts: *Henshaw v. Foster*, 9 Pick. 318, 26 Mass. 312, 1830 WL 25334 (Mass.) (in the election of governor, votes may be printed).

New Jersey: *Matthews v. Deane*, 201 N.J.Super. 583, 493 A.2d 632 (names printed on recall petitions are valid) (1984).

221 92 Cal.App.2d 157, 206 P.2d 676.

222 33 Cal.2d 814, 205 P.2d 1025.

name of a hotel used for the purpose of providing carbon copies was held not to be sufficient to show intention to adopt the letterhead as a signature, as indicated by Shenk J at 822: 'Here the defendant's letterhead was printed on its stationery at some earlier time for a purpose unconnected with the transaction in suit'. Carter J gave a strong dissenting judgment in this case, which has much to recommend it.

## *The use of a lithographed name*

**1.103** The use of printed forms to reduce wasted time is an accepted way of doing business. However, there are occasions when a manuscript signature is required under statute, more particularly with respect to the rules governing the running of a firm of solicitors. In the case of *R v. Cowper*,[223] the name of the firm of solicitors was lithographed in bulk on to a county court bill of particulars. Spaces were left blank to fill in the form as necessary. A claim was made in respect of a debt and costs. At the hearing, the registrar refused an order for costs because the solicitors had not signed the particulars in accordance with the County Court Rules, 1889, order VI, r 10. The matter was then heard before the Divisional Court, which upheld the decision of the registrar. An appeal was subsequently heard in the Court of Appeal. Lord Esher pointed out that the name of a firm was included on the particulars to ensure the court may control its officers, and asked at 535 'If that was the object, how is it affected by the objection, that the name appears in a lithograph form?' and concluded that if the forms were misused, such misuse would inevitably be found out and punished. Further, he went on to demonstrate the reason for the rule at 535:

> The whole object of the rule seems to me to be to get the document authenticated as coming from a solicitor's office, and if the solicitor has authorized the issue of the lithograph form that object is attained. He means it to be his signature and sends it forth as his, and that seems to me sufficient compliance with the Act.

**1.104** However, Fry LJ disagreed with Lord Esher. He thought that blank forms that can be filled up at any time did not offer any guarantee that the solicitor or a person authorized to act on their behalf had given their personal attention to a particular form. Also, and more compellingly, he argued, at 536, that 'the signature required is intended to be something to authenticate the particulars and the accuracy of the copies, and to make the solicitor responsible for them as an officer of the Court'. Thus attempts by solicitors to ease the burden of filling in forms has not always met with agreement from the bench, and in this case, because the members of the Court of Appeal did not agree, the decision of the Divisional Court was not changed. In comparison, a lithographed name on bonds has been held to a valid signature in the United States of America, although the position would not be any different in England and Wales.[224]

223 (1890) 24 QBD 60, 533, (1890) 59 L.J.K.B. (NS) 265, CA.

224 California: *Hewel v. Hogin*, 3 Cal.App. 248, 84 P. 1002 (the lithographic signatures of a

## *The use of a rubber stamp*

**1.105** An early record of the use of a stamp, although not made with rubber, is that of the signature of the monarch from the Tudor period in England. Apparently the signet of Mary Tudor occurs with a stamp signature of the queen, of which more than 20 specimens appear on signet warrants. Also, there are examples of rubber stamps being used instead of seals in the 19th century by various sheriffs for official documents.[225] From the case law in relation to rubber stamps, it is generally, if reluctantly in some instances, accepted that a rubber stamp is capable of being accepted as a form of signature, providing the stamp is used with the authority of the person whose signature it is: for instance, in *Macdonald v. Sun Life Assurance Company of Canada*,[226] a medical expert retained by the defence was not permitted to testify after he stated that his signature stamp had been affixed to a medical report without his authority. The question of his signature arose when it became clear that the report he referred to during his testimony differed substantially from the one served on the plaintiff and filed with the court. The court did not consider any relevant legislation, but determined the issue on the basis of existing principles.

**1.106 Wills** The case of *Jenkins v. Gainsford and Thring*[227] illustrates the problems that people suffering from ataxia encounter, and what measures they take to resolve them. Towards the end of his life, John Jenkins had great difficulty in writing and signing his name, so he had an engraving of his signature made. Thereafter, when he was required to sign a letter or other document, he would direct his amanuensis to affix an impression of his name to the document by using the engraving. Mr Jenkins left a will and executed two codicils. An affidavit by his amanuensis accompanied the codicils, stating the manner in which they were executed: he was ordered and directed by the testator to affix the signature to the codicil using the engraving, in the presence of the other subscribing witness. After the signature was affixed, the testator placed his hand on the codicil and acknowledged the signature as his own and said the codicil was to be a codicil to his will. The two witnesses then attested and subscribed the codicil. The same procedure was followed on both occasions. Sir C. Cresswell held that the codicils were duly executed. He observed that a testator has sufficiently signed by making their mark, and went on to note at 96:

---

secretary of an irrigation district were sufficient evidence of his signature to the bonds) (1906).

Missouri: *McKee v. Vernon County*, 3 Dill. 210, 16 F.Cas. 188, No. 8851 (railroad bonds are valid where the signature of the presiding justice and clerk of the county are lithographed on the bond) (1874).

Mississippi: *Town Council of Lexington v. Union National Bank*, 75 Miss. 1, 22 So. 291 (railroad bonds are valid with the signature of the clerk of the council lithographed on the bond) (1897).

225 Barnes and Hector, *Guide to Seals*, 47 note 2 and 52.

226 [2006] O.J. No. 4428 (Sup. Ct.) (QL), 2006 CanLII 41669 (ON S.C.).

227 (1863) 3 Sw & Tr 93; 164 ER 1208; (1862–3) 11 WR 854.

> Now, whether the mark is made by a pen or by some other instrument cannot make any difference, neither can it in reason make a difference that a fac-simile of the whole name was impressed on the will instead of a mere mark or X.

**1.107** The instrument or stamp was intended to stand for and represent the signature of the testator. The form the signature took was not relevant, providing the evidence surrounding the affixing of the stamp went to show that the testator intended to be bound by the content of the codicils.[228]

**1.108** However, in Scotland, the use of a stamp on a will is not acceptable in accordance with the provisions of Statute 1540, chapter 117. In *Stirling Stuart v. Stirling Crawfurd's Trustees*,[229] the testator signed a second deed by means of a stamp he was in the habit of using because he suffered from scrivener's palsy, and had great difficulty in writing.

**1.109 Voting** The case of *Bennett v. Brumfitt*,[230] was brought under s17 of the Parliamentary Voters Registration Act 1843 before the Court of Common Pleas. The usual signature of William Brumfitt was engraved in facsimile and made into a stamp, which was subsequently used to sign a notice of objection. Bovill CJ observed at 31:

> The ordinary mode of affixing a signature to a document is not by the hand alone, but by the hand coupled with some instrument, such as a pen or pencil. I see no distinction between using a pen or a pencil and using a stamp, where the impression is put upon the paper by the proper hand of the party signing.

**1.110** It is the personal act of the signatory that is relevant. Byles and Willes JJ agreed, and as to the genuineness of a signature, Keating J could not see why a signature 'is better authenticated by a signature by means of a pen than by means of an impression of a stamp affixed by the party's own hand'.[231]

**1.111 Judicial use** The development of technology permits actions that are repetitive in nature to be less onerous in their execution. Thus the use of a rubber stamp can alleviate the requirement that a manuscript signature be affixed to numerous documents by the same person in circumstances where the intention is to authenticate a document. Changes in technology included the adoption of stamps in the courts. In *Blades v. Lawrence*,[232] a case was transferred to the City of London court by the order of a Master. The order was, in the words of Blackburn

228 For almost identical facts where the deceased could no longer write because of arthritis and a stroke, see *Phillips v. Najar*, 901 S.W.2d 561 (Tex.App.-El Paso 1995).

229 (1885) 12 R. 610.

230 (1867–68) 3 LRCP 28.

231 (1867–68) 3 LRCP 28 at 32.

232 (1873–4) 9 LRQB 374; (1874) 43 LJR QB 133.

J, issued in the ordinary way 'according to the practice long established at Judge's Chambers, by the clerk of the judge, having on it the signature of the judge, stamped by the clerk'.[233] The judge in the London court inquired into the circumstances under which the order was made, and because the judge had not signed the order, he refused to hear the case and ordered the entry to be struck out. It was unanimously held by Cockburn CJ, Blackburn, Quain and Archibald JJ that such an order was properly authenticated and it was not for the judge of the London court, in the words of Cockburn CJ, 'to determine the validity or invalidity of the order bearing the proper authentication on its face'.[234] Where it was doubted that the order was genuine, the judge should have applied to a superior court to set the order aside. In this instance, the judge was ordered to pay the costs of the case.

**1.112** Consideration was given to the judicial use of rubber stamps in Ireland in the case of *The State v. His Honour Judge P. J. Roe*,[235] where it was determined that a justice of the peace may sign a committal warrant by means of a rubber stamp. Gavan Duffy P said, at 186–7:

> As to the rubber stamps, if one man may sign by a mark, another may use a rubber facsimile as a signature; but, where the device is questioned by a man entitled to call for proof, the affixing of the stamp by the Justice must be proved, either by the Justice himself or by another witness who can swear positively to the making by the Justice of the particular signature questioned; and that may not be easy evidence for a Court clerk to give, if a Justice makes a habit of stamping his name on a sheaf of documents at one time. If the fact be that pressure of work makes the use of a rubber stamp a necessity, or almost a necessity, for a very busy Justice, one would expect to see the need expressly recognised in the code, with stringent rules for the safe custody of the stamp and a peremptory veto upon any delegation of its use to a clerk or any other person.

**1.113** The acceptance of the use of a rubber stamp in legal proceedings is also illustrated in the Canadian case of *R v. Burton*,[236] in which an informant affixed a facsimile signature to an information by means of a rubber stamp, which in turn was sworn before a justice of the peace, who signed the information with a manuscript signature. The information was held to be a sufficient signature in absence of proof that the officer who signed the jurat failed to comply with the duties imposed upon him. In reaching his decision, Lacourciere J observed, at 387:

233 (1873–4) 9 LRQB 374 at 377.

234 (1873–4) 9 LRQB 374 at 376.

235 [1951] IR 172.

236 [1970] 3 C.C.C. 381, [1970] 2 O.R. 512, 8 C.R.N.S. 269 (Ont. H.C.J.).

> In my opinion the use of a rubber stamp signature by the informant is a practice that should be discouraged and indeed deprecated, as it detracts from the solemnity of an important step in the machinery of law, and may give rise to public suspicion that the officer taking the oath has done less than his duty. The partially stamped information, however, is not a nullity, in the absence of proof that the officer who signed the jurat failed to comply with the requirements set out above.

**1.114** In comparison, an Ontario Court of Appeal held in the case of *Re R v. Welsford*[237] that an information charging an accused with a summary conviction offence under a provincial statute is a nullity if the jurat bears a facsimile rubber stamp signature of the justice of the peace.

**1.115 Statute of Frauds** In *McDonald v. John Twiname Ld*[238] the plaintiff entered into an apprenticeship with the company, but an authorized representative from the company failed to sign the agreement. The name of the company was stamped on the document with a rubber stamp. In this instance, Evershed MR and Birkett LJ agreed that not only had the document had been signed by the company, but there was sufficient evidence to show they adopted, acted upon and affirmed the existence of the agreement.

**1.116 Ecclesiastical use** The ecclesiastical use of rubber stamps is demonstrated in *De Beauvais v. Green*,[239] where the bishop of Gloucester issued an order to the new incumbent to pay for repairs. One of the points raised in argument was that the bishop failed to sign the relevant order in triplicate in his own hand, as required by ss35 and 60 of the Ecclesiastical Dilapidations Act 1871, but authorized the use of a stamp for this purpose. It was held that the order by the bishop was sufficient in form to satisfy the requirements of the relevant sections.

**1.117 Solicitors Act 1974** Solicitors, in the normal course of events, are required to sign bills of costs. In the case of *Goodman v. J Eban Limited*,[240] a sole practitioner sought to recover for professional services provided to the defendant company. The solicitor affixed his name to the bill by means of a rubber stamp. The solicitor sent a bill of costs to the defendants, which was accompanied by a letter which ended in the words typewritten at the bottom of the letter 'Yours faithfully, Goodman, Monroe & Company'. Below the name, the solicitor affixed a facsimile of his signature by means of a rubber stamp. The defendants refused to pay the solicitor because the bill of costs did not satisfy the requirements of s65(2)(i) of the Solicitors Act 1932. It was held, with Denning LJ dissenting, that the bill had been signed for the purposes of s65, although, Evershed MR

237 [1967] 2 O.R. 496, [1968] 1 C.C.C. 1, 2 C.R.N.S. 5.

238 [1953] 2 QB 304 CA.

239 (1905–6) 22 TLR 816.

240 [1954] 1 QB 550; [1954] 1 All ER; [1954] 2 WLR 581, CA.

observed, at 554, that 'as a matter of good practice, the "signature" of a bill of costs, or of a letter enclosing such a bill, by means of a rubber stamp seems to me in general undesirable'. He went on to comment that the purpose of the statute was to impose a personal responsibility for any bill of costs delivered, and the client was to have the assurance by means of personal authentication that the bill was a proper bill.[241] Romer LJ noted that the rubber stamp did not, on the face of it, constitute a signature,[242] although he accepted that when the matter was considered in the light of authority and the function that a signature is intended to perform, the conclusion must be that the rubber stamp did constitute a signature. He also concluded that a repetition of the name of the firm under the typewritten name would be otiose if it was only to repeat the typed name of the firm. It was plain that Mr Goodman intended the rubber stamp to 'be regarded as a signature for the purpose of authenticating the letter'.[243] Should the client doubt its authenticity, all they had to do was ask Mr Goodman, by telephone or letter.[244] Romer LJ might have also adopted, had he been aware of it, the reasoning of Clay J in the 1934 Kentucky case of *Wurts v. Newsome*,[245] where a judge signed ballots by means of a rubber stamp. Clay J stated, at 450:

> The opportunities for fraud when a rubber stamp is used are no greater than the opportunities for fraud by forgery. It would be just as difficult to ascertain that the ballots had not been signed, and have a rubber stamp prepared, as it would be to employ one to imitate the signature of the judge who failed to sign. Besides, the statute, though designed to prevent fraud, has operated in several instances to defeat the popular will. In numerous contests that have come before this court, the successful candidate has lost by the failure of one of the judges, either through ignorance, mistake, or fraud to sign the ballots. In the circumstances we are not inclined to go further and adopt a construction so technical as to make the situation even worse. A rubber stamp identifies the

241 The signature of lawyer on a document is usually considered that the document has been read by the lawyer, as noted in the litigation following foreclosure claims as a result of the banking crisis in 2008, for which see *November Oversight Report* [Submitted under Section 125(b)(1) of Title 1 of the Emergency Economic Stabilization Act of 2008, Pub. L. No. 110–343 Examining the Consequences of Mortgage Irregularities for Financial Stability and Foreclosure Mitigation] (Congressional Oversight Panel, 16 November 2010), available at http://cybercemetery.unt.edu/archive/cop/20110402010313/http://cop.senate.gov/documents/cop-111610-report.pdf; Office of the Inspector General US Department of Housing and Urban Development, *Bank of America Corporation Foreclosure and Claims Process Review Charlotte, NC* (Memorandum No. 2012-FW-1802, 12 March 2012), available at https://www.hudoig.gov/sites/default/files/Audit_Reports/2012-FW-1802.pdf; *In Re Hill*, 437 B.R. 503 (Bankr. W.D. Pa. 2010).

242 [1954] 1 QB 550, at 563.

243 [1954] 1 QB 550, at 564.

244 [1954] 1 QB 550, at 563–564.

245 253 Ky. 38, 68 S.W.2d 448.

> ballot just as clearly as the written signature of the judge. If not placed on the ballot either by him, or someone else in his presence, and at his direction while the election is being conducted, that may be shown in a context just as it may be shown that the written signature appearing on the ballot was not his act. We therefore conclude that the signing of the ballots by a rubber stamp was a substantial compliance with the statute, and that all the ballots so signed should have been counted.

**1.118** Dissenting, Denning LJ suggested that a person must make their mark, whatever the format, by themselves. In discussing the way in which rubber stamps were used, he introduced extraneous opinion to support his assertion, at 561, which was no more than prejudice and irrelevant to the matter being dealt with: 'This is such a common knowledge that a "rubber stamp" is contemptuously used to denote the thoughtless impress of an automaton, in contrast to the reasoned attention of a sensible person'. He overlooked several points. A rubber stamp is used to sign hundreds of letters or forms for the convenience and saving in labour, as the case law illustrates, rather than the contemptuous use by a thoughtless automaton, the purpose of which is different to a solicitor's bill. Also, he clearly did not appreciate, and if he did, did not acknowledge, the fact that some people do not have the ability to sign documents. The issue was not the widespread use of rubber stamps in various other activities. In this judgment, Denning LJ refused to distinguish between the form a signature took and the function it was to perform, which has been the main thrust of judicial decision-making over the past two hundred years. Interestingly, the use of a stamp by judges and bishops during the 19th century was not raised or discussed in this case. If Denning LJ thought the personal signature of a solicitor was so necessary on a bill of costs, it may be equally as desirable when a judge orders a case to be transferred to another court, as in *Blades v. Lawrence*.[246]

**1.119** The decisions from other jurisdictions, together with the rationale articulated for accepting rubber stamps is also an instructive counterpoint to the comments by Denning LJ. In Canada, the judgment in *Goodman v. J Eban Limited* was discussed in *R v. Burton*,[247] where an informant affixed a facsimile signature to an information by means of a rubber stamp was held to be a sufficient signature in absence of proof that the officer who signed the jurat failed to comply with the duties imposed upon him. In the 1976 North Carolina case of *State of North Carolina v. Watts*,[248] the mechanical reproduction of the name of an authorized officer placed on a public record of the Division of Motor Vehicles was held to

246 (1873–4) 9 LRQB 374; (1874) 43 LJR QB 133.

247 [1970] 3 C.C.C. 381, [1970] 2 O.R. 512, 8 C.R.N.S. 269 (Ont. H.C.J.); in *R v. Blumes*, 2002 BCPC 45 (CanLII), it was not possible to determine whether the signature was an original signature, rubber stamp or facsimile signature; see also *R v. Pearce*, 2000 BCSC 0376; *R v. Parkinson* [2002] O.J. No. 5478 (Ct. J.) (QL).

248 289 N.C. 445, 222 S.E.2d 389.

be properly authenticated where the officer intended to adopt the mechanical reproduction as his signature. Branch J indicated, at 392, why the physical reality of mechanical means of rendering a signature had become relevant:

> The purpose of authentication and certification of records is to avoid the inconvenience and sometimes the impossibility of producing original public documents in court. Obviously the admission of certified records tends to expedite the trial of cases. It is just as obvious that to require the manual signing of every record certified from the Division of Motor Vehicles would be extremely time-consuming and expensive.

**1.120** The comments made by Branch J were reinforced by Hallett J in *Re United Canso Oil & Gas Ltd*,[249] where proxy forms submitted with a facsimile or mechanically rendered signature were considered to be sufficient. Hallett J explained the rationale at 289 paragraph 17:

> Today's business could not be conducted if stamped signatures were not recognized as legally binding. The affixing of a stamp conveys the intention to be bound by the document so executed just as effectively as the manual writing of a signature by hand. I would point out that no one questions the validity of millions of payroll cheques signed by facsimile signatures.

**1.121** He also addressed the fallacious argument that one form of signature was more prone to fraud than any other at 305 paragraph 64:

> In my opinion, in view of the obvious opportunities for fraud with respect to votes to be cast by registered shareholders where a bare signature is normally accepted, I cannot see any reason to differentiate between the degree of proof required by a chairman to be satisfied that a proxy has actually been executed by the registered individual shareholder (the degree of proof being virtually nothing) and the degree of proof urged upon the court by the Buckley group with respect to proxy voting of brokers for their clients. In the absence of evidence that there was no authority for the execution of proxies by brokers by facsimile signature, the proxy vote should be accepted and counted as is apparently the practice. To conclude otherwise, the chairman is presuming dishonesty on the part of the brokers who tendered the proxies on behalf of their clients. In the absence of evidence, such a conclusion is unwarranted.

249 (1980) 12 B.L.R. 130; 76 A.P.R. 282; 41 N.S.R.(2d) 282 (T.D.).

**1.122 Administrative use** The inconvenience of affixing a manuscript signature to documents was also tested in administrative proceedings in the case of *British Estate Investment Society Ltd v. Jackson* (*H M Inspector of Taxes*),[250] where an Additional Commissioner personally affixed his signature to certificates of authenticity by using a rubber stamp. The rubber stamp was retained by the Additional Commissioner, or the Clerk to the Commissioners. Danckwerts J rejected all of the arguments by British Estate, and on the matter of the stamped signature, he observed, at 86:

> Of course, this is a case, if ever there was a case, in which the signing by means of a stamped signature is proper, because everybody knows that Commissioners of this kind have to deal with numerous documents, and it is an onerous duty if they have to be signed by the writing of the Commissioner himself.[251]

**1.123** Contemporaneously, the case of *Lazarus Estates Ltd v. Beasley*[252] was heard, in which documents in the form prescribed by the Housing Repairs and Rents Act 1954 were signed with the name of the company by means of a rubber stamp. No objection was taken as to the validity of the signature in the county court, and the matter could not be addressed on appeal. However, Denning LJ could not resist commenting, at 710, that:

> The statutory forms require the documents to be 'signed' by the landlord, but the only signature on these documents (if such it can be called) was a rubber stamp 'Lazarus Estates Ltd.' without anything to verify it. There was no signature of a secretary or of any person at all on behalf of the company. There was nothing to indicate who affixed the rubber stamp. It has been held in this court that a private person can sign a document by impressing a rubber stamp with his own facsimile signature on it: *Goodman v. J Eban Limited* [[1954] 1 QB 550; [1954] 2 WLR 581; [1954] 1 All ER 763, CA], but it has not yet been held that a company can sign by its printed name affixed with a rubber stamp.

**1.124** This comment by Lord Denning was not to the point, and in the light of the extensive case law relating to this topic, from both England and Wales and the United States of America, it may be safe to indicate that Lord Denning's remarks

250 (1954–8) 37 Tax Cas 79; [1956] TR 397; 35 ATC 413; 50 R & IT 33.

251 (1954–8) 37 Tax Cas 79, at 86.

252 [1956] 1 QB 702.

on the topic are irrelevant. Of interest is the case of *Fitzpatrick v. Secretary of State for the Environment*,[253] in which enforcement notices signed with the rubber stamp of the appropriate official bearing their facsimile signature were held to be valid in accordance with the provisions of s234(2) of the Local Government Act 1972. The members of the Court of Appeal reached their decision without, it appears, reference to any relevant case law.[254]

**1.125 United States of America** The use of rubber stamps as a means of authenticating documents in the United States of America has only been tempered with the need to ensure the version of the signature in the form of an impression of a rubber stamp was used with the intent to authenticate the document. The range of uses to which rubber stamps have been put, and which judges have accepted with minor exceptions, include cheques (checks),[255] matters pertaining to the Fifth Amendment,[256] elections,[257] finance statements,[258]

253 [1990] 1 PLR 8, CA.

254 This is of interest, bearing in mind the comments by Buxton and Brooke LJJ in *Copeland v. Smith* [2000] 1 WLR 1371.

255 Pennsylvania: *Robb v. The Pennsylvania Co. for Insurance on Lives and Granting Annuities*, 40 W.N.C. 129, 3 Pa.Super. 254, 1897 WL 3989 (Pa.Super. 1897) affirmed by 186 Pa. 456, 40 A. 969; for a dissenting opinion, see 186 Pa. 456, 41 A. 49.

256 Federal 2nd circuit: *Biegeleisen v. Ross*, 158 F.3d 59 (2nd Cir. 1998) (a valid IRS levy based on a notice signed with a signature stamp rather than a manuscript signature does not violate the Due Process Clause of the Fifth Amendment).

257 Kentucky: *Wurts v. Newsome*, 253 Ky. 38, 68 S.W.2d 448 (it is a valid signature where a judge signs ballots by means of a rubber stamp) (1934).

258 Colorado: *In the Matter of Colorado Mercantile Co.*, 299 F.Supp. 55 (1969) (a financing statement submitted with a stamped signature was acceptable, even though the requirement at the time of filing was for a manual signature).

Connecticut: *In re Bengston*, 1965 WL 8262 (Bankr.D.Conn.), 3UCC Rep.Serv. 283 (a name printed in ink – understood to mean stamped with a rubber stamp – on a standard form financing statement satisfied the requirement that the secured party signed the financing statement).

Texas: *Brooks v. The State of Texas*, 599 S.W.2d 312 (a pen packet reflecting convictions for theft burglary where the facsimile signature of the clerk is affixed by means of a rubber stamp did not bar admission of the pen packet at the penalty stage) (1979).

Connecticut: *In re Deep River National Bank*, 73 Conn. 341, 47 A. 675 (the signature of Clinton B. Davis, affixed to a promissory note 'D., Treasurer' was held to be a valid signature) (1900).

when affixed to letters,[259] public documents,[260] but not receipts.[261] The judicial use of rubber stamps appears to have been widely taken up in various states, and although a federal court accepted that a search warrant signed with rubber stamp by a magistrate was held to be valid in the seventh circuit case of *United States of America v. Juarez*,[262] Tone CJ did not fully approve, at 1114:

259 Federal 6th circuit: *National Accident Society v. Spiro*, 78 F. 774, 24 C.C.A. 334 (the facsimile signature of an officer of the company affixed to a printed letter head of the company was sufficiently proven) (1897).

Wisconsin: *Kocinski v. The Home Insurance Company*, 154 Wis.2d 56, 452 N.W.2d 360 (Wis. 1990) (a facsimile signature stamped on a document with a rubber stamp satisfied the requirement that the document be subscribed).

260 Arizona: *Maricopa County v. Osborn*, 60 Ariz. 290, 136 P.2d 270 (the facsimile signature of the treasurer applied by rubber stamp was sufficient for refunding bonds) (1943).

Carolina: *Smith v. Greenville County*, 188 S.C. 349, 199 S.E. 416 (the facsimile signature using a rubber stamp by a county treasurer on a tax execution is the signature of the treasurer) (1938).

Florida: *State v. City of Fort Lauderdale*, 149 Fla. 177, 5 So.2d 263 (facsimile signatures affixed to city hospital revenue certificates and the attached coupons are valid) (1941).

New York: *Tenement House Department of City of New York v. Weil*, 76 Misc. Rep. 273, 134 N.Y.S. 1062 (an order issued under the Tenement House Law containing a facsimile signature affixed by an official by means of a rubber stamp is valid) (1912); *Brooklyn City Railroad Company v. City of New York*, 139 Misc. 691, 248 N.Y.S. 196 (a notice of claim with the signatures of an officer and of a notary public affixed to the document with a rubber stamp were sufficient) (1930).

North Dakota: *Andre v. North Dakota State Highway Commissioner*, 295 N.W.2d 128 (a record of a speeding violation with the words 'STAT. FEE JUL 24 1979 THOMAS EWING' stamped on the back of the paper was adequate for the intended purpose of informing the State Highway Department of an admission or adjudication of a traffic violation) (1980); *State of North Dakota v. Obrigewitch*, 356 N.W.2d 105, (N.D. 1984) (an order of suspension and driving record is valid where a rubber stamp was used to affix the signature of the director of the Drivers License Division of the State Highway Department).

Oklahoma: *Moss v. Arnold*, 63 Okl.Cr. 343, 75 P. 491 (the facsimile signature of the chairman of the Board of County Commissioners applied by means of a rubber stamp is sufficient to authenticate requisitions) (1938); *State of Oklahoma ex rel. Independent School District Number One of Tulsa County v. Williamson*, 1960 OK 126, 352 P.2d 394 (Okla. 1960) (the Uniform Facsimile Signature of Public Officials Act is valid and officials may use facsimile signatures on public bonds as a substitute for manuscript signatures as required by law).

Utah: *Salt Lake City v. Hanson*, 19 Utah 2d 32, 425 P.2d 773 (the signatures of a police officer and city judge to a complaint, affixed by means of a rubber stamp, are sufficient) (1967).

261 Georgia: *Bell Bros. v. Western & A. R. Co.*, 125 Ga. 510, 54 S.E. 532 (a freight receipt for a car containing cabbages signed by stencil with the name of the agent of the defendant company was not accepted because there was no proof that the agent signed the receipt, adopted the signature, or that it was his custom to sign his name to receipt by this type of stamp) (1906).

Massachusetts: *Boardman v. Spooner*, 13 Allen 353, 95 Mass. 353, 1866 WL 5009 (Mass.), 90 Am.Dec. 196 (a bill of sale of goods bearing the purchaser's name stamped upon it is not sufficient proof to show that the stamp was adopted as a signature).

262 549 F.2d 1113 (1977).

> Defendant also contends that the search warrant should be invalidated because the magistrate used a signature stamp instead of signing it personally. We do not approve the use of a signature stamp by a magistrate. Its use creates the appearance that the user lacks the sensitivity a federal judicial officer should have to the important values which the warrant is designed to protect. Nevertheless, in this case the magistrate testified unequivocally that he remembered placing the signature stamp on the warrant, and the District Court credited this testimony. We cannot say that it was clearly erroneous for the court to have done so. We therefore do not find that it was in error to refuse to declare the warrant invalid and thereby exclude the evidence seized pursuant to the warrant, despite our condemnation of the magistrate's practice.

**1.126** At a state level, the use of rubber stamps has been widely accepted,[263] and

---

Maine: *Mahoney v. Ayoob*, 124 Me. 20, 125 A. 146, 37 A.L.R. 85 (where a disclosure commissioner endorsed a capias signed with his facsimile signature impressed with a rubber stamp is not a signature because the signature was not under his hand) (1924).

263 Florida: *State of Florida v. Hickman*, Fla., 189 So.2d 254 (the facsimile signature of a justice of the peace affixed to a warrant by a rubber stamp is valid, even when affixed by the chief clerk under the authority of the justice) (1966).

Illinois: *Streff v. Colteaux*, 64 Ill.App. 179, 1896 WL 2352 (Ill.App. 1 Dist.) (a declaration may be signed with the names of the plaintiff's attorneys by means of a rubber stamp) (1896); *People of the State of Illinois v. Stephens*, 297 N.E.2d 224 (a search warrant signed by a magistrate with a rubber stamp was not invalid) (1973).

Iowa: *Loughren v. B. F. Bonniwell & Co.*, 125 Iowa 518, 101 N.W. 287, 106 Am.St.Rep. 319 (the subscription by a justice with a rubber stamp bearing the facsimile of his signature is sufficient for a notice, even when carried out by another, but with his authority) (1904).

Massachusetts: *Wheeler v. Lynde*, 1 Allen 402, 83 Mass. 402, 1861 WL 6171 (Mass.) (it is a signature where an attorney at law signs the back of a writ by means of a rubber stamp) (1861).

New Mexico: *Costilla Estates Development Co. v. Mascarenas*, 33 N.M. 356, 267 P. 74 (the signature of a court clerk by means of a rubber stamp as a method of endorsement of filing papers was held sufficient) (1928).

Pennsylvania: *Commonwealth Department of Transportation v. Ballard*, 17 Pa. Cmwlth. 310, 331 A.2d 578 (the signature of a traffic court judge by means of a rubber stamp was not inadmissible where the seal of the court was also applied to the record) (1975).

Texas: *Ex parte Spencer*, 171 Tex.Cr.R. 339, 349 S.W.2d 727 (a complaint is valid where the complainant and the deputy clerk both affixed their signatures by means of a facsimile rubber stamp) (1961); *Ex parte Britton*, 382 S.W.2d 264 (a facsimile stamped signature of the governor on extradition papers does not affect the validity of the warrant) (1964); *Parsons v. The State of Texas*, 429 S.W.2d 476 (a complaint was sufficiently signed with the facsimile signature of the complainant with a rubber stamp) (1968); *Estes v. State*, 484 S.W.2d 711 (a facsimile signature applied to a document from the Department of Corrections by means of a rubber stamp was a sufficient signature) (1972); *Huff v. The State of Texas*, 560 S.W.2d 652 (the facsimile signature of the country district clerk stamped on certified copies of a judgment and sentence is valid) (1978); *Paulus v. The State of Texas*, 633 S.W.2d 827 (Tex.Crim.App. 1981) (there was no error when an indictment is signed with the facsimile signature of the foreman of a jury by means of

Hood AJ indicated how widely rubber stamps were used in the 1943 Columbia case of *McGrady v. Munsey Trust Co.*,[264] where the chief deputy clerk personally applied a facsimile representation of their signature to a summons. Hood AJ indicated the general use of the methods in his comments at 106: 'This practice was adopted many years ago and is a matter of great convenience since more than 4,000 landlord and tenant complaints are filed in the trial court each month'. The legal and practical position of rubber stamps was put into context by Lattimore J in the 1930 Texas case of *Stork v. State*,[265] in which the facsimile signature of a justice of the peace affixed by rubber stamp to affidavit and liquor search warrant was held to be a sufficient signing. Lattimore J considered a number of cases, and stated, at 735:

> The writer is of opinion that when it appears without question, as in this case, that the magistrate in person took the affidavits of those who swore to same, and also so issued the search warrant, and that to each he affixed his name, it would be a matter of no moment whether he so affixed said name by one stroke as by the use of a stencil or rubber stamp, or whether he sat down at a typewriter and wrote his name with same upon such document, or that he wrote it out in what we commonly call longhand, provided that in each such case the facts must allow the name to have been affixed by the officer himself, or under his immediate authority and direction and in his presence.

## *A stencil-pen*

**1.127** An interesting variation of technology for appending a copy of a manuscript signature was used in the case of *Whyte v. Watt*,[266] before the Registration Appeal Court in Scotland. An objector signed a notice of objection using an instrument called a stencil-pen. The letters forming his signature were

---

a rubber stamp); *Benavides v. State of Texas*, 763 S.W.2d 587 (Tex.App. – Corpus Christi 1988) (a penitentiary packet stamped with a rubber stamp producing a facsimile of an original signature is an acceptable means of signing legal documents); *Kemp v. State of Texas*, 861 S.W.2d 44 (Tex.App. – Houston 14th Dist. 1993) (the use of a rubber stamp to produce a facsimile of a county judge's signature on a list of previous criminal records did not affect the authenticity of the signature); *In re Barber*, 982 S.W.2d 364 (Tex. 1998) (the signature of a judge affixed by a rubber stamp is a signature on a judgment, even when affixed to the document by an intermediate authority at the direction of the judge).

Utah: *State of Utah v. Montague*, 671 P.2d 187 (Utah 1983) (clerk of the court affixing an imprint of the judge's signature with authority to documents as being true originals).

Wisconsin: *Dreutzer v. Smith*, 56 Wis. 292, 14 N.W. 465 (a rubber stamp with a facsimile of the signature of the County Clerk affixed to a tax deed was considered to be writing the name) (1882).

264 32 A.2d 106.

265 114 Tex.Crim. 398, 23 S.W.2d 733.

266 (1893) 21 R. 165; see also *Henderson v. Watt* (1893) 1 S.L.T. 342.

perforated upon a prepared wax skin, stretched on a frame. He then placed the notice under the waxed skin, and passed an inked roller over the waxed skin. As the ink from the roller passed through the perforations in the waxed skin, it produced the signature on the notice. Mr Watt formed the signature; no other person was employed in the operation. When letters or words have been formed on the waxed skin by the stencil-pen in this way, up to 100 sheets of paper – or more – can be placed successively under the waxed skin, and as the inked roller passes over the waxed skin, so the letter or words are produced on the sheet of paper immediately under the waxed skin. The validity of the signature was challenged, in that it did not comply with the provisions of s4 of 19 & 20 Victoria chapter 58, Registration of Burgh Voters (Scotland) 1856, in particular, according to forms 4 and 5 of schedule A.

**1.128** Kinnear, Trayner and Kincairney LL dismissed the appeal without calling on counsel for the respondent. They followed the judgment of the English court in the case of *Bennett v. Brumfitt*,[267] and held that the provisions of the statute requiring that a notice of objection should be signed by the objector had been satisfied. It was noted that such a signature would not be sufficient to satisfy the conditions of the Statute regulating the subscription and attestation of probative deeds, but that was not necessary in order to satisfy the requirements of the Statute now under construction. Kinnear L said, at 166–7:

> The word "signed" is not a technical word but a word of ordinary language. Subscription is a method of signing. It is not the only method. We are therefore to consider whether the method of authentication described in the case can properly be called "signing." Now, upon that question, we have the advantage of a decision of the Court of Common Pleas, in the construction of a similar provision in the 6th of the Queen, chapter 18, which requires that a "notice of objection shall be signed by the objector." In *Bennett v. Brumfitt*, L. R., 3 C. P. 28, the Court held that this requirement was satisfied although the objector had not subscribed the notice but had affixed his name to it by means of a stamp on which was engraved a facsimile of his ordinary signature. I cannot suppose that when the Legislature has employed the same language in a Scots Act as in a previous English Act, it intended to prescribe one method of authentication in England and another in Scotland, and I should be very slow to differ from the learned Judges in England as to the meaning of an ordinary word in the English language.

## Signature machines

**1.129** Machines for writing multiple copies of a signature have a long history. John Isaac Hawkins (1772–1855) is credited with inventing what is generally

267 (1867–68) 3 LRCP 28.

referred to as an autopen, known at the time as a pentagraph.[268] Such devices have a long history. An 'autopen' featured in a case begun by the chef Gordon Ramsay, who took legal action against his father-in-law, Christopher Hutcheson, over a lease for a pub called the York & Albany in London. The lease was signed in 2007 for an annual rent of £640,000. Mr Ramsay's signature was affixed to the lease using a Ghostwriter Manual Feed Signature Machine. Mr Ramsay claimed that the signature was a forgery. Morgan J described how the machine worked at [75]:

> To use the machine, an operator needed a number code, to be tapped into the machine by use of a key pad, and a signature card. The signature card identified the signature which the machine would produce. It was also necessary to fit a pen to the machine. In this case, the pens which were used included a pen which produced the result of using a felt tip pen and another pen which gave the appearance of a pen with a fine knib being used. The felt tip signature was suitable for signing books or photographs and the fine knib pen was suitable for signing legal documents and cheques.

**1.130** Mr Justice Morgan decided that because Mr Hutcheson was acting as an agent for Mr Ramsay at the time, he had acted within the authority conferred on him by Mr Ramsay, and he had not exceeded his authority. Mr Ramsay was bound by the guarantee in the lease of the premises.[269] The discussion elsewhere in this book regarding the protection of the private key to a digital signature and how to guard a rubber stamp apply equally to the use of such machines.

## Mechanical marks by human action

**1.131** The application of legal principles applies to new technology in the same way as it relates to more established ways of conducting business.

### *Typewriting*

**1.132** Once the typewriter had developed sufficiently to enable a typist to type faster than a human could write, the machine began to be widely used. An early example of litigation respecting the value of a typed signature was a case involving a remonstrance in 1905 in Indiana, that of *Ardery v. Smith*.[270] In this case, an attorney had the authority to sign a remonstrance against the issue of a liquor licence for and on behalf of voters, and being afflicted with erysipelas in his right hand, he caused the names to be typed in his presence and under his

268 *Proceedings of the Institution of Civil Engineers*, 25 (1866), pp. 512–14, available at http://www.icevirtuallibrary.com/doi/pdf/10.1680/imotp.1866.23204.

269 *Ramsay v. Love* [2015] EWHC 65 (Ch).

270 35 Ind.App. 94, 73 N.E. 840.

supervision. It was held to be immaterial that the names were added by means of a typewriter. Roby J summed up the position at 841:

> In an opinion given in 1842 by William Wirt, then Attorney General, the question submitted being whether the Secretary of the Treasury was authorized by a statute requiring warrants to be drawn and signed by him to have his name impressed thereon by means of copper plate, the following language was used: 'There would be great difficulty in maintaining the proposition, as a legal one, that, when the law required signing, it means that it must be done with pen and ink. No book has laid down the proposition, or even given color to it. I believe that a signature made with straw dipped in blood would be equally valid and obligatory, and, if so, where is the legal restriction on the implement which the signer may use? If he may use one pen, why may he not use several – a polygraph, for example, or types, or a stamp? The law requires signing merely as an indication and proof of the parties' assent.' 1 Opinions of Attorneys General, 670. The quotation is an apt one, as applied to the facts now under consideration. The typewriter is a modern convenience. The signature made by it was in this case the signature of the attorney; the operator being in fact his agent, exactly as the keys and the types were his agents.

**1.133** From an evidential point of view, the person whose name was typed on the document must adopt the typed version as their signature.[271] Crane J illustrated the difficulty in the 1911 New York case of *Landeker v. Co-operative Bldg. Bank*,[272] demonstrating that it is necessary to link the application of the typewritten name

271 For Australia see *Neill v. Hewens* (1953) 89 CLR 1; for the United States of America, see Federal, 10th circuit: *Roberts v. Johnson*, 212 F.2d 672 (it must be proven to be intended to be the signature of the witness where a form designating a beneficiary is signed with a typewritten name) (1954); California: *Estate of Moore*, 92 Cal.App.2d 120, 206 P.2d 413 (a will signed with a typewritten name cannot be considered to be signed in the absence of evidence to show it was typed by the testator or that it was typed in his presence and at his direction by another) (1949); Maine: *Maine League Federal Credit Union v. Atlantic Motors*, 250 A.2d 497, 6 UUC Rep.Serv. 198 (there was no intent to adopt a typewritten name on a financing statement; it was only through inadvertence that the document was not signed with a manuscript signature) (1969); Massachusetts: *Andre v. Ellison*, 324 Mass. 665 (1949) 88 N.E.2d 340; Missouri: *First Security Bank of Brookfield v. Fastwich*, 612 S.W.2d 799 (Mo.App. 1981) (the burden of establishing the typed signature of a corporation arises when it has been put in issue by a specific denial. The burden is on the party claiming under the signature, but he is aided by the presumption that it is genuine or authorized); in the Court of First Instance of Hong Kong in the case of *Shenzhen Tian He Jian Sang Electronic Holdings Company Limited v. Hong Kong Jian Sang Electronics (Group) Limited [2008]* HKCFI 387; HCA 1587/2007, 9 May 2008, Hon Fung J held that it could not be inferred that an unsigned copy of a letter with the typed name of the second defendant was intended to be a signed copy addressed to the plaintiff.

272 130 N.Y.Supp. 780.

to proof that the name was typed with authority and intent.[273] Interestingly, a number of cases dealing with typewritten signatures are of relatively recent origin, and it is to be wondered, when reading some of the reports, whether the points ought to have been taken at all, given the long and liberal history adopted by the common law in relation to the form a signature takes and set out in this book.[274] Examples include arbitration,[275] mechanics' lien,[276] Statute of Frauds,[277]

273 See also the 1911 Californian case of *Little v. Union Oil Company of California*, 73 Cal.App. 612, 238 P. 1066; the Maryland case of *Cambridge, Inc., v. The Goodyear Tire & Rubber Company*, 471 F.Supp. 1309 (1979) where a typewritten name of a lease did not bind where it was not intended to bind as a legal signature, and the 1926 Pennsylvania case of *Tabas v. Emergency Fleet Corporation*, 9 F.2d 648 affirmed *United States Shipping Board Emergency Fleet Corporation v. Tabas*, 22 F.2d 398 where the government of the United States was not deemed to have executed a contract because its name was typed on paper in the absence of evidence to show it authorized or adopted such signature.

274 Although see the Maine case of *In re Carlstrom*, 3 UCC Rep.Serv. 766, 1966 WL 8962 (Bankr.D.Me.) where a typewritten name on a financing statement was not accepted as a signature. Note the astounding views of Conrad, Referee in Bankruptcy, negating the concept that a symbol can be considered a signature, and his hostile comments on the decision in *Benedict, Trustee in Bankruptcy of Lillian E. Hargrove d/b/a Hargrove Typesetting Services v. Lebowitz*, 346 F.2d 120 (1965).

275 Illinois: *Just Pants, an Illinois limited partnership v. Wagner*, 617 N.E.2d 246 (Ill.App. 1 Dist. 1993) (the typewritten name of an arbitrator at the end of a memorandum of decision can serve to execute and give legal effect to the contents).

276 New Jersey: *J. D. Loizeaux Lumber Company v. Davis*, 124 A.2d 593, 41 N.J. Super. 231 (the name of the plaintiff typed on a materialman's notice of intention was held to be intended to be a signing as well as to serve other functions disclosed by the printed material) (1956).

277 Federal, 9th circuit: *In the Matter of Save-On-Carpets of Arizona, Inc.*, 545 F.2d 1239 (1976) (a typewritten signature on a UCC financing statement satisfied the signature requirement of the Statute of Frauds).

Alaska: *A & G Construction Co., Inc., v. Reid Brothers Logging Co., Inc.*, Alaska, 547 P.2d 1207 (the name 'Glenn W. Reid' typed at the bottom of a letter was considered to be signed) (1976).

Florida: *Ashland Oil, Inc., v. Pickard*, Fla., 269 So.2d 714 (the typed words on notepaper with the letterhead of the company and with the word 'Harold L. Slam, President' typed at the bottom is a signature) (1972).

Maryland (1967): *Dubrowin v. Schremp*, 248 Md. 166, 235 A.2d 722.

Massachusetts: *Irving v. Goodimate, Co.*, 320 Mas. 454, 70 N.E.2d 414, 171 A.L.R. 326 (the name of the employer typed at the end of a letter to an employee is a sufficient signature) (1946).

Minnesota: *Radke v. Brendon*, 271 Minn. 35, 134 N.W.2d 887 (a prospective vendor's letter including the prospective purchaser's name and typewritten name of the vendor is tantamount to a written signature, given the intent) (1965).

Mississippi: *Dawkins and Company v. L & L Planting Company*, 602 So.2d 838 (Miss. 1992) (a letter written on a buyer's letterhead including the typewritten name of the sender is a sufficient signing to meet merchant's exception to the Statute of Frauds).

New York (1919): *Cohen v. Wolgel*, 107 Misc. Rep. 505, 176 N.Y.S. 764 affirmed 191 A.D. 883, 180 NY.S. 933.

New Mexico: *Watson v. Tom Growney Equipment, Inc.*, 721 P.2d 1302 (N.M. 1986) (a name typed on a purchase order was held to be a sufficient signature, because the mortgages,[278] pleadings,[279] secured transactions,[280] bonds,[281] taxation[282] and wills.[283]

**1.134** In New Zealand, this concept is called the 'authenticated signature fiction' and is illustrated by the case of *Bilsland v. Terry*,[284] where an agreement for the sale of land had the names of both parties set out in the document, but it was only signed with the manuscript signature of one party. It was held to be a sufficient signing to satisfy s2 of the Contracts Enforcement Act 1956. Quilliam J commented, at 50:

> Upon the authority, therefore, of the cases I have cited I find that the agreement was a sufficient memorandum in writing to satisfy the

signatory had deliberately filled out other details on the order form).

Wisconsin (1912): *Garton Toy Co. v. Buswell Lumber & Mfg. Co.*, 150 Wis. 341, 136 N.W. 147.

278 Federal 2nd circuit: *Benedict, Trustee in Bankruptcy of Lillian E. Hargrove d/b/a Hargrove Typesetting Services v. Lebowitz*, 346 F.2d 120 (1965) (the insertion of the name in the body of a financing statement was held to be a sufficient signing. The intent to authenticate was established by the act of a secretary in typing his name at his direction and subsequently filing the statement).

279 Indiana: *City of Gary v. Russell*, 112 N.E.2d 872 (a notice of claim was sufficiently signed when the plaintiff's name was typewritten at the end) (1953).

North Dakota: *Hagen v. Gresby*, 159 N.W. 3, 34 N.D. 349, 5 L.R.A. 1917B, 281 (the typewritten name and address of an attorney on a summons is sufficient. The attorney, F. B. Lambert, had not written a summons with a manuscript signature since 1896) (1916).

280 Federal 4th circuit: *Calaway v. Admiral Credit Corporation*, 407 F.2d 518 (a financing statement with a typed name was not invalid for lack of manuscript signature where a typewritten signature was provided) (1969).

Federal 5th circuit: *In the Matter of Bufkin Brothers, Inc.*, 757 F.2d 1573 (1985) (a secured creditor's typewritten corporate name on a continuation statement was sufficient to validate the statement).

Connecticut: *In re Horvath*, 1963 WL 8592 (Bankr.D.Conn.), 1UCC Rep.Serv. 624 (a typewritten name considered a signature) (1963).

Georgia: *Peoples Bank of Bartow County v. Northwest Georgia Bank*, 139 Ga.App. 264, 228 S.E.2d 181 (the printed name of the bank on a financing statement served to reinforce a manuscript signature that was not easily identified) (1976).

281 Texas: *B. F. Bridges & Son v. First Nat. Bank of Center*, 47 Tex.Civ.App. 454, 105 S.W. 1018 (a typed signature to a bond is sufficient if adopted) (1907).

282 Massachusetts: *Assessors of Boston v. Neal*, 311 Mass. 192, 40 N.E.2d 893 (an application for abatement was inadvertently not signed with a manuscript signature, but it was accompanied with a letter signed by the Treasurer of the First People's Trust, held that the application signed with a typewriter was sufficient) (1942).

283 In the 1944 Texas case of *Zaruba v. Schumaker*, 178 S.W.2d 542, a will written by the deceased on a typewriter with her typewritten name was held to be signed; compare the 1949 case in California of *Estate of Moore*, 92 Cal.App.2d 120, 206 P.2d 413 where a will signed with a typewritten name cannot be considered to be signed in the absence of evidence to show it was typed by the testator or that it was typed in his presence and at his direction by another.

284 [1972] NZLR 43.

> Contracts Enforcement Act, and is binding on the parties. I should mention that it was contended by Mr Luck that the conclusion I was invited to draw upon the basis of the authorities I have cited was plainly wrong, and that if I were to adopt it I should be introducing into the realm of conveyancing a hazard which should not be there. I realize that the rule to which I have referred is probably unknown to many conveyancers, but this alone is hardly a reason for not applying it where the facts render it applicable. The rule appears to be well established and I can see no reason why I should ignore it.

**1.135** This decision was followed in *Short v. Graeme Marsh Ltd*,[285] but not in *Carruthers v. Whitaker*[286] (*Bilsland v. Terry* was not referred to in this judgment). The *Bilsland v. Terry* and *Short v. Graeme Marsh Ltd* cases were later distinguished in *Stuart v. McInnes*,[287] where a contract for the sale of land was held not to be enforceable where neither party signed the agreement. Wilson J discussed the 'authenticated signature fiction' at 733–4:

> Although, over the years, the basis for the authenticated signature fiction seems to have changed somewhat, the line of cases in England which includes Tourret v. Cripps, Evans v. Hoare and Leeman v. Stocks has now settled the law on this topic. From these cases it is clear that, in England, the principle applies if, and only if, these conditions obtain:
>
> > (1) the contract, or the memorandum containing the terms of contract, must have been prepared by the party sought to be charged, or by his agent duly authorised in that behalf, and must have that party's name written or printed on it.
> >
> > (2) It must be handed or sent by that party, or his authorised agent, to the other party for that party to sign.
> >
> > (3) It must be shown, either from the form of the document or from the surrounding circumstances, that it is not intended to be signed by anyone other than the party to whom it is sent and that, when signed by him, it shall constitute a complete and binding contract between the parties.
>
> I think the justification for the fiction is to be found in the last condition. Where the form of the memorandum or the surrounding circumstances show the intention that the contract shall be binding on both parties although not signed by the one who prepared it, the terms of the statute are not really applicable with reference to that

285 [1974] 1 NZLR 722.

286 [1975] 2 NZLR 667.

287 [1974] 1 NZLR 729.

> one, so the fiction is introduced to meet the case. It is easy to see the justice of the result, but I confess to a regret that the solution found was to describe as a signature something that is not a signature and was never intended to be such. It might have been preferable to hold that such memoranda were outside the ambit of the statute in regard to the party whose signature was not contemplated as being necessary.

**1.136** He went on to discuss the decisions in *Bilsland v. Terry* and *Short v. Graeme Marsh Ltd* at 734–5, which he declined to follow. The same decision was reached in *Van der Veeken v. Watsons Farm (Pukepoto) Ltd,*[288] where a contract for the sale of property called for the signature of both parties, and the authenticated signature fiction was considered not relevant to the fact of this case; the decision in *Bilsland v. Terry* was also distinguished. It seems the current position in New Zealand is governed by *TA Dellaca Ltd v. PDL Industries Ltd,*[289] where the approaches taken in *Bilsland v. Terry* and *Short v. Graeme Marsh Ltd* were rejected. The members of the court favoured the approach taken by Wilson J in *Stuart v. McInnes* and Beattie J in *Van der Veeken v. Watsons Farm (Pukepoto) Ltd.* Tipping J commented, at 99: 'I agree with their observations that go further than the approach summarised by Wilson J really amounts to an unacceptable judicial repeal of the Contracts Enforcement Act 1956. The authenticated signature fiction is itself quite a significant departure from the literal terms of the Act'.

**1.137** In Canada, the use of a typed signature in combination with an authorized manuscript signature of a departmental lawyer was the issue in the case of *R v. Fredericton Housing Limited.*[290] The question was whether the typewritten signature of the Deputy Attorney General of Canada was acceptable on a statement of claim, together with the manuscript signature of a lawyer in the department. The manuscript signature 'F. J Dubrule' was affixed to the statement of claim by a solicitor in the Tax Litigation Section of the Department of Justice, of which section Mr Dubrule was the director. It was held that the signature was the signature of Mr Dubrule. It was duly authorized by him, and the typed name 'D. S. Maxwell', when it was authenticated by the subscription of the signature of Mr Dubrule, and became the signature of the Deputy Attorney General of Canada. Cattanach J made a useful observation, at 223, in discussing the difference between using a rubber stamp to affix a signature and a typewriter: 'If the typewritten name "D. S. Maxwell" is not "writing" (as I think it is) it is most certainly a mechanical method of affixing and I cannot distinguish in principle an affixing by keys striking a ribbon from a rubber stamp with ink on it'.

**1.138 Sale of property rights** The members of the Court of Appeal had occasion to consider the requirement of a signature on a document for the sale of

288 [1974] 2 NZLR 146.

289 [1992] 3 NZLR 88.

290 [1973] FC 196; [1973] CTC 160.

land in the case of *Firstpost Homes Ltd v. Johnson*.[291] In this case a director of the company reached an oral agreement with Miriam Fletcher, the owner of land in Staffordshire whereby she agreed to sell the land. A secretary typed a letter on 9 April 1993 for Mrs Fletcher to sign. Mrs Fletcher's address was typed on the top right-hand side of the letter and it was addressed to Mr Hale of Firstpost Homes Ltd, followed by the address of the company. The letter continued:

> Dear Geoff, re: Land and rear of Fulfen Farm, Burntwood Further to our recent discussions I now agree to sell you the above land shown on the enclosed plan which extends to 15·64 acres in consideration of the sum of £1,000 (One thousand pounds) per acre. Yours sincerely.

**1.139** Then there was a gap, and typed underneath the words 'M. Fletcher (Mrs)'. A plan, a copy of an Ordnance Survey plan showing the land in question, was attached to the letter by a paper clip. Mr Hale signed the plan at the foot. Mr Hale delivered the letter to Mrs Fletcher on Friday 1 April 1993 and returned on Sunday 11 April. Mrs Fletcher signed the letter and the plan. She died on 12 May 1993. The personal representatives refused to conclude the contract for the sale of the land and the company sought specific performance. His Honour Judge Farrer QC refused the application. The appeal was dismissed. In giving a substantial judgment, Peter Gibson LJ pointed out the legislature had intended to make radical changes, and the changes were intended to simplify the law and avoid disputes when enacting the Law of Property (Miscellaneous Provisions) Act 1989. While the letter indicated Mrs Fletcher intended to sell the land, it was not clear that she intended to sell the land to the company. As a result, it was the letter, and not the plan, that formed the document of sale, and only Mrs Fletcher had signed this document. It was argued by the company that the typed name and address of the company were sufficient to show it was signed by the company. However, Peter Gibson LJ rejected this submission, because it was based on previous authorities that in turn were based on earlier legislation, and not on the Law of Property (Miscellaneous Provisions) Act 1989. He considered it 'is an artificial use of language to describe the printing or the typing of the name of an addressee in the letter as the signature by the addressee when he has printed or typed the document'[292] and mentioned approvingly the comments made by Evershed MR and Denning LJ in *Goodman v. J Eban Limited*.[293] Peter Gibson LJ no longer considered the interpretation of the modern Act should be governed by the authorities in relation to the Statute of Frauds 1677 or s40 of the Law of Property Act 1925. It was decided that the company had not signed the letter, and there was, therefore, no contract in place, although this decision was 'limited to a case where the party whose signature is said to appear on a contract is only

291 [1995] 1 WLR 1567 CA.

292 [1995] 1 WLR 1567 at 1575 F-G.

293 [1954] 1 QB 550; [1954] 1 All ER 763; [1954] 2 WLR 581, CA.

names as the address of a letter prepared by him'.[294] Hutchinson and Balcombe LJJ agreed with this analysis, and Balcombe LJ reiterated the point, at 1577E, that the 'policy of the section is to avoid the possibility that one or other party may be able to go behind the document and introduce extrinsic evidence to establish a contract, which was undoubtedly a problem under the old law'. The move from form to function has certainly been halted in the case of the sale of property.[295] It is the view of Julian Farrand and Alison Clarke that the decision in *Goodman* does not provide the support that Peter Gibson LJ claimed, and the decision in *Firstpost* 'not only involved flaws in law but also enabled an unmeritorious escape from contractual obligations'.[296]

## *Telegram*

**1.140** The development of telegraphy in the early 19th century brought about the same types of dispute that occur in the era of the internet, and judges were required then, as now, to adapt old laws to new technologies. The telegram and its various technologies, including the telex, was widely used from the outset. In *Godwin v. Francis*,[297] an offer to buy a property was accepted by telegram. It was held that the telegram, together with other correspondence, was sufficient to satisfy the Statute of Frauds, and the signature of the telegraph clerk was considered a sufficient signature. In response to the argument that the instructions for the sending of the telegram cannot be a signature of the contract, because the paper was a mere instruction to the telegraph clerk, Bovill CJ responded, at 301–2:

> Assuming that argument to be correct (though I am not prepared to adopt it), that would be instructions to the company to do that which in the ordinary course of their business is done. Now, the ordinary course of business is to transmit, to write out, an exact copy of that which is intended to be conveyed, and to forward it. The acceptance of the plaintiff's offer is in the body of the document. The telegraph clerk copies it, signs it, and sends it to the plaintiff, the name of the seller appearing thereon. A correspondence ensues between the parties on the footing that there had been a binding contract for the sale of the estate; and, if the defendant had authority, it is clear that what was done did constitute a binding contract. But, independently of that, I am prepared to hold that the mere telegram written out and signed in the way indicated by the telegraph clerk, if done with the authority of the vendors, would have been a sufficient signature within the Statute of Frauds.

294 [1995] 1 WLR 1567 at 1576 E.

295 For signatures relating to the law of property, see J. Farrand and A. Clarke, *Emmet on Title* (London: Sweet & Maxwell, 2016), ch. 2 pt 2, 2.041–2.043.

296 Farrand and Clarke, *Emmet on Title*, 2.041.

297 (1870) LR 5 CP 295; 22 LT Rep NS 338.

**1.141** It was necessary to resolve the distinction between the contents of the document containing the message to be sent and subsequently presented to the telegraph office, and the document received by the recipient. In this respect, Willes J observed, at 302–3 that:

> The message was left, signed by the defendant, at the office of the Telegraph Company. A copy was sent by the company to the plaintiff, and authenticated by them in the usual way. If the message so sent had been contained in a letter sent by post, there can be no doubt that would have been a sufficient contract to satisfy the statute, That is because the General Post Office has been held to be the common agent of the parties employing it.

**1.142** Brett J also noted, at 303:

> I think there is evidence that the defendant, when he signed the instructions, intended that to operate as his signature to the contract, and that it constituted a binding contract signed by him, if he had authority to enter into it. Then, it was objected that the defendant's name appearing on the paper received by the plaintiff was insufficient, because the defendant had no power to delegate to the telegraph clerk an authority to sign his name. I think, however, it must be assumed as against him that he had authority to delegate to the clerk the power to sign for him, and that the signature so placed was binding upon him.

**1.143** A number of cases dealing with the exchange of telegrams were dealt with in a similar way as some forms of electronic signature are dealt with today: the point was not raised in argument, and therefore the issue of the efficacy of the signature not challenged, inferring an acceptance of the proof of intent of the parties in the case.[298] It is plain that the introduction of technology was not an excuse to prevent the application of legal principles to new technology. In *McBlain v. Cross*[299] it was held that the signature in a telegram was sufficient to come within the Statute of Frauds. Willes J was not going to let technology impede the way the law was interpreted, commenting, at 806 that 'If we did

298 In *Henkel v. Pape* (1870) 6 L.R.Exch. 7 and *L. Roth and Co. (Limited) v. Taysen, Townsend, and Co.* (1896–7) 12 TLR 211, CA contracts were formed by exchange of telegrams; the signature point was not raised in either case, but can be inferred that it was accepted; in *Sadgrove v. Bryden* [1907] 1 Ch 318, the words 'Consent, Shaw' sent by cablegram, which was, in turn, stamped with a 10 shilling stamp as power of attorney, was held sufficient to validate a form of proxy signed in advance but not dated in accordance with the provisions of s80 of the Stamp Act 1891; in *Behnke v. Bed Shipping Co.* [1927] 1 KB 649 a contract for the sale and purchase of a ship was conducted by letter, telegram and telephone, and it was held that a name added to a telegram is a signature where it is adopted or recognized by the party to be charged.

299 (1872) LT 804.

not hold such to be the law, the convenience which the modern invention of the electric telegraph has bestowed upon mankind would be in a great measure subverted'. In 1886, it was determined that a person may provide authority to sign a name to a memorandum of association under the Companies Act 1862,[300] and Vaughan Williams J had the foresight to issue a novel form of order in the case of *In re English, Scottish, and Australian Chartered Bank.*[301] In this case, the principal business of the bank was in Australia, but it was ordered that the bank had to be wound up in England. A scheme of reconstruction was proposed, and Vaughan Williams J directed that meetings of shareholders and creditors be held to ascertain their wishes. The majority of the creditors were in Australia, and because of the need for speed, Vaughan Williams J made an entirely new form of order directing a form of proxy to be sent by the Official Receiver by telegraph to Australia, appointing specified persons to vote for or against the scheme at the meeting to be held in London. A number of objections were taken on the result of the vote in the meeting. One of the objections was that the judge had no power to order the Australian proxies to be communicated by telegram to the meeting. The proxies ought to have been produced at the meeting. It was held that the judge had the power under s91 of the Companies Act 1862, in combination with s2 of the Joint Stock Companies Arrangement Act 1870, to direct the particulars of the Australian proxies to be communicated by telegraph, and there was no need for the proxies to be physically produced at the meeting. Lindley LJ commented, at 410: 'Now, that is an entirely new form of order. I need hardly say that it is adapted to the necessities of the time – it is ingeniously using the improved methods of communication by telegraph, which it would be folly to shut out and not use if you can do it' and Smith, LJ said, at 417:

> I wish to add a few remarks upon a point which for the first time arises in this case, that is as to whether or not the electric telegraph can be made use of to carry out what was eminently needed, and indeed was absolutely necessary to do justice in this case.

**1.144** Telegrams were as widely used in South Africa[302] and the United States of America as in any other jurisdiction. In 1869, the process involved in sending and receiving a telegram was outlined by Sargent J in the New Hampshire case of *Howley v. Whipple.*[303] In this instance, the decision centred on the requirements to provide for the proper evidentiary foundation necessary in adducing evidence of a telegram into proceedings. In addition, it also follows that telegrams may constitute adequate memorandum of the contract, and a contract can be construed

300 *In re Whitley Partners Callan's Case* (1886) 55 LJCh (NS) 540.

301 [1893] 3 Ch 385.

302 *Hersch v. Nel*, 1948 (3) S.A. 686 (A.D.); *Luttig v. Jacobs*, 1951 (4) S.A. 563 (O.P.D.) the legal effect of the signature was not discussed; *Balzun v. O'Hara* [1964] 3 All SA 368 (T).

303 48 N.H. 487 (1869).

by reference to several letters and telegrams.[304] The use of telegrams covered a range of situations, including bills,[305] judicial use[306] and the Statute of Frauds.[307] Generally, members of the judiciary have taken a robust view of telegrams, as illustrated in the 1912 Missouri case of *Leesley Bros. v. A. Rebori Fruit Co.*,[308]

304 Florida (1920): *Meek v. Briggs*, 80 Fla. 487, 86 So. 271.

305 Kentucky (1918): *Selma Savings Bank v. Webster County Bank*, 206 S.W. 870, 182 Ky. 604, 2 A.L.R. 1136.

306 Kentucky: *Blackburn v. City of Paducah*, Ky., 441 S.W.2d 395 (a telegram sent by Judge John B. Blackburn resigning from his post constituted a writing and was signed. The Board of Commissioners accepted the resignation and subsequently another police judge was appointed to fill the vacancy. When the appellant later attempted to act in this capacity, he was arrested) (1969). Clay, Commissioner, remarked, at 398, 'Perhaps we have belaboured the obvious too much. Here appellant selected the medium to the transmittal of his message, composed its content and authorized his signature thereto. It is difficult to understand how he can now question the legal efficacy of the written instrument he had drafted for the sole purpose of tendering his resignation'.

Oklahoma: *State ex rel. West v. Breckinridge*, 34 Okla. 649, 126 P. 806, 1912 OK 283 (where the resignation of the county attorney by telegram was acceptable).

307 Alabama: *McMillan, Ltd v. Warrior Drilling and Engineering Company, Inc.*, 512 So.2d 14 (Ala. 1986) (the name in telegram was a signature).

California: *Brewer v. Horst and Lachmund Company*, 127 Cal. 643, 60 P. 418, 50 L.R.A. 240 (telegrams buying and selling hops were held sufficient for purposes of Statute of Frauds) (1900).

Florida: *Heffernan v. Keith*, Fla., 127 So.2d 903 (a telegram is signed by the telegraph company with authority of the sender) (1961).

Florida: *Ashland Oil, Inc., v. Pickard*, Fla., 269 So.2d 714 (a telegram constitutes a signed memorandum) (1972).

Massachusetts (1972): *Providence Granite Co., Inc., v. Joseph Rugo, Inc., Mass.*, 291 N.E.2d 159, 362 Mass. 888.

Michigan (1890): *Ryan v. United States*, 136 U.S. 68, 10 S.Ct. 913, 34 L.Ed. 447.

Montana: *Hillstrom v. Gosnay*, Mont., 614 P.2d 466 (provided the necessary intent to authenticate the signature on a telegram is shown, the typewritten signature is a proper subscription) (1980).

Nebraska: *Hansen v. Hill*, 340 N.W.2d 8 (Neb. 1983) (a telegram accepting an offer to buy land to which the vendor's name has been affixed was considered signed under the Statute of Frauds).

New York: *Dunning & Smith v. Roberts*, 35 Barb. 463 (the manipulations of a telegraph operator, upon the oral instructions of a person to send a dispatch for him, are the equivalent to a signing by that person within the Statute of Frauds) (1862).

Texas: *Adams v. Abbot*, 151 Tex. 601 (1952), 254 S.W.2d 78 (a valid memorandum of contract may consist of letters and telegrams signed by the party to be charged and addressed to his agent or the other party to contract, or even to a third person not connected with transaction).

*Trevor v. Wood*, 9 Tiffany 307, 36 N.Y. 307, 1867 WL 6445 (N.Y.), 3 Abb.Pr.N.S. 355, 93 Am.Dec. 511, 1 Transc.App. 248 (where dealers bought and sold bullion by exchange of telegrams, the telegrams are sufficiently signed under the Statute of Frauds) (1867).

But see Vermont: *Pike Industries, Inc., v. Middlebury Associates*, 398 A.2d 280 affirmed on other grounds 436 A.2d 725, cert denied, 455 U.S. 947 (the contents of a telegram were not signed because the name of the party was not included in the body of the text) (1992).

308 162 Mo.App. 195, 144 S.W. 138.

where it was held that an exchange of two telegrams between the parties to buy and sell a carload of onion sets was held to be in substantial compliance with the Statute of Frauds. Nixon PJ remarked at 142: 'to hold otherwise would certainly embarrass present business methods and increase the expense and impair the usefulness of the telegraph as a necessary instrumentality in modern commerce'. This view was shared by Wolff, Referee in the 1961 New York case of *La Mar Hosiery Mills, Inc., v. Credit and Commodity Corporation*,[309] where he held that a name included in a telegram constituted a signature. He commented, at 190:

> It does not matter whether the telegram as delivered was copied from one written by an officer or employee of the defendant or was telephoned to the telegraph company by someone in the defendant's behalf. Precisely what happened here was not shown. The defendant could not well be heard to disclaim responsibility for the telegram and it is to the credit of the defendant that it has not attempted to do so. The telegram with the typed signature of defendant's name emanated from the defendant which is responsible for it. The signature on the telegram in suit, although typed in the office of the telegraph company, is therefore defendant's authorized signature within the requirements of the statute of frauds. In view of the way in which business is done nowadays, any other view would be unrealistic and would produce pernicious consequences, impeding the conduct of business transactions.

**1.145** The 1970 case of *Yaggy v. The B.V.D. Company, Inc.*[310] from North Carolina reinforced this point, where a telegram sent to the plaintiff accepting the latter's offer to purchase property was binding on the defendant. It was held that the defendant's name in print and affixed to the telegram by the same mechanical process employed by the telegraph company in reproducing other portions of the message constituted a signing within the Statute of Frauds. In the Pennsylvania case of *Hessenthaler v. Farzin*,[311] it was held that a mailgram that the vendor sent to a prospective purchaser of real estate confirming acceptance of sale constituted a signed writing. After revising a number of cases, Hoffman J indicated, at 993 that 'We agree with these authorities that the proper, realistic approach in these cases is to look to the *reliability* of the memorandum, rather than to insist on a formal signature'. He went on, at 994:

> The detail contained in this mailgram is such that there can be little question of its reliability. Appellants were careful to begin the mailgram by identifying themselves. They then made certain that their intention would be properly understood by declaring

309 28 Misc.2d 764, 216 N.Y.S.2d 186.

310 70 N.C.App. 590, 173 S.E.2d 496, 72 Am.Jur.2d.

311 564 A.2d 990 (Pa.Super. 1989).

> their acceptance, and identifying both the property and the consideration involved. In light of the primary declaration of identity, combined with the inclusion of the precise terms of the agreement, we are satisfied that the mailgram sufficiently reveals appellants' intention to adopt the writing as their own, and thus is sufficient to constitute a 'signed' writing for purposes of the Statute. Moreover, this result is consistent with the holdings of courts in other jurisdictions that have addressed the question of whether or not a telegram can be a signed writing for purposes of the Statute.

**1.146** Where an agent purports to act for a principal, it was determined by the Supreme Court of California in the case of *McNear v. Petroleum Export Corporation*[312] that the inclusion of the words 'Smith of Petroleum Export' at the beginning of the telegram acted as a means of identification, not authentication and was therefore not a signature.

## *Telex*

**1.147** When compared to the jurisprudence developed in Europe and the United States of America relating to the formation of contract, Japan is less concerned for contracts to be in writing and conform to a Statute of Frauds, but defines a contract as a judicial act to join two opposing wills.[313] As a result, the formation of a contract does not necessarily require either party to sign a contract. It is instructive to observe that the methods of communication do not appear to pose a problem in determining whether a contract has been formed in Japan. In the case of *Fawlty & Co Ltd v. Matsui Shoten K.K.*,[314] the plaintiff, a New Zealand company, agreed to ship meat to Kobe port. The defendant attempted to cancel the contract and refused to accept delivery, which meant the plaintiff had to sell the meat at a loss. The contract was negotiated by a mix of letters sent by airmail and exchanges by telex. The court held that there was a contract for the purchase and sale of the meat. Although the court did not have to determine whether the communications sent and received by telex were signed by the parties, nevertheless the court must have reached the conclusion that a contract had been formed in the light of the totality of the evidence, including the content of the correspondence conducted by telex. The inference is, that if signatures were necessary in Japan, it is probable that a signature sent by telex will have been acceptable.

312 280 P.R.Cal. 684.

313 N. Kashiwagi and E. A. Zaloom, 'Contract law and the Japanese negotiation process', in *The Business Guide to Japan*, ed. G. P. McAlinn (Singapore: Butterworth-Heinemann Asia, 1996), pp. 89–101, republished in K. L. Port and G. P. McAlinn, *Comparative Law: Law and the Legal Process in Japan* (2nd edn., Durham, N.C.: Carolina Academic Press, 2003), p. 459.

314 Showa 33 (Wa) No.681, 10 November 1962, translated by H. Kaneko in *Digital Evidence and Electronic Signature Law Review*, 9 (2012), pp. 109–13.

**1.148** In the English case of *Clipper Maritime Ltd v. Shirlstar Container Transport Ltd The Anemone,*[315] Staughton J had to determine whether a valid contract existed to perform a guarantee under the Statute of Frauds 1677. Clipper Maritime let their vessel *Anemone* on time charter to Afram Line Ltd. Shirlstar were in the business of leasing and operating containers. By May 1983, Shirlstar was owed US$275,000 by Transaltic, an associated company to Clipper Maritime. Owners of ships became reluctant to let their ships to such a charterer without security. The charter in respect of *Anemone* was negotiated by the owners' brokers on behalf of the charterers. It was agreed at an early stage there would be a guarantee, and the charter was eventually drawn up. The owners alleged that US$107,115.92 was due under the charter and claimed this amount from Shirlstar. Shirlstar denied they entered into a contract of indemnity. Evidence relating to the contract between the parties was partly contained in three telexes. Staughton J determined that the context in which the telexes were exchanged demonstrated the existence of a contract, even if only implied from the circumstances by which the correspondence took place.[316] Although the point did not arise, Staughton J offered extra-judicial comments in relation to the nature of the exchange of telexes in the context of s4 of the Statute of Frauds 1677: 'I reached a provisional conclusion in the course of the argument that the answerback of the sender of a telex would constitute a signature, while that of the receiver would not since it only authenticates the document and does not convey approval of the contents'.[317]

**1.149** This conclusion followed the analysis of older cases. When a person sends a telex, it can be assumed they did so either because they intended the contents to be acted upon, or had the authority so to do. Upon receipt of the answerback, the sender may wish to revoke the original document, although to retract the document effectively may be difficult. Whether a document can be effectively revoked in this way will depend upon the circumstances of the case. When the transmission of a telex is completed, the recipient will have received the document in much the same way as if the document had been sent through the post. The recipient cannot be said to approve the content until it takes such action that demonstrate its approval. A number of issues were not examined in the judgment. Although none of these issues were in dispute in this case, they could arise in the future, as pointed out by Professor Reed:

> It does not consider the effect of the cases which appear to require a mark to be made;
>
> The identification messages of telex machines (and fax machines and computers) only identify the sending *machine*, not the sender;
>
> It is quite possible to program a telex (or a fax machine or a computer's modem) to send a false identification message; and

315 [1987] 1 Lloyd's Rep 546.

316 [1987] 1 Lloyd's Rep 546 at 556(b).

317 [1987] 1 Lloyd's Rep 546 at 554(b).

> If the message is stored on disk by the recipient, it is possible to edit the contents and amend the identification message to take account of the alteration.[318] [italics in the original]

**1.150** In 2003, a case relating to the Limitation Act 1980 was heard before the Court of Appeal (Civil Division), that of *Good Challenger Navegante SA v. Metalexportimport SA (The 'Good Challenger')*.[319] This case was described by Clarke LJ as 'remarkable', because it involved an attempt by the respondent to enforce an award made by arbitrators in London against the appellant. The appellant appealed against a decision to enforce an order previously issued in 1993. In essence, there were three issues for the Court of Appeal to deal with: whether the proceedings to enforce the aware were time barred, whether there was an abuse of process, and whether the award could be enforced. There were a number of matters for the court to deal with in respect of the claim that the award had become time barred, the second of which was whether the claim was time barred in England and Wales at the relevant time as a matter of English law under s7 of the Limitation Act 1980, which provides as follows:

> An action to enforce an award, where the submission is not under seal, shall not be brought after the expiration of six years from the date on which the cause of action accrued.

**1.151** The respondents relied upon what they claimed were part payments and acknowledgments, which they said meant that the claim was not time barred under the provisions of ss29(5) and 30 of the Limitation Act 1980. The relevant document for the purposes of the appeal was whether a telex relied upon by the appellants could be considered as an acknowledgment in writing and signed by the person making it within the meaning of s30(1). The respondent relied upon two part payments by way of authorized agents, and four acknowledgements. The validity of the award was not challenged, but no payment was made immediately. Attempts were made to obtain payment during the following years, and the respondent relied upon two telexes, each between the respective agents of the parties, as acknowledgements of the obligation to pay the amount of the award. At appeal, the appellant submitted that the ordinary meaning of the word 'signed' requires the maker of the document to inscribe their name or a characteristic mark on the document in their own hand, and that there is no reason to give it any other meaning in respect of s30(1) of the Limitation Act. It would follow that the section was not satisfied where a telex contained a typed signature. There was no authority on this question in the context of s30 of the Limitation Act. The content of one telex dated 17 February 1988 is set out in the judgment of Mr Michael Crane QC, sitting as a Deputy High Court Judge in the Commercial Court.[320] The

318 Reed, 'What is a signature?', 4.1.

319 [2003] EWHC 10 (Comm), appealed [2004] 1 Lloyd's Rep 67, [2003] EWCA Civ 1668.

320 [2003] EWHC 10 (Comm) at 55–7.

telex was signed with the typewritten name 'NAVLOMAR' as authorized agent for the appellant. The question was whether the word 'NAVLOMAR' acted as a signature. The judge commented, at 61, that:

> As a matter of general principle, in my view a document is signed by the maker of it when his name or mark is attached to it in a manner which indicates, objectively, his approval of its contents. How this is done will depend upon the nature and format of the document. Thus in the case of a formal contract which prints the names of the parties and leaves a space under each name for the parties to write their names, the document will not have been signed by a party until he writes in his name in the space provided. Conversely, with a telex, where there is no such facility, the typed name of the sender at the end of the telex not only identifies the maker but leads to the inference that he has approved its contents: the typed name, therefore, constitutes his signature. Thus in my judgment each of the telexes relied on by the Claimant was signed by the sender typing in its name, or his name, at the foot of the document.

**1.152** The comments by the judge reflected the previous decisions held by numerous judges over the previous three hundred years, and were approved by Clarke LJ at 22, before discussing the language used in s30 of the Limitation Act and pointing out that the language was similar to that in s4 of the Statute of Frauds 1677.[321] There was no suggestion that the name typed on to the telex was a forgery or added without authority, and Clarke LJ articulated the reasoning of the court for accepting that the signature typed on to the telex was considered a signature under s30, at 27:

> The crucial point here is that Navlomar's typed signature appeared on the telex in circumstances in which it is evident that it was put on with Navlomar's authority so that it can be seen that Navlomar (and thus the charterers) were acknowledging the debt. The purpose of the statute is to be sure that the person said to be acknowledging the debt has in truth done so. That purpose is to my mind achieved by the conclusion reached by the judge and would be thwarted were we to accede to the charterers' submissions. We were referred to a number of other authorities but, in my judgment, none of them is directly in point or affects the conclusion of the judge. I would only add that I am pleased to be able to reach this conclusion because, although telexes are not so common now, there was a time when they were the usual form of communication between chartering brokers and their principals and any other conclusion would not be commercially sensible.

321 [2004] 1 Lloyd's Rep 67, [2003] EWCA Civ 1668 at 24.

**1.153** It followed that the claim was not time barred under English law.

**1.154** The acceptance of communications by telex in Australia occurred in 1985,[322] and there is a long history of recognition in the United States of America at the federal level.[323] Newman CJ indicated in the federal second circuit case of *Apex Oil Company, v. Vanguard Oil & Services Co.*,[324] that the hasty formation of contracts did not pose a problem for the courts. It was held that an exchange of communications by telex satisfied the merchants exception to the Statute of Frauds, and he indicated, at 423, that:

> Parties seeking the opportunity to make money with hurriedly arranged and briefly documented transactions ought not to expect appellate courts to provide them with extra protection against the risk that on occasion they will be held to the terms of an agreement that not every fact-finder would have found had been made.

**1.155** Decisions at state level in relation to the Statue of Frauds follow this trend,[325] exemplified in the early 1948 Californian case of *Joseph Denunzio Fruit Co., v. Crane*,[326] where signatures included in messages exchanged by teletype constituted a signature. O'Connor DJ observed at 128:

> As the court understands the modus operandi of the teletype machines in modern business practice, and particularly in connection with this lawsuit, Raymond R. Crane and A. B. Rains, Jr., each had a teletype machine in his office and as the machine was operated in one office, it would type the message or memorandum simultaneously in the other office; each party was readily identifiable and known to the other by the symbols or code letters used, and there is no contention that the messages did not originate in the office of one and terminate in the office of the other. The question is just what does constitute a 'signature' or 'signing' to satisfy the Statute of Frauds in California.

322 *Torrac Investments Pty Ltd v. Australian National Airlines Commission* [1985] ANZ Conv R 82.

323 Federal, 2nd circuit: *Interocean Shipping Company v. National Shipping and Training Corporation*, 523 F.2d 527 (1975) (a signature typed into a telex under authority was sufficient to bind the principle).

324 760 F.2d 417 (1985).

325 New York: *Miller v. Wells Fargo Bank International Corp.*, 406 F.Supp. 452 (1975) fn. 36, at 483 discusses the validity of a signature by way of a telex message, and raised the issue as to whether a test key on telex is capable of being a signature.

Pennsylvania: *The Ore & Chemical Corporation v. Howard Butcher Trading Corp.*, 455 F.Supp. 1150 (1978) (the exchange of telex messages between parties can constitute a written contract).

Texas: *Hideca Petroleum Corporation v. Tampimex Oil International, Ltd.*, 740 S.W.2d 838 (Tex.App. - Houston [1st Dist.] 1987) (the negotiation of sale for Dubai crude oil largely by means of exchange of telex messages).

326 79 F.Supp. 117 reversed on other grounds upon rehearing 89 F.Supp. 962.

> The court must take a realistic view of modern business practices, and can probably take judicial notice of the extensive use to which the teletype machine is being used today among business firms, particularly brokers, in the expeditious transmission of typewritten messages.

## *Facsimile*

**1.156** Documents sent by facsimile transmission have generally been accepted in common law jurisdictions.[327] The use of a facsimile transmission to send a copy of a document to a recipient was considered in the Australian case of *Molodysky v. Vema Australia Pty Ltd*,[328] where the issue of whether a facsimile transmission was considered to be service of an agreement signed by the vendor. The judge followed the test formulated in *Goodman v. J Eban Limited*[329] and concluded that the vendor intended their signature on the facsimile transmission to be effective.

**1.157** In the Singapore case of *Chua Sock Chen v. Lau Wai Ming*[330] in relation to the service of a notice to complete a transaction, Grimberg JC held that a notice to complete was properly served when sent by means of a facsimile transmission and where the original papers were subsequently sent by post to arrive the day after transmission. The judge responded to the argument that the notice sent by facsimile transmission was not a good service for the purposes of condition 29(2) and (3) the Singapore Law Society's Conditions of Sale 1981 at 1126B-C:

> I am unable to accept that contention. Neither of the two conditions I have quoted calls for the giving or servicing of notice to complete by a stipulated method. In these days of instantaneous communication it would be unrealistic and retrogressive, in the absence of clear words to the contrary under condition 29(2) and (3) by fax or telex is bad.

**1.158** Although the decision on the substance of the case was reversed on appeal, the members of the Court of Appeal offered no comments in relation to this aspect of the decision by Grimberg JC, which leads to the inference that his comments were adopted.

**1.159** A similar issue arose in England and Wales in the case of *Re a debtor (No. 2021 of 1995), ex parte, Inland Revenue Commissioners v. The debtor; Re a debtor*

327 For Poland, see Case note: Poland, I KZP 29/06, Resolution of the Polish Supreme Court, commentary by A. Lach, *Digital Evidence and Electronic Signature Law Review*, 5 (2008), pp. 147–8.

328 (1989) NSW ConvR 55-446, [1989] AUConstrLawNlr 143; note by J. Tyrril, *Australian Construction Law Newsletter*, 9 (1989), p. 24.

329 [1954] 1 QB 550; [1954] 1 All ER 763; [1954] 2 WLR 581, CA.

330 [1989] SLR 1119, the decision on the substance of the case was reversed on appeal [1992] 2 SLR 465.

*(No. 2022 of 1995), ex parte, Inland Revenue Commissioners v. The debtor.*[331] On Friday 9 June 1995 the Commissioners of Inland Revenue sent a completed form of proxy by first-class post with directions to the chairman of a meeting of creditors to vote against the debtors' proposals for voluntary arrangements. On the morning of the meeting, the Commissioners sent a facsimile transmission of the completed form of proxy to the chairman's office. Although not stated in the report of the case, it is probable that the form transmitted included the manuscript signature of the relevant official. When it was received, the chairman sought to verify the contents of the transmission by telephoning the Commissioners' office, but he was not able to speak to the officer handling the case. He refused to act upon the instructions sent by facsimile transmission. The original form of proxy arrived the following day. The Commissioners appealed the decision at first instance, where the district judge decided that the proxy sent by facsimile transmission was not signed as required by r8.2(3) of the Insolvency Rules 1986 SI 1986/1925. The question was whether the facsimile transmission of the form of proxy should have been accepted and acted upon by the chairman. In reaching his decision, Laddie J noted that given there was no direct authority on this point, he had to approach the issue from first principles. Having reviewed *Jenkins v. Gainsford and Thring*[332] and *Goodman v. J Eban Limited,*[333] he observed that:

> ... in the overwhelming majority of cases in which the chairman of a creditors' meeting received a proxy form, the form will bear a signature which he does not recognise and may well be illegible. Authenticity could only be enhanced if the creditor carrying suitable identification signed the form in person in the presence of the chairman. Even there the possibility of deception exists.[334]

**1.160** Interestingly, he went on to suggest 'that the function of a signature is to indicate, but not necessarily prove, that the document has been considered personally by the creditor and is approved of by him'.[335] Laddie J then took the matter one stage further, and made the following observation, which is directly related to the concept of an electronic signature:

> It may be said that a qualifying proxy form consists of two ingredients. First, it contains the information required to identify the creditor and his voting instructions and, secondly, the signature performing the function set out above. When the chairman receives a proxy form bearing what purports to be a signature, he is entitled to treat it as authentic unless there are surrounding circumstances which indicate otherwise.

331 [1996] 2 All ER 345, Ch D.

332 (1863) 3 Sw & Tr 93; 164 ER 1208.

333 [1954] 1 QB 550; [1954] 1 All ER 763; [1954] 2 WLR 581, CA.

334 [1996] 2 All ER 345, Ch D at 351 (b–c).

335 [1996] 2 All ER 345, Ch D at 351(d).

**1.161** In reaching the conclusion that a proxy form is acceptable when sent by facsimile transmission,[336] Laddie J noted that two things happen at the same time. The contents of the form are sent, and so is the signature applied to the form, described thus:

> The receiving fax is in effect instructed by the transmitting creditor to reproduce his signature on the proxy form which is itself being created at the receiving station. It follows that, in my view, the received fax is a proxy form signed by the principal or by someone authorized by him.[337]

**1.162** This decision was reached in November 1995 without, it seems, the benefit of the knowledge of the decision by Waller J in *Standard Bank London Ltd v. Bank of Tokyo Ltd*,[338] which was delivered on 13 March 1995. The decision by Waller J is based on a tested telex between banks, which is a slightly different concept to a facsimile transmission, because a tested telex provides for a separate method of authenticating the content of the transmission. Nevertheless, in both cases, an emphasis was placed on the fact that a document sent by such means can be considered authentic and reliable, provided the recipient was not aware of any particulars that might indicate the document cannot be trusted. A case similar to that determined by Waller J in *Standard Bank London Ltd v. Bank of Tokyo Ltd* was heard before Tay Yong Kwang JC in Singapore in 2003, in which he held, in the case of *Industrial & Commercial Bank Ltd v. Banco Ambrosiano Veneto SpA*[339] that a message using an authentication code sent through the SWIFT (Society for Worldwide Interbank Financial Telecommunication) system has the legal effect of binding the sender bank according to its contents, and where a recipient bank undertakes further checks on credit standing or other aspects, it does not detract from this proposition. The effect of the comments made by Laddie J, taken together with the comments by Waller J, suggest a move towards a responsibility by a recipient to consider all the circumstances of the means of authentication before acting upon the authority[340] – although it could be argued, in accordance with established practice between banks – that a receiving bank is entirely justified in wholly relying on an instruction based exclusively on confirmation of the test code. The practical conclusion to this question is highly significant. The Bangladesh Bank is fortunate that employees in the New York Federal Reserve and an employee in an intermediary bank questioned a series of transactions authorized via the SWIFT financial

336 Laddie J indicated that the decision he made was only in relation to Part 8 of the Insolvency Rules 1986, and said 'Different considerations may apply to faxed documents in relation to other legislation' at 352d–e.

337 [1996] 2 All ER 345, Ch D at 351(h).

338 [1995] CLC 496; [1996] 1 C.T.L.R. T-17.

339 [2003] 1 SLR 221.

340 V. Mallet and A. Chilkott, 'Bangladeshi job: how cyber heist netted $81m', *Financial Times*, 19 March/20 March 2016, p. 8.

transaction system in February 2016. Thieves had placed malicious software into the computer system of the central bank. They then initiated thirty-five transfers to the value of US$951m via the SWIFT financial transaction system. Five orders were executed to a value of US$101m, although a spelling error sent to an account in Sri Lanka enabled the bank to recover US$20m, resulting in a loss of US$81m.

**1.163** The Vice-Chancellor, Sir Andrew Morritt, was required to reach a decision on the identical point to *Industrial & Commercial Bank Ltd v. Banco Ambrosiano Veneto SpA* in the case of *PNC Telecom plc v. Thomas*,[341] as to whether the service of a notice sent by facsimile transmission for an extraordinary general meeting on a members' requisition under s368 of the Companies Act 1985 was valid. By s368, notice to call a meeting is required to be deposited at the registered office of the company. The claimant argued that the notice was not valid on three counts: because it was sent by facsimile transmission, and the use of a facsimile transmission was not permitted within the meaning of 'deposited' in s368; that the Companies Act 1985 (Electronic Communication) Order 2000 (SI 2000/3373) had made service by electronic means in respect of some sections of the 1985 Act, but not for s368, and there was a requirement to know that the notice received at the registered office was genuine, which meant that it was not permissible to send a notice by facsimile transmission. Sir Andrew referred to a number of authorities in which a facsimile transmission had been accepted by the courts, and rejected all of the arguments put forward by the claimant. He considered the deposit of the notice by facsimile transmission was valid, and robustly responded, at 94 a–b, to the illogical claim about the reliability of such a means of transmitting a document thus:

> For the reasons given by Laddie J in the last citation, there is nothing inherent in a fax transmission to make it more or less reliable than the post. It is true that a fax may be falsified by a cut and paste operation but forgery and falsification is equally possible, usually by other means, in connection with postal and personal transmission too.

**1.164** The same position with respect to facsimile transmissions holds in Canada, where, in the case of *Re United Canso Oil & Gas Ltd*,[342] proxy forms submitted with a facsimile or mechanically rendered signature were held to be sufficient. Hallett J at 289 paragraph 17 made the following point:

> Today's business could not be conducted if stamped signatures were not recognized as legally binding. The affixing of a stamp conveys the intention to be bound by the document so executed just as effectively as the manual writing of a signature by hand. I

341 [2003] BCC 202, [2004] 1 BCLC 88, [2002] EWHC 2848, 2002 WL 31676421.

342 (1980) 12 B.L.R. 130; 76 A.P.R. 282; 41 N.S.R.(2d) 282 (T.D.).

would point out that no one questions the validity of millions of payroll cheques signed by facsimile signatures.

**1.165** This view is echoed in the Singapore decision of Lim Teong Qwee JC in the case of *Masa-Katsu Japanese Restaurant Pte Ltd v. Amara Hotel Properties Pte Ltd*,[343] in which he held that a facsimile transmission of a request to extend the term of a lease was a valid form of communicating. He commented, at 18:

> The written request dated 4 October 1997 was in fact received by the landlord. It was received by fax on 10 October 1997. It was not suggested that it was received other than at the landlord's office where it could be attended to immediately. It was undoubtedly in writing when it was received. Communication by fax is not uncommon. It is fast. It is efficient. It accords with the practice of the business community. It seems to me that where as in this case a written request is to be made it is sufficiently made as much where the request is written on paper that is physically transported to the office of the person to whom the request is made as where it is transmitted by fax and received in written form at that person's office.

**1.166** Consideration was also given to a signature sent by way of facsimile transmission in the German case of GmS-OGB 1/98 before the Gemeinsamer Senat der obersten Gerichtshöfe des Bundes (Joint Senate of the Federal High Courts) in 2000. In this instance, the court had to decide whether or not a facsimile transmission sent directly from a computer (Computerfax) with a scanned signature complied with the requirements of written form for formal court pleadings. In the normal course of events, various rules of German procedural law require formal court pleadings to be signed with a manuscript signature, and a number of Federal High Courts have reached decisions on this point.[344] The court held that it was sufficient to transfer pleadings electronically in this manner, providing the documents are signed with a scanned signature, or if the document transmitted indicates that the document could not be signed personally because of the method of transmission. The members of the court reached the conclusion on the basis that the formal requirements of procedural law do not serve as an end in themselves, and the purpose of requiring court proceedings to be in written form is to identify the sender and ensure the document was sent with the sender's knowledge and intent. As a result, the intention of the sender is not seriously in doubt because of the method of

343 [1999] 2 SLR 332.

344 Federal Social Court, Beschluß vom 15.10.1996 – 14 BEg 9/96; Federal Administrative Court, Beschluß vom 19.12.1994 – 5 B 79/94.

transmission.[345] Similar decisions were made in Hungary[346] and Lithuania,[347] in which the Supreme Administrative Court in its ruling of 13 April 2006 held that the copy of an administrative decision sent by facsimile transmission constituted a proper form of notification by the governmental institution of its decision.

**1.167** In the United States of America, a federal court on the ninth circuit found itself severely constrained by a set of extremely strict rules laid down by the Bureau of Land Management in the case of *Gilmore v. Lujan*[348] respecting documents sent by facsimile transmission. In this instance, an application was sent by facsimile transmission because the original postal application had not arrived on time. The Bureau refused to accept the documents sent by facsimile transmission because the papers were not signed with a manuscript signature. Upon appeal, this decision was upheld because the signature was required to be as manuscript signature only, and no other form was permitted. The Bureau of Land Management required applications to be holographically signed in ink by each potential lessee, and machine or rubber-stamped signatures were not acceptable. The rule was altered after the case of *W. H. Gilmore*,[349] where Gilmore protested the lease was awarded to an applicant that used a rubber stamp as a signature. The regulations were deliberately altered to only permit manuscript signatures thereafter. Although the regulations required the signature to be in ink, nevertheless the Board determined, in the later case of *Jack Williams*,[350] that a signature signed with a lead pencil was adequate. Nelson CJ criticized the decision, indicating, at 142, that:

> Justice Holmes observed that citizens dealing with their government must turn square corners ... Gilmore turned all but the last millimetre, but that millimetre, whose traverse is jealously guarded by the BLM, was his undoing. Relief to Gilmore in this narrow case would expose BLM to no fraud or risk of fraud, as his bona fides are beyond question. If Gilmore and those other few luckless applicants whose documents are stored rather than delivered by the Postal Service are to get any relief, it must come at the hands of the BLM. As shown by this case, those hands are more iron than velvet. We can only suggest to BLM that the body politic would not be put at risk by the granting of relief in these narrow and rare situations.

345 M. Knopp, case note, *Digital Evidence and Electronic Signature Law Review*, 2(2005), pp. 103–4.

346 Case number BDT 2001/496.

347 *UAB 'Bite Lietuva' v. Communications Regulatory Authority* AS14–77–06.

348 947 F.2d 1409 (9th Cir. 1991).

349 41 IBLA 25 (1979).

350 91 IBLA 355 (1986).

**1.168** The use of facsimile transmissions have been challenged in other situations, such as arbitration[351] and elections,[352] although in *Bogue v. Sizemore*[353] there was no dispute about a contract disseminated by facsimile. In addition, cases have occurred under the Statute of Frauds,[354] although not always successfully.

**1.169** In Canada, forms of proxy sent by facsimile transmission were the subject matter of the British Columbia case of *Beatty v. First Exploration Fund 1987 and Company, Limited Partnership*.[355] In this case, it was held that forms of proxy sent by facsimile transmission were sufficient to meet the signature requirements under a limited partnership agreement. Hinds J indicated, at 383 that 'The faxed proxies were not themselves signed, but they bore the photographic reproduction of the original of the limited partner who executed the particular proxy'. He went on to say at 383, that 'The law has endeavoured to take cognizance of, and to be receptive to, technological advances in the means of communication. The development of that approach may be observed in a number of cases, including the following'. At 385 he addressed the argument relating to the theoretical possibility that such transmissions might be the subject of fraud, which is hardly an argument to use when the authenticity of the document in question has not been challenged:

> It was argued by counsel for the Fund that validating faxed proxies would increase the risk of fraud, create uncertainty, and give an unfair advantage to those limited partners who had access to a

351 New York: *In the Matter of American Multimedia, Inc., v. Dalton Packaging, Inc.*, 143 Misc.2d 295, 540 N.Y.S.2d 410 (an order was transmitted by facsimile machine that only contained the first of two pages of an order form, stating that all orders were subject to the terms and conditions on the reverse of the form, which was not sent. It was held that the terms did apply, because the petitioner had filed over 100 such orders in the previous three years) (1989).

352 New Jersey: *Madden v. Hegadorn*, 565 A.2d 725 (N.J.Super.L. 1989), 236 N.J.Super. 280, affirmed 571 A.2d 296 (N.J. 1989), 239 N.J.Super. 268 (a document sent by facsimile transmission containing a manuscript signature was deemed effective for filing a nomination petition, and any technical defects were cured when the candidate filed the original documents the day after the facsimile transmission).

353 241 Ill.App.3d 250, 608 N.E.2d 1246 (Ill.App.4th Dist. 1993).

354 New York: *WPP Group USA, Inc., v. The Interpublic Group of Companies, Inc.*, 644 N.Y.S.2d 205, 228 A.D.2d 296 (it was premature to decide whether the Statute of Frauds was satisfied where an unsigned facsimile transmission on the letterhead of the sender was sent) (1996). For the merchant's exception see the New York case of *Bazak International Corp. v. Mast Industries, Inc.*, 140 Ad.2d 211, 528 N.Y.S.2d 62, 6 UCC Rep.Serv.2d 375, appeal granted by 72 N.Y.2D 808, 529 N.E.2d 425, 533 N.E.2d 57 (N.Y. 1988), Order reversed by 73 N.Y.2D 113, 535 N.E.2d 633, 538 N.Y.2d 503, 57 USLW 2520, 82 A.L.R.4th 689, 7 UCC Rep.Serv.2d 1380 (N.Y. 1989) where annotated telecopies ('telecopies' is a trademark sometimes used for a facsimile machine) of headed purchase order forms signed by the alleged purchaser and sent to the alleged seller and retained without objection came within the merchant's exception to the Statute of Frauds.

355 25 B.C.L.R.2d 377 (1988).

> telecopier or fax machine. I reject that argument. Faxed proxies are, in effect, a photocopy of an original copy. They reveal what is depicted on an original copy, including an exact replica of the signature of the person who signed the original proxy. I observe no greater opportunity for the perpetration of a fraud by the use of faxed copies than by the use of original copies. The same observation applies to the matter of uncertainty.

## The writing material

**1.170** In the days before the development of techniques to identify microscopic indentations or traces of lead on paper, the material used to write on a document could cause conceptual problems. The nature of the writing material used to affix a signature was raised in the case of *Geary v. Physic.*[356] An objection was taken where a promissory note was signed using a pencil. At the trial, the Lord Chief Justice, Abbott CJ, thought the promissory note was sufficiently indorsed, and directed the members of the jury to find a verdict for the plaintiff. He also permitted the plaintiff to challenge this finding. The matter was subsequently argued before Abbott CJ, Bayley and Holroyd JJ. In his judgment, the Lord Chief Justice pointed out, 'There is no authority for saying that where the law requires a contract to be in writing, that writing must be in ink'.[357] This decision was made before the development of the forensic analysis of materials and the use of technology as a means of detecting changes to materials. Although it is now possible to detect the erasure of a manuscript signature if it were to be affixed using a pencil, the principle established by this decision remains sound. The rationale for this decision is the principle that a signature was affixed to the document with an intent that it should be acted upon. Hence the type of writing material used is irrelevant, providing it is not removed from the document. This decision may also be considered correct on the premise that the promissory note was only valid for a limited period of time, and the use of a pencil to sign the note may not have been considered relevant because there was no requirement to retain a permanent record of the note.[358]

**1.171** A similar issue arose in *Lucas v. James*,[359] where a series of remarks on a draft under-lease were written in pencil, including the words 'I agree to these terms, subject to the above observations. W. M. James'. In this instance, the plaintiff sought specific performance, while the defendant denied an agreement had been reached, arguing in part that the comments made by him on the draft, being made in pencil, were not intended to be binding. Although the claim failed

356 (1826) 5 B & C 234; 108 ER 87.

357 (1826) 5 B & C 234 at 237.

358 For a case on the use of a ballpoint pen, see J. Bing and J. Hvarre, 'Case note Denmark: U 1959.40/1H', *Digital Evidence and Electronic Signature Law Review*, 6 (2009), p. 277.

359 (1849) 7 Hare 410; 68 ER 170.

for other reasons, Sir James Wigram VC made the extra-judicial remark that these words, taken in conjunction with a previous comment made by the defendant on the same draft, would, on the face of it, bind him to the terms of the under-lease.[360] The Vice-Chancellor considered that the remarks made in pencil demonstrated a willingness to be bound by the amended document. In this instance, the use of pencil on the document was deemed perfectly acceptable as evidence of the writer's intent to agree the terms of the document.

**1.172** Whether the nature of a document that has been changed sufficiently as the result of alterations made in pencil was the subject of *Co-operative Bank plc v. Tipper*.[361] Mr and Mrs Tipper entered into a personal guarantee with the bank, but it transpired that the document erroneously described the defendants personally as both the customer (i.e. the principal debtor) and the guarantor. The bank applied to the court to rectify the error after Mr and Mrs Tipper's company went into liquidation. Mr and Mrs Tipper opposed the application of the bank on the basis that where a document is altered in a material way, the document becomes void, and therefore unenforceable. In this instance, a person unknown working for the bank used a pencil to strike out the names of Mr and Mrs Tipper and added the name and address of the company. Cooke J concluded that the proper evidential inference to draw was that the alterations constituted a drafting amendment. The changes made in pencil were not intended to alter the substance of the document, but were meant to propose that the names be put in the correct place in the document. As a result, the use of pencil did not alter the content of the document because the use of a pencil constituted a series of suggestions to correct errors in the document.

**1.173** In a case from Scotland, *Jollie v. Lennie*,[362] the testator wrote a purported will by hand in pencil on each side of a single sheet of A5 paper. The testator signed the will before a witness, who also signed. Both signatures were in pencil. The will was held to be effective.

**1.174** The use of a lead pencil has also been the subject of a number of decisions in the United States of America, include bills of exchange,[363] Statute of Frauds,[364]

360 (1849) 7 Hare 410 at 419.

361 [1996] 4 All ER 366 Ch.

362 [2014] CSOH 45, 2014 WL 978942.

363 New York: *Brown v. The Butchers & Drovers' Bank*, 6 Hill 443, 41Am.Dec. 755 (the endorsement of a bill of exchange using a lead pencil is sufficient) (1844).

Vermont: *Clossen v. Stearns*, 4 Vt. 11, 1831 WL 2104 (Vt.), 23 Am.Dec. 245 (the endorsement of a promissory note by means of a lead pencil held to be valid) (1831).

364 Missouri: *Great Western Printing Co. v. Belcher*, 127 Mo.App. 133, 104 S.W. 894 (the words 'Guaranteed. Belcher' written in lead pencil across the face of the original account is a signature, even though the signature did not include a first name) (1907).

New York: *Merritt v. Clason*, 12 Johns. 102, 7 Am.Dec. 286, 12 N.Y.S.C. 1814–15 92 affirmed as *The Executors of Clason v. Bailey*, 14 Johns. 484 (where a memorandum of a contract was written down in a note book using a lead pencil, the document is a sufficient memorandum within the Statute of Frauds) (1817).

South Carolina: *Draper v. Pattina*, 29 S.C.L. 292, 2 Speers 292, 1844 WL 2584 (S.C.App.L.) (a memorandum written using a lead pencil was not a valid objection) (1844).

wills[365] and deeds, as in the 1920 Missouri case of *Kleine v. Kleine*,[366] in which John Kleine granted his sister a lease on a portion of land, and he signed it with a lead pencil. It was held to be a valid instrument. Graves J, indicated, at 610 what he thought of Kleine and his motive for using a lead pencil in this instance:

> Kleine's testimony in the case tends to leave a bad taste in the judicial mouth. Among other things, he requested that the lease be signed with a lead pencil, and says that he 'figured' that it was no good when he signed it, 'because there was no starting point.' All this was after the sister had put her money into the improvements.

**1.175** The judge went on, at 611, to observe that:

> The real issue in the case is not the views expressed by John Kleine, to the effect that he signed the lease (in lead pencil, at his own suggestion) because he thought it invalid, owing to the absence of a starting point. He seems not only to have had that idea, but the other erroneous view, entertained by many laymen, that a deed must be signed with a pen and ink.

**1.176** His comments illustrate the frustration by many lawyers of the erroneous and endlessly inaccurate comments made by lay people in respect of legal issues relating to all manner of things.

**1.177** However, it is the use of a lead pencil on a judicial document in 1823 that serves to illustrate the fallacy about the use of lead pencil as a means of affixing a signature to a document, and also in relation to whether a document is open to attack. In the Columbia case of *United States v. Thompson*,[367] it was held that an indictment for assault and battery for violently beating a slave and signed by a Justice of the Peace with a lead pencil was not a sufficient signature. The reason given by Cranch CJ was that 'it is liable to be so easily obliterated'. This is a false conclusion based on an erroneous premise. The logic of the reasoning runs as follows: a material that can be erased was used to affix the signature to the document, ergo the signature is not valid because it is possible to erase the signature. It is correct that the material impressed on to paper by a lead pencil can be erased, but the possibility that the writing can be erased does not prevent the document from having been signed. In this instance, the document was signed with the manuscript signature of a Justice of the Peace. The evidence of the signature was clear for all to see, which meant the signature was sufficient. Had the signature been erased, then the integrity of the document would have been questioned, and, depending on the strength or weakness of the evidence tendered and tested before the court, a decision could be made as to

365 Pennsylvania: *Appeal of Knox*, 131 P. 220, 18 A. 1021, 6 L.R.A. 353, 17 Am.St.Rep. 798 (an instrument written in lead pencil was sufficient to be admitted as a will) (1890).

366 219 S.W. 610, 281 Mo. 317.

367 2 Cranch C.C. 409, 28 F.Cas. 89, 2 D.C. 409, No 16484.

the authenticity of the document, which in turn would enable the trier of fact to determine whether the document had been signed or not.

**1.178** Lawyers often use this argument relating to documents in electronic and digital format. The argument runs like this: because it is possible to forge an email, facsimile transmission or electronic signature (any form of electronic signature); ergo the email, facsimile transmission or electronic signature should not be admitted because of the possibility of forgery. Astonishingly, this argument was successfully used in the German case of AG Bonn Urteil vom 25.10.2001 3 C 193/01 Beweiskraft von Emails, JurPC Web-Dok. 332/2002, where the claimant sued the defendant for a broker's fee for acting as an intermediary for the sale of cigarettes. The claim was dismissed on the basis that there was no sufficient proof, because the emails submitted in evidence had no value as evidence because it is generally known that emails can be easily altered or forged. This argument is also fallacious. Any paper document can be forged, such as a letter from a commercial entity or a government, and lawyers are required to sift through documentary evidence regularly to test the authenticity of documents. The forgery of evidence is hardly new, and if this argument were to be accepted by judges, which it seems to be in some cases, then by logical extension, any item of documentary evidence could be excluded because it was possible to forge. If it is suggested an item of evidence is forged, the question should be raised before trial, so that the party relying on the evidence has the opportunity to adduce evidence to prove the document is genuine. Unsound arguments based on a flawed foundation have no place in a court.

## The absence of a signature

**1.179** Two further illustrations demonstrate the willingness of judges to imply a document has been signed in the absence of a manuscript signature. In the case of *Rist v. Hobson*,[368] an agreement for the sale and purchase of an estate had been drawn up but not signed by either party. The vendor sought an order for specific performance, and Sir John Leach VC reached the conclusion that where the agreement was in writing, it would be presumed the document was signed unless evidence to the contrary was adduced to rebut the presumption. It is not clear from the report whether the agreement had been committed to writing by either of the parties in this instance. However, in the later case of *Bleakley v. Smith*,[369] the agreement had been written in the hand of one of the parties. Mr Bridges agreed to sell five houses in Liverpool to John Bleakley. The only evidence to this agreement was a memorandum, written by Mr Bridges: 'July 26th, 1839. John Bleakley agrees with J R Bridges to take the property in Cable Street for the net sum of £248 10*s*'. Mr Bridges died on 10 February 1840, but had not conveyed the property. In an action against Mr Bridges's executors, the Vice-Chancellor

368 (1824) 1 Sim & St 543; 57 ER 215.

369 (1840) 11 Sim 149; 59 ER 831.

made a declaration that the memorandum was a valid and binding contract and ordered specific performance and execution of a conveyance of the properties. The Vice-Chancellor merely stated that the agreement was sufficiently signed to take it out of the Statute of Frauds. In all probability, the reason for so finding was partly because the memorandum was drawn up in the hand of Mr Bridges and he had received the purchase price. In such circumstances, there was sufficient evidence to show he intended to sell the properties. It appears that the obligation was considered to be 'entire', thus permitting an order for specific performance.

**1.180** These cases illustrate that, despite failing to comply with the formal requirements, the content of a document can be authenticated where there is sufficient evidence to show the person signing the document adopted the content.

# 2

# International initiatives

**2.1** The approach taken by a government in determining how legislation is to be enacted can affect the infrastructure of the electronic environment in a particular jurisdiction. Some jurisdictions favour the use of digital signatures carried on smart cards for the signature process, while others have developed a state public key infrastructure, with a certification authority acting as a trusted third party. Other governments have enacted legislation that seeks to be neutral, thus allowing for the changes in technology that are bound to occur over time.

## United Nations Commission on International Trade (UNCITRAL)

**2.2** Sets of uniform rules have been prepared by UNCITRAL: the Model Law on Electronic Commerce, the Model Law on Electronic Signatures,[1] and the 2005 United Nations Convention on the Use of Electronic Communications in International Contracts.[2] The Model Laws are intended to provide help, guidance and act as an instrument for national states to use in forming legislation. While states are encouraged to incorporate both the Model Law on Electronic Commerce and the Model Law on Electronic Signatures fully into their domestic legislation, changes can be made to the content. The Model Laws are complementary to each other, although many states enacted legislation relating to electronic signatures before the final version of the Model Law on Electronic Signatures was adopted. The following discussion is intended to bring the salient issues to the attention of the reader.

### Model Law on Electronic Commerce

**2.3** The objectives of the Model Law on Electronic Commerce are set out in the accompanying Guide to Enactment, as follows:

> (a) To provide a set of rules acceptable to the international community relating to electronic communications.

1 The Model Law on Electronic Commerce was adopted by the Commission on 12 June 1996, following its 605th meeting, which in turn was adopted by the General Assembly in Resolution 51/162 at its 85th plenary meeting on 16 December 1996, and includes an additional article 5 *bis* as adopted by the Commission at its 31st meeting in June 1998. The Commission at its 727th meeting on 5 July 2001 adopted the Model Law on Electronic Signatures.

2 New York (2005), adopted on 23 November 2005, entered into force on 1 March 2013.

Stephen Mason, *Electronic Signatures in Law* (London: Institute of Advanced Legal Studies, 2016), chapter 2, 'International initiatives', pp. 95–114.

(b) To illustrate how obstacles to electronic commerce can be removed by national legislators, such as rules relating to the use of 'written', 'signed' or 'original' documents, and to help create legal certainty in the electronic environment.

(c) To help remedy any disadvantages because inadequate legislation creates obstacles to international trade.

(d) To act as a means to interpret existing international conventions and other instruments that may create legal obstacles when using electronic commerce.

(e) To foster efficiency in international trade.[3]

**2.4** The Model Law is predicated upon the recognition that most legal requirements relate to documentation based on paper. It was thought that new rules might have to be developed to take into account the many distinctive differences between paper-based documents and electronic data. A new approach was established, called the 'functional equivalent approach', based on the analysis of the purposes and functions of a paper carrier. The functions a paper carrier provides for include:

(a) To provide that a document would be legible by all.

(b) To provide that a document would remain unaltered over time.

(c) To allow for the reproduction of a document so that each party would hold a copy of the same data.

(d) To allow for the authentication of data by means of a signature.

(e) To provide that a document would be in a form acceptable to public authorities and courts.[4]

**2.5** It was considered necessary that the approach would not require higher standards of security and related costs than already existed in the paper-based environment. Hence the adoption of a flexible standard, because data in digital format is not the equivalent of a paper document. Documents in paper and digital format are different in nature, and neither can perform the same functions as the other. Thus the Model Law seeks to establish the functions that a paper-based document will perform and then provides criteria that, if met, will enable electronic data to be recognized in the same way as a paper document. Part One Chapter I of the Model Law deals with electronic commerce in general. Chapter II provides for the legal requirements relating to data messages.

## *Legal recognition of data messages*

**2.6** Article 5 provides for the legal recognition of data messages as follows:

3 Introduction to the Model Law Part A, paragraphs 1–6.

4 Introduction to the Model Law Part B paragraph 16.

Article 5. Legal recognition of data messages

> Information shall not be denied legal effect, validity or enforceability solely on the grounds that it is in the form of a data message.

Article 5 bis. Incorporation by reference (as adopted by the Commission at its thirty-first session, in June 1998)

> Information shall not be denied legal effect, validity or enforceability solely on the grounds that it is not contained in the data message purporting to give rise to such legal effect, but is merely referred to in that data message.

**2.7** The provisions of article 5 establish the principle that electronic data should not be treated any differently from paper documents because of the form it takes. Article 5 bis provides guidance when reference is made to other documents in the text of another document. This occurs frequently in the paper-based world, and the aim is to ensure it can also be effective in the electronic environment. Thus the commentary in paragraph 46-2 to the Guide to Enactment suggests that advantage can be taken of the ability to have links to databases, code lists or glossaries, by making use of abbreviations. In addition, the use of embedded uniform resource locators that can direct a reader to a referenced document by way of a hypertext link is another method of referring to other, related documents.[5] An example could be where an individual or legal entity uses an individual identity certificate provided by a certificate authority.[6] This is a signed structured message that seeks to assert the existence of an association between a particular set of data that identifies a key holder with a particular public key. A certificate authority invariably incorporates the terms and conditions of use that limit its liability for the individual identity certificate by reference.

### *Writing*

**2.8** The term 'writing' is considered in article 6:

Article 6. Writing

> (1) Where the law requires information to be in writing, that requirement is met by a data message if the information contained therein is accessible so as to be usable for subsequent reference.

5 Guide to Enactment paragraph 46-5.

6 The reader should be aware that there are different classes of certificate, and it is not always clear what a particular certification authority means by a certificate and how they distinguish between types of certificate. See R. Clarke, 'Conventional public key infrastructure: an artefact ill-fitted to the needs of the information society', prepared for submission to the 'IS in the Information Society' track of the European Conference in Information Systems, Bled, Slovenia, 27–29 June 2001, available online at http://www.rogerclarke.com/II/PKIMisFit.html.

> (2) Paragraph (1) applies whether the requirement therein is in the form of an obligation or whether the law simply provides consequences for the information not being in writing.
>
> (3) The provisions of this article do not apply to the following [...]

**2.9** The purpose of article 6 is to define the basic standard that an electronic data message must meet. It is not a requirement that electronic data should conform to the functions of writing affixed to a carrier. Rather it is a provision that the electronic data should be made available by being rendered into a format that can be interpreted and read: that is, 'accessible', and the data must also be 'useable for subsequent reference'. This refers to two functions: the ability of a human to read the content of the data; and the processing of the data by a computer.

## *Signature*

**2.10** Matters pertaining to the signature are set out in article 7, as follows:

> Article 7. Signature
>
> (1) Where the law requires a signature of a person, that requirement is met in relation to a data message if:
>
> (a) a method is used to identify that person and to indicate that person's approval of the information contained in the data message; and
>
> (b) that method is as reliable as was appropriate for the purpose for which the data message was generated or communicated, in the light of all the circumstances, including any relevant agreement.
>
> (2) Paragraph (1) applies whether the requirement therein is in the form of an obligation or whether the law simply provides consequences for the absence of a signature.
>
> (3) The provisions of this article do not apply to the following [...]

**2.11** The provisions of article 7 do not claim to establish any standards or procedures to be used as substitute for a signature, because it was felt that there was a risk that the legal framework would be tied to a particular state of technological development. The aim of article 7 is to provide a basic standard of authentication between two parties, whether the parties are linked by an agreement, or where they have no previous relationship. It sets out general conditions under which electronic data can be regarded as authentic and enforceable, focusing on two of the functions of a manuscript signature, that is: to identify the author of a document and to confirm the author approved the content of the document. There are two elements to this process.

(i) The first element, set out in paragraph (1)(a), provides that where a signature is required by law, the requirement is met if a method is used to identify the person, and to indicate their approval of the information contained in the data message. The person sending the message becomes the originator of the data message.

(ii) The second element is set out in paragraph (1)(b). The method used to generate or communicate the message must be sufficiently reliable and appropriate, bearing in mind the circumstances, for its intended purpose.

**2.12** The Guide sets out a number of legal, technical and commercial factors that should be taken into account when determining whether the method used was sufficiently reliable and appropriate:

(1) the sophistication of the equipment used by each of the parties;

(2) the nature of their trade activity;

(3) the frequency at which commercial transactions take place between the parties;

(4) the kind and size of the transaction;

(5) the function of signature requirements in a given statutory and regulatory environment;

(6) the capability of communication systems;

(7) compliance with authentication procedures set forth by intermediaries;

(8) the range of authentication procedures made available by any intermediary;

(9) compliance with trade customs and practice;

(10) the existence of insurance coverage mechanisms against unauthorized messages;

(11) the importance and the value of the information contained in the data message;

(12) the availability of alternative methods of identification and the cost of implementation;

(13) the degree of acceptance or non-acceptance of the method of identification in the relevant industry or field both at the time the method was agreed upon and the time when the data message was communicated; and

(14) any other relevant factor.[7]

7 Guide to Enactment, paragraph 58.

**2.13** The legal effectiveness of the method used to apply to an electronic signature depends, in accordance with the Guide to Enactment to the Model Law on Electronic Signatures,[8] on demonstrating its reliability to the person trying the fact. However, the reliability of the method does not demonstrate a link between the owner of the electronic signature and the act of affixing the signature to a document in digital format. The Guide to Enactment to the Model Law on Electronic Commerce notes that when an electronic document is signed by means of a functional equivalent of a manuscript signature, it does not follow that the electronic data is legally valid. The relevant provisions set out in national law govern this matter.[9]

## Model Law on Electronic Signatures

**2.14** This Model Law is predicated on the principles underlying article 7 of the Model Law on Electronic Commerce, and is intended to assist states in setting out a legal framework for electronic signatures. The Model Law considers technical reliability and legal effectiveness, while setting out a number of basic rules of conduct for the parties to an electronic signature (sending party, receiving party and third-party certification authority). The objectives of the Model Law include the encouragement of facilitating the use of electronic signatures and providing equal treatment for all documents whether they are in electronic format or stored on a physical carrier.[10] In this respect, the Model Law has focused on the roles or functions relating to public key cryptography, which usually implies a trusted third party acts to certify the identity of an entity by means of an individual identity certificate. However, it should be noted that trust in a key could be established bilaterally, without the services of a trusted third party. These functions consist of the signatory function, relying function and certification function. While the signatory and relying functions remain constant, the certification function may differ, depending on the system used. While other techniques, such as biometric measurements, are not specifically covered in the Model Law, the aim has been to deal with the legal issues at an intermediate level between the generality of the Model Law on Electronic Commerce and the specific issues when considering a particular electronic signature technique.

**2.15** As the Model Law is predicated on article 7 of the Model Law on Electronic Commerce, it was not a foregone conclusion that a new Model Law would be created. Consideration was given to incorporating the new rules into the Model Law on Electronic Commerce as a new Part III, but because so many states had

8 Guide to Enactment, paragraph 76.

9 Guide to Enactment, paragraph 61; for a list of those states that have implemented and adopted the Model Law, or where Uniform legislation has been influenced by the Model Law and the principles on which it is based, see http://www.uncitral.org/uncitral/en/uncitral_texts/electronic_commerce/1996Model_status.html.

10 The history of this Model Law illustrates differences had to be resolved before the final version was agreed. The reader is referred to Part C, paragraphs 12 to 25 of the Guide that accompanies the Model Law for more information.

already implemented the Model Law on Electronic Commerce, it was felt that a separate instrument was more appropriate. To provide for consistency, the following articles have been reproduced from the Model Law on Electronic Commerce: articles 1 (Sphere of application); 2 (a), (c) and (d) (Definitions of 'data message', 'originator' and 'addressee'); 3 (Interpretation); 4 (Variation by agreement) and 7 (Signature). The notes in the Guide to Enactment make it explicit that the Model Law only offers a framework within which laws can be structured, and it is not intended to set forth all the requirements that may be necessary to implement any given electronic signature law. For instance, it does not set out the rules and regulations that may be necessary to implement electronic signature techniques. Nor does it deal with liability, leaving the national law to determine what liability a party may be subject to in accordance with applicable law. However, the Model Law does set out criteria against which an adjudicator might assess the conduct of the parties.

### *Consumer protection*

**2.16** The comments in the Guide to Enactment indicate that the Model Law has not been drafted with any special provisions in mind regarding the protection of consumers.[11] There was no reason why conditions relating to consumers should be excluded from the scope of the Model Law, especially because it was considered that the Model Law could be beneficial to a consumer. This does not prevent the consumer from being protected independently, as provided for in article 1:

> Article 1. Sphere of application
>
> This Law applies where electronic signatures are used in the context of commercial activities. It does not override any rule of law intended for the protection of consumers.
>
> It is for individual states to determine whether they should exclude or modify rules in relation to consumers and their use of electronic signatures.

### *Definitions*

**2.17** The Model Law provides a number of definitions in article 2, as described below.

**2.18 Electronic signature** The definition of an electronic signature is set out in article 2(a):

> 'Electronic signature' means data in electronic form in, affixed to or logically associated with, a data message, which may be used

11 Guide to Enactment, paragraph 91.

to identify the signatory in relation to the data message and to indicate the signatory's approval of the information contained in the data message.

**2.19** This definition is intended to include all traditional uses of a manuscript signature, and emphasizes the use of an electronic signature as a functional equivalent of a manuscript signature.[12] There are two elements to this definition of an electronic signature. The first element provides for the link between different types of electronic data: electronic signature data that is 'in, affixed to or logically associated with, a data message'.

(i) The word 'in' operates where the signature data is contained in a message or document. It can be seen when it is opened and read, or when it is printed. When used 'in' the data message, the signature data consists of additional text in the document or message.

(ii) There does not appear any difference in meaning between the words 'affixed to' and 'logically associated'. The use of the phrase 'affixed to' probably means signature data contained in a file sent as an attachment to an email. However, this example falls into the meaning 'logically associated' in any event.[13]

(iii) The phrase 'logically associated' with a message or document is where signature data is contained in a separate file from the data that has been signed. It is not visible in the data itself. The signature data can only be verified where a signature verification application is used. This uses the data that purports to have been signed, the purported signature file and the verification key to determine whether the verification is valid. The signature data will only be verified if the relevant logical association is demonstrated: if the purportedly signed data was in fact signed with the signature key corresponding to the verification key used.

**2.20** The second element provides for the purpose of the associated data, that of identifying the signatory and the signatory's approval of the content of the message. The data specifically provides for the identification of the signatory.

(i) The first part of this element permits the use of associated data that 'may be used to identify the signatory in relation to the data

12 Guide to Enactment, paragraph 93.

13 The definition of what constitutes an electronic signature was discussed on various occasions at meetings of Working Group on Electronic Commerce. A proposed change to the definition was agreed at a session in Vienna between 8 and 19 February 1999. The change is noted in A/CN.9/457 dated 25 February 1999 at paragraph 28: '"Electronic signature" means data in electronic form which (a) is included in, affixed to or logically associated with a data message'. No reason was ascribed to the inclusion of two phrases that appear to have similar meanings.

message'. The use of the word 'may' acknowledges that there is a difference between the legal notion of a signature and the different technical functions that can be used to create an electronic signature, but can also be used for other purposes.[14] Whether an electronic signature merely acts to authenticate interactions between protocols or to identify the sender, will be determined by the ability to establish a connection between the signature and the person affixing the signature to the data.

(ii) The second part of the element provides for the associated data to 'indicate the signatory's approval of the information contained in the data message'. The aim of this part of the element is to cover the traditional use of the manuscript signature. The comments in the Guide to Enactment indicate the nature of the problem: 'defining an electronic signature as capable of indicating approval of information amounts primarily to establishing a technical prerequisite for the recognition of a given technology as capable of creating an equivalent to a handwritten signature'.[15] However, it is to be observed that the method that can be used for the production of a signature with legal meaning can also be used for other purposes, such as to authenticate or identify an entity. Thus the context and intention of the method used must be taken into account before it can be inferred that a document has been 'signed'. A message or document may include data that seeks to link the person to the message or document without indicating their approval of the content.

**2.21** **Certificate** Article 2(b) provides a definition of a certificate:

> 'Certificate' means a data message or other record confirming the link between a signatory and signature creation data.

**2.22** The Guide to Enactment to the Model Law points out that a 'certificate' as defined is no different from any other meaning of a document, other than it is in digital format. The aim of such a document is to confirm facts. Thus the purpose of a certificate is to 'recognize, show or confirm a link between the signature creation data and the signatory'.[16] According to the commentary, the link is created when the signature creation data is generated. This must be wrong. The link is created when the possessor of the signature key wishes to obtain a certificate for the verification key, and perhaps accepts obligations to procure the issue of the certificate. The signature creation data is, when using asymmetric cryptography, the cryptographic key pair. The private key is the operative element

14 Guide to Enactment, paragraphs 93 and 94.

15 Guide to Enactment, paragraph 93.

16 Guide to Enactment, paragraph 96.

in the process and it is the private key that is referred to in the phrase 'signature creation data'. However, it is also meant to include the confirmation of the link between the signatory and their public key.

**2.23** **Data message** The definition provided in article 2(c) is as follows:

> 'Data message' means information generated, sent, received or stored by electronic, optical or similar means including, but not limited to, electronic data interchange (EDI), electronic mail, telegram, telex or telecopy; and acts either on its own behalf or on behalf of the person it represents.

**2.24** This definition is drafted to cover a broad range of data, including records. It does not follow that a data message has to be communicated. The definition seeks to include all forms of document not on paper, as well as future developments in technology.[17]

**2.25** **Signatory** Article 2 (d) provides the following definition of a signatory:

> 'Signatory' means a person that holds signature creation data and acts either on its own behalf or on behalf of the person it represents.

**2.26** The meaning of 'person' includes all types of person, including physical, corporate and other forms of legal entity. The digital environment permits a legal entity to have an electronic signature in its own name. A legal entity can sign documents in two ways. The method most frequently used is when authorized officers affix their manuscript signatures to a document with the requisite authority. Alternatively, the organization can use its own signature, with the impression of the seal. Whether an electronic signature has been added to digital data with authority is a matter for the law governing the relationship between the person whose actions affix the electronic signature and the legal entity.[18]

**2.27** **Certification service provider** Article 2(e) provides the following definition of a certification service provider:

> 'Certification service provider' means a person that issues certificates and may provide other services related to electronic signatures.

**2.28** The commentary mentions that the certification service provider will have to provide a certification service in order to be brought within this definition, although it can supply other services. It does not have to undertake the work directly, but can sub-contract the service. The definition does not include entities

17 Guide to Enactment, paragraphs 98 to 100.

18 Guide to Enactment, paragraphs 102 and 103.

that issue certificates for internal purposes. It is only intended to cover activities of commercial providers of such services.[19]

**2.29 Relying party** The definition of a relying party is to be found in article 2(f):

> 'Relying party' means a person that may act on the basis of a certificate or an electronic signature.

**2.30** The inclusion of what is meant by a 'relying party' is meant to provide symmetry in the definition of the various parties involved in a transaction involving an electronic signature. Interestingly, the commentary also suggests that the word 'act' should be interpreted broadly, covering a positive action and a failure to act. This issue was the subject of discussion, and concern was expressed that in some legal systems the word 'act' would not cover acts of omission.[20] The comments in the Guide to Enactment illustrate the intention is to create an obligation upon a recipient to undertake acts of due diligence, as further demonstrated by the terms of article 11:

> Article 11. Conduct of the relying party
>
> A relying party shall bear the legal consequences of its failure:
>
> (a) To take reasonable steps to verify the reliability of an electronic signature; or
>
> (b) Where an electronic signature is supported by a certificate, to take reasonable steps:
>
>> (i) To verify the validity, suspension or revocation of the certificate; and
>>
>> (ii) To observe any limitation with respect to the certificate.

**2.31** It is not certain that a recipient should be made to undertake due diligence, although there may be good reasons of public policy to enforce organizations such as banks to take steps to authenticate the identity of their customers.[21] However, taking into account the discussion of this issue elsewhere in this text, it may be appropriate for both sending and receiving parties to be aware of the risks and limitations that attend the use of electronic signatures. The comments

19 Guide to Enactment, paragraph 104.

20 Report of the Working Group on Electronic Commerce on the work of its 37th session (Vienna, 18–29 September 2000) A/CN.9/483, paragraphs 105–8.

21 When the issue of authentication is of central concern, the decision that a judge reaches can be highly contentious, for which see Shojibur Rahman v. Barclays Bank PLC, commentary by S. Mason and N. Bohm, *Digital Evidence and Electronic Signature Law Review*, 10 (2013), 169–74; Shojibur Rahman v. Barclays Bank PLC (on appeal from the judgment of Her Honour District Judge Millard dated 24 October 2012), commentary by S. Mason and N. Bohm, *Digital Evidence and Electronic Signature Law Review*, 10 (2013), 175–87; *Rahman v. Barclays Bank PLC* [2014] EWCA Civ 811.

in the Guide to Enactment suggest the recipient should bear in mind whether it is reasonable to rely on a certificate in the circumstances.[22] Furthermore, the Model Law is not intended to overrule any rules with respect to the protection of consumers, but it was thought that imposing such a duty on consumers would play a role in educating recipients about the standard of conduct expected of recipients.[23] Bearing in mind the complexity of the infrastructure surrounding different types of electronic signature, especially digital signatures, perhaps the failure to carry out an act is something that should be borne in mind when assessing the evidence in the event of a dispute, depending on the circumstances of the case.[24] This aspect of the meaning for the word 'act' should be considered in the light of the provisions of article 4:

> Article 4. Interpretation
>
> 1. In the interpretation of this Law, regard is to be had to its international origin and to the need to promote uniformity in its application and the observance of good faith.
>
> 2. Questions concerning matters governed by this Law which are not expressly settled in it are to be settled in conformity with the general principles on which this Law is based.

**2.32** The commentary indicates that article 4 is based upon the United Nations Convention on Contracts for the International Sale of Goods, and is reproduced from article 3 of the Model Law on Electronic Commerce. The aim of paragraph 1 is to ensure the interpretation of the Model Law is by reference to its international origin, with the aim of ensuring uniformity in its interpretation. It is hoped that the Law, once incorporated into national law, will not be subject only to local legislation.[25] The Model Law may act as a guide in dealing with a dispute, but national courts will be required to implement national law, especially national consumer law. Although the concept of utilizing a device to create a signature means the signing party should look to control its use and protect it from unauthorized use, it is debatable whether a duty should be imposed upon a recipient to verify the certificate and the link between the certificate, public key and identity of the sending party.

## *The requirement for a signature*

**2.33** The Model Law, by way of the provisions set out in articles 3 and 6, seeks to ensure that whatever form a signature takes, whether in electronic format or a manuscript signature placed on a physical document, it is subject to the same treatment. For an electronic signature to be acceptable, it must fulfil the

22 Guide to Enactment, paragraph 148.

23 Guide to Enactment, paragraph 149.

24 Guide to Enactment, paragraph 106.

25 Guide to Enactment, paragraphs 108 and 109.

requirements of articles 6 and 7. In addition, provisions are made for the conduct of the various parties that may be connected to an electronic signature, including that of the signatory (article 8) and the certification service provider (articles 9 and 10).[26]

## International Chamber of Commerce

**2.34** The International Chamber of Commerce produced the first version of a set of guidelines entitled 'General Usage for International Digitally Ensured Commerce' (GUIDEC) on 6 November 1997. This was revised in October 2001. The introduction to the first version of the Guide sets out one of the aims respecting electronic signatures:

> The GUIDEC aims to draw together the key elements involved in electronic commerce, to serve as an indicator of terms and an exposition of the general background to the issue. It also addresses one of the key problems in talking about electronically signed messages, in that they are not signed physically, but require the intervention of an electronic medium. This in turn alters the function of the signer, and introduces problems which a physical signature does not encounter, most especially the possibility of use of the medium by a third party. The GUIDEC therefore adopts a specific term, 'ensure', to describe what elsewhere is called a 'digital signature' or 'authentication', in an attempt to remove the element of ambiguity inherent to other terms employed.

**2.35** The revised version continued to expand on the use of digital signature technology, as indicated in the aims:

> The aim of the GUIDEC
>
> The GUIDEC framework attempts to allocate risk and liability equitably between transacting parties in accordance with existing business practice, and includes a clear description of the rights and responsibilities of subscribers, certifiers, and relying parties.
>
> The aim of the GUIDEC is to enhance the ability of the international business community to execute trustworthy digital transactions utilizing legal principles that promote reliable digital authentication and certification practices.
>
> The GUIDEC treats the core concepts, best practices and certification issues in the context of international commercial

26 For a list of legislation based on the UNCITRAL Model Law on Electronic Signatures that has been adopted or influenced by the principles on which the Model Law is based, see http://www.uncitral.org/uncitral/en/uncitral_texts/electronic_commerce/2001Model_status.html.

> law and practice. In so doing, the document assumes practices in which transacting parties are expert commercial actors, operating under the lex mercatoria. The document does not attempt to define rights and responsibilities for transactions involving consumers. Nor is it intended to outline practices for transactions in which overriding national or other public interests may demand additional transactional security, such as notarial or other public intervention, although many notarial principles are enshrined in the document. In this regard, it is also important to note that the GUIDEC does not attempt to set out rules for certification of information relating to authority, legal competence, etc., which notaries are often called upon to certify.
>
> Although the GUIDEC is organized primarily as an outline for parties involved in public key based systems (i.e. digital signatures), the fact that it draws upon existing law means most of its principles will apply for other technologies.

**2.36** The guidance, which has no legal force, sets out some best practices that might be considered when deciding to form contracts electronically. However, in the introduction to the second version, the main objective is set out in part I(1) as follows:

> The principal [*sic*] objective of the GUIDEC is to establish a general framework for the authentication of digital messages, based upon existing law and practice in different legal systems. In so doing, the GUIDEC provides a detailed explanation of principles, particularly as they relate to information system security issues, public key cryptographic techniques and emerging biometric capabilities. It also provides succinct standard practices or recommendations relating to secure authentication and processing of digital information.

**2.37** The assumptions that underpin the Guide are set out in part III:

> The movement to open network communications systems, such as the Internet, poses significant challenges to the implementation of a global electronic trading system. Among the most significant barriers to global electronic commerce over open networks are those pertaining to the security of the information involved (i.e. its integrity, availability and confidentiality). The application of security and reduction of the risk of fraud and unauthorized access is vital to the growth of the number and volume of international commercial transactions over networked computers.
>
> Appropriate information security enables a level of trust and confidence to be present in the transfer of information between

> parties. Industry recognizes the need for a reliable framework for identifying and certifying parties to a transaction and authenticating the transaction itself.

**2.38** It is interesting to note that the security of information has become paramount. It is as if the security of information has never been relevant, such as when contracts were formed by using the latest technologies, such as telegram, telex and facsimile transmissions. Part IV of the Guide traverses the UNCITRAL model laws, the now repealed European Union Directive on electronic signatures, the 1998 OECD Ottawa Ministerial Declaration, and the United States legislation, the Electronic Signatures in Global and National Commerce Act (Public Law 106-229). Parts V to VIII deal with the broad principles of electronic contracting, and parts IX and X deal with best practices, comprising authenticating a message and certification respectively.

**2.39** The provisions of part IX respecting the appropriate practice when authenticating a message are discussed within the confines of a digital signature. No other means of proving intent seems to be considered. Item 4 provides, 'A signatory **must** authenticate a message by a means **appropriate under the circumstances**' (bold in the original). First, it is to be noted that the guidance issued under the United Nations Convention on the Use of Electronic Communications in International Contracts has ameliorated the requirement that a court need to consider the reliability test. Second, it is most unusual for a person signing a message or communication to be required to authenticate a message. Authentication was not required with telegrams, so it is to be wondered why it is necessary in the digital environment. In the comment on 'clarification', to this point, the word 'must' is amplified:

> 'must': The consequence of a failure to authenticate a message properly is that the message may be disregarded. In general commercial practice and unless otherwise agreed, a message may be ignored if the manner of authenticating it either contravenes an agreement by the parties, is not suited to impart the legal efficacy intended by the parties for the message, or if reliance on the message as authenticated would not be reasonable under the circumstances.

**2.40** Even before the advent of the internet, contracts would be formed between business and individuals and business at a distance. The most striking example is that of contracts conducted by way of the post: such issues were commonplace two hundred years before the internet, and it is to be wondered why businesses need such guidance when they have been dealing with such issues for such a long period of time. Further evidence of the reliance on digital signatures and the public key infrastructure is manifest in the provisions of part X. Paragraph 1 discusses the effect of a certificate issued by a certification authority:

> A person may **rely** on a valid certificate as accurately representing the fact or facts set forth in it, if the person has no notice that the certifier has failed to satisfy a material requirement of authenticated message practice. (Bold in the original)

**2.41** This statement is bold indeed, and is predicated, as pointed out in the commentary, on the proposition that the parties 'are acting in good faith and without deception or negligence in conducting their business'. This statement on its own undermines the entire rationale of the reason for implementing the Guide, because if the parties are known to each other and recognize the communications sent between each other, there is no need for a Guide and no need for either to have digital signatures: the email address alone, together with the content, will suffice (as it does in reality) to provide sufficient evidence that the authenticity of the communications is not in doubt.[27]

## United Nations Convention on the Use of Electronic Communications in International Contracts

**2.42** This United Nations Convention was adopted in the 53rd plenary meeting of the UN on 23 November 2005. It was open for signature by all states from 16 January 2006, and 18 states had signed the Convention by 16 January 2008. The development of the Convention was based on the UN resolution 2205 (XXI) of 17 December 1966, which established the Commission on International Trade Law with the mandate to undertake the harmonization and unification of the law of international trade, and a decision in the 34th session in 2001 to prepare an international instrument dealing with issues of electronic contracting, which also aimed at removing obstacles to electronic commerce in existing uniform law conventions and trade agreements. Working Group IV (Electronic Commerce) was requested to prepare a draft Convention. In summary, the Convention covers the following, and is only relevant between commercial entities:

(i) Contracts between parties whose places of business are in different states, excluding contracts for personal, family or household purposes, amongst other forms of contract (Articles 1 and 2).

(ii) Parties may exclude the application of the Convention or derogate or vary the effect of any of its provisions (Article 3).

(iii) Location and information requirements (Articles 6 and 7).

(iv) Requirements to recognise contracts in electronic format and to recognize various requirements of form, including methods of

27 For a practical examples of where businesses in Poland would not use digital signatures, see P. Krawczyk, 'When the EU qualified electronic signature becomes an information services preventer', *Digital Evidence and Electronic Signature Law Review*, 7 (2010), 7–18.

identifying the parties and indicate intention (Articles 8 and 9).

(v) The technical issues relating to the formation of contract are covered by Articles 10, 11, 12, 13 and 14.

## Signature provisions

**2.43** Article 9(3) sets out the provisions for a signature, incorporating and extending the provisions of the Model Laws, introducing an abstract reliability test (the word 'signature' is not defined):[28]

> 3. Where the law requires that a communication or a contract should be signed by a party, or provides consequences for the absence of a signature, that requirement is met in relation to an electronic communication if:
>
> (a) A method is used to identify the party and to indicate that party's intention in respect of the information contained in the electronic communication; and
>
> (b) The method used is either:
>
> (i) As reliable as appropriate for the purpose for which the electronic communication was generated or communicated, in the light of all the circumstances, including any relevant agreement; or
>
> (ii) Proven in fact to have fulfilled the functions described in subparagraph (a) above, by itself or together with further evidence.

**2.44** It can be observed that article 9(3) changes the emphasis in respect to electronic signatures in comparison to the provisions in the Model Laws. Weight is given to the reliability of the method ('method' is not defined) used to sign a document, the purpose for which the communication is generated or communicated, and, more importantly, whether the method of signature used actually fulfilled the functions, either on its own, or if taken together with further evidence. The provisions of article 9(3) indicate that a significant change has taken place, away from the approaches taken in the Model Laws. This new approach allows for any form of electronic signature to be used, in keeping with the decisions made by judges across the globe before this Convention was agreed. The commentary to the Convention reflects this change in view.[29]

28 The text is very similar to that of s10(1)(a) and (b) of the Electronic Transactions Act 1999 (Cth) of Australia.

29 *United Nations Convention on the Use of Electronic Communications in International Contracts* (Including explanatory notes by the UNCITRAL secretariat on the United Nations Convention on the Use of Electronic Communications in International Contracts) (New York: United Nations, 2007), paragraphs 147–64.

**2.45** Of note are the comments respecting the reliability of the signature method. If not understood, the abstract reliability test could increase the risks of invalidity after the event, where the form of signature had never posed problems of authentication previously. The emphasis is on assessing the evidence when considering the methods used under article (9)(3)(a). The explanatory notes highlight the nature of the technical evidence in place to validate a particular signature. For instance, paragraph 162 provides as follows:

> 162. Legal, technical and commercial factors that may be taken into account in determining whether the method used under paragraph 3 (a) is appropriate, include the following: (a) the sophistication of the equipment used by each of the parties; (b) the nature of their trade activity; (c) the frequency at which commercial transactions take place between the parties; (d) the kind and size of the transaction; (e) the function of signature requirements in a given statutory and regulatory environment; (f) the capability of communication systems; (g) compliance with authentication procedures set forth by intermediaries; (h) the range of authentication procedures made available by any intermediary; (i) compliance with trade customs and practice; (j) the existence of insurance coverage mechanisms against unauthorized communications; (k) the importance and the value of the information contained in the electronic communication; (l) the availability of alternative methods of identification and the cost of implementation; (m) the degree of acceptance or non-acceptance of the method of identification in the relevant industry or field both at the time the method was agreed upon and the time when the electronic communication was communicated; and (n) any other relevant factor.

**2.46** The criteria is, according to the commentary at paragraph 163, proposed

> ... with a view to ensuring the correct interpretation of the principle of functional equivalence in respect of electronic signatures. The 'reliability test', which appears also in article 7, paragraph 1 (b), of the UNCITRAL Model Law on Electronic Commerce, reminds courts of the need to take into account factors other than technology, such as the purpose for which the electronic communication was generated or communicated, or a relevant agreement of the parties, in ascertaining whether the electronic signature used was sufficient to identify the signatory.

**2.47** Depending on the rules relating to admissibility, if the authenticity of the document is not in dispute between the parties, the method by which the document is generated is irrelevant: if there is a dispute, the parties generally define the issues to be adjudicated, and unless a party raises the issue of the authenticity of the document, it does not necessarily follow that the court will raise the issue on its own initiative. The practical problem relating to this issue was raised in the context of the Australian Electronic Transactions Act 1999 (Cth) in the case of *Getup Ltd v. Electoral Commissioner*,[30] which is discussed elsewhere in this text.

**2.48** Further guidance is given in paragraph 164 in an attempt to pre-empt a party from using the proposed test to prevent the signature from being admitted, even though there is no dispute that the communication was sent and received and the communication signed:

> 164. However, UNCITRAL considered that the Convention should not allow a party to invoke the 'reliability test' to repudiate its signature in cases where the actual identity of the party and its actual intention could be proved. The requirement that an electronic signature needs to be 'as reliable as appropriate' should not lead a court or trier of fact to invalidate the entire contract on the ground that the electronic signature was not appropriately reliable if there is no dispute about the identity of the person signing or the fact of signing, that is, no question as to authenticity of the electronic signature. Such a result would be particularly unfortunate, as it would allow a party to a transaction in which a signature was required to try to escape its obligations by denying that its signature (or the other party's signature) was valid—not on the ground that the purported signer did not sign, or that the document it signed had been altered, but only on the ground that the method of signature employed was not 'as reliable as appropriate' in the circumstances. In order to avoid these situations, paragraph 3 (b)(ii) validates a signature method—regardless of its reliability in principle—whenever the method used is proven in fact to have identified the signatory and indicated the signatory's intention in respect of the information contained in the electronic communication.

**2.49** This guidance is essential to understand and bring to the attention of the parties in the event of a dispute, otherwise it is conceivable that lawyers may fail to comprehend the full import of the commentary. This is of the utmost importance, because many states have enacted legislation incorporating the provisions of article 9(3) in full. However, in so doing, the provisions of the article are taken out of context. The legislation applies to all forms of electronic signature between any party, and not just commercial entities.

**2.50** The provision of the abstract reliability test merits further observations. John D. Gregory provided four reasons as to why he was sceptical of any legal

30 [2010] FCA 869 (13 August 2010); see also J. Forder, 'The inadequate legislative response to e-signatures', *Computer Law & Security Review*, 26 (2010), 418–26, at 3.3.

requirement that electronic signatures must be as reliable as appropriate in the circumstances:[31]

> The first reason for not having such a rule is that there is no such rule for handwritten signatures (or any of the other marks on paper that may constitute a signature at law). The person relying on a signature always takes the risk that the signature is not genuine, so he or she acts accordingly. That is to say, the relying party evaluates the risk that the signature is not genuine and protects himself or herself or itself accordingly.
>
> ...
>
> These precautions and judgments are not a matter of law but a matter of prudence. The law applicable to electronic signatures can be the same.
>
> ...
>
> Second, the common law does not impose any form requirement on signatures – which means it is arguable that an electronic signature is a good signature without any law reform.
>
> ...
>
> Third, ... I would submit that the law does not add any value to this lack of familiarity with an 'appropriate reliability' test. Such a test merely transfers the prudential judgment from the relying party to a judge – who may be no more competent to make it, though he or she may have the advantage of expert evidence. It may be a complicated decision.
>
> ...
>
> Fourth, a reliability requirement risks becoming a trap for the unwary, or a potential loophole for the unscrupulous.
>
> ...
>
> In short, the reliability test does not deal with what parties should reasonably be expected to ascertain – who signed what for what purpose? It adds an unforeseeable element, an optional escape method, for attacking a signature with respect to which all relevant questions are answered. And it does not help answer any of those questions independently.

**2.51** As previously mentioned, the form of the signature is not only irrelevant; it does not have a legal effect.

31 J. D. Gregory, 'Must e-signatures be reliable?', *Digital Evidence and Electronic Signature Law Review*, 10 (2013), 67–70.

# 3

# The practical issues in using electronic signatures in different jurisdictions

**3.1** The framework within which legislation is drafted invariably depends on the decisions made by politicians. While the existence of the UNCITRAL Model Law on Electronic Commerce and Model Law on Electronic Signatures have acted as a guide for many states when enacting legislation, other factors help shape the formation of legislation, such as the approach taken regionally by the European Union in the form of the now repealed Directive on electronic signatures.[1] In early reports published by the Internet Law and Policy Forum,[2] it was suggested it is possible for there to be a tension between legislation that seeks to be technologically neutral and the establishment of legal rules to provide for electronic authentication. The tension is illustrated in the judicial reaction to electronic signatures. This is because electronic signatures do not appear to be well understood in some jurisdictions (by lawyers or judges), and in what might be called civil law jurisdictions (although not exclusively), the emphasis has been on the required use of digital signatures.[3] Of interest, a number of countries have decided to specifically exclude some forms of electronic signature: that is, signatures by facsimile or by way of a scanning device.[4]

## Approaches to legislation

**3.2** There are three broad approaches to legislating for electronic signatures: the prescriptive approach, minimalist approach and two-tier approach.

1 Directive 1999/93/EC of the European Parliament and of the Council of 13 December 1999 on a Community framework for electronic signatures, OJ L13, 19.01.2000, p.12.

2 T. F. Rebel, O. Darge and W. Koenig, *Approaches of digital signature legislation* (Lecture Notes in Computer Science 1402, Berlin/Heidelberg: Springer, 1998), pp. 39–51; S. Baker and M. Yeo 'Survey of international electronic and digital signature initiatives', available online at http://www.ilpf.org/groups/survey.htm; C. Kuner, R. Barcelo, S. Baker and E. Greenwald, 'An analysis of international electronic and digital signature implementation initiatives a study prepared for the internet law & policy forum' (2000), available online at http://www.ilpf.org/groups/analysis_IEDSII.htm; 'Promoting confidence in electronic commerce: legal issues on international use of electronic authentication and signature methods' (Vienna: United Nations Commission on International Trade Law, 2009), pp. 36–43, 63–103.

3 For discussions relating to Belgium and Italy, see J. Vandendriessche, 'Hybrid signatures under Belgian law', *Digital Evidence and Electronic Signature Law Review*, 9 (2012), pp. 79–80; A. Merone, 'Electronic signatures in Italian law', *Digital Evidence and Electronic Signature Law Review*, 11 (2014), pp. 85–99.

4 Grenada: Electronic Transactions Act, 2008, s4; Jamaica: Electronic Transactions Act, 2006, s2; Saint Lucia: Electronic Transactions Act 2007, s2.

S. Mason, *Electronic Signatures in Law* (London: Institute of Advanced Legal Studies, 2016), chapter 3, 'The practical issues in using electronic signatures in different jurisdictions', pp. 115–45.

## The prescriptive approach

**3.3** A number of jurisdictions have established legislation that is prescriptive in nature. This means that a particular type of technology (encryption by way of digital signatures) is the method adopted to replace a manuscript signature in the digital environment. This approach is also referred to as the 'functional equivalent concept'. For the sake of clarity, the term 'prescriptive approach' is used, because it is a more accurate description of the approach taken by some states. This approach to legislation generally only provides that a digital signature can be acceptable as a form of electronic signature to the exclusion of all forms of electronic signature. However, this approach is ambiguous, because it neither provides for legal certainty nor for the further development of e-commerce, as claimed in the recitals of some legislation. Befuddled by technicians, many politicians have been misled into the false premise that only digital signatures can be the legal equivalent of a manuscript signature, mainly because of the incorrect assurances that digital signatures are secure and safe from interference. Attitudes change, and the Indian Information Technology Act 2000 only provided for digital signatures, but the Act has now been amended, and India can now be considered to have adopted the two-tier approach.[5] Some of the legislation listed has been drafted in such a way that it is sometimes ambiguous whether other forms of electronic signature may be acceptable. The first law passed in the Russian Federation[6] only appeared to provide for 'electronic digital signatures', although other forms of signature also appeared to be acceptable by agreement, as set out in the relevant Russian Code.[7] The new law now explicitly provides for other forms of electronic signature, thus placing the law into the two-tier approach. Although there is an emphasis on the digital signature as the functional equivalent of a manuscript signature in the laws taking this approach, the legislation sometimes permits the use of other forms of electronic signature, although it is not always clear whether other forms of electronic signature would have the same effect in law. The Electronic Transactions Act 2007 of Saint Vincent and the Grenadines illustrates this confusion. This legislation adopts the prescriptive approach with a little latitude: s22(4) provides that parties may agree to use any method of electronic signature, although where no particular method is agreed, s22(4) provides that the only form of signature that has legal force is the digital signature.

**3.4** An explicit example of a law providing for the specific type of electronic signature as a digital equivalent of the manuscript signature is s62 of the Digital Signature Act 1997 of Malaysia. The positions is as follows:

5 Information Technology (Amendment) Act, 2008.

6 Federal Law No. 63-FZ on electronic signatures, adopted by the State Duma on 25 March 2011 and approved by the Federation Council approved on 30 March 2011, which repealed Federal Law No. 1-FZ on Electronic Digital Signature.

7 V. Naumov and T. Nikiforova, 'Electronic signatures in Russian law', *Digital Evidence and Electronic Signature Law Review*, 2 (2005), pp. 62–6.

PART V

EFFECT OF DIGITAL SIGNATURE

62. (1) Where a rule of law requires a signature or provides for certain consequences in the absence of a signature, that rule shall be satisfied by a digital signature where –

(a) that digital signature is verified by reference to the public key listed in a valid certificate issued by a licensed certification authority;

(b) that digital signature was affixed by the signer with the intention of signing the message; and

(c) the recipient has no knowledge or notice that the signer –

(i) has breached a duty as a subscriber; or

(ii) does not rightfully hold the private key used to affix the digital signature.

(2) Notwithstanding any written law to the contrary –

(a) a document signed with a digital signature in accordance with this Act shall be as legally binding as a document signed with a handwritten signature, an affixed thumb-print or any other mark; and

(b) a digital signature created in accordance with this Act shall be deemed to be a legally binding signature.

**3.5** In comparison, article 14 of the Electronic Transactions Law of Saudi Arabia has the same effect, but the language used is not as explicit:

Article (14):

1. If a signature is required for any document or contract or the like, such requirement shall be deemed satisfied by an electronic signature generated in accordance with this Law. The electronic signature shall be equal to a handwritten signature, having the same legal effects.

2. Any person generating an electronic signature shall do so in accordance with the provisions of this Law and the conditions, requirements and specifications set by the Regulations, and shall take into consideration the following:

a. Take necessary precautions to prevent unlawful use of signature generating data or the personal equipment related thereto. The Regulations shall specify such precautions.

b. Notify the certification service provider of any unauthorized use of his signature in accordance with the procedures specified in the Regulations.

> 3. If an electronic signature is provided in any legal procedure, the following shall be deemed valid, unless proven otherwise or the concerned parties agree to the contrary:
>
> a. The electronic signature is the signature of the person identified in the relevant digital certificate.
>
> b. The electronic signature was provided by the person identified in the relevant digital certificate for the purpose specified therein.
>
> c. The electronic transaction has not been altered since the electronic signature was affixed thereto.
>
> 4. If an electronic signature does not satisfy the conditions and requirements set forth in this Law and the Regulations, the presumed validity established in paragraph (3) of this Article shall not apply to said signature nor to the electronic transaction associated therewith.
>
> 5. Any person relying on an electronic signature of another person shall exercise due diligence in verifying the authenticity of the signature, using relevant electronic signature verification data in accordance with the procedures set forth by the Regulations.

**3.6** Although the Ley De Firma Digital Nº 25.506 passed by Argentina in 2001[8] is more accurately described as adopting the two-tier approach, nevertheless a digital signature is considered to be the equivalent of a manuscript signature, as provided by article 3:

> ARTICULO 3º – Del requerimiento de firma. Cuando la ley requiera una firma manuscrita, esa exigencia también queda satisfecha por una firma digital. Este principio es aplicable a los casos en que la ley establece la obligación de firmar o prescribe consecuencias para su ausencia.
>
> ARTICLE 3. – On the requirement of signature. When the law requires a handwritten signature, this requirement is also met by a digital signature. This principle is applicable to those cases in which the law establishes the obligation of signing or prescribes consequences for the absence of a signature.

**3.7** As with the approach taken by Argentina, some jurisdictions adopting the two-tier approach have a tendency to require the use of digital signatures in specific situations.

8 The English translation is from the Firma Digital website at http://www.pki.gov.ar.

## The minimalist approach

**3.8** The minimalist approach to electronic signature legislation aims to be technologically neutral in determining what an electronic signature can be. The rationale is set out with clarity by the report of the expert group appointed by the Attorney General of Australia to report on a proposed legal framework for electronic commerce. The expert group conducted a wide-ranging survey of the laws that had been or were to be enacted, and concluded that it was appropriate not to take a prescriptive approach towards the legal recognition of electronic signatures for a number of reasons:

> A legislative electronic signature regime is not required
>
> Consideration of the legal issues raised by electronic commerce is sometimes complicated by the discussion of electronic signatures, a term which is used to refer to a range of technologies intended to ensure the security and certainty of electronic commerce, and in particular one of these technologies, namely digital signatures. Many jurisdictions overseas have enacted or drafted legislation to facilitate the use of electronic signatures. We have analysed a number of these enacted or proposed legislative regimes in Chapter 3. These legislative regimes go beyond ensuring the legal effect of electronic signatures and their functional equivalence with paper based signatures.
>
> It is our view that the enactment of legislation which creates a detailed legislative regime for electronic signatures needs to be considered with caution. There is the risk, particularly given the lack of any internationally uniform legislative approach, that an inappropriate legislative regime may be adopted without regard to market-oriented solutions. Given the pace of technological development and change in this area, it is more appropriate for the market to determine issues other than legal effect, such as the levels of security and reliability required for electronic signatures. Accordingly, we have recommended that legislation should deal simply with the legal effect of electronic signatures. While a number of articles in the Model Law deal with electronic signature issues that go beyond legal effect, it is our view that these issues should be left to the existing law in Australia. Whether the existing Australian law deals with these issues adequately or not, the same situation should apply to both paper based commerce and electronic commerce. At this stage we are not persuaded of the need to give a legislative advantage to electronic commerce not available to traditional means of communication. If a clear need to deal with these issues appears in the future the recommended legislation can be amended.[9]

9 'Electronic commerce: building the legal framework', report of the electronic commerce expert group to the Attorney General 31 March 1998 Executive Summary.

**3.9** The Australian government followed the recommendations of the expert group and adopted article 7 of the UNCITRAL Model Law on Electronic Commerce. This decision was made on the premise that there is no internationally uniform legislative approach to this issue, and it is important merely to deal with the legal effect of electronic signatures. By taking this approach, the Australian government decided to allow the market to determine the issues that do not have a legal effect, such as levels of security and reliability. The view taken by the expert group is reflected in the provisions of s10 of the Electronic Transactions Act 1999 (Cth) of the Commonwealth of Australia:

> 10 Signature
>
> Requirement for signature
>
> (1) If, under a law of the Commonwealth, the signature of a person is required, that requirement is taken to have been met in relation to an electronic communication if:
>
> (a) in all cases—a method is used to identify the person and to indicate the person's approval of the information communicated; and
>
> (b) in all cases—having regard to all the relevant circumstances at the time the method was used, the method was as reliable as was appropriate for the purposes for which the information was communicated; and
>
> (c) if the signature is required to be given to a Commonwealth entity, or to a person acting on behalf of a Commonwealth entity, and the entity requires that the method used as mentioned in paragraph (a) be in accordance with particular information technology requirements—the entity's requirement has been met; and
>
> (d) if the signature is required to be given to a person who is neither a Commonwealth entity nor a person acting on behalf of a Commonwealth entity—the person to whom the signature is required to be given consents to that requirement being met by way of the use of the method mentioned in paragraph (a).

**3.10** No form of electronic signature is set out. The focus is on the method used to communicate intention and to ensure it is appropriate for the purposes of the information. Hence an 'I accept' icon can be equally as effective when used to indicate the agreement for the purchase of goods or services from a trader operating a website, as the complexity associated with the use of a digital signature. The important issue is whether the intent is manifest and the method is appropriate to the particular transaction. The case of *Faulks v. Cameron*[10] is interesting from the perspective of whether the method used is appropriate to the particular transaction. In this case, involving a separation between two people, there was an exchange of emails, and the plaintiff successfully sought to submit that the email correspondence constituted a separation agreement. Inevitably whether the method is appropriate seems to be somewhat irrelevant, given the propensity of individuals to use whatever form of communication is available, without thought to the legal consequences of the actual method of communication: it was ever thus, and seems somewhat unusual that legislators should begin to impose specific technical requirements (such as the use of a digital signature) in the internet age, especially as such detailed technical requirements were not imposed in the age of the telegram.

**3.11** The Uniform Law Conference of Canada prepared two important documents that have helped shape legislation in Canada, the Uniform Electronic Evidence Act and the Uniform Electronic Commerce Act. The primary focus of the Uniform Electronic Evidence Act is to replace the concept of an original document with the proof of the reliability of a system instead of the reliability of an individual record, and using standards to demonstrate the reliability of a system.[11] The Uniform Electronic Commerce Act provides a single, media neutral, definition of an electronic signature in s1(b):

> (b) "electronic signature" means information in electronic form that a person has created or adopted in order to sign a document and that is in, attached to or associated with the document.

**3.12** Other examples of clauses adopting the minimalist approach include Guernsey, for which see s22(1):[12]

> "signature in electronic form" means a signature wholly or partly in electronic form attached to or logically associated with information in electronic or non-electronic form, and references to a signature being in electronic form shall be construed accordingly

**3.13** And the United States of America, in s106(5):[13]

> (5) ELECTRONIC SIGNATURE. – The term "electronic signature" means an electronic sound, symbol, or process, attached to or logically associated with a contract or other record and executed or adopted by a person with the intent to sign the record.

10 [2004] 32 Fam LR 417; [2004] NTSC 61.

11 It is difficult to imagine how the submission of a standard to prove a fact in a court of law is helpful. For a discussion, see S. Mason (ed.), *Electronic Evidence*, (3rd edn., London: LexisNexis Butterworths, 2012), ch. 4.

12 Electronic Transactions (Guernsey) Law, 2000.

13 Electronic Signatures in Global and National Commerce Act, 15 U.S.C. §§ 7001-7003.

**3.14** The definition of an electronic signature permits any format of electronic signature to be acceptable, and this is reflected in the case law discussed elsewhere in this text, although in the state of New York, an insurer is free to reject electronic signatures and insist upon the use of a manuscript signature when making a claim.[14]

## The two-tier approach

**3.15** The United Nations adopted the two-tier approach with the two Models Laws. Article 7 of the Model Law on Electronic Commerce provides for an electronic signature that relates to the form such a signatures takes and whether it is appropriate in the circumstances, and the Model Law on Electronic Signatures has taken one step further by incorporating the provisions of article 7 of the Model Law on Electronic Commerce and adding a provision relating to the reliability of a signature, indicating in article 6(3) the preference for the digital signature:

> Article 6 Compliance with a requirement for a signature
>
> 1. Where the law requires a signature of a person, that requirement is met in relation to a data message if an electronic signature is used that is as reliable as was appropriate for the purpose for which the data message was generated or communicated, in the light of all the circumstances, including any relevant agreement.
>
> 2. Paragraph 1 applies whether the requirement referred to therein is in the form of an obligation or whether the law simply provides consequences for the absence of a signature.
>
> 3. An electronic signature is considered to be reliable for the purpose of satisfying the requirement referred to in paragraph 1 if:
>
> > (a) The signature creation data are, within the context in which they are used, linked to the signatory and to no other person;
> >
> > (b) The signature creation data were, at the time of signing, under the control of the signatory and of no other person;
> >
> > (c) Any alteration to the electronic signature, made after the time of signing, is detectable; and
> >
> > (d) Where a purpose of the legal requirement for a signature is to provide assurance as to the integrity of the information to which it relates, any alteration made to that information after the time of signing is detectable.
>
> 4. Paragraph 3 does not limit the ability of any person:

14 *DWP Pain Free Medical P.C. v. Progressive Northeastern Ins. Co.*, 14 Misc.3d 800, 831 N.Y.S.2d 849.

> (a) To establish in any other way, for the purpose of satisfying the requirement referred to in paragraph 1, the reliability of an electronic signature; or
>
> (b) To adduce evidence of the non-reliability of an electronic signature.

**3.16** The provision of certainty as to the legal effect that follows the use of an electronic signature is left for the enacting state, although the Model Law seeks to expressly establish the legal effects that will result where the technical characteristics set out in article 6(3)(a) to (d) apply, and which a digital signature is capable of conforming to.

**3.17** The European Union Regulation (EU) No 910/2014 of the European Parliament and of the Council of 23 July 2014 on electronic identification and trust services for electronic transactions in the internal market and repealing Directive 1999/93/EC[15] is one such approach, in which the Regulation distinguishes between an electronic signature, advanced electronic signature, and qualified electronic signature. The two-tier approach has also been adopted by Singapore in the Electronic Transactions Act Ch 88.[16] This legislation also differentiates between electronic signatures and secure electronic signatures. The Act provides that an electronic signature can be proved in any manner, as provided for in the amended version of s8, closely following article 7 of the Model Law on Electronic Commerce:

> 8. Where a rule of law requires a signature, or provides for certain consequences if a document or a record is not signed, that requirement is satisfied in relation to an electronic record if —
>
> (a) a method is used to identify the person and to indicate that person's intention in respect of the information contained in the electronic record; and
>
> (b) the method used is either —
>
> (i) as reliable as appropriate for the purpose for which the electronic record was generated or communicated, in the light of all the circumstances, including any relevant agreement; or
>
> (ii) proven in fact to have fulfilled the functions described in paragraph (a), by itself or together with further evidence.

**3.18** This amended definition includes the abstract reliability test in s8(b)(i), but also overrides the test in s8(b)(ii) where it is proven that the form of electronic signature has actually fulfilled the functions, regardless of the test.

15 OJ L257, 28.8.2014, p. 73–114.

16 This act repeals the Electronic Transactions Act Ch 16 of 2010, which in turn repealed the Electronic Transactions Act 1998.

The removal of the word 'symbol' and substitution of the word 'method' does not alter the meaning, thus the type of electronic signature can extend to any form of electronic data, as indicated by the decision of Prakash J in *SM Integrated Transware Ltd v. Schenker Singapore (Pte) Ltd* with respect to the name forming part of an email address.[17] The definition of a secure electronic signature in s18, in contrast, very similar to the advanced electronic signature set out in article 2(2) of the repealed European Union Directive on electronic signatures.

**3.19** China has also adopted the two-tier approach in the Electronic Signatures Law of the People's Republic of China of 2015.[18] Article 2 provides a definition of electronic signature and data message, both of which are widely drafted:

> "Electronic signature" in this law means data in electronic form in or affixed to a data message, which may be used to identify the signatory in relation to the data message and to indicate the signatory's approval of the information contained in the data message.
>
> "Data message" means information generated, sent, received or stored by electronic, optical, magnetic or similar means.

**3.20** Confusingly, article 3 provides that the parties are free to determine whether to use electronic signatures in civil activities, which implies that the type of signature referred to in article 2 is a digital signature, although digital signatures are clearly referred to in chapter 3 article 13, even if the word 'digital' is not used:

> Article 13: An electronic signature is deemed to be a reliable electronic signature if the following requirements are met:
>
> (1) The signature creation data, when used to an electronic signature, is linked to the signatory and to no other person;
>
> (2) The signature creation data is under the control of the signatory and of no other person when signing;
>
> (3) Any alteration to an electronic signature, made after the time of signing, is detectable;
>
> (4) Any alteration to the content or form of a data message, made after the time of signing, is detectable.

**3.21** Although article 14 provides that 'The reliable electronic signature has the same legal effect as the hand-written signature or seal', nevertheless this

17 [2005] 2 SLR 651, [2005] SGHC 58.

18 Order No. 24 of the President of the People's Republic of China, promulgated on and effective since 4 April 2015, amending the 2004 law. M. Wang and M. Wang, 'Introduction to the Electronic Signatures Law of the People's Republic of China' together with an unofficial translation, *Digital Evidence and Electronic Signature Law Review*, 2 (200), 79–85; C. Cao, 'A note to China's new law on electronic signatures', *Digital Evidence and Electronic Signature Law Review*, 13 (forthcoming 2016).

approach has not prevented judges concluding that data sent by way of text messages between mobile telephones is capable of being admitted into evidence, as in *Yang Chunning v. Han Ying*.[19]

# Digital signature presumptions

**3.22** Where a law adopts the aim of substituting an electronic signature as a functional equivalent of a manuscript signature, that is, the digital signature, a number of presumptions may be included in the legislation. Illustrated below are some of the presumptions set out in various laws, illustrating the need to take care to fully understand the provisions of individual laws when entering or advising on the validity of electronic signatures between jurisdictions. Perhaps the law in Puerto Rico sums up the position:[20]

> § 8703a. Challengeable assumptions
>
> A valid electronic signature generates the following challengeable assumptions:
>
> > (a) There is the challengeable assumption that the document has not been modified from the time it had been signed, if it is possible to use a device to verify the electronic signature and the contents of an electronic document that is able to successfully corroborate the signature and the contents thereof.
> >
> > (b) There is the challengeable assumption that the electronic signature belongs to the signer who holds the electronic signature certificate containing the data for the verification of the corresponding signature.
> >
> > (c) There is the challengeable assumption that the electronic signature was added by the signer to an electronic document with the intent to sign the same.
> >
> > (d) There is the challengeable assumption that the information contained in an electronic signature certificate in effect is correct.

## Default form of signature

**3.23** Of interest are the provisions set out in s13(1) of the South Africa Electronic Communications and Transactions Act, 2002 and s6(1) of the

19 (2005) hai min chu zi NO.4670, Beijing Hai Dian District People's Court. For a translation of this case with a commentary, see *Digital Evidence and Electronic Signature Law Review*, 5 (2008), pp. 103–5.

20 Puerto Rico Ley de Firmas Electrónicas de Puerto Rico, Ley número 359 de 16 de Septiembre 2004 (Electronic Signature Act 359/2004); 3 L.P.R.A. § 8701.

Zambia Electronic Communications and Transactions Act, 2009. Both are identical, and relate to the legal position where a law requires a signature, but where no particular type of signature is specified in the legislation. The default position is as follows:

> 13. (1) Where the signature of a person is required by law and such law does not specify the type of signature, that requirement in relation to a data message is met only if an advanced electronic signature is used.

## Validity of the signature

**3.24** In some jurisdictions a digital signature is only valid when certain criteria are met, including that the certificate that identifies the owner of the private key was issued or recognized by a certification authority licensed by the government, as provided by article 9 of the Argentinean Ley De Firma Digital Nº 25.506:

> ARTICULO 9º - Validez. Una firma digital es válida si cumple con los siguientes requisitos:
>
> a) Haber sido creada durante el período de vigencia del certificado digital válido del firmante;
>
> b) Ser debidamente verificada por la referencia a los datos de verificación de firma digital indicados en dicho certificado según el procedimiento de verificación correspondiente;
>
> c) Que dicho certificado haya sido emitido o reconocido, según el artículo 16 de la presente, por un certificador licenciado.
>
> ARTICLE 9. – Validity. A digital signature is valid if it complies with the following requirements:
>
> a) That it was created during the period of time in which the signing party's digital certificate was valid;
>
> b) That it has been duly verified by reference to the digital signature verification data indicated in this certificate according to the corresponding verification procedure;
>
> c) That such certificate was issued or recognized, according to article 16 of the present law, by a licensed certification authority.

**3.25** In China, a 'reliable' electronic signature has the same legal effect as a manuscript signature or a seal in accordance with the provisions of article 14 of the Electronic Signatures Law of the People's Republic of China of 2015, although the provisions of article 13 will also have to be met.

**3.26** In addition to considering practical matters, such as obtaining evidence of the application of electronic signatures in cross-border transactions, it is necessary to pay careful attention to the legislation and regulations surrounding digital signatures in the jurisdictions in which the parties intend to exchange documents or contracts.

## Integrity of the digital signature

**3.27** Article 8 of the Argentine Ley De Firma Digital Nº 25.506 establishes a presumption that the verification procedures applied to a digital signature demonstrate it has not been modified:

> ARTICULO 8º – Presunción de integridad. Si el resultado de un procedimiento de verificación de una firma digital aplicado a un documento digital es verdadero, se presume, salvo prueba en contrario, que este documento digital no ha sido modificado desde el momento de su firma.
>
> ARTICLE 8. – Integrity presumption. If the result of the verification procedure of a digital signature applied to a digital document is true, it is presumed, unless otherwise specified, that this digital document has not been modified as from the moment it was signed.

## Presumption the user affixed the digital signature

**3.28** Some legislation tends to avoid setting the presumptions relating to an electronic signature, especially of a digital signature, although a number of countries have provided that a message is to be attributed to the sender in given circumstances, and Israel has made such a presumption explicit in article 3 of Electronic Signature Law, 5761 – 2001:

> 3. An electronic message signed with a secure electronic signature is admissible in any legal procedure, and will constitute prima-facie evidence that:
>
> (1) the signature is that of the owner of the signing device;
>
> (2) the electronic message is that which was signed by the owner of the signing device.

**3.29** By article 3 of the Japanese Law Concerning Electronic Signatures and Certification Services (Law No.102 of 2000), a record shall be genuinely complete when signed by the sender:

> Chapter 2: Presumption of the authenticity of an electro-magnetic record
>
> Article 3:
>
> An electro-magnetic record which is made in order to express information (with the exception of one drawn by a public official in the exercise of his official functions) shall be presumed to be authentic if an electronic signature (limited to those that, if based

on the proper control of the codes and objects necessary to perform the signature, only that person can substantially perform) is performed by the principal in relation to information recorded in the electro-magnetic record.[21]

**3.30** This provision highlights the need for a user to control their private key very carefully, as well as provide for the proper security of their computer to prevent a signature from being misused. In Argentina, any person using a digital signature will be presumed to have sent it, even where it is sent automatically, according to article 10 of the Argentine Ley De Firma Digital Nº 25.506:

> ARTICULO 10. – Remitente. Presunción. Cuando un documento digital sea enviado en forma automática por un dispositivo programado y lleve la firma digital del remitente se presumirá, salvo prueba en contrario, que el documento firmado proviene del remitente.
>
> ARTICLE 10. – Sender presumption. When a digital document is sent automatically by a programmed device and bears the sender's digital signature it shall be presumed, unless otherwise specified, that the signed document was originated by the sender.

**3.31** This position is also set out in the Electronic Transactions Order 2000 of Brunei Darussalam, which has a two-tier model. The Electronic Transactions Order provides for electronic signatures, as defined in s2:

> 'electronic signature' means any letters, characters, numbers or other symbols in digital form attached to or logically associated with an electronic record, and executed or adopted with the intention of authenticating or approving the electronic record;

**3.32** An electronic signature is capable of satisfying a rule of law that requires a signature, as provided in s8:

> Electronic signatures.
>
> 8. (1) Where any rule of law requires a signature, or provides for certain consequences if a document is not signed, an electronic signature satisfies that rule of law.
>
> (2) An electronic signature may be proved in any manner, including by showing that a procedure existed by which it is necessary for a party, in order to proceed further with a transaction, to have executed a symbol or security procedure for the purpose of verifying that an electronic record is that of such party.

**3.33** However, there is also provision for a secure electronic signature, as provided by s17 in Part V of the Order:

21 Taken from the translation available at http://www.meti.go.jp.

> Secure electronic signature
>
> 17. If, through the application of a prescribed security procedure or a commercially reasonable security procedure agreed to by the parties involved, it can be verified that all electronic signature was, at the time it was made —
>
> (a) unique to the person using it;
>
> (b) capable of identifying such person;
>
> (c) created in a manner or using a means under the sole control of the person using it; and
>
> (d) linked to the electronic record to which it relates in a manner such that if the record was changed the electronic signature would be invalidated, such signature shall be treated as a secure electronic signature.

**3.34** The Order appears to distinguish between a secure electronic signature and a digital signature, because the term digital signature is defined in s2 and references are made to the effect of digital signatures in Part VI, although s18(4) provides that a secure electronic signature can comprise a digital signature. The importance of the secure electronic signature is revealed in the presumptions set out in s18:

> Presumptions relating to secure electronic records and signatures.
>
> 18. (1) In any proceedings involving a secure electronic record, it shall be presumed, unless evidence to the contrary is adduced, that the secure electronic record has not been altered since the specific point in time to which the secure status relates.
>
> (2) In any proceedings involving a secure electronic signature, it shall be presumed, unless evidence to the contrary is adduced, that —
>
>> (a) the secure electronic signature is the signature of the person with whom it correlates; and
>>
>> (b) the secure electronic signature was affixed by that person with the intention of signing or approving the electronic record.
>
> (3) In the absence of a secure electronic record or a secure electronic signature, nothing in this Part shall create any presumption relating to the authenticity and integrity of the electronic record or an electronic signature.

**3.35** This clause demonstrates that the user of a secure electronic signature is presumed to have affixed the signature to any electronic data and that there is a direct link between the user and the signature.

**3.36** The Singapore Electronic Transactions Act Ch 88 also provides a presumption that the signature is that of the person with whom it is associated, and a further presumption that the person affixed their signature with the intention of signing or approving the document sent, as provided for in s19(2):

> (2) In any proceedings involving a secure electronic signature, it shall be presumed, unless evidence to the contrary is adduced, that –
>
> > (a) the secure electronic signature is the signature of the person to whom it correlates; and
> >
> > (b) the secure electronic signature was affixed by that person with the intention of signing or approving the electronic record.

**3.37** The nexus between the digital signature and the act of affixing it to a document or message is the subject of a rebuttable presumption in s9 of the Electronic Commerce Act of 2000, Republic Act No 8792 of the Philippines:

> Sec. 9. Presumption Relating to Electronic Signatures. – In any proceedings involving an electronic signature, it shall be presumed that –
>
> > (a) The electronic signature is the signature of the person to whom it correlates; and
> >
> > (b) The electronic signature was affixed by that person with the intention of signing or approving the electronic document unless the person relying on the electronically signed electronic document knows or has notice of defects in or unreliability of the signature or reliance on the electronic signature is not reasonable under the circumstances.

**3.38** In this instance, it appears that the recipient may act upon receipt of an electronic document or message where an electronic signature has been affixed, whilst s9(b) implies that the recipient may be required to take action and thereby become a verifying party before relying on the signature. However, the provision is that a recipient only needs to take any action where they know or have notice of any defects or unreliability that would make it unreasonable to rely on the signature. The provision is not a mandatory requirement to authenticate the electronic signature. However, if the recipient were to rely on the signature to their detriment in circumstances that they should have been aware that they might not be able to trust the signature, then they will have the burden of proving its authenticity in accordance with the provisions of s11(b).

**3.39** Article 6(3) of the Bahrain Legislative Decree No 28 of 2002 with respect to electronic transactions has a similar provision, although the presumption is rebuttable and does not apply to any other form of electronic signature:

3. In any legal proceedings involving an electronic signature that is associated with an Accredited Certificate, it shall be presumed unless the parties have agreed otherwise or unless evidence to the contrary is adduced that:

(i) such electronic signature is the signature of the person to whom it correlates;

(ii) such electronic signature was affixed by that person to whom it correlates for the purpose of signing such electronic record;

(iii) the electronic record that is signed with such signature has not been altered since the time at which the electronic signature was affixed.

4. If the electronic signature is not made with the use of an Accredited Certificate, the presumption of an authenticity created under the provisions of the preceding Paragraph shall not be attached to the electronic signature or record.

**3.40** The presumption that where a person obtains a digital signature, they are presumed to have affixed the signature, is a good example of the reversal of the burden of proof. Normally, the relying party must prove the signature was that of the signatory. Where a digital signature is used, the claimant can prove that a particular verification key serves to verify the signature, but all it demonstrates is that some corresponding signature key was used to make the signature. It does not prove the person whose key it was caused the signature to be affixed. By making it clear to the person obtaining a digital signature that they will have to prove they did not use their private key, the law puts an emphatic and clear duty on the signing party to put robust security measures in place to protect the private key. This means, in circumstances where a digital signature is used, that where the signatory claims they did not affix the signature to the document or communication, the signatory is, in effect, refusing to be bound by a promise because they claim a third party sent the communication or document without permission or authorization, which in turn means their defence is that they were either unable to provide for the proper security of their private key (bearing in mind the risks discussed elsewhere in this text, this would be a good defence), or they were negligent.[22]

## Presumption of ownership

**3.41** In article 7 of the Ley De Firma Digital Nº 25.506 of Argentina, it is presumed that a digital signature belongs to the holder of the certificate:

22 For the Russian banking cases and digital signatures, see O. I. Kudryavtseva, 'The use of electronic digital signatures in banking relationships in the Russian Federation', *Digital Evidence and Electronic Signature Law Review*, 5 (2008), pp. 51–7; A. Dolzhich, 'Digital evidence and e-signature in the Russian Federation: a change in trend', *Digital Evidence and Electronic Signature Law Review*, 6 (2009), pp. 181–3.

> ARTICULO 7º – Presunción de autoría. Se presume, salvo prueba en contrario, que toda firma digital pertenece al titular del certificado digital que permite la verificación de dicha firma.
>
> ARTICLE 7. – Authorship presumption. Unless it is otherwise proved, every digital signature is presumed to belong to the holder of the digital certificate that permits the verification of the digital signature in question.

**3.42** A similar presumption is also included in article 3 of the Israeli law:[23]

> 3. An electronic message signed with a secure electronic signature is admissible in any legal procedure, and will constitute prima-facie evidence that:
>
> (1) the signature is that of the owner of the signing device;
>
> (2) the electronic message is that which was signed by the owner of the signing device.

**3.43** It is refreshing to observe that some politicians in some countries are willing to make the implicit explicit.

# Certification authorities

**3.44** It is a matter of public policy whether a state sets up an implementation scheme to provide for a technical framework for electronic authentication, or permits a voluntary scheme to operate. A scheme may include some or all of the following: the provision of national and international standards for products and services relating to electronic authentication; the provision of a framework to regulate the supervision, accreditation and certification of some or all authentication products and services. Where such a framework is in place, it may be one that is established by the state or a voluntary accreditation scheme, and the provision of guidelines, best practice and other matters that relate to the provision of authentication infrastructures.

## Licensed certification authorities

**3.45** The states of Latin America have, to a large extent, adopted a licensing system for certification authorities. For instance, the Argentine government started a public key infrastructure project in 1996, which includes a fully operational root certification authority, a licensed certification authority (the Ministry of Economy) and other bodies that have started to issue licenses. Chapter III of the Ley De Firma Digital Nº 25.506 establishes the regime for a certification authorities, and article 17 provides for certification authorities to be licensed:

23 Electronic Signature Law, 5761 – 2001.

> ARTICULO 17. - Del certificador licenciado. Se entiende por certificador licenciado a toda persona de existencia ideal, registro público de contratos u organismo público que expide certificados, presta otros servicios en relación con la firma digital y cuenta con una licencia para ello, otorgada por el ente licenciante.
>
> La actividad de los certificadores licenciados no pertenecientes al sector público se prestará en régimen de competencia. El arancel de los servicios prestados por los certificadores licenciados será establecido libremente por éstos.
>
> ARTICLE 17. - Of the licensed certification authority. A licensed certification authority is any person, public registry of contracts or a government agency which issues certificates and renders other services related to digital signatures and holds a license for this purpose, issued by the Licensing Institution.
>
> The activity of the licensed certification authority which does not belong to the public sector shall be governed by a competitive regime. The licensed certification authorities shall freely establish their fees.

**3.46** The provisions relating to the certification authority include its functions,[24] methods for becoming licensed,[25] the duties,[26] rights and duties of the holder of a digital certificate,[27] provisions relating to the control of the licensing regime,[28] and matters relating to the Application Authority, auditing and the formation of an Advisory Commission.[29]

**3.47** Malaysia has opted for a compulsory licensing regime, as set out in Part II to the Digital Signature Act 1997 (note the provisions relating to electronic signatures in the Electronic Commerce Act 2006). The advantages of a compulsory licensing regime can be seen in the provisions of Part IV of the Act, which set out the duties of licensed certification authorities and subscribers, including the need of both parties to use trustworthy systems,[30] the conditions that must be fulfilled when issuing a certificate,[31] the warranties and obligations a certification authority must adhere to[32] and the duties of the subscriber.[33] Of particular note is the duty of the subscriber as set out in clause 43:

24 Article 19.

25 Article 20.

26 Article 21.

27 Chapter IV articles 24 and 25.

28 Chapter V.

29 Chapters VI, VII and VIII.

30 Section 27.

31 Section 29.

32 Sections 34 to 37.

33 Sections 30 to 42.

> 43. By accepting a certificate issued by a licensed certification authority, the subscriber named in the certificate assumes a duty to exercise reasonable care to retain control of the private key and prevent its disclosure to any person not authorised to create the subscriber's digital signature.

**3.48** The duty of the subscribing party to provide for the proper security of their private key, enforced by contractual measures as between the certification authority and subscribing party, is thus enshrined in law in Malaysia. Taiwan has also established a compulsory licensing regime by article 11 of the Electronic Signatures Law 2001.[34]

### Voluntary licensing

**3.49** The government of Singapore has adopted a voluntary licensing regime, and certification authorities can apply to be licensed by the Controller of Certification Authorities in accordance with the Electronic Transactions (Certifications Authority) Regulations 2010, issued under the authority of the third schedule of the Electronic Transactions Act 2010. However, all certification authorities, whether they are licenced or not, are subject to the relevant provisions of the Act. In particular, Part II to the third schedule sets out the duties that affect every certification authority.

## Recognition of foreign certificates

**3.50** Legislation either remains silent on the matter of the recognition of foreign certificates, or expressly provides for the recognition of foreign certificates with requirements attached. Where recognition is not mentioned in legislation, the inclusion or exclusion of evidence relating to the certificate will be a matter for procedural rules and the exercise of the judicial function. In addition, the effect of any terms relating to applicable law, jurisdiction and time and place of when and where the contract was formed will also be the subject of substantial law and decisions by the courts. Where legislation expressly provides for the recognition of certificates issued by certification authorities beyond the boundary of a nation state, the provisions may merely give legal effect to the certificate, or require the certification authority to conform to requirements laid down in the legislation. An example of such a requirement is provided for in article 16 of the Ley De Firma Digital Nº 25.506 of Argentina, which provides as follows:

> ARTICULO 16. – Reconocimiento de certificados extranjeros. Los certificados digitales emitidos por certificadores extranjeros

34 P.-H. Ou and A. Tsai, with N. Kaiser, 'The e-signature in Taiwan: consent, integrity and accessibility', *Digital Evidence and Electronic Signature Law Review*, 13 (forthcoming 2016).

podrán ser reconocidos en los mismos términos y condiciones exigidos en la ley y sus normas reglamentarias cuando:

a) Reúnan las condiciones que establece la presente ley y la reglamentación correspondiente para los certificados emitidos por certificadores nacionales y se encuentre vigente un acuerdo de reciprocidad firmado por la República Argentina y el país de origen del certificador extranjero, o

b) Tales certificados sean reconocidos por un certificador licenciado en el país, que garantice su validez y vigencia conforme a la presente ley. A fin de tener efectos, este reconocimiento deberá ser validado por la autoridad de aplicación.

ARTICLE 16. - Recognition of foreign certificates. Digital certificates issued by foreign certification authorities shall be considered valid in the same terms and conditions required by law and its regulation, when:

a) They meet the conditions established by the present law and its corresponding regulation decree for the certificates issued by national certification authorities and there is in force a reciprocity agreement signed by the Argentine Republic and the country of origin of the foreign certification authority; or

b) They are recognized by a local licensed certification authority that guarantees their validity in accordance with the present law. In order to have effect, the Application Authority should validate this recognition.

**3.51** Similar provisions apply in the Dominican Republic, and article 43 of the law in Colombia makes an almost identical requirement:

Artículo 43. Certificaciones recíprocas. Los certificados de firmas digitales emitidos por entidades de certificación extranjeras, podrán ser reconocidos en los mismos términos y condiciones exigidos en la ley para la emisión de certificados por parte de las entidades de certificación nacionales, siempre y cuando tales certificados sean reconocidos por una entidad de certificación autorizada que garantice en la misma forma que lo hace con sus propios certificados, la regularidad de los detalles del certificado, así como su validez y vigencia.

Article 43. Reciprocal certification. The digital signature certificates issued by foreign certification entities may be recognized in the same terms and conditions required by the law for the issuance of local certificates by national certification entities; provided said certificates are recognized by an authorized certification entity who

> guarantees equally as it does with its own certificates, the regularity of the details in the foreign certificate, as well as its validity and effect.

**3.52** The European Union will also recognise certificates or classes of certificates that are issued as qualified certificates from foreign certification authorities under the provisions of the Regulation, as provided in article 14:

> International aspects
>
> 1. Trust services provided by trust service providers established in a third country shall be recognised as legally equivalent to qualified trust services provided by qualified trust service providers established in the Union where the trust services originating from the third country are recognised under an agreement concluded between the Union and the third country in question or an international organisation in accordance with Article 218 TFEU.
>
> 2. Agreements referred to in paragraph 1 shall ensure, in particular, that:
>
> > (a) the requirements applicable to qualified trust service providers established in the Union and the qualified trust services they provide are met by the trust service providers in the third country or international organisations with which the agreement is concluded, and by the trust services they provide;
> >
> > (b) the qualified trust services provided by qualified trust service providers established in the Union are recognised as legally equivalent to trust services provided by trust service providers in the third country or international organisation with which the agreement is concluded.

**3.53** A number of other jurisdictions have similar provisions to the European Union, including Bermuda[35] and Brunei Darussalam.[36] Provision for the recognition of foreign certificates is included in s19 of the Information Technology Act 2000 passed in India:[37]

> 19. Recognition of foreign Certifying Authorities.
>
> (1) Subject to such conditions and restrictions as may be specified by regulations, the Controller may with the previous approval of the Central Government, and by notification in the Official Gazette, recognise any foreign Certifying Authority as a Certifying Authority for the purposes of this Act.

35 Section 21, Electronic Transactions Act 1999.

36 Section 43, Electronic Transactions Order, 2000.

37 The Information Technology (Certifying Authority) Regulations 2001 were passed in July 2001 under the provisions of s89 of the Act.

> (2) Where any Certifying Authority is recognised under sub-section (1), the Digital Signature Certificate issued by such Certifying Authority shall be valid for the purposes of this Act.

**3.54** A similar provision is provided in s40 of the Electronic Communications and Transactions Act 2002 passed by South Africa, as well as under article 15 of the Electronic Signatures Law 2001 passed by Taiwan, subject to permission from the competent authority.

# Liability

**3.55** Various provisions are made in legislation for the liability of the certification authority, the holder of the digital signature and, to a lesser extent, the recipient of a digital signature. Where legislation fails to deal adequately, or at all, with the issues of liability, the general law that applies to these issues will be considered by national courts.

## Liability of the certification authority

**3.56** The Electronic Transactions Order 2000 passed by Brunei Darussalam provides for a presumption in relation to the information listed in a certificate issued by a certification authority, which few other jurisdictions have implemented. With the exception of information that has not been verified by the certification authority, the information will be presumed to be correct, as provided in s21:

> Presumptions regarding certificates.
>
> 21. It shall be presumed, unless evidence to the contrary is adduced, that the information listed in a certificate issued by a licensed certification authority is correct, except for information identified as subscriber information which has not been verified, if the certificate was accepted by the subscriber.

**3.57** Thus any contract term that purports to negate this aspect of a certificate will have no effect in Brunei Darussalam, and any certification authority attempting to avoid this provision by refraining from verifying information provided by an applicant will probably negate the requirements of their certification practice statement, or, if there is no such provision in their certification practice statement, any certificate they issue without verifying the information supplied by the applicant will mean the certificate has very little value. Also, the Order provides a further assurance of reliance in s23:

> Reliance on certificates foreseeable.
>
> 23. It is foreseeable that persons relying on a digital signature will also rely on a valid certificate containing the public key by which the digital signature can be verified.

**3.58** By comparison, article 42 of the law in the Dominican Republic excludes the foreseeability as a requirement:

> Art. 42.- Responsabilidad de la entidad de certificación.
>
> Salvo acuerdo entre las partes, las entidades de certificación responderán por los daños y perjuicios que causen a toda persona.
>
> ARTICLE 42. – Liability of the certifying entity.
>
> Excepting by agreement between the parties, the certifying entities shall be liable for the damages and harm which they cause to any person.

**3.59** In Barbados, the certification service provider has a significant liability by s20 of the Barbados Electronic Transactions Act, 2001, an authorized certification service provider is liable to the recipient, where the recipient relies on the certificate, for the following:

> (1) By issuing an accredited certificate, an authorized certification service provider is liable to any person who reasonably relied on the certificate for
>
> > (a) the accuracy of all information in the accredited certificate as from the date on which it was issued, unless the authorized certification service provider has stated otherwise in the accredited certificate;
> >
> > (b) assurance that the person identified in the accredited certificate held, at the time the accredited certificate was issued, the signature creation device corresponding to the signature verification device given or identified in the accredited certificate;
> >
> > (c) assurance that the signature creation device and the signature verification device functioned together in a complementary manner, where the service provider generates both devices, unless the person who relied on the accredited certificate knows or ought reasonably to have known that the authorization of the certificate service provides has been revoked.

## Liability of the sender

**3.60** Where legislation provides for digital signatures, such as the Ley De Firma Digital Nº 25.506 of Argentina, the provisions relating to the holder of a digital certificate are expressed in the form of duties in article 25:

> ARTICULO 25. – Obligaciones del titular del certificado digital. Son obligaciones del titular de un certificado digital:

> a) Mantener el control exclusivo de sus datos de creación de firma digital, no compartirlos, e impedir su divulgación;
>
> b) Utilizar un dispositivo de creación de firma digital técnicamente confiable;
>
> c) Solicitar la revocación de su certificado al certificador licenciado ante cualquier circunstancia que pueda haber comprometido la privacidad de sus datos de creación de firma;
>
> d) Informar sin demora al certificador licenciado el cambio de alguno de los datos contenidos en el certificado digital que hubiera sido objeto de verificación.
>
> ARTICLE 25. - Duties of the digital certificate holder. These are duties of the holder of a digital certificate:
>
> a) To keep exclusive control of his digital signature creation data, not to share it, and to prevent it from being publicly known;
>
> b) To use a technically reliable digital signature creation device;
>
> c) To request the licensed certification authority to revoke his certificate if faced with any circumstance which might have compromised the privacy of his signature creation data;
>
> d) To inform the licensed certification authority without delay of any change in any of the data which has been subject to verification contained in the digital certificate.

**3.61** In China, article 27 of the Electronic Signatures Law provides for the liability of the signing party:

> Where the signatory knows that the signature creation data has been compromised or may have been compromised, but fails to notify the relevant parties without undue delay and to cease to utilize the signature creation data, or where the signatory does not provide genuine, complete and accurate information to the certification service provider, or is responsible for any other faults, he shall be responsible for any damages suffered by the relevant relying parties and the certification service provider.

**3.62** The liability is contingent upon the signing party being aware that the signature creation data has been compromised or may have been compromised, although article 15 requires the signatory to exercise reasonable care to protect the signature creation data. The Dominican Republic has provided a slightly more detailed approach to the duties of a signing party in article 53:

> Art. 53. - Deberes de los suscriptores. Son deberes de los suscriptores:
>
> > a) Recibir de las claves por parte de la entidad de certificación o generar las claves, utilizando un sistema de

seguridad exigido por la entidad de certificación;

b) Suministrar información completa, precisa y verídica a la entidad de certificación;

c) Aceptar los certificados emitidos por la entidad de certificación, demostrando aprobación de sus contenidos mediante el envío de éstos a una o más personas o solicitando la publicación de éstos en repositorios;

d) Mantener el control de la clave privada y reservada del conocimiento de terceras personas;

e) Efectuar oportunamente las correspondientes solicitudes de suspensión o revocación.

Párrafo. - Un suscriptor cesa en la obligación de cumplir con los anteriores deberes a partir de la publicación de un aviso de revocación del correspondiente certificado por parte de la entidad de certificado.

ARTICLE 53. - Duties of the signers. The duties of the signers are:

a) To receive the passwords from the certifying entity, or to generate the passwords, using a security system required by the certifying entity;

b) To provide complete, precise, and accurate information to the certifying entity;

c) To accept the certificates issued by the certifying entity, demonstrating approval of its contents by means of the sending of same to one or more persons or requesting the publication of same in repositories;

d) To maintain the control of the private reserved password from the knowledge of third persons;

e) To perform opportunely the corresponding requests for suspension or revocation.

Paragraph. - A signer ceases to be obligated to comply with the abovegoing duties as of the publication of a notice of revocation of the corresponding certificate by the certifying entity.

**3.63** The provisions of article 53 set out, in slightly more explicit detail, the duties expected of a person where they decide to obtain and use a digital signature, the definition of which includes a link to the password, as defined in article 2(i) as:

i) Firma digital: Se entenderá como un valor numérico que se adhiere a un mensaje de datos y que, utilizando un procedimiento matemático conocido, vinculado a la clave del iniciador y al texto del mensaje, permite determinar que este valor se ha obtenido exclusivamente con la clave del iniciador y el texto del mensaje, y

> que el mensaje inicial no ha sido modificado después de efectuada la transmisión;
>
> i) Digital signature: It will be understood as a numerical value attached to a data message and which, by using a known mathematical procedure, linked to the password of the initiator and to the text of[38] the message, allows one to determine that this value has been obtained exclusively with the inititator's password and the text of the message, and that the initial message has not been modified after the transmission has been effected;

**3.64** The liability of a sender, once their duties are set out, is provided for in article 55:

> Art. 55. – Responsabilidad de los suscriptores.
>
> Los suscriptores serán responsables por la falsedad o error en la información suministrada a la entidad de certificación y que es objeto material del contenido del certificado. También serán responsables en los casos en los cuales no den oportuno aviso de revocación o suspensión de certificados en los casos indicados anteriormente.
>
> ARTICLE 55. – Liability of the signers. The signers shall be liable for falseness or error in the information supplied to the certifying entity and which is the material object of the contents of the certificate. They shall also be liable in those cases in which they do not give prompt notice of revocation or suspension of certificates in the cases indicated above.

**3.65** In comparison, the Australian Commonwealth Electronic Transaction Act provides for a presumption in s15:

> 15 Attribution of electronic communications
>
> (1) For the purpose of a law of the Commonwealth, unless otherwise agreed between the purported originator and the addressee of an electronic communication, the purported originator of the electronic communication is bound only if the communication was sent by the purported originator or with the authority of the purported originator.

**3.66** This provision only binds the sending party where the originator accepts they sent the communication, or authorized the sending of the communication. There is no presumption that the electronic signature is that of the sending party. It seems, therefore, that the recipient is required to prove the signing party signed; but it may be that proof of verification puts an evidential burden

38 The word 'ot' in the original translated text altered to read 'of.'

on the purported signing party to introduce evidence that they did not sign the communication.

## Liability of the recipient

**3.67** Where a person or legal entity relies on a signature, it is for them to prove the signature is not a forgery in circumstances where the signature is challenged by the purported signing party.[39] In terms of electronic signatures, this is illustrated by s24 of the Saint Vincent and the Grenadines Electronic Transactions Act 2007, which provides: 'A person relying on an electronic signature shall bear the legal consequences of his failure to take reasonable steps to verify the reliability of an electronic signature'. Arguably, this is such a well-established rule that it is not necessary to set out what actions a recipient needs to follow in order to rely on an electronic signature. By way of example, the provisions of article 21 of the Dubai Law of Electronic transactions and Commerce No 2/2002 do go some way to set out such a duty:

> 1. A person is entitled to rely on an Electronic Signature or an Electronic Certificate to the extent that it is reasonable to do so.
>
> 2. Where an Electronic Signature is supported by a Certificate, the Relying Party in respect of such signature shall bear the legal consequences of its failure to take reasonable and necessary steps to verify the validity and enforceability of the Certificate, as to whether it is suspended or revoked, and of observing any limitations with respect to the Certificate.
>
> 3. In determining whether it was reasonable for a person to rely on an Electronic Signature or a Certificate, regard shall be had, if appropriate, to:
>
> > a. the nature of the underlying transaction which was intended to be supported by the Electronic Signature;
> >
> > b. the value or importance of the underlying transaction, if this is known;
> >
> > c. whether the Relying Party in respect of the Electronic Signature or certificate has taken appropriate steps to determine the reliability of the Electronic Signature or the Certificate;
> >
> > d. whether the Relying Party in respect of the Electronic Signature or certificate took reasonable steps to verify if the Electronic Signature was supported by a Certificate, or if it should be expected to be so supported;
> >
> > e. whether the Relying Party in respect of the Electronic Signature or Certificate knew or ought to have known

39 For case law where electronic signatures are forged, see chapter 6.

> that the Electronic Signature or the Certificate had been compromised or revoked;
>
> f. any agreement or course of dealing between the Originator and the Relying Party, or any trade usage which may be applicable;
>
> g. any other relevant factor.
>
> 4. If reliance on the Electronic Signature or the Certificate is not reasonable in the circumstances, having regard to the factors in paragraph (2) of this Article, the party relying on the Electronic Signature or Certificate assumes the risk of the Electronic Signature or the Certificate not being valid.

**3.68** Exceptions in the commercial arena includes IdenTrust and Bolero, both of which operate a system that binds the three parties (user, certification authority and receiving party) to a relationship governed by contractual terms.

**3.69** The Argentine government, in article 23, have responded by imposing a mild form of limitation on the recipient of a digital signature by way of a rule against relying on the validity of the certificate:

> ARTICULO 23. - Desconocimiento de la validez de un certificado digital. Un certificado digital no es válido si es utilizado:
>
> a) Para alguna finalidad diferente a los fines para los cuales fue extendido;
>
> b) Para operaciones que superen el valor máximo autorizado cuando corresponda;
>
> c) Una vez revocado.
>
> ARTICLE 23. - Lack of recognition of the validity of a digital certificate. A digital certificate is not valid if it is used:
>
> a) For a purpose different from that for which it was issued;
>
> b) For transactions that exceed the maximum value authorized when applicable;
>
> c) Once it has been revoked.

**3.70** In comparison, the provisions of the Singapore Electronic Transactions Act Ch 88 permits the recipient to presume that the document or message that is signed with a digital signature has been affixed by the person or entity to whom the digital signature is associated with, although it is a presumption that can be rebutted, as provided in s5 of the third schedule:

> Unreliable digital signatures
>
> 5. Unless otherwise provided by law or contract, a person relying on a digitally signed electronic record assumes the risk that the digital signature is invalid as a signature or an authentication of

> the signed electronic record, if reliance on the digital signature is not reasonable under the circumstances having regard to the following factors:
>
> > (a) facts which the person relying on the digitally signed electronic record knows or has notice of, including all facts listed in the certificate or incorporated in it by reference;
> >
> > (b) the value or importance of the digitally signed electronic record, if known;
> >
> > (c) the course of dealing between the person relying on the digitally signed electronic record and the subscriber and any available indicia of reliability or unreliability apart from the digital signature; and
> >
> > (d) any usage of trade, particularly trade conducted by trustworthy systems or other electronic means.

**3.71** The provisions of this section have, it appears, been influenced by article 13 of the UNCITRAL Model Law on Electronic Commerce. Whilst the provisions of this section appear to be reasonable, the reference in s5(a) of the phrase 'including all facts listed in the certificate or incorporated in it by reference' seems to imply that to rely on the signature, the recipient will have to consider becoming a verifying party before relying on the signature. Section 22 of the Electronic Transactions Order 2000 issued by Brunei Darussalam has an almost identical provision to that mentioned above.

**3.72** Where the certification authority is regulated, as in Malaysia, s63 of the Digital Signature Act 1997 takes a pragmatic view where a recipient is not sure of the authenticity of the signature:

> 63. (1) Unless otherwise provided by law or contract, the recipient of a digital signature assumes the risk that a digital signature is forged, if reliance on the digital signature is not reasonable under the circumstances.
>
> (2) Where the recipient determines not to rely on a digital signature under this section, the recipient shall promptly notify the signer of its determination not to rely on a digital signature and the grounds for that determination.

**3.73** The provisions of this section appear to have taken into account the comments made by Romer LJ in *Goodman v. J Eban Limited*, where he pointed out that 'If in fact his clients entertained any doubt as to the authenticity of the letter, nothing could be easier than to ask him, by telephone or letter, to confirm it.'[40] If in doubt, the recipient is advised to make a telephone call, send an email or use such old fashioned technology as a facsimile transmission or the postal services to confirm the signature with the person that sent the message or document. By

40 [1954] 1 QB 550 at 564.

confirming the signature in this fashion, the recipient does not have to consider becoming a verifying party, and the terms 'verifying party' and 'relying party' used by certification authorities thereby become meaningless.

# 4

# The European Union

**4.1** The European Union took an active stance on issues relating to the information society by 1996. In September 1996, the European Parliament passed a resolution asking the Commission to prepare proposals covering security and confidentiality, authentication and to safeguard privacy,[1] and in November 1996 the Council of Ministers requested the Member States and the Commission to prepare consistent measures to ensure the integrity and authentication of electronically transmitted documents.[2] Further initiatives continued, with the OECD adopting 'Guidelines for cryptography policy' on 27 March 1997,[3] which set out general principles to guide countries in formulating policies related to the use of cryptography. A European Ministerial Conference took place in Bonn in July 1997, entitled 'Global information networks: realising the potential', which led to the Bonn Ministerial Declaration, the objective of which was 'to broaden the common understanding of the use of Global Information Networks, to identify barriers to their use, to discuss possible solutions and to undertake an open dialogue on further possibilities for European and international co-operation'. The Declaration covered the topic of electronic signatures, specifically digital signatures.

**4.2** The Commission subsequently produced a communication in response to the resolution from the Parliament, 'Ensuring security and trust in electronic communications: towards a European framework for digital signatures and encryption'.[4] This document made it explicit that the only method of electronic signatures that was under consideration was that of the digital signature. In arguing the case, assertions were made in the Executive Summary without reference to any evidence, or the accuracy of the premise upon which the assertion was made, such as: 'As cryptographic services and products are more and more demanded', and 'As, in addition, they need a specific regulatory framework to take

1 European Parliament Resolution A4-244/96, 19.9.96, OJ320, p.164, 28.10.96 Europe and the global information society – Recommendations to the European Council.

2 Council Resolution 96/C 376/01 of 21 November 1996 on new policy-priorities regarding the information society, OJ No C 376, 12.12.96, p. 1.

3 Conference conclusions, 'A borderless world: realising the potential of global electronic commerce', 7–9 October 1998, Ottawa, Canada (Directorate for Science, Technology and Industry Steering Committee for the Preparation of the Ottawa Ministerial Conference, SG/EC(98)14/REV6); A global action plan for electronic commerce prepared by business with recommendations from governments, 7–9 October 1998, Ottawa, Canada (Directorate for Science, Technology and Industry Steering Committee for the Preparation of the Ottawa Ministerial Conference, SG/EC(98)11/REV2).

4 Communication from the Commission, 'Ensuring security and trust in electronic communications: towards a European framework for digital signatures and encryption', COM(97) 503 Final, 8 October 1997.

S. Mason, *Electronic Signatures in Law* (London: Institute of Advanced Legal Studies, 2016), chapter 4, 'The European Union', pp. 147–66.

into account their legal implications'. One comment made was factually incorrect: 'Digital signatures could even bring significant law enforcement benefits as they allow for example messages to be attributed to a particular reader and/or sender' because no form of electronic signature, including the digital signature, is capable of proving the person whose private key was used was the person who caused the digital signature to be affixed to a document or communication. On the subject of digital signatures, it was asserted that the failure of digital signatures to be offered as a service was predicated on 'the absence of legal recognition of digital signatures'.[5] There was a fear amongst some that the European Union needed to regulate electronic signatures, especially as some nation states had already begun to pass laws on the topic.

**4.3** On 1 December 1997, the Council invited the Commission to submit a proposal for a European Parliament and Council Directive on digital signatures. The proposal was to be offered as soon as possible. A draft proposal was produced by May 1998,[6] and submitted by the Commission on 16 June 1998.[7] The Council consulted the Economic and Social Committee on 30 July 1998[8] and the Committee of the Regions, which had reviewed the proposal by early 1999.[9] By 14 April 1999, the proposal had been reviewed and a number of amendments were proposed by the Parliament.[10] Apparently there was a difference of opinion over what legal effect an electronic signature would have when created using products (secure signature-creation devices) that meet a minimum level of technical security.[11] This matter was the subject of debate at the Council meeting of 27 November 1998. The security requirements relating to these products were enumerated in Annex III of the Directive. The opposition to setting out such criteria was voiced in the main by the United Kingdom and the Netherlands. The reason for the objection was the concern that the industry could not meet the conditions laid down in the Annex. At the time, it was suggested that the matters might be resolved by making the contents of Annex III a strong recommendation, or by reducing the requirements relating to the products.[12] In the event, the

5 Part II, paragraph 3.

6 Proposal for a European Parliament and Council Directive on a common framework for electronic signatures, COM(1998) 297 final 13.05.1998.

7 Proposal for a European Parliament and Council Directive on a common framework for electronic signatures, OJ C 325, 23.10.98, p. 5.

8 Opinion of the Economic and Social Committee on the 'Proposal for a European Parliament and Council Directive on a common framework for electronic signatures', OJ C 40, 15.2.1999, p. 29.

9 Opinion of the Committee of the Regions on the 'Proposal for a European Parliament and Council Directive on a common framework for electronic signatures', OJ C 93, 6.4.1999, p. 33.

10 Electronic signatures, Proposal for a European Parliament and Council Directive on a common framework for electronic signatures, OJ C 104, 14.4.1999, p. 49.

11 Recital 15 and definition in Article 2.

12 J. Dumortier and P. Van Eecke, 'The European draft directive on a common framework for electronic signatures', *CLSR*, 15 (1999), pp. 106–12, 111–12.

content of Annex III was split between requirements and recommendations for secure signature-creation devices. The views expressed by some countries may also have influenced the decision to revise the meaning of an electronic signature and produce more than one version of an electronic signature, which seems a somewhat bizarre concept, because a document is either signed or it is not signed.

**4.4** The Directive was adopted by the European Parliament and Council on 13 December 1999, and came into force on 19 January 2000.[13] Member states were required to implement the Directive by 19 July 2001,[14] and a review of the operation of the Directive was prepared and delivered to the European Parliament and to the Council by 19 July 2003.[15] A further development took place in 2005 with the establishment of an Expert Group on electronic commerce with a remit to set up working groups to study specific subjects on the basis of the mandate, and to invite experts and observers with specific knowledge to participate in the work of the Group and the working groups,[16] and in 2011 it was decided to review the Directive again.[17] There have been a number of European Union studies in relation to electronic signatures that shaped the landscape in the EU (set out at the end of this chapter), and it was decided to revise the Directive in the light of the need to widen the scope to include electronic identification and trust services for electronic transactions.[18]

## The Regulation

**4.5** The Directive is repealed with effect from 1 July 2016 by article 50 of Regulation (EU) No 910/2014 of the European Parliament and of the Council of 23 July 2014 on electronic identification and trust services for electronic transactions in the internal market and repealing Directive 1999/93/EC.[19] A

13 Directive 1999/93/EC of the European Parliament and of the Council of 13 December 1999 on a Community framework for electronic signatures, OJ L 13, 19.01.2000, p.12.

14 Article 13(1).

15 Article 12(1). The contract to prepare a review for the Commission was prepared by J. Dumortier and P. Van Eecke, *The Implementation of the European Directive on Electronic Signatures Status Report* (Landwell and Interdisciplinary Centre for Law & Information Technology, Katholieke Universiteit Leuven, 2002).

16 Commission Decision of 24 October 2005 establishing an expert group on electronic commerce (2005/752/EC), OJ L 282, 26.10.2005, p. 20.

17 Commission from the Commission to the European Parliament, the Council, the European Economic and Social Committee and the Committee of the Regions, A Digital Agenda for Europe /* COM/2010/0245 f/2 */ (2.1.2).

18 Proposal for a Regulation of the European Parliament and of the Council on electronic identification and trust services for electronic transactions in the internal market (Text with EEA relevance){SWD(2012) 135}{SWD(2012) 136} Brussels, 4.6.2012, COM(2012) 238 final.

19 OJ L257, 28.8.2014, pp. 73–114.

regulation is a binding legislative act that must be applied in its entirety across the member states of the EU in accordance with article 288 of the consolidated version of the Treaty on the Functioning of the European Union.[20] This means that the legislation in place across all member states of the European Union will be amended and repealed in due course. What is striking about this Regulation is the transfer of power to the executive in the form of a substantial amount of delegated legislation that has been authorized under the Regulation, for which see the list at the end of this chapter.

**4.6** The purpose of the Regulation is broadly set out in recital 1:

> Building trust in the online environment is key to economic and social development. Lack of trust, in particular because of a perceived lack of legal certainty, makes consumers, businesses and public authorities hesitate to carry out transactions electronically and to adopt new services.

**4.7** The provisions of article 1 set out the content of the Regulation:

> Subject matter
>
> With a view to ensuring the proper functioning of the internal market while aiming at an adequate level of security of electronic identification means and trust services this Regulation:
>
> (a) lays down the conditions under which Member States recognise electronic identification means of natural and legal persons falling under a notified electronic identification scheme of another Member State;
>
> (b) lays down rules for trust services, in particular for electronic transactions; and
>
> (c) establishes a legal framework for electronic signatures, electronic seals, electronic time stamps, electronic documents, electronic registered delivery services and certificate services for website authentication.

**4.8** The Regulation covers far more than electronic signatures. The discussion in this chapter is restricted to electronic signatures.[21] As with the Directive, the Regulation provides for three types of electronic signature under article 3: electronic signature; advanced electronic signature, and a qualified electronic signature.

**4.9** There is a significant difference between the types of signature, and one that is not readily imported into a legal framework based on common law. The legal effects of electronic signatures are set out in article 25:

20 OJ C 326, 26.10.2012, pp. 171–2.

21 The Regulation includes electronic seals, time stamps and registered delivery services.

> Legal effects of electronic signatures
>
> 1. An electronic signature shall not be denied legal effect and admissibility as evidence in legal proceedings solely on the grounds that it is in an electronic form or that it does not meet the requirements for qualified electronic signatures.
>
> 2. A qualified electronic signature shall have the equivalent legal effect of a handwritten signature.
>
> 3. A qualified electronic signature based on a qualified certificate issued in one Member State shall be recognised as a qualified electronic signature in all other Member States.

**4.10** Article 18 provides that the Regulation should be applied in accordance with national rules on liability, and continues: 'Therefore, it does not affect those national rules on, for example, definition of damages or relevant applicable procedural rules, including the burden of proof'. In addition, article 46 provides that 'An electronic document shall not be denied legal effect and admissibility as evidence in legal proceedings solely on the grounds that it is in electronic form.' For which see the case of I Up 505/2003,[22] decided by the Supreme Court of the Republic of Slovenia in 2003 regarding the status of an email, and two cases from Finland from 2004, discussed in earlier editions of this text.[23]

## The electronic signature

**4.11** The Regulation provides the definition of an electronic signature in article 3(10):

> 'electronic signature' means data in electronic form which is attached to or logically associated with other data in electronic form and which is used by the signatory to sign;

**4.12** The definition is very broad, in keeping with the wide nature of what is capable of constituting a signature in digital terms, and therefore includes any means that is capable of demonstrating proof of intent. This definition will include any of the forms of electronic signature discussed elsewhere in this text. The elements of an electronic signature comprise:

> (i) Data in electronic form.
>
> (ii) The data must be attached to or logically associated with other electronic data.
>
> (iii) The electronic signature is to be used by the signatory to sign the data.

22 For a case note, see *Digital Evidence and Electronic Signature Law Review*, 4 (2007), p. 97.

23 Combined cases 106/04/JH (140/04/JH and 147/04/JH, judgment MAO: 161/04, 162/04, 163/04 of 27.8.2004) available online in Finnish at http://www.finlex.fi.

**4.13** The process of authentication is between software protocols, not between human beings and it is not clear whether the authentication relates to the origin of the data, or acts to verify the identity of a person or entity.

## The advanced electronic signature

**4.14** An advanced electronic signature is a more elaborate construct than an electronic signature. There is no definition of an advanced electronic signature, but article 3(11), taken with the provisions of article 26, sets out a number of characteristics relating to performance:

> 'advanced electronic signature' means an electronic signature which meets the requirements set out in Article 26;

**4.15** Article 26 reads:

> An advanced electronic signature shall meet the following requirements:
>
> (a) it is uniquely linked to the signatory;
>
> (b) it is capable of identifying the signatory;
>
> (c) it is created using electronic signature creation data that the signatory can, with a high level of confidence, use under his sole control; and
>
> (d) it is linked to the data signed therewith in such a way that any subsequent change in the data is detectable.

**4.16** Aside from a minor change in one word in article 26(d), the most significant alteration is in the re-drafting of 26(c), which previously read, under the Directive: 'it is created using means that the signatory can maintain under his sole control'. In essence, an advanced electronic signature is a digital signature in all but name. An advanced electronic signature is required to meet the requirements laid down in Annex I (article 28), and devices that create qualified electronic signatures must meet the requirements laid down in Annex II. Each of the four attributes noted above are discussed below.

### *Uniquely linked to the signatory*

**4.17** No form of electronic signature can conform to this part of the requirement. For instance, a user relinquishes control over their scanned signature once it has been sent. A digital signature is not linked to the person creating it: the unique link is made with the private key, not the user. Nobody is capable of committing a private key to memory,[24] because it is far too complicated. Below is an example of

24 'Guidelines on memory and the law recommendations from the scientific study of human memory' (The British Psychological Society Research Board, 2008), http://www.forcescience.org/articles/Memory&TheLaw.pdf.

a private key in TXT format (2048 bits), by way of example:[25]

```
Private-Key: (2048 bit) modulus:
00:dd:3c:f6:9a:be:d2:66:20:0c:7d:0c:ae:bc:18:cc:f4:e8:89:8d:16
:b3:5c:16:75:06:33:f9:08:4f:d6:9b:f4:6b:e7:4d:0f:44:af:8b:87:d-
c:79:78:93:e8:e4:20:19:df:f0:0d:04:4d:2c:4c:ad:19:b0:31:8c:6a:
4d:a6:d6:0e:e8:ae:e2:37:75:8d:d5:1e:a2:31:15:3c:f4:4d:ad:5d:f8
:d0:23:c2:72:de:e2:73:9b:ef:f7:84:25:b0:cf:92:4d:39:4a:18:41:-
ac:91:81:28:ac:5b:f2:7d:74:e2:8f:f9:a7:c1:c0:b1:93:dd:cd:b1:4c:2
3:23:63:27:30:4c:da:8e:72:e4:0d:77:c2:22:e2:b4:43:bb:9d:ca:36:
59:fc:98:91:0c:da:c4:2c:34:03:0c:e5:91:51:e2:23:20:ae:68:5e:30
:8f:9e:f5:a5:2c:e4:bf:ab:2f:fb:82:03:31:b4:ff:5e:90:a8:f0:be:b0:4d
:aa:f3:af:2c:27:42:c8:7e:7a:d2:c3:e8:5b:53:8d:86:db:ae:f6:7c:45:
03:35:b6:52:9d:a0:c1:e0:da:ac:6b:68:05:7e:f8:73:41:62:63:56:b
3:47:6e:11:d8:d4:6c:92:be:65:aa:f2:a5:72:3d:4e:d9:d2:e2:8d:42:-
92:3e:cf:39:f9:63:89
publicExponent: 65537 (0x10001)
privateExponent:
5c:a2:77:1b:6a:45:0c:af:e4:aa:c3:91:b2:7e:ab:ea:ec:27:14:25:6a:2
a:67:d8:ce:25:1a:e4:09:11:f2:31:10:b1:43:c9:dd:d7:a7:13:d7:14:
21:91:c5:15:27:ff:cd:8d:64:d5:e5:3e:64:48:a2:95:ec:d9:3f:75:8e:2
2:d9:11:42:90:c3:e9:fb:de:3d:ba:69:d4:db:b5:eb:84:68:f1:92:ad:3
6:71:04:b4:4a:f6:03:2f:5f:6c:ac:b0:ed:30:5a:89:94:c8:82:ea:55:eb
:62:e8:09:0b:d0:d2:40:b8:a7:2e:70:71:aa:59:58:14:21:ae:20:d6:1
6:84:d2:29:5c:9b:a7:56:50:3a:10:0b:c6:70:2b:97:dd:f8:fa:73:74:2
2:5f:d6:ce:0d:75:45:8a:61:5d:86:25:cb:ad:19:06:fe:8e:a4:f9:0d:3
5:2a:02:04:93:ec:df:0c:db:ca:f0:8c:ae:a7:54:c2:37:a1:11:7b:9f:40
:54:a4:fd:31:a4:  f9:ee:60:3c:8f:3b:0e:b1:e2:10:6d:f0:36:50:63:27:
6e:cc:85:c1:5d:10:4a:36:23:5d:bf:c7:ee:9b:af:3f:e6:49:47:c6:9e:b
8:00:b0:d9:d2:de:07:46:43:14:2f:de:7c:51:57:a5:8d:4b:13:04:54:
25:3b:d5
prime1:
00:fd:5a:b3:5d:5c:e5:cf:c2:b7:e9:54:93:30:f1:21:07:9c:c1:01:35:6
4:7e:90:93:a7:13:d1:89:7b:58:2b:56:29:61:5e:3f:8d:25:23:be:f4:f
8:84:ff:2e:a1:83:42:f8:19:44:32:2f:7c:2e:d9:f1:64:88:74:57:8a:ea:
1c:3b:12:70:0a:be:86:28:3b:4c:d5:72:79:22:c7:d2:5a:0a:31:98:29
:c0:51:26:6c:42:03:9c:43:83:d2:72:ab:7d:3f:fd:2b:db:0f:62:0b:c1:
```

25 This example is from Symeon (Simos) Xenitellis, 'The open-source PKI book: a guide to PKIs and open-source implementations' and quoted under GNU Free Documentation License, Version 1.3, 3 November 2008 published by the Free Software Foundation: http://ospkibook.sourceforge.net/docs/OSPKI-2.4.7/OSPKI-html/sample-key-components.htm. For an example of a private key in PEM format, see http://ospkibook.sourceforge.net/docs/OSPKI-2.4.7/OSPKI-html/sample-priv-key.htm.

e3:7c:2c:2c:4b:54:ba:36:98:c3:75:b1:8f:69:4b:5b:62:e2:cb:45:8a:
98:1f

prime2:

00:df:8c:67:d5:09:4e:3a:11:c1:9f:d6:7c:a9:88:e8:0d:88:6f:72:3
f:9a:f3:db:43:f5:e3:0f:85:eb:1f:40:5c:26:6f:31:49:82:4a:ec:7c:6
7:17:22:89:c5:99:67:55:ca:06:de:e8:3a:22:85:cf:86:21:82:2a:f-
d:03:f8:8e:03:24:b0:4d:40:0e:f7:33:25:29:1e:f7:66:5f:13:6
8:b6:d2:5b:a8:54:17:e2:b4:1a:50:11:13:49:3b:40:65:69:b7:
cf:00:bb:39:36:cb:0a:36:62:e4:59:2d:94:d8:11:c2:6e:fe:03:c-
c:35:f0:89:00:77:ec:a3:ce:2f:57

exponent1:

00:c2:f9:01:1d:f1:76:fe:1b:48:b3:6d:1d:d5:45:4b:f8:f2:be:6
9:72:b0:82:e2:3a:6f:12:c6:67:7a:1f:d1:41:fe:98:6b:12:97:49
:a4:a7:b9:18:64:29:89:b6:4c:30:c6:83:93:42:d7:de:46:a3:f-
c:ac:34:82:ec:38:00:90:77:39:6a:36:2a:87:4e:00:c-
c:d1:5a:c6:34:68:f8:cd:c8:18:80:94:68:e7:4a:9d:77:74:15:d6
:b3:64:ca:50:85:14:30:7e:86:97:e1:09:51:4e:02:ea:6f:b0:0d:65:
3c:cc:f5:66:e6:9d:8a:17:af:1d:7b:91:99:53:de:5b

exponent2:

00:9b:be:7b:5c:8d:d6:25:58:d7:98:1f:5b:cc:d5:a8:2e:3d:7e:b-
f:8f:16:ca:8c:59:a5:c6:a2:ba:ff:5b:4f:80:a3:-
fa:55:d1:4b:e8:1d:28:72:be:48:7e:c9:df:1d:82:44:75:52:f9:6
1:ff:49:50:92:b7:67:b3:c1:80:f1:bb:26:ef:79:b0:e8:4f:44:e4
:2a:20:a3:05:64:1a:1b:30:9a:26:a6:5a:f8:f3:87:2b:49:25:b-
d:2f:bd:96:7d:3f:ea:4e:77:f6:9f:79:b5:f5:f1:50:80:c7:6c:65:f8:4c:
2c:db:54:6e:be:80:98:97:d3:2b:33:61:f7:a1:9f:93

coefficient:

00:90:c8:8a:b9:61:c2:b1:5c:82:69:bd:d1:51:fe:97:03:d8:1d:de:
a6:23:be:61:0b:02:d7:c2:4c:81:ad:4b:5b:51:e4:f8:05:21:5f:86:7
a:78:22:56:85:9c:fe:19:23:f1:20:47:67:3d:67:d7:12:cd:ec:a0:d-
f:f3:24:94:d3:a3:03:82:00:74:0b:68:1d:5b:88:49:fa:05:c9:2b:2f:a0
:7f:79:85:e4:a9:a3:0e:d9:29:8c:61:d0:cc:f1:7a:bc:e7:bd:d3:bc:b9:
35:02:ef:54:51:97:52:af:c5:20:96:71:07:c9:17:00:6d:ab:7d:27:c9:
74:71:26:d8:ce

**4.18** This means that private keys are retained on a computer, disk or smart card. It is not possible to create an electronic signature that can be uniquely linked to the signatory. Professor Sorge disagrees with this analysis:

> 'Mason ... states the unique link of a signature to a person was impossible to achieve, as the required private key cannot be memorized and must be stored in a computer or on a smart card. The consequence is that third parties cannot be excluded from signature generation with absolute certainty. Following this

> opinion, advanced electronic signatures would not be possible at all – a result that was obviously not intended by the legislator. As a consequence, the problem pointed out by Mason is not considered in most legal literature.'[26]

**4.19** His argument is first, that because the politicians responsible for enacting the Directive did not intend that this characteristic would not be effective, it follows that the analysis set out in previous editions of this text is wrong. The second limb of the argument is that because the problem is not considered in most of the legal literature, it follows that the point is therefore irrelevant. Professor Sorge did not cite Lorna Brazell, who said, in relation to this precise point regarding the digital signature:

> ' ... the signature is not uniquely linked to the signatory: it is uniquely linked only to the signatory's private key. In the real world, no one is ever going to keep their private key in their head, inaccessible to others. The number is simply too long.'[27]

**4.20** These are strange arguments. First, it is pertinent to observe that where the text of the legislation is defective, it is for the politicians responsible for enacting the legislation to rectify the mistake. Second, Professor Sorge argues that because the 'consensus' is that some commentators ignore this important point, it follows that it is not relevant. In science, consensus counts for little – although the consensus was, at one time, that the sun orbited the earth – yet such harmony among the learned did not mean the assumption was true. What is important are facts and logic.

### *Capable of identifying the signatory*

**4.21** Any form of electronic signature is capable of identifying the person that signed it.

### *Created using electronic signature creation data that the signatory can, with a high level of confidence, use under his sole control*

**4.22** Any form of electronic signature can be created under the sole control of the user, but when a private key to a digital signature is used, a recipient will not know whether it was the owner that actually used the private key. A digital signature does not authenticate the purported signer. A digital signature authenticates that a certain private key was used to create the relevant digital signature.

26 C. Sorge, 'The legal classification of identity-based signatures', *Computer Law & Security Review*, 30 (2014), pp. 126–36 at p. 130.

27 L. Brazell, *Electronic Signatures and Identities: Law and Regulation* (2nd edn, London: Sweet & Maxwell, 2008), pp. 135–6.

**4.23** It is also arguable whether the signatory can ever maintain that the electronic signature is under their sole control when located on a computer, given that computers are not trustworthy, because their design is open, complex, flexible and the software that runs them is not perfect, and the ease by which a key on a computer can be misused.[28] The case law discussed elsewhere in this text illustrates this point – especially where forms of electronic signature have been retained on a main frame, and others have used the signature for improper purposes or without authority. As pointed out by Petr Švéda and Václav Matyáš Jr.,[29] a trustworthy signature system will need to incorporate a 'restrictive configuration' that would only provide a few elementary tasks in order to assure functional integrity. This means that such a computer would not be able to be used for any other purpose. It would also need a special dedicated machine that was used only for the purpose of signature creation and verification,[30] and to provide for trust, this type of system would have to be under the direct control of the user. Where electronic signatures only use software, especially when the private key of a digital signature is placed on a personal computer, the problem for the person whose key it is, is that they cannot be absolutely sure that they signed what they see on the screen. In addition, they 'cannot be sure that no further signature processes will be executed in the background when using his private key'.[31]

**4.24** If the private key is loaded on a smart card (which is increasingly the case for bank cards, for instance), the ease by which a smart card can be stolen or 'borrowed' by another person is so significant as to undermine the suggestion that the signature can remain under the sole control of the person whose signature it is.[32] Even the members of the Forum of European Supervisory Authorities for Electronic Signatures accept this. The concept of 'sole control' was discussed in a 2004 paper:[33]

28 For further information, see P. A. Loscocco, S. D. Smalley, P. A. Muckelbauer, R. C. Taylor, S. J. Turner and J. F. Farrell, 'The inevitability of failure: the flawed assumption of security in modern computing environments' (National Security Agency, 14 November 1998).

29 P. Švéda and V. Matyáš Jr., 'Digital signatures and electronic documents: a cautionary tale revisited', *Upgrade*, III (2004), pp. 35–45, 37.

30 However, even if a secure signature creation device was used under the provisions of Annex III, there is a significant flaw: the device signs a binary string which the human user has no means of verifying. This is highly significant, for which see N. Bohm, 'Watch what you sign!', *Digital Evidence and Electronic Signature Law Review*, 3 (2006), pp. 45–9.

31 Švéda and Matyáš Jr., 'Digital signatures and electronic documents', p. 37.

32 S. C. Rennie and J. R. Rudland, 'Differences in medical students' attitudes to academic misconduct and reported behaviour across the years – a questionnaire study', *J Med Ethics*, 29 (2003), pp. 97–102, in which medical students admitted they would forge signatures on work submitted.

33 'Working paper on advanced electronic signatures' (Forum of European Supervisory Authorities for Electronic Signatures, 12 October 2004).

c) 'sole control'

Creation and storage of signature-creation data

Most requirements on the creation and storage of signature-creation data have their foundation in Annex III and Annex II j who do not apply on advanced electronic signatures. However, the advanced electronic signature must be 'created using means that the signatory can maintain under his sole control'. This does not require the use of a special hardware device as a signature-creation device, but it requires – especially in the case where the private key is stored in software – the use of security measures by the signatory to maintain his control over the key (e.g. encryption of the file which stores the private key, restriction of access to the computer and this file).

What does 'sole control' mean in the context of (automatically signing) systems which are maintained by several system administrators (this is also relevant for systems that sign qualified certificates)? If the certificate is issued to a certain natural person, the security concept and the configuration of the server must ensure that only this person has control over the private key. How the person executes her control is defined in the security concept. If the certificate is issued to a legal person (which is not possible in most countries) the personnel of the legal person maintains 'sole control' over the private key by its security concept.

**4.25** In a 2005 paper 'Public statement on server based signature services',[34] the members of the Forum elaborated on 'sole control' in relation to server-based signature services:

Sole control

The meaning of 'sole control' in Article 2 of the Directive has been discussed in the FESA working paper on advanced electronic signatures. According to that paper, the use of special hardware as signature creation device is not required. However, the signatory must take measures to maintain control over his key. The security concept and the system configuration of the server must ensure that only the signatory, who is either a natural or a legal person, has control over the corresponding signature creation data.

If signatures are created automatically at a server, the signatory is usually not present in person. However, the signatory has control over security measures, and has the responsibility to select suitable security measures.

34 'Public statement on server based signature services' (Forum of European Supervisory Authorities for Electronic Signatures, 17 October 2005), now noted on the Forum website as 'outdated', although no reason is given.

> For server based signature services, the signatory is not present in person either. But neither can he select suitable security measures. He can only choose whether or not to enlist the services. The signatory can decide whether or not security measures taken by the service provider are sufficient for him. For making this decision, the signatory needs at least access to a comprehensible version of the security concept and confidence that the service provider sticks to the security concept (confidence can be strengthened by audits performed by a trusted third party like an independent auditor or a supervisory authority).
>
> In addition, sole control requires certain cryptographic qualities of algorithms and of signature creation data that have been discussed in the working paper mentioned above.
>
> Under these premises, FESA members believe that sole control at least of the signature creation data can be achieved and that advanced electronic signatures can be created by a server based signature service.

**4.26** The authors of these papers indicate the tenuous nature of the digital environment, and how it cannot be under the sole control of anybody. In addition, the authors of the second paper include a footnote to the final sentence, thus: 'Note that according to German law, "sole control" implies physical control and that therefore in Germany, server based signature services cannot be used for creating advanced electronic signatures and definitely not for creating qualified electronic signatures'. The position in Germany must be correct, otherwise the meaning of 'sole control' becomes distorted beyond measure.

**4.27** Birgit Pfitzmann demonstrated the weakness of a device such as a smart card in 1996, in that smart cards tend to communicate through another device under the control of a third party, such as a point-of-sale terminal or ATM. This means the person signing does not have any control over what message is actually signed. This in turn means that 'this arrangement cannot provide the authenticity function, or at least no better than blank signatures can'.[35] Further, Petr Švéda and Václav Matyáš Jr. indicate that they 'know of no technology that can make a hardware device fully resistant to penetration by a skilled and determined attacker' and pointed out that many 'successful attacks have occurred because smart cards were exposed to more sophisticated attackers than designers anticipated'.[36]

**4.28** A smart card does not solve the problem. This is because the signatory trusts the computer to correctly reveal what data is being sent to the card for signature. Malicious software could operate so as to sign documents without the knowledge of the signing party, because the smart card does not have its own

35 B. Pfitzmann, *Digital Signature Schemes General Framework and Fail-Stop Signatures* (Berlin: Springer-Verlag, 1996), 1.4.

36 Švéda and Matyáš Jr., 'Digital signatures and electronic documents', p. 37.

keyboard or display. No doubt the design of smart cards will change and improve, but the ability of intelligent people to overcome the security will always ensure smart cards and the systems that interact with them will be undermined in some way.

**4.29** Thus a signatory will not know whether the 'means' was working correctly, or what it was doing, or what changes (such as security fixes and upgrades) were happening to it over time, and so it seems impossible to obtain 'sole control' of the technology. The organization issuing the 'means' may be able to assure the signatory that the 'means' will operate correctly and be under the issuer's 'control', but then the signatory must trust the issuer. In turn, the issuer will have to trust the manufacturer, developer and any other person in the chain.

**4.30** It seems that the European Union has accepted this criticism,[37] and amended the relevant clause from:

> (c) it is created using means that the signatory can maintain under his sole control;

**4.31** To read:

> (c) it is created using electronic signature creation data that the signatory can, with a high level of confidence, use under his sole control;

**4.32** It is refreshing to note the change to this provision, although there is no guidance to the citizen as to how they determine the level of confidence.

### *Linked to the data signed therewith in such a way that any subsequent change in the data is detectable*

**4.33** The only form of electronic signature that is capable of complying with this element is the private key of digital signature, which acts to encrypt the date, but even a digital signature is not immune from attack. This provision applies to the advanced electronic signature and the qualified electronic signature.

## Qualified electronic signature

**4.34** A qualified electronic signature is defined in article 3(12):

> 'qualified electronic signature' means an advanced electronic signature that is created by a qualified electronic signature creation device, and which is based on a qualified certificate for electronic signatures;

37 Stephen Mason, 'Informal debate on the issues relating to terminology and clarification of concept in respect of the EU e-signature legislation', *SCRIPTed*, 9 (2012), pp. 64–85, and previous editions of this text.

**4.35** A qualified electronic signature consists of three component parts: an advanced electronic signature, a qualified certificate and a qualified electronic signature creation device that must comply with the requirements set out in Annexes I and II.

## Service providers

**4.36** The Regulation provides, under article 3(19) and (20) for 'trust service providers' and 'qualified trust service providers'. Recital 35 provides that all trust service providers are subject to the requirements of the Regulation:

> All trust service providers should be subject to the requirements of this Regulation, in particular those on security and liability to ensure due diligence, transparency and accountability of their operations and services. However, taking into account the type of services provided by trust service providers, it is appropriate to distinguish as far as those requirements are concerned between qualified and non-qualified trust service providers.

**4.37** The duties of trust service providers are covered in depth by the Regulation, but this text does not explore the status of trust service providers.

## Liability

**4.38** Liability in general is provided for in article 11:

> 1. The notifying Member State shall be liable for damage caused intentionally or negligently to any natural or legal person due to a failure to comply with its obligations under points (d) and (f) of Article 7 in a cross-border transaction.
>
> 2. The party issuing the electronic identification means shall be liable for damage caused intentionally or negligently to any natural or legal person due to a failure to comply with the obligation referred to in point (e) of Article 7 in a cross- border transaction.
>
> 3. The party operating the authentication procedure shall be liable for damage caused intentionally or negligently to any natural or legal person due to a failure to ensure the correct operation of the authentication referred to in point (f) of Article 7 in a cross-border transaction.
>
> 4. Paragraphs 1, 2 and 3 shall be applied in accordance with national rules on liability.
>
> 5. Paragraphs 1, 2 and 3 are without prejudice to the liability under national law of parties to a transaction in which electronic

> identification means falling under the electronic identification scheme notified pursuant to Article 9(1) are used.

**4.39** The position on liability and burden of proof in respect of trust service providers is set out in article 13:

> 1. Without prejudice to paragraph 2, trust service providers shall be liable for damage caused intentionally or negligently to any natural or legal person due to a failure to comply with the obligations under this Regulation.
>
> The burden of proving intention or negligence of a non-qualified trust service provider shall lie with the natural or legal person claiming the damage referred to in the first subparagraph.
>
> The intention or negligence of a qualified trust service provider shall be presumed unless that qualified trust service provider proves that the damage referred to in the first subparagraph occurred without the intention or negligence of that qualified trust service provider.
>
> 2. Where trust service providers duly inform their customers in advance of the limitations on the use of the services they provide and where those limitations are recognisable to third parties, trust service providers shall not be liable for damages arising from the use of services exceeding the indicated limitations.
>
> 3. Paragraphs 1 and 2 shall be applied in accordance with national rules on liability.

## Relying party

**4.40** A relying party is defined in article 3(6):

> 'relying party' means a natural or legal person that relies upon an electronic identification or a trust service;

**4.41** The only reference to the need for a relying party to assure themselves of the validity of a signature is in recital 57:

> (57) To ensure legal certainty as regards the validity of the signature, it is essential to specify the components of a qualified electronic signature, which should be assessed by the relying party carrying out the validation. Moreover, specifying the requirements for qualified trust service providers that can provide a qualified validation service to relying parties unwilling or unable to carry out the validation of qualified electronic signatures themselves, should stimulate the private and public sector to invest in such

> services. Both elements should make qualified electronic signature validation easy and convenient for all parties at Union level.

**4.42** Interestingly, the recital acknowledges the central risk regarding the complexity of validating a digital signature, as discussed elsewhere in this text, and article 33 expressly provides for such a service:

> Qualified validation service for qualified electronic signatures
>
> 1. A qualified validation service for qualified electronic signatures may only be provided by a qualified trust service provider who:
>
> (a) provides validation in compliance with Article 32(1); and
>
> (b) allows relying parties to receive the result of the validation process in an automated manner, which is reliable, efficient and bears the advanced electronic signature or advanced electronic seal of the provider of the qualified validation service.
>
> 2. The Commission may, by means of implementing acts, establish reference numbers of standards for qualified validation service referred to in paragraph 1. Compliance with the requirements laid down in paragraph 1 shall be presumed where the validation service for a qualified electronic signature meets those standards. Those implementing acts shall be adopted in accordance with the examination procedure referred to in Article 48(2).

**4.43** What is missing in the provisions of article 32(1) is the assurance that the signature was affixed by the person whose signature it purports to be.

## Review of the Regulation

**4.44** The Regulation is to be reviewed no later than 1 July 2020 in accordance with the provisions of article 49.

## References

### Delegated legislation under the Regulation

Commission Implementing Decision (EU) 2016/650 of 25 April 2016 laying down standards for the security assessment of qualified signature and seal creation devices pursuant to Articles 30(3) and 39(2) of Regulation (EU) No 910/2014 of the European Parliament and of the Council on electronic identification and trust services for electronic transactions in the internal market (Text with EEA relevance) C/2016/2303, OJ L109, 26.4.2016, p. 40–42

Commission Implementing Decision (EU) 2015/1984 of 3 November 2015 defining the circumstances, formats and procedures of notification pursuant to Article 9(5) of Regulation (EU) No 910/2014 of the European Parliament and of the Council on electronic identification and trust services for electronic transactions in the internal market (notified under document C(2015) 7369) (Text with EEA relevance), OJ L289, 5.11.2015, p. 18–25

Commission Implementing Decision (EU) 2015/1505 of 8 September 2015 laying down technical specifications and formats relating to trusted lists pursuant to Article 22(5) of Regulation (EU) No 910/2014 of the European Parliament and of the Council on electronic identification and trust services for electronic transactions in the internal market (Text with EEA relevance), OJ L235, 9.9.2015, p. 26–36

Commission Implementing Regulation (EU) 2015/1502 of 8 September 2015 on setting out minimum technical specifications and procedures for assurance levels for electronic identification means pursuant to Article 8(3) of Regulation (EU) No 910/2014 of the European Parliament and of the Council on electronic identification and trust services for electronic transactions in the internal market (Text with EEA relevance), OJ L235, 9.9.2015, p. 7–20

Commission Implementing Decision (EU) 2015/1506 of 8 September 2015 laying down specifications relating to formats of advanced electronic signatures and advanced seals to be recognised by public sector bodies pursuant to Articles 27(5) and 37(5) of Regulation (EU) No 910/2014 of the European Parliament and of the Council on electronic identification and trust services for electronic transactions in the internal market (Text with EEA relevance), OJ L235, 9.9.2015, p. 37–41

Commission Implementing Regulation (EU) 2015/1501 of 8 September 2015 on the interoperability framework pursuant to Article 12(8) of Regulation (EU) No 910/2014 of the European Parliament and of the Council on electronic identification and trust services for electronic transactions in the internal market (Text with EEA relevance), OJ L235, 9.9.2015, p. 1–6

Commission Implementing Regulation (EU) 2015/806 of 22 May 2015 laying down specifications relating to the form of the EU trust mark for qualified trust services (Text with EEA relevance) C/2015/3364, OJ L128, 23.5.2015, p. 13–15

Commission Implementing Decision (EU) 2015/296 of 24 February 2015 establishing procedural arrangements for cooperation between Member States on electronic identification pursuant to Article 12(7) of Regulation (EU) No 910/2014 of the European Parliament and of the Council on electronic identification and trust services for electronic transactions in the internal market Text with EEA relevance, OJ L53, 25.2.2015, p. 14–20

## Standards

The authority to provide for stems from Directive 98/34 of the European Parliament and of the Council laying down a procedure for the provision of information in the fields of technical standards and regulations and of rules on information services, OJ L 204 of 21.7.1998, p.37, as amended by Directive 98/48 of the European Parliament and of the Council, OJ L 217 of 5.8.1998, p. 18.

Three European Standards Organisations are recognized: CEN, CENELEC and ETSI (Commission Decision of 14 July 2003 on the publications of reference of generally recognised standards for electronic signature products in accordance with Directive 1999/93/EC of the European Parliament and of the Council 2003/511/EC, OJ L 175 15.7.2003, p. 45).

The following standards are set out in the Annex:

CWA 14167-1 Security Requirements for Trustworthy Systems Managing Certificates for Electronic Signatures – Part 1: System Security Requirements; CWA 14167-2 Security Requirements for Trustworthy Systems Managing Certificates for Electronic Signatures – Part 2

Cryptographic Module for CSP signing operations with backup – Protection profile (CMCSOB-PP) and CWA 14169 Secure Signature-creation devices 'EAL 4+'

See also the 'Standardisation Mandate to the European Standardisation Organisation CEN, CENELEC and ETSI in the field of Information and Communication Technologies applied to electronic signatures,' M/460 (European Commission, Enterprise and Industry Directorate-General, Innovation Policy, ICT for Competitiveness and Innovation, Brussels, 22 December 2009).

## EU Reports

*2002*

J. Dumortier and P. Van Eecke, *The Implementation of the European Directive on Electronic Signatures Status Report* (Landwell and Interdisciplinary Centre for Law & Information Technology, Katholieke Universiteit Leuven, 2002)

*2003*

J. Dumortier, S. Kelm, H. Nilsson, G. Skouma and P. Van Eecke, *The Legal and Market Aspects of Electronic Signatures* (Interdisciplinary Centre for Law & Information Technology, Katholieke Universiteit Leuven, 2003)

*2006*

Report on the operation of Directive 1999/93/EC on a Community framework for electronic signatures, COM(2006) 120 final, 15.3.2006

Rambøll Management, *Benchmarking of existing national legal e-business practices, from the point of view of enterprises (e-signature, e-invoicing and e-contracts)* (European Commission, Directorate-General for Enterprise and Industry, Draft Final Report, November 2006)

K.U.Leuven-ICRI (Interdisciplinary Centre for Law & ICT) and Lawfort, *Legal study on Legal and Administrative Practices Regarding the Validity and Mutual Recognition of Electronic Documents, with a View to Identifying the Existing Barriers for Enterprises* (D3.6 – Final Report, November 2006), prepared for the DG Enterprise and Industry, and D3.4 – First Interim Report (country reports, July 2006)

*2007*

S. Lacroix, O. Delos, P. van Eecke, M. Custers and W. Janin, *Study on the Standardisation Aspects of e-Signature* (EU DG Information Society and Media, final report dated 22 November 2007)

*2008*

'Action plan on e-signatures and e-identification to facilitate the provision of crossborder public services in the Single Market Brussels', 28.11.2008 COM(2008) 798 final

*2009*

H. Graux, *Study on electronic documents and electronic delivery for the purpose of the implementation of Art. 8 of the Services Directive* (European Commission Internal Market Directorate-General, version 1.3, 24 February 2009)

R. Cimander, M. Hansen and H. Kubicek, *Electronic Signatures as Obstacle for Cross-Border E-Procurement in Europe Lessons from the PROCURE-project* (Institut für Informationsmanagement Bremen GmbH, June 2009)

H. Graux, C. Staffe and E. Meyvis, *European Federated Validation Service Study Solution Profile – A-SIT Signature Verification Service* (IDABC European eGovernment Services, July 2009)

H. Graux and C. Staffe, *Study on European Federated Validation Service (EFVS): Feasibility and Global Implementation Plan* (IDABC European eGovernment Services, September 2009)

H. Graux, G. Lambert, B. Jossin and E. Meyvis, *Study on Mutual Recognition of e-signatures: update of Country Profiles Analysis & Assessment Report* (IDABC European eGovernment Services, October 2009)

E. Coscia, M. Megliola and C. Rubattino, eProcurement Map (IDABC Programme and ePractice, v2.0, October 2009)

J. Millard, J. Shahin, K. Pedersen, N. Huijboom and T. van den Broek, *i2010 eGovernment Action Plan Progress Study Final Report* (SMART 2008/0042, November 2009)

'Standardisation mandate to the European Standardisation Organisation CEN, CENELEC and ETSI in the field of information and communication technologies applied to electronic signatures', M/460 (European Commission, Enterprise and Industry Directorate-General, Innovation Policy, ICT for Competitiveness and Innovation, Brussels, 22 December 2009)

*2010*

H. Graux, O. Delos and S. Lacroix, *Completion of the Framework for Signature Validation Services* (IDABC European eGovernment Services, March 2010)

SEALED, time.lex and Siemens, 'Study on cross-border interoperability of e-signatures (CROBIES)' (Version 1.0, 31 July 2010)

*2011*

A. Rosenkötter, A. Hoffmann, A. Gyulai-Schmidt, A. Fritz and E. Kühn, *Digital Internal Market Study* (Directorate General for Internal Policies, Policy Department A: Economic and Scientific Policy, Internal Market and Consumer Protection, IP/A/IMCO/ST/2011-04, June 2011)

*2012*

L. A. Remotti, A. F. van Veenstra, M. van Lieshout, L. Kool, G. Rumpf, B. Ipektsidis and T. Damvakeraki, *EU online Trustmarks – Building Digital Confidence in Europe, Final Report* (A study prepared for the European Commission DG

Communications Networks, Content & Technology, 2012, Contract number: SMART 2011/0022)

H. Graux, M. De Soete, P. Van Eecke, O. Delos, T. Debusschere, M. Hansen, M. Sel and R. Genhini, *Study to support the implementation of a pan-European framework on electronic identification and trust services for electronic transactions in the internal market* (SMART 2012/0001)

*2013*

DLA Piper, SEALED, Time.lex, Pricewaterhousecoopers, SGA, *Feasibility study on an electronic identification, authentication and signature policy (IAS) Final Report* (Luxembourg, Publications Office of the European Union, 2013)

# 5

# England and Wales, Northern Ireland and Scotland

## The Electronic Communications Act 2000

**5.1** The first draft of a bill, the Electronic Communications Bill, was published in July 1999. This Bill was withdrawn when it attracted a great deal of wrath regarding key escrow (which is now expressly excluded in the Act by s14) and provisions that were later incorporated into the Regulation of Investigatory Powers Act 2000. The Electronic Communications Act received the royal assent on 25 May 2000, and extends to Northern Ireland.[1] The Act is in three parts:

> Part 1: Cryptography service providers. This part of the Act provides for the establishment of a statutory register of approved providers of cryptography support services. It has not been implemented, and a voluntary scheme is in place.[2] Further, by the terms of s16(4), Part I was repealed on 25 May 2005 because no order was made under s16(2) by the end of the period of five years beginning with the day on which the Act was passed.
>
> Part II: Facilitation of electronic commerce, data storage, etc. This part is concerned with the legal recognition and admissibility of electronic signatures; permits the removal of statutory restrictions, which impose a requirement that a transaction must be in writing, and facilitates the use of electronic means to store information in an electronic format.
>
> Part III: Miscellaneous and supplemental. This part makes a number of amendments to the Telecommunications Act 1984 regarding the modification of telecommunications licences, and also covers the usual matters including interpretation; the short title, commencement and the territorial extent of the Act.

**5.2** Sections 7, 11 and 12 came into force on 25 July 2000 in accordance with the provisions of the Electronic Communications Act 2000 (Commencement No 1) Order 2000 (SI 2000 No 1798); section 4(2) was amended by section 82, Schedule 4(10) of the Regulation of Investigatory Powers Act 2000, and section 15(1) was amended by section 406(1), Schedule 17(158) of the Communications Act 2003, and sections 11 and 12 were repealed by section 406(7), Schedule 19(1) of the Communications Act 2003. The Act was amended in 2016 by

1 Section 16(5).

2 tScheme, available online at http://www.tscheme.org.

S. Mason, *Electronic Signatures in Law* (London: Institute of Advanced Legal Studies, 2016), chapter 5, 'England and Wales, Northern Ireland and Scotland', pp. 167–79.

The Electronic Identification and Trust Services for Electronic Transactions Regulations 2016 (SI 2016 No 696).[3]

**5.3** Unless there is a specific statutory requirement for a document to be signed, English law does not require any document to be signed to be both valid and effective. Thus in many instances, it was possible to sign a document with an electronic signature before the passing of the Act. The signature at the end of an e-mail, as in the case of *Hall v. Cognos Limited*[4] was sufficient, providing the person signing the document intended to sign it and intended their signature to affect the authenticity of the document. If the identity of the person signing the document is in doubt, further evidence can be adduced to identify the person who affixed their signature to the document.

## The international context

**5.4** The Explanatory Notes to the Act were prepared by the Department of Trade and Industry. The commentary, at paragraph 19, suggested the Bill was consistent with the EU Electronic Signatures Directive, although it only implemented some of the provisions of the Directive – a Statutory Instrument was subsequently passed to implement the Directive in full.[5] It was also suggested that the Bill was compatible with the Cryptography Guidelines published by the Organization for Economic Co-operation and Development on 19 March 1997, the United Nations Commission on International Trade Law Model Law of Electronic Commerce, and the draft Uniform Rules on Electronic Signatures and Certification Authorities.

## The definition of an electronic signature

**5.5** The amended definition of an electronic signature[6] reads in s 7(2) as follows:

> (2) For the purposes of this section an electronic signature is so much of anything in electronic form as-
>
> > (a) is incorporated into or otherwise logically associated with any electronic communication or electronic data; and
> >
> > (b) purports to be used by the individual creating it to sign.

3 Made on 30 June 2016; laid before Parliament 1 July 2016; into force on 22 July 2016.

4 Industrial Tribunal Case No 1803325/97.

5 The Electronic Signatures Regulations 2002 (SI 2002 No 318 (made on 13 February 2002, laid before Parliament 14 February 2002, in force on 8 March 2002). These Regulations are revoked by Regulation 4 of the Electronic Identification and Trust Services for Electronic Transactions Regulations 2016 (SI 2016 No 696).

6 Amended by The Electronic Identification and Trust Services for Electronic Transactions Regulations 2016 (SI 2016 No 696) (made on 30 June 2016; laid before Parliament 1 July 2016; in force on 22 July 2016).

**5.6** An electronic communication is defined in s15(1):[7]

> 'electronic communication' means a communication transmitted (whether from one person to another, from one device to another or from a person to a device or vice versa) -
>
> (a) an electronic communications network; or
>
> (b) by other means but while in an electronic form;

**5.7** While an electronic signature does not have the same characteristics as a manuscript signature, it is the equivalent of a manuscript signature when it performs a similar function. The better view is to consider an electronic signature as a link between protocols of electronic devices that communicate via software, each with the other. The attention should be focused on the treatment of messages before they are transmitted and after they are received. By way of example, consider the steps taken in relation to a document in electronic format:

> (i) Alice uses a computer to type a letter. She has two options. She can print it out and sign it manually before arranging for it to be delivered to its destination. This can be by means of the post, hand delivery or any other method. When the document is produced in printed format and is signed with a manuscript signature, the electronic version remains (unless expunged), but no longer governs the content. The paper version becomes the document that will govern the relationship between the parties. Alternatively, Alice can decide to sign the letter with the private key of a digital signature.
>
> (ii) Signing the letter with the private key of a digital signature follows a protocol. The letter is in the form of a number of bits. For instance, Alice may instruct the software in her computer to perform a mathematical calculation on the file. She will do this by typing in a password to reveal the file containing the private key and clicking an icon to instruct the software to carry out the necessary actions. The program will then decrypt the private key with the password and calculate the signature. The calculation, called a signature, is then associated with the document by the computer. There is a direct association between the software in which the file has been created and the mathematical calculation that is used to sign the document. The signature is proof in mathematical terms that a value, known as a secret key, was present in the computer at the time the calculation was made. Thus there is an association between the secret key and the signing of the document, although it must be remembered that the encryption key is just a value, which must have been available to the system that originated the signature. It does not identify the

7 As amended by s406(1), Schedule 17(158) of the Communications Act 2003.

individual. Thus it does not follow that Alice caused the software to undertake the mathematical calculation. There is no nexus between the signing of the document by the software and any action on the part of Alice (it would be different if Alice accepts that it was her action that caused the connection to occur). A problem may occur if a person gains access to the computer by means of malicious software, such as, for instance, a Trojan horse that causes the software to display one message on the screen, while signing another document. It is possible for a third party to have written a suitable plug-in that infiltrates the computer, permitting a person to enter the computer remotely without authority and use the private key to sign documents without Alice's consent or her knowledge. Should the computer have been taken over in this way, the status of the computer changes from being trusted to un-trusted. However, the owner or user may not be aware that the computer cannot be trusted.[8]

(iii) Consider another scenario. Alice creates a document and then saves it. Assume Alice attaches it to an e-mail to be sent at a time in the future. Assume the document is automatically signed with the private key of a digital signature as Alice sends it, without any action. It does not follow that the signature appended automatically can authenticate that is was Alice who signed the document.[9]

(iv) It is possible in principle to produce an electronic signature that can be trusted, and link the individual to the document. By having a computer that is not connected to any external connections, and never has been so connected at any time, and that incorporates no components that have ever been incorporated in a machine which has ever had any external connections, and by retaining complete physical control over access to the computer by anyone except Alice, it is possible to provide for the nexus between the electronic signature and Alice. However, this then requires the user to rely on the security of the software and hardware, which in turn poses even more problems.[10]

8 For cases where the digital signatures of companies have been used by criminals to transfer funds from company bank accounts, see O.I. Kudryavtseva, 'The use of electronic digital signatures in banking relationships in the Russian Federation', *Digital Evidence and Electronic Signature Law Review*, 5 (2008), pp. 51–7, and O.I. Kudryavtseva, Case note: Resolution of the Federal Arbitration Court of Moscow Region of 5 November 2003 N КГ-А 40/8531-03-П, *Digital Evidence and Electronic Signature Law Review*, 5 (2008), pp. 149–51.

9 To a certain extent, this matter will be dealt with by the organization. Access controls will be included in the infrastructure to determine which messages should be signed and by whom. The only problem is if an insider with sufficient rights of access alters the configurations.

10 It is also possible to retain control by placing the computer in a safe, and burying the safe below six feet of earth. The debate then concerns whether the worms can be trusted.

**5.8** An electronic signature can be the equivalent of a manuscript signature where it performs a similar function, even though the two types of signature are conceptually different. The manuscript signature exists in the corporeal world and requires the physical application of matter to alter the surface of a carrier. An electronic signature can only be defined within the operational boundaries of the binary numbers used by computers.

## The elements of an electronic signature

### *So much of anything in electronic form*

**5.9** This is a wide-ranging provision that should ensure new concepts yet to be invented are covered by the term 'electronic form'.

### *Incorporation or logical association*

**5.10** The first element, 'so much of anything in electronic form' must either be incorporated or logically associated with any electronic communication or electronic data. This part of the requirement differs slightly from article 3(10) of the Regulation, which refers to 'attached to or logically associated with'. However, the meaning of the word 'attached' is defined as 'joined functionally', which implies a similarity to the meaning of 'incorporated', which in turn is defined as to 'be included as part of a whole' or 'embodied'.[11] This seems to be a semantic difference that does not affect meaning. The signature could be incorporated by reference to the way it is created. For instance, with a digital signature, incorporation is possible when the software takes part of the plaintext and encrypts it (creating the message authentication code), so the recipient can check if the message has been altered. In effect, the message authentication code is a separate part of the message, but is also incorporated into the message by taking the message and encoding it. Alternatively, a biometric measurement can be attached to a message. This is where the biometric measurement, if used, must be logically associated with the message, otherwise it will not serve any function. Although the discussion above is predicated on particular methods of producing electronic signatures, the underlying principles are the same for all methods, including a name typed into an e-mail or an e-mail address, although the functions of an electronic signature may differ between products and methods.

### *Purports to be used by the individual creating it to sign*

**5.11** In this revised sub-clause merely recognises that it does not follow that where an electronic signature was affixed to data, it follows that the person whose signature it purports to be was the person that caused the signature to be affixed.

11 *Oxford English Dictionary*, 2nd edition on CD-ROM (v. 4.0).

**5.12** In the context of the Act, the meaning of authenticity relates to the single issue of verifying the person or entity, as provided for in s15(2):

> (2) In this Act-
>
> (a) references to the authenticity of any communication or data are references to any one or more of the following-
>
> > (i) whether the communication or data comes from a particular person or other source;
> >
> > (ii) whether it is accurately timed and dated;
> >
> > (iii) whether it is intended to have legal effect;
>
> and
>
> (b) references to the integrity of any communication or data are references to whether there has been any tampering with or other modification of the communication or data.

**5.13** This definition relates to the evidential issues regarding the authentication of the communication or data. Where an electronic signature is in issue, whichever party has the burden of proof will be required to submit evidence in response to the guidance set out in s15(2), together with any other extrinsic evidence that may be necessary to support the evidential burden.

**5.14** An electronic signature will have to be admissible before it can become legally effective.[12] In addition, it does not follow that the communication will have a legal effect unless it is intended to have such an effect,[13] and the provisions of s7 do not address whether the signature is genuine. Section 7(1) of the Act provides for the admissibility of the electronic signature in two ways:

> 7(1) In any legal proceedings-
>
> > (a) an electronic signature incorporated into or logically associated with a particular electronic communication or particular electronic data, and
> >
> > (b) the certification by any person of such a signature,
>
> shall each be admissible in evidence in relation to any question as to the authenticity of the communication or data or as to the integrity of the communication or data.

**5.15** First, an electronic signature is admissible under the provisions of s7(1)(a) where it is incorporated into or logically associated with a particular electronic communication or data. Alternatively, in accordance with the provisions of s7(1)(b), the authenticity or the integrity of the communication or

12 Law Commission, 'Electronic commerce: formal requirements in commercial transactions advice from the Law Commission' (2001), 3.27.

13 Section 15(2)(a)(iii).

data can be admissible where any person certifies the signature. The certificate would normally be provided by an entity such as a trusted third party, although it does not follow that such a certificate has to be provided by a trusted third party. For instance, it is perfectly possible for Bob to certify that Alice signed an e-mail she sent when she typed her name at the bottom of the text. It seems, therefore, that if a recipient receives an electronic communication which is signed with an electronic signature, and the certifying certificate relating to the electronic signature can be verified, the communication in question is admissible in evidence, subject to the provisions of s15(2) of the Act.[14]

**5.16** The certification by any person mentioned in s7(1)(b) is satisfactory if the statement made includes the criteria set out in s7(3), as amended:

> (3) For the purposes of this section an electronic signature incorporated into or associated with a particular electronic communication or particular electronic data is certified by any person if that person (whether before or after the making of the communication) has made a statement confirming that-
>
> (a) the signature,
>
> (b) a means of producing, communicating or verifying the signature, or
>
> (c) a procedure applied to the signature,
>
> is (either alone or in combination with other factors) a valid means of signing.

**5.17** The person or organization certifying the electronic signature may need to certify before or after or both before and after sending the communication, that the signature is authentic and the integrity of the data or communication is therefore not to be questioned. From a practical point of view, the certification process will probably occur before the sending of the communication, although there may be circumstances where the certification process can occur after the communication is sent. The actual certification will probably be an assertion, that ought to be substantiated by suitable evidence, by the person or organization certifying the signature that there is an association that links the verification key (if a digital signature) with an entity, and certifies that the use of the verification key is a valid way of verifying whether a private key issued to the person named was used in creating the signature. The link between the components of the key pair, if this were to be challenged, would have to be the subject of expert evidence. It is possible for a certificate in isolation to be sufficient in some instances. In all probability, where a party seeks to adduce evidence of a certificate as establishing the authenticity or integrity of the communication or message or both, additional evidence may be required. It is the provision of this extrinsic evidence that is

14 It should be noted that all this evidence would have been admissible anyway, just as it has been in the past.

necessary to provide evidence of the user's identity. From the practical point of view, it may be difficult to obtain such evidence if the communication in question is the subject of legal action years after it was sent. Even if such a certificate is accepted as evidence of the facts contained in the certificate, it will not link the act of signing with the individual or entity whose signature it is. Whether the certification is provided electronically or physically, it may have to be the subject of proof that part of the content of the certificate is acceptable as to the truth of the content, because the information relating to the subscribing party will be a hearsay statement in relation to any facts not within the knowledge of the certification service provider. It should be noted that the provisions of s7 do not consider whether the signature is genuine, or if it demonstrates the necessary intent by the signing party. The section, in dealing with admissibility, leaves the question of evidential weight to the adjudicator.

## Other forms of electronic signature and the electronic seal

**5.18** The Regulation, which is directly applicable, also provides for the advanced electronic signature and the qualified electronic signature. These forms of signature are discussed in the chapter on the European Union. The concept of the electronic seal has also been introduced by the Regulation (by article 3(25)), including the advanced electronic seal (article 3(26)) and qualified electronic seal (article 3(27)). These have been included in the Act by the incorporation of new section 7A dealing with electronic seals and related certificates.

## The power to modify legislation

**5.19** There are many thousands of references in statutes and statutory instruments which require the use of paper or can be interpreted to require the use of paper, as well as the use of manuscript signatures. Amending such provisions with an overall catch-all clause was not possible, nor desirable. However, it is pertinent to observe a comment by the Law Commission in relation to this issue:[15]

> While section 7 deals with admissibility, it does not provide that electronic signatures will satisfy a statutory signature requirement. It does not, therefore, assist in determining to what extent existing statutory signature requirements are capable of being satisfied electronically.

**5.20** In any event, power has been delegated to Ministers to modify, by order made by statutory instrument, the provisions of any enactment or subordinate legislation, or instruments made under such legislation, for which they are responsible. The government recognizes the need for a coordinated approach between departments in enacting such subordinate legislation. Following the recommendation noted in paragraph 10.45 to the Performance and Innovation

15 Law Commission, 'Electronic commerce: formal requirements in commercial transactions advice from the Law Commission' (2001), 3.27.

Unit Report 'e-commerce@its.best.uk' (September 1999), the Central IT Unit in the Cabinet Office was given the task of developing guidelines to ensure Departments follow a consistent approach.

**5.21** The authority granted to Ministers is provided by s8(1). Ministers have the power to modify by statutory instrument the provisions of:[16]

> (a) any enactment or subordinate legislation, or
>
> (b) any scheme, licence, authorisation or approval issued, granted or given by or under any enactment or subordinate legislation,
>
> in such manner as he may think fit for the purpose of authorising or facilitating the use of electronic communications or electronic storage (instead of other forms of communication or storage) for any purpose mentioned in subsection (2).

## *Limitation of powers*

**5.22** The power granted to the Minister is limited by the terms of s8(3), where consideration must be given to the arrangements for record keeping. Changes must not be made that make the new arrangements for record keeping less satisfactory than before the changes were made. A further limitation is set out in s8(6), which provides that an order 'shall not require the use of electronic communications or electronic storage for any purpose'. This subsection is qualified by s8(6)(b), which permits a period of notice to expire before effect is given to a variation or withdrawal of an election or other decision.

## *Purposes for which modification can be made*

**5.23** Modification of an enactment can be made for the following purposes, by permitting the use of electronic means as follows:

> (a) The doing of things that may need to be evidenced in writing or where a document, notice or instrument is required.[17]
>
> (b) Alternative means of delivery where the post or other specified means of delivery is required.[18]
>
> (c) Where there is a requirement for a matter to be authorized by a person's signature or seal, or where it is required to be delivered as a deed or witnessed.[19]

16 By s8(7), matters under the care and control of the Commissioners of the Inland Revenue or Customs and Excise are not included, because there are corresponding powers in s132 of the Finance Act 1999, which have already been exercised by way of statutory instruments relating to electronic tax and VAT returns.

17 Section 8(2)(a).

18 Section 8(2)(b).

19 Section 8(2)(c).

> (d) Where a statement may be required to be made under oath or to be contained in a statutory declaration.[20]
>
> (e) Where records have to be kept, maintained or preserved in relation to any account, record, notice instrument or other document.[21]
>
> (f) The provision, production or publication relating to any information or other matter.[22]
>
> (g) The making of any payment.[23]

### *The provisions a Minister may make*

**5.24** The Act provides the Minister with a power to provide for a range of issues when drafting a statutory instrument. The list is set out in s8(4). The provisions of s8(4)(g) cross refer to s8(5). These two sections provide Ministers with the powers to determine such issues as matters relating to the legal presumption and the burden of proof. Section 8(4)(g) reads as follows:

> (g) provision, in relation to cases in which the use of electronic communications or electronic storage is so authorised, for the determination of any of the matters mentioned in subsection (5), or as to the manner in which they may be proved in legal proceedings;

**5.25** Section 8(5) provides:

> (5) The matters referred to in subsection (4)(g) are-
>
> (a) whether a thing has been done using an electronic communication or electronic storage;
>
> (b) the time at which, or date on which, a thing done using any such communication or storage was done;
>
> (c) the place where a thing done using such communication or storage was done;
>
> (d) the person by whom such a thing was done; and
>
> (e) the contents, authenticity or integrity of any electronic data.

**5.26** These two sections, taken together, indicate a Minister has a great deal of control over how electronic communications are to be handled, and what presumptions will apply when using electronic communications. The combined

20 Section 8(2)(d).

21 Section 8(2)(e).

22 Section 8(2)(f).

23 Section 8(2)(g).

effect of s8(4) and s8(5) permits a Minister to impose rebuttable or irrebuttable presumptions, with the potential for shifting the risks from the receiving party to the purported signing party. This has the potential for doing great injustice, and as a result causing much harm to the prospects of electronic commerce. Arguably, the power is wider than just replacing paper documents with an electronic equivalent. An example would be replacing the circulation of statutory accounts to shareholders by post or as attachments to an e-mail, with an electronic notice of their availability at a nominated uniform resource locator.

**5.27** The Electronic Communications Act 2000 as amended has not altered the underlying flexibility of the meaning of a signature. An electronic signature does not have to be in the specific form of digital signature for it to be accepted as a signature. By typing a name to an electronic document, all the person needs to do is intend the name they type to act as a means of authentication, and intend the recipient to act upon the content of the document. The act of typing a name in this fashion comes within the provisions of s7(2) of the Electronic Communications Act 2000, because the typed signature is incorporated with the content of the document for the purpose of establishing the authenticity of the communication.[24] No further requirements are necessary to make a typed signature admissible. Whether a name in an e-mail address can be construed as a form of electronic signature is discussed at length elsewhere in this text in relation to the case of *J Pereira Fernandes SA v. Mehta.*[25]

## Regulation of Investigatory Powers

**5.28** The Regulation of Investigatory Powers Act 2000 (RIPA), which extends to Northern Ireland, received the Royal Assent on 28 July 2000. For the purposes of this text, the powers relating to the disclosure of a key are relevant. The power to require disclosure is provided in s49, but of importance is what is the meaning of a key. What constitutes a key is widely defined, and includes codes and passwords. The definition in s56(1) is as follows:

> in relation to any electronic data, means any key, code, password, algorithm or other data the use of which (with or without other keys) -
>
> (a) allows access to the electronic data, or
>
> (b) facilitates the putting of data into an intelligible form;

24 In *Golden Ocean Group Limited v. Salgaocar Mining Industries PVT Ltd* [2011] EWHC 56 (Comm), Mr Justice Christopher Clarke indicated at 103 that 'an e-mail, the text of which begins "Paul/Peter", may be regarded as signed by Peter because by that form of wording Peter signifies that he is addressing Paul and authenticates the content of the whole of what follows'.

25 [2006] 1 WLR 1543; [2006] 2 All ER 891; [2006] 1 All ER (Comm) 885; [2006] All ER (D) 264 (Apr); [2006] IP & T 546; *The Times* 16 May 2006; [2006] EWHC 813 (Ch).

**5.29** In the context of digital signatures, any person or organization that obtains and uses private keys should ensure the key is only suitable for the purposes of a digital signature, and it cannot be used for any other purpose.[26] If a key can be used for purposes other than a digital signature, it may be the subject of a s49 notice. Also, it will be important to ensure keys used for digital signatures are stored separately from any other types of private key used for other purposes.

## Possession of a key

**5.30** A person has possession of a key in accordance with the provisions of s56(2). A person may be deemed to have a key, even they do not have the key. The definition is as follows:

> References in this Part to a person's having information (including a key to protected information) in his possession include references-
>
> (a) to its being in the possession of a person who is under his control so far as that information is concerned;
>
> (b) to his having an immediate right of access to it, or an immediate right to have it transmitted or otherwise supplied to him; and
>
> (c) to its being, or being contained in, anything which he or a person under his control is entitled, in exercise of any statutory power and without otherwise taking possession of it, to detain, inspect or search.

**5.31** This is a fairly important provision, because the officers of an organization, whatever the legal form the organization takes, are the ones responsible for the proper management of the private key.[27] This is because any s49 notice served will be served on an officer or senior manager. Control must, therefore, be exercised over the acquisition and use of private keys. For instance, a person at the highest level in an organization should be made responsible for this issue. Considerations in whether to use private keys will cover, but not be limited to:

(a) Deciding if information sent electronically needs to be encrypted. If it does, whether there are more appropriate means of delivering the information to the intended recipient.

(b) Deciding if documents or messages need to be digitally signed.

26 It is possible for encrypted data to be encoded in such a way that it can be decoded in two separate ways, one to reveal the secret message and the other to reveal an innocuous message: D. Grover, 'Dual encryption and plausible deniability', *Computer Law & Security Report*, 20 (2004), pp. 37–40.

27 R.J. Anderson, *Security Engineering: A Guide to Building Dependable Distributed Systems* (2nd edn, Indianapolis: Wiley, 2008), ch. 25 for a discussion on the principles involved in this process.

If so, then the next question is whether a risk analysis has been conducted to determine the likely costs of resolving a dispute if a signature has been misused, bearing in mind the discussion elsewhere in this text relating to liability.

(c) If private keys are to be used, whatever the purpose, sufficient consideration must be given to storage, access for appropriately authorized officers and employees, and the provision of checks and balances to provide for security.

## Exclusion of electronic signatures

**5.32** Where a key is used only for the purpose of generating a digital signature, it does not have to be disclosed in response to a notice, providing it has not been used for any other purpose.[28] It might be useful to recall that a key pair has more than the single function of producing a digital signature. The same key pair can be used to encrypt a message, depending on the algorithm used. An electronic signature is defined in s56(2) and means:

> anything in electronic form which-
>
> (a) is incorporated into or logically associated with, any electronic communication or other data;
>
> (b) is generated by the signatory or other source of the communication or data; and
>
> (c) is used for the purpose of facilitating, by means of a link between the signatory or other source and the communication or data, the establishment of the authenticity of the communication or data, the establishment of its integrity, or both;

**5.33** This exemption may be less effective than it seems. In a commercial context, where more than one person may properly have access to a key, the person served with the notice may not be able to be sure that a key, despite being intended for signature purposes, has never been used to decrypt a message encrypted with the corresponding public key. Although it is arguably for the prosecution to prove that a key has been used for such a purpose, and is therefore subject to seizure, the mere assertion of this fact by the person demanding access to the key would place the recipient of the notice in a position of impossible difficulty in resisting the demand.[29]

28 Section 49(9).

29 For more detail, see S. Mason, ed., *Electronic Evidence* (3rd edn., London: LexisNexis Butterworths, 2012), ch. 6.

# 6

# Introduction to the electronic signature

**6.1** While it is possible for an electronic signature to perform the same functions as a manuscript signature, the document to be signed does not exist as a physical object in the same way as the content of a document rendered on to a paper carrier.[1] It is not necessarily intended that an electronic signature should be manifest in a physical form, which leads to the conclusion that the quality and extent of the evidence to provide intent becomes vitally important in the event it is disputed that an electronic signature was affixed to a document or communication.[2]

**6.2** It does not follow that lawyers are even aware of electronic signatures,[3] or the fact that electronic signatures can be used instead of manuscript signatures, and challenges have been made, claiming that an electronic signature should not be used instead of a manuscript signature.[4] For instance, in the Californian case of *Ni v. Slocum, as Chief Elections Officer*[5] electronic signatures were not permitted on an initiative petition without a change of law, and in Missouri, the City did not agree to conduct transactions by electronic means.[6] Compare these decisions to (i) the decision of the Supreme Court of Utah in *Anderson v. Bell*,[7] where an electronic signature satisfied the signature requirement for

1 On occasion, arguments will be made that a manuscript signature must be used, especially in criminal proceedings. Judges tend to take a robust approach to such submissions, for which see, by way of example, *United States of America v. Mariner*, 2012 WL 60827, where the indictment only contained electronic signatures.

2 By way of example, see a case from the Court of Appeal, Fourth District, Division 2, California: *Ruiz v. Moss Bross. Auto Group, Inc.*, 232 Cal.App.4th 836 (2014), 181 Cal.Rptr.3d 781, 14 Cal. Daily Op. Serv. 14,270, 2014 Daily Journal D.A.R. 16,951, where Moss Bros failed to prove Ruiz signed an agreement electronically.

3 The judge had to alert the lawyers to the case of *Harding v. Brisbane City Council* [2008] QPEC 75 (16 October 2008) in *Morgan v. Toowoomba Regional Council (No 2)* 2011 [2011] QPEC 61 2011, 2011 WL 2159617 – even though the first edition of this text was published in 2003.

4 Case translation: Sweden, Case No. 11534-13, *Digital Evidence and Electronic Signature Law Review*, 12 (2015), pp. 103–6.

5 196 Cal.App.4th 1636 (2011), 127 Cal.Rptr.3d 620, 11 Cal. Daily Op. Serv. 8306, 2011 Daily Journal D.A.R. 9936; a loan document signed with a digital signature could not be enforced under the provisions of the Administration of Justice Act § 478: Case translation: Denmark, U.2014.52 V, 6 September 2013, with a commentary by Professor Lars Bo Langsted, 11 *Digital Evidence and Electronic Signature Law Review* (2014), 147 – 148; Case translation: Denmark, U.2014.712Ø, 13 November 2013, *Digital Evidence and Electronic Signature Law Review*, 11 (2014), pp. 149–50.

6 *WCT & D, LLC, v. City of Kansas City, Missouri*, --- S.W.3d ---- (2015), 2015 WL 8231576.

7 234 P.3d 1147 (Utah 2010), 234 P.3d 1147 (2010).

S. Mason, *Electronic Signatures in Law* (London: Institute of Advanced Legal Studies, 2016), chapter 6, 'Introduction to the electronic signature', pp. 181–200.

nomination petitions that the Utah Code imposes on those who wish to run for statewide office but do not affiliate with a registered political party; (ii) the decision in *Benjamin v. Walker*,[8] where the Supreme Court of Appeals of West Virginia determined that an electronic receipt containing a unique transaction identifier is a sufficient signature of the contributor within the meaning of the West Virginia Code Chapter 3 Elections §3-12-9(b) regarding qualifying contributions, and (iii) *Thompson Brothers (Construction) Ltd. v. Alberta (Appeals Commission for Alberta Workers' Compensation)*,[9] where the electronic signatures of counsel are accepted in Alberta, Canada. A similar question arose in England and Wales in *FHG Publications Ltd v. Tee-Hillman*,[10] in the County Court at Southampton on 21 November 2000. In this case, FHG sent a single Statement of Truth accompanying a batch of proceedings to be issued. They were all sent electronically, and duly signed by an individual whose name was also printed on the document. The claim form received by Tee-Hillman had only the name of the solicitors inserted in its Statement of Truth, as issued by the Claims Production Centre. Tee-Hillman paid the sum in dispute on 31 August, but refused to pay any costs, arguing although FHG had provided a single Statement of Truth satisfying paragraph of Practice Direction 7C para 1.4(5), it was necessary for an individual's signature to be present on the claim form received by him. It appeared that a copy of the electronic signature had not been transferred to the claim form by the Claims Production Centre. The application was dismissed.

# Digital documents

## Information relating to the carrier

**6.3** When a manuscript signature is affixed to a physical carrier, two changes occur. First, the signature alters the carrier physically with the addition of a substance, such as ink, to the surface. Second, the signature increases the amount of information about the carrier, and thereby the document. An electronic signature, on the other hand, only tends to alter the information relating to the digital data. It does not necessarily alter the carrier in the same way as a manuscript signature, although an inline Pretty Good Privacy signature, for instance, is read with the message. The information associated with the carrier is termed the metadata. The metadata refers to the data about data. It is a digest of the structure and subject matter of a resource. For instance, the metadata in relation to a piece of paper may be:

8 786 S.E.2d 200 (2016).

9 2012 CarswellAlta 874, 2012 ABCA 150, [2012] A.W.L.D. 3031, [2012] A.W.L.D. 3036, [2012] A.W.L.D. 3098, 216 A.C.W.S. (3d) 576, 522 A.R. 184, 544 W.A.C. 184.

10 [2001] C.L.Y. 662.

> Explicit from perusing the paper itself, such as the title of the document, the date, who wrote it, who received it and where the document is located.
>
> Implicit, which includes such characteristics as the types of type used, such as bold, underline or italic; perhaps the document is located in a coloured file to denote a particular type of document; labels may also act as pointers to allow the person using the document to deal with it in a particular manner, such as a confidential file, for instance.

**6.4** With digital documents, the implicit data needs to be made explicit if it is to be used to help interpret the purpose of the document. Such data can include, and be taken automatically from the originating application software, or supplied by the person that originally created the record. As a result, a digital record will normally contain two main types of information, the content of the document and its internal structure, and the metadata, which describes the record and each of the constituent parts.

## The nature of a document in digital form

**6.5** A digital document can be evident as a physical document, where it is created using a computer and produced in physical format by being printed. However, it must be noted that the nexus between the printed document and the document stored in digital format will alter. First, the printed form of the document will capture the content of the document at the time it is printed. The physical manifestation of the electronic document (a contract or a will, for instance) can then be marked with a manuscript signature, and it then becomes a document in the physical sense. The information about the physical carrier will then alter over time. However, unless the metadata relating to the document stored in digital form is retained in such a way as to link the document, as printed, with the act of printing, the nexus between the printed version of the document and the electronic version may change. Such alterations to the metadata will take place when the original document stored in digital form is deleted or the content is modified or re-written. In such circumstances, the content on the printed carrier may differ from the content stored in digital form. While this will not matter when a standard letter, by way of example, is altered to change the name and address of the recipient, it will be of substantial concern when the document is a contract, and the printed version differs from the digital version. The information relating to the content of the document, the metadata, might then become a crucial aspect of the evidence.[11] Alternatively, a person cannot observe a digital document that is stored in a digital form without using a computer with a screen. Even when a document is apparent to the eye on a screen, the viewer

11 For case law on the importance of metadata, see S. Mason, ed., *Electronic Evidence* (3rd edn., London: LexisNexis Butterworths, 2012), 2.09–2.10.

is not looking at the underlying digital format of the carrier. This is because it is in binary form, which in turn is translated into a readable format on the screen.

**6.6** Reference to electronic documents in this text will primarily be references to documents stored in digital format that are invisible to the human eye.

## Signing without authority

**6.7** The legal response to signing a document in electronic format without authority remains as for physical signatures. An electronic signature can, of course, be affixed without the authority of a person, as in the case of *Securities and Exchange Commission v. Penthouse International, Inc., n/k/a/ PHSL Worldwide, Inc.*,[12] where the electronic signature (the type of electronic signature is not made clear) of Robert C. Guccione, the principal executive officer and principal financial officer of Penthouse, was affixed to a certificate without his permission.[13]

**6.8** Depending on the facts, a person can ratify the signature. The Supreme Court, New York County, New York concluded that where a personal assistant electronically signs a document for the purchase of property using dedicated electronic signature software without explicit authority, the signature is capable of being ratified by the principal.[14] In the Ohio case of *Cleveland Metropolitan Bar Association v. Brown-Daniels*,[15] Barbara Brown-Daniels used the electronic password and signature of Donald R. Murphy, an attorney with whom she began to work with after a court suspended her electronic-filing privileges. The court determined that Ms Brown-Daniels used Mr Murphy's signature with his permission before he terminated their association, but her use of his authentication and signature after termination of their association was unauthorized.

## Delegating the use of an electronic signature

**6.9** Another can be a delegated person to sign a document, as in the Australian case of *Whittaker v. Child Support Registrar*[16] where a person affixed the scanned electronic signature of another to a letter with authority. However,

12 390 F.Supp.2d 344 (2005), Fed. Sec. L. Rep. P 93,565; see also the Kansas case of *Robinson v. City of Arkansas*, 912 F.Supp.2d 1045 (D.Kan. 2012).

13 The enforcement action was settled by final judgments entered before the Honorable Robert W. Sweet of the United States District Court for the Southern District of New York on 27 April 2007, https://www.sec.gov/litigation/litreleases/2007/lr20110.htm; see also the Ontario case of *Baird v. College of Chiropractors of Ontario* 2015 ONSC 1484.

14 *In the Matter of an Article 75 Proceeding ADHY Investments Properties, LLC, Petitioner v. Garrison Lifestyle Pierce Hill LLC*, 41 Misc.3d 1211(A), 980 N.Y.S.2d 274, 2013 N.Y. Slip Op. 51634(U).

15 985 N.E.2d 1289 (Ohio 2013), 135 Ohio St.3d 278.

16 [2010] FCA 43 (5 February 2010).

the indiscriminate use of a signature that is subject to professional regulations can lead to sanctions, as illustrated in the Ohio case of *Disciplinary Counsel v. Lorenzon.*[17] In 2008, Mr Lorenzon entered into an agreement with Consumer Law Group, P.A., a law firm in Florida that negotiates debt on behalf of consumers. Mr Lorenzon was paid US$1,000 annually to serve as local counsel for Consumer Law. He was required to execute a contract with each Ohio client. To simplify the execution of the contracts, Mr Lorenzon provided Consumer Law with his electronic signature and Ohio attorney registration number. Mr Lorenzon later discovered that Consumer Law had used his name, electronic signature and attorney-registration number to enter into contracts without his knowledge. He was subsequently charged with violations of the Ohio Rules of Professional Conduct. The Supreme Court of Ohio upheld the decision of the Panel and Board, in that Mr Lorenzon was found guilty of infringing Rule 8.4(h) of the Professional Conduct Rules for permitting his electronic signature and attorney-registration number to be used without restriction.

## Forged signatures

**6.10** The use of electronic signatures can facilitate the smooth running of an organization, but sometimes undue pressures can be made on employees to such an extent that they carry out actions that they ought not to contemplate. This is illustrated in the Canadian case of *Re: Jade Truman Kaiser Mason,*[18] where Mr Mason affixed the electronic signature of customer on to electronic documents without their knowledge, although it is not clear what form the electronic signatures took in this case.

**6.11** An early case where the PIN to a corporate bank account was used without authority occurred in the Australian employment case of *H. Sayner and Joblink Plus Limited – re Termination of employment,*[19] where Joblink had an electronic transfer policy, which stated that a member of the Board must enter a code into the system when transferring funds electronically. The codes were written on a piece of paper, placed in a sealed envelope and left with the Finance Manager to store in a safe location and to be opened in an emergency. The envelope had a direction written on the outside to the effect that the envelope was not to be opened except in an emergency in the event that neither Ms Esther Halliday, the Chair of the Board, or other members of the Board were able to attend the office to transfer money. Ms Sayner used the corporate PIN to pay for a holiday for the then Finance Manager, Mr Helanath Disanayake and his family to the Novotel Opal Cove Resort at Coffs Harbour using Joblink funds in the amount of A$2,241.50. This expenditure was improper and not approved by the Board.

17 978 N.E.2d 183 (Ohio 2012), 133 Ohio St.3d 332.

18 2012 CanLII 42180 (CA MFDAC); 2012 CanLII 42181 (CA MFDAC).

19 PR950280 [2004] AIRC 748 (30 July 2004).

**6.12** When forms of electronic signature are placed on a hard drive in such a way that there is no mechanism to prevent others from using the electronic signature of another person, they are exposed to being used without authority, as in the Canadian case of *Adamo v. College of Physicians and Surgeons of Ontario*,[20] where the electronic signature of another doctor was affixed to a falsified record without authority. Similar examples occurred in Australia in the cases of *Salfinger v. Niugini Mining (Australia) Pty Ltd (No. 3)*[21] which concerned the forgery of purported assignments where Heerey J concluded that Mr Salfinger had access to Mr McCordic's electronic signature, and concluded that Mr Salfinger affixed Mr McCordic's electronic signature to a document without his authority, and in *Re Macartney and Tax Agents' Board of Victoria*,[22] where the applicant applied to the Victorian Tax Agents' Board for registration as a tax agent. He was a qualified accountant, aged 64. At the time of making the application, he was about to lose his position with his employer. To support his application, he had to provide a statement of relevant employment. The statement was not to be signed by the applicant. Before he left his employment, he obtained a copy of the letterhead of the firm he was working for, together with an electronic signature of one of the partners of the firm. He then produced a statement of employment using the letterhead and electronic signature and sent it to the board. On appeal, McDonald, Deputy President, concluded that the actions of the applicant were such that he was not of good fame, integrity and character, and was not a fit and proper person to prepare income tax returns and transact business on behalf of income tax matters. He was suspended from applying for registration as a tax agent for a period of three months.

**6.13** A further case that illustrates the ease by which documents can be forged is *Djordje Mitic v. Eco Pro Australia Pty Ltd*,[23] where Djordje Mitic claimed that the termination of his employment by Eco Pro was unlawful. Part of the evidence was in the form of a letter dated 14 July 2008, which contained the signature of Mr Bikkemberg and his own signature. Djordje Mitic disclosed the letter before the proceedings. The content of the letter was similar to a letter dated 7 July 2008, except that it was not confined to a period of employment for six months, and expressed entitlements in annual terms. Both letters contained errors of a typographical and formatting nature of which appear to arise from an imperfect knowledge of the English language. The evidence from Mr Bikkemberg tended to establish that the signature at the bottom of the letter of 14 July 2008 was electronically created on 20 August 2008. Mr Bikkemberg wrote the letter dated 20 August to Mr Mitic. This letter was, in turn, forwarded by Mr Noel to Mr Mitic as an attachment to an email on 22 January 2009. The letter contained Mr Bikkemberg's electronic signature in electronic form. It is not clear from the judgment whether this was a scanned version of Mr Bikkemberg's manuscript

20 2007 CanLII 9873 (ON S.C.D.C.).

21 [2007] FCA 1532 (8 October 2007).

22 [2008] AATA 210.

23 [2009] AIRC 503 (26 May 2009).

signature. The recipient could therefore cut and paste the signature. The judge commented that the letter of 14 July was not professionally prepared, for example it had the addressee's street number next to his name on the line above the street name. There was insufficient evidence for the judge to establish whether a letter of offer dated 14 July 2008 was ever authorized by Mr Bikkemberg and provided to Mr Mitic, but on the balance of probabilities, the judge concluded that no such letter existed at the time.[24]

**6.14** At issue in the case of *Williams Group Australia Pty Ltd v. Crocker*[25] before the Supreme Court of New South Wales was the use of an electronic signature affixed to a guarantee allegedly given by a director of a company to secure the terms of a trade credit agreement. *Williams Group* began to use a commercial electronic signing system to permit directors to sign documents electronically. Before using the system, Mr Crocker had to provide a username and password to enable him to obtain access to the system before uploading his signature. Unfortunately, it is not certain what form the signature took, because it is not mentioned in the judgment. In early July 2012, IDH Modular submitted an application for commercial credit to *Williams Group*. The form included a deed of guarantee and indemnity. The application included signatures attributed to each of the three directors on both the application form and the deed of guarantee and indemnity. The signatures were dated 28 June 2012. Ms Harrison was noted as having witnessed the signatures. It was common ground that the two signatures attributed to Mr Crocker (on the application form and on the deed of guarantee and indemnity) were placed on those documents electronically using the electronic signing system. It is also common ground that Mr Crocker's signature was affixed to the document on 2 July 2012 from the Murwillumbah office, although it was Mr Crocker's evidence, which was not contested, that he was not in Murwillumbah at that time. *Williams Group* eventually accepted that Mr Crocker did not place his signature on the documents, but contended that he was liable under the guarantee, either because he authorized an employee to affix his signature, or in the alternative he subsequently ratified it, or in the further alternative his conduct after the event was such that he accepted the guarantee. There was insufficient evidence for any of these arguments to be sustained, and McCallum J dismissed the claim. See also the New Zealand case of *Gong v. Zhang*,[26] where one of the issues was whether an electronic signature was used without authority; and a further example of a forged electronic signature in the context of employment is provided in the British Columbia case of *Caravel Management Corp. v. Roberts*,[27] where a senior employee used the electronic signature of an authorized signatory to steal.

24 See the Australian case of *Tassone v. Kirkham* [2014] SADC 134, 2014 WL 3889065 for an example of one person using another person's email account to send defamatory comments to others.

25 [2015] NSWSC 1907.

26 [2014] NZHC 2838.

27 2014 CarswellBC 2249, 2014 BCSC 1419, [2014] B.C.W.L.D. 6492, [2014] B.C.W.L.D. 6586, [2014] B.C.W.L.D. 6591, [2014] B.C.W.L.D. 6594, 243 A.C.W.S. (3d) 766.

**6.15** In the case of *In re Edward Henry Josephson and Alissa R. Josephson, Debtors*[28] before the United States Bankruptcy Court in District of Montana, R. Clifton Caughron, an attorney, inserted both debtors' electronic signatures to an Addendum preceded by "/s/". The signatures were affixed without their authority. It was found that Mr Caughron violated the provisions of Local Bankruptcy Rule 9011-1(a) and Rule 9011(b) by falsely representing that the debtors signed the Addendum. Apparently this was not the first time that Mr Caughron was sanctioned under Rule 9011 of forging the electronic signatures of his clients.[29] In *Teltschik v. Williams & Jensen, PLLC*,[30] an attorney by the name of Meredith Kelley signed a conciliation agreement in her own name, ostensibly as attorney to Corwin Teltschik, although it was not clear in what capacity she signed. This particular issue did not have a great deal of apparent significance in the light of the facts of the case.

**6.16** In *Liberty Mortgage Corporation v. Fiscus*,[31] Vickie Casper-Fiscus, wife of Ray Fiscus, without his knowledge or authorization, signed his name on a General Power of Attorney, a Limited Power of Attorney, and a Power of Attorney (Real Estate), which together purported to appoint her as her husband's lawful attorney. Her daughter from a previous marriage notarized the documents. Using the powers through the forged documents, the wife then raised money on the property. It appears that the forged signature was probably a manuscript signature, but the wife also signed his name on the tax return without his knowledge. It transpired that this was an electronic signature, because he had authorized electronic filing with the tax authorities.

**6.17** Case law that covers criminal proceedings that includes the forgery of electronic signatures in the United States of America include a prosecution that arose from the establishment of One Fund after two bombs were detonated near the finish line of the Boston Marathon on 15 April 2013.[32] One Branden E. Mattier and his half-brother Domunique D. Grice were convicted of various offences arising from a false claim to the fund. Mattier signed a claim form as a representative for his aunt. His signature was notarized. Attached to the claim form was a letter, purporting to be from Dr. Peter A. Burke, chief of trauma services at Boston Medical Center, with his purported signature. He created the letter using forms obtained from the internet. The letter, dated 2 May 2013, claimed that both of his aunt's legs had been amputated as a result of

28 2008 WL 113861; for similar cases before the United States Bankruptcy Court, S.D. Texas, Houston Division, see *In re Stomberg*, 487 B.R. 775 (2013) and *In re Bradley*, 495 B.R. 747 (2013); and for a case before the United States Bankruptcy Appellate Panel of the Ninth Circuit, see *In re Singh*, 2014 WL 842102.

29 2008 WL 113861 at 4.

30 683 F.Supp.2d 33 (2010).

31 --- P.3d ----2016, WL 285970189, UCC Rep.Serv.2d 815, 2016 CO 31.

32 *Commonwealth v. Mattier*, 50 N.E.3d 157, 474 Mass. 261 (2016); for an example in England and Wales, see *Regina v. George Katcharian, Ian Yorkshire, Cemel Esmene* [2013] EWCA Crim 2447, 2013 WL 6865176.

injuries from the bombings. It was thought that this was a fraudulent claim, and One Fund and conducted an internal investigation, which established that his aunt died in 2000. The claim was rejected, and the administrators alerted the Attorney General's office of the false claim. In *Birge v. State of Indiana*,[33] Deborah Birge provided her driver's license information, but she signed the name "Charles Tippet" in the signature box of the electronic signature product for medication.

## Evidence of intent to sign

**6.18** An issue that can exercise the minds of the adjudicator is how to determine the actual act that constitutes the acceptance by the sender of the electronic signature, and when the act occurred. In the case of a manuscript signature, the person furnishes evidence of their intent by physically writing on a carrier, and providing there is sufficient text to link the person to the document, the proof of intent is demonstrated.[34] The question of intent is illustrated in the New Zealand case of *MFT Properties Limited v. Country Club Apartments Limited*.[35] In this case, which regarded negotiations by email, one email was signed 'Gary'. It was not in dispute that this referred to Mr Gary McNabb, the sole director of MFT. The issue was whether he was expressing a personal view during the course of negotiations or whether he was expressing an intention to bind MFT to the reduced rent it had been receiving. Woolford J concluded, at [39], that:

> The name 'Gary' sufficiently identifies Mr McNabb but I am of the view that it does not evidence his intention to bind MFT to the contents of the document.

**6.19** However, in the digital context, the moment of authentication may not be when the person actually types in their name or adopts the signature text at the end of the email or put in automatically when a new email is begun where the program is set up to include a signature at the end of the email.

### The automatic inclusion of the signature

**6.20** The problems with the automatic inclusion of the signature block in facsimile transmissions, email and SWIFT communications have caused some differences in opinions between judges.

33 25 N.E.3d 828 (2014).

34 For an example of failure to prove the electronic signature, see the Californian case of *Rosas v. Macy's, Inc.*, 2012 WL 3656274; where an electronic signature was not in issue; see Case note: France, CA Douai, 8e ch., 1re sect., 2 mai 2013, n° 12/05299: JurisData n° 2013-008597, *Digital Evidence and Electronic Signature Law Review*, 11 (2014), pp. 180–1.

35 HC Auckland CIV-2010-404-005913 [2011] NZHC 422 (13 April 2011).

## *Facsimile transmission*

**6.21** Historically, it is useful to consider the cases of facsimile transmission first. The practice of programming the machine to include the name of the sender on the top or bottom of each page automatically was challenged in the New York case of *Parma Tile Mosaic & Marble Co., Inc., v. Estate of Fred Short, d/b/a Sime Construction Co.*[36] In this instance, it was held that the automatic imprinting by the facsimile machine of the name of the sender at the top of each page transmitted did not satisfy the requirement that writing shall be subscribed. Smith J offered the following opinion:[37]

> The act of identifying and sending a document to a particular destination does not, by itself, constitute a signing authenticating the contents of the document for Statute of Frauds purposes and reject plaintiff's argument that such an inference is warranted here. It is undisputed that MRLS' fax machine, after being programmed to do so, automatically imprinted 'MRLS Construction' on every page transmitted, without regard to the applicability of the Statute of Frauds to a particular document. We also reject plaintiff's contention that the intentional act of programming a fax machine, by itself, sufficiently demonstrates to the recipient the sender's apparent intention to authenticate every document subsequently faxed. The intent to authenticate the particular writing at issue must be demonstrated.

**6.22** In previous editions of this text, it was suggested that this decision by the members of the Court of Appeals in New York did not accord with the case law (see their references at 635) and the argument that no contract was made (at 635) did not necessarily follow from the nature of the document sent by facsimile transmission. The decision in this case remains arguable on the facts. Miller J reached the same conclusion in the New Zealand case of *Welsch v. Gatchell*.[38] Having analysed a number of electronic signature cases. He said, at [63]:

> It follows from what I have said that a name written on a fax may amount to a signature. But a fax header printed using the machine's capacity to add writing to the document as it is copied and sent cannot serve as a signature unless, perhaps, there is evidence that is was specifically inserted for the transaction concerned. A fax header identifies the owner of the sending machine, the sending

36 155 Misc.2d 950, 590 N.Y.S.2d 1019 (Supp. 1992), *motion for summary judgment affirmed*, 209 A.D.2d 495, 619 N.Y.S.2d 628 *reversed* 663 N.E.2d 633 (N.Y. 1996), 640 N.Y.S.2d 477 (Ct.App. 1996), 87 N.Y.2D 524.

37 663 N.E.2d 633 (N.Y. 1996) at 635.

38 CIV 2005-406-279 [2007] NZHC 1898, [2009] 1 NZLR 241, (2007) 8 NZCPR 708, (2007) 5 NZ ConvC 194,549 (21 June 2007).

> number and the time of despatch. There is no reason to suppose that it serves the added purpose of a signature, because every fax does not require a signature. And where the header is added automatically, it cannot qualify as a signature because it was not affixed to the particular writing with the intention that by adding his or her name the sender would adopt its contents.

**6.23** In this case, a contract for the sale of land was formed orally and by facsimile. The sale of land requires the adoption of the contract by way of a signature. The document was not signed, which means there was no evidence to demonstrate an intent to be bound by the transaction, because the name and number printed automatically only acted to identify the person sending and receiving the document.

## *Email*

**6.24** An identical legal question arises in the case of email, and it begins with the early Missouri case of *International Casings Group, Inc., v. Premium Standard Farms, Inc.*[39] A new contract for the purchase of hog casings was partly established by an exchange of emails between the parties. Kent Pummill signed some of his emails 'Kent', and some he sent without adding his name, while Tom Sanscki sent all of his emails without any form of salutation. Having concluded there was sufficient evidence to establish the existence of a contract that contained all the essential terms, Laughrey DJ rehearsed the statutory provisions governing electronic signatures, and concluded that the signatures satisfied the UCC Statute of Frauds, providing each person had the intention to authenticate the document. The judge appeared to make it clear that where an email includes the name of the sender in the header or at the bottom of the email, the act of pressing the send icon on a computer constituted the authentication of the document and it was a valid electronic signature under the Missouri and North Carolina Electronic Transactions Act. The comments made by Laughrey DJ are recorded at 873:

> There is overwhelming evidence that Sanecki's and Pummill's emails are authentic and that the information contained in them was intended by each to accurately reflect their communications with the other. Although they do not all contain a typed name at the bottom of the emails, each email contains a header with the name of the sender. Given the testimony at the preliminary hearing, it is clear that Sanecki and Pummill, by hitting the send button, intended to presently authenticate and adopt the content of the emails as their own writing. This is enough to satisfy the UCC given the breadth of the definition of signature, as well as the UETA which specifically refers to a 'process attached to or logically associated with a record'. The judge took the opportunity

39 358 F.Supp.2d 863 (W.D.Mo. 2005), 2005 WL 486784.

to list relevant case law at 874, and distinguished the decision in *Toghiyany d/b/a First Class Refurbishing v. Amerigas Propane, Inc*[40] where emails were held not to include a signature. Examining the *Toghiyany* decision, Laughrey DJ noted that the contract was not enforceable because it lacked a term of duration; the definition of 'signature' in the UCC did not apply to *Toghiyany* because the sale was not governed by the UCC, and the case was decided before the Missouri UETA was passed.

**6.25** Contrast this case with the later decision of the Supreme Court, Appellate Division, First Department, New York in the case of *Bayerische Landesbank v. 45 John Street LLC*,[41] where the court held that an email containing the reprinted name in a signature block did not constitute a sufficient writing under Statute of Frauds. There is no indication whether the court inferred that the signature block was not capable of being proof of intent to sign. In Texas, Godbey J considered the use of automatically attached signatures in *Williamson v. The Bank of New York Mellon*.[42] The judge noted, at 710, that '[t]he question of whether automatically attached signature blocks qualify as signatures under Rule 11 is murkier', concluding that although the signature block can be generated automatically, nevertheless such a signature is valid.[43] The judge said, at 710–11:

> The Court respectfully disagrees with *Cunningham* and concludes, for three reasons, that the Texas Supreme Court would disagree as well.
>
> First, McInnis's email client did not create a signature block of its own volition. Rather, McInnis must have generated his signature block at some point in the past. He then directed his email client to attach the signature block to his subsequent outgoing email. The Court concludes that these actions affirmatively show intent to sign the record as required by TUETA. There is no fundamental difference between, on one hand, manually typing a signature block into a series of emails and, on the other, typing the block once and instructing a computer program to append it to future messages.

**6.26** The judge acknowledged that the information had to be typed into the facsimile machine in *Parma Tile Mosaic & Marble Co., Inc., v. Estate of Fred Short,*

40 309 F.3d 1088 (8th Cir. 2002).

41 102 A.D.3d 587 (2013), 960 N.Y.S.2d 64, 2013 N.Y. Slip Op. 00419.

42 947 F.Supp.2d 704 (2013).

43 Disagreeing with the contrary decision by the Court of Appeals on Texas in the case of *Cunningham v. Zurich American Insurance Company*, 352 S.W.3d 519 (2011). For technical reasons, the court did not reach a conclusion in the New York case of *Mark Bruce International, LLC v. Blank Rome LLP*, 2011 WL 1742017, 866 N.Y.S.2d 92, 2008 N.Y. Slip Op. 51081(U), *affirmed* 60 A.D.3d 550 (2009), 876 N.Y.S.2d 19, 2009 N.Y. Slip Op. 02254.

*d/b/a Sime Construction Co.*,[44] yet concluded that the name of the company did not constitute a signature. In *Williamson v. The Bank of New York Mellon*,[45] Godbey J also agreed that the signature block in the email had to be typed in by a human, and the human had to instruct the software code to attach the signature block to each email sent out – in this case, the signature acted as an electronic signature to bind the sender. Perhaps these cases can be distinguished. In the case of a facsimile transmission, the information typed into the machine is included automatically on each sheet that is sent. To remove the information would mean resetting the machine. In the case of an email (and depending on how the email client works), it is usually possible for a person to delete or amend the signature block when writing a new email or when replying to an email. Given the greater flexibility with email, these decisions can be reconciled.

## *SWIFT communications*

**6.27** In Singapore in 2003, Tay Yong Kwang JC held in the case of *Industrial & Commercial Bank Ltd v. Banco Ambrosiano Veneto SpA*[46] that a message using an authentication code sent through the SWIFT (Society for Worldwide Interbank Financial Telecommunication) system has the legal effect of binding the sender bank according to its contents, and where a recipient bank undertakes further checks on credit standing or other aspects, it does not detract from this proposition. In England, Blair J reached the same conclusion in *WS Tankship II BV v. The Kwangju Bank Ltd.*[47] A guarantee was issued by Kwangju Bank, but the guarantee was not signed. Even the words 'Kwangju Bank' did not appear. The bank was referred to as 'we' in the guarantee. The case for the bank was that the guarantee was therefore not signed, and the bank was not bound. Blair J rejected this argument at [154], because the bank accepted that the guarantee was properly issued, fully authorized and intended to be relied upon by the beneficiary. In addition, it was sent by conventional means by way of the secure messaging system used between banks – that is, using a digital signature – and the words 'Kwangju Bank Ltd' were contained in the header to the SWIFT message. Blair J continued, at [155]:

> It is argued on behalf of Kwangju Bank that this is not text which it typed in, but an output message header, that is, text generated by the SWIFT messaging system. That may be correct, but the name appears, and in my opinion it is a sufficient signature for the purposes of the Statute of Frauds. The words 'Kwangju Bank Ltd'

44 155 Misc.2d 950, 590 N.Y.S.2d 1019 (Supp. 1992), *motion for summary judgment affirmed*, 209 A.D.2d 495, 619 N.Y.S.2d 628 *reversed* 663 N.E.2d 633 (N.Y. 1996), 640 N.Y.S.2d 477 (Ct.App. 1996), 87 N.Y.2D 524.

45 947 F.Supp.2d 704 (2013).

46 [2003] 1 SLR 221.

47 [2011] EWHC 3103 (Comm).

> appear in the header, because the bank caused them to be there by sending the message. They were 'voluntarily affixed' in the words of the old cases (c.f. *J Pereira Fernandes SA v. Mehta* [2006] 1WLR 1543 dealing with email addresses). Whether or not automatically generated by the system, and whether or not stated in whole, or abbreviated (in fact the name of the bank appeared here in complete form), this is in my judgment a sufficient signature for the purposes of the Statute of Frauds. The position is analogous to that considered by Christopher Clarke J in *Golden Ocean Group Ltd v. Salgaocar Mining Industries Pvt Ltd* [2011] EWHC 56 (Comm) who at [103] observed that 'an email, the text of which begins "Paul/Peter", may be regarded as signed by Peter because by that form of wording Peter signifies that he is addressing Paul and authenticates the content of the whole of what follows'. Therefore, I reject Kwangju Bank's submissions in this regard.

**6.28** One commentator who agrees with the decision in this case also suggests it is arguable that the reasoning is wrong. Richard Bethell-Jones suggests that 'The automatic insertion of a name in a header is hardly something that any person (including a company) would regard as having the solemn authenticating properties of a "signature"'.[48] It is suggested that this argument is to ignore the underlying rationale of the SWIFT system between banks.

**6.29** Jeffrey Cole J made similar observations on this precise point in the Illinois case of *Princeton Industrial, Products, Inc., v. Precision Metals Corp.*,[49] in which he said, at 820–1:

> It would seem that, for PMC, nothing can be done through email unless the individual sending the email goes through the physical process of typing her name at the bottom. It's not clear how a recipient or anyone could distinguish between a physically keystroked name and one that is attached to the sender's email automatically. So, for PMC, all electronic commerce would be held hostage to swearing contests over whether an individual typed their name or it was generated automatically by their email account. One might say that's ridiculous or, as Judge Cardozo more artfully put it in regards to the statute of frauds:
>
>> The statute must not be pressed to the extreme of a literal and rigid logic. Some compromise is inevitable if words are to fulfill their function as symbols of things and of ideas. How many identifying tokens we are to exact, the reason and common sense of the situation must tell us.

48 R. Bethell-Jones, 'Digital signatures and the statutory signature requirement', *Lloyds Maritime and Commercial Law Quarterly*, 2 (2012), pp. 184–8 at p. 186.

49 120 F.Supp.3d 812 (2015), 87 UCC Rep.Serv.2d 460.

> *Marks v. Cowdin*, 226 N.Y. 138, 143–144, 123 N.E. 139, 141 (1919). History – as well as reason and common sense – tells us we have sufficient identifying tokens here.
>
> ...
>
> Thus, contrary to what PMC seems to be driving at, Ms. Schleifer's intent can be satisfied and shown without her having to testify at a trial. Otherwise, most signatures on most contracts, electronic or otherwise, would have to be tested at trial. And every contractual obligation could be avoided; in other words, fraud could be accomplished by the 'extreme ... literal and rigid' application of the statute of frauds that PMC appears to be espousing.

**6.30** Approaching the question from the point of view of how the technology is set up is one way of helping to determine this particular issue. Arguably, if an organization authorizes an employee to insert the name, address and contact details of the legal entity into an email client, then it must be appropriate for the organization to put recipients on notice that they can or cannot use this information as a form of signature, or to prove intent, or that the recipient cannot rely on such information to bind the company for any legal purpose. When reaching judgments on such issues, it cannot be correct to ignore the way the technology is set up and used, although the question of intent remains.[50]

## Attachments to emails

**6.31** The issue of intent to sign is of relevance to attachments, as noted by Wall MJ in the New York case of *Pepco Energy Services, Inc., v. Geiringer*,[51] in which the judge granted the plaintiff's motion for summary judgment. In this instance, the defendant argued that a letter attached to an email was executed, despite the lack of a signature. The argument was based on the proposition that the name typed in the letter was a form of signature, and if it was not a form of signature, then the name in the email constituted an electronic signature that acted to sign the letter. The judge rejected these arguments. First, he indicated that the name typed on the letter was not capable of being a signature;[52] the name, title and corporate

50 The English case of *J Pereira Fernandes SA v. Mehta* [2006] 1 WLR 1543; [2006] 2 All ER 891; [2006] 1 All ER (Comm) 885; [2006] All ER (D) 264 (Apr); [2006] IP & T 546; *The Times* 16 May 2006; [2006] EWHC 813 (Ch) and the Singaporean case of *SM Integrated Transware Ltd v. Schenker Singapore (Pte) Ltd* [2005] 2 SLR 651, [2005] SGHC 58 are discussed elsewhere.

51 The letter is replicated in full in the Order discussed and set out in *Pepco Energy Services, Inc., v. Geiringer*, 2009 WL 3644295 (E.D.N.Y.) at 12; the order was reconsidered at the request of the defendant in *Pepco Energy Services, Inc., v. Geiringer*, 2010 WL 318284 (E.D.N.Y.), where the judge considered the electronic signature in more detail.

52 See the New York cases of 1911: *Landeker v. Co-operative Bldg. Bank*, 130 N.Y.Supp. 780 and 1919: *Cohen v. Wolgel*, 107 Misc. Rep. 505, 176 N.Y.S. 764 *affirmed* 191 A.D. 883, 180 NY.S. 933 where, in construing statutes that have been repealed but replaced with similar statutes, a typewritten name was considered to be a signature.

affiliation typed at the bottom of the letter appeared in a format that would normally appear under a manuscript signature, and there was no evidence to indicate that the letter was intended to be signed – in fact, there was evidence to demonstrate that there was no intent to sign the letter.

**6.32** A similar question arose in *SN4, LLC, v. Anchor Bank, FSB*[53] before the Court of Appeals of Minnesota. In this instance, a series of emails were exchanged between the parties relating to the sale and purchase of real estate. SN4 argued that Anchor Bank 'signed' the contract as the result of signatures in two relevant emails. The court rejected this argument. Both parties anticipated that they would enter into a written contract signed with manuscript signatures, a point stated explicitly in the relevant email exchanges. The court concluded, at 569, that:

> ... no reasonable fact-finder could determine that Nemec and Berg's electronic signatures are logically associated with the purported July 18th agreement attached to their emails. Although the evidence indicates that Nemec and Berg intended to electronically sign their email messages, the evidence is insufficient to establish that they intended to electronically sign the email attachment.

**6.33** In terms of the evidence of the sequence of the application of electronic signatures, the timing of the insertion of an electronic signature can be significant, as in *R v. Delalla*[54] before the Supreme Court of British Columbia. In this case, an information was quashed because the Justice of the Peace who laid the information signed the attestation electronically 12 seconds before the informant signed his attestation.

## Partial document with separate signature page

**6.34** As technology is developed and used, so individuals will adjust their behaviour and adapt accordingly. It is undoubtedly the experience of many lawyers across the world that some clients will expect them to work at an impossibly fast pace when negotiating and entering into contractual relationships. The need for speed has increased significantly since the world became networked digitally. For this reason, contracts will be formed and real estate purchased solely relying of documents in digital format. In most cases, a document in digital format is a perfectly acceptable way of entering into legal relations. However, the digital environment often means that our concept of a 'document' has had to change. Technically, there is only digital data, but for the purposes of this discussion, we only know of documents on paper – thus we associate a contract as recorded on paper and signed with manuscript signatures on the relevant page. In developing the terms of a contract, the signature page is often left until the document is

53 848 N.W.2d 559 (Minn.App. 2014).

54 2015 BCSC 592. Compare *R v. McGrath* 2015 BCPC 5, [2015] B.C.W.L.D. 1815, [2015] B.C.J. No. 136, 119 W.C.B. (2d) 55 where the information was declared to be valid.

finished to the satisfaction of the parties. What can then occur will depend on the parties and the advice they receive from their lawyers. A number of options arise: the signature page is signed with the manuscript signature of each party who happen to be together; the signature page, containing a number of signatures for people across continents is signed by each on a separate piece of paper and then scanned; perhaps each signatory appends a digital signature at different times to the document. Whatever method is used, it is highly likely that the document and the signature pages might well be separate documents. In such circumstances, it then becomes necessary to undertake appropriate measures to prevent additional pages from being added to the agreement that have not been agreed, and for the signature pages, or signatures generally, to be properly associated with the agreement,[55] and for draft signature pages to be dealt with appropriately.[56] In Scotland, this particular issue is now dealt with by the Legal Writings (Counterparts and Delivery) (Scotland) Act 2015.[57]

**6.35** This cannot be the proper working mechanism in criminal matters. Morse J rejected an 'e-ticket' in the New York case of *People v. Rose*,[58] where computer-generated simplified traffic information and supporting depositions were generated by a device. At the time, the e-ticket was 'signed' before any information was placed on the ticket. This meant the arresting officer was signing an essentially blank document.

## Forms of electronic signature

**6.36** Electronic signatures are manifest in a variety of forms, all of which can demonstrate the intent of the signing party to authenticate the data. Unfortunately, the terms 'electronic signature' and 'digital signature' tend to be

55 For which see *Garguilo v. Gershinson* [2012] EWLandRA 2011_0377 in the context of a lease; *Gopaul v. Naidoo* [2014] EWHC 2684 (QB) regarding the undertaking of the redevelopment of two properties by conversion into six flats.

56 For draft signatures, see *Mercury Tax Group Ltd, R (on the application of) v HM Commissioners of Revenue & Customs* [2009] BTC 3, [2008] EWHC 2721 (Admin), [2008] STI 2670, [2009] Lloyd's Rep FC 135, [2009] STC 743; *Execution of documents by virtual means* (16 February 2010) http://www.lawsociety.org.uk/support-services/advice/practice-notes/execution-of-documents-by-virtual-means/; *Note on execution of documents at a virtual signing or closing* (The Law Society Company Law Committee and The City of London Law Society Company Law and Financial Law Committees, May 2009 (including minor amendments – February 2010)) http://www.citysolicitors.org.uk/attachments/article/121/20100226-Advice-prepared-on-guidance-on-execution-of-documents-at-a-virtual-signing-or-closing.pdf; *Practice Note: Execution of a document using an electronic signature* (21 July 2016), available at http://www.lawsociety.org.uk/support-services/advice/practice-notes/execution-of-a-document-using-an-electronic-signature/.

57 H. MacQueen and C. Garland, 'Signatures in Scots law: form, effect, and burden of proof', *Juridical Review* (2015), pp. 107–34.

58 11 Misc.3d 200 (2005), 805 N.Y.S.2d 506, 2005 N.Y. Slip Op. 25526.

used interchangeably.[59] This creates confusion.[60] In essence, a digital signature is data appended to, or a cryptographic transformation of, a data unit that allows a recipient of the data to prove the source and integrity of the data unit. The digital signature mechanism defines two processes, that of the purported signing of a data unit by the person initiating the signature, which is a private action, and verifying a signed data unit by using the procedures and information publicly available. A digital signature is a signature that is specifically based on asymmetric cryptography, coupled with a one-way hash function. A digital signature is a particular type of signature that is usually brought about by the use of a public key infrastructure.[61] A digital signature is not a plain sequence of numbers.[62] It is often asserted that the digital signature provides a higher degree of certainty for the recipient. However, little attention is paid to illustrating the significant technical and legal obstacles to this assertion, or that the verification process is opaque, that a digital signature can be removed from a document in electronic format without trace,[63] and that a public key infrastructure provides for encryption, not the process of signing.

**6.37** By comparison, the term 'electronic signature' is anything in electronic form that can be used to demonstrate a signing entity intended their signature

59 This is also pointed out in paragraph 2.2 of the Final Report of the EESSI Expert Team dated 20 July 1999 European Electronic Signature Standardization Initiative, and on page 16 of OECD, A Global action plan for electronic commerce prepared by business with recommendations from governments, 7–9 October 1998, Ottawa, Canada (Directorate for Science, Technology and Industry Steering Committee for the Preparation of the Ottawa Ministerial Conference, SG/EC(98)11/REV2); see also GUIDEC II, 'General Usage for International Digitally Ensured Commerce' for further discussion of the terms. GUIDEC II does not use the term 'electronic signature' but 'digital signature', thus adding to the confusion. In addition, the Draft Guide to Enactment of the UNCITRAL Model Law on Electronic Signatures, dated 12 – 23 March 2001 (A/CN.9/WG.IV/WP.88) also appears to refer to digital signatures and electronic signatures interchangeably, see paragraphs 31 to 62. The European Union adds to the confusion even more by refusing to refer to the term 'digital signature' in the Directive for electronic signatures. Yet further confusion is rendered with the title of at least one legal text book: D. Campbell (ed.), *E-Commerce and the Law of Digital Signatures* (Dobbs Ferry, N.Y.: Oceana Publications, 2005); A. Srivastava, *Electronic Signatures for B2B Contracts: Evidence from Australia* (Springer, 2013), although such confusion does not occur, however, in A. Srivastava, 'Businesses' perception of electronic signatures: an Australian study', *Digital Evidence and Electronic Signature Law Review*, 6 (2009), pp. 45–65.

60 Also noted by C. Adams and S. Lloyd, *Understanding PKI Concepts, Standards, and Deployment Considerations* (2nd edn., Boston, M.A.: Addison-Wesley, 2002), pp. 184–5.

61 See also paragraph 33 to UNCITRAL Model Law on Electronic Signatures, Guide to Enactment.

62 In *Ontario Workplace Safety and Insurance Appeals Tribunal* Decision No. 2877/07R 2008 CarswellOnt 8624, 2008 ONWSIAT 3111, an NSR (a seven-digit number), where 'NSR' stands for 'no signature required', is incorrectly described as a digital signature.

63 A. McCullagh, W. Caelli and P. Little, 'Signature stripping: a digital dilemma' *Journal of Information, Law and Technology*, 1 (2001), http://www2.warwick.ac.uk/fac/soc/law/elj/jilt/2001_1/mccullagh.

to have legal effect, as illustrated in the Connecticut case of *Peruta v. Outback Steakhouse of Florida, Inc.*,[64] where an employee gave evidence that tips were declared by putting the information into a computer when they left the restaurant and filled out a 'checkout form'. It was a matter of law to be decided by the court at trial whether such an act constituted an electronic signature, but a glance at the Connecticut Uniform Electronic Transactions Act, especially Sec. 1-272, 'Legal recognition of electronic records, electronic signatures and electronic contracts', taken together with the definition of an electronic signature at Sec. 1-267(8), would appear that such an action was an electronic signature. An electronic signature, especially when defined in legislation, tends to represent a generic response to the concept of authentication, and is to be understood in such a context. A signature can be manifest in different forms,[65] and the term 'electronic signature' is used to reflect methods other than the use of a public key infrastructure to sign a message or document, such as the typing of a name on an electronic document, or the capture of the dynamics of a manuscript signature.

**6.38** For the sake of clarity, the term 'electronic signature' is used to denote the generic concept of a signature that is brought about by the use of a computer or computer-like device, and includes a digital signature as one form of electronic signature.[66] We should also be alert to new forms of electronic signature as they are developed and used.[67] However, this does not prevent the terms used to describe electronic signatures from adding to or increasing the confusion for failing to describe the form of electronic signature at issue. This is illustrated in the Zimbabwean case of *Tedco Mgmt Svcs (PVT) Ltd v. Grain Marketing Board*,[68] in which an employee stole a total of $204,818.61 by adding the electronic signature of an authorized signatory to a series of cheques. The signatures were described as 'machine' signatures printed from the computer, which implies that the company caused authorized images of manuscript signatures to be scanned and stored on a computer. Another illustration is the Texas case of *In re Piranha, Inc., Debtor, Berger v. Piranha, Inc.*,[69] where an electronic signature was attached to a form sent to the Securities and Exchange Commission purporting to be the resignation of a director. It was established that the legislation did not prevent the person whose signature was used from challenging the signature and

64 50 Conn.Supp. 51, 913 A.2d 1160 (Conn.Super. 2006).

65 The use of 's/' instead of '/s/' when indicating the electronic signature of an attorney is irrelevant: Federal, 3rd Circuit, *Xu v. Naqvi*, 537 Fed.Appx. 76 (2013), 112 A.F.T.R.2d 2013-6538, 2013-2 USTC P 50,556.

66 In the British Columbia case of *Ghaed v. Telus Communications Co.* 2013 BCSC 1675, a digital signature is referred to, but it is debatable whether this particular form of signature was in operation by Dr Ghaed, given his lack of technical knowledge.

67 J. Friedman, 'Signing your next deal with your Twitter @username: the legal uses of identity based cryptography', *Canadian Journal of Law and Technology*, 13 (2015), pp. 33–56.

68 1996 (1) ZLR 109 (SC).

69 297 B.R. 78 (N.D.Tex. 2003), 2003 WL 21468504 (N.D. Tex.), *affirmed* 83 Fed.Appx. 19.

contending he did not execute, adopt or authorize its use, but the report does not make it clear what type of electronic signature was under discussion, although consideration of the relevant regulation[70] appears to indicate that it was a typed name.[71]

**6.39** Examples of electronic signatures are discussed in the following chapters.

70 Part 232—Regulation S-T—General Rules and Regulations for Electronic Filings § 232.302 Signatures.

71 Other examples include:

Florida: *Florida Department of Agriculture and Consumer Services v. Haire*, 836 So.2d 1040 (Fla.App. 4 Dist. 2003); the corrected opinion is *Haire v. Florida Department of Agriculture and Consumer Services,* Nos SC03-446 & Sc03-552, February 12, 2004, available online at http://archive.law.fsu.edu/library/flsupct/sc03-446/op-sc03-446-corrected.pdf.

New York: *People of the State of New York v. Rose*, 11 Misc.3d 200, 805 N.Y.S.2d 506; *People of the State of New York v. Cortella*, 12 Misc.3d 666, 814 N.Y.S.2d 514 - (both cases were in relation to the use of an electronic signature of a police officer on an electronically generated traffic deposition (which was accepted), but concern was expressed that the signature was already in the document before the document was completed by the officer).

Texas: *Gunda Corporation, LLC, v. Yazhari*, 2013 WL 440577 (in this case it might have been a scanned signature, a copy of which was held by the organization, which in turn will mean the organization will need to prove that the signature could not be used by any other person with access to the system).

Utah: *Anderson v. Bell*, 234 P.3d 1147 (the use of electronic signatures of registered voters to enable a candidate to stand for election as governor).

Missouri: *Mead v. Moloney Securities Co., Inc.*, 274 S.W.3d 537 (electronic signature on a form sent to the Financial Industry Regulatory Authority).

Pennsylvania: *Walter v. Magee-Women's Hospital of UPMC Health System*, 876 A.2d 400.

# 7

# Electronic sound

**7.1** It is possible to record sounds digitally when a person speaks to software code. In the United States of America, electronic signatures are defined by s 106(5) of the Electronic Signatures in Global and National Commerce Act, 106-229, which provides:

> Electronic signature. – The term 'electronic signature' means an electronic sound, symbol, or process, attached to or logically associated with a contract or other record and executed or adopted by a person with the intent to sign the record.

**7.2** In the June 2007 9th circuit case of *Shroyer v. New Cingular Wireless Services, Inc.*,[1] a person indicated their assent, and thereby executed an electronic signature over the telephone, by selecting the answer 'Yes' in response to the statement 'You agree to the terms as stated in the Wireless Service Agreement and terms of service.' Although the judgment of the Court of Appeals did not explicitly indicate that this form of electronic signature is valid under the Act, nevertheless this decision is in keeping with the definition of electronic signature, and is a perfectly acceptable form of electronic signature. In December 2007, the Court of Appeals in Kansas also reached a similar conclusion. In the case of *In the Matter of the Marriage of Takusagawa*,[2] the appellant argued that the provisions of the Kansas Statute of Frauds required a written signature where an agreement to the transfer of land was part of the divorce settlement. The trial judge approved the terms of an oral separation agreement on the final day of the hearing, and the details of the agreement were put on the record. Both parties stated under oath that what was recorded by the court was their understanding of the terms of the agreement. The transcript indicated that the judge asked the appellant 'Ma'am, is that your understanding of the agreement?' The appellant replied 'Yes'.[3] It is certain that the appellant did not affix her manuscript signature to any document. The issue was whether the oral response to a judge was a form of signature. The judge who wrote the judgment of the court, Leben J, cited the 1921 decision of the Supreme Court of Kansas in *Whitlow v. Board of Education*,[4] in which the members of the school board voted at a meeting to sell some land. When the appellant handed her cheque over in payment and to complete the transaction, the members of the board refused to complete the sale. The minutes of the meeting indicated that a motion to sell the land to Josephine Whitlow was

1 498 F.3d 976.

2 38 Kan.App.2d 401, 166 P.3d 440.

3 38 Kan.App.2d 401 at 410.

4 108 Kan. 604, 196 P. 772.

S. Mason, *Electronic Signatures in Law* (London: Institute of Advanced Legal Studies, 2016), chapter 7, 'Electronic sound', pp. 201–3.

made and passed, and that the members of the board authorized the president of the board to sign a deed in exchange for payment. The Supreme Court of Kansas rejected the argument of the school board that the Statute of Frauds prevented the agreement being enforced because the minutes of the board had not been signed. It was determined that the minutes as recorded by the clerk were an authentic record that the law required the board to keep. In this respect, the minutes constituted a sufficient memorandum of the contract to bind the board under the Statute of Frauds. In this instance, a signature was not necessary where a public record was maintained by law, which in turn provided authentication of the formation and terms of the contract. The members of the court considered that a properly certified transcript of a court hearing was superior to the minutes recorded by the clerk to the school board, and found that a signature was not necessary where 'a court transcript providing the terms of the agreement and the oral assent of the party to be charged with the agreement that has been fairly stated on the record of the proceeding.'[5] However, the discussion did not end at this point. Leben J then went on to consider the provisions of the Uniform Electronic Transactions Act K. S. A. 2006 Supp 16-1601, on the assumption that the transcript of the agreement was recorded on equipment that required electricity to enable it to work. Based on this assumption, the judge then considered ss 16-1602(f), (h) and (i), which reads as follows:

> (f) "Electronic" means relating to technology having electrical, digital, magnetic, wireless, optical, electromagnetic or similar capabilities.
>
> ........
>
> (h) "Electronic record" means a record created, generated, sent, communicated, received or stored by electronic means.
>
> (i) "Electronic signature" means an electronic sound, symbol or process attached to or logically associated with a record and executed or adopted by a person with the intent to sign the record.

**7.3** He concluded that where a party makes an oral statement in legal proceedings before a judge, and '... assuming that the court reporter's equipment was consistent with modern practice, it would appear that the electronic capture of Mieko's oral assent that this was the agreement would satisfy the statute of frauds. No more is needed to show that Mieko made or adopted the agreement'.[6] This line of reasoning is far from convincing, and arguably stretches the meaning of electronic signature beyond the terms of the statute.[7] The final claim to

5 38 Kan.App.2d 401 at 409.

6 38 Kan.App.2d 401 at 410.

7 The same could be argued if a will is recorded on tape, and not written down, as in the case of *In the Matter of the Estate of Reed v. Buckley*, 672 P.2d 829 (Wyo. 1983); in *Franklin County Cooperative v. MFC Services (A.A.L.)*, 441 So.2d 1376 (Miss. 1983) it was determined by the Supreme Court of Mississippi that the statement 'OK, we will take care of it' made

support the thesis that both parties entered into a binding agreement in court is more convincing: that an oral settlement placed on the record and acknowledged by the parties in open court should be sufficient to satisfy the requirement of the Statute of Frauds, especially because the law in Kansas allowed for oral separation agreements in divorce proceedings, and such agreements can be incorporated into the decree of divorce if approved by the judge.

**7.4** Where one party to a conversation records what is said without the knowledge of the other party or parties, it does not follow that promises made, including a statement that might be construed as an electronic signature, will be valid. In the case of *Sawyer v. Mills*,[8] heard at appeal before the Supreme Court of Kentucky, Barbara Sawyer and her husband recorded a conversation with Mr Mills, in which he made promises to make certain payments. Among other things, it was determined that any contract formed during this conversation was not enforceable under the provision of the Statute of Frauds. Further, the court considered that the agreement by Mr Mills did not constitute an electronic signature just because it was identifiable and was identified at trial as being his. In explaining this in giving the opinion of the court, Nobel J said, at 8:

> There must be intent to attach or logically associate the electronic signature to the agreement, that is, an intent to execute the contract. That was impossible here, because the medium on which the alleged agreement and electronic signature were recorded (the audio tape) was used surreptitiously. Mills did not know he was being recorded when he went to the Sawyers' art studio. Thus, Mills's identifiable voice on the tape, even if construed as an electronic signature, was procured without Mills's knowledge or intent, and would be tantamount to a forgery which cannot be used to demonstrate a valid contract.

**7.5** Although the comments made by Mr Mills were capable of being construed as an electronic signature, the text of the statute envisages more than a mere spoken assent that is recorded in secret. The statute requires the electronic equivalent of a signature, that is, an electronic sound, symbol, or process that demonstrates an intention to enter the agreement. Furthermore, the parties put the agreement into writing. Mr Mills refused to sign the written contract. This refusal to sign by Mr Mills demonstrated that he did not intend to execute or adopt anything he said in the conversation.

---

over the telephone had the capacity of proving intent to enter a contract when the words are subsequently written down in a memorandum.

8 Ky., 295 S.W.3d 79.

# 8

# The 'I accept' and 'wrap' methods of indicating intent

## Click wrap

**8.1** Clicking the 'I accept' or 'I agree' icon (also known as 'click wrap') to confirm the intention to enter a contract when buying goods or services electronically is now a very popular method of demonstrating intent. In the United States of America, the phrase 'wrap' has become common.[1] The action of clicking an icon is capable of providing evidence of the process that is executed or adopted by the person clicking on the icon – that is, the user is required to undertake a positive activity.[2] This is certainly implied in the Canadian case of *Rudder v. Microsoft Corp*,[3] and has been widely accepted in the United States of America implicitly,[4] and explicitly in respect of the formation of commercial online contracts and

1 N. C. Kim, *Wrap Contracts Foundations and Ramifications* (New York: Oxford University Press, 2013); S. Blount, *Electronic Contracts* (2nd edn., Chatswood, NSW: LexisNexis Butterworths Australia, 2015).

2 Although technically literate people are capable of installing software and by-passing the need to click on the 'I agree' icon, for which see *Aral v. Earthlink, Inc.*, 134 Cal.App.4th 544, 36 Cal.Rptr.3d 229 (determined by members of the Court of Appeal, Second District, Division 4, California, to be a contract of adhesion); where there are a succession of changes to the terms uploaded on to a website, it is incumbent on the issuer of such terms to ensure they retain evidence to prove when a person clicked to acknowledge the new terms were received, as in the Maryland case of *Harold H. Huggins Realty, Inc., v. FNC, INC.*, 575 F.Supp.2d 696; in *Rogers v. Dell Computer Corporation*, 127 P.3d 560 (Okla. 2005), Dell failed to provide evidence to demonstrate where the contract was formed.

3 (1999), 2 C.P.R. (4th) 474, 47 C.C.L.T. (2d) 168 (Ont. Sup. Ct.), FSR (1996) 367. See also *Kanitz v. Rogers Cable Inc.*, (2002), 58 O.R. (3d) 299 (Sup. Ct.).

4 Federal 6th circuit: *CompuServe, Incorporated v. Patterson*, 89 F.3d 1257 (6th Cir. 1996).

California: *America Online, Inc., v. Superior Court of Alameda County*, 90 Cal.App.4th 1 (2001), 108 Cal. Rptr.2d 699, 01 Cal. Daily Op. Serv. 5191, Daily Journal D.A.R. 6367; *Koresko v. RealNetworks, Inc.*, 291 F.Supp.2d 1157 (E.D.Cal. 2003).

Florida: *America Online, Inc., v. Booker*, 781 So.2d 423 (Fla.App. 3 Dist. 2001).

Illinois: *In re RealNetworks, Inc., Privacy Litigation*, 2000 WL 631341 (N.D.Ill.); *Lieschke v. Realnetworks, Inc.*, 2000 WL 198424 (ND Ill.); *DeJohn v. The .TV Corporation Int'l*, 245 F.Supp.2d 913 (C.D.Ill. 2003).

New Jersey: *Caspi v. Microsoft Network, L.L.C.*, 323 N.J. Super. 188, 732 A.2d 528 (N.J.Super.A.D. 1999).

Texas: *Barnett v. Network Solutions, Inc.*, 38 S.W.3d 200 (Tex.App.-Eastland 2001).

Washington: *M. A. Mortenson Company, Inc., v. Timberline Software Corporation*, 970 P.2d 803 (Wash.App. Div. 1 1999) affirmed *M. A. Mortenson Company, Inc., v. Timberline Software Corporation*, 998 P.2d 305 (Wash. 2000) (clicking the 'I accept' icon was part of the formation of a 'layered contract'; note the dissenting opinion of Sanders J, and also the majority of the members of the Supreme Court of Kansas also disagreed with the analysis, for which see *Wachter Manufacturing Company v. Dexter & Chaney, Inc.*, 144 P.3d 747 (Kans. 2006), although note the dissenting opinion of Luckert, J).

S. Mason, *Electronic Signatures in Law* (London: Institute of Advanced Legal Studies, 2016), chapter 8, 'The "I accept" and "wrap" methods of indicating intent', pp. 205–14.

software agreements,[5] in the formation of employment contracts,[6] in respect of requiring children to upload written work to identify plagiarism,[7] where a child

5 Federal: *Treiber & Straub, Inc., d/b/a Treiber & Straub Jewelers v. United Parcel Service, Inc.*, 474 F.3d 379 (7th Cir. 2007).

10th Circuit: *Hancock v. American Telephone and Telegraph Company, Inc.*, 701 F.3d 1248 (2012), 90 Fed. R. Evid. Serv. 103.

California: *Hotmail Corporation v. Van$ Money Pie Inc.*, 1998 WL 388389, 47 U.S.P.Q.2d 1020; *Comb v. PayPal, Inc.*, 218 F.Supp.2d 1165 (N.D.Cal. 2002).

Carolina: *Bergenstock v. Legalzoon.com, Inc.*, 2015 WL 3866703

Colombia: *Forrest v. Verizon Communications, Inc.*, 805 A.2d 1007 (D.C. 2002).

Florida: *Siedle v. National Association of Securities Dealers*, 248 F.Supp.2d 1140 (M.D.Fla. 2002); *Salco Distributors, LLC v. iCode, Inc., 2006* WL 449156 (M.D.Fla.).

Illinois: *Mudd-Lyman Sales and Service Corporation v. United Parcel Service, Inc.*, 236 F.Supp.2d 907.

Indiana: *Adsit Company, Inc., v. Gustin*, 874 N.E.2d 1018 (Ind.App. 2007); *Appliance Zone, LLC v. Nextag, Inc.*, 2009 WL 5200572 (S.D.Ind.), 93 U.S.P.Q.2d 1540.

Kansas: *Mortgage Plus, Inc., v. DocMagic, Inc., d/b/a Document Systems, Inc.*, 2004 WL 2331918 (D.Kan.), 55 UCC Rep.Serv.2d 58.

Maine: *Stenzel v. Dell, Inc.*, 870 A.2d 133 (Me. 2005).

Maryland: *Blue Bird, LLC v. Nolan*, No. 302920-V (Md. Cir. Ct. Oct. 23, 2008).

Massachusetts: *I.Lan Systems, Inc., v. Netscout Service Level Corp.*, 183 F.Supp.2d 328 (D.Mass. 2002) (Young CJ, indicated at 338 'The only issue before the Court is whether click wrap license agreements are an appropriate way to form contracts, and the Court holds that they are.'); *Hughes v. McMenamon*, 204 F.Supp.2d 178 (D.Mass. 2002).

Missouri: *Davidson & Associates, Inc., v. Internet Gateway*, 334 F.Supp.2d 1164 (E.D.Mo. 2004); *Burcham v. Expedia, Inc.*, 2009 WL 586513 (E.D.Mo.).

New Jersey: *Bergraft v. e-Bay, Inc.*, (N.J. Super. Ct. Oct. 1, 2003) the Order is available online from the website of Professor Eric Goldman (http://eric_goldman.tripod.com/caselaw/begraftvebay.pdf).

New York: *Moore v. Microsoft Corporation*, 293 A.D.2d 587, 741 N.Y.S.2d 91, 48 UCC Rep.Serv.2d; *Person v. Google Inc.*, 456 F.Supp.2d 488 (S.D.N.Y. 2006); *Universal Grading Service v. eBay, Inc.*, 2009 WL 2029796 (E.D.N.Y.); *Scherillo v. Dun & Bradstreet, Inc.*, 684 F.Supp.2d 313; *5381 Partners, LLC v. Sharesale.com, Inc.*, 2013 WL 5328324; *Nicosia v. Amazon, Inc.*, 84 F.Supp.3d 142 (2015); *Whitt v. Prosper Funding LLC*, 2015 WL 4254062.

Pennsylvania: *Bragg v. Linden Research, Inc.*, 487 F.Supp.2d 593 (E.D.Pa. 2007); *Feldman v. Google, Inc.*, 513 F.Supp.2d 229 (E.D.Pa. 2007); *Novak d/b/a Petswarehouse. Com v. Tucows, Inc.*, 2007 WL 922306 (E.D.N.Y.).

Rhode Island: *Groff v. America Online, Inc.*, 1998 WL 307001 (R.I.Super.) (this is an unpublished opinion); *Bar-Ayal v. Time Warner Cable, Inc., 2006* WL 2990032 (S.D.N.Y.).

Texas: *Recursion Software, Inc., v. Interactive Intelligence, Inc.*, 425 F.Supp.2d 756 (N.D.Tex. 2006); *RealPage, Inc., v. EPS, Inc.*, 560 F.Supp.2d 539, 545 (E.D.Tex. 2007); *In re Online Travel Company Hotel Booking Antitrust Litigation*, 953 F.Supp.2d 713 (2013), 2013-1 Trade Cases P 78,428.

Washington: *Dix v. ICT Group, Inc.*, 125 Wash.App. 929, 106 P.3d 841 (Wash.App. Div. 3 2005), affirmed 160 Wash.2d 826, 161 P.3d 1016; *Riensche v. Cingular Wireless, LLC*, 2006 WL 3827477 (W.D.Wash.).

6 Ohio: *Bell v. Hollywood Entertainment Corporation*, 2006 WL 2192053 (Ohio App. 8 Dist.).

Pennsylvania: *Verizon Communications, Inc., v. Pizzirani*, 462 F.Supp.2d 648 (E.D.Pa. 2006).

7 Virginia: *A.V. ex rel. Vanderhye v. iParadigms, L.L.C.*, 544 F.Supp.2d 473 (E.D. Va. Mar. 11, 2008) (reversed in part on other grounds in *A.V. ex rel. Vanderhye v. iParadigms, L.L.C.*, 562 F.3d 630 (4th Cir 2009)).

continues to use a website after initiating legal action against the website,[8] where a player agrees to waive the right to take legal action against an athletic league,[9] and where an agent clicks to accept the terms,[10] although breaching the terms of use of a website does not necessarily mean the person breaking the terms has committed a crime under the provisions of the Computer Fraud and Abuse Act, 18 U.S.C. §1030.[11]

**8.2** The Texas case of *Via Viente Taiwan, L.P. v. United Parcel Service, Inc.*[12] is an example of how judges in the US tend to approach the matter. In this case, the defendant entered into a contract to ship the beverages made by the plaintiff to Taiwan. For UPS to do this effectively, it was necessary to upload the relevant UPS software to the plaintiff's network, which included a software license agreement. The hearing before Schell DJ had to determine whether the parties entered into a valid binding contract, and if so, whether the forum selection clause was valid. The plaintiffs argued that the license agreement was not valid. Schell DJ disagreed. He pointed out that the actions of the employees of the plaintiff belied their argument, in that, first, the Carrier Agreement required the plaintiffs to use the UPS online software program, and that the relevant software had to be installed by a UPS representative, which incorporated a set-up process which included terms of service that had to be agreed with the click of an icon. None of this could be achieved without the agreement of employees of the plaintiff, and the judge indicated that it would be difficult to believe that the plaintiff would permit a UPS technician to have unsupervised access to the computers to install the program. The judge said that 'Not only would such a sequence of events be difficult to believe, but it runs contrary to the Defendant's ordinary procedures.'[13] In this instance, the judge roundly rejected the arguments of the plaintiff. In taking a robust approach to the fact that technology was now a significant part of office life, the judge reached the conclusion that a 'click wrap' agreement was perfectly in keeping with the times.[14] In *Scarcella v. America Online*, on an application by America Online to dismiss the claim of the plaintiff in a small claims action because of lack of jurisdiction, the judge at first instance outlined the process

8 Illinois: *E.K.D., by her next friend v. Facebook, Inc.*, 885 F.Supp.2d 894 (2012)

9 *Stephenson v. Food Bank for New York City*, 21 Misc.3d 1132 (A), 875 N.Y.S.2d 824, 2008 WL 4934625 (N.Y.Sup.), 2008 N.Y. Sip Op. 52322(U).

10 *Siebert v. Amateur Athletic Union of the United States, Inc.*, 422 F.Supp.2d 1033 (D.Minn. 2006).

11 *United States of America v. Drew*, 259 F.R.D. 449 (the accused, with others, set up a fictitious profile of a male in a social networking website; then they contacted Megan Meier (aged 13 years) under the pseudonym 'Josh Evans'. They flirted with her over a number of days before sending a message that 'the world would be a better place without her in it.' Megan subsequently killed herself.

12 2009 WL 3908729 (E.D. Tex.).

13 2009 WL 3908729 (E.D. Tex.) at 2.

14 798 N.Y.S.2d 348, 2004 WL 2093429 (N.Y. City Civ. Ct. 2004) *affirmed* 11 Misc.3d 19, 811 N.Y.S.2d 858 (2005).

by which customers agreed the terms of a Member Agreement. Neither court commented on the validity or otherwise of the enforceability of the action of clicking the 'I Agree' icon, but interestingly America Online stated on the website 'if you are eager to just go and explore the service ... That's OK'. The claimant argued that by enabling a potential customer to bypass the action of agreeing the terms, this was deceptive.

**8.3** For a 'click wrap' contract to be enforceable, it is necessary that the party to whom the contract is directed is notified that a contract exists, and that it is intended to apply to them. In the 9th circuit case of *Knutson v. Sirius XM Radio, Inc.*,[15] Mr Knutson, in purchasing a motor vehicle from Toyota, was not aware that a trial subscription to Sirius XM satellite radio that accompanied the purchase of the vehicle also meant that Sirius intended him to be bound by the terms of a contract that he was not aware existed.

**8.4** In England and Wales, the Law Commission has suggested that this form of signature is the technological equivalent of a manuscript signature using a cross.[16] It is suggested that this analysis is sound. This analysis is also in keeping with the decisions made by judges over the past two hundred years regarding the form that a manuscript signature may take. In English law, the validity of the signature depends on the function it performs, not necessarily the form a signature takes. Even if the act of clicking on an icon to order goods or services is deemed to be less secure than that provided by a manuscript signature, it does not follow that the reliability of the signature will affect its validity. Should a dispute occur between a buyer and a seller where one of the issues relates to the pressing of the icon, and the parties fail to resolve the matter, they will have to contemplate taking legal action. Before the matter reaches a court, both parties will have to pay particular attention to the quantity and quality of the evidence available to them. In all probability, the reliability of the signature will depend on the ability of one or both of the parties to adduce sufficient forensic evidence of a high enough quality to demonstrate whether the icon was clicked or not. Even if the relying party can prove that the icon was clicked, it will not follow that the purported buyer clicked it. The nexus between the action of clicking the icon and the identity of the person who purported to order the items may be difficult to resolve, bearing in mind the security risks associated with using the internet.

**8.5** The first instance decision in the case of *Bassano v. Toft*[17] is an example where the use of the 'I accept' icon was upheld in England under the provisions of the Consumer Credit Act 1974. It was argued by counsel for Mrs Bassano that the loan agreement was not executed by her in a manner that complied with the Act. The judge disagreed, indicating, at [43], that:

15 771 F.3d 559, 14 Cal. Daily Op. Serv. 12,769, 2014 Daily Journal D.A.R. 15,058.

16 Law Commission, 'Electronic commerce: formal requirements in commercial transactions advice from the Law Commission' (2001), 3.37; see also 3.36 and 3.38.

17 [2014] EWHC 377 (QB), [2014] Bus LR D9.

> s61 of the Act requires the agreement to be signed in the prescribed form, and the form prescribed at the time was that required by The Consumer Credit (Agreements) Regulations 2010 (SI 2010 No 1014). The only relevant prescription was in regulation 4(3)(a), which provides that the signature must be in a space indicated in the document for that purpose and dated. Regulation 4(5) recognises that a regulated agreement may be concluded electronically by regulation 4(5), and that the document may contain 'information about the process or means of providing, communicating or verifying the signature to be made by the debtor.' There was therefore nothing in the Consumer Credit Act 1974 to suggest that regulated agreements were capable of being signed by an electronic signature.

**8.6** This type of conflicting evidence, coupled with a denial that the email communications were sent by the sender, occurred in Germany in the three cases of OLG Köln, 19 U 16/02; LG Konstanz, 2 O 141/01 A; AG Erfurt, 28 C 2354/01.[18] The three individual defendants were asked to pay for items bought in internet auctions. The winning bids were sent from email accounts where the user can write the email on the website of the provider of the address. Each of the defendants had access to the address by means of a password, but denied taking part in the bidding process. All three cases were dismissed, because the relying party failed to prove to the satisfaction of the courts that the defendants sent the declarations, which meant the plaintiff failed to prove that a contract had been concluded. By the same token, exactly the same problem may occur with the use of digital signatures. Whether a user denies clicking on an icon or using their private key to sign a document or message, the problem will be the same: proving that the sending party carried out the action. In this respect, the difference between a digital signature and clicking an icon is a narrow one.

**8.7** Proof is central to the question. In the US case of *Kerr v. Dillard Stores Services, Inc.*,[19] the issue was whether an employee had clicked the 'I accept' icon in respect of an arbitration agreement. In this instance, the employer required employees to consent to arbitration by executing the arbitration agreement by way of an intranet computer system. For months, the employee had made it clear that they did not wish to sign the arbitration agreement, and refused to do so. Evidence was given to demonstrate how easy it was for a supervisor to reset an employee's password: indeed, this is just what a supervisor did in front of the plaintiff when the plaintiff had failed to log on to find out when she was next on duty. On the same day that the supervisor logged on to change the plaintiff's password, the computer system sent an internal email to the plaintiff, indicating

18 M. Knopp, Case Note, OLG Köln, Ur19 U 16/02; LG Konstanz, 2 O 141/01 A; AG Erfurt, 28 C 2354/01, *Digital Evidence and Electronic Signature Law Review*, 2 (2005), pp. 105–6; for a translation of Ur19 U 16/02, see H. Picot and M. Kast, *Digital Evidence and Electronic Signature Law Review*, 5 (2008), pp. 108–9.

19 2008 WL 2152046 (D. Kan.), 2009 WL 2525582 (D.Kan.); 2009 U.S. Dist. LEXIS 11792.

that the agreement had been 'signed'. The employee was adamant that they had not executed the agreement, and Vratil J concluded that it was unlikely that the plaintiff would not have spontaneously reversed her decision in front of the supervisor, and that the supervisor could have clicked on the 'I accept' icon as the plaintiff watched. The judge set out the problem:[20]

> The problem with Dillard's position is that it did not have adequate procedures to maintain the security of intranet passwords, to restrict authorized access to the screen which permitted electronic execution of the arbitration agreement, to determine whether electronic signatures were genuine or to determine who opened individual emails. While the record establishes that Champlin and plaintiff were at the kiosk on April 28, it does not show that they were there at precisely 3:26:20 p.m. Therefore, it is not inconceivable Champlin or a supervisor logged on to plaintiff's account and executed the agreement. The Court recognizes that defendants' burden of proof is not absolute certainty, but merely a preponderance of the evidence. At the same time, Dillard's has not demonstrated the efficacy of its security procedures with regard to electronic signatures. Therefore, its version of events is no more likely true than plaintiff's. For these reasons, this case basically turns on the burden of proof. Dillard's has the burden of proof and its evidence that plaintiff executed the arbitration agreement is not persuasive. On this record, the Court cannot find that it is more likely than not true that plaintiff executed the electronic agreement to arbitrate.

**8.8** This case illustrates how important proof is in the context of digital evidence.[21]

**8.9** In passing, Professor Preston notes that 'wrap' contracts are now considered to be enforceable without further inquiry, and the trend among judges in the US demonstrates a 'circularity of judicial review: one court finds a new kind of contract enforceable, and other courts then assume enforceability because "everyone is doing it" without performing a thorough analysis of the

20 2009 U.S. Dist. LEXIS 11792.

21 See California: *Martin v. Snappel Beverage Corp.*, 2005 WL 1580398; New York: *Zaltz v. Jdate*, 952 F.Supp.2d 439 (2013).

Massachusetts: *Ajemian, coadministrator, v. YAHOO!, Inc*,. 987 N.E.2d 604 (Yahoo could not provide any evidence that the 'accept' icon was clicked when opening an account).

New York: *Novak d/b/a Petswarehouse.Com v. Tucows, Inc* 2007 WL 922306 (E.D.N.Y.) and *The Prudential Insurance Company of America v. Dukoff and Estate of Shari Dukoff*, 674 F.Supp.2d 401; *Bynum v. Maplebear Inc.*, --- F.Supp.3d ---- (2016), 2016 WL 552058 (where a third-party electronic signature service was used to gather digital data to demonstrate the clicking on the agreement to agree the terms).

Washington: *Kwan v. Clearwire Corporation*, 2012 WL 32380.

earlier opinions and distinguishing the facts',[22] and cites Matheson, CJ in the case of *Hancock v. American Telephone & Telegraph Company, Inc.*,[23] where the judge states, at 1255, that 'Clickwrap agreements are increasingly common and "have routinely been upheld."' New terms to describe the methods devised to enforce contract terms on websites include 'sign-in-wraps' and 'scrollwrap'.[24]

**8.10** In the Queensland case of *Harding v. Brisbane City Council*,[25] the applicant used an online facility to appeal against a planning application. The person submitting the request was required to include details of a form of 'identification' as part of the submission process. Mr Harding typed in the number of his driving licence, but he made an error, and one of the numbers he typed in was incorrect. His application was rejected. At the appeal, the judge was required to determine, amongst other things, whether the input of an incorrect number merited the rejection of the submission. It did not. Robin QC DCJ held at [18] that:

> I think a common sense approach should be taken by which erroneous reproduction of more than a couple of digits (in the absence of special circumstances, such as the same number (exclusively) repeated – which may indicate some hardware or software malfunction) might be seen as creating some concern as to the signature, having regard to s 14(a) & (b) of the Act; on a commonsense approach in the present context, one wrong digit does not create any real concern.

**8.11** This discrepancy did not vitiate the submission as a properly made one. Robin QC DCJ was not correct in concluding that the driving licence constituted a 'signature'. The signature comprised the act of clicking of the 'accept' icon, and not the submission of the numbers identifying the driving licence.[26] The numbers identifying the driving licence acted as an additional item of evidence to demonstrate to the Council that the person making the submission was who they claimed to be, which is a different issue entirely.

## Browse wrap

**8.12** There is a category in the United States of America commonly called 'browse wrap' agreements, although there is some controversy with how judges

22 C. B. Preston, '"Please note: you have waived everything': can notice redeem online contracts?', *American University Law Review*, 64 (2015), pp. 535–90, at p. 543, including the further citations noted in the article.

23 701 F.3d 1248 (10th Cir. 2012).

24 New York: *Berkson v. Gogo, LLC*, 97 F.Supp.3d 359 (2015).

25 [2008] QPEC 75 (16 October 2008).

26 The 'I accept' icon was accepted in *eBay International AG v. Creative Festival Entertainment Pty Ltd* (ACN 098 183 281) [2006] FCA 1768.

apply the distinction between 'click wrap' and 'browse wrap' in case law.[27] Judges have also had to deal with cases that look like 'browse wrap', but are 'click wrap',[28] and what can be described as hybrid cases,[29] as described by Holwell, J at 838 in the case of *Fjeja v. Facebook, Inc.*:[30]

> Facebook's Terms of Use are somewhat like a browsewrap agreement in that the terms are only visible via a hyperlink, but also somewhat like a clickwrap agreement in that the user must do something else—click "Sign Up"—to assent to the hyperlinked terms. Yet, unlike some clickwrap agreements, the user can click to assent whether or not the user has been presented with the terms.

**8.13** In this case, the judge held that the user was bound by the terms and conditions, and said, at 839–40:

> The mechanics of the internet surely remain unfamiliar, even obtuse to many people. But it is not too much to expect that an internet user whose social networking was so prolific that losing Facebook access allegedly caused him mental anguish would understand that the hyperlinked phrase "Terms of Use" is really a sign that says "Click Here for Terms of Use." So understood, at least for those to whom the internet is in an indispensable part of daily life, clicking the hyperlinked phrase is the 21st-century equivalent of turning over the cruise ticket. In both cases, the consumer is prompted to examine terms of sale that are located somewhere else. Whether or not the consumer bothers to look is irrelevant.
>
> ...
>
> Here, Fteja was informed of the consequences of his assenting click and he was shown, immediately below, where to click to understand those consequences. That was enough.

27 For which see Preston, '"Please note: you have waived everything"'; M. A. Lemley, 'Terms of use', *Minnesota Law Review*, 91 (2006), pp. 459–83. For the position in Canada, see S. Sigel, T. Ling and J. Izenberg, '1998 electronic commerce: the validity of webwrap contracts', Uniform Law Conference of Canada, http://www.ulcc.ca/en/1998-halifax-ns/395-civil-section-documents/1660-validity-of-webwrap-contracts-1999; I. Gupta, 'Are websites adequately communicating terms and conditions link in a browse-wrap agreement?', *European Journal of Law and Technology*, 3 (2012), http://ejlt.org/article/view/47/239.

28 California: *Savetsky v. Pre-Paid Legal Services, Inc., d/b/a LegalShield*, 2015 WL 4593744 (previous hearing reported at 2015 WL 604767.

29 The Court of Appeals of Texas concluded the facts in *Hotels.com, L.P. v. Canales*, 195 S.W.3d 147, 195 S.W.3d 147 (2006) illustrated a similar hybrid approach. In this case, the terms did not apply to the main plaintiff because of entering a contract over the telephone, but the terms applied to those plaintiffs that had used the website.

30 841 F.Supp.2d 829 (2012).

**8.14** 'Browse wrap' agreements are where one party aims to impose terms of use or sale on another party where a visitor demonstrates assent by using the website. The potential customer is not required to indicate acceptance of any terms by any positive action, but the user must have had actual or constructive knowledge of the terms and conditions for them to be effective.[31] This form of electronic signature comprises the process of using the website, thereby indicating knowledge of the relevant terms,[32] although for such terms to be effective, or for constructive notice to apply, they must be conspicuous,[33] intend to apply,[34] and the party with the burden of proof must demonstrate how a visitor

31 Or the product if in Illinois: *Schafer v. AT & T Wireless Services, Inc.*, 2005 WL 850459 (S.D.Ill.).

32 California: *Cairo, Inc., v. CrossMedia Services, Inc.*, 2005 WL 756610 (N.D.Cal.); *Fagerstrom v. Amazon.com, Inc.*, 2015 WL 6393948 (an appeal was filed on 23 November 2015).
Florida: *Brueggemann v. NCOA Select, Inc.*, 2009 WL 1873651 (S.D.Fla.).
Missouri: *Major v. McCallister*, 302 S.W.3d 227 (2009)
New York: *Druyan v. Jagger*, 508 F.Supp.2d 228 (S.D.N.Y. 2007).
New Mexico: *Fiser v. Dell Computer Corporation, a/k/a Dell, Inc.*, 142 N.M. 331, 165 P.3d 328, 63 UCC Rep.Serv.2d 449, 2007 -NMCA- 087
Texas: *American Airlines, Inc., v. Farechase, Inc.*, Case No. 067-194022-02 (Texas, 67th Dist., Mar. 8, 2003).

33 Federal: *Specht v. Netscape Communications Corporation*, 150 F.Supp.2d 585 (S.D.N.Y. 2001) *affirmed* 306 F.3d 17 (2nd Cir. 2002); *Nguyen v. Barnes & Nobel*, Inc., 763 F.3d 1171 (9th Cir. 2014), 14 Cal. Daily Op. Serv. 9479, 2014 Daily Journal D.A.R. 11,191.
California: *Pollstar v. Gigmania Ltd.*, 170 F.Supp.2d 974 (E.D.Cal. 2000); *Be In, Inc., v. Google Inc.*, 2013 WL 5568706; *Friedman v. Guthy-Renler LLC*, 2015 WL 857800; *Tompkins v. 23andMe, Inc.*, 2014 WL 2903752; *Long v. Provide Commerce, Inc.*, 245 Cal.App.4th 855 (2016), 200 Cal.Rptr.3d 117, 16 Cal. Daily Op. Serv. 2897, 2016 Daily Journal D.A.R. 2630.
Illinois: *Hubbert v. Dell Corporation*, 835 N.E.2d 113 (Ill.App. 5 Dist. 2005); *PDC Laboratories, Inc., v. Hach Company*, 2009 WL 2605270 (C.D.Ill.); *Hussein v. Coinabul, LLC*, 2014 WL 7261240; *Sgouros v. TransUnion Corp.*, 2015 WL 507584 (where it was determined that the agreement was neither a click wrap nor a browse wrap agreement).
Massachusetts: *Small Justice LLC v. Xcentric Ventures, LLC*, 99 F.Supp.3d 190 (2015), 114 U.S.P.Q.2d 1321.
Nevada: *In re Zappos.com, Inc., Customer Data Security Breach Litigation*, 893 F.Supp.2d 1058 (2012), 95 A.L.R.6th 721.
New Jersey: *Syndicate 1245 at Lloyd's v. Walnut Advisory Corporation*, 2011 WL 5825979; *Liberty Syndicates at Lloyd's v. Walnut Advisory Corporation*, 2011 WL 5825777; *Hoffman v. Supplements Togo Management, LLC*, 18 A.3d 210, 84 A.L.R.6th 763.
New York: *Hines v. Overstock.com, Inc.*, 668 F.Supp.2d 362, 367 (E.D.N.Y. 2009) affirmed, 380 F.App'x 22 (2d Cir. 2010); *Register.com, Inc., v. Verio, Inc.*, 126 F.Supp.2d 238 (S.D.N.Y. 2000) *affirmed*, 356 F.3d 393 (2nd Cir. 2004).
Rhode Island: *DeFontes v. Dell Computers Corporation*, 2004 WL 253560 (R.I.Super.) (this is an unpublished opinion) affirmed *DeFontes v. Dell, Inc.*, 984 A.2d 1061; *Hodosh, Lyon & Hammer, Ltd., v. Barracuda Networks, Inc.*, 2016 WL 705272.
Texas: *Southwest Airlines Co. v. Farechase, Inc.*, 318 F.Supp.2d 435 (N.D.Tex. 2004); *Southwest Airlines Co. v. BoardFirst, L.L.C.*, 2007 WL 4823761 (N.D. Tex.).
Virginia: *Cvent, Inc., v. Eventbrite, Inc.*, 739 F.Supp.2d 927, 96 U.S.P.Q.2d 1798.

34 Pennsylvania: *Collegesource, Inc., v. Academyone, Inc.*, 2012 WL 5269213, 2012-2 Trade Cases P 78,129.

is made aware of the terms.[35] A party might fail because they cannot demonstrate a number of issues of relevance, such as that the agreement actually existed on its website at the material time; that any agreement applied to the actual product in dispute, or that the defendants agreed to its terms.[36]

35 New York: *Edme v. Internet Brands, Inc.*, 968 F.Supp.2d 519 (2013), 41 Media L. Rep. 2696.

36 Florida: *IT Strategies Group, Inc., v. The Allday Consulting Group, L.L.C.*, 975 F.Supp.2d 1267 (2013).

# 9

# Personal Identification Number (PIN) and password

**9.1** The PIN[1] is possibly the oldest form of electronic signature, and has become a very widely used form of authentication,[2] especially to obtain access to a bank account through the use of an ATM (automated teller machine or automatic teller machine or automated banking machine or cash machine), or to confirm a transaction with a credit card or debit card.[3] Invariably, a claim by the user that they did not authorize one or more transactions conducted on the account will require the relying party – that is, the bank, with the burden of proof – to prove the account holder authorized the transaction. The fact a withdrawal or other form of transaction took place may not be in issue, and in any event, the bank can adduce the evidence under the relevant business records or the Bankers' Books exemptions. The burden remains the same, whatever the technology used.[4] Cormac Herley, P.C. van Oorschot and Andrew S. Patrick report that:[5]

> In the UK 'chip and PIN' initiative, signatures authorizing financial transactions are replaced by consumer entry of a 4-digit PIN. The vendor motivation for adopting the new system is an offloading of liability. Users become responsible for all approved transactions

1 In *United States of America v. Miller*, 70 F.3d 1353 (D.C. Cir. 1995), Karen LeCraft Henderson J referred to the PIN at 1355 as acting 'as a sort of electronic signature authorizing an ATM to release available funds'.

2 In *United States v. Lawrence*, 557 Fed.Appx. 520 (2014), 113 A.F.T.R.2d 2014-1138, 2014-1 USTC P 50,195, a PIN is used by the Internal Revenue Service as a form of electronic signature, which can also be affixed by an agent.

3 For instance, the use of PIN was explicitly recognized as a type of electronic signature by the Civil Chamber of the Supreme Court of Lithuania in its ruling in the case of *Ž.Š. v. AB Lietuva taupomasis bankas*, civil case no. 3K-3-390/2002; for a case note, see S. Trofimovs, *Digital Evidence and Electronic Signature Law Review*, 5 (2008), pp. 143–5, and for a translation, see S. Trofimovs, *Digital Evidence and Electronic Signature Law Review*, 6 (2009), pp. 255–62.

4 See also M. Silalahi Nuth, 'Unauthorized use of bank cards with or without the PIN: a lost case for the customer?', *Digital Evidence and Electronic Signature Law Review*, 9 (2012), pp. 95–101; case translation: Norway, Journal number 04-016794TVI-TRON, *Bernt Petter Jørgensen v DnB NOR Bank ASA by the Chairman of the Board* (Trondheim District Court, 24 September 2004), *Digital Evidence and Electronic Signature Law Review*, 9 (2012), pp. 117–23; case translation: Republic of Turkey, Case number: 2009/11485, judgment number: 2011/4033, by Av. Burcu Orhan Holmgren, *Digital Evidence and Electronic Signature Law Review*, 9 (2012), pp. 124–7.

5 C. Herley, P.C. van Oorschot and A.S. Patrick, 'Passwords: if we're so smart, why are we still using them?', in R. Dingledine and P. Golle (eds.), *Financial Cryptography and Data Security, 13th International Conference, FC 2009, Accra Beach, Barbados, February 23–26, 2009* (Berlin/Heidelberg: Springer, 2009), pre-publication version available online at http://research.microsoft.com/pubs/80199/fc09.pdf.

S. Mason, *Electronic Signatures in Law* (London: Institute of Advanced Legal Studies, 2016), chapter 9, 'Personal Identification Number (PIN) and password', pp. 215–22.

> where authorization relied on a correct PIN, whereas for traditional magnetic-stripe technology with signatures, users are liable for losses in disputed transactions only if they are shown to be negligent or involved in fraud. (From a legal perspective in countries like the UK, liability related to signature forgery falls on the relying party. PIN-authorized transactions apparently fall outside the scope of such statutory protection, and banks assert that use of a PIN implies cardholder negligence.) Consumers may be particularly unhappy to learn this detail of the new technology in light of prior demonstrations that chip and PIN readers can leak user PINs.

**9.2** The statement 'users become responsible for all approved transactions where authorization relied on a correct PIN' is incorrect. Whatever the form of technology that is used, the relying party has the burden of proof. The bank must prove that it had the mandate of the customer to undertake an action on the account, regardless of the nature of the technology. A PIN is merely one form of electronic signature, and the law has not changed because of the nature of the technology used by the banks. The participants at this conference will possibly not have understood the nuances of the legal process and the difficulty that a customer might have in challenging the evidence produced by the bank to prove that the customer caused the PIN to be entered into an ATM, for instance. Judges tend to refrain from ordering banks to adduce additional evidence in banking cases, and an added problem is that there is a presumption in England and Wales that 'In the absence of evidence to the contrary, the courts will presume that mechanical instruments were in order at the material time', formulated by the Law Commission in 1997.[6] Judges have implied that the words 'mechanical instruments' include computers and computer-like devices, even though computers and computer-like devices are not mechanical instruments. Judges have also, although not exclusively, used the term 'reliable' in relation to computers. With such a presumption in place, a customer taking legal action against a bank for the recovery of money stolen by a thief will have a significant problem in persuading a judge that the bank should adduce sufficient evidence to prove the customer used the PIN.[7]

**9.3** The central concern is usually whether it was the customer or somebody else that was responsible for withdrawals made from the customer's account

6 Law Commission, *Evidence in Criminal Proceedings: Hearsay and Related Topics* (1997), 13.13; for the United States of America, see C.M. Barger, 'Challenging judicial notice of facts on the internet under Federal Rule of Evidence 201', *University of San Francisco Law Review*, 48 (2013), pp. 43–70.

7 S. Mason, *When Bank Systems Fail – Debit cards, credit cards, ATMs, mobile and online banking: your rights and what to do when things go wrong* (2nd edn., St Albans: PP Publishing, 2014); S. Mason (ed.), *Electronic Evidence* (3rd edn., London: LexisNexis Butterworths, 2012), ch. 5, 'Mechanical instruments: the presumption of being in order'; S. Mason, 'Electronic evidence: a proposal to reform the presumption of reliability and hearsay', *Computer Law & Security Review*, 30 (2014), pp. 80–4.

using the correct PIN or password. The United States case of *Judd v. Citibank*[8] illustrates the nature of the problem. In 1980, Dorothy Judd discovered two withdrawals were made from her account by use of a cash card and PIN in the sum of US$800 when she was at work. Marmarellis J indicated that the case turned on issues of evidence, burden and credibility. He determined the issue by considering whether the plaintiff had proven her case by a fair preponderance of the credible evidence. In this instance, the issue was whether to believe the person or the printout of the transactions from the machine. The judge determined that the plaintiff had proved her case 'by a fair preponderance of the credible evidence' and judgment was awarded in the amount of the loss plus interest and disbursements.

**9.4** Further cases followed in 1981. In *Feldman v. Citibank, N.A.; Pickman v. Citibank, N.A.*[9] (two cases brought into one hearing), Ms Pickman discovered debits recorded against her account on various occasions: US$150.00 on 6 February 1981; US$150.00 on 3 May; two amounts of US$150.00 each on 9 May; US$150.00 and an additional US$20.00 on 10 May 1981. In each instance, the records of the bank indicated that the money was withdrawn by the use of a card issued to her. The record of the judgment is not abundantly clear in respect of the evidence Ms Pickman gave to the court. It is recorded at 44 that Ms Pickman did not notice the first unauthorized withdrawal that took place on 6 February 1981, and only discovered it after a cheque was returned because of insufficient funds in the account in May, thereby alerting her to the withdrawals that were recorded by the bank in May. However, at 45 [3], it is noted that Ms Pickman actually noticed the unauthorized transaction when she received her bank statement for February, but did not pursue her claims until she noticed the additional withdrawals in May, which in turn alerted her to the February loss. The judge based his judgment on this second description. LeVine J referred to the Final Report (1977) of the National Commission on Electronic Fund Transfers, in particular the recommendation that where a customer fails to notify the bank of a disputed transaction, the customer will be liable for any subsequent unauthorized use that could have been prevented, had the customer alerted the bank to the problem in a timely manner. The judge decided to apply the recommendation of the Commission, and determined that because Ms Pickman did not contact the bank within 30 days of receiving her bank statement for February to dispute the unauthorized transaction, she could only recover for the first unauthorized withdrawal, but not subsequent unauthorized withdrawals, because of her failure to inform the bank of the first unauthorized withdrawal, and her inaction precluded the bank from discovering a weakness in its security system.

**9.5** In the case of Mr Feldman, the court took judicial notice of news reports in the media of a number of methods used by thieves to steal money from ATMs, including where money was stolen by deceiving the customer into cooperating

8 N.Y.City Civ.Ct., 435 N.Y.S.2d 210.

9 N.Y.City Civ.Ct., 443 N.Y.S.2d 43.

with the thief. The scheme operated as follows: it appears that two ATMs would be placed by the bank in a vestibule, and a telephone would be located between the machines – the telephone was put in place for the use of the customer to communicate with employees of the bank. A customer enters the area where the ATMs are located, where they might see a person (the perpetrator of the deception) using the telephone, ostensibly speaking to an employee of the bank to inform them that one of the machines (the machine they appear to be complaining about, and which they appear to be using) was not working. The customer would not, naturally, give much attention to the person speaking over the telephone. The thief observes the customer enter their PIN into the machine. At this moment, the thief distracts the customer by telling him that the other machine is not functioning properly, but the bank employee has advised the perpetrator to enter another card into the machine to resolve the problem. The customer unwittingly accedes to the request, and inserts his card into the second machine. This action enables the thief to insert the customer's PIN into the machine and effect a withdrawal on the customer's account. It was Mr Feldman's evidence that there was no other person in the area at the time he withdrew money from the ATM, but the records indicated that US$20.00 was withdrawn on machine number 1 at 7:31:11 (the withdrawal he made), and a further US$200.00 was withdrawn on machine number 2 at 7:31:48. Astonishingly, despite the evidence of the plaintiff, the judge accepted the evidence of the security provisions described by the Operational Supervisor from the bank, and determined that Mr Feldman was liable for the unauthorized ATM transaction because he had 'unwittingly' allowed a thief to withdraw from his account.

**9.6** It is of interest to compare the liability of *Feldman* (decided on 16 September 1981) to the case of *Ognibene v. Citibank, N.A.*[10] (decided on 9 December 1981) where the same method of theft was used as in *Feldman*. Three withdrawals were made on 16 August 1981 from two adjacent ATMs, the first, by the plaintiff at 5:41 for US$20.00, then two further withdrawals at 5:42 for US$200.00 and 5:43 for US$200.00. Thorpe J described it at 846 as 'a scam which [the] defendant has been aware of for some time'. In this case, the judge indicated that the rights, liabilities and responsibilities of the banks were set out in federal legislation contained in 15 U.S.C. 1693, commonly called the Electronic Fund Transfer Act. At the time of this litigation, New York had not enacted legislation which governed such disputes, so the federal law applied. Under the legislation, the burden was on the customer to show a transaction was not authorized, and the bank had the burden of proving that the transfer was authorized. The judge concluded that Mr Ognibene met his burden of proof. In essence, the bank argued that although the customer was deceived, the evidence of the customer that he had permitted the card to be used met the banks' burden of proof in relation to authorization. This argument was roundly and rightly rejected, partly because the customer did not furnish the PIN to the thief, but because the thief observed

10 N.Y.City Civ.Ct., 446 N.Y.S.2d 845.

the customer key in the PIN on a machine in the premises of the bank, and obtained his card by deception. The judge indicated, at 848, that:

> On the contrary, the unauthorized person was able to obtain the code because of the bank's own negligence. Since the bank had knowledge of the scam and its operational details (including the central role of the customer service telephone), it was negligent in failing to provide plaintiff-customer with information sufficient to alert him to the danger when he found himself in the position of a potential victim.

**9.7** In June 1981, after the method had come to the attention of the bank, Citibank had cause to place signs in areas where ATMs were located. The signs were approximately two and a half inches in diameter, containing a circle in red, upon which was written the words 'Do Not Let Your Citicard Be Used For Any Transaction But Your Own'. Thorpe J indicated that this was not adequate, because it failed to give the reason behind the warning. As a footnote, the problem of thefts from ATMs and bank accounts became such a problem, that in the following year, the Attorney General of New York initiated legal action against Citibank, seeking relief for 'repeated or persistent fraud or illegality in transaction of business' by the bank.[11]

**9.8** In England and Wales, PC John Munden was charged with attempting to obtain money by deception after he complained that he was not responsible for making six transactions from ATM machines, all of which appeared on his statement in September 1992. He was subsequently prosecuted at Mildenhall Magistrates' Court in Suffolk in February 1994 and convicted. He appealed against his conviction before Turner J, sitting with two magistrates at Bury St Edmunds Crown Court. It appears that the defence attempted to obtain information about the computer systems, records and operational procedures of Halifax Building Society, but the Halifax apparently refused to provide such evidence, except in the form of a report by a third party. In these circumstances, the court decided that PC Munden's conviction could not stand, and he was acquitted. In Germany, an appeal from a civil action was brought before the Bundesgerichtshof (the Federal Supreme Court) in 2004.[12] In this instance, the plaintiff's purse was stolen. It contained her cash card, and an hour or so later, cash was withdrawn at two different ATMs using the correct PIN.[13] The plaintiff took action against

11 *State of New York, by Abrams v. Citibank, N.A.*, 537 F.Supp. 1192 (1982); in *Porter v. Citibank, N.A.*, 123 Misc.2d 28, 472 N.Y.S.2d 582 (N.Y.City Civ.Ct. 1984), where the customer used their card, but no money was dispensed, employees of the bank testified that on average cash machines were out of balance once or twice a week.

12 5 October 2004, XI ZR 210/03, published BGHZ 160, 308-321 Bundesgerichtshof (Federal Court of Justice); for a translation and commentaries by M. Eßer and T. Kritter, see *Digital Evidence and Electronic Signature Law Review*, 6(2009), pp. 248–54.

13 It has since been demonstrated that any PIN can be used to obtain money from an ATM, with no need for the thief to have the correct PIN, for which see S.J. Murdoch, S. Drimer,

her bank to recover the money, and the bank refused to reimburse the customer, because, it was alleged, of her negligence, which excluded the bank's liability under its general terms and conditions for the issue of cash cards. The court of first instance found for the plaintiff, and a regional court reversed the decision on appeal. The plaintiff appealed to the Federal Supreme court on a point of law. The only issue before the Federal Supreme Court concerned the burden of proof. The decision of the regional court was confirmed. It was held that the rules on prima facie evidence applied. This was because the facts proved in the matter (the withdrawal of cash in conjunction with a stolen bank card and the use of the correct PIN) characteristically resulted from a different set of facts (the storage of the PIN with the card). The court also held that in order to prove her case, the plaintiff had to show that the same result could occur in another way, in order to rebut the prima facie evidence.

**9.9** In comparison, two judges in separate jurisdictions have reached different conclusions on similar facts. In the Greek case of 5526/1999,[14] the claimant's bank cash card was stolen from his car, amongst other items. Although the claimant immediately informed the police and the bank, the bank failed to put a stop on the account in time, and funds were subsequently debited from his account. The bank sought to enforce the terms and conditions that applied to the issuance of the card, relying on the strict liability of the customer where the card was used without authority. In this instance, the term was considered unfair, because it was contrary to the main principle of the allocation of fault in Greek law, and second, because such terms are contrary to good faith. The customer was not held to be at fault.

**9.10** Compare this decision to the South African case of *Diners Club SA (Pty) Ltd v. Singh*[15] where Levinsohn J held, at 659, that a contract term by which the customer was liable, irrespective of who used the PIN, was not against public policy. This is a very wide and sweeping decision that cannot be maintained in the light of the relative ease by which a PIN can be obtained without the consent or authority of the cardholder. In the Papua New Guinea District Court, Seneka J found for Mathew Roni against the Bank of South Pacific.[16] Mr Roni discovered the loss of his Save Card, and informed the bank immediately he knew of the loss. It was not in dispute that the bank put a stop to all withdrawals, but it subsequently transpired that a number of transactions occurred after the time the bank put a stop on the account, some of the transaction took place almost at

---

R. Anderson and M. Bond, 'Chip and PIN is broken', 2010 IEEE Symposium on Security and Privacy (this was awarded the Best Practical Paper) available online at http://www.cl.cam.ac.uk/~sjm217/papers/oakland10chipbroken.pdf.

14 Court of First Instance of Athens constituted by one judge 5526/1999; for a translation into English see A. Fylla, Case note – Greece, *Digital Evidence and Electronic Signature Law Review*, 4 (2007), pp. 89–90.

15 2004 (3) SA 630 (D).

16 *Roni v. Kagure* [2004] PGDC 1; DC84 (1 January 2004).

almost the same time in separate geographical locations using the correct PIN. The judge reached the conclusion that the bank was negligent.

**9.11** In situations such as those illustrated above, the nature of the evidence and the methods that third parties can use to obtain the correct PIN will be highly relevant in reaching a decision between two conflicting claims. However, not every dispute is about unauthorized transactions. Transactions can occur with the authority of the user, but the user may dispute the amount they authorized, as in the Danish case of U.2000.1853V, where, at a restaurant with late-night opening hours, A authorized two Dankort card payments as he swiped his debit card through one of N's card terminals, entered his PIN, and agreed the amount that appeared on the display. The court was satisfied that one of the payments was erroneously accepted in the sum of DKK 10,500 instead of DKK 105. N was therefore ordered to pay back the difference. The court accepted, as a starting point, that when the appellant entered his PIN and approved an amount in the sum of DKK 10,500, the appellant made a binding payment to the respondent. However, that action did not rule out that it could be proved that payment of a higher amount was made by mistake.[17]

**9.12** It might also be usefully observed that where legislation requires a document to be signed in a specific manner, the use of a PIN will not be accepted as a substitute manuscript signature.[18]

**9.13** In respect of the use of passwords as a form of electronic signature, the Canada Business Corporations Act R.S.C. 1985, c. C-44 was amended to permit some transactions to occur in electronic form. In *Re Newbridge Networks Corp.*,[19] the applicant corporation applied for an order approving an electronic voting procedure for approximately 4,300 option-holders throughout Canada and the world. The decision was issued before the Electronic Commerce Act, S.O. 2000, c. 17 came into force in Ontario, but Farley J considered actual and proposed amendments to the relevant federal and provincial statutes. The judge found those amendments overly restrictive and too focused on the present state of technology. Instead, he looked behind the mechanics of the procedure to the underlying requirements of reliability, safeguarding and notice, and observed that statutory provisions should retain the flexibility to accommodate future technological change. In the particular circumstances, the electronic notice and voting procedures were the functional equivalent of receiving notice and being able to vote by postal mail. Farley J observed, at 6, that 'on balance the electronic procedure envisaged is a safer and more reliable system than is that which relies on the mails or other delivery systems' with built-in password integrity and instantaneous delivery. The court equated the use of a password signifying the user's choice with the traditional form of signing a paper proxy vote.

17 For a full report of this case, see *Digital Evidence and Electronic Signature Law Review*, 4 (2007), p. 98.

18 *Charles Parsons (Vic) Pty Ltd and Collector of Customs* [1995] AATA 171; (1995) 37 ALD 779 (28 June 1995).

19 (2000), 48 O.R. (3d) 47, [2000] O.J. No. 1346 (QL) (Sup. Ct.) (QL).

**9.14** Of interest is a decision that accepts the proposition that the unique number issued by a bank can be a signature. In the New Jersey case of *Spevack, Cameron & Boyd v. National Community Bank of New Jersey*,[20] the unique account number assigned by a bank to a depositor was determined to be as complete a signature as the depositor's written or printed name. Bilder (retired and temporarily assigned on recall) observed, at 1169, that a signature may take many forms, and there was no reason why a bank account number could not be one of them:

> In this computer age the use of numbers as a means of identification has become pervasive. Indeed, numbers are more readily recognized and handled than signatures. The 'signature' used by Homequity was its account number at Midlantic, the bank in which it deposited the check. That 'signature' accurately identified the payee and the funds were properly credited to the payee's account. In fact, had Homequity written a name without the account number, the bank would have had to look up the number that corresponded with the same. In keeping with the electronic age, it is the numbers which have the primary significance.

**9.15** The problems with the PIN and banking applications represents an ever-changing struggle between clever thieves who implement new strategies to steal, and the banks in overcoming the threats as they are discovered.[21] Arguably, one of the problems that employees of banks face when trying to persuade directors to spend money on security is the collective lack of understanding of the problem.[22]

20 677 A.2d 1168 (N.J.Super.A.D. 1996), 291 N.J.Super. 577. Note the 1844 New York case of *Brown v. The Butchers & Drovers' Bank*, 6 Hill 443, 41 Am.Dec. 755 where a person writing '1. 2. 8.' on the back of a bill of exchange as a substitute for his name served to endorse the bill.

21 S. Mason and T.S. Reiniger, '"Trust" between machines? Establishing identity between humans and software code, or whether you know it is a dog, and if so, which dog?', *Computer and Telecommunications Law Review*, 21 (2015), pp. 135–48; Mason, *When Bank Systems Fail*; S. Mason, 'Electronic banking and how courts approach the evidence', *Computer Law & Security Review*, 29 (2013), pp. 144–51; R. Porkess and S. Mason, 'Looking at debit and credit card fraud', *Teaching Statistics*, 34 (2012), pp. 87–91 (also in German: 'Betrug mit Kundenkarten und Kreditkarten', *Stochastik in der Schule*, 34 (2014), s. 15–18); S. Mason, 'Debit cards, ATMs and negligence of the bank and customer', *Butterworths Journal of International Banking and Financial Law*, 27 (2012), pp. 163–73; S. Mason, 'UK credit card fraud: the scale of the problem', *e-Finance & Payments Law & Policy*, 6 (2012), pp. 14–16.

22 M. Arnold, 'Bank directors lack technology know-how', *Gulf News*, 2 Nov. 2015, B6.

# 10

# Typing a name into an electronic document

**10.1** The use of electronic signatures pre-dates any form of legislation, and in the latter decade of the 20th century, adjudicators found themselves applying well-established legal principles to new technologies when presented in the form of electronic signatures, just as judges in the 19th century were confronted with the increasing use of printing, typewriting and telegrams: all, it must be said, without the need for special legislation to be enacted. Case law applying electronic signature statutes in the United States of America indicates that the act of typing a name into a document on screen was considered just as acceptable a method of proving intent as any other form of signature,[1] although this form of electronic signature is not uniformly accepted in all jurisdictions for all purposes.[2] However, reports of cases dealing with electronic signatures sometimes indicate that the lawyers and judges do not appear to be familiar with signatures.[3] In *Wright v. Direct Capital Securities, Inc.*,[4] the plaintiff typed his name into an agreement, knowing he was typing his name into the form as an electronic signature. The defendants wanted to enforce the provisions of the agreement by compelling the plaintiff to deal with the matter by arbitration. At a hearing before the trial judge to compel arbitration, it is reported (at 2) that the trial judge concluded 'there was no legal precedent allowing it to rely upon such a "signature" as evidence of intent to arbitrate'. No relevant case law or electronic signature legislation appeared to have been referred to or cited, and although the members of the Court of Appeal appeared to accept the typed signature as a form of electronic signature by inference, there is no explicit discussion of the case law or legal principles.

**10.2** Lawyers and judges are beginning to accept that typing a name into a document such as an email is a valid method of signing a document, as in *Orton v.*

1 Uniform Electronic Transactions Act, s 2(8) definition of electronic signature, Official Comment 7; in *Buckles Management, LLC, v. Investordigs, LLC*, 728 F.Supp.2d 1145 (D.Colo. 2010) Babcock J held that the signature in an email was not valid where the party charged was not the signatory, and the party charged did not adopt the signature.

2 For instance, see the following case translations from Denmark: U.2001.252Ø (Request for dissolution; Bankruptcy Court; signature; sufficiency of electronic signature with name typed on document) and U.2001.1980/1H (Request for dissolution; Bankruptcy Court; requirement for manuscript signature; sufficiency of electronic signature with name typed on document), *Digital Evidence and Electronic Signature Law Review*, 6 (2009), pp. 232–4.

3 In the Australian case of *Philip Laming v. TicketXpress Pty Ltd* PR941462 [2003] AIRC 1503 (3 December 2003), Hamilton, Deputy President of the Australian Industrial Relations Commission indicated, incorrectly, at [2] that 'Emails do not contain signatures, even electronic signatures, and the only readily identifiable marking may be the email address'.

4 2010 WL 659073 (Cal.App. 4 Dist.) (this case is noted as Nonpublished/Noncitable).

S. Mason, *Electronic Signatures in Law* (London: Institute of Advanced Legal Studies, 2016), chapter 10, 'Typing a name into an electronic document', pp. 223–54.

*Collins*,[5] where the word 'Putsmans' was deliberately typed in an email after the customary salutation 'Yours faithfully'). Mr Peter Prescott QC, sitting as a Deputy Judge, said, at [21]:

> I have no doubt that its purpose would be recognized throughout the profession. Anyone would think: 'Putsmans are signing off on this document'. It was intended to signify that document was being sent out with the authority of the defendants' legal representative.

**10.3** The main area of contention is to argue whether an email or series of emails constitutes the necessary evidence that an agreement has been reached.

# Acts by lawyer as agent

**10.4** With the appropriate authority, an agent is capable of binding their principal in the electronic world as in the physical world. That this applies to attorneys is illustrated in the Tennessee case of *Waddle v. Elrod*,[6] where the Supreme Court determined that the emails exchanged between counsel with their name typed at the bottom of the email satisfied the signature requirement of the Statute of Frauds. The position is the same in New Zealand,[7] and in the United States: Michigan,[8] New York[9] and Texas.[10]

# Interest in real property

## Australia

**10.5** The Supreme Court of the Northern Territory in Australia had cause to consider the effectiveness of an electronic signature under Australia's electronic transactions legislation in an action for an adjustment of property interests under Division 3 of Part 2 of the De Facto Relationships Act 1991 (NT). In *Faulks*

5 [2007] 3 All ER 863, [2007] 1 WLR 2953, [2007] EWHC 803 (Ch); *Green (Liquidator of Stealth Construction Ltd) v. Ireland* [2011] EWHC 1305 (Ch) [2011] BPIR 1173 where it was accepted that typing a name into an email is sufficient for the purposes of s2 Law Property (Miscellaneous Provisions) Act 1989; *Lindsay v. O'Loughnane* [2012] BCC 153, [2010] EWHC 529 (QB).

6 367 S.W.3d 217 (2012).

7 *Cox v. Coughlan* [2014] NZHC 164 (14 February 2014).

8 *Wessel v. Wessel*, 2014 WL 325237, unpublished opinion.

9 *Williamson v. Delsener*, 59 A.D.3d 291 (2009), 874 N.Y.S.2d 41, 2009 N.Y. Slip Op. 01333; *Jackson v. New York City Department of Education*, 2012 WL 1986593; *Forcelli v. Gelco Corporation*, 109 A.D.3d 244 (2013), 972 N.Y.S.2d 570, 2013 N.Y. Slip Op. 05437; *Maria McBridge Productions, Inc., v. Badger*, 46 Misc.3d 1221(A) (2015), 46 Misc.3d 1221(A) (2015) Unreported Disposition.

10 *Williamson v. The Bank of New York Mellon*, 947 F.Supp.2d 704 (2013).

*v. Cameron*,[11] the parties lived together in a relationship for some two years before they separated. In 2003, the plaintiff informed her former partner that she was in the process of preparing a separation statement. The defendant had, by this time, moved out of the country, and the only means of communication the plaintiff had with her former partner was by email, because he did not provide a postal address. One of the issues in this case was whether a separation agreement between two partners had been formed for the purposes of the Act. Section 45(2) of the Act provides that where the court is satisfied that there is a separation agreement between the partners, is in writing and signed by the other partner, the court may make an order under Division 3 or 5 of Part 2, but may not make an order that is inconsistent with the terms of the agreement. In her application, the plaintiff submitted that the email correspondence constituted a separation agreement, or in the alternative, if the court did not consider the email correspondence constituted a separation agreement, regard should be given to what was agreed by this form of correspondence. First, the judge reached the conclusion that, even though the evidence was not overwhelming, there was an agreement between the former partners, and that it was enforceable at common law. The second issue was whether the email correspondence had been signed. The defendant typed his name at the bottom of the text 'Regards, Angus,' and in applying the provisions of s9 of the Electronic Transactions (Northern Territory) Act 2000 (NT) to the name typed at the bottom of the email, Acting Master Young concluded, at 64:

> I am satisfied that the printed signature on the defendant's emails identifies him and indicates his approval of the information communicated, that the method was as reliable as was appropriate and that the plaintiff consented to the method. I am satisfied that the agreement is 'signed' for the purposes of s45(2).

**10.6** The case of *Kavia Holdings Pty Limited v. Suntrack Holdings Pty Limited*[12] was an action for the option to renew a lease before the Supreme Court of New South Wales. Pembroke J determined that the text of the relevant email did not amount to a notice within the meaning of clause 7 of the lease. In relation to the formality of a signature, he said, in passing at [33], the following:

> In my view the inclusion of the sender's name on the email amounted to 'signing' for the purpose of the clause. The requirement for signing is intended to identify the sender and authenticate the communication. That is sufficiently achieved in an email by the setting out of the sender's name together with the email address from which the email is dispatched. The name of the sender and his email address are readily and rapidly verifiable. Any

11 [2004] 32 Fam LR 417; [2004] NTSC 61.

12 [2011] NSWSC 716.

other conclusion would produce a capricious and commercially inconvenient result that might have wide-reaching and unintended consequences in modern-day trade and commerce.

## Canada

**10.7** The exchange of emails regarding the offer and acceptable of buying a property was considered by Rideout J in *Girouard v. Druet*.[13] The Court of Appeal of New Brunswick reversed the decision on appeal[14] because, the court concluded, the parties did not have the requisite intention to enter into a binding contract for the purchase and sale of the condominium unit. The signature issue was not determined because it not necessary to reach a conclusion in this matter, although Robertson and Richard JJA entered into a rambling discussion about electronic signatures at [24] to [30]. One highly respected Canadian commentator noted of this discussion: 'I wonder if all the verbiage of the CA was necessary'.[15]

## United States of America

**10.8** In 2006, the Missouri Court of Appeals concluded that the typed signatures in an exchange of email communications constituted signatures for the purpose of terminating a lease.[16] In a case before Foster J in the Massachusetts Land Court, *St. John's Holdings, LLC v. Two Electronics, LLC*,[17] the parties negotiated over a contract for the sale of land. St John's Holdings took legal action to enforce its rights as a buyer of a property pursuant to a binding letter of intent to purchase. Part of the evidence was an exchange of emails and text messages between the parties' real estate brokers. The plaintiff argued that these exchanges constituted an agreement on all essential terms that satisfied the Statute of Frauds. Foster J, at 8, considered that the 'way in which the parties handled the transaction was sufficient for them to appreciate that the text message would memorialize the contractual offer and acceptance'. The judge then inferred that the name 'Tim' added to the end of a text message in the context of the exchanges between the parties was intended to be authenticated by the sender as a deliberate choice to type his name at the conclusion of his text message.

13 2011 NBQB 204 (in French on CanLII), the English text is at [2011] N.B.J. No. 260, and [2011] A.N.-B.no 260.

14 *Druet v. Girouard* 2012 NBCA 40.

15 J. Gregory, 'Email transactions in land – in New Brunswick', 30 April 2012, http://www.slaw.ca/2012/04/30/email-transactions-in-land-in-new-brunswick/.

16 *Crestwood Shops, L.L.C., v. Hilkene*, 197 S.W.3d 641 (Mo.App. WD. 2006).

17 2016 WL 1460477.

## Loan of money

### Australia

**10.9** In the case of *Stuart v. Hishon*,[18] Ms Hishon loaned money to Mr Stuart and subsequently initiated proceedings to recover A$28,216.17 plus interest, being the outstanding and unpaid balance of monies owing to her pursuant to a loan of A$83,760.87 made by Ms Hishon to him in July 1996. Prior to the litigation, a series of email correspondence occurred between the parties regarding the payment of the loan, and Mr Stuart ended each email with 'Tom'. Counsel for Mr Stuart argued that it was necessary to provide evidence to establish that Mr Stuart placed the printed name on his email intending it to be an acknowledgment of the debt, and that no such evidence existed. Harrison J did not accept this argument, stating, at [34], that 'Mr Stuart typed his name on the foot of the email. He signed it by doing so. It would be an almost lethal assault on common sense to take any other view'.

### China

**10.10** In China, the court of first instance case of *Yang Chunning v. Han Ying*,[19] Mr Yang claimed that the defendant Miss Han asked to borrow RMB 11,000 from him. Yang agreed to lend the money to Miss Han, but Miss Han failed to return the money. As evidence, Mr Yang exhibited several text messages sent from Miss Han's mobile telephone about the loan. It was confirmed that the messages were transmitted from Miss Han's mobile telephone number. In this case, the judge supported the plaintiff's claim based on the evidence of the mobile telephone message between the parties. The court judged that these messages, as a form of electronic text according to the Electronic Signature Law, could serve as evidence to support Mr Yang's claim.

### United States of America

**10.11** In the Texas case of *Parks v. Seybold*[20] before the Court of Appeals, the Gaming Management Corporation executed a note payable to Scott Seybold in the amount of US$10,000, plus 15 per cent interest. Clyde Parks wrote the note by hand, and he signed it in his capacity as vice-president of the corporation. The corporation ceased to exist, and Mr Seybold sought full payment on the note. The parties subsequently exchanged a number of emails, and the court agreed with the trial judge that the emails constituted writing, and the inclusion of the words 'Thank you, Clyde' above an automatic signature block served to demonstrated that he signed the emails.

18 [2013] NSWSC 766.

19 (2005) hai min chu zi NO.4670, Beijing Hai Dian District People's Court; for a translation of this case, see *Digital Evidence and Electronic Signature Law Review*, 5 (2008), pp. 103–5.

20 2015 WL 4481768.

# Employment

## England and Wales

**10.12** In England and Wales, the first case of this nature occurred in the Industrial Tribunal case of *Hall v. Cognos Limited.*[21] Cognos employed Mr Hall as a sales executive under the terms of the Standard Employment Agreement used by Cognos. He was provided with a motor car for business and personal use. Mr Hall was reimbursed for all reasonable expenses incurred for travel, accommodation and other costs in accordance with the relevant policy, which the chairman determined was incorporated into the contract. The policy stated that all expenses over six months old would not be paid. Mr Hall failed to submit any travel expenses between 1 December 1995 and 3 June 1996. By January 1997 Mr Hall wanted his expenses to be paid. A series of emails was exchanged on 15 January between Mr Hall, Sarah McGoun (of HR) and Keith Schroeder, Mr Hall's line manager. Mr Hall asked if he could submit a late expenses claim to Ms McGoun. Ms McGoun in turn referred Mr Hall to Keith Schroeder, and Mr Schroeder, in response to the question as to 'whether [the late submission] is OK with you?' replied, 'Yes, it is OK.' Mr Hall subsequently submitted his expenses, although he did not provide all the necessary forms immediately. He also inflated his claims. His employers refused to make any payment and dismissed him.

**10.13** Counsel for Cognos argued that because an email was not in writing and signed, the exchange of emails did not have any effect on the terms of the employment agreement. Mr C. T. Grazin, the chairman sitting on his own, declined to accept this proposition, attractive as it appeared to him. He held that the emails were in writing and signed once they were printed out. Despite there being no reference or discussion to any relevant case law or the statutory definitions of 'writing' and 'document,' the chairman concluded at 5:

> I am satisfied that an email is 'in writing and signed by the parties' once it is printed out. The position might (it is not necessary to make any finding on this point) be different if the email was only retained temporarily on the computer's hard disk storage system. The documents that were, however, produced from the computer are clearly in writing and bear the signatures of both 'Sarah' and 'Keith'. The fact that those signatures are printed, rather than handwritten, is not in my view material. For those reasons, I reject Mr Pym's submission that the relevant email messages are incapable, as a matter of law, of having any modifying effect on the specific contract between the parties.

**10.14** A further argument put forward on behalf of Cognos was that Mr Schroeder did not have the authority to respond to Mr Hall's request, nor was he authorized to agree to it. This was rejected on the basis that as Mr Hall's line manager, Mr

21 Industrial Tribunal Case No 1803325/97.

Schroeder was vested with the appropriate authority to deal with such a request, and as a result, Mr Hall could rely on Mr Schroeder's response. This meant Mr Schroeder's response acted to bind Cognos. As a result, the exchange of emails between Mr Hall and his line manager acted to vary the policy, and Cognos was obliged to pay Mr Hall his reasonable expenses.

## United States of America

**10.15** Organizations are increasingly requiring potential employees to apply for jobs electronically, and sometimes by way of a third party company that operates an online service. The procedures and technology are not always perfect, despite assertions to the contrary by those that create and operate such systems. An example is that of the Californian case of *Adams v. Quiksilver, Inc.*,[22] where Lynn Adams, when applying for a job with her former employer, was requested to type her name into an electronic form for the purpose of a background check. The employer relied on her signature to enforce an arbitration agreement, which was also included in the form, although the employee was not aware the form contained such an agreement. The employee gave evidence to the effect that she did not type her name into the form, partly because she did not complete the form, and partly because her name was already typed in the form before she received it as an attachment to an email. The employer had engaged a third party to provide a service to deal with the entire recruitment process online. The third party company asserted that it was impossible for the form to be sent to the applicant, because the entire process was meant to be online, and only available through their website. The employer filed a motion to compel arbitration. Wilkinson J heard the application, and also had a brief evidentiary hearing to establish whether the employee had made the electronic signature, as asserted. The judge determined the electronic signature had been added and granted the motion. The employee appealed the decision. The members of the Court of Appeal agreed that there was no evidence to indicate that the employee had typed in her electronic signature to the form. It was for the employer, relying on the signature, to prove that the employee had filled in her name on the form. The evidence from the employer in contradiction of the evidence from the employee was far from sufficient to prove their case. This is an important case, because it illustrates the weakness of the evidence that was submitted by the employer to prove its case.[23] For this reason, it is difficult to understand why the report is marked 'nonpublished/noncitable'.

22 2010 WL 602515 (Cal.App. 4 Dist.).

23 For a discussion of authenticating evidence in legal proceedings in the United States of America, see K. Chasse, 'The admissibility of electronic business records', *Canadian Journal of Law and Technology*, 18 (2011), pp. 105–91; B.W. Esler and J.J. Schwerha IV, 'United States of America', in S. Mason (ed.), *Electronic Evidence* (3rd edn., London: LexisNexis Butterworths, 2012); G.L. Paul, *Foundations of Digital Evidence* (n.p.: American Bar Association, 2008); for a general discussion on the authentication of electronic evidence and the presumption that machines are working properly, see Mason (ed.), *Electronic Evidence*, chs. 4 and 5.

# Contract

## England and Wales

**10.16** The members of the Court of Appeal Civil Division in *Nicholas Prestige Homes v. Neal*[24] did not concern themselves with the question of the signature in emails in this particular case. It was concluded that a contract was formed with the exchange of emails regarding the commission on a sale of property. By implication, the names typed at the end of the email, 'Marc Taylor' and 'Sally' were construed as valid signatures.[25]

## Israel

**10.17** Whether a signature contained in an email constitutes a valid contract in Israel was considered by Noa Grossman J in *Computer Sky Edv v. Prime Medical Company Ltd.*[26] It was held that a contract that was signed through email correspondence is valid. In essence, the reasoning of the decision was as follows: negotiations are also carried out today through electronic communications. An offer, a request for an offer and the reception of an offer can all be performed via email correspondence. The correspondence as a whole is what creates the actual agreement. Unlike a printed contract that incorporates the parties' will into one document, a contract reached by way of reciprocating electronic communications is a mosaic of all the parties' communications.

## Lithuania

**10.18** Two rulings of the Lithuanian courts, in the Court of Appeal[27] and in the Supreme Court of Lithuania[28] accept email communications (typed by the name) as evidence in civil proceedings, although it is not certain whether names written in the emails will be accepted as a form of electronic signature.

## Scotland

**10.19** The nature of the electronic signature was not specifically at issue in *Baillie Estates Ltd v. Du Pont (UK) Ltd*,[29] where Hodge L concluded that an exchange of emails constituted a valid contract, notwithstanding the apparent informality

24 [2010] EWCA Civ 1552; [2010] All ER (D) 22 (Dec).

25 An exchange of emails constituted an agreement in *Bieber v. Teathers Ltd (In Liquidation)* [2014] EWHC 4205 (Ch), 2014 WL 6862668, and as with *Nicholas Prestige Homes v. Neal* 2010] EWCA Civ 1552; [2010] All ER (D) 22 (Dec), the nature of the signatures was not considered.

26 Tel Aviv Peace Court Civil Case 29488/04, (4 August 2005, unpublished decision).

27 10 April 2006, case No. 2A- 95/2006.

28 6 March 2006, case No. 3K-3-169/2006.

29 2009 GWD 25-399, [2009] ScotCS CSOH_95, [2009] CSOH 95.

of the content of the emails exchanged, because the exchange demonstrated an agreement to enter into a contract. By inference, it is possible to observe that the named typed at the bottom of each email constituted an electronic signature.

## South Africa

**10.20** A contract can be varied by an exchange of emails that includes the name of the person sending the email where their name appears in the email, as in the case of *Spring Forest Trading v. Wilberry*,[30] where the parties agreed to cancel a contract by exchange of emails. Wilberry argued, among other things, that the form of the electronic signature was relevant in establishing the an agreement was not reached to cancel the contract because it was necessary to use an advanced electronic signature, as contemplated in s 13(1) of the Electronic Communications and Transactions Act 25 of 2002. In delivering the unanimous judgment of the Supreme Court of Appeal, Cachalia JA rejected this argument on the basis that this was a misreading of the legislation, and that the section did not apply in this case. The judge said, at [28]:

> The typewritten names of the parties at the foot of the emails, which were used to identify the users, constitute 'data' that is logically associated with the data in the body of the emails, as envisaged in the definition of an 'electronic signature'. They therefore satisfy the requirement of a signature and had the effect of authenticating the information contained in the emails.

**10.21** This finding is also consistent with the approach taken by the courts in South Africa, as noted by the judge at [26]:

> The approach of the courts to signatures has therefore been pragmatic, not formalistic. They look to whether the method of the signature used fulfils the function of a signature – to authenticate the identity of the signatory – rather than insist on the form of the signature used.

## United States of America

**10.22** Under the hearsay provisions for evidence in the United States of America, a third party statement is not admissible into evidence. The advent of email as a method of communication has led to some new and interesting challenges, as exemplified in the federal 9th circuit case of *Sea-Land Service, Inc., v. Lozen International, LLC.*[31] Sea-Land agreed to transport containers of grapes from Mexico to England. The containers were to travel for part of the journey by rail. Sea-Land's railroad agent placed the containers on the wrong train, and the

30 (725/13) [2014] ZASCA 178; 2015 (2) SA 118 (SCA) (21 November 2014).

31 285 F.3d 808 (9th Cir. 2002).

grapes did not arrive at the port in sufficient time for the sailing of the vessel they were due to be transported in. Sea-Land began the action to recover the full amount of its contract with Lozen, and Lozen counterclaimed for breach of contract and for loss of cargo, because it had to sell the grapes domestically at a lower price. At the hearing for summary judgment, the judge excluded an internal email written by an employee of Sea-Land and forwarded to Lozen by another employee of Sea-Land. On appeal, it was held that the email was not hearsay as an admission of a party opponent. Graber CJ indicated the position at 821:

> The original email, an internal company memorandum, closes with a electronic 'signature' attesting that the message was authored by 'Mike Jacques', Sea-Land's 'Rail Reefer Services Coordinator' at the time the email was written. Jacques is listed as one of Sea-Land's employees in Exhibit 9, a letter from Sea-Land to Lozen that the district court *did* admit into evidence. The original email also appears to concern a matter within the scope of Jacques' employment.
>
> More importantly, however, Jacques' original email was forwarded to Lozen by Laurie Martines, a second Sea-Land employee. She copied the entire body of Jacques' internal memorandum into her email and prefaced it with the statement 'Yikes, Pls note the rail screwed us up ....', Martinez thereby incorporated and adopted the contents of Jacques' original message, because of her remark 'manifested an adoption or belief in [the] truth' on the information contained in the original email.

**10.23** The name typed into a medical insurance form for a patient was accepted as an electronic signature where the patient reviewed and approved the information, and authorized the signature to be typed on the form;[32] the exchange of emails with names typed in the body of the emails served to amend a real estate contract.[33] There are occasions when a document is intended to be signed, but for some reason the contract is performed without a relevant signature. This occurred in *Brighton Investment Limited v. Har-Zvi*,[34] where Brighton was not able to produce an executed copy of a Memorandum of Understanding. Discussions between the parties had been conducted by email. In giving judgment, Garry J indicated the nature of the email exchange that took place between the parties, at 1223:

> In their email communications, Levy and defendant discussed multiple business deals using a telegraphic style and irregular syntax that cannot readily be understood without explanatory extrinsic information.

32 *Long v. Time Insurance Co.*, 572 F.Supp.2d 907 (S.D.Ohio 2008).

33 *Sims v. Stapleton Realty, Ltd.*, 305 Wis.2d 655, 2007 WL 2386494 (Wis.App.).

34 88 A.D.3d 1220 (2011), 932 N.Y.S.2d 214, 2011 N.Y. Slip Op. 07555.

> ...
>
> Given this lack of clarity in the parties' written communications, their intent must be determined by assessing whether the totality of the circumstances, including their course of conduct after June 2005, consistently indicated their mutual belief that an agreement had been reached.

**10.24** In this instance, the objective evidence established that the parties intended to be bound. The evidence comprised the exchange of emails and the subsequent course of conduct of both parties.

## Guarantees and debt

### Australia

**10.25** That email correspondence is used extensively for business has become a fact that judges now take for granted. Users intend that email correspondence be effective, and although lawyers will be instructed to argue the contrary, courts will continue to find, providing the evidence makes it clear, that the parties intend their email correspondence to be acted upon and to be bound by what is written. Such a case occurred before the Federal Circuit Court of Australia in *Austral-Asia Freight Pty Ltd v. Turner.*[35] An exchange of emails occurred in respect of a debt claimed in two amounts, one of A$33,884.02 and the other of A$2,859.14, in respect of two different companies. Hartnett J concluded, at [30], that there was an objectively manifested intention to be legally bound, it was conveyed in sufficient writing, and the name typed at the end of the emails constituted a signature for the purposes of s 126 of the Instruments Act 1958 (Vic).

### New Zealand

**10.26** In *Sanson v. Parval Marketing Limited,*[36] upheld on appeal under *Gachot v. Sanson,*[37] it was accepted that the first name of a person typed into an email is capable of forming part of the evidence to demonstrate the assignment of a guarantee. Asher J commented at [42]:

> I do not consider that the Parkers, in particular Mr Len Parker, would have been content with a guarantee from HMM, a company registered in the British Virgin Islands and of no established worth. Mr Gachot, on the other hand, was at the helm of a successful international brand and was clearly a man of some substance,

35 [2013] FCCA 298 (2013), 2013 WL 2253153.

36 HC AK CIV 2006-404-7231 [2008] NZHC 87 (11 February 2008).

37 [2009] NZCA (CA95/2008) 86.

> living in a Commonwealth jurisdiction. I have no doubt, viewing the exchange objectively, that the guarantee was from Mr Gachot personally and not from his company HMM. The relevant emails in June and September 2006 were exchanged with Mr Gachot personally, being addressed to 'Bertrand Gachot' at b@hype.com. In his 20 June 2006 email, Mr Gachot signed himself 'Bertrand Gachot, CEO HMM Int', but the 2 September 2006 email that he sent is worded in the first person and signed 'Bertrand' without reference to his company.

# Insurance

## United States of America

**10.27** The first two cases of names typed into a digital document that appeared to have reached the courts in the United States are from the insurance sector, illustrating, perhaps, that this particular sector, in seeking to extend the use the new technology, was the first to be caught up in spurious claims relating to the application of the law to the technology: many people may have forgotten or not even been aware of the history of judicial decision making in respect of emerging technologies during the 19th century. In 1990, insurance agents brought an action against an insurer in the case of *Wilkens v. Iowa Insurance Commissioner*,[38] alleging that the insurer failed to comply with section 515.52 of the Iowa Code, in that an agent, Larry Hertel, countersigned insurance policies by typing his name into the document on the computer. The Insurance Commissioner considered that signatures generated on a computer met the requirements of the statute, and the members of the Court of Appeals of Iowa agreed. Section 4.1(7) of the 1989 Iowa Code provided, at the material time, the following:

> *Written – in writing – signature.* The words "written" and "in writing" may include any mode of representing words or letters in general use. A signature, when required by law, must be made by the writing or markings of the person whose signature is required. If a person is unable due to a physical handicap to make a written signature of mark, that person may [make substitutions] in lieu of a signature required by law ....

**10.28** Sackett J giving the judgment of the court indicated, at 3, that the sole issue was proving intent, not the method or technology used to effect the signature:

> We find the fact that the signature is computer-generated rather than hand-signed does not defeat the purpose of the act. The

38 457 N.W.2d 1 (Iowa App. 1990).

> issue is not how the name is placed on a sheet of paper; rather the issue is whether the person whose name is affixed intends to be bound. No one argues that the agent whose name was affixed did not intend to be bound. We find the signature requirements of the statute were met.

**10.29** This litigation was followed in 1993 with the South Carolina case of *Cylburn v. Allstate Insurance Company*.[39] In this instance, the plaintiff took legal action against his insurer for breach of contract. The plaintiff's house burned down approximately two years after he stopped paying insurance premium payments. The plaintiff claimed that the policy had not been legally cancelled, which meant he had been denied insurance cover. The arguments in the case primarily focused on the interpretation of the South Carolina Code, in particular § 38-75-730(b), where cancellation arises when premiums are not paid – the cancellation is not effective unless the insured is provided with written notice of cancellation not fewer than ten days before the proposed effective date of cancellation. At the trial, the members of the jury concluded that the defendant had sent notice of cancellation of the policy to the plaintiff for failing to pay the premium. However, the jury were also asked to decide whether the insurance company had sent a written notice to their insurance agent, indicating the policy was cancelled. It appears that the insurance company sent computer disks to its agents to bring them up-to-date with changes, and the members of the jury decided that this method of providing written notice was not sufficient. On appeal, it was decided, after a brief indication that other forms of technology, such as videotapes and tape recordings were considered as 'writings,' that the computer disk sent by postal mail to the agent was equally as acceptable. Blatt SDJ indicated, at 956–7, that the form of technology was hardly a problem in reaching a decision based on sound legal principles:

> The storage of information on tape recordings and videotapes is not that much different from that on floppy diskettes for computers, but rather is more a difference in the devices used to read the information. The information can be retrieved and printed as 'hardcopy' on paper. In today's 'paperless' society of computer-generated information, the court is not prepared, in the absence of some legislative provision or otherwise, to find that a computer floppy diskette would not constitute a 'writing' within the meaning of [S.C.Code 1976] § 38-75-730.

**10.30** The nature of the evidence in such cases is important, and any organization relying on any form of technology, including specialized electronic signature software, will need to gather sufficient evidence of the signing process, as illustrated in the Louisiana case of *Bonck v. White and Progressive Security*

39 826 F.Supp. 955 (D.S.C. 1993).

*Insurance Company*,[40] where the evidence of the electronic signature of Wendi Bonck was insufficient to grant summary judgment.

# Public administration, judiciary and the police

## England and Wales

**10.31** In *Badre v. Court of Florence, Italy*,[41] an extradition order was made in enforcement of a European Arrest Warrant. The electronic signature on the certificate issued by the Serious Organised Crime Agency was challenged, because, it was argued, it was not subscribed with a physical signature in ink, but with an electronic signature in the form of letters and a number: 'GW (200820)'. There was no other dispute about the content of the certificate. It was accepted that in all other respects the document produced was a proper certificate. The certificate was issued under the provisions of s2(7) and (8) of the Extradition Act 2003. The purpose of the certificate is to assert the authority to issue an arrest warrant under the Act. Counsel for the appellant submitted that the provision of a proper certificate under s2 of the Act is a precursor to the validity of the warrant and the subsequent jurisdiction of the court. When a certificate is issued, the requested person may be lawfully arrested. The powers of the court follow on from such an arrest. If the arrest cannot be shown to be lawful, the court has no jurisdiction. Mr Summers argued that a machine purported to issue the certificate in this case. McCombe LJ rejected this argument, indicating that it seemed clear that the designated authority provided the certificate. The official causing the certificate to be issued used their initials GW and an identifying code as a means of authentication. The electronic form of the signature on the certificate did not act to detract from the validity of it. The judge then went on to observe, at [16], that a manuscript signature would be preferable:

> It is perhaps unfortunate that the electronic age has produced more haste and less speed, because it has thrown up this technical argument where none existed before. It must surely be the easiest task in the world to produce a signature in ink, or at least the full name and designation of the individual certifying and perhaps an official stamp or rubric confirming that that individual does indeed certify the contents of the document to lend some additional force of authority to the certificate that is being produced. I would hope that SOCA would consider either reverting to the old practice of producing these certificates, properly signed by a real person, in the form that was actually used

40 115 So.3d 651 (La.App. 4 Cir. 2013); see also California: *Coffey v. Beverages & More, Inc.*, 2014 WL 1691552; Mississippi: *Buckhalter v. Penney Corporation, Inc.*, 2012 WL 4468455.

41 [2014] EWHC 614 (Admin), [2014] A.C.D. 93.

in an earlier warrant in this case (subsequently withdrawn); or at least better identifying the individual making the certification on the face of the document.

**10.32** An identical point was taken in *The Queen on the Application of Neculai Jugan v. Deta Court of First Instance, Romania*,[42] where a certificate was issued pursuant to s2(7) of the Extradition Act 2003. It was dated 28 May 2013, and below the date were the words 'Signed LT' in type, and underneath that '#101782'. The appellant contended that this was not a valid signature, which meant that an essential procedural requirement had not been made out. This argument was rejected on the basis that a witness gave written evidence confirming the signature and the authenticity of the certificate.

## Scotland

**10.33** Many police forces in the United Kingdom now use digital systems to implement and record decisions, as in the case of *HM Advocate v. Purves*,[43] as explained by Maciver S at [7]:

> I found from that evidence that the procedure within Lothian and Borders Police is that the applications from various officers for directed surveillance are dealt with by a secure online system which meets that Force's requirements in respect of security and accessibility. A password system is used which means that only selected and appropriate individuals can access the system and once authorization has been given by a detective superintendent the authorization cannot be altered. The applying officer makes his application by typing the grounds for his request in his online application and that is read on screen by a detective superintendent or superior rank who, having considered the application, either grants or refuses authorization. If authorization is granted as in this case, the reasons for authorization are typed personally by the superintendent and thus entered into the secure system.

**10.34** In this instance, the solicitor advocate for the first accused argued that the authorization for directed surveillance granted by the police superintendent in terms of the Regulation of Investigatory Powers (Scotland) Act 2000 was not in writing until it was printed off, and it could not therefore be a valid authorization until that time, and that when it was printed off, it did not have the signature of the authorizing superintendent and was also defective on that account.[44] The

42 [2014] EWHC 460 (Admin), 2014 WL 640434.

43 2009 GWD 30-479, [2009] HCJ 2, 2009 SLT 969, [2009] ScotHC HCJ_2, 2010 SCL 88.

44 Interestingly, there was no mention in the judgment of the content of the chapter written by Iain G. Mitchell QC, 'Scotland', in Mason (ed.), *Electronic Evidence* – the first edition was published in 2007.

Sheriff rejected both arguments. As a matter of general principle, he dismissed the first argument at [11]:

> I found on a simple basis of commonsense and reality, that it must be accepted and understood that in every phase of life, society has moved forward, and specifically in this connection has moved on from only producing documents in pen and ink, and that the development is normal and acceptable. I did not find it an acceptable or reasonable argument that an online document which had not yet been printed off but which had been typed and was viewable on a screen was not to be regarded as being 'in writing'. I came to the view that such a document, having been prepared in this case by Detective Superintendent Doneghan personally by depressing the keys on his personal computer and by the use of a secure system, was in fact a written document and was preserved for future use within Lothian and Borders Police online system. I consider it to be a flawed argument to suggest that that document could not be regarded as a written document until it was actually printed off and could be held in the hand for reading purposes.

**10.35** Regarding the issue of whether the authorization was signed, there is no requirement for the document to be signed under the provisions of the statute, which follows that the authorization was valid.

## United States of America

**10.36** Challenges involving the name typed into an email began to occur in 1997. The first challenge appears to be the Massachusetts case of *Doherty v. Registry of Motor Vehicles*,[45] relating to public documents and concerning the interpretation of revisions to the relevant code. The plaintiff's driving license was suspended by the Massachusetts State Police following his arrest for operating a motor vehicle while under the influence of intoxicating liquor and for refusing to take a breathalyser test. The police officer submitted his report to the Registry of Motor Vehicles in the form of an email. When submitting a report, an officer is required to make such reports under the penalties of perjury. The plaintiff contended that because the email did not contain the officer's manuscript signature, the Registrar of Motor Vehicles could not act on the content of the email. The relevant text is taken from the memorandum of decision as follows:

> The report is not signed by anyone. At the bottom of the report, there are statements indicating the identity of various state police

45 No 97/CV0050 (Suffolk, SS Massachusetts District Court, May 28, 1997), available online at http://www.loundy.com/CASES/Doherty_v_RMV.html; electronic signatures are used routinely in traffic offences, for which see the Canadian cases of *R v. Eged*, 2009 BCPC 180 (CanLII) and *City of London v. Caza*, 2010 ONSC 1548 (CanLII) by way of example.

> troopers and their functions. The report states that 'Thomas Kelley' is the officer before whom the refusal was made and that 'Tpr. Kevin Hogaboom' is the other person who witnessed the refusal. At the bottom of the report there is the following statement: 'This is the report of TROOPER THOMAS KELLEY and was made by TROOPER THOMAS KELLEY under the penalties of perjury. Data entry and transmission were done by KELLY, THOMAS by or at the direction of TROOPER THOMAS KELLEY'.

**10.37** Agnes J held that the email was signed where the statement was made under the penalties of perjury, even where the report did not contain a manuscript signature:

> I conclude that a police officer who files or transmits (or who has another file or transmit) a report that is required by law to be made to the Registry of Motor Vehicles or to some other agency or individual by means of Email or some other electronic method in which there is a statement that identifies the officer making the report and a statement that it is 'made under the penalties of perjury' has 'signed' the document and is subject to a prosecution for perjury if the report is wilfully false in a material manner even though the report does not contain a handwritten signature.

**10.38** In reaching his decision, he considered the effect of the legislation, which was amended in 1995, and relevant case law. Amongst other conclusions, he noted that the legislature removed the requirement that the police officer's report had to be in writing; that the format of the report may be approved by the registrar, and the legislature inserted a new phrase to permit the mode of communication to include electronic means of transmission. In essence, the changes were meant to give effect to the use of email in such circumstances. A similar case was brought before the court in New York in relation to the pre-programmed insertion of the electronic signature of the issuing officer regarding a simplified traffic information charging a person for driving while intoxicated.[46] The defendant claimed that the charging documents failed to comply with the requirements of New York State Criminal Procedure Law, s100.40 'Local criminal court accusatory instruments; sufficiency on face' in that the signature was not properly validated because no signature was actually made and there was no evidence of any other acknowledgement or affirmation by the officer in relation to the authentication of the information. The judge, Fryer J, indicated that the officer met all the requirements by personally preparing the information, served it on the defendant, and provided a verified supporting deposition.

**10.39** Lawyers and members of the judiciary use electronic signatures. This is demonstrated in the Florida case of *Florida Department of Agriculture and*

46 *People of the State of New York v. Patanian*, 20 Misc.3d 298, 857 N.Y.S.2d 482.

*Consumer Services v. Haire,*[47] in which it was decided that a judge might affix an electronic signature to a warrant. Warner J observed, at 1059–60:

> When a judge issuing a warrant directs the use of an electronic signature, it is clear that the judge is attesting to the act of issuing the warrant. Accordingly, we find no prohibition to the use of an electronic signature, so long as it is the judge who authorizes and is in control of its use.
>
> The record here, however, discloses that in one instance an issuing magistrate authorized the Department to affix his signature to search warrants. We disapprove of a procedure which would permit the Department itself to prepare and electrically sign warrants with the judge's signature. However, technologically there is no reason why the Department could not provide the judge with software, expertise, and assistance to issue such warrants without the judge actually permitting the Department to electronically sign the warrants on the judge's behalf.

**10.40** The Supreme Court of Arizona reached a similar conclusion that the name of a judge typed in a judgment constitutes a signature in the case of *Haywood Securities, Inc., v. Ehrlich,*[48] in which Ryan J indicated that nothing in the Rules of Civil Procedure or case law prohibited judgments from being signed electronically, and commented at 741 that 'the defining characteristic of the requirement that a judgment be "signed" is that the document has affixed to it in some form the name of the judge that evidences *an intention of authentication*' (italics in the original). In the case of *Kloian, d/b/a Arbor Management Company v. Domino's Pizza, L.L.C.,*[49] the Supreme Court of Michigan also considered the names of attorneys typed at the bottom of emails constituted electronic signatures, and upheld an initial settlement agreement negotiated between the parties and agreed through their lawyers by exchange of emails.

## Statute of Frauds

**10.41** Email is a particularly useful means of communicating and negotiating the terms of contracts. Aside from the question as to whether the content of an exchange of emails is sufficient to demonstrate the formation of a contract, one of the issues is whether the exchange of electronic communications were signed,[50]

47 836 So.2d 1040 (Fla.App. 4 Dist. 2003), rehearing denied *Haire v. Florida Department of Agriculture and Consumer Services,* 870 So.2d 774 (2004), 29 Fla. L. Weekly S67.

48 149 P.3d 738 (Ariz. 2007).

49 733 N.W.2d 766 (Mich.App. 2006).

50 Kentucky: *Commonwealth Aluminum Corporation v. Stanley Metal Associates,* 186 F.Supp.2d 770 (W.D.Ky. 2001) (correspondence between a manufacturer and supplier comprising a series of letters, facsimile transmissions and emails, held to satisfy the Statute of Frauds.

and if so, whether the emails were sufficiently signed under the relevant Statute of Frauds, or whether the signatures in an exchange of emails between the parties clearly identified the parties.[51] Of interest is where some judges do not indicate what form of signature is referred to in a judgment. In the Wisconsin case of *Alliance Laundry Systems, LLC v. Thyssenkrupp Materials, NA*,[52] an exchange of emails took place that may have been deemed to constitute sufficient to form a contract with a value greater than US$500, which therefore required the agreement to be in writing, in accordance with the Uniform Commercial Code. In a hearing where the buyer applied for summary judgment, Lynn Adelman J indicated that an electronic signature constituted a signature under the provisions of the Uniform Commercial Code. In this instance, it is presumed that the electronic signature was in the form of names typed into the respective emails that were exchanged.

## Canada

**10.42** In Canada, an electronic signature in an email was held to constitute a signature under the Statute of Frauds 1677.[53]

## England and Wales

**10.43** In England and Wales, Clarke J indicated in *Golden Ocean Group Limited v. Salgaocar Mining Industries PVT Ltd* at 103[54] that 'an email, the text of which begins "Paul/Peter", may be regarded as signed by Peter because by that form of wording Peter signifies that he is addressing Paul and authenticates the content of the whole of what follows'. On appeal,[55] it was common ground between Clarke

---

By implication, the signatures on the emails must have been acceptable to the court).

New York: *Page v. Muze, Inc.*, 270 A.D.2d 401; 705 N.Y.S.2d 383; 2000 N.Y. Slip Op. 02646 (an unsigned email made an equivocal reference to terms and was not shown to have satisfied the subscription requirement); *Sel-Lab Marketing, Inc., v. Dial Corp.*, 48 UCC Rep.Serv.2d 482, 2002 WL 1974056 (S.D.N.Y.) (an exchange of emails did not conform to the Statue of Frauds partly on the grounds that only one of the emails was signed, but not by the party to be charged. The judge did not appear to consider whether the name in the email address could be an electronic signature); *Al-Bawaba.com, Inc., v. Nstein Technologies Corp.*, 19 Misc.3d 1125(A), 2008 WL 1869751 (N.Y.Sup.), 2008 N.Y. Slip Op. 50853(U) (the first name of the sender typed into the bottom of an email provided evidence of the intent to authenticate the email).

51 In the Californian case of *Carimati di Carimate v. GinsGlobal Index Funds*, 2009 WL 3233538 (C.D.Cal.), Matz J indicated that the signatures in an exchange of emails between the parties clearly identified the parties. Although this was a motion by the defendants to dismiss the causes of action, which the judge denied, the judge felt the need to indicate that this was the correct position under the Delaware statute.

52 570 F.Supp.2d 1061, 66 UCC Rep.Serv.2d 427.

53 *Leoppky v. Meston*, 2008 ABQB 45 (CanLII).

54 [2011] EWHC 56 (Comm).

55 *Golden Ocean Group Ltd v. Salgaocar Mining Industries PVT Ltd* [2012] 1 Lloyd's Rep 542, [2012] 3 All ER 842, [2012] EWCA Civ 265, [2012] 2 All ER (Comm) 978, [2012] 1 WLR 3674, [2012] 1 CLC 497, [2012] WLR(D) 70.

J and the members of the Civil Division of the Court of Appeal that an electronic signature is sufficient and that a first name, initials[56] or a nickname will suffice. It was argued by Mr Kendrick on behalf of Golden Ocean that the affixing of the first name 'Guy' to an email was not done in a manner that indicated that it was intended to authenticate the document. On this point, Tomlinson LJ said, at [32]:

> I do not accept Mr Kendrick's first argument. Chartering brokers may communicate with one another in a familiar manner but that does not detract from the seriousness of the business they are conducting. In my judgment Mr Hindley put his name, Guy, on the email so as to indicate that it came with his authority and that he took responsibility for the contents. It is an assent to its terms. I have no doubt that that is a sufficient authentication.

## United States of America

**10.44** Two federal cases were decided in 2002 and 2005 respectively. The facts pre-date the passing of the Electronic Signatures in Global and National Commerce Act, 15 U.S.C. § 7001–7003. In the seventh circuit case of *Cloud Corporation v. Hasbro, Inc.*,[57] in an action for breach of contract, the contract was modified by an exchange of email communications during 1996 between employees of each company, in which it was decided that the sender's name in an email satisfied the requirements of the Illinois Statute of Frauds. The report of this case is inconclusive respecting the form in which the signature took. Posner CJ for the court stated, at 296, that '... we conclude without having to rely on the Federal Act that the sender's name on an email satisfies the signature requirements of the statute of frauds', but it is not clear whether the judge refers to the name of the employee typed in the body of the text, possibly at the end of the email, or whether it is a reference to the name contained in the email address. In reaching this conclusion, Posner CJ considered the federal eighth circuit case of *Toghiyany d/b/a First Class Refurbishing v. Amerigas Propane, Inc.*,[58] in which it was concluded that emails did not include a signature. The report of this case is ambiguous, and Posner CJ commented on this at 296 '... it is unclear whether the court thought the absence of a signature fatal or thought that it was that absence combined with the absence of an essential term – the duration of the contract – that triggered the statute of frauds'.

56 *Regions Bank v. Cabinett Works L.L.C.*, 92 So.3d 945 (2012), 11-748 (La.App. 5 Cir. 4/10/12) concerned an agreement to settle a dispute by way of an exchange of emails. The Court of Appeal of Louisiana concluded that the initials of a lawyer 'DCM' at the end of an email did not establish an indication that the initials and names on the emails that the bank's counsel sent to the guarantor's counsel were adopted as electronic signatures.

57 314 F.3d 289 (7th Cir. 2002).

58 309 F.3d 1088 (8th Cir. 2002).

**10.45** The second federal case is *Lamle v. Mattle, Inc.,*[59] in which the name of an employee added to an email sent in 1997 was held to be a valid writing and signature to satisfy California's Statute of Frauds. It was observed that if the email had been sent after 1 January 2000, there would have been no question of its sufficiency under the Uniform Electronic Transactions Act, Cal. Civ. Code §§ 1633.7. The case was therefore decided on the basis of Californian common law, and Dyk CJ observed at 1362 that 'We can see no meaningful difference between a typewritten signature on a telegram and an email'. This observation must be right.

**10.46** Prior to the federal court cases noted above, the case of *Shattuck v. Klotzbach*[60] came before the Superior Court at Plymouth in Massachusetts. The parties discussed the sale of a property by an exchange of emails. In an action to enforce the contract, it was held that the emails contained sufficient terms concerning the purchase and sale of the property to form an agreement.[61] In addition, it was also held that the names of the parties typed at the end of each email was a signature, and where the husband signed on behalf of his wife where both husband and wife were aware of the negotiations, his signature was valid for his wife. Murphy J indicated, at 361, that 'Taken as a whole, a reasonable trier of fact could conclude that the emails sent by the defendant were "signed" with the intent to authenticate the information contained therein as his act'.[62] This was followed by the New York case of *On Line Power Technologies, Inc., v. Square D Company,*[63] where it was held that an exchange of emails provided sufficient evidence to suggest the parties intended to enter into an agreement for the payment of commissions, and it was made clear that the emails contained valid electronic signatures under N.Y. State Technology Law § 104 (2003) and 15 U.S.C. § 7001 (2003). The form of the signature is not clear. The description given is that the name 'Steven J. Maling, NE Regional Service Sales Manager for Square D' was included in the relevant emails, and the emails originated from the email address of the company. There are three possibilities: the name was typed at the end of the email, or it was included in the email address or it was both typed at the end of the email and included as part of the email address. Another New York case was also heard in the same year, that of *Rosenfeld v. Zerneck,*[64] where it was held that the content of an exchange of emails was not sufficient to create a binding

59 394 F.3d 1355 (Fed. Cir. 2005).

60 14 Mass. L. Rptr 360; 2001 WL 1839720 (Mass. Super.).

61 The Court of Appeals of Texas agreed with the trial court that the description of a property contained in three emails, with typed signatures, satisfied the Statute of Frauds in *Dittman v. Cerone*, 2013 WL 5970356.

62 For a contrary view, see *Vista Developers Corp., v. VFP Realty LLC*, 17 Misc.3d 914, 2007 N.Y. Slip Op. 27418 in that electronic signatures were not held to constitute a writing for the purposes of contracts concerning conveyances of real estate, which are dealt with separately and exclusively in the General Obligations Law, § 5-703.

63 2004 WL 1171405 (S.D.N.Y.).

64 776 N.Y.S.2d 458 (Sup. 2004).

agreement to buy and sell property, but Kramer J recognized that a name typed at the end of an email constitutes an electronic signature and satisfies the Statute of Frauds. The further New York case of *Bazak International Corp. v. Tarrant Apparel Group*[65] concerned allegations of breach of contract and unjust enrichment, in which it was confirmed that where the name of the sender is typed at the bottom of an email and typed on the company's letterhead, the signature satisfies the requirements of the statute.

**10.47** There will be occasions when an exchange of emails is capable of confirming the existence of an oral contract, thus bringing it within the Statute of Frauds in some jurisdictions, as in the Illinois case of *Polyad Company v. Indopco Inc.*,[66] where an exchange of emails with the sender's name in the email was held to constitute an electronic signature.

# Wills

**10.48** There are circumstances when a will has been considered for probate as a result of being written on a computer, and it is conceivable that a court may be required to consider the content of an email that is clearly testamentary in character – perhaps an email sent by a service man or woman while on active duty.[67] One state in the United States of America has enacted legislation to enable an electronic will.[68]

## Australia

**10.49** There have been a number of cases in Australia where wills have only been made in electronic format. Aside from deciding whether the electronic will is valid, the judges have also had to decide whether a will is signed where the deceased typed their name into the document. In the case of *In the will of Mark Edwin Trethewey*,[69] Beach J concluded that typing their name at the foot of the document was the equivalent of a signature in the circumstances of the case.[70]

65 378 F.Supp.2d 377 (S.D.N.Y. 2005).

66 2007 WL 2893638 (N.D. Ill.).

67 Jeremy Malcolm, a lawyer in Australia signed his will using digital signatures; see Angus Kidman, 'Australian makes digital will', *ZDNet Australia*, 20 Jan. 2004, available online at http://www.zdnet.com/article/australian-makes-digital-will/; *Digital Evidence and Electronic Signature Law Review*, 1 (2004), p. 90; M.C. Wood-Bodley, 'Wills, data messages, and the Electronic Communications and Transactions Act', *The South African Law Journal*, 21 (2004), pp. 526–8; a paper by W.H. Hurlburt QC, 'Electronic wills and powers of attorney: has their day come?' (Alberta Law Reform Institute) no longer appears to be available online.

68 Nevada: NRS 133.085 Electronic will.

69 [2002] VSC 83 (14 March 2002).

70 In *Mahlo v. Hehir* [2011] QSC 243 (19 August 2011), McMurdo J concluded that he was not satisfied that Dr Mahlo intended that an electronic document should form her will,

**10.50** The late Daniel Yazbek prepared a Microsoft Word document, entitled 'Will.doc' on his computer between 11 and 14 July 2009. The police later found it on his computer. Acob Yazbek, one of Daniel's brothers, claimed that this document was an informal testamentary document that formed Daniel's will. The defendants, Daniel's parents, say their son died intestate. The primary issue in dispute was whether the electronic document, 'Will.doc', or a printed out paper copy of Will.doc, satisfied the requirements of s8 of the Succession Act 2006 (NSW) sufficiently for the court to declare either to be Daniel's last will.[71] The judge, Slattery J, determined that the document was probably created by Mr Yazbek, as set out at [26]:

> The name 'Daniel Yazbek' at the end of Will.doc was not in the form of an electronic signature, reproducing his handwriting. The words of his name were typed like the rest of Will.doc. The internal evidence of Will.doc strongly supports the inference that Daniel created it. Daniel's password could have been discovered by other users by trial and error methods. But there was no suggestion in the evidence that any other individual was either in a position to access Daniel's laptop or had any motive to create documents such as Will.doc on Daniel's laptop.

**10.51** It was not in contest that Will.doc was not executed or witnessed in conformity with the formal requirements of s6(1) of the Succession Act, although Mr and Mrs Yazbek did not concede that the printed out document may not have been executed in accordance with s6(1). The judge determined that the document, whether in electronic format or in paper format was a document, and therefore came within the provisions of s8 of the Succession Act; that Will.doc purported to state Daniel's testamentary intention, and that it was intended to be his will.[72] Although the printed version of the document was not signed with a manuscript signature, nevertheless the judge concluded, at [116], that the act of typing his name on the second page of the electronic document after the final salutation represented a degree of adoption of Will.doc as operative and therefore valid.

## Canada

**10.52** An early example of a will prepared in digital format is the Quebec case of *Rioux v. Coulombe*,[73] where the police found a note after the testatrix committed suicide on 4 May 1996 that led to the discovery of a diskette, with the following

because she knew that in writing a new will, she had to do more than type or modify a document upon her computer. She understood that she had to sign it.

71 *Alan Yazbek v. Ghosn Yazbek* [2012] NSWSC 594 (1 June 2012).

72 *Alan Yazbek v. Ghosn Yazbek* [2012] NSWSC 594 at [79]–[81]; [82]–[90]; [113]–[120].

73 (1996), E.T.R. (2d) 201 (Qc. Sup. Ct.).

text written by hand on the label: 'Cecu est mon testament/Jacqueline Rioux/1er février 1996' ('This is my will/Jacqueline Rioux/1 February 1996'). A single electronic file was stored on the disk, comprising directions of a testamentary nature. There was no signature in the document. The file had been last saved on 16 April 1996 at 10:25 am. On the same day, the testator wrote in her diary that she had made a will on her computer, bearing the date 1 February 1996. Michaud, greffier (master) of the Quebec Superior Court, decided that the text did not meet the requirements of article 726 of the Code civil du Québec, requiring a holograph testament.[74] However, he found the electronic will to be valid under the dispensing power of Quebec. In so doing, he failed to address any of the evidential issues that arose out of the circumstances.[75]

**10.53** In the case of *Buckmeyer Estate (Re)*,[76] the executor proffered three documents for admission to probate: a will dated 5 May 2007, an email dated 23 August 2007, and an amendment to the will dated 27 August 2007. The will was properly proven. The issue to be determined was whether the email and the amendment were testamentary documents and whether s37 of The Wills Act, 1996, S.S. 1996 c. W-14.1 applied. The email was from the deceased, John Buckmeyer to the executor (johnbuckmeyer@hotmail.com to dave.gibson@sasktel.net). The subject was 'John's arrangements'. The email consisted of two pages. It was accepted that he wrote the email, and that it contained his electronic signature. The content indicated that he was very sick and in his last days, and stated that he wanted to give the executor more information and express his wishes clearly before he died. The deceased listed his credit accounts, gave a direction with respect to his cremation, where his ashes were to be sent and directions with respect to funeral services. Ottenbreit J considered the provisions of the Electronic Information and Documents Act 2000, S.S. 2000 c. E-7.22 in respect of the electronic signature in the email. The judge, it is respectfully suggested, correctly indicated that the issue was whether the content of the email complied with the provisions of the Wills Act. The issue was whether the content of the email constituted a disposition intended to take effect on death, reflecting testamentary intention, and an essential element for a clause to be considered testamentary is the disposal of property. In this instance, Ottenbreit J decided that the purpose of the email was to provide additional information to the executor in carrying out his duties. It was not a testamentary document and therefore not admitted to probate.

74 Brown J considered the meaning of the word 'holograph' in detail in the case of *In the Matter of the Estate of Reed v. Buckley*, 672 P.2d 829 (Wyo. 1983) at 831–2, and reached the logical conclusion that a tape recording could not be considered to be in writing. It follows that a will drafted using digital data cannot be a holographic will.

75 N. Kasirer, 'From written record to memory in the law of wills', *Ottawa Law Review*, 29 (1997–8), pp. 39–61, suggested, at p. 44, that the Master was somewhat perfunctory in deciding that the diskette and the text recorded did not constitute a holographic will, missing the opportunity of testing the elasticity of the ordinary rules of form, and he went on to discuss the evidential problems that were not addressed (pp. 44–8).

76 2008 SKQB 260 (CanLII).

## South Africa

**10.54** Such matters were covered in the South African case of *Macdonald v. The Master*,[77] where the deceased committed suicide on or about 14 December 2000 and left in his own handwriting four notes dated 13 December 2000 on a bedside table next to the bed on which he was lying. One of the notes read as follows:

> I, Malcom Scott MacDonald, ID 5609065240106, do hereby declare that my last will and testament can be found on my PC at IBM under directory C:/WINDOWS/MYSTUFF/MYWILL/PERSONAL.

**10.55** The deceased was employed as a senior IT specialist with IBM Global Services. The evidence before the court was that the personal computer allocated to the deceased was controlled by a password that only the deceased knew. Each employee with a personal computer at IBM was required to change their password every month, to record the password on a piece of paper, seal it in an envelope, and hand it over to an employee whose job was to safeguard the passwords by keeping them in a locked facility. Only three senior members of staff had the right to request the password. On 14 December 2000, Mr Dimmick, the Professional Development Manager with a right to obtain the password, obtained access to the computer and printed the contents on to paper. The document purported to be his last will and testament. It was handed to his widow. The file was then deleted. The document had the following heading: LAST WILL AND TESTAMENT FROM MALCOLM SCOTT MACDONALD. The first paragraph read:

> I, the undersigned, Malcolm Scott Macdonald (ID 5609065240106), divorced, do hereby revoke all wills, codicils and other testamentary acts heretofore made by me and declare the following to be my last will and testament.

**10.56** The document then appointed an executor and set out the disposition of the deceased's property, but it was neither dated nor signed by any witnesses or the deceased. The Master refused to accept the will, because it failed to comply with the provisions of s2(1)(a), in that it is necessary for a will to be in writing, signed, attested by two competent witnesses, and the testator must initial every page. Hattingh J set out the requirements necessary for the will to be accepted at 70 F-G:

> In order to be successful with their application under this section, the applicants must, on a balance of probabilities, establish:
>
> (a) the documents, annexures A and F were drafted by the deceased;
>
> (b) that the deceased had died since the drafting of the documents; and

77 2002 (5) SA 64; S. Snail and N. Hall, 'Electronic wills in South Africa', *Digital Evidence and Electronic Signature Law Review*, 7 (2010), pp. 67–70.

(c) the documents were intended by the deceased to be his will.

**10.57** It was necessary to decide whether the requirements of section 2(3) had been satisfied, which reads:

> If a court is satisfied that a document or the amendment of a document drafted or executed by a person who has died since the drafting or execution thereof, was intended to be his will or an amendment of his will, the court shall order the Master to accept that document, or that document as amended, for the purpose of the Administration of Estates Act, 1965 (Act No. 66 of 1965), as a will, although it does not comply with all the formalities for the execution or amendment of wills referred to in subsection (1).

**10.58** Hattingh J commented that the legislature introduced s2(3) with the intention of eliminating injustice and inequity where a person failed to comply with the formalities set out in s2(1). It was necessary to determine whether the deceased drafted the documents. Of the two approaches that could be adopted (the document must be drafted in the deceased's handwriting, or the document may be typed by the deceased or even dictated by the deceased), the judge adopted the liberal approach, commenting at 71A-B that:

> The retention of the formal requirements of s2(1) and the peremptory nature of s2(3) do not justify a strict interpretation of s2(3). Not only is this inconsistent with the very purpose of s2(3), namely to prevent the last wishes of a testator from being nullified by a non-compliance with technical formalities, but it also does not take cognizance of the realities of the technological world we live in.[78]

**10.59** The second point, that the deceased had died since the drafting of the documents, was accepted, as was the third point, that the testator intended the draft will to be his last will and testament. Hattingh J usefully set out the factors at 72C-G that were of importance in reaching his decision:

> (a) the documents are a clear indication of the deceased's intention that they should be regarded as his will and testament;
>
> (b) the documents are not preliminary sketches or notes for discussion with an attorney or anybody else to draft a will, but his final wishes;
>
> (c) there is no element of suspicion of fraud attached to the documents and their reproduction;
>
> (d) there is no suspicion that there could have been any tampering with the computer or the documents;

78 Hattingh J gave detailed reasons for trusting the digital data and the surrounding circumstances at 71G-J.

(e) not only did the documents exist on the computer, but there was indeed clear reference by the testator to these specific documents in his notes;

(f) there was a clear indication by the deceased where this document could be found on his computer;

(g) only the deceased had access, by way of secret password, to put the documents on the computer;

(h) only the deceased could have typed the said documents;

(i) they could only be extracted upon the instructions of the deceased in his own handwriting and only with the deceased's own secret code.

**10.60** In this case, Hattingh J concluded, at 72I-J, that s2(3) called 'for an approach which promotes an extensive or flexible interpretation. This is also in accordance with the spirit of the technological age ...'. Although the testator did not sign his name in the document, it could be argued that the password served a similar function.

## United States of America

**10.61** The Tennessee case of *Taylor v. Holt*[79] also serves to illustrate the fluid notion of an electronic signature, and the circumstances surrounding the making of a purported electronic will. Steve Godfrey prepared his last will and testament on his computer and affixed his computer-generated signature at the end, described in the report as his 'stylized cursive signature'. Two neighbours witnessed the will by each signing their name below the signature applied by Mr Godfrey, and dated the document next to their respective signatures. He died approximately one week later. Doris Holt, Mr Godfrey's girlfriend, submitted the will for probate. Mr Godfrey's sister filed a complaint alleging, in part, that the will was not signed and claiming that Mr Godfrey had died intestate. Doris Holt was granted summary judgment on the basis that there were no undisputed material facts and that all the legal requirements concerning the execution and witnessing of the will had been met. This decision was upheld on appeal. Swiney J, delivering the opinion of the Court of Appeals, noted, at 833:

> In the case at hand, Deceased did make a mark that was intended to operate as his signature. Deceased made a mark by using his computer to affix his computer-generated signature, and, as indicated by the affidavits of both witnesses, this was done in the presence of the witnesses. The computer-generated signature made by Deceased falls into the category of 'any other symbol or methodology executed or adopted by a party with intention to authenticate a writing or record', and, if made in the presence of two

79 134 S.W.3d 830 (Tenn.Ct.App. 2003).

> attesting witnesses, as it was in this case, is sufficient to constitute proper execution of a will. Further, we note that Deceased simply used a computer rather than an ink pen as the tool to make his signature, and, therefore, complied with Tenn. Code Ann. § 32-1-104 by signing the will himself.

**10.62** The phrase 'stylized cursive signature' could mean that it was a biodynamic version of a manuscript signature; alternatively, he could have inserted a file with his scanned signature; and as a further alternative, he could have typed his name using the keyboard, then altered the font to change the look of the signature. The report also does not indicate the form of signature used by the witnesses, but it is probable that they merely typed their names into the document, using the keyboard. If this was the case, and if it becomes generally acceptable to sign a will using an electronic signature, it is possible to foresee that it will be necessary to consider what evidence there is to confirm the witnesses whose names were placed on the will actually attended the signing of the will and affixed their electronic signatures to the document. If such a state of affairs becomes the norm, it is probable that in proving probate, the witnesses will have to give evidence, which may serve to defeat the witnessing of the will.

**10.63** In reaching its decision, the members of the court considered the formalities for the execution and witnessing of a will in Tennessee, as provided for in the Tennessee Code § 32-1-104, which states:

> 32-1-104. Will other than holographic or nuncupative. —
>
> The execution of a will, other than a holographic or nuncupative will, must be by the signature of the testator and of at least two (2) witnesses as follows:
>
> (1) The testator shall signify to the attesting witnesses that the instrument is the testator's will and either:
>
> (A) The testator sign;
>
> (B) Acknowledge the testator's signature already made; or
>
> (C) At the testator's direction and in the testator's presence have someone else sign the testator's name; and
>
> (D) In any of the above cases the act must be done in the presence of two (2) or more attesting witnesses.
>
> (2) The attesting witnesses must sign:
>
> (A) In the presence of the testator; and
>
> (B) In the presence of each other.

**10.64** On the face of these provisions, it seems possible to sign a will with an electronic signature, and the members of the court prayed in aid the definition of a signature under § 1-3-105(27) as it then was of the Tennessee Code. One commentator[80] has argued that this decision is correct, because of the definition of 'signature' in the Tennessee Code permits all forms of signature, including electronic signatures:

> 1-3-105. Definition of terms used in code.
>
> (31) "Signature" or "signed" includes a mark, the name being written near the mark and witnessed, or any other symbol or methodology executed or adopted by a party with intention to authenticate a writing or record, regardless of being witnessed;

**10.65** The rational is that because the Tennessee statute of wills does not alter the meaning of these words, the electronic signature is acceptable in this instance. However, this decision was reached in 2003, after the passing of Senate Bill No. 376.[81] The Uniform Electronic Transactions Act, § 47-10-103 limits the scope of the use of electronic signatures, and specifically excludes wills:

> 47-10-103. SCOPE.
>
> (a) Except as otherwise provided in subsection (b), this act applies to electronic records and electronic signatures relating to a transaction.
>
> (b) This act does not apply to a transaction to the extent it is governed by:
>
> > (1) A law governing the creation and execution of wills, codicils, or testamentary trusts;

**10.66** It appears that the members of the court interpreted some of the legislation, but failed to consider all of the relevant legislation, which means this decision cannot be very persuasive.[82]

80 C.M. Ross, 'Probate – *Taylor v. Holt*: the Tennessee Court of Appeals allows a computer generated signature to validate a testamentary will', *The University of Memphis Law Review*, 35 (2005), pp. 603–18, at p. 613.

81 Public Acts, 2001, Chapter No. 72 Senate Bill No. 376, passed on 9 April 2001 and approved on 11 April 2001; Uniform Electronic Transactions Act, Tenn. Code Ann. §§ 47-10-101 to 47-10-123.

82 In 2007, the Borgarting lagmannsrett (Court of Appeal for the region near Oslo) in Norway was required to determine whether an electronic copy of a testament that was lost could be admitted into probate in the case of LB-2006-27667, for which see J. Bing, translation and commentary, *Digital Evidence and Electronic Signature Law Review*, 5 (2008), pp. 134–40.

# Constitution of legal entity

## Australia

**10.67** In *Islamic Council of South Australia Inc v. Australian Federation of Islamic Councils Inc*,[83] Brereton J observed at [22] that the constitution of the organization did not explicitly require that a request be signed, but went on to observe that 'if it were necessary that it be formally signed, the word "Ramzi" was subscribed to the email with the intent of authenticating the communications, and constitutes a signature notwithstanding that it appears in typewritten and not handwritten form'.

# Amending boilerplate contractual terms

**10.68** The findings in the above cases, especially those cases that revolve around the exchange of emails, are significant. Even if the Industrial Tribunal decision of *Hall v. Cognos Limited* from England and Wales is not binding on any court, it remains a good decision. This is partly because the format of the document is irrelevant. First, the effect the case law should have on the advice that a lawyer gives their clients is highly pertinent, whether dealing with commercial contracts, employment contracts or any other form of relationship that is possible to create or vary in writing. Consider, by way of example, a standard clause added to most contracts in the following terms:

> The contract shall not be altered unless done so in writing and signed by both parties.

**10.69** If the words 'in writing and signed' remain as a standard element in such a clause, it will leave open the probability that contracts, no matter how long they have taken to negotiate, or their apparent length, are susceptible to being varied by an exchange of emails, perhaps between two fairly junior employees, or a person posing as an employee using the company email address.[84] This may well occur because most organizations have now lost control of their means of communication, because all, or virtually all, employees in some sectors have the ability to communicate with the outside world by means of email and other forms of technology, contrary to the position before the introduction of such facilities. This problem will be mitigated to a certain extent in contracts which provide

83 [2009] NSWSC 211.

84 As occurred in *CSX Transportation, Inc., v. Recovery Express, Inc.*, 415 F.Supp.2d 6 (D.Mass. 2006); D. Fosbrook and A.C. Laing, *The A-Z of Contract Clauses* (5th edn., London: Sweet & Maxwell, 2010) have prepared a number of boilerplate clauses at A.541 to A.572, but with the exception of A.568, all the combinations are written in such a way that the contract might be altered by an exchange of emails, although some of the examples will require one or more signatures of authorized representatives.

a list of nominated personnel within each organization who have the authority to agree alterations and variations. In such circumstances, if a junior employee agrees an alteration without reference to those who are authorized to agree such changes, any dispute will centre on what, if any, authority was vested in the junior employee, and whether their actions acted to bind the organization. From the point of view of the organization, it is imperative to ensure that its employees are made aware of the effect that a promise can have if made by exchange of email. To mitigate this problem, it may be wise to establish whether the parties are content for a contract to be altered by exchange of emails, and if not, to include an amended version of the standard clause, such as, by way of example:

> The contract shall not be altered unless done so in writing on paper and signed with the manuscript signature of both parties.

**10.70** The *Hall v. Cognos Limited* case illustrates the ease by which a contract can be varied, as does *C&S Associates UK Ltd v. Enterprise Insurance Company Plc*,[85] the Ohio case of *In re National Century Financial Enterprises, Inc., Amedisys, Inc., v. JP Morgan Chase Manhattan Bank, as Trustees*,[86] and New York case of *Stevens v. Publicis, S.A.*.[87] In the *Amedisys* case, a regular exchange of emails took place between employees of Amedisys and National Century over the amount of funding Amedisys would need from week to week. It was held that the exchange of email messages were sufficient to satisfy a clause in an agreement between the parties specifying that its terms could be modified only in writing. The clause read:

> Section 10.6 Amendments; Waivers; Consents
>
> No modification, amendment or waiver of, or with respect to, any provision of this Agreement, and all other agreements, instruments and documents thereto, nor consent to any departure by the Seller or the Subservicer from any of the terms or conditions thereof, shall be effective unless it shall be in writing and signed by each of the parties hereto. Any waiver or consent shall be effective only in the specific instance and for the purpose for which it is given ....

**10.71** After a brief discussion on the meaning of what constituted 'writing,' the Calkoun BJ stated the decision of the court at 596:

> In this case, Amedisys sent a weekly email to NCFE to notify how much funding Amedisys wanted for that week. Further, Amedisys was provided, on a weekly basis, with reconciliation reports showing its requested funding amounts. The Court finds that

85 [2015] EWHC 3757 (Comm).

86 310 B.R. 580 (Bkrtcy.S.D.Ohio 2004).

87 50 A.D.3d 253, 854 N.T.S.2d 690, 2008 N.Y. Slip Op. 02880.

> these weekly emails and reconciliation reports satisfy the writing and signature requirements of the Sale Agreement. Further, the Court finds that these emails modified the Sale Agreement where Amedisys received funds from the sale of the accounts receivable on its terms when it so directed the NCFE Defendants instead of receiving funds automatically upon the sale of the accounts receivable.

**10.72** A further point centres on whether the use of email is appropriate and reasonable in the circumstances. Whether the use of email is a reasonable means of communication between two parties, or any number of parties, will depend on arrange of factors, as indicated by Marrero DJ in *Bazak International Corp. v. Tarrant Apparel Group*, where he commented, at 387–8:

> Nonetheless, whether email is an appropriate and reasonably expected form of communication between the two particular parties before the court is a question of fact. Here, the issue's resolution requires a factual inquiry into trade usage and course of dealing ... Neither party directly addresses whether email is an appropriate method of communication in the re-sale trade generally or in Tarrant and Bazak's particular relationship. Yet later email correspondence from Tarrant to Bazak (the 'GMAC email') provides evidence in light of which a reasonable jury could find that the parties did accept email as an appropriate form of communication.

**10.73** This view corresponds with that expounded in *Campbell v. General Dynamics Government Systems Corporation*,[88] although this issue was never debated with other forms of communication, such as the use of telegrams or telex.[89]

88 321 F.Supp.2d 142 (D.Mass. 2004), *affirmed* 407 F.3d 546 (1st Cir. 2005).

89 The position is reinforced in the case of *Basis Technology Corporation v. Amazon.com, Inc.*, 71 Mass.App.Ct. 29; 878 N.E.2d 952 (Mass.App.Ct. 2008).

# 11

# The name in an email address

**11.1** The name in an email address is capable of identifying a person, especially where an email address in an organization, whether public or private, is allocated by setting out the name of the person followed by the domain name of the organization. There are other variations that can be used, such as when an email address describes the office or function of the person, rather than their name. However, even this, if allocated to a single person, can also function to identify an individual. The link between the prefix of the email address and the person responsible for sending the email can be problematic: for instance, the sender may be able to choose the first part, and may decide to adopt letters or numbers or a combination of letters and numbers with a view to obfuscating their identity. Further, the sender might hide the true email address. If it was not obvious who the sender was, and if correspondence ensues and a dispute occurs, it will be a matter of establishing what, if any, evidence there is pertaining to the source of the relevant emails as a preliminary point. It has been held in a number of jurisdictions that the name in an email address, or the combination of the name and the domain name in an email address can be a form of electronic signature.

## *Limitation Act*

**11.2** The case of *McGuren v. Simpson*[1] raised the issue as to whether correspondence by email was capable of constituting an acknowledgement that was in writing and signed for the purposes of the Limitation Act 1969 (NSW). Mr Simpson and Ms McGuren were in a relationship between 1992 and 2000. Mr Simpson received a cheque for A$23,000 when he was in prison in November 1993 in respect of a claim for damages for personal injuries he suffered in a motor vehicle accident. He endorsed the cheque in favour of Ms McGuren's sister to enable her to bank the cheque in her account on behalf of Ms McGuren (Ms McGuren did not want to pay the cheque into her own account, otherwise it would have affected the state benefits she was receiving at the time). Mr Simpson claimed that the defendant used the money almost entirely for her own purposes and he sought recovery of the money from Ms McGuren. Ms McGuren asserted that she used the money in accordance with his instructions and with his approval. Mr Simpson's main item of evidence was in the form of an email sent to him by Ms McGuren. It read in part:

> Date: Wed, 29 Sep 1999 14 16.20+1000
>
> To: "Rob – yahoo"<Robert-john-simpson@yahoo.com.au>

1 [2004] NSWSC 35.

S. Mason, *Electronic Signatures in Law* (London: Institute of Advanced Legal Studies, 2016), chapter 11, 'The name in an email address', pp. 255–85.

> From: "McGuren, Kim" Kim.Mcguran@air.gov.au
>
> I am going to try and book a cab for 6pm at childcare does that suit you?
>
> It probably won't turn up but I may as well book it. So, what do you want to do: split up, – go to counselling or – just blame each other for every thing since everything is obviously the other persons fault, for the rest of our lives? Yes, I spent the money and I shouldn't have and yes, you have been violent and you shouldn't have so what now??

**11.3** Master Harrison dealt with an appeal from a Local Court Magistrate, and the main issue to determine was whether Mr Simpson's cause of action was statute barred under s14 of the Limitation Act 1969 (NSW). The time limit is extended under the provisions of s54 where the person against whom the cause of action lies confirms the cause of action by acknowledging it to the person who holds the action, providing the acknowledgment is in writing and signed by the maker. Mr Simpson's case was that Ms McGuren acknowledged the cause of action in the email she sent when she wrote the words 'Yes, I spent the money and I shouldn't have'. The Magistrate previously determined that the email was an electronic communication within the meaning of s9(1) of the Electronic Transaction Act 2000 (NSW). However, the Act was not in force at the time the email was sent, which meant the provisions of the Act did not apply to the email, hence the Magistrate's decision was incorrect. Master Harrison dealt with the problem in the context of the common law. First, he concluded that the email constituted a written document. In so doing, he noted the expansive approach taken in other jurisdictions [at 20], and decided to construe the Act to take into account the changes in technology [at 21], a view taken by judges in England and Wales and the USA in the 19th century: 'It is my view that ..... s 54 of the Act ought to be read to accommodate technological change and that, accordingly, the email sent by the plaintiff constitutes a written document'. Second, he agreed with the decision of the Magistrate, that the email address was a signature for the purpose of s54(4) of the Limitation Act 1969 (NSW), at [22]:

> As Ms McGuren's name appears in the email and she expressly acknowledges in the email as an authenticated expression of a prior agreement, the email is recognisable as a note of a concluded agreement. Accordingly, the Magistrate was correct at law to conclude that Ms McGuren signed the email and that the requirements of s 54(4) of the Act were met. It was open to the Magistrate to find that Ms McGuren acknowledged the claim and she has admitted her legal liability to pay Mr Simpson that which he seeks to recover.

## Statute of Frauds

**11.4** The question arose in the English case of *J Pereira Fernandes SA v. Mehta*[2] whether the name forming part of an email address could be construed as a signature. J Pereira Fernandes SA is a Portuguese company that supplied bedding products in July 2002 to Bedcare (UK) Limited, a company of which Mr Mehta was a director. Bedcare failed to pay for the products it had received, and was wound up on a Petition by J Pereira Fernandes SA by an Order made on 7 March 2005. The cause of the appeal before HH Judge Pelling QC, sitting as a judge of the Chancery Division, related to the presentation of a winding up petition by J Pereira Fernandes SA on 12 January 2005. On 20 February 2005, an email was sent from the email address 'Nelmehta@aol.com' to Ian Simpson & Co, solicitors acting for J Pereira Fernandes SA.[3] Mr Mehta's name was not typed at the end of the email. On 9 November 2005, District Judge Harrison gave summary judgment to J Pereira Fernandes SA in the sum of £24,985.53 and ordered Mr Mehta to pay the costs of the claim, which were summarily assessed in the sum of £1,080.00. Mr Mehta was subsequently given permission to appeal by Holman J on 20 February 2006. The email contained the following text:

> ... I would be grateful if you could kindly consider the following.
>
> If the hearing of the Petition can be adjourned for a period of 7 days subject to the following:
>
> a. A Personal Guarantee to be given in the amount of £25,000 in favour of your client – together with a list of my personal assets provided to you by my solicitor
>
> b. A repayment schedule to be redrawn over a period of six months with a payment of £5,000.00 drawn from my personal funds to be made before the adjourned hearing
>
> I am also prepared to give a company undertaking not to sell market or dispose of any company assets without prior consent from your client pending the signing of the Personal Guarantee.

**11.5** The email address that appeared on this particular email also appeared on other emails sent to Ian Simpson & Co by Mr Mehta, which included his name typed at the end of the email. There were two matters of relevance to consider:

2 [2006] 1 WLR 1543; [2006] 2 All ER 891; [2006] 1 All ER (Comm) 885; [2006] All ER (D) 264 (Apr); [2006] IP & T 546; *The Times* 16 May 2006; [2006] EWHC 813 (Ch).Note: the case is cited as *Mehta v J Pereira Fernandes SA* on the British and Irish Legal Information Institute website, but *J Pereira Fernandes SA v. Mehta* in the All England Law Reports. The citation from the All England Law Reports has been adopted.

3 In the reports, it is said that Mr Mehta caused one of his members of staff to send the email. The email was sent on Tuesday 20 February 2005 at 20:30. It was subsequently confirmed in May 2006 to Ian Simpson & Co by the Insolvency Service in Manchester that no employee or salary records were recorded as being delivered up for Bedcare (UK) Limited (information provided by Ian Simpson & Co to the author).

whether the e-mail could be considered a sufficient note or memorandum, and if so, whether it was signed by the party charged, that is, by him, or by somebody else on his behalf. The email was a rare example of a document that is brought into the purview of s4 of the Statute of Frauds 1677.[4] This is because s4 now only applies to contracts of guarantee, and the content of this email provided a guarantee, in that Mr Mehta offered to personally cover debts owed by the company. Section 4 reads:[5]

> Noe action shall be brought ... whereby to charge the defendant upon any speciall promise to answere for the debt default or miscarriages of another person ... unlesse the agreement upon which such action shall be brought or some memorandum or note thereof shall be in writeing and signed by the partie to be charged therewith or some other person thereunto by him lawfully authorized.

**11.6** Harrison DJ, in giving summary judgment, considered that the email did amount to a note or memorandum of guarantee, although he did not explicitly comment on whether the names in the email address could amount to a signature. Judge Pelling QC agreed with Harrison DJ on this point, and also held the email to be a note or memorandum that brought it within s4 of the statute. He commented on the purpose of the statute as follows at [16]:[6]

> The purpose of the statute of frauds is to protect people from being held liable on informal communications because they may be made without sufficient consideration or expressed ambiguously or because such a communication might be fraudulently alleged against the party to be charged. That being so, the logic underlying the authorities I have referred to would appear to be that where (as in this case) there is an offer in writing made by the

4 For a history of the Statute, see W.S. Holdsworth, *A History of English Law Volume VI* (London: Methuen & Co, 1924), pp. 379–97. Holdsworth considered the Statute was out of date when he wrote this text, at 396: '... the prevailing feeling both in the legal and the commercial world is, and has for a long time been, that these clauses have outlived their usefulness, and are quite out of place amid the changed legal and commercial conditions of to-day.'; see also E. Rabel, 'The Statute of Frauds and comparative legal history', *Law Quarterly Review*, 63 (1947), pp. 174–7, in which he concluded, at 187, 'The case against the Statute of Frauds has been proved time and again by outstanding authorities, even before the Sixth Interim Report of the English Law Revision Committee of 1937 solemnly pronounced sentence for repeal. An examination of the historical background on which the Statute arose can but support the views expressed by the Revision Committee and the conclusion that the Statute essentially belongs to distant times, far removed from the conditions of modern life'.

5 *Halsbury's Statutes of England and Wales Volume 11(1)* (4th edn., 2010 reissue), 7; Chronological Table of the Statutes Part 1 (HMSO).

6 [2006] 2 All ER 891 at 16.

> party to be bound which contains the essential terms of what is offered *and* the party to be bound accepts that his offer has been accepted unconditionally, albeit orally, there is a sufficient note or memorandum to satisfy s 4.

**11.7** The second question to consider was whether the email had been signed. Solicitors for J Pereira Fernandes SA already had a number of emails from Mr Mehta in which he included his name typed at the bottom of the text. In this respect, the evidence of a number of communications from the same address demonstrated that they were authentic. Mr Mehta did not dispute the email was sent.

**11.8** The evidence upon which a decision could be made in *Fernandes* was more substantial than the evidence that Prakash J dealt with in *SM Integrated Transware Ltd v. Schenker Singapore (Pte) Ltd.*[7] In this instance, Judge Pelling QC took the view that the email address was similar to an automatically generated name and facsimile number of the sender of a facsimile transmission, although his comments, at [19], noted that a human being had to type the data into the software:

> As is well known to anyone who uses email on a regular basis, what is relied upon is not inserted by the sender of the email in any active sense. It is inserted automatically. My knowledge of the technicalities of email is not sufficiently detailed to enable me to know whether it is inserted by the ISP with whom the sender or the recipient has his email account. However, I accept Mr Aslett's submission that as a matter of obvious inference, if it is inserted by the latter it can only be from information supplied by the former. Mr Mehta suggested that the address was inserted by his employee. I do not see how this could be so and certainly Mr Mehta was not able to give me a coherent explanation of how that might be so. It is possible that Mr Mehta's employee was authorized to use Mr Mehta's e mail account remotely but, even if that is so, I do not see how that can impact on any of the issues I have to resolve since it is not in dispute that the email was sent on the instructions of Mr Mehta and the method by which the sender address came to be inserted would not be affected even if that was the position.

**11.9** That such information is considered in judgments to be 'automatic' illustrates a misunderstanding. A human being has to put the information into the machine. The facsimile number of the sender is put into the machine by a person, as is the name in an email address or the 'signature block' of an email.[8]

7 [2005] 2 SLR 651, [2005] SGHC 58.

8 Considered in the New York case of *Parma Tile Mosaic & Marble Co., Inc., v. Estate of Fred Short, d/b/a Sime Construction Co.*, 155 Misc.2d 950, 590 N.Y.S.2d 1019 (Supp. 1992), *motion for summary judgment affirmed*, 209 A.D.2d 495, 619 N.Y.S.2d 628 *reversed* 663

**11.10** Counsel for J Pereira Fernandes SA submitted that the intent to sign was not relevant, and mentioned *Elpis Maritime Co. Ltd. v. Marti Chartering Co. Inc.*,[9] which had different facts to the case in point, and also emphasised the decision in *Evans v. Hoare*,[10] where the name and address were relied upon to serve as a signature. However, the judge pointed out that in *Evans v. Hoare*, Cave J considered, at 597, that the place of the signature was not relevant: 'Whether the name occurs in the body of the memorandum, or at the beginning, or at the end, if it is intended for a signature there is a memorandum of the agreement within the meaning of the statute'. Judge Pelling QC then went on to indicate that the name of the party to be bound must be intended for a signature. In reaching this conclusion, the judge did not refer to the comments made by Cave J (at 597–8) after the text he quoted, which are highly significant:

> In the present case it is true that the name of the defendants occurs in the agreement; but it is suggested on behalf of the defendants that it was only put in to shew who the persons were to whom the letter was addressed. The answer is that there is the name, and it was inserted by the defendants' agent in a contract which was undoubtedly intended by the defendants to be binding on the plaintiff; and, therefore, the fact that it is only in the form of an address is immaterial. A case was referred to in the argument, *Schneider v. Norris*, in which a printed bill-head was held to amount to a signature within the meaning of the statute. That is a stronger case than the present. The printed heading there was not put into the document for the purpose of constituting a memorandum of the contract; but it was so used with the assent of the party sought to be charged, and it therefore was held to have the effect of a signature. This shews that it is unimportant how the name came to be inserted in the document. (reference omitted)

**11.11** The judge considered that the approach he took was supported by the decision in *Caton v. Caton*,[11] where Richard Bewley Caton, aged 78 in 1852, a clergyman of the Church of England, proposed marriage to Mrs Harriet Henley, a widow of about 60 years of age. Both parties owned property, and Mr Emmet, a solicitor, was requested to draw up the settlement upon the basis of a draft written by the Reverend Caton. After the settlement was prepared, the Reverend Caton first suggested to Mrs Henley it was too long, and later suggested they could save expense by not executing the settlement at all. Mrs Henley agreed

N.E.2d 633 (N.Y. 1996), 640 N.Y.S.2d 477 (Ct.App. 1996), 87 N.Y.2D 524; see also the New Zealand case of *Welsch v. Gatchell* [2007] NZHC 1898; [2009] 1 NZLR 241; (2007) 8 NZCPR 708; (2007) 5 NZ ConvC 194,549 (21 June 2007).

9 [1992] 1 AC 21, HL.

10 [1892] 1 QB 593; (1892) 66 LTRep NS 345.

11 (1867) LR 2 HL 127.

not to execute the settlement on his promise that he would strictly and faithfully carry out the terms of the memorandum, and leave certain property to her in his will. Despite the remonstrations of Mr Emmet that Mrs Henley ought to insist upon entering the settlement before marriage, Mrs Henley married the Reverend on 7 February 1853. The Reverend Caton took possession of Mrs Henley's property and paid her £80 a year. Mrs Henley's fortune was estimated to be about £14,904. At the time of their marriage, the Reverend showed Mrs Henley a will that appeared to be in conformity with the promise he made. It was duly executed. He died on 24 January 1864, when it then transpired that he had made a new will, without the knowledge of Mrs Caton, revoking all others, leaving her with less than she otherwise expected. Mrs Caton took legal action to enforce the marriage settlement. The agreement began with the introductory words 'in the event of a marriage between the under-named parties' and the initials of the Reverend Caton appeared four times with reference to particular instructions. Stuart VC found for Mrs Caton at first instance, a decision that was reversed on appeal by Cranworth LC. Upon further appeal to the House of Lords, the appeal was dismissed. The sole question was whether, where the Reverend's initials appeared on the document, they served to apply to the entire document. It was determined that the document was a mere draft of proposal for a settlement, and there was insufficient evidence to show the initials of the Reverend applied to the entire document. On the position of the initials, Lord Chelmsford LC said at 139:

> The cases on this point cited in the course of the argument establish that the mere circumstances of the name of a party being written by himself in the body of a memorandum of agreement will not of itself constitute a signature. It must be inserted in the writing in such a manner as to have the effect of 'authenticating the instrument', or 'so as to govern the whole instrument', to use the words of Sir *William Grant*, in the case of *Ogilvie v. Foljambe* [(1817) 3 Mer 53; 36 ER 21], or in the language of Mr. Justice *Coleridge*, in *Lobb and Knight v. Stanley* [(1844) 5 QB 574; 114 ER 1366], 'so as to govern what follows'. Now I cannot think that the occurrence of Mr. *Caton's* name in the manner in which it appears can possibly be taken to govern the entire memorandum, although the whole of it is in his handwriting. (Italics in the original)

**11.12** He continued at 139–40:

> The name of the party, and its application to the whole of the instrument, can alone satisfy the requisites of a signature. In the memorandum in question, Mr. *Caton's* name is incidentally introduced with reference to a particular purpose, or as matter of description, and as this mention of his name would clearly be insufficient in itself, it cannot have any new effect given to it by the introductory words of the memorandum.

**11.13** Lord Westbury indicated, at 143 that what is alleged to constitute the signature must:

> ... be so placed as to shew that it was intended to relate and refer to, and that in fact it does relate and refer to, every part of the instrument. ... it must govern every part of the instrument. It must shew that every part of the instrument emanates from the individual so signing, and that the signature was intended to have that effect. It follows, therefore, that if a signature be found in an instrument incidentally only, or having relation and reference only to a portion of the instrument, the signature cannot have legal effect and force which it must have in order to comply with the statute, and to give authenticity to the whole of the memorandum.

**11.14** This case might be compared to the decision in the case decided by the Master of the Rolls, *De Biel v. Thomson*[12] and subsequently affirmed by the Lord Chancellor and reaffirmed upon further appeal, *Hammersley v. De Biel, an infant, by Blake*,[13] where an extremely vague promise, the evidence of which was very tenuous, was upheld under the Statute of Frauds.

**11.15** Earlier cases on the physical position of the signature also emphasizes the need to consider the intent behind the signature, as commented on by the Lord Chief Baron in *Stokes v. Moore*,[14] where the defendant prepared instructions for the renewal of a lease, written in his own hand and with his name appearing in the body of the draft. It was held, first, not to be a sufficient memorandum of agreement, and second, not considered signed by the defendant. The Lord Chief Baron discussed this at 222:

> The purport of the statute is manifest, to avoid all parol agreements, and that none should have effect, but those signed in the manner therein specified. It is argued that the name being inserted in any part of the writing is a sufficient signature. The meaning of the statute is, that is should amount to an *acknowledgment by the party* that it is his agreement, and if the name does not give such authenticity to the instrument, it does not amount to what the statute requires. (Italics in the original)

**11.16** Eyre B also commented at 223:

> The signature is to have the effect of giving authenticity to the whole instrument, and if the name is inserted *so as to have that effect*, I do not think it signifies much, in what part of the instrument it is to be found: it is perhaps difficult, except in the case of a letter with a postscript, to find an instance where a name inserted in the

12 3 Beav. 469.

13 [1845] 12 Clark & Finnelly 45; 8 ER 1312.

14 (1786) 1 Cox 219; 29 ER 1137.

> middle of a writing can well have that effect; and there the name being generally found in a particular place by the common usage of mankind, it may very probably have the effect of a legal signature, and the extend to the whole; but I do not understand how a name inserted in the body of an instrument and *applicable to particular purposes*, can amount to such an authentication as is required by the statute .... (Italics in the original)

**11.17** In *Ogilvie v. Foljambe*,[15] a letter written by the plaintiff relating to the sale of a lease situated in Grosvenor Place began 'Mr Ogilvie has the pleasure to acquaint Mr Foljambe ....' In this instance, Sir William Grant MR held the name governed all that followed in the letter. His comments are noted at 62:

> Another question is, whether, taking the agreement to be sufficiently explicit in terms, it has the signature which is required by the statute. It is admitted that, provided the name be inserted in such manner as to have the effect of authenticating the instrument, the provision of the act is complied with, and it does not much signify in what part of the instrument the name is to be found.

**11.18** In *Holmes v. Mackrell*,[16] a promissory note written in the hand of the defendant with his name written on top, but not signed at the end, was held to be a sufficient signature for the document. One submission argued by S. Temple QC for the defendant was that the signature must be at the foot of the document, to which Crowder J responded, at 792 'Is it the less the signature of the party, because he writes his name at the top of it?'. Counsel in turn responded to this question 'In the case of a will, it is true, the signature under Car. 2, c. 3, s.5, might be in any part of it: but, even there, it must have been made with the design of authenticating the instrument.' In his judgment at 796, Crowder J intimated why this issue was of some importance:

> In the case of a note written in the third person, the name at the commencement serves to authenticate the document just as well as a formal signature at the foot of it. If, then, the signature is sufficient, what does the defendant say here? In effect he says, – 'I have given two promissory notes for 510*l*., and I am now liable upon them'. That is a plain and deliberate and unconditional acknowledgment of a debt, and it is clear from the case of *Tanner v. Smart*, 6 B. & C. 603, 9 D. R. 549, and the authorities which have followed it, that, where there is an absolute and unconditional acknowledgment of an existing debt, a promise to pay is to be inferred. It seems to me that the acknowledgment here is one from which a promise to pay must necessarily be inferred.

15 (1817) 3 Mer 53; 36 ER 21.

16 (1858) 3 C.B. (N.S.) 789; 140 ER 953.

**11.19** It appears that judges, when dealing with cases where a promise was made that affected an innocent party, and the person making the promise subsequently sought to avoid being held to their promise by arguing a technical point that the promise was not signed, thus making it unenforceable, were, generally, not willing to allow the person making the promise to succeed on such a technicality. Two of the most notable English cases, *Lobb and Knight v. Stanley*[17] and *Tourret v. Cripps,*[18] neither of which was cited or discussed in *Fernandes*, illustrates that similar situations had arisen in the past, and lawyers and judges have previously been required to deal with similar factual situations as in *Fernandes.* In *Lobb,* Stanley, a certified bankrupt, gave a written promise signed by him after his bankruptcy. Three undated letters were produced, one of which read 'Mr Stanley begs to inform Mr Lobb ...'. It was considered sufficient that he began the text with his name, and his name governed the promise that followed.[19] In *Tourret v. Cripps,*[20] Mr R. L. Cripps wrote in his own hand on a sheet of memorandum paper an offer to lease parts of 14 and 15 Mortimer Street, Cavendish Square. The memorandum was not signed by him, but contained, at its head, the words 'From Richd. L Cripps' and his address. Tourret, who initiated an action against Cripps for specific performance, accepted the offer. His printed name served as a signature to hold him to the promise he made.

**11.20** In *Orton v. Collins,*[21] Peter Prescott QC sitting as a Deputy Judge made the following observations in relation to *Mehta v. J Pereira Fernandes S.A.* at [21]:

> Mr Zelin doubted whether simply typing 'Putsmans' on the email amounted to a signature that complied with the Practice Direction, citing *Nilesh Mehta v. J Pereira Fernandes S.A.* [2006] EWHC 813 (Ch), but wisely he did not waste much time on the point. In that case the signature was alleged to be constituted by the words 'From: Nelmehta@aol.com' appearing in the email header. It was a mere statement of the sender's email address and it would have been generated automatically after the message was transmitted. *It was not put there by the sender with the intention of authenticating the document.* In contrast, in our case the word 'Putsmans' was deliberately typed in (what is more, after the customary salutation 'Yours faithfully'). I have no doubt that its purpose would be recognised throughout the profession. Anyone would think: 'Putsmans are signing off on this document'. It was intended to

17 (1844) 5 QB 574; 114 ER 1366.

18 (1879) 48 L J Ch 567; 27 WR 706.

19 This case was specifically mentioned by Phipson that a 'signature under the Statute of Frauds may be by surname only' (S.L. Phipson, *The Law of Evidence* (6th edn, London: Sweet and Maxwell, 1921), p. 516).

20 (1879) 48 L J Ch 567; 27 WR 706. These cases were reviewed by Buckley J in *Hucklesby v. Hook* 82 LT 117.

21 [2007] EWHC 803 (Ch), [2007] 1 WLR 2953.

> signify that document was being sent out with the authority of the defendants' legal representative.' (Emphasis added).

**11.21** However, the judge seems to have taken it as granted that the word 'Putsmans' was deliberately typed in without any evidence on the point. The word, together with 'Yours faithfully' could have been part of the email template that was automatically generated when the email was created.

**11.22** The position of a name in a document has also exercised the judicial mind in the United States of America.[22] For instance, in Illinois, a warrant of attorney was held to be executed even when the defendants failed to sign a retail instalment contract on the reverse side, because a signature had been affixed to the face of the document,[23] and a number of cases have been taken under the Statute of Frauds.[24] The inclusion of a name in a document can serve two purposes: to establish that the person has signed the document, and as a means of identifying a party. For instance, Lord Millett commented, at [176] in *"Starsin", Owners of cargo & Ors v. "Starsin", Owners and/or demise charterers of*: [25]

> Where a contract is contained in a signed and written document, the process of ascertaining the identity of the parties and the capacity in which they entered into the contract must begin with the signatures and any accompanying statement which describes the capacity in which the persons who appended their signatures did so. This may require interpretation, and to this extent the process may without inaccuracy be described as a process of construction. But it is not of the same order as the process of construing the detailed terms and conditions of the contract. These describe the incidents of the contract and the nature and extent of the parties' obligations to each other. But the identity of

22 For further cases relating to individual States, see R.A. Lord, *Williston on Contracts*, vol. 10 (4th edn., n.p.: Thompson West, 1990), ch. 29, 29:35 note 30.

23 *The First National Bank of Elgin v. Husted*, 205 N.E.2d 780 1965.

24 Federal (1828): *Barry v. Coombe*, 26 U.S. 640, 1 Pet. 640, 1828 WL 2995 (U.S.Dist.Col.), 7 L.Ed. 295 (statement of account written by Robert Barry, with his name at the top and signed by Griffith Coombe and the bottom, held to be sufficient particulars of the property to be sold and signed by both parties).

California (1897): *California Canneries Company v. Scatena*, 117 Cal. 447, 49 P. 462, 49 A.Jur. 380, 112 A.L.R. 937 (the place of signature was irrelevant).

Illinois: *McConnell v. Brillhart*, 17 Ill. 354, 1856 WL 5329 (Ill.), 65 Am.Dec. 661, 7 Peck (IL) 354.

Massachusetts (1896): *New England Dressed Meat & Wool Co., v. Standard Worsted Co.*, 165 Mass. 328, 43 N.E. 112, 52 Am.St.Rep. 516.

New York: *JSO Associates, Inc., v. Price*, 2008 WL 904703 (N.Y. Sup.), 239 N.Y.L.J. 72, 2008 N.Y. Slip Op. 30862 (U).

25 [2003] UKHL 12 (13 March 2003), [2003] 1 CLC 921, [2003] UKHL 12, 2003 AMC 913, [2003] 1 Lloyd's Rep 571, [2003] 2 WLR 711, [2003] 1 All ER (Comm) 625, [2004] 1 AC 715, [2003] 2 All ER 785, [2003] 1 LLR 571.

> the parties themselves is not an incident of the contract. Where a signature is accompanied by a description of the capacity in which the signatory has appended his signature the description is not a term or condition of the contract. It is part of the signature and so part of the factual evidence of the identity of the party which is undertaking contractual liabilities under the contract.

**11.23** This point is further illustrated in the 1916 case from Virginia of *Sutherland v. Munsey*.[26] The facts are that Lafayette Sutherland and his wife Mary intended to sell their property in the county of Russell in Virginia to J. G. Muncy and H. Hardway of Russell & Wise Co. The buyers prepared an agreement for the sale and purchase of the real estate, continuing the name of the parties as follows:

> This agreement made and entered into this the 18 day of August, 1910, by and between Lafayette Sutherland, Virginia, and Mary G. Sutherland, his wife of the county of Russell and State of Virginia, parties of the first part, and J. G. Muncy and H. Hardway of Russell & Wise Co., Va. as parties of the second part.

**11.24** Mr and Mrs Sutherland signed the document at the end by means of their respective marks. The buyers refused to complete, and Mr and Mrs Sutherland took action for specific performance. In an appeal from the Circuit Court, Russell County, it was held that the writing of the names at the beginning of the document were there for the purposes of identification, not as a signature. Harrison J provided the opinion of the court at 884:

> It is, we think, clear that the names of the appellees, in the connection in which we find them, were not designed as signatures, nor written there for the purpose of authenticating the instrument, but were written in that connection for an entirely different purpose – that of identification. The language is in the usual form of introduction to such an instrument, and the entire instrument, including the location of the names of all the parties, is in the usual form – the form that would have been used if the paper been drawn tentatively without the intention of signing it. It was necessary to identify the parties to this instrument, and the names of the appellees appear with the names of all the parties, in that portion of the instrument where the names of the parties are usually mentioned for the purpose of identification.

**11.25** In comparison, Judge Pelling QC sought to distinguish the case of an email. His view is set out at [28] and [29]:

26 119 Va. 791, 89 S.E. 882.

> However, that is not the issue in this case. Here the issue is whether the automatic insertion of a person's email address after the document has been transmitted by either the sending and/or receiving ISP constitutes a signature for the purposes of s 4.
>
> 29. In my judgment the inclusion of an email address in such circumstances is a clear example of the inclusion of a name which is incidental in the sense identified by Lord Westbury in the absence of evidence of a contrary intention. Its appearance divorced from the main body of the text of the message emphasizes this to be so. Absent evidence to the contrary, in my view it is not possible to hold that the automatic insertion of an e mail address is, to use Cave J's language, '*intended for a signature*'. To conclude that the automatic insertion of an email address in the circumstances I have described constituted a signature for the purposes of s 4 would I think undermine or potentially undermine what I understand to be the Act's purpose, would be contrary to the underlying principle to be derived from the cases to which I have referred and would have widespread and wholly unintended legal and commercial effects. In those circumstances, I conclude that the e mail referred to at [3] above did not bear a signature sufficient to satisfy the requirements of s 4. (Italics in the original)

**11.26** In this particular instance, the judge made observations about the technicalities of email in the absence of expert evidence, as did Lyberopoulos J, the President of the court in the Greek case 1327/2001 – Payment Order.[27] It seems that the judge assumed that the ISP adds the email address to the document.[28] He then concluded, in the absence of any relevant technical evidence, that the email address could not, therefore, be intended as a signature. It is suggested that this approach is arguable. It is possible to distinguish the decision by Hall VC in *Tourret v. Cripps*[29] on the basis that Cripps wrote the content by hand. The decision must be correct, taking into account the handwritten text, the printed words 'From Richd. L Cripps', and the address printed on the paper. Hall VC might have speculated as to the purpose of having stationery printed, and whether each time a letter or note is sent, the use of the information printed on the letter was sufficient evidence to demonstrate an intent to sign. In this instance, as in other cases, the judge looked to the entire document for evidence

27 English translation by M.G. Rachavelias, 'Case translation – Greece', *Digital Evidence and Electronic Signature Law Review*, 3 (2006), pp. 104–7; G. Skouma, 'Case note', *Digital Evidence and Electronic Signature Law Review*, 1 (2004), pp. 83–6.

28 In *Golden Ocean Group Limited v. Salgaocar Mining Industries PVT Ltd* [2011] EWHC 56 (Comm), Mr Justice Christopher Clarke indicated, at 103, that 'There is authority that the insertion of a person's email address by an internet service provider after the document has been transmitted is, absent evidence to the contrary, incidental'.

29 (1879) 48 L J Ch 567; 27 WR 706. These cases were reviewed by Buckley J in *Hucklesby v. Hook* 82 LT 117.

to indicate intent, and taking into account the message written on the letter, together with the name printed on the top of the stationery, Hall VC considered that this was sufficient to hold the man to his promise. However, to distinguish *Tourret* from *Fernandes* in this way is far from satisfactory. This is because the facts in *Tourret* comprised a mix of text written by hand with pre-printed text. With networked communications, such a mix is impossible. The very nature of networked communications means that content must be typed - or cut and pasted - so to argue that the decision in *Tourret* is significantly different because of the additional of text written by hand cannot be right.

**11.27** Also, Judge Pelling QC did not consider the email as a complete document. The problem with this analysis is that the information contained in the 'From', 'To', 'Sent' and 'Subject' part of the email cannot be disconnected from the body. The information is neither separate when presented visually on a screen, nor when printed out on paper. In addition, the source code (usually hidden) is also an integral part of the email, and this set of metadata is of considerable evidential value, as argued by the applicant in the pleadings in the case of Tribunale Mondovì, 7 giugno 2004, n. 375 (decr.), *Giur. It. 2005, 1026.*[30] Further, should the method used to cause an email address to be attached to a particular email be of relevance, then other factors ought to be considered, including the mechanism by which the application software brings the disparate objects together to permit the user to view the email on screen, because each object will be in a different storage location on the computer.

**11.28** A similar issue relating to email correspondence confronted Phelan J in the Canadian case of *Dursol-Fabrik Otto Durst GmbH & Co. c. Dursol North America Inc.*,[31] decided after the decision by Judge Pelling QC, in proceedings for contempt of court where the defendant and his company were the subject of a number of orders prohibiting the marketing and selling of goods. One of the issues to determine was whether the defendant, Robert Scott, used email correspondence to market and sell products. In his evidence, he claimed he was ignorant of two email addresses in issue and how the signature that appeared at the end of emails worked. The evidence indicated he sent out emails that identified him in his corporate capacity. In this case, the court heard appropriate technical evidence as well as the evidence from the defendant. The judge did not believe the defendant because his evidence was both contradictory and inconsistent. In reaching his decision, the judge made some interesting and highly pertinent remarks at 56 about the use of email and the practical aspects of using email that bear repeating:

> Even if one accepted Scott's explanation, which I do not, he was a business man who used computers constantly to transact business. He took no steps to deal with his address and signature. In today's world such ignorance, or, more importantly, the refusal to secure

30 For a translation of the pleadings, see G.P. Coppola, 'Case note', *Digital Evidence and Electronic Signature Law Review*, 4 (2007), pp. 86–8.

31 2006 FC 1115.

> the technical assistance to deal with these types of matters, is not acceptable. Scott exhibited recklessness and a complete disregard for the obligations he had under this Court's Orders.

**11.29** The technical evidence demonstrated that, contrary to the defendant's assertions, he could see the default signature he set up, thus contradicting his claim that he was not aware his signature appeared at the end of the email. Further, it was also established that the defendant had a number of different email addresses, and had the option of using whichever address he chose when sending and responding to correspondence. The judge rejected the contention that the defendant's claimed lack of knowledge of email addresses and signatures was a mitigating factor in disobeying a court order.

**11.30** One further point might be usefully considered, and that is the purpose of the email address, which is of the utmost significance. The address acts to ensure the communication reaches the person it is addressed to, otherwise, an email address, even if different by one letter, number or dot is unforgiving. It will not reach its destination, unlike a letter sent by way of post, where a human being can extract information from the envelope and use their knowledge to effect delivery of an envelope incorrectly addressed. It is also suggested that the 'From' address is also used with the intent to identify the sender (it being the function of the 'Reply-to' address to indicate where, by default, a reply will be sent). If it follows that the 'From' line of an email acts to designate the sender, then the act of signature is the irrevocable despatch of the email. Additional technical evidence may be adduced to demonstrate a connection to the person that sent, or caused to be sent, a document in electronic format, taking into account all of the data associated with the document, including the metadata, client software, and any other technical information that may not be obvious on the face of the document as presented on the screen to a recipient without further exploration of the technical attributes of the software. In this respect, it is difficult to see how the email address can be considered to have merely appeared or is incidental: it is a crucial element of the document. This, it is suggested, also corresponds to the advice offered by the Law Commission:[32]

> 3.37 We do not believe that there is any doubt that clicking on a website button to confirm an order demonstrates the intent to enter into that contract. That will satisfy the principal function of a signature: namely, demonstrating an authenticating intention. We suggest that the click can reasonably be regarded as the technological equivalent of a manuscript 'X' signature. In our view, clicking is therefore capable of satisfying a statutory signature requirement (in those rare cases in which such a requirement is imposed in the contract formation context).

32 Law Commission, 'Electronic commerce: formal requirements in commercial transactions advice from the Law Commission' (2001).

> 3.38 It might be said that the click differs from other accepted forms of signature in that it does not produce a visible signature. However:-
>
> (1) The general trend in English law is that the validity of a signature depends on its satisfying the function of a signature, not on its being a form of signature already recognised by the law.
>
> (2) In combination with the information which will be available as to the email address of the 'clicker', a click is capable of satisfying the second and third functions identified in paragraph 2.6. The combination could be regarded as analogous to signing by way of a stamp.
>
> (3) Some old authorities did suggest that a signature was required to be a 'mark' which would, by definition, be visible. We believe it is unlikely that the courts would regard such authorities as binding in modern conditions.
>
> (4) On most websites the purchaser's details will appear on screen (whether entered by the purchaser on that occasion, or automatically as a result of previous transactions). Sometimes this will involve the use of an individual password. The combination of the details, any password, and the click could be regarded as analogous to a manuscript signature or a typed signature.
>
> (5) The vendor's system may display or record the click in a visible form.
>
> (6) The click may generate writing; the record of the transaction in the vendor's system and any confirmatory response to the purchaser.
>
> (7) Even if a click is less secure than a manuscript signature, reliability is not essential to validity.
>
> Conclusions on signatures
>
> 3.39 Digital signatures, scanned manuscript signatures, typing one's name (or initials) and clicking on a website button are, in our view, all methods of signature which are generally capable of satisfying a statutory signature requirement. We say that on the basis that it is function, rather than form, which is determinative of the validity of a signature.

**11.31** It is the action of clicking the 'send' icon, or causing an agent to click the 'send' icon, that is the act of authentication. This view accords with the comments offered in the Law Commission Report, where it is suggested that the clicking of an icon probably constitutes the technological equivalent of signing with mark, and is therefore a signature. Further, the action of clicking the 'send' icon tends to be the irrevocable dispatch of the communication (although if the person is quick enough, they may, depending on the software, stop the software from sending the email), and can be similar to, or the equivalent of, the act of writing a manuscript signature or affixing a stamp to a document. In this respect, the information contained in the email address serves the same function as the use of headed notepaper in *Tourret v. Cripps*. Cripps took a sheet of headed notepaper and wrote a promise on the paper. In this instance, Mehta either himself or through an agent, caused an email to be written (or cut and paste content) containing a promise. Instead of taking out a physical piece of notepaper and writing on it, he or his agent used a machine, namely a computer. The information contained in the email address served the same purpose as the name and address on the notepaper used by Cripps. Conceptually, there is no difference between the two: the cases are merely separated by time and the technology – that is, Mehta did not add any content by writing by hand. Prakash J gave her reasons for accepting the name in an email address based upon the same principle in *SM Integrated Transware Ltd v. Schenker Singapore (Pte) Ltd*[33] at 92:

> There is no doubt that at the time he sent them out, he intended the recipients of the various messages to know that they had come from him. Despite that, he did not find it necessary to identify himself as the sender by appending his name at the end of any of the emails whether the messages were sent to his colleagues or to third parties like Mr Heng. I can only infer that his omission to type in his name was due to his knowledge that his name appeared at the head of every message next to his email address so clearly that there could be no doubt that he was intended to be identified as the sender of such message.

**11.32** In analysing this case, Professor Ter Kah Lang indicated that the judge only addressed the identification function of the email address, not the intent to authenticate. Had the judge considered authentication, Professor Ter Kah Lang suggests that the conclusion might have been different.[34] Simon Blount also agrees with this analysis. However, he suggests that if Tan was saying that he did not need to sign his emails because he knew his name was already part of the email address, the decision may be correct, although in such case the author is then intended to be bound by every word sent in the email.[35]

**11.33** In the later New York case of *JSO Associates, Inc., v. Price*,[36] Bucaria J reached the same decision. In this instance the name of Edward Price appeared

33 [2005] 2 SLR 651, [2005] SGHC 58.

34 T.K. Lang, 'Have you signed your electronic contract?', *Computer Law & Security Review*, 27 (2011), pp. 75–82 at p. 77.

35 S. Blount, *Electronic Contracts* (2nd edn., Chatswood, NSW: LexisNexis Butterworths, 2015), p. 35.

36 2008 WL 904703 (N.Y. Sup.), 239 N.Y.L.J. 72, 2008 N.Y. Slip Op. 30862 (U).

in the email address at the top, but he did not type his name at the bottom of the text. The judge took the view that it was necessary to be assured that the email was sent by the person that purported to send it, or at least it was sent with their authority. Bucaria J then went on to refer to the Court of Appeal case of *Morris Cohon & Co. v. Russell*,[37] quoting the following text from 574, and indicating that although the technology had changed, the rationale had not:

> The Statute of Frauds was designed to guard against the peril of perjury; to prevent the enforcement of unfounded fraudulent claims. But ... the Statute of Frauds was not enacted to afford persons a means of evading just obligations; nor was it intended to supply a cloak of immunity to hedging litigants lacking integrity; nor was it adopted to enable defendants to interpose the Statute as a bar to a contract fairly, and admittedly made.

**11.34** The source and authenticity of the email were not questioned, and thus it was determined that the email had been signed – the name appeared as the sender of the email, and half an hour later, the sender sent a further email in which the name was typed into the bottom of the text.[38]

**11.35** Judge Pelling QC mentioned the Electronic Communications Act 2000, but no consideration was given to the provisions of s7,[39] or whether s7 applied to the facts of this case. Arguably, an email address is brought within the ambit of the Act as a form of electronic signature. First, the question is whether the email address can be considered a signature for the purposes of the Act, and the provisions of s7(2)(a) have to be considered. Section 7(2) provides:

> (2) For the purposes of this section an electronic signature is so much of anything in electronic form as-
>
> > (a) is incorporated into or otherwise logically associated with any electronic communication or electronic data; and
> >
> > (b) purports to be so incorporated or associated for the purpose of being used in establishing the authenticity of the communication or data, the integrity of the communication or data, or both.

37 23 N.Y.2d 569.

38 Although the nature of the electronic signature was not in issue in *Lindsay v. O'Loughnane* [2012] BCC 153, [2010] EWHC 529 (QB), nevertheless Mr Justice Flaux assessed all the evidence in relation to relevant emails to determine that emails were sent and signed at [54–9].

39 The judge stated, at [30], that it was his understanding that the Electronic Communications Act 2000 was enacted to give effect to Directive 2000/31/EC on certain legal aspects of information society services, in particular electronic commerce, in the Internal Market (Directive on electronic commerce) (OJ L 187/1, 17.7.2000). The aim of the Act was to implement the provisions of Directive 1999/93/EC of the European Parliament and of the Council of 13 December 1999 on a Community framework for electronic signatures, OJ L 13, 19.01.2000, p.12, as set out in Note 19 of the Explanatory Notes to the Act.

**11.36** As discussed above, an email will not arrive at its destination without a correct address, and if a person sending an email wishes the person receiving the email to reply, they must also use an accurate 'reply-to' email address, otherwise the recipient will not be able to respond. It is suggested above that there is a purpose for including a name or other form of description (such as the use of a title in lieu of a name) in the address of an email: to identify the sender. Also, technically, an email includes the various addresses in the email. Without an address, there would be no purpose in sending or receiving email correspondence. If the email address is not logically incorporated into the body of the text to be sent, the content will not be sent or received. To relate the email address to the provisions of s 7(2), it is necessary to consider the elements of an electronic signature.

> So much of anything in electronic form: This is such a wide-ranging provision that the address associated with an email must come with the term, just as the hidden metadata must also come within the term. Without the email address, the email could not be sent and received.
>
> Incorporation or logical association for the purpose of establishing authenticity or integrity: The thing in electronic form must be incorporated or logically associated with the communication or data for the purpose of being used to establish the authenticity or the integrity of the communication or data, or both. For the thing to be an electronic signature, it must be affixed to the data for a purpose: that is, to authenticate the communication or data or provide for the identity of the communication or data.

**11.37** An email address clearly comes within the requirements of this provision: it is in electronic form, and the name included in the email address is included for the purpose of establishing the authenticity of the content. If the name were a nickname or pseudonym, rather than a proper name or part of a proper name, the same conclusion would apply, based on the previous decisions at common law. If it is accepted that the email address, or the name of the person in an email address can be considered an electronic signature, it can be admitted into evidence under the provisions of s7(1).[40]

**11.38** Finally, the Law Commission considered the nature of the evidence required to demonstrate the intent to authenticate. An objective test was proposed:

> 3.29 Because signatures affect many areas of personal and commercial life, it is essential that the courts develop a straightforward approach. We believe this should be by way of a purely

40 Judge Pelling QC expressed the view, at [30], that typing a name into the main body of an email can constitute an electronic signature, which is correct.

objective test: namely, would the conduct of the signatory indicate an authenticating intention to a reasonable person? This approach is consistent with the authorities, flexible and would, over time, produce the greatest certainty.

**11.39** It is suggested that this is test cannot be right, because an objective test would need to be based on an analysis of the surrounding circumstances, including the technology, and the average person using the technology probably varies widely in terms of their technical understanding and ability, partly because the technology changes so rapidly. It is suggested that a subjective test is more appropriate.[41] This is the view taken by Flemming DJP in *Chisnall and Chisnall v. Sturgeon and Sturgeon*,[42] where he held that the signing of a contract for the sale of an erf was achieved by a mark or marks with the function of making the document an act of the signer, and of signifying assent to the content of the document. He indicated at 645F, that 'An enquiry concerning assent must, of course, not be into what the signatory subjectively planned but what his acts signify to the other party'. This is what the English authorities have also held up to this point. A subjective test will allow a judge to consider both the surrounding circumstances and what was in the mind of the sender at the moment they are deemed to sign. If the facts of *J Pereira Fernandes SA v. Mehta* are considered in this light, the conclusion must that the email in question was signed. The surrounding circumstances in this case, as in *SM Integrated Transware Ltd v. Schenker Singapore (Pte) Ltd*, were as follows:

(i) The email was from Mr Mehta.

(ii) Mr Mehta knew that his email address would appear in the email, which went to show that it came from him; it also enabled the recipient to respond; as a result, the email address was his unique mark.

(iii) There was a course of correspondence between the parties by email.

(iv) The email contained a promise made by Mr Mehta or under his authority.

(v) Mr Mehta admitted the email was sent, which indicated that he adopted the content of the email.

**11.40** In summary, it is suggested that the requirement for a signature is not dependent and should not be limited by technology, and this is borne out by the case law from the past.[43] Lawyers and judges have been required to consider how

41 The subjective test is proposed by Mr Pépin Aslett, counsel for J Pereira Fernandes SA, Nicholas Bohm and the author.

42 1993 (2) SA 642 (W).

43 In *R Mercury Tax Group Ltd, R (on the application of) v. HM Commissioners of Revenue & Customs* [2008] EWHC 2721 (Admin) the signature pages of a trust deed, an option

new technologies effect the underlying legal principles. The decisions reached in the past remain relevant: the conclusion was, and remains, that any form of mark, whatever the technology used, has the capacity to demonstrate intent, and this should be no different when considering electronic signatures. Taking this into account, the decision by Judge Pelling QC is open to question. In addition, the judge suggested, in reaching this decision, that to conclude otherwise would lead to 'widespread and wholly unintended legal and commercial effects'. Arguably, this decision has led to the opposite: there is now uncertainty, especially amongst lay people, who cannot be expected to understand that this decision only refers to s4 of the Statute of Frauds, and only to guarantees. This decision is incompatible with the previous decisions on identical facts, albeit in applying the legal principles to different technologies, and sends a signal out that implies that a person may no longer be held to their promise for the lack of typing their name into the body of an email.[44] Notwithstanding this observation, this decision is generally accepted as being correct, sometimes with no discussion,[45] and sometimes with some discussion, but without covering much of the case law discussed above.[46] Professor Ter Kah Lang set out the issue at 79: that there is a fundamental distinction between identifying the sender by means of the pre-printed letterhead, and the intent of the signatory to adopt the name as authenticating the document. Miller J commented on this point in *Welsh*

agreement and a sale/purchase agreement were signed some time before the final versions were complete, and were then attached, without the consent of those who signed the pages, to final versions that were different to the draft versions. This case caused the Law Society Company Law Committee, the City of London Law Society Company and Financial Law Sub-Committees to form a Joint Working Party and draft 'Guidance on execution of documents at a virtual signing or closing'; see also E. Walton, 'Guidance on the execution of documents at "virtual" signings following the *Mercury* case', *Butterworths Journal of International Banking and Financial Law*, 24 (2009), pp. 327–9.

44 Judges in both the High Court and Court of Appeal (Civil Division) took a different view where it appears there was no signature at all in the case of *Decouvreur v. Jordan*, The Times 25 May 1987 (or 27 May 1987) CA, 1987 WL 493255; an appeal was dismissed before a court comprising Fox and Nourse LJJ and Sir Denys Buckley, where judgment for the plaintiff had been given by Mr Justice Farquharson in the sum of £15,000 on a claim against the second defendant under a contract of guarantee. The report states that 'Any writing by which the guarantor of a debt could be identified in a memorandum of the guarantee and which showed an intention to adopt the guarantee sufficed as a signature for the purposes of the Statute of Frauds 1677'. See C. Freedman and J. Hardy, 'J Pereira Fernandes SA v. Mehta: a 21st-century email meets a 17th century statute', *Computer Law & Security Report*, 21 (2007), pp. 77–81. In *Kloian, d/b/a Arbor Management Company v. Domino's Pizza, L.L.C.*, 733 N.W.2d 766 (Mich.App. 2006) the members of the Court of Appeal in Michigan declined to accept that a name typed at the top in the heading of an email acted as a means of signature in circumstance where the statute required a subscription – that is, a signature at the bottom of the document.

45 L. Brazell, *Electronic Signatures and Identities Law and Regulation* (2nd edn., London: Sweet & Maxwell, 2008), 2-027; G. Andrews and R. Millett, *Law of Guarantees* (6th edn., London: Sweet & Maxwell, 2011), p. 82; H. MacQueen and C. Garland, 'Signatures in Scots law: form, effect, and burden of proof', *Juridical Review* (2015), pp. 107–34.

46 Lang, 'Have you signed your electronic contract?'; Blount, *Electronic Contracts*.

*v. Gatchell*[47] at [75], although arguments could abound if one party specifies a particular type of electronic signature is required:

> An electronic signature will not prove adequate unless the Court is satisfied that its insertion was intended to signify adoption of the electronic note or memorandum of which it forms part or with which it is otherwise associated. That suggests that it would be prudent for those who wish to rely on an electronic writing and signature to warn the party to be charged that the writing is a contract that will bind that party when he or she attaches an electronic signature to it, and to specify what form of electronic signature is required.

**11.41** Whether the name typed into an email can satisfy the provisions of s4 of the Statute of Frauds is open to debate. What is disappointing is the lack of consideration of the decisions by senior judges from the 19th century when faced with identical facts in slightly different formats. The common law is supposed to be based on precedent, yet pertinent decisions by senior judges have either been missed or ignored in this debate.

## Civil Procedure

**11.42** In the Greek case of 1327/2001 – Payment Order,[48] a Greek company entered an oral agreement with a Czech company situated in Prague, by which the Czech company agreed to provide lodging arrangements for groups of Greek tourists sent by the Greek company. The invoice of the Greek company was not paid on time. There was an exchange of emails between employees of the companies, and the Czech company recognized the debt in an email dated 27 July 2000, sending a further email on 12 September 2000 in which it was made clear that the company intended to pay the invoice and reiterated the promises made in the earlier email. For the emails to be admissible in evidence, they had to come within the meaning of a 'private document' as defined in articles 443 and 444 of the Greek Civil Procedure Code:

> Article 443 Civil Procedure Code: Elements of private documents. A private document has conclusive power only when it has the manuscript signature of its editor or, instead of a signature, a mark that he (the editor) drew on the document and is verified by a notary or any other public authority, which confirms that the mark is placed instead of the signature and that the editor declared that he cannot sign.

47 [2007] NZHC 1898; [2009] 1 NZLR 241; (2007) 8 NZCPR 708; (2007) 5 NZ ConvC 194,549 (21 June 2007).

48 English translation by M.G. Rachavelias, 'Case translation – Greece', *Digital Evidence and Electronic Signature Law Review*, 3 (2006), pp. 104–7; G. Skouma, 'Case note', *Digital Evidence and Electronic Signature Law Review*, 1 (2004), pp. 83–6.

> Article 444 Civil Procedure Code: Official books of merchants and other professionals. The definition of private documents also contains
>
> (1) the books that merchants and professionals are obliged to keep under commercial law or other statutes
>
> (2) the books that lawyers, notaries, doctors, pharmacists and nurses are obliged to keep under current statutes
>
> (3) photographic and cinematic representations, recordings and any other mechanical representation.

**11.43** The President of the Court, Lyberopoulos J, identified a number of criteria that were specific to email that might lend the email to being defined as a private document: first, the method by which a user authenticated themselves to an Internet Service Provider in the process of setting up an email account, leading to the conclusion that the account holder had access to the account; second, the use of a unique email address, and finally the form or layout of the content of the document. The judge concluded that the email address constituted proof of the identity of the sender, which meant an email could be considered a private document under the provisions of the Code. The comments of the judge, as translated, indicated his line of thinking:

> ... each user electronic address is unique, in that it is chosen by the sender himself, and has the characteristic of a manuscript signature, even though it does not have the traditional form of a signature. The above-mentioned are valid regardless of where the sender's electronic address appears in relation to the text that it accompanies when it appears on the screen of the computer, or its mechanical representation on paper; this follows because it is necessary to take into consideration that the authentication of the sender and the binding to his will of the content that is included in the electronic message...[49]

**11.44** The judge was also satisfied that the email was authentic and the evidence demonstrated that it was sent by the person whose name was in the email address, thus complying with the provisions of article 445 of the Civil Procedure Code. With respect to the status of the email correspondence, it was held that the original copies of the communication were the files as stored in the hard disk of the computer, and the emails were capable of being printed on paper and ratified by an attorney at law. These conclusions do not answer all of the legal issues relating to this form of evidence, because it appears the judge made a number of assumptions about the veracity of the technology and how it works that cannot be reconciled with the reality, and in the absence of appropriate expert evidence. The applicant applied to the court to order the defendant to pay the sums due by

49 Rachavelias, Case Translation – Greece, p. 105.

way of special proceedings of a payment order, which is subject to articles 623-34 of the Civil Procedure Code. A party to whom a debt is owed can make the application, on the condition that the obligation of payment and the amount is proved. In this case, Lyberopoulos J held that the email address was a signature under the provisions of articles 443 and 444(3) of the Civil Procedure Code. Another court reached the same conclusion in 2013.[50]

**11.45** In comparison, the members of the Court of Appeal in Michigan declined to accept that a name typed at the top in the heading of an email acted as an electronic signature in the case of *Kloian, d/b/a Arbor Management Company v. Domino's Pizza,*[51] under Rule 2.507(G) (as it now is: at the time of the case, it was Rule 2.507(H)) of the Michigan Court Rules of 1985, Chapter 2 Civil Procedure (updated 11 January 2011)). The Rule provides as follows:

> Agreements to be in writing. An agreement or consent between the parties or their attorneys respecting the proceedings in an action, subsequently denied by either party, is not binding unless it was made in open court, or unless evidence of the agreement is in writing, subscribed by the party against whom the agreement is offered or by that party's attorney.

**11.46** The members of the court distinguished between the phrase 'in writing and signed' and 'writing, subscribed'. The meaning of 'subscribed' in Webster's College Dictionary (2001) was referred to at 773: '"Subscribe" means "to append, as one's signature, *at the bottom of a document* or the like; sign."' (Italics in the original). This meant that the email agreeing to a modified settlement did not satisfy the requirement that it had been subscribed. The first two meanings given to the work 'subscribe' in the Oxford English Dictionary are both considered rare:[52]

> 1.1 trans. To write (one's name or mark) on, orig. at the bottom of, a document, esp. as a witness or consenting party; to sign (one's name) to. Now rare.
>
> b.1.b To write, set down, or inscribe below or at the conclusion of something. Now rare.

**11.47** The editors of the Oxford English Dictionary may consider the meaning as determined by the members of the Court of Appeal in Michigan to be rare, but the rarity of the meaning of 'subscribe' is arguably irrelevant if the meaning is clear and appropriate for the purpose. In this respect, lawyers might like to take note of this decision, although the comments by Bucaria J in *JSO Associates, Inc., v.*

50 M.G. Rachavelias, 'Case translation: Greece, Payment Order 5845/2013', *Digital Evidence and Electronic Signature Law Review*, 11 (2014), pp. 177–9.

51 L.L.C., 733 N.W.2d 766 (Mich.App. 2006).

52 *Oxford English Dictionary*, 2nd edition on CD-ROM (v. 4.0).

*Price*[53] bear consideration from the point of view of the technology under debate, in that the judge might have reached a different conclusion, given identical facts. In this instance, the judge was discussing the need for a signature to be placed at the end of a memorandum. In reference to the decision in *Steinberg v. Universal Machinenfabrik GMBH*,[54] in which an indecipherable scrawl at the top of the memorandum was held not to be sufficient to satisfy the writing to be at the end of the document, Bucaria J commented at 27:

> However, Steinberg was decided in a different technological era, when email and home computers had not even entered the public imagination. Moreover, the requirement of a signature at the bottom was to minimize the opportunity for fraudulent additions to the memorandum, a practice which is not feasible with electronic communication.

## Legal fees arrangement

**11.48** In Israel, Hagai Brenner J determined, in a claim for legal fees in the case of *Atias v. Salfan Ltd*,[55] that there was no basis for the defendant's claim that a legal fees agreement between her and the plaintiff was not signed. The plaintiff sent an email to the defendant in which he summarized their joint understanding of the legal fees. The defendant confirmed that understating in a reply message, and used an expression that literally translates to 'No problem'. A legal fees agreement is not required to be in writing (although recommended) and the email correspondence between the two parties was determined to be sufficient proof of the existence of the agreement. In the absence of any other information, such as whether the defendant also signed her name in the reply email, it may be inferred that Hagai Brenner J reached the decision based on the email address of the defendant.

## Summary proceedings

**11.49** In Italy, in the case of Tribunale Mondovì, 7 giugno 2004, n. 375 (decr.), *Giur. It. 2005, 1026*, a lawyer sought payment of fees in the sum of €3,304.80 in respect of assistance provided to a client in criminal proceedings before the Mondovì Criminal Court. The defendant acknowledged the debt in an email dated 29 April 2004, and promised that payment would occur by no later than 1 May 2004. Having failed to make the payment, the lawyer took action to recover the debt. In his pleadings, the lawyer set out the arguments to show that the email was a document in writing and signed with an electronic signature. To demonstrate the email was a document, he prayed in aid the provisions of

53 2008 WL 904703 (N.Y. Sup.), 239 N.Y.L.J. 72, 2008 N.Y. Slip Op. 30862 (U).

54 24 A.D.2d 886, 264 N.Y.S.2d 757.

55 Tel Aviv Peace Court Civil Case 24210/06 (5 July 2006, unpublished decision).

article 1(1)(b), of Presidential Decree 445/2000, that an electronic document is 'an electronic representation of legally relevant acts, facts or data', and article 8, which provides for the validity of such a document, providing that 'the electronic document, whoever made it, the registration on electronic support and the transmission with electronic instruments, are valid and relevant for any legal effect, if they conform to the provisions of this Decree'. To demonstrate the email was signed with an electronic signature, the lawyer pointed to the address of the sender, which goes to show that person who wrote the email must have inserted a username and a password. He then turned his attention to the provisions of article 10(2) of the Decree, which provides that 'The electronic document, signed with an electronic signature, satisfies the legal requirement of written form', and then questioned whether the email was signed. Article 1(1)(cc) of the Decree specifies that an electronic signature is 'a set of data in an electronic form, which is attached or logically connected to other electronic data, used as a method of authentication'. The argument thus ran:

> To say that an email has been signed with an 'electronic signature' (a 'simple' one, as opposed to a 'digital' signature, which is a particular type of qualified electronic signature, which guarantees a higher authenticity and, consequently, is a certified private document under Article 1, first Paragraph, sub-section n and 10, Paragraph 3 of the Decree) it shall contain a set of data in electronic form which may be connected with other data used as a method of authentication (the law refers to an undersigning, but this is a judicial fiction, as electronic data cannot be signed: the same applies to digital signatures and other electronic signatures).

**11.50** The judge upheld the motion and issued a summary judgment, as requested. In issuing the summary judgment, it is implied that the judge accepted the email address as an electronic signature. The use of a password and username suggested that the person that sent the email had authenticated himself or herself sufficiently accurately with the Internet Service Provider. This evidence emphasises a degree of authentication that serves to provide for the authenticity of the email, although it does not seem to have been questioned in this case.[56]

## Civil Law Act

**11.51** In Singapore, whether the name in an email address could be an electronic signature was raised in the case of *SM Integrated Transware Ltd v. Schenker Singapore (Pte) Ltd.*[57] In this instance, Prakash J determined that it was possible

56 For a translation of the pleadings, see G.P. Coppola, 'Case note', *Digital Evidence and Electronic Signature Law Review*, 4 (2007), pp. 86–8.

57 [2005] 2 SLR 651, [2005] SGHC 58; T.K. Leng, 'Concluding leases by email', *Computer Law & Security Report*, 21 (2005), pp. 423–6.

for an email address to be a form of electronic signature for the purposes of s6(d) of the Civil Law Act (Cap 43, 1994 Rev Ed). In this case, SM Integrated entered into negotiations to provide warehousing space and logistics services to Schenker. Schenker intended to enter a contract with a third party to handle dangerous goods, which in turn meant Schenker needed more storage facilities than it actually had. SM Integrated and Schenker prepared a draft agreement by way of meetings and the exchange of email correspondence, the content of which included reference to the transaction and the terms of the draft agreement. The agreement was never signed. Schenker subsequently failed to enter a contract with the third party, and because it no longer required the additional storage space, it declined to sign the draft agreement. SM Integrated initiated an action for damages suffered as a result of the alleged repudiation of the proposed lease, claiming that a combination of the draft agreement and the correspondence by email relating to the terms of the agreement demonstrated that an agreement had been formed. Schenker took the view that there was no contract, because the negotiations failed to produce a final agreement, but even if a valid contract existed, it did not satisfy the requirements of Electronic Transactions Act 1998 (Cap 88 of 1999), in that is was neither in writing nor signed.

**11.52** The arguments put forward by Schenker were not accepted. It was held that all the essential terms had been agreed, which meant an agreement for the lease did exist, and that if any conditions precedent of relevance existed, they will have been satisfied but the repudiation of the lease by Schenker. In her reasons for judgment, Prakash J gave careful consideration to the issue of whether or not the correspondence by email that passed between the parties was capable of satisfying the statute of frauds requirements of the s6(d) of the Civil Law Act (Cap 43, 1994 Rev Ed), which states:

> Contracts which must be evidenced in writing
>
> 6. No action shall be brought against –
>
> (d) any person upon any contract for the sale or other disposition of immovable property, or any interest in such property;
>
> unless the promise or agreement upon which such action is brought, or some memorandum or note thereof, is in writing and signed by the party to be charged therewith or some other person lawfully authorised by him.

**11.53** Counsel for Schenker argued that the signature and writing requirements regarding this particular type of contract were not capable of being satisfied electronically because of the provisions of s4(1)(d) of the Electronic Transactions Act 1998 (as it was then), which stated that the Act does not apply to 'any contract for the sale or other disposition of immovable property, or any interest in such property'. This argument was rejected. It was held that the provisions of the Act required judges to construe its terms in accordance with the terms set out in section 3, particularly s3(b):

> Purposes and construction
>
> 3. This Act shall be construed consistently with what is commercially reasonable under the circumstances and to give effect to the following purposes:
>
> (a) to facilitate electronic communications by means of reliable electronic records;
>
> (b) to facilitate electronic commerce, eliminate barriers to electronic commerce resulting from uncertainties over writing and signature requirements, and to promote the development of the legal and business infrastructure necessary to implement secure electronic commerce;

**11.54** In reaching a decision on this matter, it was reasonable to consider the position at common law and by construing the provisions of s6(d) Civil Law Act 1994, not by 'blindly relying on s4(1)(d) of the ETA'.[58] It was also held that the communications exchanged by email were in writing.[59] Apart from the legal basis of the decision that the emails were in writing, Prakash J, at [81], took a realistic and sound approach by making it clear that, despite the claim that the emails did not constitute writing, the facts did not correspond to such a contention:

> 81. In this case, the parties readily admitted that they had sent and received each other's email messages. No one argued or testified that the printed copies of the emails that appeared in the bundle of documents were not true copies of the emails that they had seen on screen and responded to electronically. Neither Mr Tan nor Mr Luth objected to the contents of the printed copies of their respective email messages. In fact, they confirmed that they had sent out those various messages and attached the printouts as exhibits to their respective affidavits. Mr Tan did not resile from any of his emails. He did not deny receiving the email messages and attachments sent by Mr Tan and Ms Yong (in particular he did not deny receiving Ms Yong's email of 27 January 2003 and the draft LSA that was an attachment to that email). He specifically confirmed he had sent out his response in the email of 4 February 2003 and commented in court on the contents of that email.

**11.55** Arguments that email and other documents created in digital format do not constitute 'writing' are disingenuous. The law is often derided for not responding to the development of new technologies, yet the comments made by judges in the 19th century indicated they were perfectly willing and able to apply legal principles to new forms of technology. It is widely recognized that digital data is the mainstay of many businesses and government across the world, and

58 [2005] 2 SLR 651, paragraph 76.

59 [2005] 2 SLR 651, paragraphs 77–85.

to suggest that evidence from such sources is not admissible because it is not a 'writing' is bordering on the preposterous.

**11.56** Mr Tan did not append his name at the bottom of the email, so the only evidence of a signature comprised the content of the heading: 'From "Tan Tian Tye"<tian-tye.tan@schenker.com.>' The name in the email address was considered a signature, and in reaching this conclusion, Prakash J referred to the Massachusetts case of *Shattuck v. Klotzbach*,[60] and the seventh circuit case of *Cloud Corporation v. Hasbro, Inc.*[61] In her judgment, Prakash J provided a clear exposition of the underlying principles that were established in the English and American courts in the 19th century:

> 91. I am satisfied that the common law does not require handwritten signatures for the purpose of satisfying the signature requirements of s 6(d) of the CLA. A typewritten or printed form is sufficient. In my view, no real distinction can be drawn between a typewritten form and a signature that has been typed onto an email and forwarded with the email to the intended recipient of that message.
>
> 92. One minor difficulty in this case is that Mr Tan did not append his name at the bottom of any of his email messages. All his email messages, however, including the message dated 4 February 2003 and sent to Ms Yong, had, near the start thereof, a line reading "**From**: "Tan Tian Tye" <tian-tye.tan @schenker.com>". Mr Tan confirmed in court that he had sent out those messages. There is no doubt that at the time he sent them out, he intended the recipients of the various messages to know that they had come from him. Despite that, he did not find it necessary to identify himself as the sender by appending his name at the end of any of the emails whether the messages were sent to his colleagues or to third parties like Mr Heng. I can only infer that his omission to type in his name was due to his knowledge that his name appeared at the head of every message next to his email address so clearly that there could be no doubt that he was intended to be identified as the sender of such message. Therefore, I hold that the signature requirement of s6(d) is satisfied by the inscription of Mr Tan's name next to his email address at the top of the email of 4 February 2003.
>
> 93. I recognize that one person's email facility can, in some cases, be accessed by a third party who can then send out messages which purport to be authentic messages from the owner of that email address. If that happened, the owner of the address would be entitled to dispute the authenticity of the messages purportedly

60 14 Mass. L. Rptr 360; 2001 WL 1839720 (Mass. Super.).

61 314 F.3d 289 (7th Cir. 2002).

> sent by him. That is not the case here. Further, such dispute would be as to the person who initiated the message and would not be decided on the basis of whether the message bore a signature.

**11.57** In the same year, Lai Kew Chai J referred to the decision of Judith Prakash J in the bankruptcy proceedings of *Wee Soon Kim Anthony v. Lim Chor Pee*.[62] Although the judge did not have to consider the email correspondence in this case, having determined that the exchange did not form a valid agreement because there was no meeting of the minds, nevertheless he commented, at [39], that he considered the exchange of email correspondence was likely to satisfy the written record and signature requirements of s111 of the Legal Profession Act (Cap 161, 2001 Rev Ed).[63]

## Means of authentication

**11.58** It was held in the United States of America in the federal eleventh circuit criminal case of *United States of America v. Siddiqui*,[64] that an email was correctly authenticated under the requirements of Federal Rules of Evidence 901(a), because a number of internal factors supported the authenticity of the email, including the email address: 'msiddiquo@jajuar1.usouthal.edu', the use of a nickname of the sender, 'Mo,' written at the end of the email, and pertinent content.[65] With respect to the content of an email address, Wilson DJ observed by in footnote 4 in the case of *Poly USA, Inc., v. Trex Company, Inc.*:[66]

> In its initial supporting brief, Poly claimed that when Beladakis signed the May 28, 2004, emailed document that it became binding on both parties because Trex 'signed' the document with an electronic signature by sending it through a Trex email account. See 15 U.S.C. § 7006 ('The term "electronic signature" means an electronic sound, symbol, or process, attached to or logically associated with a contract or other record and executed or adopted by a person with the intent to sign the record.'). Poly

62 [2005] 4 SLR 367, [2005] SGHC 159.

63 Note also *Singh Chiranjeev v. Joseph Mathew* [2008] SGHC 222, [2009] 2 SLR 73.

64 235 F.3d 1318 (11th Cir. 2000).

65 See also: Missouri: *International Casings Group, Inc., v. Premium Standard Farms, Inc.*, 358 F.Supp.2d 863 (W.D.Mo. 2005), 2005 WL 486784.

New York: *Medical Self Care, Inc., v. National Broadcasting Company, Inc.*, 2003 WL 1622181 (S.D.N.Y.) in a Memorandum Opinion, Swain J determined that an email containing the text 'ConAgra is OK' constituted written consent authorizing SelfCare to assign its remaining advertising time to ConAgra. It is not clear if the person sending the email typed their name at the bottom of the email. If not, the judge implied acceptance of the authenticity of the email from the email address alone; *JSO Associates, Inc., v. Price*, 2008 WL 904703 (N.Y. Sup.), 239 N.Y.L.J. 72, 2008 N.Y. Slip Op. 30862 (U) (email address accepted as a signature).

66 W.D. Va. No. 5:05-CV-0031 (March 1, 2006).

> did not pursue this argument at the hearing nor in its additional briefing. Nevertheless, the court finds the use of a Trex email account to send an email does not necessarily constitute an electronic signature under 15 U.S.C. § 7006 and, moreover, that Trex did not intend to electronically sign the emailed document by sending it from a Trex email account. Thus, the May 28 emailed document was not binding.

**11.59** In commenting upon the suggestion that an email address can demonstrate proof of intent, although rejecting that it could in this particular case, the judge made the pertinent observation that the use of the email address does not necessarily constitute an electronic signature where there is no intention to sign. This must be correct, and whether an email address is capable of constituting a form of electronic signature will depend on the facts of each case.

# 12

# A manuscript signature that has been scanned

**12.1** A variation of the biodynamic version of a manuscript signature is where a manuscript signature is scanned from the paper carrier and transformed into digital format, which makes it very easy to use by the recipient for the purposes of forgery.[1] The files containing the representation of the signature can then be attached to a document. This version of a signature is used widely in commerce, especially when marketing materials are sent through the postal system and addressed to hundreds of thousands, if not millions, of addresses. It could be argued that when sending a document by facsimile transmission, that the recipient of the document has in their possession this version of the manuscript signature: the entire document is scanned and transmitted, together with the content. Arguably, this is the form of signature that was discussed in the case of *Re a debtor (No 2021 of 1995), Ex p, Inland Revenue Commissioners v. The debtor; Re a debtor (No 2022 of 1995), Ex p, Inland Revenue Commissioners v. The debtor*[2] where a completed form of proxy was sent by facsimile transmission. Although the report does not clearly state the proxy form, as transmitted, contained the manuscript signature of the relevant official from the Commissioners of Inland Revenue, it can be inferred that a manuscript signature had been appended to the original form of proxy that was sent by facsimile transmission. Laddie J offered an opinion in relation to this point at 351f-g:

> For example, it is possible to instruct a printing machine to print a signature by electronic signal sent over a network or via a modem. Similarly, it is now possible with standard personal computer equipment and readily available popular word processing software to compose, say, a letter on a computer screen, incorporate within it the author's signature which has been scanned into the computer and is stored in electronic form, and to send the whole document including the signature by fax modem to a remote fax. The fax received at the remote station may well be the only hard copy of the document. It seems to me that such a document has been 'signed' by the author.

**12.2** This observation must be correct. Providing the sending party intended the recipient to accept such a signature as a method of authentication and to act upon the content of the document transmitted, the method used to transmit the signature remains merely a method by which the document or message is communicated. The means of communication used should not

1 See chapter 6 for examples of forged electronic signatures.

2 [1996] 2 All ER 345, Ch D.

S. Mason, *Electronic Signatures in Law* (London: Institute of Advanced Legal Studies, 2016), chapter 12, 'A manuscript signature that has been scanned', pp. 287–89.

affect the legal consequences that follow the delivery and subsequent receipt of the document.[3]

## Mortgage redemption

**12.3** In 2006, a registration judge in Denmark refused to cancel a mortgage because the signatures were not added by means of a manuscript signature. The Danish Western High Court upheld this decision in case U.2006.1341V. The facts were that a mortgage bank N delivered a mortgage for the purpose of cancellation. The scanned signatures of A and B were affixed to the cancellation endorsement. By a notice circulated to all judicial districts, N had authorized A and B to jointly endorse the mortgage by means of scanned manuscript signatures. The endorsements were added or attached to the original mortgage. The registration judge refused to cancel the mortgage because the signatures were not added by means of a manuscript signature in accordance with s9(1) of the Danish Registration of Property Act. The Danish Western High Court upheld this decision, and took the view that under s261(2) of the Danish Administration of Justice Act, the endorsement must be signed, and in accordance with established case law, pleadings must be available in their original form, and photocopies or facsimiles are therefore not sufficient. In addition, the registry took the view that, on grounds of due process, manuscript signatures are still required on documents to be registered (or cancelled), and that any change of this state of the law should, if necessary, be clarified by the legislature in the same way as the provisions on digital signatures.[4]

## Writing

**12.4** In a case before the German Federal Supreme Court (Bundesgerichtshof), file number XI ZB 40/06, NJW 2006, 3784 regarding Sec. 130 ZPO: (10.10.2006), it was held that scanned manuscript signature is not sufficient to be qualified as 'in writing' under s130(6) ZPO if the signature is printed on a document and then sent by facsimile transmission. This ruling appears to prevent the admission into evidence of a document twice removed from the source. First, the signature is scanned and then printed on the document, then the document is sent on by means of facsimile transmission. As an item of evidence, such a document might be highly suspect in the absence of a clear acknowledgment by the person whose signature it is that they were entirely responsible for the entire process or they authorized another person to produce the document and transmit it, and they adopted the content of the document as their own.

3 For a discussion of cases involving scanned images of manuscript signatures in Belgium, see J. Vandendriessche, 'An overview of some recent case law in Belgium in relation to electronic signature', *Digital Evidence and Electronic Signature Law Review*, 7 (2010), pp. 90–100.

4 For a case report, see *Digital Evidence and Electronic Signature Law Review*, 4 (2007), p. 99.

## Employment

**12.5** In France, the case of Cour de Cassation, soc., 17 mai 2006, 04-46706[5] also considered the legal effect of a scanned signature. In this instance, an employee of the Association of the La Réunion Marine Park was dismissed on 27 January 2002. A claim for unfair dismissal was issued. The only relevant issue for present purposes was that the dismissal letter had not been signed, but took the form of a letter bearing a signature that had been scanned. On 25 May 2004, the Court of Appeal of Saint-Denis de la Réunion held that a scanned manuscript signature did not constitute an electronic signature, as defined by article 1316 – 4 of the French Civil Code, but nevertheless considered that the dismissal letter had been validly signed. Upon appeal to the Cour de Cassation, the supreme French civil court, the employee argued that the Court of Appeal should have decided that the dismissal letter was not admissible, as the Court of Appeal had found the signature had been rendered into digital format earlier. On this point, the Cour de Cassation held that the fact that the signature had been put into digital format on the dismissal letter might affect the formal process of the dismissal procedure, but it did not in itself deprive the dismissal of substantive justifiable grounds. The Cour de Cassation appeared to leave open the question of whether or not the electronic signature did affect the dismissal procedure. In this instance, the Cour de Cassation held that there were justifiable substantive grounds for the dismissal.

5 The decision in French is available at http://www.legifrance.gouv.fr.

# 13

# Biodynamic version of a manuscript signature

**13.1** There are products available that permit a person to produce a biodynamic version of their manuscript signature. For instance, some delivery companies use hand-held devices that require the recipient of an item of post or parcel to sign on a screen acknowledging receipt of the mail – the electronic signature recorded on this particular device has been the subject of a data protection application in Canada, for which see the relevant chapter in this text.

**13.2** Another method of obtaining a digital version of a manuscript signature is where a person can write their manuscript signature by using a special pen and pad. The signature is reproduced on the computer screen, and a series of measurements record the behaviour of the person as they perform the action. The measurements include the speed, rhythm, pattern, habit, stroke sequence and dynamics that are unique to the individual at the time they write their signature.[1] The subsequent electronic file can then be attached to any document in electronic format to provide a measurement of a signature represented in graphic form on the screen. While it appears that this concept might be usefully applied in the electronic environment, the drawbacks are as significant as for any other form of generating electronic signatures, including linking the evidence in a coherent fashion to prove a person signed a particular document,[2] and problems relating to the protection of personal data.[3]

## Electoral register

**13.3** In Australia, the Electoral Commissioner rejected the biodynamic version of a manuscript signature (biodynamic signature) in the case of *Getup Ltd v.*

1 Such a device seems to be used by the Queensland Police Services, for which see *Bismark v. Queensland Police Service District Court of Queensland* [2014] QDC 152 2014, WL 8104519 in which such a device is used by the appellant.

2 The nature of the evidence was discussed by Chin DJ in *Labajo v. Best Buy Stores, L.P.*, 478 F.Supp.2d 523 (S.D.N.Y. 2007) at 530, although this report was in respect of a motion for judgment on the pleadings and before discovery, so the defendants would have had the opportunity of obtaining more coherent evidence for the trial; F. Luan, S. Ma, K. Cheng and X. Dong, 'On-line handwritten signature verification algorithm based on time sequence', *International Journal of Information and Systems Sciences*, 1 (2005), pp. 229–36; R.P. Gonçalves, A.B. Augusto and M.E. Correia, 'Time/space based biometric handwritten signature verification', *10th Iberian Conference on Information Systems and Technologies (CISTI), 2015* (n.p.: IEEE, 2015), pp. 743–8.

3 The data protection issues relating to such products are dealt with elsewhere in this text. See R.J. Anderson, *Security Engineering: A Guide to Building Dependable Distributed Systems* (2nd edn, Indianapolis, IN: Wiley, 2008), 15.9 for an indication about what can go wrong with biometric systems, and J. Grijpink, 'Privacy law: biometrics and privacy', *Computer Law & Security Review*, 17 (2001), pp. 154–60.

S. Mason, *Electronic Signatures in Law* (London: Institute of Advanced Legal Studies, 2016), chapter 13, 'Biodynamic version of a manuscript signature', pp. 291–4.

*Electoral Commissioner*[4] prior to the Australian election in August 2010. Ms Trevitt used her biodynamic signature to enrol as a voter over the internet before the election took place. Lawyers for the Commissioner wrote to Ms Trevitt, indicating 'that the electronic signature on the claim form was not sufficient'.[5] Her attempt to register her vote was rejected. The main point at issue was whether the form of signature used was appropriate, in accordance with the provisions of s10(1)(b) of the Electronic Transactions Act 1999 (Cth). Perram J considered s10(1)(a) and (b), and whether this Act applied to the Commonwealth Electoral Act 1918 (Cth). Section 10(1) provides as follows:

> (1) If, under a law of the Commonwealth, the signature of a person is required, that requirement is taken to have been met in relation to an electronic communication if:
>
> > (a) in all cases – a method is used to identify the person and to indicate the person's approval of the information communicated; and
> >
> > (b) in all cases – having regard to all the relevant circumstances at the time the method was used, the method was as reliable as was appropriate for the purposes for which the information was communicated;

**13.4** Ms Trevitt affixed her electronic signature to the form with a biodynamic signature. It was argued by counsel for the Commissioner that it was for the Commissioner to form an opinion about the reliability of the method in accordance with the purpose. The judge did not agree with this argument. He set out his reasoning at 14–15:

> The provision does not mention anyone forming an opinion. In particular, because s 10(1)(b) is pitched at a very high level of generality it understandably eschews identifying any of the parties to the communication at all. Even assuming the provision should be read as requiring someone to hold an opinion it is silent as to whether it is to be held by the sender or the recipient or both. Further, as Mr Kirk, who appeared with Ms Rao for the applicants, pointed out, the breadth of the requirement that the issue be considered in light of all of the relevant circumstances bespoke the possibility that not all of the circumstances might be known to the participants to the communication. Such a view of the provision counted against it being read as requiring the formation of an opinion by one or other of the persons involved in its application.

4 [2010] FCA 869 (13 August 2010).

5 [2010] FCA 869 (13 August 2010) [8].

> 15. I do not see a way around those concerns. To accede to the notion that s 10(1)(b) required the Commissioner to form an opinion would involve, so it seems to me, an intolerably strained construction of its plain words. Further, it would be a construction which necessarily identified the recipient as the person whose opinion mattered. That reading of s 10(1)(b) might have very serious consequences in a range of cases yet to come and about which nothing can be known. In those circumstances, I do not read s 10(1)(b) in a manner for which the Commissioner contends. This has the consequence that the provision sets a standard which, in this instance, is to be ascertained and applied by the Court.

**13.5** Perram J then considered the nature of the evidence, the possibility of forgery and the fact that the Commissioner accepted other forms of signature (whether they are sent by facsimile transmission and scanned versions of manuscript signatures), and concluded, at 17 that:

> In that circumstance, I cannot accept the slightly pixilated nature of Ms Trevitt's signature rendered it unreliable for the Commissioner's purposes, not at least while he continues to accept faxed or emailed claim forms.

**13.6** This particular point was raised in a previous edition of this text in relation to article 9(3) of the United Nations Convention on the Use of Electronic Communications in International Contracts, and the abstract reliability test is discussed elsewhere in this text.

## Contract formation

**13.7** At issue in the US case of *American Family Life Assurance Company of Columbus v. Biles*[6] was whether the signature of the late David Biles was a forgery. The method used by Mr Biles to apply his signature to a life insurance policy was by way of a proprietary biodynamic version of his manuscript signature, using a pad and computer. Of interest was the approach taken by the two document examiners in the case. Robert G. Foley gave evidence for the plaintiff,[7] and William J. Flynn gave evidence for the defendant.[8] Mr Foley compared the photocopies presented to him by the plaintiff of the images of two signatures affixed to the document. Mr Flynn, in contrast, examined the data files used to create the

6 2011 WL 4014463 2011 (S.D.Miss.) and 2011 WL 5325622 (S.D.Miss.).

7 *American Family Life Assurance Company of Columbus v. Biles*, 2011 WL 5835356 (S.D.Miss.) (affidavit of Robert G. Foley); *American Family Life Assurance Company of Columbus v. Biles*, 2011 WL 7909386 (S.D.Miss.) (supplemental affidavit of Robert G. Foley).

8 *American Family Life Assurance Company of Columbus v. Biles*, 2011 WL 5835357 (S.D.Miss.) (affidavit of William J. Flynn).

images representing the electronic signature. One of the reasons for the hearings was an application to strike the affidavit of Robert G. Foley on the basis that his examination was not appropriate, given that he ought to have examined the data files. Lee DJ ordered a *Daubert*[9] hearing to determine whether to agree to exclude Mr Foley's evidence.[10] At the subsequent hearing, the defendants sought to exclude the evidence of Mr Flynn. After hearing the evidence, the judge concluded that the challenge to Mr Foley's reliability was well taken, because his opinion was not based on the examination of the best evidence available.[11] The implication is that when electronic signatures of this nature are challenged, it is important to ensure the adjudicator is aware of the need for the examination of the digital data, and that a comparison of the images produced by the digital data is not appropriate.[12]

9 *Daubert v. Merrell Dow Pharmaceuticals*, 509 U.S. 579 (1993).

10 *American Family Life Assurance Company of Columbus v. Biles*, 2011 WL 4014463 2011 (S.D.Miss.).

11 *American Family Life Assurance Company of Columbus v. Biles*, 2011 WL 5325622 (S.D.Miss.); *American Family Life Assurance Company of Columbus v. Glenda C. Biles, Individually, Natural Mother of David Biles, Deceased, and Administratrix of Estate of David Biles, Deceased*, 714 F.3d 887 (5th Cir. 2013) (appeal on the enforcement of the arbitration agreement).

12 H.H. Harralson, 'Forensic document examination of electronically captured signatures', *Digital Evidence and Electronic Signature Law Review*, 9 (2012), pp. 67–73.

# 14

# Digital signatures

## Technical overview of digital signatures

**14.1** Cryptography is the method of hiding the contents of a message, used from ancient times to the present. Encryption (or enciphering) is the process by which a plaintext (or cleartext) message is disguised sufficiently to hide the substance of the content. As well as ordinary text, a plaintext message can be a stream of binary digits, a text file, a bitmap, a recording of sound in digital format, audio images of a video or film and any other information formed into digital bits. When a message has been encrypted, it is known as ciphertext or a cryptogram. The opposite procedure, that of turning the ciphertext back into plaintext, is called decryption (or deciphering).[1] In essence, contemporary cryptographic systems change one set of symbols that have meaning (binary data) into a second set of symbols that has no meaning, by means of a mathematical process. Cryptography is usually required to undertake a number of functions, the most important of which is authenticity, rather than secrecy. These functions are discussed below.

(i) Authenticity: When sending or receiving information or placing an order, both parties need to have assurance of the origin of the message. The aim is to corroborate the identity of the software that sent the data. The identity of a person cannot be corroborated, because a person is not part of the communications process – the process only involves communications between software.

(ii) Integrity: It is helpful to demonstrate the integrity of the message, because it is important to know if the content of the message has been tampered with.

(iii) Honesty: To provide an assurance, to the extent that is technically possible, that demonstrates that the software emanates from a known source, such that the purported sender has been honest about the actions that have been caused to be undertaken. The purpose is an attempt to bind human users to specific actions in such a way that if they deny taking the action, they either demonstrate an intention to deceive, or they have been negligent in failing to secure the use of their private key adequately. This is called 'non-repudiation' in the security industry. There are different types of non-repudiation: non-repudiation of origin,

1 Encipher and decipher are terms used in the ISO 7498-2 standard.

S. Mason, *Electronic Signatures in Law* (London: Institute of Advanced Legal Studies, 2016), chapter 14, 'Digital signatures', pp. 295–337.

which prevents the entity that sent the message or document from denying that they sent it, and non-repudiation of receipt, where an entity cannot deny have not received a message or document. Other types of non-repudiation include non-repudiation of creation, non-repudiation of delivery and non-repudiation of approval.[2] This topic is dealt with at greater length in the chapter on evidence.

(iv) Confidentiality: Another purpose is to provide for the confidentiality of a document. In the digital environment, cryptography is used as a substitute for a manuscript signature, and is often described as a digital signature. To understand how a document can be signed with a digital signature, it is necessary to be aware of how cryptography works, for which see the discussion below.

## Algorithms and keys

**14.2** The plaintext of a message is encrypted and decrypted by the use of a cryptographic algorithm (also called a cipher). There tend to be two related functions, one for encryption and another for decryption. In most instances, the secrecy of the algorithm will not matter, because modern cryptography uses a key. However, it is possible to have what is called a restricted algorithm, because the security of the algorithm is based on ensuring the way it works is kept a secret. There are drawbacks to the use of restricted algorithms. If a user leaves the group that share the algorithm, or should the secret be revealed for any reason, then the algorithm must be changed. Further, there is no quality control or standardization, which means the algorithms can be easy to break. By using a key, a strong algorithm does not need to be secret and can be used by millions of users. As a result, there is no need to constantly develop new algorithms. A key can comprise a number of values. This range of values is called a keyspace. A key can be used to encrypt and decrypt a message, or there can be two separate keys, one to encrypt a message and another for decrypting the message. To complete the picture, a cryptosystem comprises an algorithm, all possible messages, all possible cryptograms and all possible keys.

## Control of the key

**14.3** To decrypt the ciphertext, the recipient needs to know both the decryption algorithm and the decryption key. The way a key is controlled, managed and distributed is crucial. This is why the principle laid down by Auguste Kerckhoffs von Niuewenhof remains a fundamental rule of cryptanalysis: the security of a

2 C. Adams and S. Lloyd, *Understanding PKI Concepts, Standards, and Deployment Considerations* (2nd edn., Boston: Addison-Wesley, 2002), p. 51.

cryptosystem must depend on keeping the key secret.[3] This issue is discussed more fully when considering the weaknesses relating to cryptosystems.

## Disguising the message

**14.4** There are two types of mathematical families that permit the message to be disguised: symmetric cryptographic systems and asymmetric cryptographic systems.

### *Conventional or symmetric cryptographic systems*

**14.5** As the name infers, the encryption key can be computed from the decryption key, and the decryption key can be computed from the encryption key. In practice, these two keys are often identical when used in symmetric systems. The symmetric system is also referred to as secret-key algorithms, single-key algorithms, one-key algorithms or shared key ciphers. Two people can use the same system to send and receive encrypted messages to each other. Both the sender and the receiver must agree on the key before they can communicate. This system can have very long keys, which means a message can be very secure. The effectiveness of this system depends on the key, and is suitable for closed user groups where there is a strong element of mutual trust between the users, such as banks, the military, and intelligence agencies. However, a disadvantage is that the key must be kept secure and secret. Two people must have the key to communicate. If encrypted messages are to pass between large numbers of people, a large number of keys will have to be distributed. The security of the system depends on those people with access to the keys to ensure they are kept secure and secret. Also, from the point of view of managing the keys, it is important for pairs of users to have different keys to reduce the risks of compromise when large numbers of people share a key. Some symmetric algorithms work on the plaintext, one digit at a time. These are called stream ciphers. Others work in groups of digits on the plaintext. The groups of digits are called blocks, and the algorithms are called block algorithms or block ciphers. How an algorithm and the cipher work is important, because of their strengths and weaknesses. If an algorithm or cipher is easy to attack, then an application should not use it, and if losses occur because of the failure of either, then a successful legal action may be possible because it could be argued that the system was designed and possibly implemented negligently.

**14.6** Sending a message that has been encrypted only provides for the security of the content. It does not attribute the message to the source from which the message was sent. It is possible for an interceptor to intercept the message and send a substitute message in place of the original message. If a forger sends the message, the recipient will not be aware that the sender of the message has used

3 A. Kerckhoffs, 'La Cryptographie militaire', *Journal des Sciences Militaires*, 9 (1883), pp. 5–38, although this principle applied to a time when all systems were symmetric.

the key improperly. Authentication seeks to corroborate the integrity of the message and authenticity of the sender. There are two types of authentication.

> (i) One-way authentication is where one party is authenticated to another party, such as a person using an ATM when they wish to withdraw cash or make a deposit. The user identifies themselves by using their PIN, and the card is authenticated cryptographically.
>
> (ii) Two-way authentication, where both parties to a message seek to verify the attribution of data that purports to identify each other or the message or both, such as virtual private networks.

**14.7** The process of authentication also uses a secret key. This is called the message authentication code or data authentication code. This mechanism can provide authentication without the need for secrecy. In symmetric cryptographic systems, the aim is for the originator and the legitimate recipient to be the only two entities that can create or check the message authentication code. This is an example of how the message authentication code can work:[4]

> Alice sends a message in plaintext to Bob. The software on the computer that Alice uses encrypts the message by using a block algorithm or cipher. All of the ciphertext blocks are then discarded with the exception of the last block. The last block is the message authentication code. (Note: If Alice wants to provide for both the integrity and the privacy of the message, the message can also be encrypted again.)
>
> Bob receives the message. The software on his computer computes what the message authentication code should have been. If Eve intercepted and altered the message, Bob will realise this, because the incorrect plaintext is re-encrypted, producing an incorrect message authentication code. If the plaintext has been altered, the ciphertext blocks will be different, especially the last ciphertext block. If the plaintext has not been altered, the re-encrypted plaintext will not have changed, and Bob can be sure that Alice has sent the plaintext message.

**14.8** However, this does not prevent Eve from listening in to Alice when she sends the message to Bob. Eve can then record every message, together with the message authentication code. Alternatively, she can delete the message sent by Alice, repeat old messages or change the order in which the messages are sent. Thus the message authentication code needs to include a scheme by which each message is numbered sequentially.

4 Alice, Bob, Carol, Dave and interloper Eve are used widely in cryptology. See 'The Alice and Bob after dinner speech' given at the Zürich Seminar, April 1984 by John Gordon by invitation of Professor John Massey, available online at http://web.mit.edu/jemorris/humor/alice-and-bob.

## *Asymmetric cryptographic systems (Public key)*

**14.9** Using a symmetric cryptographic system with large numbers of users is difficult. Keys cannot be distributed over the open communications network, so they have to be distributed in other ways. When a member leaves the group, all the other members have to redistribute new keys. Thus, assuming a separate key is used for each pair in a group, and if there are 10 people members of the group, 45 different keys will be required. The development of the asymmetric cryptographic system, or public key,[5] helps to resolve this problem. With this system, keys only have one purpose: one key to encrypt and one key to decrypt. Given a large enough key, the decryption key cannot be calculated from the encryption key within a useful length of time (perhaps several centuries). The algorithms used in the system are commonly called 'public key' because the encryption key is usually made public. Anybody can use the encryption key to encrypt a plaintext message, but only the person with the decryption key that corresponds to the encryption key can decrypt the message. The encryption key is called the public key or public encryption key, and the decryption key is called the private key, secret key or private decryption key. The system can work in two ways.

## An individual creates and controls their own public key

**14.10** The user can generate a pair of keys using what is called a trapdoor one-way function, containing the mathematical equivalent of a secret trapdoor. For the purposes of understanding the concept, this algorithm is easy to compute in one direction and difficult to compute in the opposite direction, unless you know the secret.[6]

**14.11** Sending a message using public key cryptography:

> Alice and Bob decide to exchange messages that are encrypted.
>
> Alice generates her own public and private keys using the software on her computer. Although she keeps the private key secret, she gives Bob her public key.
>
> Bob writes his message and encrypts it using Alice's public key. He sends it to Alice.
>
> Alice decrypts Bob's message using her private key.

5 The concept of public key cryptography was invented twice during the 20th century. By James H. Ellis, Clifford Cocks and Malcolm J. Williamson at British Intelligence GCHQ, whose work remained classified until December 1997. Then two researchers at Stanford University, Whitfield Diffie and Martin Hellman, proposed the concept in 1976. Development of the principles can also be attributed to R. C. Merkle, R. L. Rivest, A. Shamir and L. A. Adleman.

6 It has yet to be proven that a mathematical function can have a one-way function (see F. Piper, S. Blake-Wilson and J. Mitchell, *Digital Signatures: Security & Controls* (Rolling Meadows, IL: Information Systems Audit and Control Foundation, 1999), p. 16).

**14.12** This method of encrypting and decrypting messages means the private keys do not have to be distributed securely. In addition, it is possible for Alice to place her public key in a public database. The protocol then looks like this:

> Bob goes to the database and obtains Alice's public key.
>
> Bob writes Alice a message and uses her public key to encrypt the message. Bob then sends the message to her.
>
> Alice decrypts the message using her private key upon receipt.

**14.13** There are problems in relation to the methods by which an individual creates and controls their own keys.[7] An interceptor may intend to disrupt Alice's life by interrupting her ability to receive and send encrypted messages. It is possible for an interceptor to intercept, modify, delete and substitute a false message between the parties. Such an attack cannot be solved by the use of cryptography. This is how such an attack can work:

> Alice sends her public key to Bob. Eve intercepts this key. Eve then sends her key to Bob.
>
> Bob sends his public key to Alice. Again, Eve intercepts this key and sends her key to Alice.
>
> When Alice sends a message to Bob, she encrypts it using what she thinks is Bob's public key. Eve intercepts this message and decrypts it with her private key. Having carried out whatever action she intends with the message, she then re-encrypts it with Bob's public key and sends it on to Bob.
>
> The same process occurs when Bob sends a message to Alice.

## Authenticating a signature using public key cryptography

**14.14** The underlying rationale of public key cryptography is that a message can be attributed to a particular entity. First, Alice can use a key generation algorithm to generate a key pair: a private signing key and the public signature verification key, or she can use her existing key pair. She then publishes her public key on a database. Thereafter the example continues:

> Alice writes a message and wants to send it to Bob with her digital signature. The software on her computer computes a digital signature from her private key and the content of the message.
>
> Alice sends her message and the digital signature to Bob. The signature may be, but does not need to be, separate from the

7 In *Maughan v. Wilmot* [2016] EWHC 29 (Fam), 2016 WL 2394, the husband created his own digital signature to attach to emails.

message.[8] The signature operates in the same way as a message authentication code.

Upon receipt of the message, Bob uses Alice's public key to verify that the corresponding private key signed the message.

**14.15** However, given this scenario, it is generally noted in the technical literature that Bob cannot be sure that the public key in the database is that of Alice. This means this mechanism does not resolve the issue of identifying the sender of the message. A person could generate their own public and private keys, post the public key on a database and claim it belongs to Alice. Bob might think he is sending messages to Alice, but in fact his message might posted to an interceptor. In addition, the interceptor could use their own private key to send messages to Bob, which he would assume came from Alice. There is further a problem with this method of adding a signature to a message, which in turn is inherent in any system that uses cryptography in the electronic environment to create a signature. The signature is not computed by Alice, but by the software on her computer. Thus there is no direct evidence to show Alice appended the signature to the message. This is, naturally, an identical problem with all forms of electronic signature and communication over networked communications – for instance, the same point can be made about the origin of an email. The recipient cannot be certain that an email comes from the purported source, yet the vast majority of emails that are sent and received are trusted. This is because the correspondents either know each other in the physical world, or even if they have not met, then they become familiar with each other in the virtual world by way of an exchange of correspondence and other signs, such as looking at websites and asking others that are trusted to indicate whether the person they have yet to meet is indeed the person they claim to be.

## Public key infrastructure

**14.16** The concept of the public key infrastructure tries to resolve the problem by linking a public key to a named individual or legal entity.[9] The notion behind a public key infrastructure is to have organizations called trusted intermediaries, trusted third parties, trust service providers or certification authorities ('Certificate Authority'), that act to certify the connection between a person and

8 This can be important, for which see N. Bohm, 'Watch what you sign!', *Digital Evidence and Electronic Signature Law Review*, 3 (2006), pp. 45–9.

9 R.J. Anderson, *Security Engineering: A Guide to Building Dependable Distributed Systems* (2nd edn, Indianapolis, IN: Wiley, 2008), at 21.4.5.7 notes there is some confusion between 'public (key infrastructure)' and '(public key) infrastructure'. He defines the first as an open system where the infrastructure can be used by any new application that is subsequently developed. He calls this open public key infrastructure. New applications cannot be used in the second, which he calls a closed public key infrastructure. For the flaws in PKI, see C. Ellison, 'Improvements on conventional PKI wisdom', *Proceedings of the 1st Annual PKI Research Workshop* (Gaithersburg, MD: NIST, 2002), available online at http://www.cs.dartmouth.edu/~pki02/.

their public key. In theory, the trusted third party guarantees the authenticity of the public key by issuing an individual identity certificate (usually abbreviated to 'certificate'), which binds a name string to a public key. This in turn seeks to create a link between the provision of a key and the identity of the natural person or legal entity to which the key has been issued. It should be emphasized that users, when using a public key infrastructure, should aim to continue to generate their own key pairs. Where a third party generates the key pair on behalf of a user, the degree of security exercised over the key pair is reduced.

**14.17** The certification authority issues an individual identity certificate, which includes the following characteristics: data identifying the certification authority; data identifying the subscriber that includes the subscriber's public key, and it is signed with the Certification Authority's private key. The individual identity certificate may also contain other information, such as the level of inquiry carried out before issuing the certificate.

**14.18** To acquire such a certificate, Alice will provide the certification authority with a copy of her public key and proof of her identity. The degree of proof of identity will differ, depending on the level of liability Alice wants to cover. When Alice sends a message to Bob, she also sends him a copy of her certificate. Alternatively, when she publishes her verification key, she publishes the certificate. The software on Bob's computer will decrypt the message according to the key he has been given. It will then be for Bob in most circumstances to undertake his own due diligence, perhaps by checking the certificate revocation list to ensure the public key has not been revoked or has expired, or sending an email to Alice (or contacting her by telephone) to confirm that she sent the communication. If Bob does not act to verify the information contained in the certificate, but contacts Alice directly, his due diligence will not involve the organization that issues the certificate.

## Difficulties with public key infrastructure

**14.19** The purported advantage to the relying party of using the 'standard model' public key infrastructure digital signature is not that the signature provides greater security, but arises from persuading the subscribing party that because it is apparently more secure, the user takes responsibility for every use of the private key, by whomsoever made. It must be emphasized that the greater security of the mechanism does not necessarily offer the subscribing party any protection against attacks. The key might be stolen, or the software might sign something other than what is presented on the screen. The industry implies that the system has a 'non-repudiation' property, and it is this property that justifies the imposition of a non-repudiation term on the subscribing party. This cannot be right, because if the system genuinely possessed a non-repudiation property, it would not be necessary to impose such a term. Given that digital signatures in a public key infrastructure do not possess such a property, and the inability to create false digital signatures is based on complex theoretic assumptions,[10] the acceptance of such a term invariably involves an acceptance of risk by the user. However, the nature and extent of the risk is not made clear, and it is highly improbable that ordinary users will have the knowledge, skills and resources to manage such a risk.[11]

## Authenticating the sender

**14.20** There are various methods of obtaining sufficient evidence to demonstrate, with a degree of probability, that an electronic signature came from the person it purports to have been sent by. The aim is to gather sufficient evidence to be assured that the person sending the signature is the person they claim. Attempts are made, using various mechanisms, to obtain information from a combination of the following:[12]

> Proof by knowledge: what the person knows.
>
> Proof by possession: what the person owns.
>
> Proof by characteristics: what the person is.

**14.21** When combined, the techniques relating to authentication can provide a higher level of authentication than a single method. In many instances, the method by which a person seeks to authenticate themselves is by a combination of hardware and software. A software component can retrieve and verify passwords. A token, such as a smart card, can be placed in a slot in a computer or in a separate 'reader'. Stewart Brymer and James Ness have reassured solicitors in Scotland about the trust to be put into such readers:[13]

> Can I trust it?
>
> Linked to the move from a 'wet signature' is the issue of trust. How can I trust or interrogate the authenticity of a digital signature?

10 B. Pfitzmann, 'Fail-stop signatures: principles and applications', in *Proceedings of the Eighth World Conference on Computer Security, Audit and Control* (New York: Elsevier, 1991), pp. 125–34; B. Pfitzmann, *Digital Signature Schemes: General Framework and Fail-Stop Signatures* (Berlin: Springer, 1996).

11 A. Jøsang and B. AlFayyadh, 'Robust WYSIWYS: a method for ensuring that what you see is what you sign', in L. Brankovic and M. Miller (eds.), *Proceedings of the Sixth Australasian Conference on Information security – Volume 81* (Australian Computer Society, 2008), pp. 53–8; Bohm, 'Watch what you sign!'; D. Davis, 'Compliance defects in public-key cryptography', *Proceedings of the Sixth USENIX UNIX Security Symposium* (San Jose, CA, 1996).

12 For an analysis of the strengths and weaknesses of each, see R.E. Smith, *Authentication From Passwords to Public Keys* (Boston, MA: Addison-Wesley, 2002), 1.6.

13 S. Brymer and J. Ness, 'Using your secure digital signature', *The Journal of the Law Society of Scotland*, 14 March 2016, online at http://www.journalonline.co.uk/Magazine/61-3/1021468.aspx.

> The real question is – on what basis have you been trusting or interrogating the authenticity of wet signatures? The reality is that rarely are wet signatures verified in any meaningful way.
>
> We trust them because they are presented to us in a context that causes us to believe that they are what they are, set against the background of spending three months negotiating terms we agreed on the telephone, confirmed by email and followed up with a paper document which reflects those terms. Naturally, we are reasonably entitled to trust that the document bears appropriate wet signatures.
>
> The same is true of the Society's digital signature, but in this case, provided you have the software and card reader installed, the signature will automatically declare itself 'valid' and you can further interrogate the signature by double-clicking it.

**14.22** Both are vulnerable to attacks.[14]

**14.23** Identification can also be achieved by using a biometric measurement.

## *The ideal attributes of a signature in electronic form*

**14.24** Whether a signature is in manuscript form or electronic form, the purpose for affixing the signature will not alter. However, when a signature is in electronic format, more considerations will apply to the signature. Whilst it is abundantly clear that a manuscript signature can be forged, or can be transferred from one piece of paper to another,[15] or that documents can be altered after they have been signed, digital signatures can help to resist attacks of these kinds. The attributes below set out the requirements of a digital signature:

> (i) The signature must be authentic. In this respect the method ought, ideally, to provide for the authentication of the origin of the data and the integrity of the message.
>
> (ii) Ideally, there ought to be a technical method in place that prevents the person appending the signature to the document from

14 S. Drimer, S.J. Murdoch and R. Anderson, 'Optimised to fail: card readers for online banking', in R. Dingledine and P. Golle (eds.), *Financial Cryptography and Data Security, 13th International Conference, FC 2009, Accra Beach, Barbados, February 23-26, 2009* (Berlin/Heidelberg: Springer, 2009), pp. 184–200; N. Bohm and S. Mason, 'Identity and its verification' *Computer Law & Security Review*, 26 (2010), pp. 43–51.

15 For examples where the cutting and pasting of manuscript signatures have been upheld in the United States of America, see: Iowa: *Ferguson v. Stilwill*, 224 N.W.2d 11 (the signature of the Illinois Secretary of State, cut from an instrument and attached to a certificate of conviction was sufficient in the absence of evidence to show the act of pasting was not authorized) (1974); Maine: *Richardson v. Bachelder*, 19 Me. 82, 1841 WL 932 (Me.), 1 App. 82 (an attorney affixed the signature of the magistrate, which was physically on a slip of paper, to the writ, the writ was held to be properly issued, the magistrate having recognized and adopted it).

claiming later that they did not sign it. This is virtually impossible to achieve in the electronic environment. Care must be taken to distinguish between the degree of probability that a system can be designed to prevent a person from making such a claim, and any suggestion of a presumption that purports to bind the user to a signature that is verified.[16]

(iii) The signature should not be capable of being forged, in that the private key is secure.

(iv) Where a signature is added to a message that comprises a legal act, the signature and its link to the relevant document should remain verifiable for as long as it is of legal importance.

(v) The signature cannot be re-used.

(vi) The document that has been signed cannot be altered without rendering the signature unverifiable.[17]

**14.25** In the digital environment, it is considered technically possible to achieve all of these attributes – in theory,[18] but it must be emphasized that the connection between the human and the machine cannot be bridged, and the technology is fallible.[19] Practical problems, which are discussed below, continue to exist with the implementation of a digital signature. However, the essential functions set out above can, largely, be met by the application of cryptography to the formation of a digital signature. As with manuscript signatures, there are always risks attached to the use of any form of electronic signature, and the user, whether a sending party or a receiving party, should make themselves aware of the risks before using any form of electronic signature for high value transactions.

**14.26** There is one further meaning that an electronic signature cannot, without education and training, provide. This is the addition of what is termed 'social meaning', or what can also be described as the 'significance of the act'. A ceremony is attached to the signing of a document, and when a person affixes their manuscript signature to a document, the importance of the act is reinforced by the physical nature of the act, because 'People intuitively understand that they are legally responsible for the documents to which they attach their autographs'.[20]

16 For an analysis of the means by which a computer can be affected by malicious software, see D. Bilar, 'Known knowns, known unknowns and unknown unknowns: anti-virus issues, malicious software and internet attacks for non-technical audiences', *Digital Evidence and Electronic Signature Law Review*, 6 (2009), pp. 123–31.

17 J. Dumortier, P. Van Eecke and I. Anné, *The Legal Aspects of Digital Signatures* (Leuven: Interdisciplinary Centre for Law & Information Technology, 1998), Report I Part III B, 59; B. Schneier, *Applied Cryptography* (2nd edn, Indianapolis, IN: Wiley, 1996), 2.6.

18 J. Lopez, R. Oppliger and G. Pernu, 'Why have public key infrastructures failed so far?', *Internet Research*, 15 (2005), pp. 544–56.

19 A.L. Young and M. Yung, *Malicious Cryptography: Exposing Cryptovirology* (Indianapolis, IN: Wiley, 2004).

20 Dumortier, Van Eecke and Anné, *The Legal Aspects of Digital Signatures*, p. 77.

The function of attaching an electronic signature to a document or message is not understood in the same way as the use of manuscript signatures, partly because the signature can be applied to the document without any action by the individual to whom the signature is attributed, or without their knowledge.[21]

## Methods of authentication

### *Authentication using secret codes*

**14.27** Secret codes or passwords have been used for some time, especially in banking. The code usually consists of a combination of digits or characters or both. The principle is based on ensuring the code is unique and only known to the user and the issuer. There is a shared secret between the two parties. The user identifies themselves by using the code, and the issuer, if the code is correct, assumes the person entering a transaction is the person to whom the code is assigned.[22] Secret codes tend to be most appropriate when used in a closed community, as opposed to the open structure of the internet, because a secret code cannot guarantee the identity of the person using the code. However, it should be noted that the evidence of a shared secret will not necessarily be sufficient to satisfy the relying party that an authorized user used the code. Evidence of the procedures and systems used by the relying party will not be sufficient to prove to a third party, such as a court, that it was the user that added the code. It is posited that a secret code cannot be considered strictly as a signature, because the use of the code tends only to be used for the single characteristic of authenticating the user,[23] but two courts have decided otherwise, with respect, correctly, given the facts.[24] However, secret codes can be used as additional tools in a protocol, such as the generation of a key. The aim in generating a key is to be as unpredictable as possible, and one method of initiating the generation process is to use a secret key, such as a password. Another way of generating a key would be to use a pseudo-random number generator.

21 E.Y. Chou, 'Paperless and soulless: e-signatures diminish the signer's presence and decrease acceptance', *Social Psychological and Personality Science*, 6 (2015), pp. 343–51.

22 Thieves have successfully infiltrated a number of banks across the world to steal significant sums of money, for which see 'SWIFT attackers' malware linked to more financial attacks', *Symantec Security Response*, 26 May 2016 at http://www.symantec.com/connect/blogs/swift-attackers-malware-linked-more-financial-attacks; one legal action has already been initiated before the United States District Court, Southern District of New York: *Banco del Austro, S.A., v. Wells Fargo Bank, N.A.*, Case No. 1:16-cv-00628 (LAK).

23 Anderson, *Security Engineering*, 10.4 for a study of the problems relating to ATMs; Dumortier, Van Eecke and Anné, *The Legal Aspects of Digital Signatures*, pp. 60–3.

24 *Standard Bank London Ltd v. Bank of Tokyo Ltd* [1995] CLC 496; [1996] 1 C.T.L.R. T-17 and *Industrial & Commercial Bank Ltd v. Banco Ambrosiano Veneto SpA* [2003] 1 SLR 221, where a message using an authentication code sent through the SWIFT (Society for Worldwide Interbank Financial Telecommunication) system has the legal effect of binding the sender bank according to its contents, and where a recipient bank undertakes further checks on credit standing or other aspects, it does not detract from this proposition.

## *Authentication using biometric measurements*

**14.28** Using a biometric measurement is the method by which it is possible to authenticate an individual through the measurement of physical characteristics. A biometric measurement has the ability to identify a person because the image is reduced to digital format. Such a measurement represents a unique characteristic of that individual, but it cannot be a secret. Human characteristics comprise a number of attributes, some of which lend themselves to being measured:

> (i) Appearance, such as height, weight, colour of skin, hair and eyes, visible physical markings, gender, facial hair, wearing of spectacles.
>
> (ii) Social behavioural traits, including voice recognition, style of speech, visible handicaps.
>
> (iii) Natural physiography, such as iris patterns, retinal scan, fingerprint or thumbprint verification, capillary patterns in earlobes, two or three dimensional facial recognition, vein check and hand geometry, DNA patterns.
>
> (iv) Bio-dynamics, such as signature verification and the dynamics when using the keys on a keyboard.[25]

**14.29** There are significant difficulties with the use of biometric measurements, including the range of tolerances to reduce false negatives and increase false positives, or vice versa. The manufacturer of the device usually sets the tolerances, and a great many devices do not work as claimed.[26] The most prominent biometric system presently used to authenticate an individual is the recognition of their fingerprints, although voice recognition and facial recognition systems are in use – such as in passports in airports. To offer an outline of some of the issues, if a face recognition system is installed, the purpose of the installation is important. If it is to help recognise terrorists in airports, then biometric measurements need to be obtained of those terrorists that the authorities wish to identify. Unless a photograph exists of the person, then one must call into question the expense of installing such a system. A further problem relates to the accuracy of the software. In the unlikely event that the software is accurate to 90 per cent, one in ten people will be identified incorrectly as a terrorist.

**14.30 Fingerprints** Most fingerprint systems use optical or capacitive sensors for capturing the details of a fingerprint, such as branching and end points of the ridges. An optical sensor detects differences in reflection, whilst capacitive sensors detect differences in capacitance. Other systems use thermal sensors and ultrasound sensors. The process can be described thus: the image of the fingerprint is captured, features are then extracted from the image, and they are stored as templates on a database. Some systems encrypt templates and only

25 Anderson, *Security Engineering*, ch. 15.

26 Anderson, *Security Engineering*, ch. 15.

manage the compressed images. Although widely used, there are problems associated with fingerprint scanners. Such systems can be undermined in a number of ways:

(i) A person can be forced to press their finger against a scanner by a criminal.

(ii) An impostor can use their own fingerprint and challenge the false rejection rate and false acceptance rate. Fingerprints tend to be categorized as 'loops', 'whorls' and 'arches', amongst other descriptions. If the impostor knows the category of the registered fingerprint and has a pattern similar to that of the registered one, there is a possibility that the scanner may not reject the false fingerprint.

(iii) A person may have their finger cut off, so a criminal can use the severed finger to defeat the scanning device.[27] This can be avoided where a device also gauges the temperature of the finger.

(iv) The use of an artificial clone of the original fingerprint, where a fingerprint is copied by making a mould of the registered fingerprint, which is cheap to replicate and seems to be effective against many fingerprint devices.[28]

(v) Other attacks will work, depending on the nature of the fingerprint system, such as making a noise or flashing a light against the scanner. Other techniques that can cause the scanner to stop working within the tolerances to the environment include heating up, cooling down, changing the humidity, and hitting or causing the scanner to vibrate.

**14.31** Regardless of how easy it may be to defeat fingerprint reading systems, they seem to be most effective when used as a deterrence factor, especially in

27 Biometric ATMs are now widespread in India: thumbprints are scanned to enable a customer to obtain access to their account. Whether customers have had their thumbs cut off by thieves is not known: J. Leahy, 'Citigroup gives Indian poor a hand with thumbprint ATMs,' *Financial Times*, 2–3 December, 2006, p. 15. See the example of Mr Kumaran, who had the tip of his index finger chopped off by thieves because the security system installed in his S-Class Mercedes Benz utilized the measurements of both the index fingers and thumbs of the owner. The immobiliser system caused the engine in the vehicle to cut out after a few minutes unless the owner pressed their finger or thumb on to the sensor (J. Kent, 'Malaysia car thieves steal finger', *BBC News Kuala Lumpur*, 31 March 2005, available online at http://news.bbc.co.uk/1/hi/world/asia-pacific/4396831.stm).

28 T. Matsumoto, H. Matsumoto, K. Yamada and S. Hoshino, 'Impact of artificial "gummy" fingers on fingerprint systems', paper prepared for Proceedings of SPIE Vol 4677 Optical Security and Counterfeit Deterrence Techniques IV, 24–25 January 2002, available online at http://cryptome.org/gummy.htm; note the comments on tests run by others as a result of this research in Anderson, *Security Engineering*, 15.5; see also D. Chek Ling Ngo, A. Beng Jin Teoh and J. Hu (eds.), *Biometric Security* (Newcastle: Cambridge Scholars Publishing, 2015).

reducing false claims by people on state benefits.[29]

**14.32** In summary, it is possible to use a measurement of a biometric characteristic to authenticate an individual, but the use of such a measurement can only be used effectively in a closed system. There are many problems associated with the use of biometric measurements in an open system that have yet to be resolved. For instance, where a document is authenticated using a biometric measurement, the person relying on the measurement to authenticate the document will need to check the data against a database of biometric measurements. Unless there was such a depository in an open user community, the relying party will not be able to verify the source of the biometric measurement. Further, where human characteristics are reduced to digital form by a biometric system, the system becomes susceptible to being deceived by the 'replay' of the relevant numerical information, even without the presence of the individual, unless the system as a whole can successfully be made secure against such an attack. Securing a database of biometric measurements is difficult to achieve in practice in distributed systems. A significant disadvantage of biometric measurements is the ease by which the measurement can be replicated by third parties for ulterior motives. Thus if biometric measurements are to be used, they can only be used effectively if they can prove two things: first, that the measurement actually was taken from the identified person at the time the measurement was taken, and second, that the measurement matches the data stored in the database.

## Types of infrastructure for asymmetric cryptographic systems

**14.33** There are, in broad terms, two types of infrastructure that provide for the signing of electronic documents by means of a digital signature: Pretty Good Privacy (PGP) software, and public key cryptography. The discussion in this chapter will focus on the issues relating to the provision of key pairs that are provided and maintained by commercial organizations. However, it is to be noted that key pairs generated and used by individuals using PGP will also be subject to many of the issues discussed in this chapter.

**14.34** The type of structure will affect the nature and extent of the legal liability that participants are exposed to. This in turn will determine how participants manage their legal liability. The two categories are:

> (i) A closed environment, where there is only one domain for all communications. This domain can be located in a single place for a single enterprise, or comprise a collection of enterprises, each of which operate under the same set of technical and operational procedures. One example may be a multi-national company that operates in several jurisdictions and maintains an intra-company domain across the world. Another example may be a group of end

29 Anderson, *Security Engineering*, 15.9.

users (both sending and receiving parties) that enter a network with one or more certification authorities by which liability is allocated according to agreed contractual terms between the parties. IdenTrust and Bolero are examples.[30]

(ii) An open environment, where a sender enters into an agreement with a certification authority to provide a certificate for a verification key, and where the receiving parties are not known by either the sending party or certification authority in advance. The role of trusted third parties, also called certification authorities, is to provide certificates that link the identity of the owner to the public key. These bodies can be public or private, licensed or unlicensed. Whether a certification authority is in the hands of a public or private body, and whether is it licensed or unlicensed, it must be trustworthy.

## Management of the key and certificate

**14.35** The foundation of the public key infrastructure rests on asymmetric cryptography, with a public and private key pair. The public key is usually distributed in the form of a certificate, whilst the private key is a separate item with its own distinct structure that should be protected from being disclosed to unauthorized third parties when in it is transported, used and stored. Once a person subscribes to a digital signature, a range of issues that are referred to as life-cycle management, amongst other terms, must be addressed. Regardless of the name given to the process, procedures and processes must be in place to create the certificate and key pair, verify the identity of the applicant, distribute the certificate and cancel the certificate at the end of its period of validity or before, should it be compromised. The quality of software, design of the network and management of the security system all affect the way the keys and certificate are managed and stored. This is important, because a digital signature is not computed by the user, but by software. The software on a computer will carry out the task on the instructions of a user, but the software is not in a position to identify whether the instructions come from a legitimate user or the signals from unauthorized malicious software that has successfully embedded itself in the user's computer.

### *Identifying an applicant*

**14.36** It should be recalled that an individual could generate their own public and private key pair, using software on their computer. The individual then provides the certification authority with evidence of their identity. The type of evidence and degree of proof will depend on the nature of the type of certifying certificate required. In any event, the identity of the person or entity must be

30 IdenTrust: http://www.identrust.com, Bolero: http://www.bolero.net.

bound to the public key. When confirming the identity of a person or legal entity, a certification authority will tend to be expected to comply with the requirements from a recognized body.[31]

## *The certificate*

**14.37** When the certification authority has verified the identity of the individual or entity to their satisfaction, they will issue a certificate. This is a software record that affirms the connection of a public key to an identified person or corporate entity. It does not follow that a certification authority will undertake this task. There are a number of reasons for this. First, the cost of developing a suitable administrative infrastructure with the relevant expertise will be expensive. It may not, therefore, be possible to justify the cost in commercial terms. Second, there are a number of organizations that already have the relevant expertise, such as banks and credit reference agencies. Whilst the database these organizations use may be imperfect, nevertheless it makes sound economic sense not to replicate a service that already exists. This usually means there is an added layer of contact where a certification authority issues a certificate. First, the registration authority will take steps to verify the identity of the person or legal entity seeking a certificate. Upon confirmation of identity by the registration authority, the certification authority will then issue a certificate. Thus an additional layer of complexity is added to the mix surrounding the link between the person or legal entity seeking a certificate and the subsequent granting of the certificate. The next point to ponder is the entity that generates the registration authority's key. Whoever generates the registration authority's key will also be involved in the contractual matrix. In all probability, a contractual relationship will exist between the certification authority and the registration authority, and the contract will provide for the liability and warranties between each entity. Where liability will fall in the event of a dispute will depend on the particular circumstances of the case.

## *The generation of the key pair belonging to the subscribing party*

**14.38** It is good practice for the subscribing party to generate their own key pair. Where the subscribing party generates a key pair, there is, theoretically, less of a risk of the private key being compromised. However, many subscribing parties will not have the software to generate their own key pair. This means a third party will be requested to generate a key pair on their behalf. There are two aspects to this that demonstrate a level of vulnerability that may be undesirable. The party generating the key pair will have to be trusted not to compromise the key, and the key pair will be vulnerable to attack or compromise when transported to the user.[32]

31 For an overview, see Piper, Blake-Wilson and Mitchell, *Digital Signatures*, ch. 5 and Adams and Lloyd, *Understanding PKI Concepts*, Part II.

32 Adams and Lloyd, *Understanding PKI Concepts*, pp. 92–4; F. Piper and S. Murphy, *Cryptography: A Very Short Introduction* (Oxford: Oxford University Press, 2002), pp. 109–10.

## *Validating the public key*

**14.39** Either the certification authority or the registration authority should carry out checks that the public key is actually that of the applicant, and that the applicant has the corresponding private key. The check is simple: it needs to be determined whether the subscriber can make a signature that can be verified by the public key. If carried out, such a check can protect both the subscribing party and the authority that undertakes the task, because it can ensure the subscribing party has submitted the correct key and the authority can demonstrate it undertook care to investigate and verify for itself that the public key was that of the applicant, thus making sure it did not certify an incorrect or invalid key.

## *Distributing the certificate*

**14.40** Once the certification authority has created a certificate, it is important for both the authority and the subscribing party to ensure the content of the certificate is accurate and relates to the correct entity. The certificate is usually sent electronically, which can present difficulties:

> (i) Where the subscribing party signs to acknowledge receipt of the certificate, they will not necessarily agree its content. Where a certificate has been created by an impostor, evidence of receipt will be just that: evidence that the certificate was received. In an ideal world, the subscribing party should be required to indicate they received and accept the content of the certificate by using another certified signing key.
>
> (ii) Before the certificate is issued, the certificate authority must decide whether to wait until it has received acceptance from the subscribing party by which the subscribing party acknowledges receipt of the certificate before it is delivered, or to issue the certificate and ask for a receipt. If the subscribing party does not send a receipt to the certification authority, then the certificate may have to be revoked immediately.[33]

**14.41** It becomes clear that certification authorities must produce security policies that deal with some, if not all, of these issues. They should be made publicly available, and may well be incorporated into any contract that is formed between the certification authority and the subscribing party. Two types of document are often created: a certificate policy and a certificate practice statement. The names of these documents will differ between authorities, as will the division between them of their subject matter. Audit trails are also important to check that the methods and procedures that control the process function correctly. Such audit trails must be secure and, ideally, be capable of being verified by an independent third party.[34]

33 Piper, Blake-Wilson and Mitchell, *Digital Signatures*, pp. 36–7.

34 Piper, Blake-Wilson and Mitchell, *Digital Signatures*, pp. 36–7; Adams and Lloyd, *Understanding PKI Concepts*, p. 96.

## *Distributing certification authority keys*

**14.42** Individuals or entities wishing to use the public keys of different organizations or individuals may well have to visit each certificate authority to obtain the relevant public key. To help reduce the effort that is required to do this, certificate authorities may cross-certify the public keys of other certification authorities. There are two types of cross-certification:

(i) Where two certification authorities are part of the same domain. For instance, there are two levels within a given certification authority – the higher level may certify the lower level. This is called intradomain cross-certification.

(ii) Where certification authorities are different entities, the process is called interdomain cross-certification.

**14.43** Cross-certification can occur in two ways. One certification authority can cross-certify another unilaterally. Alternatively, two certification authorities can undertake a mutual cross-certification exercise. A cross-certificate can be issued to a certification authority, or a certification authority can issue it. The process of cross-certification is where a certificate authority gives copies of its keys to another certification authority. This is achieved either by handing over the key or by issuing special 'authority certificates', the purpose of which is to bind each certificate authority to its public key.

**14.44** A further mechanism is to have a hierarchy of certification authorities, where higher-level authorities certify low-level authorities. In this case, the prospective user needs to verify the highest level certificate first, usually called a root certification authority, then to check the trail and validity of every authority certificate that leads to the certificate the user wants to trust or use.[35] On a final note, when a person buys a computer with software already installed, there are a number of certificates already installed in their browsers. As a result, the user, without realising it, 'trusts' whoever uploaded the software to the computer to include appropriate authorities' certificates.[36] The certificates can be deleted, and new ones added if the user knows how to do this. If the user does not update their browser, the certificates will eventually expire and produce sometimes rather obscure error messages when signatures are verified. In addition, unless the user is aware of the complexities of the hierarchy of certification authorities, it is possible for a malicious party to insert a fraudulent certificate into chain of certificates, and appear to be trusted.[37]

35 Adams and Lloyd, *Understanding PKI Concepts*, pp. 132–45 for a detailed discussion; Piper, Blake-Wilson and Mitchell, *Digital Signatures*, pp. 37–8.

36 S. Mason and T.S. Reiniger, '"Trust" between machines? Establishing identity between humans and software code, or whether you know it is a dog, and if so, which dog?', *Computer and Telecommunications Law Review*, 21 (2015), pp. 135–48.

37 N. Ferguson, B. Schneier and T. Kohno, *Cryptography Engineering: Design Principles and Practical Applications* (Indianapolis, IN: Wiley, 2010), 18.3.1 for an example of where a software fault had the capacity to undermine the security of an entire system; for

## *Revocation of a certificate*

**14.45** The certificate is used to bind the name of a person or entity with their public key. However, just as with physical seals, there may be many reasons for revoking a certificate (or seal) before the expiry date. In the past, the owner of the seal would put notices up in such public places as churches and markets, warning people not to reply on the seal.[38] In the digital age, such notices are placed over the internet. The reasons for revoking a certificate include, but are not limited to:

> (i) The user is aware that the private key corresponding to the certificate has been lost or compromised.
>
> (ii) The certificate holder asks for the certificate to be revoked.
>
> (iii) The certification authority revokes a certificate where the holder breaches a term of the agreement.
>
> (iv) Where the certificate was issued in error.

**14.46** There are a range of technical solutions to providing public knowledge of certificates that have been revoked, but the most well-known is the certificate revocation list.[39] A certification revocation list is a signed data structure that contains a list of those certificates that have been revoked. Where a list exists, there are a number of important issues that must be addressed:

> (i) The difference in time between the command to revoke the certificate and the last time the certificate was used.
>
> (ii) The reliability of the revocation procedure; in other words, whether it can be relied upon to provide a definitive answer that can be trusted (in addition, the accuracy of the clocks that determine the time the revocation was actually uploaded to the certification revocation list – whether it was the certification authority time or the relying party time, and at whose risk – consider the possibility that the relying party deliberately sets their clock at a different time, for instance to Greenwich Mean Time or British Standard Time, to confuse the evidence).
>
> (iii) The number of revocation commands that the revocation system can handle at any one time.[40]

---

examples, especially Secure Socket Lawyer (SSL) certificates, see http://wiki.cacert.org/Risk/History; *Carbanak APT: The Great Bank Robbery* (v 2.1, Kaspersky, 2015), online at http://25zbkz3k00wn2tp5092n6di7b5k.wpengine.netdna-cdn.com/files/2015/02/Carbanak_APT_eng.pdf.

38 As described by Wills J in *The Staple of England v. The Governor and Company of the Bank of England* (1888) 21 QBD 160 at 167.

39 Adams and Lloyd, *Understanding PKI Concepts*, pp. 107–26.

40 Ferguson, Schneier and Kohno, *Cryptography Engineering*, 19.8.

**14.47** If a certification authority does not have a revocation list, the person seeking to determine whether to rely on a certificate needs to know how they can establish whether a key has been revoked or compromised.

## *Expiry of keys*

**14.48** Certificates have a fixed period of validity, in the same way that a royal seal matrix had, and they expire in due course. One technical question relates to how the life of the key is computed. Ellison and Schneier contend that the key has a 'theft lifetime' as a function of the vulnerability of the sub-system that stores the key. Other factors that also should be taken into account include the threat of physical and network exposure to attacks and how attractive the key is to an attacker.[41] There are three options available when a certificate expires: (i) no action is taken; (ii) the certificate is renewed and the same public key is placed into a new certificate with a new period of validity, (iii) a new pair of public and private keys are generated and a new certificate is generated to provide for a certificate update.[42]

## *The duties of a user*

**14.49** There are a number of points that people or organizations that use private keys should be aware of, as set out below.

**14.50 Management of private keys** The user must manage their private keys effectively and take measures that are appropriate to prevent the unauthorized use of the keys, and to protect them securely against any other form of attack, such as theft or misuse by a third party that gains access to the system by way of malicious software or other method. This duty is often included in electronic signature legislation.

**14.51 Storage of private keys after expiry** When deciding whether to use private keys, their use should be carefully monitored, because different types of algorithm are used for different purposes. Thus in the United Kingdom, consideration must be given to the possibility that a private key may be the subject of a s49 notice under the Regulation of Investigatory Powers Act 2000, and the safe storage of keys that have expired.

**14.52 Disposal of equipment with private keys** Particular care should be taken when disposing of the hardware that contains the private keys. For instance, in the European Union, the Directive on waste electrical and electronic

41 C. Ellison and B. Schneier, 'Ten risks of PKI: what you're not being told about public key infrastructure', *Computer Security Journal*, 16 (2006), p. 6, available at https://www.schneier.com/cryptography/paperfiles/paper-pki.pdf.

42 Adams and Lloyd, *Understanding PKI Concepts*, pp. 101–2.

equipment requires all electrical and electronic equipment to be reused, recycled and subject to any other form of recovery to reduce the disposal of waste.[43]

### *Internal management*

**14.53** The internal management of a certification authority, which the individual user may not be familiar with, can affect the trust to be placed in the certificates issued. Such issues include, but are not limited to, the following:

(i) The level and extent of the checks made on employees.

(ii) How to verify the identity of the employees that control the keys.

(iii) Policies on how keys are stored.

(iv) The mechanisms in place to verify that the relevant policies are followed.

(v) Whether the internal management of the certificate system is properly carried out.

(vi) The level and extent of any insurance cover may also have a bearing on the suitability of different types of certificate issued.

## Barriers to the use of the public key infrastructure

**14.54** There are a variety of problems that affect those vendors that purvey digital signature services. For an industry in its infancy, perhaps this is to be expected. However, given the extent to which government and non-governmental agencies attempt to reach universal standards of various kinds, it does seem somewhat bizarre that some of the problems even exist. For instance:

(i) There is no standard in the industry relating to the provision of a directory service. A number of models exist and competing standards are under consideration, as well as the development of proprietary solutions.

(ii) Vendors do not implement some functions, and when they are implemented, they may be implemented in a different manner

43 Directive 2002/96/EC of the European Parliament and of the Council of 27 January 2003 on waste electrical and electronic equipment OJ L 37 13.3.2003, p. 24; Directive 2003/108/EC of the European Parliament and of the Council of 8 December 2003 amending Directive 2002/96/EC on waste electrical and electronic equipment (WEEE), OJ L345, 31.12.2003, p. 106–107; Directive 2008/34/EC of the European Parliament and of the Council of 11 March 2008 amending Directive 2002/96/EC on waste electrical and electronic equipment (WEEE), as regards the implementing powers conferred on the Commission, OJ L81, 20.3.2008, pp. 65–6.

to another vendor. This leads to problems with interoperability between the systems of different vendors.[44]

(iii) The performance of the repository service where the certificate revocation lists is held may be a problem. At present there are a limited number of vendors that operate a public key infrastructure, and the numbers of people using those that are available are in the minority. Whether the systems in place are capable of expanding with greater use in the future is open to debate.

(iv) The number of people that have any knowledge of public key cryptography is small. The numbers of personnel required are not limited to administrative personnel, but include people in senior positions that can develop the relevant policy documents, such as certification practice statements and interdomain interoperability agreements. The public key infrastructure strategy must also be considered and documented.[45]

**14.55** In addition, there are weaknesses that can affect the use of the signature, such as that the data to be signed can be modified; a personal identity number can be obtained; the person affixing a signature might sign different data than intended, and an attacker can interfere with the software code as it communicated between component parts: in essence, the signatory has to trust the writer of the software that it will work as intended.[46]

## What a public key infrastructure can and cannot do

**14.56** Depending on how it is used, a public key infrastructure has its uses.[47] However, it is very important to be clear about what a digital signature can and cannot do.

### What a digital signature is capable of doing

**14.57** The uses to which cryptography can be put within a public key infrastructure include demonstrating the integrity of the message and providing for the confidentiality of a document, although using digital signatures within

44 P. Krawczyk, 'When the EU qualified electronic signature becomes an information services preventer', *Digital Evidence and Electronic Signature Law Review*, 7 (2010), pp. 7–18.

45 Adams and Lloyd, *Understanding PKI Concepts*, ch. 25.

46 A. Spalka, A.B. Cremers and H. Langweg, 'Trojan horse attacks on software for electronic signatures', *Informatica*, 26 (2002), pp. 191–204; H. Langweg, *Malware Attacks on Electronic Signatures Revisited* (2006) available at ftp://ftp.cryptopro.ru/pub/TrustedPass/110519/Theory/_hanno_research_gi06p.pdf.

47 Ferguson, Schneier and Kohno, *Cryptography Engineering*, at 19.9, 'So what is a PKI good for?', the authors conclude that 'there are few advantages to PKIs'.

a public key infrastructure will not act to correct human behaviour.[48] At best, a public key infrastructure provides encryption, not the process of signing. A digital signature only authenticates that a certain private key was used to create the relevant digital signature.

## What no form electronic signature is capable of doing

**14.58** A digital signature can provide for the authenticity of information. It binds key pairs with names. The recipient of a message or document with which a digital signature is associated can confirm the binding of the verification key with the name of the person whose private key has been used. But the recipient cannot determine whether the sending party authorized the use of the digital signature: this is also true of any other form of electronic signature. The private key of a digital signature is protected by a password or passphrase. The most important point to be aware of is this: *the private key of a digital signature is only as good as the password that protects it.* This means that when the password is inserted into a computer to provide access to the private key of a digital signature, it proves any of the following:

> (i) The person to whom the private key was issued might have been the person that inserted this information into the software, and therefore the recipient can infer that the private key of the digital signature is capable of proving that the person to whom the private key was issued was physically at the keyboard at the time of the session; or
>
> (ii) a person (perhaps the owner of the private key or her secretary) instructed the software to retain the password information in the computer memory, so that any person (*whether they were sitting in front of the computer or whether they obtained control of the computer remotely*) that obtains access to the private key can use the password, which in turn does not prove that the person to whom the private key was issued is physically at the keyboard at the time of the session (the recipient of the correspondence is not to know whether it was the person whose key it was, or her secretary, or an impostor), although it can be concluded that the

48 Davis, 'Compliance defects in public-key cryptography', paragraph 1; Adams and Lloyd, *Understanding PKI Concepts*, ch. 14 for a useful and more detailed discussion; B. Reynis and U. Bechini, 'European civil law notaries ready to launch international digital deeds', *Digital Evidence and Electronic Signature Law Review*, 4 (2007), pp. 14–18; J. Decker, 'The e-notarization initiative, Pennsylvania, USA', *Digital Evidence and Electronic Signature Law Review*, 5 (2008), pp. 73–7; T.S. Reiniger, 'The proposed international e-identity assurance standard for electronic notarization', *Digital Evidence and Electronic Signature Law Review*, 5 (2008), pp. 78–80; this article is followed by the text of 'The draft International Electronic Notarization Assurance Standard', *Digital Evidence and Electronic Signature Law Review*, 5 (2008), pp. 81–97.

use of the password proved the computer stored this information; or

(iii) that a person (whoever they may be) who used the password, actually knew the password.

**14.59** The recipient relies on one small item to persuade it that the sender is the person whom they claim to be: the password that enables the sender to cause a computer to affix the private key of a digital signature to the document. In reality, the reliance rests on the quality of the digital evidence[49] that ties a presumed identity to a presumed act, and in turn the integrity of the password, the software code and the security in place to protect the password and private key. The problems with passwords are so well-known that Dan Geer merely stated the obvious in a talk at the UNC Charlotte Cyber Security Symposium in 2013:[50] 'Everyone in this room knows how and why passwords are a problem'.

**14.60** It is generally recognized that the password is an exceedingly weak mechanism, as indicated by P. C. van Oorschot and Julie Thorpe:[51]

49 Bearing in mind that computers and networks are not secure, for which see in the legal context, R.R. Jueneman and R.J. Robertson, Jr., 'Biometrics and digital signatures in electronic commerce', *Jurimetrics Journal*, 38 (2008), pp. 427–57; note also the further technical problems in P. Švéda and V. Matyáš Jr., 'Digital signatures and electronic documents: a cautionary tale revisited', *Upgrade*, 5 (2004), pp. 35–45.

50 D. Geer, 'Tradeoffs in cyber security', a talk at the UNC Charlotte Cyber Security Symposium (2013), 9 October 2013, available at http://geer.tinho.net/geer.uncc.9x13.txt; see also J. Bonneau and E. Shutova, 'Linguistic properties of multi-word passphrases', in J. Blythe (ed.), *Financial Cryptography and Data Security Volume 7398* (Berlin/Heidelberg: Springer, 2012), pp. 1–12; J. Bonneau, C. Herley, P.C. van Oorschot and F. Stajano, *The quest to replace passwords: a framework for comparative evaluation of Web authentication schemes* (University of Cambridge Computer Laboratory Technical Report 817, 2012), available at https://www.cl.cam.ac.uk/techreports/UCAM-CL-TR-817.pdf; D. Goodwin, 'Anatomy of a hack: How crackers ransack passwords like "qeadzcwrsfxv1331"', *arstechnica*, 21 May 2013, at http://arstechnica.com/security/2013/05/how-crackers-make-minced-meat-out-of-your-passwords/; A. Belenko and D. Sklyarov, '"Secure password managers" and "military-grade encryption" on smartphones: oh, really?', (n.d.), available at http://www.elcomsoft.co.uk/WP/BH-EU-2012-WP.pdf.

51 P.C. van Oorschot and J. Thorpe, 'On the security of graphical password schemes', available online at https://scs.carleton.ca/sites/default/files/tr/TR-05-11.pdf. There is a considerable amount of material on this topic, together with the associated subject of memory and the human need to write down complex passwords (which could have a bearing on whether a human can be made liable for writing down passwords that the vendor or bank insists must be long and difficult to remember), for which see the following short list of more recent references, all of which in turn refer to other sources: K. Helkala and N. Kalstad Svendsen, 'The security and memorability of passwords generated by using an association element and a personal factor', in P. Laund (ed.), *Information Security Technology for Application* (Lecture Notes in Computer Science 7161, Berlin/Heidelberg: Springer, 2012), pp. 114–30; J. Bonneau, *Guessing human-chosen secrets* (University of Cambridge Computer Laboratory Technical Report 819, 2012); J. Bonneau and S. Preibusch, 'The password thicket: technical and market failures in human authentication on the web', Ninth Workshop on the Economics of Information Security (WEIS 2010), available from

> The ubiquitous use of textual passwords for user authentication has a well-known weakness: users tend to choose passwords with predictable characteristics, related to how easy they are to remember. This often means passwords which have 'meaning' to the user. Unfortunately, many of these 'higher probability' passwords fall into a tiny subset of the full password space. Although its boundaries vary depending on its exact definition and the probabilities involved, we refer to this smaller subset as the probable password space.
>
> Ideally, users would choose passwords equi-probably from a large subset of the overall password space, to increase the cost of a dictionary attack, i.e., a brute-force guessing attack involving candidate guesses from a prioritized list of 'likely passwords'. If a password scheme's probability distribution is non-uniform, its entropy is reduced.

**14.61** Given the willingness of people to use the same passwords for a variety of purposes[52] and to purportedly share their passwords (or perhaps an imagined password) with strangers,[53] or provide their password in return for a pen,[54] a bar of chocolate,[55] the chance to win tickets to the theatre,[56] or the opportunity to win chocolate Easter eggs,[57] it is to be wondered why the digital signature is considered to be so important by some legislators. The weaknesses are also

http://www.jbonneau.com/publications.html and http://preibusch.de/publications/password_market/; W. Moncur and G. Leplâtre, 'PINs, passwords and human memory', *Digital Evidence and Electronic Signature Law Review*, 6 (2009), pp. 116–22; M.A. Conway and E.A. Holmes, *Guidelines on Memory and the Law: Recommendations from the Scientific Study of Human Memory* (The British Psychological Society Research Board, 2008), http://www.forcescience.org/articles/Memory&TheLaw.pdf; M. Geuss, 'How a criminal ring defeated secure chip-and-PIN credit cards', *arstechnica*, 20 October 2015, http://arstechnica.co.uk/tech-policy/2015/10/how-a-criminal-ring-defeated-the-secure-chip-and-pin-credit-cards/; C. Herley, P.C. van Oorschot and A.S. Patrick, 'Passwords: if we're so smart, why are we still using them?, in Dingledine and Golle (eds.), *Financial Cryptography and Data Security* (the authors report that transactions by way of a PIN reverse the burden of proof, but this is not correct).

52 For instance, see the UK Office of Communications (Ofcom) report dated 23 April 2013, available at http://media.ofcom.org.uk/news/2013/uk-adults-taking-online-password-security-risks/.

53 M. Kelly, 'Chocolate the key to uncovering PC passwords,' *The Register*, 17 April 2007.

54 J. Leyden, 'Office workers give away passwords for a cheap pen', *The Register*, 18 April 2003.

55 'Passwords revealed by sweet deal,' *BBC News*, 20 April 2004; J. Leyden, 'Women love chocolate more than password security', *The Register*, 16 April 2008.

56 'How to sell your self for a song,' *BBC News*, 24 March 2005.

57 'Easter eggs bypass security,' *OUT-LAW News*, 18 April 2006, available online at http://www.out-law.com/page-6843.

explored by Petr Petr Švéda and Václav Matyáš Jr.[58] The authors illustrate, at paragraph 3, that when a person has the private key of a digital signature on their computer, the user or owner 'cannot be sure that no further signature processes will be executed in the background when using his private key', and they make the point in paragraph 4 that 'It is very hard to build a system or an application that does not compromise its security. There are a lot of potential problems – e.g., it can be misused, one of the components can fail, as well as the signing application, keys stored on hard disk or in memory are vulnerable'. They go on to indicate, at 4.1:

> At the time of writing, we know of no technology that can make a hardware device fully resistant to penetration by a skilled and determined attacker from a powerful organization. A lot of experts believe that absolute protection will remain unattainable. So the total cost of breaking a hardware device has to be much more than the value of stored and protected information.

**14.62** It is noted elsewhere that the 'advanced electronic signature', a creature of the previous EU Directive on electronic signatures, was predicated on the use of smart cards, yet the authors of this paper are clear in their own mind that the evidence demonstrates how vulnerable smart cards are, at 4.2:[59]

> A smart card is a simple and inexpensive security module. It consists of multiple components combined with a single chip that uses external power supply and clock. When a card is used as a personalized trusted device it generates a key pair locally, stores the private key locally, and only publishes the corresponding public key. The biggest problem with smart cards is that they lack a direct communication channel to the user. None of current available smart cards has a really trustworthy user interface. The user is completely dependent on potentially untrusted devices to get some information about his transactions. For example if the personal computer to which the smart card has been connected is compromised, it might ask the smart card to sign a completely different message to that which the user sees.

58 *Švéda* and Matyáš Jr., 'Digital signatures and electronic documents'; P.A. Loscocco, S.D. Smalley, P.A. Muckelbauer, R.C. Taylor, S.J. Turner and J.F. Farrell, 'The inevitability of failure: the flawed assumption of security in modern computing environments', in *21st National Information Systems Security Conference: building the information security bridge to the 21st century* (Gaithersburg, MD: National Institute of Standards and Technology, 1998), pp. 303–14, available at http://babel.hathitrust.org/cgi/pt?id=coo.319240839778 13;view=1up;seq=5 – the individual paper is available at https://www.cs.utah.edu/flux/fluke/html/inevit-abs.html.

59 K. Schmeh, *Cryptography and Public Key Infrastructure on the Internet* (Indianapolis, IN: Wiley, 2001), has a different view, although acknowledges attacks are possible (15.2.3).

> Many successful attacks have occurred because smart cards were exposed to more sophisticated attackers than designers anticipated, where design principles for tamper resistant smart cards are also discussed. The smart card without trustworthy user interface is a typical example of an architectural error. Many attacks are also possible due to protocol and application programming interface failures. (reference omitted)

**14.63** In summary, it is necessary to ensure the person receiving data signed with the private key of a digital signature understands the difference between trusting the signature and trusting the owner of the signature.

## The weakest link

**14.64** Although an emphasis has been made in this text upon the reliance placed upon the activities of certification authorities and other participants in the public key infrastructure (registration authorities, directory services listing public keys, certification revocation list services, time stamping, to name but a few), comparatively little discussion has been given to the weakest link in the chain of a digital signature. If Bob wants Alice to use a digital signature to authenticate her messages, he has to persuade Alice that it is essential that when he receives a message or document from her, he can be completely assured, whether he decides to become a verifying party or not, that it was Alice, and only Alice, that caused the digital signature to be affixed to the document or message. He therefore has to persuade Alice that she must take good care of her private key, such that she accepts the risk of being held responsible for unauthorised use of it by others. If Alice asks, not without reason, 'What's in it for me?' there seems to be no answer. Whether Bob decides to undertake the sometimes gargantuan task of carrying out the verification procedure or not, if he cannot satisfy himself that Alice kept her private key absolutely safe, he cannot be sure that Alice affixed the digital signature to the message. So he will try to insist that Alice carries the blame anyway.

**14.65** In any event, the recipient of a digital signature can be certain that:

> The person (whomsoever they might be) that keyed in the password that protects the private key of the digital signature, knew the password.

**14.66** Or in the alternative, the recipient of a digital signature can be certain that:

> The person that caused the private key to be attached to an email or document called up the private key and clicked on the 'password' icon (they did not need to know the password) because the software was instructed to remember the password.

**14.67** There seems to be an unquestioning reliance on the use of digital signatures that has no bearing on the risks associated with the use of the technology. This reliance is also manifest in the assumption made that a digital signature proves the person whose signature it is, and was the person that caused the computer to affix the signature to the document, as in the Portuguese case of (Evora) Ac. RE 13-12-2005 (R.982/2005), in which an email was sent with a digital signature attached. In this instance, it was determined that the digital signature served to authenticate the document, guaranteed the identity of the sender, and the integrity of the message. Whilst a digital signature is capable of identifying the sender, it cannot guarantee the sender caused the digital signature to be affixed to the message. Thus the most important point to be aware of is this: the private key of a digital signature is only as good as the password that protects it and any additional mechanism used to protect the private key, as Richard E. Smith has pointed out:[60]

> Public key cryptography succeeds only as long as a private key's owner can keep it under control – always available when needed but never disclosed to anyone else.

**14.68** It will be argued by some that the private key to a digital signature can be secured by a combination of a password and the biometric measurement of a fingerprint, for instance. This 'solution' relies on the technology (secret) of the biometric scanner that is chosen to fulfil this role, and does not take into account the various methods by which the mechanism can be compromised.

## The burden of managing the private key

**14.69** The user of a digital signature is expected to keep their private key secure. Failure to do so will mean a mischievous member of staff or a malicious third party can append a digital signature to a document or message for nefarious purposes. The management of the private key acts to underpin the efficacy of a digital signature. Some of the issues to which a recipient must give consideration include those set out below.

### *Bypassing passwords*

**14.70** Depending on the nature of the application software on any given computer or system, where a user has set their security setting to 'High' they will have to enter their password every time they wish to enter their private key to affix the private key of a digital signature to a document or message. Where the security setting is set to the default, 'Low', the messages will be automatically signed without any further intervention by the user. Given this scenario, any person with access to a computer or device containing a digital signature in a

60 R.E. Smith, *Authentication: From Passwords to Public Keys* (Boston, MA: Addison-Wesley, 2002), p. 431.

powered-up state will be able to send messages or documents with a digital signature affixed.

**14.71** Another alternative is for the user to retain their private key in memory during the login session. A user must either enter their password every time they wish to use their private key to affix a digital signature to a document or message, or they retain their private key in memory during the login session. If a user keeps the private key in memory, it exposes the key to being stolen. Examples include leaving the computer unattended, thus permitting a third party to take sufficient action to steal the key. Alternately, if the private key is on a laptop computer and the laptop computer is stolen, it may be possible for the thief to obtain access to the private key. Further, malicious software has been developed to steal passwords and private keys.[61] Finally, even if the private key is stored on an encrypted smart card, it must be used with a computer to sign a message or document, and the computer may have been maliciously programmed to sign a document or message other than the one the user intends to sign.[62]

**14.72 Quality of password** There are a number of issues surrounding the question of passwords, as noted above, and they are well documented. The entire edifice of the public key infrastructure and the security of the private key rests to a very large extent on the quality of the password used to protect it, and attempts are made to replace passwords.[63] Most of us prefer to use passwords that are easy to remember, which in turn makes a password easy to guess and vulnerable to attack. If the user does not have an effective control over the quality of the passwords used,[64] the system will be vulnerable to an offline guessing attack.[65]

**14.73** If a recipient of a digital signature intends to rely on the purported authority of the signature, they have a range of options:

61 H. Shinotsuka, 'How attackers steal private keys from digital certificates', Symantec official blog, 22 February 2013, at http://www.symantec.com/connect/blogs/how-attackers-steal-private-keys-digital-certificates.

62 See Young and Yung, *Malicious Cryptography* for further examples of how the technology can be used for malicious purposes; note the discussion on this issue by M. Rückert and D. Schröder, 'Security of verifiably encrypted signatures', *in Pairing-Based Cryptography – Pairing 2009* (Lecture Notes in Computer Science 5671, Berlin/Heidelberg: Springer, 2009), pp. 17–34.

63 J. Bonneau, C. Herley, P. C. van Oorschot and F. Stajano, *The Quest to Replace Passwords: A Framework for Comparative Evaluation of Web Authentication Schemes* (University of Cambridge Computer Laboratory Technical Report 817, 2012), available at https://www.cl.cam.ac.uk/techreports/UCAM-CL-TR-817.pdf.

64 K. Solic, H. Ocevcic and D. Blazevic, 'Survey on password quality and confidentiality', *Automatika*, 56 (2015), pp. 69–75; I. Urbina, 'The secret life of passwords', *The New York Times Magazine*, 19 November 2014, available at http://www.nytimes.com/2014/11/19/magazine/the-secret-life-of-passwords.html?_r=1.

65 Davis, 'Compliance defects in public-key cryptography'; H. Roßnagel and J. Zibuschka, 'Integrating qualified electronic signatures with password legacy systems', *Digital Evidence and Electronic Signature Law Review*, 4 (2007), pp. 7–13.

(i) To rely on the signature without taking any affirmative action. In some jurisdictions, the electronic signature legislation lays down a duty on the recipient to verify the signature, although the duty is invariably set at a high level of generality. It is conceivable that judges will take into account the arrangements between the sender and recipient before reaching a conclusive judgment. For instance, if a recipient relied on a digital signature attached to a high-value contract, a court may well consider it is appropriate in the circumstances that a recipient takes reasonable steps to authenticate and verify the digital signature, and to ensure the sending party duly authorized it.

(ii) To rely on the signature after undertaking steps to verify and authenticate the various certificates in the chain (that is, assuming the recipient has a trusted copy of the public key of the Root Certification Authority), and checking the authenticity and reliability of any time stamps (the time the time stamp is generated should not be independent of the time the digital signature data is generated),[66] thus becoming a verifying party. Should a dispute occur, one of the questions that will need to be addressed is to what extent the actions taken by the verifying party were adequate in the circumstances of the case, including their state of knowledge at the time.

(iii) Ignore the infrastructure surrounding the use of the digital signature, and require the sending party to confirm their intentions by an alternative method, or to confirm, using another medium (such as letter, facsimile transmission or telephone) that the communication was sent by them.

**14.74** As a result of the foregoing discussion, it becomes clear that public key cryptography is more suitable for server-to-server security, rather than for use on a desktop.

## Case law relating to digital signatures

**14.75** Below are cases dealing with digital signatures across a number of jurisdictions.

66 J. Stapleton, P. Doyle and S. Teppler, 'The digital signature paradox' (an updated version of a paper of the same name that was originally published in the *Proceedings of the 2005 IEEE Workshop on Information Assurance and Security*), available online at http://www.proofspace.com/newsletter/articles/0807/pdf/0807_02.pdf.

## Judicial use

**14.76** In the United States of America, judges may begin to use digital signatures to affix the judicial seal to digital data.[67]

## Administrative proceedings

**14.77** The determination to implement digital signatures in some jurisdictions is illustrated in the case of LJN: AW6886, Rechtbank Maastricht, 05/860 WSFBSF K1[68] from the Netherlands. The plaintiff, a student, applied for a student grant for students living away from home. The Informatie Beheer Groep (IGB), the Dutch institution responsible for the processing of the various grants, informed her that she would receive the higher grant from 1 March 2005. She was already in receipt of a grant for students living at home, which is lower than the amount received when living away from home. The plaintiff did not agree with this decision, having lived away from home since 1 January 2005, and had properly informed the IBG of this. She sent two emails to the IBG in which she explained her situation and set out her complaint, and objected to the decision of the IBG. The IBG rejected her notice of objection, and thereupon the plaintiff initiated legal action.

**14.78** In reaching its decision, the court had to decide whether the email could be considered a proper notice of objection. Article 2:13 of the Dutch General Administrative Law Act allows for notices of objection to be sent electronically, providing the provisions of part 2.3 of the General Administrative Law Act are taken into account. Article 6.5 of the Act states that a notice of objection has to be signed. Article 2.16 of part 2.3 of the Act states that this can be electronically if the method of authentication is trustworthy enough, having regard to the nature and the content of the electronic message and the purpose for which it is being used. The email was sent by way of a Hotmail account, which, it was held, failed to meet the requirements of the legislation. Even though the IBG considered emails sent by Hotmail as a proper notice of objection, the court held that they did not have the freedom to do so, since the requirements of the law were disregarded, although no reason is given as to why, taking into account the nature, content and purpose of the email, it was necessary to send the email with a digital signature.

## Banking

**14.79** In the Russian Federation, corporate customers who wish to undertake banking transactions online are required to accept the specific terms of a separate agreement in order to use such facilities, and the customer is required to have a

67 T. Reiniger and J.R. Francoeur, 'Justice and sheriff: practical and authoritative methods for the electronic issuance of officially certified documents in the United States', *Digital Evidence and Electronic Signature Law Review*, 7 (2010), pp. 42–52; note fn. 21 and the relevant text.

68 Available online at http://zoeken.rechtspraak.nl/resultpage.aspx?snelzoeken=true&searchtype=kenmerken&vrije_tekst=AW6886.

digital signature in order to operate an online bank account.[69] There have been a number of examples where corporations have discovered that funds (in one case almost 63 million roubles) were transferred electronically without their knowledge, and the customer has initiated legal action to recover the funds from the bank. In each instance, the transfer was authorized by the use of the private key of the digital signature of the person nominated by the corporation to possess the signature. One such case is that of an appeal to the Federal Arbitration Court of Moscow Region of 5 November 2003 N КГ-А 40/8531-03-П.[70] The plaintiff was Open Joint Stock Company of Intertoll and International Electric Communication 'Rostelecom', and the defendant was the Joint Stock Commercial Savings Bank of the Russian Federation. In this instance, on 2 August 1999, 29,580,850 roubles were debited from the customer's account by electronic payment order. The customer affirmed that they had not issued instructions to the bank to debit the amount. The appeal court rejected the plaintiff's claim. Taking into account the expert opinion, the appeal court indicated that the

> lower courts reasonably concluded that the evidence testified to the fact that there were signs of the electronic payment order transfer, and the electronic digital signature affixed to the disputed payment order was correct and belonged to the vice general director of the plaintiff. The examination also indicated that the system in place did not permit the communication session to begin without producing the client's main key, or to send documents from the client's computer on behalf of the other client, or to process documents that were not signed with a duly registered electronic digital signature.[71]

**14.80** As pointed out by Olga I. Kudryavtseva in her discussion of this case, keeping the private key of an electronic digital signature secret is demanding, and there has been an increase in litigation over this issue in the Russian Federation.

## Submission of electronic applications to court

**14.81** In some jurisdictions, such as many states in the United States of America, courts have accepted the submission of documents electronically for some time, while other jurisdictions are just beginning to make suitable arrangements.

69 For background information and additional case law, see O.I. Kudryavtseva, 'Russia' in S. Mason (ed.), *International Electronic Evidence* (London: British Institute of International and Comparative Law, 2008); O.I. Kudryavtseva, 'The use of electronic digital signatures in banking relationships in the Russian Federation', *Digital Evidence and Electronic Signature Law Review*, 5 (2008), pp. 51–7; A. Dolzhich, 'Digital evidence and e-signature in the Russian Federation: a change in trend', *Digital Evidence and Electronic Signature Law Review*, 6 (2009), pp. 181–3.

70 The facts are set out and the case discussed by O.I. Kudryavtseva in 'Case note: Russian Federation', *Digital Evidence and Electronic Signature Law Review*, 5 (2008), pp. 149–51.

71 Kudryavtseva, 'Case note: Russian Federation', p. 150.

Once legislation was passed to enable the use of electronic signatures in some jurisdictions, various attempts were made to submit applications and other responses to courts electronically, not always with success.[72] An interesting aspect of using digital signatures arises with respect to the monetary value of the certificates that accompany the signature. The Certification Authorities issue certificates linked to a monetary value to limit liability on the certificate. When submitting documents to a court, it would hardly seem necessary to link the digital signature to the monetary value placed on the certificate, because the content of the document is the item of value, and the court does not rely on the monetary value of the certificate to accept documents electronically. However, this issue arose in the German case of FG Münster 11 K 990/05 F (Electronically signed statement of claim – On the interpretation of the term 'monetary limitation') before the Finance Court of Münster in Westphalia on 23 March 2006. Counsel for the plaintiff filed a statement of claim together with other documents by way of an email with a qualified electronic signature in accordance with the German Signature Act (Signaturgesetz). The corresponding signature certificate contained a monetary limitation of €100. The court dismissed the case, because the procedural rules required the claim to be filed with a valid qualified electronic signature, and an electronic signature containing a monetary limitation was not a qualified electronic signature under the signature act that was capable of replacing a manuscript signature on a written statement of claim. The plaintiff argued that the monetary limitation corresponding to the certificate only applied to the conclusion of contracts and not to other declarations signed with the corresponding qualified electronic signature. However, it was held that the term 'monetary limitation' implies a mechanism designed to protect the user against any financial consequences, and not just the conclusion of contracts exceeding the amount for which the certificate was covered. As a result, and because the minimum legal court fees before the financial courts exceed €100, a qualified electronic signature limited to €100 could not be used to file a statement of claim by way of -mail. This decision caused some consternation in Germany, as pointed out by Martin Eßer:[73]

> This decision may not only cause confusion and uncertainty for lawyers using qualified electronic signatures with monetary limitations, but may also increase scepticism towards electronic signatures with the public. The opinion of the members of the

72 A. Nordén, 'Case note: Sweden Case no 2572-2573-2002', *Digital Evidence and Electronic Signature Law Review*, 1 (2004), p. 80; P. Bazin, 'Case notes: Élections *municipales de la Commune d'Entre-Deux-Monts*, Case No 235784, Conseil d'Etat, 28 December 2001 and *Société Chalets Boisson v. M. X.*, Case No 00-46467, Cour de Cassation, chambre civile 2, 30 April 2003', *Digital Evidence and Electronic Signature Law Review*, 1 (2004), pp. 81–2; C.A. Rohrmann, 'Case note – Brazil' and 'Comments about the Brazilian Supreme Court electronic signature case law', *Digital Evidence and Electronic Signature Law Review*, 3 (2006), pp. 98–100.

73 M. Eßer, 'Case note – Germany', *Digital Evidence and Electronic Signature Law Review*, 3 (2006), pp. 111–12.

Financial Court may not convince the members of the Appeal Court, because the court disregarded two persuasive and systematic arguments:

First, the purpose of the signature is to ensure the originator's identity and the integrity of the signed and submitted document. A monetary limitation is not necessary to put this characteristic of the signature into question. Even though the signature contains a monetary limitation, this does not have any effect on the integrity and authenticity, as both can still be verified by the recipient.

Secondly, the monetary limitation has to be legally qualified as a declaration of will of the originator. As such it has to be interpreted by the recipient – the court – like every other declaration of will. The court has to examine in good faith the objective intention of the originator pursuant to the general principles emanating from sections 133 and 157 of the German Civil Code (Bürgerliches Gesetzbuch – BGB). According to these principles, the court should have come to the conclusion that a monetary limitation only applies to financial transactions, and not to the transmission of a statement of claim to a court. The transmission of a statement of claim is not a financial transaction and the plaintiff's lawyer does not intend to conclude any contract with the court. Therefore any monetary limitation should not have been taken into consideration by the court.

**14.82** The Federal Finance Court (Bundesfinanzhof) subsequently heard the appeal to this decision,[74] and it was held that if such a signature contained a monetary restriction that restricts the kind of transactions it can be used for, the restriction does not impair the validity of the signature for the purposes of legal appeals.

**14.83** Other cases relating to electronic filing into court include the Brazilian case of Apelação Cível (Civil Appeal) N. 2006.01.99.025080-7/GO of 19 September 2006, the Tribunal Regional Federal – 1a. Região (Federal Appeal Court of the 1st Region) in which it was decided that litigation relating to tax should not be dismissed because a digital signature was used to send documents electronically. The members of the court accepted that the digital signature was valid, following the Medida Provisória Nº 2.200-2. In Hungary, the decision in case number BH2006/324, which was a libel case (press rectification lawsuit), held that documents in electronic format can be considered as drawn up in writing and capable of generating legal effects only if they are furnished with an identifiable signature pursuant to the applicable legal provisions, that is, with an advanced electronic signature. This finding was extended to contracts.

74 File number XI R 22/06; BB 2007, 92 (leading record only, otherwise not published at the time of this revision); M. Eßer, 'Case note Germany, 19 February 2009, IV R 97/06', *Digital Evidence and Electronic Signature Law Review*, 6 (2009), p. 278.

**14.84** In Colombia, during 2002, Mr Samper was subject to unsolicited bulk email sent for marketing purposes by a company owned by Mr Tapias, and after failing to stop the unwanted emails from being sent, he eventually took legal action against those responsible. The writ was served on the defendants by email. The proceedings were assigned to the Municipal Court of Rovira, Tolima.[75] The case of *Juan Carlos Samper Posada v. Jaime Tapias, Hector Cediel and others*[76] is of interest for two reasons. First, the defendant argued that the court was not competent to hear the case because the court was located in Rovira, and the facts occurred in the city of Bogotá, and that the parties lived in Bogotá. Alexander Díaz García J dealt with this objection swiftly:[77]

> The court however considered that the defendant has not understood that all behaviour based on information technology has a virtual component, and may not be uniquely limited to the material venue. The court expressed its surprise that a person somewhat familiar with the new technologies should argue that the venue may only be determined by the territorial element, taking into consideration the virtual element of information technologies.

**14.85** In reaching his decision on this point, the judge took the view that the characteristics of the new technology and the services offered are not limited to a physical and formal venue. In addition, s95 of the Colombian Statute of the Administration of Justice (Law 270 of 1996) contemplated the use of the new technologies in the service of justice:

> Los juzgados, tribunales y corporaciones judiciales podrán utilizar cualesquier medios técnicos, electrónicos, informáticos y telemáticos para el cumplimiento de sus funciones. Los documentos emitidos por los citados medios, cualquiera que sea su soporte, gozarán de la validez y eficacia de un documento original siempre que quede garantizada su autenticidad, integridad y el cumplimiento de los requisitos exigidos por las leyes procesales. Los procesos que se tramitan con soporte informático garantizarán la identificación y el ejercicio de la función jurisdiccional por el órgano que la ejerce, así como la confidencialidad, privacidad, y seguridad de los datos de carácter personal que contengan en los términos que establezca la ley.
>
> Judges, courts and other judicial corporations are allowed to use any technical, electronic and telematic means in order to accomplish their duties. Every document issued by the mentioned

75 Rovira is a town in the region of Tolima, and the events took place in Bogotá.

76 Decisión 73-624-40-89-002-2003-053-00.

77 V. Frigeri and M.F. Quinche, 'Case note', *Digital Evidence and Electronic Signature Law Review*, 2 (2005), pp. 65–72, at p. 66.

> means, whatever its support should be, will be considered as valid as an original document, as long as its authenticity, integrity and the fulfilment of procedural law's requirements are guaranteed. Every procedure handled with technical supports, will guarantee the identification and the authorities' jurisdictional duty, as the confidentiality, privacy and security of the personal data included, according to the terms set forth by the law.

**14.86** The further point was observed that documents issued by such methods are as valid and efficient as an original document as long as the originality, authenticity and integrity of the document are guaranteed, and the procedural requirements set forth by the applicable regulations are met. The judge concluded the matter by observing that 'The venue for Constitutional Judges comprises all the national territory and the applicable regulation does not exclude this court's venue in the cyberspace, taking into account the facts under discussion took place in cyberspace'.[78] The defendant also argued that the documents sent by the court required a digital signature. However, this was also dismissed, based on the provisions of article 6 of Law 527 of 1999 regarding the validity of an email, which provides:

> Artículo 6°. Escrito. Cuando cualquier norma requiera que la información conste por escrito, ese requisito quedará satisfecho con un mensaje de datos, si la información que éste contiene es accesible para su posterior consulta.
>
> Lo dispuesto en este artículo se aplicará tanto si el requisito establecido en cualquier norma constituye una obligación, como si las normas prevén consecuencias en el caso de que la información no conste por escrito.

> Article 6th. Written. Whenever any regulation requires the information to be in writing, such requirement will be satisfied by a data message; if the information such message contains is accessible for its later consultation.
>
> The provisions in this article will apply both, if the requirement established in any regulation constitutes an obligation, and if the regulations anticipate consequences in case the information is not in writing.

**14.87** Where the regulation requires that the information be sent in writing, an email will suffice, providing the email is available to the parties for further consultation. In this instance, the emails were available to both parties. Furthermore, it was observed that the law only requires the use of digital signatures in certain circumstances, and where a digital signature was not

78 Frigeri and Quinche, 'Case note', p. 67.

used, the law provided the requirements to assure the content of the message is original. It was held that the absence of a digital signature did not affect the correspondence sent by the court, and in any event, the court could not affix a digital signature to an email, because it did not have the facilities.

**14.88** In the Czech Republic, the Constitutional Court had cause to determine the validity of papers sent to the court electronically in case number IV. ÚS 319/05, issued on 24 April 2006. By way of introduction,[79] an application to a civil court in the Czech Republic can be submitted in writing, orally in the form of a deposition, in electronic form, by way of telegraph or by facsimile transmission. Where an application is submitted by facsimile transmission or in electronic form, the application must be supplemented by presenting the original application within a fixed period of time, or an application must be completed in writing which has the same wording as the application previously submitted in the electronic form or facsimile transmission. An application that has not been supplemented in accordance with the Civil Procedure Code will not be taken into consideration by the court. In this case, the members of the court upheld the ability to use a digital signature in respect of section 11 of the Electronic Signatures Act for the purposes of the signing of applications sent to the courts. The Constitutional Court, in considering the historical and systematic interpretation of the Civil Procedure Code, together with the comparative interpretation of other codes such as the Criminal Procedure Code and the Administrative Procedure Code, reached the conclusion that an application may be submitted to the court in electronic form without any original supplements if it is accompanied by an advanced electronic signature and qualified certificate issued by an accredited certification service provider in accordance with section 11 of the Electronic Signatures Act. It also held valid that applications submitted in electronic form without such a signature must be supplemented by presenting the original of application within a fixed period of time. The decision reflected the intended purpose of the legislation to make it easier to send applications to the court in electronic form. This decision was followed by a decision of the Supreme Court of the Czech Republic, case number 5 Tdo 1059/2006, issued on 20 September 2006, in which it was held that applications to the court relating to criminal procedure that are submitted in electronic form, cannot be taken into consideration unless provided with a recognized electronic signature in accordance with section 11 of the Electronic Signatures Act.

**14.89** In 2003, an appeal in the case of *AS Valga Külmutusvagunite Depoo (in bankruptcy)*[80] was head before the Administrative Chamber of Tallinn Circuit Court in Estonia, regarding the ruling filed by *AS Valga Külmutusvagunite Depoo (in bankruptcy)*[81] against a Tallinn Administrative Court Ruling of 17 March 2003.

79 For more information, see J. Matejka and P. Kuhn, 'Czech Republic', in S. Mason (ed.), *International Electronic Evidence* (London: British Institute of International and Comparative Law, 2008).

80 Administrative matter no 2-3/466/03.

81 Administrative matter no 3-366/2002.

The appellant submitted a response to the court by email on 27 February 2003. The email was signed with a digital signature, in compliance with clause 3(1) of the Digital Signatures Act (Digitaalallkirja seadus Vastu võetud 8. märtsil 2000. a. (RT I 2000, 26, 150)):

> Digitaalallkirjal on samad *õiguslikud* tagajärjed nagu omakäelisel allkirjal, kui seadusega ei ole neid tagajärgi piiratud ning on tõendatud allkirja vastavus käesoleva seaduse § 2 lõike 3 nõuetele.
>
> A digital signature has the same legal consequences as a handwritten signature if law does not restrict these consequences and if the compliance of the signature with the requirements of subsection 2 (3) of this Act is proved.

**14.90** The court refused to acknowledge that the submission had been made, because it was not in the form required by the rules of procedure, and it required the appellant to submit a properly compiled and signed response on paper with a manuscript signature. This decision was the subject of the appeal. In reversing the decision of the lower court, the members of the Administrative Chamber of Tallinn Circuit Court considered the legal effect of a digital signature was the equivalent of a manuscript signature, as provided by clause 3(1) of the Digital Signatures Act, and there was no reason why the information sent by email could not be accepted. The Tallinn Administrative Court ruling of 17 March 2003 in administrative matter no 3-366/2002 was annulled, and the matter referred back to the court of first instance in order to continue the performance of the acts set out in article 33 of the Code of Administrative Court Procedure.[82]

**14.91** One case from Germany has already been mentioned above. There have been a number of cases in different jurisdictions in Germany relating to the filing of applications and appeals to court by email, and they have all concluded that the law requires the application to be submitted with a digital signature. The cases cover a range of courts:

> Federal Finance Court (BFH - Bundesfinanzhof), file number VII B 138/05; BFH/NV 2006, 104 regarding new Sec. 52a FGO: (14.09.2005). For an appeal to be submitted in due form it must contain a qualified electronic signature if submitted electronically, otherwise it is inadmissible. In this case the appeal was submitted by an ordinary, signed, email and was thus held to be inadmissible.
>
> Higher Administrative Court Rheinland-Pfalz (OVG Rheinland-Pfalz - Oberverwaltungsgericht), file number 10 A 11741/05, NVwZ-RR 2006, 519 re new Sec. 55a VwGO: (21.04.2006). An electronically submitted document had no legal effect and is not suited to meet a procedural deadline if it is not provided with a

82 V. Näslund, 'Case report', *Digital Evidence and Electronic Signature Law Review*, 1 (2004), pp. 75–9.

qualified electronic signature. In this case, the deadline for appeal was not met for that reason.

Higher Administrative Court Bavaria (Bayerischer VGH – Verwaltungsgerichtshof), unpublished, file number 12 ZB 05.2821 regarding old Sec. 86a VwGO: (08.11.2005) Old Sec. 86a VwGO also required a qualified electronic signature for an appeal submitted in electronic form to be admissible. In this case the appellant submitted an appeal by ordinary, signed, email which was not sufficient. The appeal did not qualify as 'in writing' under Sec. 152 VwGO. See also Higher Administrative Court Hesse (Hessischer VGH – Verwaltungsgerichtshof), file number 1 TG 1668/05, DÖV 2006, 438 regarding old Sec. 86a VwGO: (03.11.2005), reaching the same conclusion as the previous case.

Administrative Court Sigmaringen (VG Sigmaringen – Verwaltungsgericht), VBlBW 2005, 154, file number 5 K 1313/05 regarding old Sec. 86a VwGO: (27.12.2004). If submitted in electronic form, an objection against an administrative decision must be provided with a qualified electronic signature to be admissible, otherwise it is not qualified as 'in writing' under Sec. 70 VwGO. In this case the objection sent by ordinary email was not sufficient.

**14.92** The reasoning behind this line of cases is demonstrated by the case of 10 A 11741/05, a decision of the Higher Administrative Court of Rhineland-Palatinate (OVG Rheinland-Pfalz) dated 21 April 2006, where a claim by a soldier in a dispute over service hours was not accepted by a lower administrative court. In this instance, the soldier filed an appeal through his lawyer to the Higher Administrative Court. The document setting out the grounds of appeal was sent as an attachment to an email without a qualified electronic signature, as defined by s3(3) of SigG (*Signaturgesetz,* German Signature Act), and as required by the procedural rule of s55(a)(1)(3) VWGO. The appeal was rejected because the document sent to the court did not have a qualified electronic signature. The court indicated that the history of the legislative process demonstrated the need for a qualified electronic signature. Section 55a VwGO replaced the old Section 86a VwGO on 1 April 2005, and under the provisions of the amended section 86a VwGO, the use of a qualified electronic signature was not an imperative formality, but a procedural rule. However, the wording of the new section 55a VwGO meant the court had to conclude that the use of a qualified electronic signature was a mandatory formal requirement. The decisions reached by judges in Germany are startling, as any lawyer from a common law background will acknowledge, but the conclusions judges are required to reach because of the law also concern many German lawyers.[83]

83 M. Eßer, 'Case note – Germany', *Digital Evidence and Electronic Signature Law Review*, 4 (2007), pp. 91–2.

**14.93** In the past in Switzerland, the Federal Court has decided that a complaint sent by facsimile transmission would not meet the required formality of writing set forth by law and was therefore not accepted (BGE 121 II 252; 112 Ia 173); it also reached the same conclusion in connection with complaints handed in by email (1P.254/2005 of 30 August 2005). These decisions may now be treated differently as a result of the provisions of article 42(4) BGG (Bundesgerichtsgesetz; Federal Act of the Swiss Supreme Court of 17 June 2005, into force 1 January 2007). This article allows the electronic filing of briefs with the Swiss Supreme Court if a certified digital signature is used.[84]

## Contract

**14.94** The legislation in Argentina follows the functional equivalent concept, and the legislation itself is discussed in more detail elsewhere. Two cases have occurred that illustrate the way the law has been interpreted and applied. In the case of *Huberman Fernando Pablo c/Industrias Audiovisuales Argentinas SA s/ despido*,[85] it was decided that an email sent by an employee did not constitute an acceptable method of a resignation without the inclusion of a digital signature, and in *Cooperativa de Vivienda Crédito y Consumo Fiduciaria LTDA c/Becerra Leguizamón Hugo Ramón s/incidente de apelación*,[86] it was decided that an email without a digital signature attached is not recognized as a document signed by the parties under the terms of Law 25.506. The decisions in both cases reflect the fact that only digital signatures are recognized as an equivalent to a manuscript signature in the absence of an agreement between the parties that another form of electronic signature is acceptable.

**14.95** In France, it appears that a digital signature was affixed to a contract for a subscription to a telephone line formed over the internet. The contract was enforceable.[87]

## Signing health records

**14.96** The practical problems of ensuring that when a digital signature is used, the person whose signature it is was the person that has used the signature is clearly highlighted in the case of Conseil d'Etat, 26 Mars 2004, No. 255265, *Fédération Nationale des Infirmiers*. Although the word 'digital signature' is not

84 C. Gasser and S. Peters, 'Submission of evidence through digital documents in Swiss civil litigation', *Digital Evidence and Electronic Signature Law Review*, 3 (2006), pp. 84–8; C. Gasser, 'Digital evidence in the new Swiss Federal Code of Civil Procedure', *Digital Evidence and Electronic Signature Law Review*, 6 (2009), pp. 195–6.

85 29884/02 S. 56885 – CNTRAB – SALA VI – Buenos Aires, 23 de febrero de 2004 (published in http://www.elDial.com.ar (subscription required)).

86 CNCOM – SALA A 16645/2006 – Buenos Aires Junio 27 de 2006 (Published in http://www.elDial.com.ar (subscription required)).

87 L. Ramkhalawan, 'Case translation: France, jugement du 19 décembre 2014', *Digital Evidence and Electronic Signature Law Review*, 12 (2015), pp. 71–5.

used in the outline of this case, it is highly probable that the signature referred to is a digital signature, because they are placed on cards, and the insertion of two cards simultaneously helps to ensure that the holder of the digital signature is the person who 'signs' with the signature. In this instance, the National Union of Nurses (the Fédération Nationale des Infirmiers) sought a ruling that guidelines (a *circulaire*) dated 26 January 2003 of the National Health Insurance Body (La Caisse Nationale d'Assurance Maladie) concerning the electronic transmission of healthcare forms by nurses and midwives for the reimbursement or payment of nursing services were null and void. Arguments were submitted concerning the extent of the power of the Caisse Nationale d'Assurance Maladie to issue the guidelines. In terms of an electronic signature, the practical problem at issue was that, according to the guidelines, the signature of the healthcare form affixed in an electronic form should occur by the simultaneous reading of the patient's individual electronic card and that of the health professional. It appears that the National Union of Nurses issued the challenge on the ground that it is not always possible for the two cards to be inserted at the same time, and therefore in practice, the signature would not comply with article R 161-43 of the Social Security Code. A subsequent decree was introduced on 28 April 2003, which permitted the reading of the individual electronic card and the medical professional card to take place at separate times. However, the decree was introduced subsequent to the guidelines and therefore this raised the question of the legality of the guidelines. The Conseil d'Etat declared the guidelines of 20 January 2003 null and void.

## European Patent Office

**14.97** The European Patent Office sets out the rules regarding electronic signatures and authentication in Decision of the President of the EPO dated 26 February 2009 concerning the electronic filing of documents.[88] In *ERICSSON/ Electronic filing of appeals T1427/09*,[89] an electronic signature was affixed to the electronic filing of an appeal, but not in the correct name. This was an application for an appeal against the decision of the examining division, sent on 9 March 2009, refusing European patent application 01962282.8. The notice of appeal and the statement setting out the grounds of appeal in this case were filed electronically on 11 May 2009 and 17 June 2009 respectively. The notice of appeal dated 11 May 2009 included the name of Mr Friedrich Kühn, a European Patent Attorney. There was no manuscript signature. The electronic filing of this document was certified by a signature authentication showing that both the sender certificate and the signer certificate underlying the filing were issued to I. Elfving. Mr Kühn provided a manuscript signature to the statement setting out the grounds of appeal dated 17 June 2009. However, the electronic filing of this statement was certified by a signature authentication showing that both the

88 [2009] OJ EPO 182.

89 [2010] E.P.O.R. 22.

sender certificate and the signer certificate underlying the filing were issued to R. Ahlund. The reference to a 'sender certificate' and a 'signer certificate' appears to indicate that a digital signature was affixed to the notice.

**14.98** In Decision of the President of the EPO dated 26 February 2009 concerning the electronic filing of documents,[90] article 8(2) provides that the authenticity of documents filed in appeal proceedings are to be confirmed by the use of an enhanced electronic signature of a person authorized to act in the proceedings in question. Neither I. Elfving nor R. Ahlund were authorized to act in the proceedings. As a result, the notice of appeal and the statement setting out the grounds of appeal were deemed not to be signed. The appellant was therefore invited to file signed copies of the documents within two months in accordance with Rule 50(3) of the European Patent Convention.

90 [2009] OJ EPO 182.

# 15

# Liability

**15.1** The number of possible parties linked to an electronic signature will differ, depending on the type of signature used. The number of links in the chain, and how secure those links are, will give rise to different levels and types of liability, although some of the parties may be considered to be too far removed from the creation of the signature to incur any liability, whether contractual or non-contractual.[1]

## Liability: links in the chain

**15.2** There are a number of ways in which liability may arise, and the following discussion serves to illustrate some of the problems that could occur.

### A biodynamic version of a manuscript signature

**15.3** A biodynamic version of a manuscript signature is created using a proprietary pad that measures the various dynamics of the signature as it is written. Thus the reliability of the software, how secure it is, how it interacts with the software on the user's computer and what methods are used to provide for the security of the measurements are open to scrutiny. The person or organization using such technology will then have to consider the security of the biodynamic measurements, including how they are to be stored, how they are to be destroyed, who has access to the measurements and how they are used. Once the measurements are attached to a document or message, the recipient may use the measurements as they see fit.

### A scanned manuscript signature

**15.4** A manuscript signature that has been scanned represents a considerable risk if the original document is not properly protected, and when the file of the signature is attached to a document, enabling a third party to use it improperly.[2] It must be emphasised that this risk is manifest for every document in existence that has an original manuscript signature affixed to it, but the potential for misuse is probably low in comparison to other methods of forgery used by criminals.

1 Whether a party has a contractual or non-contractual claim (or both) will depend on the facts of a case, and this chapter does not deal with the law relating to contractual or non-contractual claims.

2 By way of example, see *Djordje Mitic v. Eco Pro Australia Pty Ltd* [2009] AIRC 503 (26 May 2009) where one of the parties appeared to have used the scanned signature of another party, apparently as part of a forgery of a letter.

S. Mason, *Electronic Signatures in Law* (London: Institute of Advanced Legal Studies, 2016), chapter 15, 'Liability', pp. 339–49.

One further risk relating to this form of signature was the subject of research at the University of Derby in England. A study conducted by Nazia Mehrban and Ian James Turner at the Faculty of Education, Health and Science looked at a number of manuscript signatures and scanned versions of the same signatures. They compared the two for some of the features that make a signature unique. It was found that there were up to ten differences between the two signatures. It was observed that many features that make manuscript signatures difficult to forge (stroke order, pooling of ink, stroke direction) are not present in the scanned version of a signature. This means that somebody intent on forging a signature can more easily copy from a scanned version of a signature and more easily pass the manuscript signature of another as their own if the only reference material available to the person relying on the signature is a scanned signature. It was also found that the type of pen used also appears to have an influence on the number of differences observed. Ballpoint pens proved to be the best, followed by fountain pens. Apparently roller ball pens were the worst.[3]

## A typed name

**15.5** Typing a name on an electronic document represents the easiest way of authenticating a message, whilst also providing for the weakest evidence. Clearly, anybody can type the name of another person or organization into an electronic document with the intention of causing the recipient to believe the message originates from a person or entity other than the person that originated the document or message. Such an action may intend to deceive or misrepresent some fact.

## Participants in the public key infrastructure

**15.6** A number of people or organizations that use the public key infrastructure are likely to find themselves liable in one way or another. Those most at risk are:

(i) The sender of a signed message, where an individual or legal entity obtains an individual identity certificate in which their identity will be associated to the value of a public key, which in turn is linked to the value of a private key under their control.

(ii) The certification authority that issues the individual identity certificate. It must be emphasized that there will probably be more than one certification authority involved in any one transaction.

(iii) The registration authority (where used by a certification authority), which undertakes to confirm the identity of an individual or legal entity.

3 N. Mehrban and I.J. Turner, 'A comparison of the identifying features in original signatures and electronically scanned signatures', *Journal of the American Society of Questioned Document Examiners*, 11 (2008), pp. 1–7.

(iv) A receiving party, where they receive an electronic communication that has been signed electronically, and act in reliance on a relevant individual identity certificate by using the public key affirmed in the certificate and associated with the identity of the sender, thus verifying that the communication was signed using the corresponding private key, which in turn implies that the communication originated from the sender.

### Digital signatures – public key infrastructure

**15.7** Applying a signature using public key cryptography can involve a number of parties. For instance, a key pair may be issued by one party and an individual identity certificate by another. Even where the same authority issues both, checking the identity of the person or organization that applied for a digital signature may be undertaken by yet another organization, a registration authority. Thereafter, the subscribing party retains the private key, whilst the public key is held in a public depositary by the certification authority. The subscribing party has the duty of securing the private key, whilst the terms of Certificate Practice Statements attempt to require the recipient to undertake due diligence before relying upon the sender's digital signature. Potential liability lies with the certification authority for not keeping the certificate revocation list up-to-date, with the registration authority for not checking the identity of a subscribing party properly, and with the subscribing party for not securing their private key properly. Note also that certificates are packaged with wrappers. For example, PKCS #12 wrapping (PKCS stands for Public Key Cryptography Standards) is a standard that supports the direct transfer of personal information, enabling the user to move the certificate and corresponding private keys from one computer to another.[4] Other certificates have different types of wrappers, and a further complication is that the industry standard X.509 certificate is available in different formats, including RSA and DSA variants.[5]

## How liability can be incurred

**15.8** Electronic signatures are difficult to secure (for instance, the act of typing a name into a document is not necessarily, in the absence of corroborating evidence, the best evidence that the person caused their name to be typed into the document or email), and digital signatures expose the participants to a range of acts and omissions. The following list serves to indicate the main areas where liability may arise (it is not meant to be exhaustive):

4 RFC 2986, available at https://tools.ietf.org/html/rfc2986.

5 See R. Green, 'Certificates', for an interesting discussion about some of these issues, available from http://mindprod.com/jgloss/certificate.html.

(i) The person whose signature is used may not have authorized the use of the signature. A number of cases are noted in chapter 6.

(ii) The private key of the digital signature of the signing party may have been compromised, permitting an unauthorised person to gain access to and use the key without authority.

(iii) A communication was sent with an electronic signature affixed, but the sender did not intend the communication to have any legal effect.

(iv) A communication was sent with the electronic signature affixed, but the sender was coerced into sending the communication with the electronic signature against their will.

(v) A communication was sent with the electronic signature affixed, but the sender revoked the certifying certificate.

(vi) A communication was sent with the electronic signature affixed, but when the sender realised they did not want to be bound by the promise, they revoked the certifying certificate of the digital signature immediately.

(vii) A certificate linked to the private key of a digital signature may have been issued to an impostor, or it may incorrectly link the identity of one person or legal entity with a public key that has been allotted to another.

(viii) Where a certification authority fails upon request to suspend or revoke a private key that has been compromised, or is dilatory in so doing.

(ix) Where the private key of the certification authority is compromised, leading to the creation of fraudulent certificates.

(x) A breach in security occurs that leads to the possibility that information can be stolen.

(xi) Where attribute certificates are incorrectly generated or allocated, or where a certificate is not issued or where there is a delay in issuing a certificate.

(xii) Where access to the certificate repository or certificate revocation list of the certification authority is interrupted or compromised, thereby preventing a recipient being able to verify whether a certificate has been revoked.

(xiii) Where a certificate has been suspended or revoked incorrectly.

(xiv) Where the certificate authority publishes erroneous information.

(xv) In the event a duplicate key is generated.

**15.9** The most likely dispute arising from the use of key pairs within a public key infrastructure will probably be to do with the actual transaction itself, rather than any problems relating to the failing of the certification authority. Where there is a dispute about a failure of the certification authority, the amount of liability the certification authority impose contractually will probably be far less than the value of the underlying transaction, although this will not prevent a challenge on the basis that the limit is unreasonable.[6]

## Types of loss

**15.10** The following is merely a list of examples that could occur, all of which will have both criminal and civil ramifications.

> (i) The relying party Alice claims for loss flowing from having acted in the belief that she contracted with Bob when Alice did not, in fact contract with Bob.
>
> (ii) Alice claims for her loss flowing from being held liable for entering a contract with Bob, when Alice did not enter the contract but the revocation of Alice's private key was published too late.
>
> (iii) Alice tries, unsuccessfully, to enter a contract with Bob, but fails to do so successfully because the certification authority's certificate failed correctly to embody Alice's public key.

**15.11** The first two claims depend on whether liability attaches to a subscriber for signatures made by others. This is a critical question that underlies most of the other examples, but depends on the resolution of issues on which the industry and government participants in the debate remain somewhat silent.

## Assumptions in public key infrastructure

**15.12** The rationale behind the public key infrastructure is this: when a certification authority issues a certificate, it bases the issuance of the certificate on its Certificate Practice Statement and terms of trade. A contractual relationship is formed between the certification authority and the customer who buys the certificate. While the certificate purports to verify the identity of an individual person or legal entity, it is the merchant or person receiving the certificate that

6 For a more detailed discussion of the liability of certification services providers, see G. Dimitrov, *Liability of Certification Service Providers: How the Providers of Certification Services Related to Electronic Signatures Could Manage their Liabilities* (Saarbruecken: VDM Verlag, 2008).

relies on the content of the certificate.[7] The logic is as follows:[8]

> (i) The individual or entity provides the certification authority with sufficient evidence acceptable to the certification authority or registration authority to demonstrate that they are who they say they are. Depending on the level of the certificate obtained, this information could be the name, address and the number of a driving licence. For certificates that will support high value transactions, the person or entity seeking a certificate may be required to provide more robust evidence, including physically appearing before a notary public.
>
> (ii) The certification authority provides the user with a certificate.
>
> (iii) The individual or entity is then given a keyholder's name.
>
> (iv) The keyholder is the person or entity that obtained the certificate.
>
> (v) This is all the recipient needs to know.

**15.13** There are a number of flaws with this logic. For instance, John Smith of York may wish to enter a contract with a company who is not aware of his identity. The company cannot distinguish, when it looks at the certificate, how many John Smiths live in York and whether this particular John Smith is the person identified with the certificate. Unless the certificate provides the company with a unique identifier identifying this particular John Smith (which they may or may not provide), and the company wishes to confirm John Smith's identity, it must consider other ways of doing so. If a certification authority were to undertake to positively identify a subscribing party, the information that might be needed to satisfy the recipient may be so extensive that few individuals or legal entities would consider subscribing for such a certificate.[9] In conclusion, a certification authority provides a very narrow promise when issuing a certifying certificate. It

7 See T.J. Smedinghoff, *Certification Authority Liability Analysis* (Washington, DC: American Bankers Association, 1998), available at http://papers.ssrn.com/sol3/papers.cfm?abstract_id=2602207 for a discussion of the issues relating to the liability of certification authorities in the North American context.

8 C. Ellison and B. Schneier, 'Ten risks of PKI: what you're not being told about public key infrastructure', *Computer Security Journal*, 16 (2000); for two responses to this article, see B. Laurie, 'Seven and a half non-risks of PKI: what you shouldn't be told about public key infrastructure', at https://groups.google.com/forum/#!topic/jyu.ohjelmointi.coderpunks/PtWHnFue9Zk and A. Pérez, 'Ten risks of PKI', available at https://sites.google.com/site/aramperez/home/10-risks-of-pki; 'PKI Assessment Guidelines', C.4.2 'Attribution presumptions in digital signature statutes'.

9 For a useful discussion, see C. Ellison, 'Improvements on conventional PKI wisdom', *Proceedings of the 1st Annual PKI Research Workshop* (Gaithersburg, MD: NIST, 2002), pp. 165–75, available online at http://www.cs.dartmouth.edu/~pki02/; N. Bohm and S. Mason, 'Identity and its verification', *Computer Law & Security Review*, 26 (2010), pp. 43–51.

does not appear that certification authorities seek first to establish the identity of a person and then go on to verify that identity. It is important to understand that verification is not the same as identification.[10]

**15.14** The certification authority generally does not share a secret with the person to whom they provide a certificate. Many certification authorities use the information collected by a credit bureau to identify the identity of the applicant. This means the identification process is based on the accuracy of the data collected by the credit bureau and the effectiveness of the credit bureau in keeping the information up-to-date. Another issue is whether the recipient of the electronic signature trusts the originator's certification authority.

## Risks associated with the use of digital signatures[11]

### Issuing a certificate to an impostor

**15.15** A number of certification authorities have issued false SSL (Secure Socket Layer) certificates that support the security of websites.[12] The issuing of false certificates illustrates the weakness of how certificates are created and issued, and also how important the certificates are in relation to the operation of the internet. It is not known whether false certificates have been issued that are associated with digital signatures that are used by people or legal entities. The 2001 example of VeriSign issuing two Class 3 Software Publisher certificates incorrectly has been cited in previous editions of this text by way of example.[13] A more significant incident occurred in 2011, when DigiNotar B.V., a Dutch certificate authority owned by VASCO Data Security International, Inc, was placed into voluntary bankruptcy as a result of the discovery that the company

10 J. Grijpink and C. Prins, 'Digital anonymity on the internet', *Computer Law & Security Report*, 17 (2001), pp. 379–89, at p. 381(a).

11 F. Piper, S. Blake-Wilson and John Mitchell, *Digital Signatures: Security & Controls* (Rolling Meadows, IL: Information Systems Audit and Control Foundation, 1999), ch. 4; N. Ferguson, B. Schneier and T. Kohno, *Cryptography Engineering: Design Principles and Practical Applications* (Indianapolis, IN: Wiley, 2010), ch. 19.

12 See the CAcert Wiki for a list of fraudulent certificates that have been issued (the aim of this website is to maintain a list of attacks with reasonably authoritative references): http://wiki.cacert.org/Risk/History.

13 The 'VeriSign security alert fraud detected in Authenticode signing certificates', 22 March 200, is no longer available, nor is G.L. Guerin, 'Microsoft, VeriSign, and certification revocation'; for the CERT Advisory, see http://www.lafn.org/faq/virus/fraud_certificate.html; for the Microsoft Security Bulletin MS01-017, see https://technet.microsoft.com/library/security/ms01-017; U. S. Department of Energy Computer Incident Advisory Capability, L-062: Erroneous Verisign-Issued Digital Certificates for Microsoft; F. Gomes, 'Security Alert: Fraudulent Digital Certificates' (SANS Institute, 2003), available online at http://www.sans.org/reading_room/whitepapers/certificates/security-alert-fraudulent-digital-certificates_679.

had issued several hundred fraudulent certificates.[14] The company also issued certificates for the PKIoverheid program on behalf of the government in The Netherlands. A hacker obtained access to the DigiNotar computer systems and issued an unknown number of false certificates. On 2 September 2011, after being informed of the results of the investigation of the DigiNotar systems by Fox-IT, the Dutch government stopped trusting certificates issued by DigiNotar[15] and regained control over the company's intermediate certificate to manage an orderly transition, replacing untrusted certificates with new ones from another provider.[16] The fact that false certificates have been issued illustrates the weaknesses inherent in the trust placed in software code[17] – because it is software code that controls the entire edifice of everything digital – and it is imperative for lawyers to more fully understand the technical issues by adopting a realistically sceptical approach to understanding the nature of software.[18]

## Certificate revocation list

**15.16** There are two technical issues that affect the ability to download a suitably recent certificate revocation list: how the certification authority tells you where to obtain the relevant certificate revocation list, and whether your computer carries out the functions you require. There are many different ways to obtain a certificate revocation list, and because there is no standard within the industry, no one method is mandatory.[19] Regardless of the method used, the significant issues for every recipient, which they may not be aware of, are as follows:

> (i) The certificate revocation list should be digitally signed by the certificate authority using its root certificate to prevent a certificate revocation list from being forged.

14 'VASCO announces bankruptcy filing by DigiNotar B.V.' (n.d.), https://www.vasco.com/about-vasco/press/2011/news_vasco_announces_bankruptcy_filing_by_diginotar_bv.html.

15 *Factsheet: Fraudulently issued security certificate discovered*, 5 September 2011, version 2.2, https://www.ncsc.nl/english/current-topics/factsheets/factsheet-fraudulently-issued-security-certificate-discovered.html; *Black Tulip Report of the investigation into the DigiNotar Certificate Authority breach* (Fox-IT BV, PR-110202, 13 August 2012, version 1.0), available at https://www.rijksoverheid.nl/documenten/rapporten/2012/08/13/black-tulip-update.

16 *Overheid zegt vertrouwen in de certificaten van Diginotar op, Nieuwsbericht* (3 September 2011), at https://www.rijksoverheid.nl/actueel/nieuws/2011/09/03/overheid-zegt-vertrouwen-in-de-certificaten-van-diginotar-op.

17 S. Mason and T.S. Reiniger, '"Trust" between machines? Establishing identity between humans and software code, or whether you know it is a dog, and if so, which dog?', *Computer and Telecommunications Law Review*, 21 (2015), pp. 135–48.

18 Note the comments by N. van Eijk in 'The DigiNotar case: internet security is no abstract matter', *Computers & Law*, 23 (2013), pp. 21–2.

19 C. Adams and S. Lloyd, *Understanding PKI Concepts, Standards, and Deployment Considerations* (2nd edn., Boston, MA: Addison-Wesley, 2002), pp. 107–26.

(ii) The certificate revocation list is dated by the certification authority, which means that every certificate revocation list expires.

(iii) Every certificate revocation list has a higher sequence than the one issued previously, to prevent forgery.

(iv) The person wishing to check a particular certificate must know where to find a suitably recent certificate revocation list.

(v) The certificate revocation list must actually be able to be obtained by a relying party.

(vi) The contents of the certificate revocation list must be authenticated.

**15.17** Any duty that is to be imposed on a certification authority should take into account the complexity of these issues. If Microsoft designed the software to take a user to the address where the certificate revocation list existed only if the address was provided by the certification authority with the certificate, then establishing the responsibility for passing this knowledge on to a recipient will be a necessary perquisite to any possible defence by a certification authority. Apparently, VeriSign did not issue Class 3 Software Publisher certificates with an address for the certificate revocation list. This appears to mean that, at the time of the incident, the user of the relevant Microsoft software was not able to retrieve the certificate revocation list of a given certifying certificate issued by VeriSign. At the time of this incident, Guerin concluded that Microsoft did not have software that had a working revocation infrastructure. Microsoft did not agree with this analysis, and published a rebuttal that is no longer available,[20] to which Guerin rebutted the points raised by Microsoft in his article, which is no longer available. The report located on U.S. Department of Energy Computer Incident Advisory Capability website, referring to 'L-062: Erroneous Verisign-Issued Digital Certificates for Microsoft' no longer appears to be available. However, if a vendor of software such as Microsoft did not have a working revocation infrastructure in place in the past, then it could be argued that past certificates can hardly be said to be reliable. This means the evidential weight to be given to a certificate must be considered against these practical problems, otherwise the evidence may be so poor as to make the concept of a certificate irrelevant. Arguably, a court should take such practical issues into account when deciding whether a duty of care should be imposed on a certification authority.[21]

## Other risks

**15.18** Other types of risk include, in no particular order:

20 However, Microsoft published 'Response to inaccurate Crypto-Gram article on VeriSign certificates' at https://technet.microsoft.com/en-us/library/cc751324.aspx.

21 See S. Mason (ed.), *Electronic Evidence* (3rd edn., London: LexisNexis Butterworths, 2012), ch. 5 for a detailed consideration that machines are presumed to be working properly.

1. The fraudulent substitution of a public key for that of a genuine user, where an impostor substitutes his or her own public key for that of the genuine user. There is no attempt to recreate the certificate of the genuine user. The attacker can sign a document with a false public key that identifies the genuine user incorrectly.[22]

2. The theft of keys, perhaps where a thief puts a website up and directs the subscriber to the website, and then asks them to give the relevant passwords, or where hackers break into the system and overcome the security system to replace crucial pieces of software with code in the browser or signing tools to enable them to use the certificate or private key of the digital signature.

3. The failure of security, where the extent of the security measures in place, either on the computer or the system upon which the certificate is located, is an important factor in evaluating the possibility that a system can be compromised.[23]

4. Side-channel attacks, where a hacker can, by carefully measuring the amount of time it takes the system to perform the operations of a private key, obtain the fixed Diffie-Hellman exponents, factor RSA keys and break other cryptographic systems. Such an attack is possible because other variables relating to the performance of the hardware and software can be monitored by the hacker to exploit measurements in timing to find the entire key. Such an attack is computationally inexpensive against a vulnerable system.[24] A hacker can also exploit the variation in voltage consumed in order to derive information about the private key number.[25] For instance, some computational processes run so slowly that it is possible to see the mathematical functions performed by the software. Smart cards are also vulnerable to this type of attack. The card is plugged into a reader or encoder and the information contained on the memory is protected by secondary protection. Where the reader or encoder is powered by a battery that is running low in power,

22 F. Piper and M. Robshaw, 'Cryptography – a snapshot of where we stand', *Information Security Bulletin*, June 2001, p. 21.

23 One example of a virus and what it can do to a system is discussed by R. Perry, 'The BadTrans virus and e-conveyancing', *Computers and Law*, 12 (2002), pp. 8–9.

24 P.C. Kocher, 'Timing attacks on implementations of Diffie-Hellman, RSA, DSS, and other systems', available at https://www.rambus.com/timing-attacks-on-implementations-of-diffie-hellman-rsa-dss-and-other-systems/; E. Bangerter, D. Gullasch and S. Krenn, 'Cache games – bringing access-based cache attacks on AES to practice' (2010), available at https://eprint.iacr.org/2010/594.pdf.

25 Piper and Robshaw, 'Cryptography', p. 22; J. Kelsey, B. Schneier, D. Wagner and C. Hall, 'Side channel cryptanalysis of product ciphers', *Journal of Computer Security*, 8 (2000), pp. 141–58 available online at https://www.schneier.com/academic/paperfiles/paper-side-channel2.pdf.

it is possible to obtain access to the memory by bypassing the security mechanism on the card.

5. A certification revocation list that is not up-to-date or cannot be identified for the recipient of the digital signature to establish whether the data in the certificate has been modified.

6. Subverting the 'root' key – certification authorities use root public keys. Thus, if an attacker can add their own public key to the root key list, the attacker can issue its own certificates. These certificates will be treated exactly like legitimate certificates.

7. Obtaining access to the certification authority's private key – the secret key of the certification authority is vulnerable to attack. If the private key is stolen, the thief can produce an unlimited number of ostensibly valid, but forged certificates.

**15.19** From the available case law, it seems that litigation usually centres on whether a person used their electronic signature (such as the ATM PIN cases and digital signature cases from the Russian Federation), or whether a third party used the signature to steal money. The more complex methods outlined in this chapter will probably be rare events, if only because thieves tend to use the shortest and easiest methods to steal money or goods.

# 16

# Evidence and digital signatures

**16.1** In the event an electronic signature becomes the subject of a dispute, the normal considerations will apply regarding the submission of evidence into legal proceedings, including any rules relating to the authentication of the evidence, the weight to be given to the evidence and whether it is necessary to help the adjudicator in reaching a decision by providing for expert witnesses. This chapter aims to alert the reader to some of the issues that might arise in relation to digital signatures in particular.

## The evidence forming a digital signature

**16.2** A certificate is issued with a digital signature,[1] which is a signed data structure that binds a public key to an identity. This certificate will purport to bind the public key to the information contained in the certificate. The subscribing party provides some of the information contained in the certificate, which may or may not be verified by the certification authority, and the certification authority is responsible for the remaining information. The subscriber will have a pair of keys, private and public. The key pairs may be generated by the keying material available to the subscribing party in their computer, by a registration authority, by the certification authority or by a trusted third party key generation facility.

**16.3** Individuals can create their own private and public key pairs, or key generating organizations can undertake this task. The creation and certification processes are distinct. The same issues discussed in this chapter will apply to keys not certified by a third party, with the added complication that the level of authenticity may be lower because proving who the public key belonged to might be more difficult for any person wishing to rely on an uncertified key. How the key pair is generated may also be problematic if there is evidence that the software used to generate key pairs has flaws, such as being liable to generate weak keys.

### Continuity of evidence forming a digital signature

**16.4** The links in the continuity of evidence that bind a signature in digital format may be complex. The example of the digital signature illustrates the complexity of the process and the number of participants. With a digital signature the following set of links may not be unusual:

1 The use of the word 'certificate' is shorthand for an individual identity certificate.

S. Mason, *Electronic Signatures in Law* (London: Institute of Advanced Legal Studies, 2016), chapter 16, 'Evidence and digital signatures', pp. 351–86.

> First link: A subscriber enters a contract with a trusted third party key generation facility to generate a key pair. This key pair must then be distributed safely: the private and public keys to the subscribing party, and the public key to the certification authority.
>
> Second link: The certification authority creates the certificate. The subscribing party's public key must be incorporated into the certificate. This is the act of binding the subject name (the subscribing party) with their public key. This certificate is then digitally signed with the private key of the certification authority that issues the certificate.
>
> Third link: Once the certificate has been generated, it must be distributed. The methods used include physical delivery, posting the certificate in a public repository database to permit recipients to obtain access to the certificate over the internet, and distribution by means of email.

**16.5** When a subscribing party uses their digital signature, a certification authority requires the receiving party to undertake a certain amount of due diligence to rely on the promise made in the certificate. Individual certification authorities attempt to impose a varying range of obligations on a recipient. In some jurisdictions, the law requires a recipient to undertake an exercise in due diligence, although where a law provides for such a requirement, it is usually drafted in general terms. By way of example, s24 of the Electronic Transactions Act 2006 of Antigua and Barbuda provides as follows:

> 24. A person relying on an electronic signature shall bear the legal consequences of his failure to—
>
> (a) take reasonable steps to verify the reliability of an electronic signature; or
>
> (b) where an electronic signature is supported by a certificate, take reasonable steps to—
>
> (i) verify the validity, suspension or revocation of the certificate; or
>
> (ii) observe any limitation with respect to the certificate.

**16.6** For the purpose of this discussion, it will be useful to indicate the range of actions a recipient might be required to undertake if they were obliged to verify the certificate used by the sending party.

## Verifying the integrity of a certificate

**16.7** A recipient can go through a list of checks to assure themselves that the certificate links the sending party to the document or message that was signed.

## *Verify the certificate path*

**16.8** To trust the certificate sent by Alice, Bob must check all of the certificates back to the root or foundation certificate. Only by checking back to the foundation certificate can Bob determine whether he can trust the public key in Alice's certificate in relation to the purpose for which he will use it. The certificate attached to the message or document and the corresponding public key can only be trusted if every certificate and their corresponding keys in the path from the foundation key to Alice's key can be trusted. There are two phases to this exercise:

> (i) Constructing the path, which requires Bob to bring together all the relevant certificates to form a complete path. This process may be complicated and time-consuming, because there may be a number of certification authorities in the chain, all of which have cross-certified their respective certificates. The assumption is that Bob can retrieve all of the certificates he needs to scrutinize them and put the chain of certificates together in a logical sequence. Bob must also check the issuing certificate of each of the certification authorities in the chain against a certificate revocation list.[2]
>
> Validating the path, where Bob must decide whether the path between each certificate is valid. This involves undertaking the mathematical computation to verify each digital signature; checking the validity period of each certificate for date of expiry; making sure each certificate has not been revoked, by checking the relevant certification revocation list, and then considering other issues such as the policies that apply to the certificate, any restrictions on the use of the key and if there are any other constraints on the use of the certificate.[3]

2 Microsoft offer guidance on this point, but fail to illustrate the complexity of searching all of the certificates in a chain, and how to identify where the chain begins and ends. See 'How to tell if a digital signature is trustworthy' online at https://support.office.com/en-us/article/How-to-tell-if-a-digital-signature-is-trustworthy-0464f8ab-fefa-4bc7-af0d-e07a12f7097e?CorrelationId=7de8c7fc-375e-4cd2-8f10-26d4824fa4b3&ui=en-US&rs=en-US&ad=US; to understand the complexity of the task, see E. Barker, *Recommendation for Obtaining Assurances for Digital Signature Applications* SP 800-89 (National Institute of Standards and Technology, November 2006), also M.H.M. Schellekens, *Electronic Signatures Authentication Technology from a Legal Perspective* (The Hague: T.M.C. Asser Press, 2004), pp. 30–2, K. Schmeh, *Cryptography and Public Key Infrastructure on the Internet* (Indianapolis, IN: Wiley, 2001), 19.3.1–19.3.2, and D. Davis, 'Compliance defects in public key cryptography', Proceedings of the 6th conference on USENIX Security Symposium, Focusing on Applications of Cryptography – Volume 6 (San Jose, CA: Usenix Association, 1996), pp. 171–8, for a discussion of some of the defects of PKI, relevant now as they were in 1996, available online at http://world.std.com/~dtd/.

3 C. Adams and S. Lloyd, *Understanding PKI Concepts, Standards, and Deployment Considerations* (2nd edn., Boston, MA: Addison-Wesley, 2002), pp. 147–9.

## *Other validation requirements*

**16.9** Once Bob has checked and validated the certificates and certificate path, he must then consider the following checks:

> (i) Establish the integrity of the certificate by ensuring the digital signature on the certificate is properly verified.
>
> (ii) The certificate validity period must be checked to ensure it is valid on the date and the time Bob intends to rely on it.
>
> (iii) Check the certificate has not been revoked. There are various methods to implement a certificate revocation list. There are a number of variations, including, but not limited to, certificate revocation lists (which is a signed data structure that contain a list of revoked certificates); certification authority revocation lists, used to revoke the public key certificates of certification authorities and online certificate status protocol, which is a protocol that permits Bob to receive a response to his request for information.
>
> (iv) Check Alice has used the certificate in accordance with the constraints set out in the certificate, including the relevant agreements and certification policies.

**16.10** As a result, when determining the nature of the evidence, it is necessary to ascertain the source of the information and the uses to which the relevant document is put. It is worth recalling the nature of the promise made to a receiving party when a sending party affixes a digital signature to a document or message:

> *Bob receives a message digitally signed by Alice with Alice's digital signature certificate attached. Alice's public key is incorporated into the certificate. The certificate purports to bind Alice's name with her public key, and in turn the certificate purports to assure Bob that the message was signed using a key verifiable by a key certified in a certificate issued to Alice.*

**16.11** The nature of this promise is well illustrated by the following comment from the Select Committee on Trade and Industry, Seventh Report, House of Commons Session 1998–99, paragraph 12:

> Written signatures are tightly associated with people and weakly associated with documents, whilst digital signatures are tightly bound to documents and weakly bound to individuals (or identities).

**16.12** The crucial point to remember is that a digital signature does not, of itself, provide evidence that the sending party actually caused the private key of the digital signature to be affixed to the message or document. This proposition is relevant in respect of any form of electronic signature. Where a certification authority is involved within the framework of a public key infrastructure, all the certification authority can do is give evidence about how the certificate was formed, where the information was obtained, and if they verified the information, what methods were used to verify the information. Thus a certification authority can give evidence as to the formation of the certificate, but the certificate cannot be adduced as evidence of the truth of the facts stated within it.

### Assertions can differ

**16.13** Much will depend on whether the recipient is taking legal action against the certification authority, or the purported signer. This, in turn, depends on what statement the purported signing party makes about the signature. For instance, the statement might be, 'Yes, that was signed with my private key, but not by me or with my authority'. In which case, the certification authority is not involved, because there was nothing wrong with its certificate. However, it might be, 'That was signed with a key having nothing to do with me'. In this case, the claim is against the certification authority that certified the verification key. If the certification authority admits it signed the relevant certificate, then it is irrelevant if the recipient becomes a verifying party and takes action to undertake due diligence. The issue is whether it is liable for any errors. If the certification authority denies signing the certificate, then the issue may depend on which certification authority cross-signed the relevant certificate. It will be difficult for a certification authority to admit it is their certificate, but claim that it should not be trusted because the verifying party (if the recipient chooses to become a verifying party) followed the chain of certificates. It cannot be for a certification authority to determine whether a recipient should have trusted its signature or not.

## Assessment of evidence

### 'Non-repudiation'

**16.14** By way of an introduction, there is a term, 'non-repudiation', that has become part of the vocabulary of digital signatures. This is a dangerous expression, and one that lawyers should take particular care in understanding. It does not mean the system for non-repudiation is perfect, although some technical authors (and lawyers and academics[4]) continue to assert that digital

4 'Data encryption' (The Parliamentary Office of Science and Technology, no. 270, October 2006), incorrectly states on p. 2 that digital signatures '... can also be used for non-repudiation: if a party digitally signs an electronic document, they cannot later deny this'; R. Low and E. Foo, 'The susceptibility of digital signatures to fraud in the National Electronic Conveyancing System: an analysis', *Australian Property Law Journal*, 17 (2009), pp. 303–25 incorrectly comment, at p. 307, that 'When the recipient receives the coded summary and

signatures are better than they actually are. By way of example, Klaus Schmeh states that:

> The purpose of a digital signature is to ensure non-repudiation. This means that Alice cannot contest her completed signature in retrospect. When all is said and done, a digital signature is an excellent way of meeting this requirement.[5]

**16.15** Francisco Jordan-Fernádez and Jordi Buch i Tarrats observe that:

> The most important benefit electronic signatures brings to e-commerce and all electronic transactional systems is that they cannot be repudiated. This service provides evidentiary value that proves that the data has been created by a specific entity and has not been altered since the date of its creation, thereby guaranteeing its irrefutability.[6]

**16.16** Professor Sorge states:

> The private key, which is to be kept secret, is used by the signatory to sign messages; signatures can be verified with the corresponding public key. Successful verification of a digital signature guarantees integrity and authenticity of the corresponding message. Non-repudiation is also achieved, i.e. it can be proven that the message was signed by the signatory.[7]

---

the certificate, the recipient can use the CA's public key to verify the CA's signature on the certificate. If that is successful, the recipient can have confidence that the sender's public key is what it purports to be, that is, the sender's public key actually did come from the sender'; R. Wacks, *Privacy: A Very Short Introduction* (Oxford University Press, 2010) incorrectly states at pp. 25–6 that 'The advantage of a public key system is that if you are able to decrypt the message, you know that it could only have been created by the sender'; M. Bromby, 'Identification, trust and privacy: how biometrics can aid certification of digital signatures, *International Review of Law, Computers & Technology*, 24 (2010), pp. 133–41 incorrectly states 'Parties involved in such an electronic communication cannot deny their involvement subsequently' at p. 135; A. Tauber, P. Kustor and B. Karning, 'Cross-border certified electronic mailing: a European perspective', *Computer Law & Security Review*, 29 (2013), pp. 28–39, in which the authors fail to indicate the issues relating to 'non-repudiation'.

5 Schmeh, *Cryptography*, 16.1.1.

6 'Electronic signature today: a manufacturer's viewpoint', *Upgrade*, 5 (2004), pp. 23–7 at p. 24. See also an early paper by R. Clarke, 'Conventional public key infrastructure: an artefact ill-fitted to the needs of the information society', prepared for submission to the 'IS in the Information Society' track of the European Conference on Information Systems (ECIS 2001), Bled, Slovenia, 27–29 June 2001, available at http://www.rogerclarke.com/II/PKIMisFit.html.

7 C. Sorge, 'The legal classification of identity-based signatures', *Computer Law & Security Review*, 30 (2014), pp. 126–36, at p. 126.

**16.17** None of these statements are correct.

**16.18** When engineers use the term non-repudiation in an engineering sense, they mean that there is a degree of probability or certainty that the protocol can demonstrate that one item of software communicated with another item of software, or to put it another way, 'Nonrepudiation provides proof of the integrity and origin of data that can be verified by a third party'.[8] Many technicians assert that non-repudiation is a fact: that is, once the software proves that a message or document was sent and received, it follows that a human being caused the message to be sent. Such an assertion is not logical, and is misleading. This reasoning is often extended from the engineering domain into the legal domain, by asserting that if the system can demonstrate that one item of software communicated with another item of software, that is, that digital data comprising a message or document was sent or received, it is for the purported sender to demonstrate that they caused it to be sent. The purpose of the concept is to bind users to specific actions in such a way that if they deny taking the action, they either demonstrate an intention to deceive, or they have been negligent in failing to secure the use of their private key adequately. The use of the term is inherently misleading. The logic is as follows:

> It is proven that certain items of software communicated, each with the other. (A message was sent from Alice's computer to Bob's computer, and Alice's private key was affixed to the communication).
>
> It follows that the purported sender caused the software to communicate. (Ergo, Alice affixed the private key to the message).

**16.19** The purpose of the term non-repudiation is to provide for causation, which it cannot. It is possible that Alice's computer, from which the message was purported to have been sent, was located in San Antonio. At the material time, Alice might have been physically located in Irkutsh, and did not have access to the internet, ruling out that she could obtain access to her computer remotely to undertake the requisite action.

**16.20** It is generally assumed that non-repudiation has a legal effect: that is, a person cannot deny causing the software to send a message or document. However, a signature can be challenged for a number of reasons. The most pertinent is where the purported sender claims that they did not cause the electronic signature to be affixed to the message or document, as in the case of Dara O'Reilly, whose digital signature was used on two occasions in India in a

8 United States General Accounting Office, Report to the Chairman, Subcommittee on Government Efficiency, Financial Management and Intergovernmental Relations, Committee on Government Reform, House of Representatives, 'Information security: advances and remaining challenges to adoption of public key infrastructure technology', GAO-01-277 (2001), p. 18.

complex property transaction. He denied using the digital signature.[9] In effect, there is a claim that the signature is a forgery. In such circumstances, the fact that a message or document was sent might not be at issue. The dispute often turns on whether the sender caused the signature to be affixed to the message or document.[10] In such instances, it is for the party relying on the signature to prove the message or document was sent, and that the purported sender caused their electronic signature to be affixed.

**16.21** Other examples where the signature may be in dispute are where the sender accepts the message or document was sent with an electronic signature, but the signature was obtained as a result of unconscionable conduct by a party to a transaction, fraud instigated by a third party, or undue influence exerted by a third party, amongst other reasons recognised in law. It will be for the adjudicator to determine whether a particular argument is credible. That the sender caused the signature to be affixed to a message or document may not be in issue.

**16.22** It is important to ensure the technical meaning does not override the need to restrain the meaning within a legal context. Where engineers use the term, it should not be mistaken that they are using it in a legal context, despite a general misunderstanding in the view of some engineers that the term should have a legal meaning. Even where the evidence demonstrates that a message or document was sent or received with an electronic signature affixed, it does not follow that the message was sent by the person whose username or password (or both username and password) was used at the material time, nor signed by them. Carl Ellison of Intel Laboratories in his paper 'Improvements on conventional PKI wisdom' has dismissed these arguments by technicians about non-repudiation.[11] The comments in paragraph 3.4.3 entitled 'Not Achievable' demonstrate the vacuity of the link between evidence that software has communicated with software, and the assertion that such evidence is therefore proof that a particular person caused a machine to undertake a particular action:

> The main problem with the theory of non-repudiation is that it is not technically achievable. That is, the intention is to bind a human being to a digitally signed document. With a holographic signature

9 D. McDonald, 'Sean Quinn aide at centre of mystery over $90m asset', *Irish Independent*, 23 August 2012, available at http://www.independent.ie/business/irish/sean-quinn-aide-at-centre-of-mystery-over-90m-asset-26889961.html.

10 For the cases where private keys were used without the authority or authorization of the person to whom the private key was linked, see the banking cases from the Russian Federation: O.I. Kudryavtseva, 'Russia', in S. Mason (ed.), *International Electronic Evidence* (London: British Institute of International and Comparative Law, 2008); O.I. Kudryavtseva, 'The use of electronic digital signatures in banking relationships in the Russian Federation', *Digital Evidence and Electronic Signature Law Review*, 5 (2008), pp. 51–7; Resolution of the Federal Arbitration Court of Moscow Region of 5 November 2003 N КГ-А 40/8531-03-П, *Digital Evidence and Electronic Signature Law Review*, 5 (2008), pp. 149–51.

11 First Annual PKI Research Workshop – April 2002, available online at http://www.cs.dartmouth.edu/~pki02/.

on a paper document, the human's hand came in contact with the paper of the document. With a digital signature there is machinery between the human and the signed document: at least a keyboard, software (to display the document and to drive the signature process) and a key storage and use facility (e.g., a smart card).

No one has demonstrated, in the normal computer for home or office use, the prevention of introduction of hostile software. To the contrary, we have seen a steady increase in such incursions over the years.

There are secure facilities for key storage and use, but no mechanism that an average home or small business user would choose to buy has been proved secure.

Meanwhile, computers are not restricted to isolated rooms with card access entry, raised floors, guards outside the glass walls, etc., that they might have been in the 1970s when much of this thinking about public key cryptography had its nascence. Computers are not only everywhere; they are unprotected to a continually increasing degree. Therefore, even if the computer has no hostile software and its private key is kept in a truly secure facility, access to the keyboard of that computer is not limited to the person certified to be associated with that private key.

What might make this process of non-repudiation work would be hardware that would serve as a witness to a signature, providing tamper-proof evidence of the actions of a human being (e.g., through videotape), of what that human was reading and of the human's positive action to assent to the displayed document. Such a log of human behavior could then be presented in court to prove the claim of non-repudiation.

Of course, if such hardware were available, then we would not need digital signatures, much less the assumption of non-repudiation on digital signatures.

**16.23** This point is also considered in a slightly different way by Niels Ferguson, Bruce Schneier and Tadayoshi Kohno:[12]

> In theory, a PKI should provide you with nonrepudiation. Once Alice has signed a message with her key, she should not be able to later deny that she signed the message. A key server system can never provide this; the central server has access to the same key that Alice uses and can therefore forge an arbitrary message to make it look as if Alice sent it. In real life, nonrepudiation doesn't

12 N. Ferguson, B. Schneier and T. Kohno, *Cryptography Engineering: Design Principles and Practical Applications*, (Indianapolis, IN: Wiley, 2010), 19.9 bullet point 3.

> work because people cannot store their secret keys sufficiently well. If Alice wants to deny that she signed a message, she is simply going to claim that a virus infected her machine and stole her private key.

**16.24** In 2000, Carl Ellison and Bruce Schneier wrote on the same topic:[13]

> Alice's digital signature does not prove that Alice signed the message, only that her private key did. When writing about non-repudiation, cryptographic theorists often ignore a messy detail that lies between Alice and her key: her computer. If her computer were appropriately infected, the malicious code could use her key to sign documents without her knowledge or permission. Even if she needed to give explicit approval for each signature (for example, via a fingerprint scanner), the malicious code could wait until she approved a signature and sign its own message instead of hers. If the private key is not in tamper-resistant hardware, the malicious code can steal the key as soon as it's used.
>
> While it's legitimate to ignore such details in cryptographic research literature, it is just plain wrong to assume that real computer systems implement the theoretical ideal. Our computers may contain viruses. They may be accessible to passers-by who could plant malicious code or manually sign messages with our keys. Should we then need to deny some signature, we would have the burden of proving the negative — that we didn't make the signature in question against the presumption that we did.

**16.25** Where the party whose private key is used denies they caused the private key to be affixed to the data, it is for the party relying on the signature to prove the signing party caused the private key to sign the data. The burden of proof will depend on the pleadings and what presumptions, if any, apply.

**16.26** The term 'cryptographic non-repudiation' means being able to prove that where a digital signature verifies a public key, then the associated private key made that signature: it does not prove that the person whose private key is used caused the private key to make the signature.[14] However, non-repudiation is of no benefit without a secure time stamping service to demonstrate that a particular event occurred at a given time and date, or that a specific item of data existed before a specific date. This technical meaning of the term has begun to be used in a legal sense by vendors of the public key infrastructure, which in turn has tended to confuse legislators.[15]

13 C. Ellison and B. Schneier, 'Risks of PKI: e-commerce', *Communications of the ACM*, 43 (2000), p. 152.

14 Adams and Lloyd, *Understanding PKI Concepts*, pp. 32–3, 51–3.

15 B. Schneier, *Secrets & Lies: Digital Security in a Networked World* (Indianapolis, IN: Wiley,

## Rejecting electronic signatures

**16.27** A fundamental issue with respect to electronic signatures is the connection between the mental state of the person who may wish to be bound by the affixing of the electronic signature to a communication or document, and the act of affixing the electronic signature. The following issues are pertinent when establishing a nexus between the electronic communication and the electronic signature:

Whether the genuine user intended to be bound by the contents of the electronic document.

If another person used the private key (or form of electronic signature) without authorization, how they obtained access to the key.

Who should bear responsibility for the unauthorized use.

**16.28** The party challenging the admissibility of the electronic signature may be making either one or all of the following claims:

The security used by the sender was not sufficient to prevent a third party from gaining access to their computer or system and making improper use of their key or password.

The procedures and technical abilities (such as the means of producing, communicating or verifying the signature) of the trusted third party or card issuer were at fault.

Another organization in the chain that links the sending of the certificate and its receipt by the relying party, other than the trusted third party, was at fault.

**16.29** There is no doubt that the technology can, to a high degree of probability, prove that an electronic signature was affixed to a communication, but it cannot prove who made the signature. Given the state of the technology, it may be reasonable to infer that the holder named in the certificate (or the person whose name is typed at the bottom of an email) affixed the electronic signature to the communication. However, the inference is weaker where there is little or no security in place on the computer or system upon which the private key sits.[16]

## Reliability of certifying certificates

**16.30** Regardless of the technical meaning of the term 'non-repudiation', there are a number of problems that affect the reliability of systems that are used to affix digital signatures to an electronic communication:

---

2000), p. 235 and A. McCullagh and W. Caelli, 'Non-repudiation in the digital environment', http://firstmonday.org/htbin/cgiwrap/bin/ojs/index.php/fm/article/view/778/687.

16 M. Sneddon, *Legal liability and e-transactions* (Canberra: National Office for the Information Economy, 2000), paragraph 3.2 (b)(i), available online at http://unpan1.un.org/intradoc/groups/public/documents/apcity/unpan014676.pdf.

(i) The confusing design on the screen, which can lead a user to activate the signing function without knowing the significance others attach to the signature.

(ii) The software application may be set to send a receipt, but the recipient may not know the original sender sent the receipt. This also raises the question as to whether the receipt is authentic.

(iii) A design flaw in the public key infrastructure.

(iv) The open nature of the internet, which means hackers could insert malicious software into computers that can be designed to steal private keys or relay the keystrokes of the user, thereby obtaining the passwords used to obtain access to a private key.

**16.31** The general rule with respect to signed documents is this: a person is normally bound by their signature to a document, even if they fail to read and understand the content. Where a party relies on a signed document and wishes to enforce it against the signing party, the relying party must prove the signature is that of the signing party, or the signing party authorized the document. This is the case where the signing party claims they did not sign the document, or if they did sign the document, they signed the document under duress, or because of the fraud of a third party. It is not for the signing party to prove that they did not authorise the document or sign it.

**16.32** A person has a defence where they have been misled into signing a document that is essentially different to that which they intended to sign, a state of affairs that has usually, but not always, been induced by a fraud perpetrated upon the party signing the document.[17] However, this does not mean that a person should fail to exercise care when they affix their signature to a document in the absence of a fundamental mistake as to the content of the document. This occurred in *Saunders v. Anglia Building Society*,[18] where Mrs Gallie signed what she understood was a deed of gift of her house to her nephew, but it was, in fact, a deed of assignment to a third party. Mrs Gallie raised the defence that she thought the effect of the document was to give her house to her nephew, but in fact it assigned her rights to a fraudulent third party. The members of the House of Lords agreed that the identity of the person to whom the house was assigned did not make the deed totally different in character to the document Mrs Gallie intended to sign, and her defence failed. Lord Hodson offered the following observations 1019E respecting the use of a signature:

> Want of care on the part of the person who signs a document which he afterwards seeks to disown is relevant. The burden of proving non est factum is on the party disowning his signature;

17 In *United Dominions Trust Ltd v. Western* [1976] QB 513 a party signed a blank hire-purchase proposal form, and the dealer inserted incorrect figures before sending it to the finance company.

18 [1971] AC 1004; [1970] 3 WLR 1078; 114 SJ 885; [1970] 3 All ER 961.

> this includes proof that he or she took care. There is no burden on the opposite party to prove want of care. The word 'negligence' in this connection does not involve the proposition that want of care is irrelevant unless there can be found a specific duty to the opposite party to take care.

**16.33** In his judgment, Viscount Dilhorne agreed with the comments made by Lord Hodson, and commented, at 1023(E):

> In every case the person who signs the document must exercise reasonable care, and what amounts to reasonable care will depend on the circumstances of the case and the nature of the document which it is thought is being signed. It is reasonable to expect that more care should be exercised if the document is thought to be of an important character than if it is not.

## The burden of proof – UNCITRAL

**16.34** It has been suggested that the technical meaning of 'non-repudiation' has the effect of either shifting the onus of proof from the recipient of the alleged electronic signature, or denying the right of the user of the certifying certificate to repudiate the certificate.[19] Whilst it is clear that 'non-repudiation' has different meanings in the legal sense and the technical sense, there is a further difference between the two. That is, the technical meaning relates to events that have taken place after the signature has taken place, and has no relation to the actual mechanism of the affixing of the digital certificate.
**16.35** The development of the two sets of uniform rules prepared by UNCITRAL, the Model Law on Electronic Commerce and the Model Law on Electronic Signatures, have influenced the legislation relating to electronic signatures implemented by states.[20] In particular, both Model laws provide for the duties of the participants when using electronic signatures.

### Model Law on Electronic Commerce

**16.36** Of relevance are the provisions of article 13 to the Model Law. Note 83 to the Guide to Enactment indicates that article 13 originates in article 5 of the UNCITRAL Model Law on International Credit Transfers. This defines the

19 McCullagh and Caelli, 'Non-repudiation in the digital environment'.

20 The Model Law on Electronic Commerce was adopted by the Commission on 12 June 1996, following its 605th meeting, which in turn was adopted by the General Assembly in Resolution 51/162 at its 85th plenary meeting on 16 December 1996, and includes an additional article 5 *bis* as adopted by the Commission at its 31st meeting in June 1998. The Model Law on Electronic Signatures was adopted by the Commission at its 727th meeting on 5 July 2001.

obligations of the sender of a payment order. Bearing in mind such a transfer would normally be subject to a contractual agreement between the parties, setting out the technical procedures agreed between each party (and any other parties in the chain) for such a transfer, it seems improbable that such a provision should affect a public key infrastructure which uses the open network of the internet. However, the text of article 13 is of interest, because the Model Law on Electronic Signatures was developed on the premise that it could have been incorporated into an extended version of the Model Law on Electronic Commerce. Article 13 provides for a presumption that presumably must be rebuttable relating to the originator of a data message:[21]

> *Article 13. Attribution of data messages*
>
> (1) A data message is that of the originator if it was sent by the originator itself.
>
> (2) As between the originator and the addressee, a data message is deemed to be that of the originator if it was sent:
>
>> (a) by a person who had the authority to act on behalf of the originator in respect of that data message; or
>>
>> (b) by an information system programmed by, or on behalf of, the originator to operate automatically.
>
> (3) As between the originator and the addressee, an addressee is entitled to regard a data message as being that of the originator, and to act on that assumption, if:
>
>> (a) in order to ascertain whether the data message was that of the originator, the addressee properly applied a procedure previously agreed to by the originator for that purpose; or
>>
>> (b) the data message as received by the addressee resulted from the actions of a person whose relationship with the originator or with any agent of the originator enabled that person to gain access to a method used by the originator to identify data messages as its own.
>
> ...
>
> (5) Where a data message is that of the originator or is deemed to be that of the originator, or the addressee is entitled to act on that assumption, then, as between the originator and the addressee, the addressee is entitled to regard the data message as received as being what the originator intended to send, and to act on that assumption. The addressee is not so entitled when it knew or should have known, had it exercised reasonable care or used any agreed procedure, that the transmission resulted in any error in the data message as received.

21 Guide to Enactment paragraph 65.

**16.37** It is pertinent to observe the points made in the notes to Enactment in relation to the provisions of article 13. Guidance note 83 states that it is not the purpose of article 13 to assign responsibility between the parties, rather the purpose of the Article is to deal

> ... with attribution of data messages by establishing a presumption that under certain circumstances a data message would be considered as a message of the originator, and goes on to qualify that presumption in case the addressee knew or ought to have known that the data message was not that of the originator.

**16.38** Earlier drafts of article 13 included, according to Guidance note 92, an additional paragraph, '... expressing the principle that the attribution of authorship of a data message to the originator should not interfere with the legal consequences of that message, which should be determined by other applicable rules of national law'. Whilst the article does not expressly make this point, nevertheless it seems clear from the provisions of article 13(1) that the onus of proof appears to alter between the parties. The logic can be described as follows:

> If a user chooses to publish a verification key, it is assumed that when it is used, it will have been used by the user. It is presumed that the user, once they have a digital signature, will ensure that only they or a person authorized to use the signature will use it.
>
> Where a recipient wishes to rely upon the digital signature, provided they carry out adequate procedures to demonstrate the authenticity of the certifying certificate under article 13 (3)(b) and (5)[22] (i.e. undertake the verifying procedures set out for a digital signature), the recipient, thereupon becoming a verifying party, is permitted to assume the digital signature is that of the sender. In this instance, the recipient is under a duty to carry out such procedures. By undertaking such actions, the verifying party may be taken to have accepted there is a direct link between the certificate (if a digital signature is used) and the sender. It can be argued that the verifying party will be deemed to have satisfied themselves that they could rely on the relationship between the certificate and the affixing of the signature to the message, above and beyond the promise made by the certification authority, that can only promise that the message was signed using a certificate issued to the user.

**16.39** However, should the sender dispute they sent the message with the electronic signature attached, it must be, in the ordinary course of events, for the recipient to prove the sender sent the message.

22 The provisions of Article 13(3)(a) will not apply unless the originating party agreed with the receiving party in advance what, if any, procedure the recipient should undertake before relying on the signature.

## Model Law on Electronic Signatures

**16.40** Further guidance is also available from the Model Law on Electronic Signatures. The Model Law does not deal in detail about the issues of liability that may affect the participants of an electronic signature, but it does consider the relationship between signatory and the certification authority by outlining the expected conduct that each should undertake in their respective roles.[23] The provisions of article 8 refer to the conduct of the signatory, as follows:

> Conduct of the signatory
>
> 1. Where signature creation data can be used to create a signature that has legal effect, each signatory shall:
>
> (a) Exercise reasonable care to avoid unauthorized use of its signature creation data;
>
> (b) Without undue delay, utilize means made available by the certification service provider pursuant to article 9 of this Law, or otherwise use reasonable efforts, to notify any person that may reasonably be expected by the signatory to rely on or to provide services in support of the electronic signature if:
>
> (i) The signatory knows that the signature creation data have been compromised; or
>
> (ii) The circumstances known to the signatory give rise to a substantial risk that the signature creation data may have been compromised;
>
> (c) Where a certificate is used to support the electronic signature, exercise reasonable care to ensure the accuracy and completeness of all material representations made by the signatory that are relevant to the certificate throughout its life cycle or that are to be included in the certificate.
>
> 2. A signatory shall bear the legal consequences of its failure to satisfy the requirements of paragraph 1.

**16.41** There is a requirement that where a party decides to use an electronic signature, especially when in digital format using the public key infrastructure, they are expected to take reasonable care to protect the signature creation data and prevent unauthorized use of the signature creation data. The aim in drafting the provisions of articles 8, 9 and 11 is to provide a minimal 'code of conduct' for the parties involved with the use of an electronic signature.[24] Subparagraphs (a) and (c) apply to all forms of electronic signature, whilst subparagraph (c)

23 Guide to Enactment paragraph 77 also states that the issues relating to liability are left to applicable law.

24 Guide to Enactment paragraph 137.

only applies to digital certificates supported by a certificate. The use of the word 'reasonable' in this article illustrates the need for individual states to define what will be considered reasonable in the light of a dispute occurring. The provision of paragraph 2 leaves it to a national court to determine what, if any, legal consequences will follow where a signing party fails to take care under the provisions of paragraph 1(a) or fails to inform receiving parties where their signature creation device has been used without authority or compromised.

**16.42** A similar duty is held to be necessary for the relying party (a person only becomes a relying party if they decide to verify the signature and certificate) as set out in article 11:

> Conduct of the relying party
>
> A relying party shall bear the legal consequences of its failure:
>
> > (a) To take reasonable steps to verify the reliability of an electronic signature; or
> >
> > (b) Where an electronic signature is supported by a certificate, to take reasonable steps:
> >
> > (i) To verify the validity, suspension or revocation of the certificate; and
> >
> > (ii) To observe any limitation with respect to the certificate.

**16.43** Interestingly, article 2(f) of the Model Law does not distinguish between a recipient that relies on an electronic signature and a recipient that undertakes to verify the authenticity of an electronic signature. The meaning of a relying party is 'a person that may act on the basis of a certificate or an electronic signature'. Thus a relying party may decide to act on the basis of an electronic signature, but is not required to undertake any verification procedures. Note 148 in the Guide to Enactment identifies and separates two issues: whether the electronic signature is valid, and whether it is reasonable for a recipient to rely on an electronic signature that does not reach the standard set out in article 6. The note indicates that the intention is for the recipient to bear in mind whether and to what extent they should rely on the signature. The validity of the signature should not depend on the conduct of the recipient, although it is debatable whether certification authorities, in drafting their terms of trade and certification practice statements, have fully grasped this point (or if they have, they ignore it). A close look at the provisions of article 6 will help to illuminate the underlying foundations relating to the validity of an electronic signature:

> Compliance with a requirement for a signature
>
> 1. Where the law requires a signature of a person, that requirement is met in relation to a data message if an electronic signature is used that is as reliable as was appropriate for the purpose for which the data message was generated or communicated, in the light of all the circumstances, including any relevant agreement.

2. Paragraph 1 applies whether the requirement referred to therein is in the form of an obligation or whether the law simply provides consequences for the absence of a signature.

3. An electronic signature is considered to be reliable for the purpose of satisfying the requirement referred to in paragraph 1 if:

(a) The signature creation data are, within the context in which they are used, linked to the signatory and to no other person;

(b) The signature creation data were, at the time of signing, under the control of the signatory and of no other person;

(c) Any alteration to the electronic signature, made after the time of signing, is detectable; and

(d) Where a purpose of the legal requirement for a signature is to provide assurance as to the integrity of the information to which it relates, any alteration made to that information after the time of signing is detectable.

4. Paragraph 3 does not limit the ability of any person:

(a) To establish in any other way, for the purpose of satisfying the requirement referred to in paragraph 1, the reliability of an electronic signature; or

(b) To adduce evidence of the non-reliability of an electronic signature.

**16.44** The provisions of this article are considered central to the Model Law, and add to article 7 of the Model Law on Electronic Commerce. The intention is to offer guidance as to how the test of reliability in paragraph 1(b) of article 7 can be satisfied.[25] Article 7 of the Model Law on Electronic Commerce reads as follows:

*Article 7. Signature*

(1) Where the law requires a signature of a person, that requirement is met in relation to a data message if:

(a) a method is used to identify that person and to indicate that person's approval of the information contained in the data message; and

(b) that method is as reliable as was appropriate for the purpose for which the data message was generated or communicated, in the light of all the circumstances, including any relevant agreement.

(2) Paragraph (1) applies whether the requirement therein is in the form of an obligation or whether the law simply provides consequences for the absence of a signature.

25 Guide to Enactment paragraph 115.

**16.45** The intention behind the drafting of article 6 is to establish criteria that would apply to the technical form of an electronic signature that establishes certain legal effects. Legal effects would follow from electronic signature techniques that were recognized as reliable, and there would be no legal effect where an electronic signature technique was of lesser reliability than a reliable technique.[26] The provision of article 7 paragraph 1(a) of the Model Law on Electronic Commerce will produce a legal effect, no matter what form the electronic signature takes. However, it follows that what will constitute a reliable method of signature in the light of the circumstances will depend on what the trier of a fact will determine after the signature was used – perhaps months, if not years after its use. As a result, the intention behind the drafting article 6(3) in the Model Law on Electronic Signatures is to create a benefit in favour of particular types of techniques for affixing electronic signatures to a document or message. Thus the intention is to provide for the legal effect of, primarily, a digital signature, although it is left to the individual state to establish the legal effects and whether a presumption should apply.[27] The aim of article 6 is to provide for a presumption that the signatory, when they affix their electronic signature to a document or message, is presumed to have approved the linking of their identity with the data contained in the document or message.[28] It is not a presumption that the person who has signed the data is in fact the signatory.[29] Legal effects will only flow from the affixing of the signature if the nature of the document or message and surrounding circumstances indicate such an inference should be so drawn.[30]

**16.46** The third party to a digital signature is the certification authority. The Model Law, in article 9, sets out the type of conduct expected of a certification authority.

> Conduct of the certification service provider
>
> 1. Where a certification service provider provides services to support an electronic signature that may be used for legal effect as a signature, that certification service provider shall:
>
> > (a) Act in accordance with representations made by it with respect to its policies and practices;
> >
> > (b) Exercise reasonable care to ensure the accuracy and

26 Guide to Enactment paragraph 118.

27 Guide to Enactment paragraph 119.

28 This encompasses the use of corporate signature creation data, where several employees share the same method of creating a corporate signature. As a signature is created, so the data must be capable of identifying the particular individual that created the signature data (Guide to Enactment paragraph 121).

29 This point is made in paragraph 78 to the Guide to Enactment, although the observation is made that 'At best, the digital signature provides assurance that it is attributable to the signatory'.

30 Guide to Enactment paragraph, 120.

completeness of all material representations made by it that are relevant to the certificate throughout its life cycle or that are included in the certificate;

(c) Provide reasonably accessible means that enable a relying party to ascertain from the certificate:

(i) The identity of the certification service provider;

(ii) That the signatory that is identified in the certificate had control of the signature creation data at the time when the certificate was issued;

(iii) That signature creation data were valid at or before the time when the certificate was issued;

(d) Provide reasonably accessible means that enable a relying party to ascertain, where relevant, from the certificate or otherwise:

(i) The method used to identify the signatory;

(ii) Any limitation on the purpose or value for which the signature creation data or the certificate may be used;

(iii) That the signature creation data are valid and have not been compromised;

(iv) Any limitation on the scope or extent of liability stipulated by the certification service provider;

(v) Whether means exist for the signatory to give notice pursuant to article 8, paragraph 1 (b), of this Law;

(vi) Whether a timely revocation service is offered;

(e) Where services under subparagraph (d) (v) are offered, provide a means for a signatory to give notice pursuant to article 8, paragraph 1 (b), of this Law and, where services under subparagraph (d) (vi) are offered, ensure the availability of a timely revocation service;

(f) Utilize trustworthy systems, procedures and human resources in performing its services.

2. A certification service provider shall bear the legal consequences of its failure to satisfy the requirements of paragraph 1.

**16.47** A certification authority is expected to undertake its obligations as described in its own terms and policies. Paragraph 1(c) sets out what is considered to be one of the essential contents of the Model Law, and in relation to digital signatures, it is necessary to be able to associate the signatory with the public key as well as with the private key.[31] Note 146 of the Guide to Enactment indicates that it was originally considered necessary to address the issues of liability, but it has now been left to individual states to determine.

## The burden of proof

**16.48** In the light of the guidance provided by the UNCITRAL Model Laws, it seems self-evident that there is a need to consider how to allocate liability for an electronic signature between the participating parties. A person has total control over the use of their manuscript signature, and the legal rules that apply to manuscript signatures reflect this physical reality. However, once the accepted format of the signature changes, so it may be considered appropriate, depending on the nature of the transaction, for the legal rules that apply to the new format of signature to reflect the different range of risks associated with the new manifestation of signature. Consider the example of Charles Goodman, the solicitor who used a rubber stamp to sign a letter that accompanied his bill of costs.[32] Although the control of the rubber stamp was not the subject of judicial comment, Evershed MR noted at 554, that Mr Goodman '... kept the stamp locked up in his own room so as to be available only for his own use'. Although neither Mr Goodman's actions nor the comment by Evershed MR make an explicit point about taking reasonable care of the rubber stamp, nevertheless the implication that the rubber stamp should be kept safe is obvious. It is clear that Mr Goodman took reasonable care to ensure only he had access to the rubber stamp, and the observation by Evershed MR implied that this made the use of the rubber stamp acceptable as a method of authenticating documents. If Evershed MR had considered the matter further, he might have reached the conclusion that there is a reasonable expectation in circumstances where a person decides to use a rubber stamp as a form of signature, that they can be expected, as a rule of law, to provide for the security of the use of the signature, and to take appropriate steps to guard against its use by unauthorized persons.

**16.49** Williams J discussed this point in the case of *Robb v. The Pennsylvania Co. for Insurance on Lives and Granting Annuities*,[33] discussed below. The matter of the security of a rubber stamp was also mentioned briefly in *British Estate Investment Society Ltd v. Jackson (H M Inspector of Taxes)*[34] where an Additional Commissioner regularly used a rubber stamp to sign significant volumes of documents. In his judgment, Danckwerts J mentioned the measures taken in the office to provide for the safety and unauthorized use of the rubber stamp.[35]

31 Guide to Enactment, paragraph 143.

32 *Goodman v. J Eban Limited* [1954] 1 QB 550; [1954] 1 All ER 763; [1954] 2 WLR 581, CA.

33 40 W.N.C. 129, 3 Pa.Super. 254, 1897 WL 3989 (Pa.Super. 1897) affirmed by186 Pa. 456, 40 A. 969, for dissenting opinion, see 186 Pa. 456, 41 A. 49.

34 (1954 – 1958) 37 Tax Cas 79; [1956] TR 397; 35 ATC 413; 50 R & IT 33.

35 (1954 – 1958) 37 Tax Cas 79 at 87.

Once again, there is no explicit mention of the need for a signing party to provide for the security of the rubber stamp and to protect it against misuse. However, the action of the signing party in providing for the security of the rubber stamp suggests that, even without a rule of law requiring them to take steps to secure the rubber stamp, they took such precautions because the nature of the instrument thus created permits others to use a recognized means of identifying and authenticating a document. If this train of thought is accepted, a number of points can be made in support of the requirements required by the UNCITRAL Model Laws and the contractual obligations that certification authorities seek to impose on subscribing parties and receiving parties, as follows:

> (i) The evidence from Charles Goodman in *Goodman v. J Eban Limited* and of the Additional Commissioner in *British Estate Investment Society Ltd v. Jackson (H M Inspector of Taxes)* demonstrates that when the signing party acquired a rubber stamp as a means of affixing their signature to a document, they took appropriate precautions to safeguard it from misuse and theft.
>
> (ii) The comments by Evershed MR[36] and Danckwerts J[37] imply that the authorized use of the rubber stamp rested on the care with which the signing party took of the item, and because the security of the rubber stamp was assured, the signature affixed to the document by the rubber stamp was authentic and therefore valid.
>
> (iii) In the event the recipient doubted the authenticity of the signature, they can undertake their own form of due diligence to verify the authenticity and validity of the signature. This point was made by Romer LJ at 564 in *Goodman v. J Eban Limited* where he pointed out that 'If in fact his clients entertained any doubt as to the authenticity of the letter, nothing could be easier than to ask him, by telephone or letter, to confirm it.' Whilst the point made by Romer LJ is an explicit instruction as to what action the recipient could take, the comment was not necessarily meant to form a legal rule.

**16.50** Although none of the comments made by the judges in these two cases are sufficient to form a rule of law in relation to such matters, nevertheless they recognized that where technology is used to provide a substitute for so physical an act as the affixing of a manuscript signature to a document, new considerations relating to the presumptions that should apply to alternative methods of applying a signature must be considered.

**16.51** In light of the decision of Waller J in *Standard Bank London Limited v. Bank of Tokyo Limited*,[38] it appears that this train of thought may have already been

36 *Goodman v. J Eban Limited* [1954] 1 QB 550 at 554.

37 *British Estate Investment Society Ltd v. Jackson (H M Inspector of Taxes)* (1954 – 1958) 37 Tax Cas 79 at 87.

38 [1995] CLC 496; [1996] 1 CTLR T-17.

adopted in England and Wales. In this case, the Bank of Tokyo in Kuala Lumpur arranged for three tested telexes to be sent to Standard, containing a secret code confirming and authenticating the authorized signatory of three letters of credit with a total face value of US$19.8m, and confirming that the Bank of Tokyo accepted all responsibilities and liabilities under those letters of credit. Evidence was adduced to indicate that banks not only used this system with confidence, but also used it to avoid arguments about authority. In this instance, the tested telexes were sent fraudulently.

**16.52** The main thrust of the Bank of Tokyo's case was this: because they could establish that a thief must have been working in their tested telex department, Standard could only rely upon the apparent authority of the tested telexes. As a result, it argued that there was a lower test to establish the lack of apparent authority. Waller J disagreed with this argument at 502C, because the issue was not reliance on apparent authority:

> Standard rely first on a general representation by BOT that if a telex comes by tested telex that telex will be duly authorised by BOT (that representation on any view is authorised);
>
> second they rely on the use of the tested telex mechanism itself as representing that the telex is authorised as the previous representation stated that it would be; and
>
> thirdly they rely on the statement in the telex as being the authorised statement of BOT.

**16.53** The Bank of Tokyo was found liable for negligent misrepresentation because the tested telexes could not have been sent without negligence on the bank's part. Whether Standard had a duty to inquire into the authenticity of the tested telexes depended on the circumstances of each case.[39] Tested telexes contain codes or tests, which are secret between the sender and the recipient. This allows the recipient to accept without question that the telex was sent by and with the authority of the sender. The tested telexes in this instance were sent through other banks, because the Bank of Tokyo in Kuala Lumpur did not have a means of directly authenticating telexes between itself and Standard. By sending tested telexes, banks intend the receiving bank to act on the content without further instructions. This means the receiving bank requires the sending bank to confirm the person signing the document is an authorized signatory, verify the signatory is authorized to sign the particular document, and provide sufficient evidence to satisfy the recipient that the sending bank authorized the sending of the telex.

**16.54** Superficially, there is a similarity between the circumstances of this case and the public key infrastructure, where the authentication process has to go through so many channels. However, there is a distinction between a tested telex produced in a bank and the public key infrastructure. The authority of a telex

39 [1995] CLC 496 at 501H.

is reliant upon internal systems within the bank.[40] No third party is involved in identifying the sender of the telex or authenticating the codes or text sent. In addition, the tested telex is sent through other banks over apparently secure lines of communication. Conversely, the public key infrastructure operates over the internet, which was designed to be open and is, therefore, insecure. The link between the identity and authentication of a user of an electronic signature is not as cohesive as between such trusted parties as banks. There are significantly more links, which neither party has control over, in the chain between the sending party and receiving party of an electronic signature. As a result, it can be argued that there is a distinction between what can be termed a 'secure or closed communication system' and an 'open communications system'. Clearly the burden of proving that an electronic signature was used without authority must be borne by either the user or the relying party. In this instance, Waller J took the view that the sender was in full control of the environment in which the tested telex was sent, and decided that the burden should fall on the sender.

**16.55** In the context of an open insecure network, however, different criteria might, based upon the protection of the consumer, be applied by the courts. Private individuals are encouraged to use inherently insecure personal computers for digital signatures at the request of parties that intend to rely on such signatures, such as governments and commercial entities. It will be interesting to know if the government carries out the duties of a verifying party each time a subject communicates with a department electronically.

## The recipient's procedural and due diligence burden

**16.56** Whether it is for the user, when using an electronic signature, to bear such a burden, is debatable. If it is accepted that the recipient is required to establish whether they could rely on the certificate in all the circumstances, they may be required to provide any or all of the evidence discussed above in relation to verifying the integrity of a certificate, depending on the nature of the challenge. Providing the recipient has carried out all the relevant checks required, it is possible to argue that it has discharged what can be described as a procedural and due diligence burden and has become a verifying party.

## The sending party: the burden of proof of security and integrity

**16.57** Once the recipient, if required so to do, has satisfied a judge that it has discharged the procedural and due diligence burden, the user will need to address the issue of the security and integrity of their computer or system, amongst other topics of relevance in the circumstances. This can be described as the burden

40 A message using an authentication code sent through the SWIFT (Society for Worldwide Interbank Financial Telecommunication) system has the legal effect of binding the sender bank according to its contents: *Industrial & Commercial Bank Ltd v. Banco Ambrosiano Veneto SpA* [2003] 1 SLR 221.

of proof of security and integrity, which comprises both a persuasive burden (or burden of proof on the pleadings) and the evidential burden of adducing evidence. In discussing this aspect, it is useful to compare identical problems that have exercised the minds of people in the past, and what mechanisms were put in place to provide for the integrity of the method of proving intent.

**16.58** In the case of the impression of a seal, the use of a seal became so common by the 14th century that consideration had to be given to provide for additional evidence, other than the impression of a seal affixed to the document, that the seal impression was not a forgery or added without authority. The sovereign might have a number of seals for different purposes: a signet for the secretary; a privy seal, which was in between the secretary and the Chancellor; the great seal, controlled by the Chancellor to authenticate the most formal of acts, and a finger ring, later called a privy signet, for the personal affairs of the monarch.[41] Care was taken to destroy seal matrices in a public ceremony, as occurred when Edward III ascended the throne and had the great seal used by his father and grandfather broken into tiny pieces in his presence.[42] However, the physical object of the impression of a seal can be undermined, just as any other form of authentication. For instance, the seal itself might be forged, or the seal of a dead person used, as in the case of Hannibal when he forged letters in the name of the dead Roman consul Marcellus after removing the signet ring from his body.[43] For instance, it was an offence to forge the royal seal. By the Statute of Edward III, counterfeiting the great and privy seals were treasonable offences, and one man who forged the seal of Henry II was only saved from being hanged by the king's mercy.[44] At common law it was a felony and regarded as a capital offence, and there are three medieval cases of this nature.

**16.59** A person could challenge a document where the seal was not right, or the right seal was attached to the wrong document. As seals became more common, the other issue was the degree of forgery for ordinary seals. There is evidence that illustrates people took their seal very seriously. In 1190, for instance, Adam, son of Peter de Birkin broke his seal and replaced it. He went to the length of repeating a grant he had previously made to the abbey of Rievaulx.[45] There then developed a means of countersigning the main seal with the use of a secret seal as a counter-seal to one of the great seals. The great seal would be in the possession and under the control of the officer of state, and the secret seal in the possession of the owner, thus providing a double check to the authenticity of the document, because the second seal may be imprinted on to the great seal, providing two

41 P.M. Barnes and L.C. Hector, *A Guide to Seals in the Public Record Office* (2nd edn., London: HMSO, 1968), p. 8; P. Chaplais, *English Diplomatic Practice in the Middle Ages* (London: Hambledon and London, 2003), pp. 97–8.

42 P.D.A. Harvey and A. McGuinness, *A guide to British medieval seals* (University of Toronto Press, 1996), p. 34.

43 Chaplais, *English Diplomatic Practice*, p. 6.

44 Harvey and McGuinness, *A guide to British medieval seals*, pp. 33, 98–9.

45 Barnes and Hector, *A Guide to Seals in the Public Record Office*, pp. 29–30.

seal impressions on the same seal. The concerns for the security of the seal were sometimes carried to what seems like extraordinary lengths, but were probably routine. In 1214 the chapter seal of Salisbury cathedral was in the care of two cannons, but by 1353 it was kept in a chest with three locks, and was only used in the presence of all three cannons, each of whom held a key. By the Statute of Acton Burnell in 1283, debts could be registered before the mayor, who issued a recognisance with a special seal supplied by the crown. However, in 1285, the Statute of Merchants amended the previous statute, and ordered that the seal must be contained in two parts, the larger to be retained by the mayor, and the smaller to be retained by the clerk – indicating, in the opinion of one scholar, that there had probably been a scandal.[46] In the late 13th century, the seal of the corporation of Winchester was placed in a box with three locks, and the keys retained by two counsellors and one ordinary person, and this box in turn was itself kept in a chest with two keys, held by one counsellor and one other.[47]

**16.60** Conceptually, there is little difference between the seal matrix and a rubber stamp, and the nature of the security in place to prevent unauthorized use is identical. In this respect, the 1897 Pennsylvania case of *Robb v. The Pennsylvania Co. for Insurance on Lives and Granting Annuities*[48] is highly instructive. This case pre-dates the use of electronic signatures in any form by one hundred years, yet the difference in time does not diminish the issues, even if they were articulated with different concepts and language by the judges at the time. In this case, money had been paid out on two cheques signed with the facsimile signature of the bank depositor by means of a rubber stamp. Mr Robb did not authorize either cheque. In 1893, Mr Robb, as the president of a commercial corporation, had occasion to send out a large number of invitations to a banquet. To save himself the trouble of signing each invitation, he had a rubber stamp made with a facsimile of his signature. After retiring, he rented a private office, and with the rent came the services of an office boy. He employed the boy on various errands, including sending him to the bank to draw money on cheques. It can be inferred from the report that he used the rubber stamp to sign cheques. He kept the rubber stamp in a compartment inside a fireproof safe. He locked the compartment and put the key to the compartment in a drawer in the safe, behind some papers, and covered it up. He then locked the drawer, and placed the key into an unlocked drawer in the safe. He then locked the safe, and put the key in a little box, which he put in a wooden drawer or box, and this was kept on top of another safe. The plaintiff surmised that the office boy had watched his moves at some time in the past. The majority of the judges found that Mr Robb was not negligent in the use of the rubber stamp. The basis of their decision centred on whether he was negligent in failing to exercise care in preventing the rubber stamp from

46 T.F.T. Plucknett, *Legislation of Edward I* (Oxford: Clarendon, 1949), p. 140, quoted in Harvey and McGuinness, *A guide to British medieval seals*, p. 111.

47 Harvey and McGuinness, *A guide to British medieval seals*, pp. 58–62, 98–9.

48 40 W.N.C. 129, 3 Pa.Super. 254, 1897 WL 3989 (Pa.Super. 1897) affirmed by 186 Pa. 456, 40 A. 969, for dissenting opinion, see 186 Pa. 456, 41 A. 49.

falling into the wrong hands. Rice PJ rejected the proposition that Mr Robb was bound to keep the stamp in a place that prevented any person from obtaining it without authority. However, no attempt was made by the majority judges to explain how the bank was in a position to challenge the signature, given that the signature was identical each time the rubber stamp was used, with the exception that the impression will vary in quality depending on the amount of ink used and the pressure applied to the stamp as the signature is affixed to the cheque. The majority held that the bank was liable for the cheques. Williams J wrote a dissenting judgment that raises the modern issues, using different language, but germane nevertheless. His entire opinion is printed in the law report on page 49. The major part of his opinion, with which Sterrett CJ concurred, raises important issues that are relevant to digital signatures in particular:

> It is conceded that Mr Robb caused the stamp to be made with which this check was executed. He says he only intended to use it for a particular purpose, but it is perfectly apparent that he intended his signature produced by this stamp should be recognized as his by his friends and acquaintances who should receive it, as it certainly would be. The signatures made by it as they are presented to us in the paper books, when placed by the side of admittedly genuine signatures, are indistinguishable from them. Now, this stamp belonged to him, was made under his direction, and for his use. It was intended for the rapid production of his signature. It was in his possession. He was bound to take care of it as safely as of his own signature made by himself with his own hand. He was bound to do this at his peril. There is no question of reasonable or sufficient care in this case. As with the signed check, so with this stamp signature. When he put it in his safe, and left the key where it was possible for any one to get it, and so gain admission to the safe, he exposed himself to the loss that might follow, and that loss is his. He seeks in this action to put his own proper loss upon the bank that paid the checks, by alleging that the checks were forged. But they were not forged. The signature was his. He prepared it. All that can be said is that he did not affix it to the checks. But he had prepared it so that any one could affix it to a check or any other paper, and when so affixed it was absolutely impossible to tell that it had not been done by him. There would be some justification for his claim upon the bank if he had advised the banker that he had prepared such a signature that might by a possibility be clandestinely gotten from his possession, and given him an impression made by it, and pointed out, if he could have done so, how it might be distinguished from his signature as made by a pen; but he did nothing of the kind. If the bank is not protected by his signature made by means of his own private stamp, if it is bound at its peril to know and discriminate between his signature made

> with his pen and that made with his private stamp, then he has, by the use of the stamp, very greatly increased the responsibility and peril of the bank without so much as giving it notice or affording the slightest intimation of the necessity for additional vigilance in scrutinizing checks purporting to bear his signature. Upon every rule of commercial law, and upon every consideration of equity and good conscience, the judgment entered in the court below in this case should be reversed, and judgment should be entered here in favour of the defendant.

**16.61** It was for the bank, relying on the signature, to prove it was genuine. The image of the signature was genuine, but Mr Robb had neither applied it, nor authorized the signature to be applied to the cheque. In this respect, it was a forgery, and in the words of Wills J in *The Staple of England v. The Governor and Company of the Bank of England*:[49]

> A forgery can give no title, and those that rely upon it must be able to shew some extraneous ground – such as that of estoppel – why they should be entitled to act upon it.

**16.62** In *The Staple of England*, the bank were held liable for failing to make proper enquiries as to title where the company gave the safe keeping of the Company seal to their clerk (a solicitor), and the clerk, without authority, affixed the seal to a power of attorney that enabled him to sell funds of the Company for his own benefit. The seal and the rubber stamp have the same problem: the need to prevent unauthorized use. Although the use of rubber stamps was not new at the time of this case, nevertheless Mr Robb failed to notify the bank that he was using a mechanical reproduction of his manuscript signature. Arguably, if the bank had been made aware of this practice, as suggested by Williams J, it might have refused to honour such cheques, or if it accepted them, the bank might have taken additional care to ensure with each cheque that he had affixed the signature with the intention of signing it.

**16.63** There is a difference of degree between securing a physical object such as a rubber stamp and a digital signature, but in the event of a dispute, it follows that it is the holder of the certificate and private key who is in the best position to prove either that the security in place was adequate, such that the certificate and private key could not be used improperly. The user will possibly be in physical control of the following (this list is not exhaustive):

> The hardware and the software of the computer or system upon which the private key sits.
>
> The security in place in relation to the computer or system, the use of the system by employees and the control of any tokens used to store the private key.

49 (1888) 21 QBD 160 at 166.

> The ability of the user to revoke their private key promptly after finding out that their system or private key was compromised.

**16.64** If the user wishes to argue their security was so poor that an unauthorized third party could have gained access to the system to send an electronic communication with an electronic signature attached without authority, the user will undoubtedly be admitting breach of contract with the vendor from whom they obtained the certifying certificate. They are also probably admitting they were negligent. This is the central conundrum any user of a digital signature faces. The flexible nature of the need to implement suitable precautions relating to securing a seal was recognized by Wills J, and in a prescient comment, he indicated in *The Staple of England* at 168, that:

> The precautions which appear to be natural in one century may appear pedantic and unnecessary in another ... there can be no inflexible and unvarying rule of law as to that which is essentially a mixed question of fact and law...

## The persuasive and evidential burden of demonstrating weaknesses in the infrastructure

**16.65** Once a communication leaves the user's computer or system, they relinquish control of the document or message. If the user can demonstrate the effectiveness of the security and integrity of their computer or system, the next link is the network over which the communication passes and the public key infrastructure that supports such items as digital signatures, although these considerations also apply to ATMs and online banking systems, for instance. Evidence might be required from a number of organizations in the chain (discussed in more detail below), including the registration authority and the effectiveness of the registration procedure, the methods of management the certification authority uses to control its infrastructure, and the effectiveness or otherwise of any third party supplier whose product or service is included in the chain.

**16.66** If the recipient can demonstrate the due diligence they carried out was reasonable in the circumstances, and the user can demonstrate, to the required standard, the security and integrity of their computer or system, the question then becomes: which party to the proceedings has the persuasive and evidential burden of demonstrating any weaknesses in the infrastructure. The burden of proof will inevitably be on the party that asserts the problem lies with third parties in the chain. It seems that all the recipient needs to do is to demonstrate procedural and due diligence. Thereafter, it is for the sender to either demonstrate lack of security, or that the fault occurred as the result of failure by third parties in the chain, unlike the burden in proving a manuscript signature.

## Burden of proof – the Jitsuin

**16.67** Since the eighth century, a similar system of authentication to that of the electronic signature has existed in the physical world, by which a signing party deposits an imprint of their mark with a trusted third party, and relying parties can rest assured that when the mark is used, they can rely on the authentication of the person by the mark. This is the Jitsuin (original seal) of Japan. Other seals include the Ginko-In (bank seal) for banking purposes, and Mitome-In (approval seal) for use in everyday circumstances, such as signing for a delivery of post. The seal is called an insho, and the word 'inkan' describes the impression of the seal. The purpose of a name seal is to confirm a person's intention to enter a transaction and to act as a form of identification. The use of Mitome-In in Japan is so much part of everyday life that foreigners, although they are permitted in some situations to use a manuscript signature instead of a name seal, are advised to obtain such a seal if they are going to remain in the country for any length of time.[50]

**16.68** Jitsuin are used instead of manuscript signatures to execute important documents. For instance, the Jitsuin Seal Registration Certificate is required as an attachment to the document of application for the transfer of registration in the real property registry at the Legal Affairs Bureau. The importance attached to the Jitsuin Seal Registration Certificate under Japanese Law is such that the transfer of the registration is essential for the perfection of the transfer of title of a real property. The Jitsuin is endowed with a legal presumption that is founded partly on the common understanding that a name seal either cannot be forged, or is difficult to forge, and partly on a very long history of use.

### *Registering a Jitsuin*

**16.69** Jitsuin are required to conform to specific criteria:

> (i) The name on the seal must conform to the registered name; the seal must have a border surrounding the name (and the border must not be missing or chipped); machine-made, mass-produced seals are not acceptable; the seal must be made of a material that cannot be altered easily, and the diameter must be greater than 8mm square but smaller than 25mm square.
>
> (ii) Only the owner of a seal or a representative can apply to register a Jitsuin, and the applicant has to be over the age of 15 years.
>
> (iii) A Jitsuin must be registered at the offices of the local government, whether village, town or city.

**16.70** Upon applying for a registered seal (Jitsuin) and Seal Registration Certificate (inkan toroku shomeisho) some local offices will send the applicant a letter of

50 For a further explanation, see G.P. McAlinn (ed.), *Japanese Business Law* (Leiden: Wolters Kluwer, 2007), pp. 202–4.

verification for the purpose of identification. Alternatively, the usual range of documents will be required to be produced when the applicant attends the office. The registration takes place when the applicant attends the office with their seal, during which their identity is checked. Where a representative registers the seal, they will be required to provide a Letter of Attorney or a Letter of Advice Giving Right of Representation, which must be signed and sealed by the owner of the seal. After registering the seal, the applicant is given a Seal Registration Card (inkan torokusho, a plastic card) rather than a Seal Registration Certificate.

## *The Seal Registration Certificate*

**16.71** The Seal Registration Certificate includes the following information: an impression of the registered seal; the name of the seal holder; the date of birth of the seal holder; the gender of the seal holder; the address of the seal holder. The registration of the Jitsuin is tied to a particular geographical locality, so if the seal holder moves to another part of Japan or leaves Japan for good, the seal registration becomes null and void, and a new registration process must be undertaken at the new location. Where a Jitsuin is lost, the process is to attend the office that issued the Seal Registration Certificate and initiate the procedure to delete the registration. There is no procedure to notify relying parties that the Jitsuin has been stolen or lost.

## *The legal presumption of the Seal Registration Certificate*

**16.72** A Seal Registration Certificate proves the seal holder has adopted the impression of the seal that is recorded in the Certificate. The Civil Procedure Law provides for a legal presumption relating to the authenticity of a private document, as follows: 'A private document shall be presumed to be authentically executed if it bears the signature or seal of the principal or his representative'.[51] It appears that this presumption is rebuttable. This discussion is restricted to private documents, and does not include government documents.[52] For this presumption to operate, the party bearing the burden of proof is required to prove that the registered owner of the seal intended to affix an impression of their seal on the document. This intention may itself be presumed if the relying party proves that the seal impressed on the document and the impression of the adopted seal held by the owner is the same. However, the relying party must also prove that the signing party has in fact adopted the seal. This fact is proved by using the Seal Registration Certificate, because the Seal Registration Certificate bears the adopted seal and the name of the signing party, thus it is easy for the relying party to prove that the signing party adopted the seal.[53] Once it is

51 Civil Procedure Law (Law No 109 of 1998) Article 228(4).

52 Civil Procedure Law (Law No 109 of 1998) Article 228 and 228(2) and (3).

53 This chain of presumption is reinforced by the provisions of Civil Procedure Law (Law No 109 of 1998) Article 229, which states: 'The authenticity of execution of documents may also be proved by a comparison of specimen of handwriting or seal impression'.

established that the signing party intended to affix an impression of their seal by operation of this presumption, the presumption under the Civil Procedure Law takes effect, and the document in question is presumed to be authentically executed.

**16.73** This explanation demonstrates there are two levels of presumption, a process known as the 'Two Phase Presumption'. It involves the following steps.

> If the impression of the seal and the adopted seal held by the signing party are the same, then it is presumed that:
>
>> The signing party intended to affix the seal impression, which in turn creates the presumption that:
>>
>>> The document bearing the seal impression was authentically executed.

**16.74** It is to be noted that there is no statutory requirement of due diligence in order to utilize this presumption.

## *Rebutting the presumption*

**16.75** The owner of the seal can rebut these presumptions. However, it is difficult to effectively prove that the document was not authentically executed, which is tantamount to trying to prove a negative. Of recent, this presumption has been found to pose problems in an age when it is very easy to forge name seals with the availability of advanced technology. This problem reached national importance following a series of thefts from deposit accounts held in banks using forged or stolen seals. The problem is partly explained by Matsushita Shuli:[54]

> Door-picking artist quietly breaks and enters victim's house and nicks bank account passbook. The passbook, especially old ones, usually carries the seal image on the first page. The joker scans

54 Obtaining information about this problem in the English language is difficult. A budget committee at Congress was arranged to discuss 'The problem of seal impression' on 27 February 2003, by Mr Toshimasa Yamada of the Democratic Party and Mr Hideo Usui of the Liberal Democratic Party, but links to this item no longer appear to be live. The Japanese Bankers Association (http://www.zenginkyo.or.jp/en/) does not have any documents in English about this issue, but by typing in the words 'deposits stolen seal', a number of documents that refer to the problem of theft will be discovered. Slightly more information was possible to obtain from the article by Matsushita Shuli (from which the quote is taken), 'A futile effort to prop up hopeless *Hanko* system?' CNET Asia, 14 August 2006, but the article no longer appears to be available online; but see M. Negishi, 'Security concerns jeopardize future of age-old tradition of "hanko" seals', *The Japan Times*, undated, available at http://www.japantimes.co.jp/news/2004/01/14/business/security-concerns-jeopardize-future-of-age-old-tradition-of-hanko-seals/#.V0xESulvf8t. The most recent news item is 'UPDATE 1-Molex probing unauthorized loans at Japan unit', 9 April 2010 2:36pm EDT, Reuters, online at http://www.reuters.com/article/idUSSGE6380JJ20100409; 'Huge Local Fraud Case, ebiz in Japan', 20 April 2010, Japan.Inc, online at http://www.japaninc.com/tt562_huge-local-fraud-case.

> this image and prints it on the withdrawal slip with color printer. The bank teller accepts this slip and passbook as authentic, and victim's account will be emptied. Sometimes, the scanned digital image goes to hanko carving machine, too.
>
> The real cause of trouble: It's the stamped image of one's hanko that is stored in the databases of government offices, banks and other public institutions. Not the particulars of physical hanko itself! And any image can be flawlessly reproduced in this era of digital processing. QED.

**16.76** The Jitsuin and the Seal Registration Certificate have been a very effective method of providing for the authenticity and intention of a person when entering into a legally binding agreement. A trusted third party undertakes to certify the nexus between the applicant and the Jitsuin. The presumption worked well in a society where the accurate copying of name seals was difficult for the would-be thief.[55] However, with the advent of modern means of duplication, a tension has begun to be manifest between the assurance that an individual can prove their identity and thereby authenticate a document with the use of a Seal Registration Certificate in combination with a Jitsuin, and the failure to require the relying party to take steps to authenticate the identity of the person who claims the name seal is their adopted Jitsuin. The Seal Registration Certificate proves the seal holder has adopted the impression of the seal that is recorded in the Certificate. In modern Japan, the failure to balance the presumption that accompanies the use of a Jitsuin, with an accompanying duty to take steps to require the person using the name seal to provide the certificate of authenticity, has meant ordinary consumers suffer the loss. This is an example where advances in technology have caused problems in a system of authentication that has worked well over an extended period of time in Japanese history. Whilst a change to the law will not follow immediately, when a change does occur, a cultural shift will also have to take place, in which the relying party will have to take reasonable steps to verify the signing party.

## Burden of proof - standards

**16.77** Technical specifications, known as standards, are a voluntary means of providing for interoperability between equipment and processes. It does not follow that the same standards will be implemented for the same product, and when a vendor implements a standard, it may not be implemented consistently with other vendors.[56] It is conceivable that, in the event of a dispute, the party

55 N. Kawawa, 'The Japanese law on unauthorized on-line credit card and banking transactions: are current legal principles with respect to unauthorized transactions adequate to protect consumers against information technology crimes in contemporary society?', *Digital Evidence and Electronic Signature Law Review*, 10 (2013), pp. 71–80 for a general overview of the position in Japan.

56 For an example relating to qualified electronic signatures in Poland where companies

bearing the burden of proof may have recourse to apply their mind to the relevant standards and to determine whether the standards were complied with, and if not, why not. In this respect, consideration will have to be given to whether any relevant standards were tested and certified by an approved certification laboratory in accordance with the Common Criteria for Information Technology Security Evaluation.

## Burden of proof – summary

**16.78** In the context of electronic signatures, and digital signatures in particular, there is a clear lesson to be understood. In the physical world where the signature-creation device is difficult to replicate accurately, a tri-part method of providing assurance can be very effective. The owner of the Japanese seal provides evidence of their identity to satisfy a nominated authority sufficiently for the authority to create a certificate to link the seal to the owner. The authority retains the evidence of the link, and the relying party can rest assured that the person with the seal, if authenticated with a certificate, is who they say they are. The flaw in this model, in an age when a name seal is easy to duplicate, is to fail to impose a duty on the relying party to undertake sufficient due diligence to satisfy themselves that the holder of the seal is the person whose name seal is registered.

**16.79** The use of a rubber stamp as a form of signature has similar properties to the name seal, but without the properties of the Jitsuin. In the cases of *Goodman v. J Eban Limited*[57] and *British Estate Investment Society Ltd v. Jackson (H M Inspector of Taxes)*[58] the respective recipients of the stamped documents did not question the authenticity of the stamped signature, but sought to challenge the format of the signature. The underlying assumptions about the security of a rubber stamp were not fully articulated; that is, the owner of such a stamp is expected to keep it secure and prevent any unauthorized use. If the recipient was in any doubt as to the authenticity of the document signed with a rubber stamp, they could always take steps to verify the integrity of the document. While observations about the security were made in passing by the judges and did not lay down a rule of law, nevertheless they represent underlying assumptions about the risks to be attached to the use of a means of providing authentication to a document, which may not always be under the control of the owner, at least in cases where the means in question are adopted for the convenience and advantage of the user, rather than the recipient.

**16.80** The risks for the participants when using electronic signatures is, to a certain extent, similar to that of the Jitsuin and rubber stamp, depending on

chose different signature formats from the standards available, which in turn prevented any possible intra-country interoperability for years, see P. Krawczyk, 'When the EU qualified electronic signature becomes an information services preventer', *Digital Evidence and Electronic Signature Law Review*, 7 (2010), pp. 7–18.

57 [1954] 1 QB 550; [1954] 1 All ER 763; [1954] 2 WLR 581, CA.

58 (1954–1958) 37 Tax Cas 79; [1956] TR 397; 35 ATC 413; 50 R & IT 33.

the type of electronic signature used. In the context of the digital signature, the trusted third party allocates the risks and responsibilities. In general, a subscribing party or receiving party that relies on such technology is either fully aware of the limitations associated with the use of a digital signature, or they have no concept of the issues, and they use a digital signature in ignorance of the risks they may face if their reliance were to be tested. Statute provides that where a trusted third party with a contractual relationship with its customer (a bank) debits the account of a customer with the payment of a cheque the customer did not sign, the bank has no authority to take the money and therefore must credit the account with the amount charged.[59] The allocation of risk with the Jitsuin is under threat because of the ease by which a name seal can be forged.

**16.81** It was judges during the 19th century who created the protection for those customers that affixed their manuscript signature to a cheque. All the politicians did was to codify the rule developed by judges.[60] While it will be important to take into account the suggestion made by Romer LJ in *Goodman v. J Eban Limited*[61] where he suggested the recipient of a document stamped with a rubber stamp can take action to authenticate the document, the action and effort required to check that the writer of a letter intended to affix their signature by means of a rubber stamp is far less than the magnitude of the task facing a recipient of, in particular, a digital signature. The terms and content of the certification practice policies of the certification authorities demonstrate the complexity of the task faced by a recipient if they are expected to verify a digital signature.

## Presumptions

**16.82** The aim of a presumption is to reduce the need prove every item of evidence adduced in court, or to reduce the need for evidence in relation to some issues. Some presumptions are considered irrebuttable. Where an irrebuttable presumption operates, once a party has proved a fact or had one fact admitted, another fact will be presumed, and the other party cannot call evidence to the contrary. With a rebuttable presumption, after the proof of admission of the presumption is admitted into evidence, the court can presume another fact as a result. However, the other party then has the persuasive or evidential burden to disprove the presumed fact. One presumption that applies to computers is the

59 Bills of Exchange Act 1882 s24; Directive 2007/64/EC of the European Parliament and of the Council of 13 November 2007 on payment services in the internal market amending Directives 97/7/EC, 2002/65/EC, 2005/60/EC and 2006/48/EC and repealing Directive 97/5/EC (Text with EEA relevance) OJ L 319, 5.12.2007, p. 1–36, implemented by The Payment Services Regulations 2009 (SI 209/2009) as amended by The Payment Services (Amendment) Regulations 2009 (SI 2475/2009).

60 N. Bohm, I. Brown and B. Gladman, 'Electronic commerce: who carries the risk of fraud?', *Journal of Information, Law and Technology*, 3 (2000), http://www2.warwick.ac.uk/fac/soc/law/elj/jilt/2000_3/bohm, paragraph 2.

61 [1954] 1 QB 550 at 564.

presumption that a machine is presumed to be in working order. In the context of digital evidence, however, it is pertinent to be aware of the imperfections inherent in the way computers function, and how digital evidence is prone to alteration. Evidence derived from a computer must be admissible, authentic, accurate and complete in the same way as any other form of evidence. However, computers are also very volatile, in that a document, record or log can be altered very easily without leaving an obvious trace. Bearing in mind that much of the evidence accumulated about the use of an electronic signature will be by way of software code between a series of computers, all of which will be connected to the internet, the problems of relying on evidence generated by computers increase.[62]

62 See Mason, *Electronic Evidence*, ch. 5 for a detailed consideration of this presumption.

# 17

# Data protection

**17.1** Electronic signatures come in various forms, and to illustrate a simple but disturbing way in which documents are used, one can look to the activities of some local councils in England. When a person applies for planning permission, they are required to submit a planning application, and their manuscript signature is affixed to the document. The documents that accompany a planning application are open to the public to view. However, some local authorities scan the applications and publish the application into pdf format before uploading the entire document on to a website, thus exposing a number of manuscript signatures to being viewed by the entire world. This action enables would-be thieves to obtain a perfect specimen of a manuscript signature that could be used for nefarious purposes in the future. This is just one of the problems that affect electronic signatures and the application of the principles of data protection. This state of affairs in England illustrates that rules put into place to provide for openness in pre-digital times are not always appropriate in the digital age. In this instance, the application of a rule requiring openness at a time when paper was paramount has been uncritically transposed into the digital age without thought to the wider repercussions.

## The legal framework

### Organisation for Economic Cooperation and Development

**17.2** In the international context, the Organisation for Economic Cooperation and Development developed a set of guidelines, part of which included the need to consider the issues relating to the protection of personal data.[1] Principle 5, 'Protection of privacy and personal data', sets out the expectation:

> The fundamental rights of individuals to privacy, including secrecy of communications and protection of personal data, should be respected in national cryptography policies and in the implementation and use of cryptographic methods.

**17.3** In discussing the issues relating to privacy, the guidelines expressly note the difference between cryptographic keys used for confidentiality and those used for authentication. Any user that intends to use a private key for the

1 *Cryptography Guidelines: Recommendation of the Council* (OECD, 27 March 1997. See also *OECD Guidelines on the Protection of Privacy and Transborder Flows of Personal Data* (OECD, 2013) and *Guidelines for Consumer Protection in the Context of Electronic Commerce* (OECD, 1999).

S. Mason, *Electronic Signatures in Law* (London: Institute of Advanced Legal Studies, 2016), chapter 17, 'Data protection', pp. 387–95.

purposes of authentication must be made aware of the difference, and undertake to ensure only the relevant algorithms are used for the purpose of generating a private key. Failure so to do may enable malicious individuals to use the private key not only to impersonate an individual, but also to send incriminating material electronically that can be associated with the innocent holder of the private key.[2]

# Guidelines

## PKI Assessment Guidelines

**17.4** The PKI Assessment Guidelines[3] consider some of the issues. In particular, the authors assume correctly that many end users, both consumers and businesses, will not be knowledgeable about the technology that underpins public key cryptography. Additionally, it is also thought that it cannot be presumed that:[4]

> ... all or even most certificate owners and users regularly read and understand the complex and often lengthy legal documents that usually govern the contractual relationships amongst the various parties in a PKI.

**17.5** Thus the guidelines emphasise the need of assessors take particular note of the method by which a certification authority or registration authority incorporates the use of information practices into the contract with a subscribing party, and how personal data is to be used where a recipient decides to become a verifying party. It is suggested that participants within the public key infrastructure (certification authorities, registration authorities and the repository) should take reasonable steps to make subscribing parties aware of the links within the infrastructure and how their personal data is used.[5]

## CARAT Guidelines

**17.6** The National Automated Clearing House Association developed a set of guidelines for constructing policies for the use of public key certificates, consideration of which was given to the issue of confidentiality.[6] The guidance

2 *Guidelines for Cryptography Policy* (OECD, 1997). See also OECD Ministerial Conference, 'A borderless world: realising the potential of global electronic commerce', Action plan for electronic commerce, 7–9 October 1998, Ottawa, Canada (SG/EC(98)9/REV5).

3 PKI Assessment Guidelines (v1.0 10 May 2003) (Information Security Committee, Electronic Commerce Division, Section of Science and Technology Information Security Committee American Bar Association) C.5.

4 PKI Assessment Guidelines C.5.

5 C.5.1.1.

6 'Guidelines for constructing policies governing the use of identity-based public key certificates' (National Automated Clearing House Association, The Internet Council,

offered is that a certificate policy should provide that information in certificates is not confidential. The guide distinguishes between the types of privacy that should be considered in relation to electronic transactions:

> Data privacy, which refers to the privacy and accuracy of the data that a subscribing party knows is being collected.
>
> Transactional privacy, which refers to the privacy and accuracy of transactional data the subscribing party may not be aware of that is being collected. It does not follow that transactional data will be collected as it is generated. The point is, that where such data is collected, the subscribing party has the same right to privacy even where they are not aware that the data is being collected.[7]

**17.7** The advice offered is to follow the OECD guidelines, as well as follow the laws in a prevailing jurisdiction. The issue of jurisdiction, which is not discussed in this text, was also an issue discussed by the PKI Assessment Guidelines.

## Australia

**17.8** In Australia, the Officer of the Federal Privacy Commissioner prepared a document in 2002 entitled *Privacy and Public Key Infrastructure: Guidelines for Agencies using PKI to communicate or transact with individuals.*[8] The document sets out the risks, both actual and potential. The first is whether the amount of information gathered is relevant to the level of certificate being issued or requested at the registration stage, contained in Public Key Certificates, (which are also normally publicly available, in that it is conceivable that the transactions carried out by an individual may be tracked), and included in Public Key Directories and Certificate Revocation Lists, which in turn may enable the directories to be scanned for information and downloaded with a view of using the data in ways that interferes with the privacy of individuals. On page 19 the following comment is offered: 'The issue to consider, from a privacy perspective, is whether PKI applications require the publication of a public key directory. If publication is considered necessary then a privacy protective option is to allow individual clients to opt out of having their public keys listed in the directory. This is similar to the way telephone subscribers may opt out of having their phone number published in the phone directory'. Another issue concerns logs

---

Certification Authority Rating and Trust (CARAT) Task Force, 14 January 2000) available online from http://civics.typepad.com/files/carat_final_011400-1-1.pdf.

7 Part E paragraph 2.8, 2.

8 An electronic version is available at http://www.rogerclarke.com/DV/OAPC-2001.pdf; V. Liu, 'Release of Guidelines by the Privacy Commissioner for Agencies using PKI: implications for Agencies, government contractors and private sector organisations', *Computers and Law: Journal for the Australian and New Zealand Societies for Computers and the Law*, 47 (2002), pp. 24–31, online at http://www5.austlii.edu.au/au/journals/ANZCompuLawJl/2002/9.pdf.

and ephemeral data which are stored by servers hosting public key directories, Certificate Revocation Lists and other PKI transactions and maintained by CAs and agencies: such logs will normally retain details of when a certificate was viewed and what online transactions the individual entered into. It is a legitimate expectation that a relevant organization may maintain records of such activities; nevertheless, the logs could be used to monitor transactions and compile profiles of individuals using such services.

**17.9** The Federal Privacy Commissioner offers nine guidelines, each of which includes a commentary. They are:

> Guideline 1 – Agency Client Choice on the Use of PKI Applications
>
> Agencies should allow their clients to choose whether to use PKI for a particular transaction and to offer them alternative means of service delivery. The alternative need not always be an online alternative. In providing this choice agencies should advise their clients of the privacy risks and advantages associated with their use of PKI and alternative methods for that transaction.
>
> Guideline 2 – Awareness and Education
>
> Agencies and their contracted PKI service providers should co-operate closely to ensure that their clients are fully informed of the proper use of PKI and of the risks and responsibilities associated with the use of PKI, including the secure management of private keys.
>
> Guideline 3 – Privacy Impact Assessments (PIAs)
>
> Agencies should undertake a Privacy Impact Assessment before implementing a new PKI system or significantly revising or extending an existing PKI system.
>
> Guideline 4 – Evidence of Identity
>
> When developing PKI applications or contracting with PKI services providers, agencies should ensure that only minimum Evidence of Identity that is necessary for, or directly related, to the process is collected.
>
> In addition, where a client wishes to obtain more than one certificate then the client should be given a range of options including:
>
>> consenting to use a Gatekeeper certificate of equal or higher value to apply for a new certificate;
>>
>> consenting to the re-use of Evidence of Identity documentation previously provided by the client;
>>
>> or providing documentation on registration for an additional certificate.

Guideline 5 – Aggregation of Personal Information

In the course of PKI transactions with clients, agencies and their contracted PKI service providers should ensure that no detailed history of client transactions is created or used by the agency or contracted PKI service provider, except to the extent that this is required for system maintenance or evidentiary purposes.

Agencies and contracted PKI service providers, should not use PKI transactions to collect personal information that is not necessary, or directly related to, the PKI business transaction.

Guideline 6 – Single or Multiple Certificates

Agencies should allow clients to use more than one certificate, where these are fit for the purpose of the relevant application. Agencies should also recognise certificates they have not issued where these certificates are fit for the purpose of the relevant application.

Guideline 7 – Subscriber Generation of Keys

Where an agency issues certificates or contracts for their issue, the agency should allow its clients the option of generating their own keys, provided that the agency is satisfied that subscriber key generation can be implemented securely.

Guideline 8 – Public Key Directories

Agency clients should be allowed to opt out of including their public keys in a public key directory (PKD) where the PKD is published.

Guideline 9 – Pseudonymity and Anonymity

Agencies should provide their clients with anonymous and pseudonymous options for transacting with them, to the extent that this is not inconsistent with the objectives and operation of the relevant online application.

## European Union

**17.10** The Article 29 Data Protection Working Party adopted a *Working document on biometrics*.[9] A biodynamic version of a manuscript signature was determined to come within the provisions of the relevant data protection Directive, because the use of the data implied the processing of personal data. It was determined that it the data came within the provisions of the relevant Directive on data protection. A further document entitled *Opinion 3/2012 on developments in biometric technologies* was published on 27 April 2012.[10] The

9 12168/02/EN WP 80.

10 00720/12/EN WP193.

Opinion expressed the view that technologies using biodynamic data should be subject to appropriate security, and duly outlined the principles. Reference was made to biodynamic versions of a manuscript signature on page 27, and the data protection risks associated with the use of such methods of applying a signature were set out:

> Accuracy: People may not always sign in the same manner, so they could face problems during the enrolment process as well as when verifying their identity.
>
> Impact: Biometrics based on behavioural characteristics such a signature may not be unique over time and can be changed by the data subject. Changes of signature can also have a physiological origin and can preclude a successful verification resulting in the need of alternative procedures in order to verify the identity of the individuals.
>
> Anti-spoofing: While the graphical image of a traditional signature can be easily replicated and forged by a trained human, photocopy or with computer graphics software, a dynamic signature is more secure because the verification process checks also dynamic characteristics which are complex and unique to the handwriting style of a person.

## Practical issues[11]

### Generating the private key

**17.11** The most secure private key is that which is generated within the total control of the person who intends to use it. Thus a key pair can be generated from a personal computer, but the exposure to attack depends not on where they were generated, but on where the keys are stored, and personal computers are very weak from this point of view, especially when connected to a network. If a trusted third party generated the key pair for a person, then the user would have to be assured that the private key would be only be available to them. In addition, further assurances would have to be made by the key generator respecting the security process, because it is very easy for a person to use the private key to impersonate the legitimate owner to the detriment of the actual owner.

11 The author is indebted to the early work of G. Greenleaf and R. Clarke, 'Privacy implications of digital signatures', joint address, IBC Conference on Digital Signatures, Sydney, 12 March 1997, available online at http://www.rogerclarke.com/DV/DigSig.html, whose structure is followed in this section; see also M.H.M. Schellekens, *Electronic Signatures: Authentication Technology from a Legal Perspective* (The Hague: T.M.C. Asser Press, 2004), ch. 5.

### Storage of the private key

**17.12** Where an individual decides to take advantage of the ability to have and use a digital signature, the next issue they must consider is how the private key is stored, backed up and how the copies are stored. Any breach of security will increase the risks associated with the private key being used by a malicious person or organization to the detriment of the owner of the private key, should the security of the private key be so poor as to make it relatively easy to obtain for illicit purposes.

### Revocation of private keys

**17.13** The act of revoking a private key will require the person with the private key to identify themselves to the certification authority. The authentication of the user will invariably be intrusive, but necessary if the key is to be revoked effectively and in a timely manner.

### Data required for the certificate

**17.14** Clearly either the certification authority or registration authority will require the intended subscriber to provide them with sufficient personal data to identify themselves to obtain and use a digital signature. Either or both organizations will be required to deal with the data in a manner appropriate to the jurisdiction within which the subscribing party is situated.

## Case law

### Biodynamic versions of a manuscript signature

**17.15** The Office of the Privacy Commissioner of Canada dealt with an application of the use of biodynamic versions of a manuscript signature in PIPEDA Case Finding #71.[12] In separate complaints, two recipients of parcels objected to the practice of a courier company that demanded they sign for the parcel by providing an electronic signature upon delivery, and then posted the signatures on the company website without consent. The facts are summarised in the report:

> When asked to sign electronically for receipt of a parcel, the first complainant expressed his preference for signing a paper receipt, but was told that unless he provided an electronic signature he would not receive his parcel. The complainant provided his electronic signature under protest and took possession of his parcel. He later made email inquiries of the company to determine

12 2002 CanLII 42333 (P.C.C.).

whether electronic signatures were indeed mandatory under company policy or whether allowances were made for persons who preferred to sign paper. Replies indicated only that obtaining electronic signatures was company policy.

After agreeing to provide a signature electronically to indicate receipt of a delivery by the company in question, the second complainant discovered that this electronic signature had been placed in the tracking section of the company website, along with his name and address and the delivery status of the parcel in question. When he asked that his electronic signature be removed, a company representative told him it was not possible.

**17.16** The investigation by the office of the Commissioner revealed the following:

The company stores signatures obtained from parcel recipients in its tracking system, which is accessible at the company's website, and uses them in providing an online tracking service for its customers.

By keying in the appropriate parcel identification number (PIN), a website user gains access to information about the corresponding shipment – specifically, name and address of the intended recipient, delivery status of the parcel and, once delivery is completed, the recipient's electronic signature.

It is sometimes possible, by varying a digit of the PIN within a reasonable range, to gain access to names, addresses, and electronic signatures pertaining to other shipments – that is, the personal information of others.

There was no evidence that the company had in any way informed the complainants of its intention to use their electronic signature on its website for online tracking purposes or sought consent for such use.

At the time of the complaints, it was not company policy to remove signatures from the online tracking system at the request of individuals.

**17.17** The Commissioner's office determined that it had jurisdiction under the provisions of the Personal Information Protection and Electronic Documents Act (PIPEDA). The Act applies to any federal work, undertaking or business, and the Commissioner had jurisdiction because inter-provincial courier companies are federal works, undertakings or businesses as defined in the Act. The relevant Principles were: Principle 4.3 of Schedule 1, that states that the knowledge and consent of the individual are required for the collection, use, or disclosure of personal information, except where inappropriate; Principle 4.3.3, that states that an organization must not, as a condition of the supply of a product or service, require an individual to consent to the collection, use, or disclosure of personal information beyond that required to fulfil the explicitly specified and legitimate purposes, and section 5(3) that states that an organization may collect, use, or disclose personal information only for purposes that a reasonable person would consider appropriate in the circumstances.

**17.18** On the matter of use, the Commissioner determined that the company had neither informed nor sought the consent of people in respect of any use it intended to make of their electronic signatures beyond the immediate purpose of indicating receipt. There was no evidence that the company had ever obtained consent to place electronic signatures on its website and using them for the purpose of providing a tracking service to its customers.

**17.19** The Commissioner found the company had been in contravention of Principle 4.3 and section 5(3), because a reasonable person would not have considered such use appropriate in any circumstances, especially given the demonstrated potential for unauthorized disclosure of the signatures. In addition, the company was in breach of Principle 4.3.3, because the ostensible and immediate purpose for the collection had been to indicate receipt of a parcel, but that purpose could have been fulfilled by other means, such as a signature on paper. For this reason, it cannot be said that an electronic signature was a requirement for the fulfilment of the purpose. As a result, it was determined that the electronic signatures had not been required to fulfil explicitly specified and legitimate purposes and that the company had therefore not been justified in demanding them as a condition of service.

## A name typed in an email

**17.20** The question of whether a name typed in an email can be considered to be confidential will depend on the circumstances. The Information and Privacy Commissioner of Ontario, Canada considered, given the facts of Order MO-3140, Appeal MA14-303,[13] that an electronic signature typed in an email was confidential. In this instance, a person filed a request by email about the conduct of a councillor. The councillor in turn requested to see a copy of the email. It was granted. The individual who sent the email to the region appealed the decision to provide the Councillor making the request with a copy of the email. The adjudicator ordered the provision of the disclosure of the information that was not personal, and ordered that the electronic signature be not given.

13 2014 CanLII 79320 (ONIPC).

# Index

Lightning Source UK Ltd.
Milton Keynes UK
UKOW05f0933140517
301123UK00001B/7/P

9 781911 507000